# Student Teaching:
## EARLY CHILDHOOD
## PRACTICUM GUIDE

**7TH EDITION**

Jeanne M. Machado, Emerita
San Jose City College

Helen Meyer-Botnarescue, Ph.D., Emerita
California State University—East Bay

 WADSWORTH
CENGAGE Learning

Australia • Brazil • Japan • Korea • Mexico • Singapore • Spain • United Kingdom • United States

**Student Teaching: Early Childhood Practicum Guide, Seventh Edition**
Jeanne Machado, Emerita
Helen Botnarescue, Ph.D., Emerita

Executive Editor: Linda Schreiber-Ganster

Senior Developmental Editor: Lisa Kalner Williams

Assistant Editor: Caitlin Cox

Editorial Assistant: Linda Stewart

Media Editor: Dennis Fitzgerald

Marketing Manager: Kara Kindstrom

Marketing Assistant: Dimitri Hagnéré

Marketing Communications Manager: Martha Pffeifer

Content Project Manager: Samen Iqbal

Creative Director: Rob Hugel

Art Director: Maria Epes

Print Buyer: Paula Vang

Rights Acquisitions Account Manager, Text: Bob Kauser

Rights Acquisitions Account Manager, Image: Leitha Etheridge-Sims

Production Service: Lindsay Burt, MPS Limited, A Macmillan Company

Text Designer: Lee Anne Dollison

Photo Researcher: Joshua Brown

Copy Editor: Richard Camp

Cover Designer: Bartay Studios

Cover Image: © Cengage Learning, ECE Photo Library

Compositor: MPS Limited, A Macmillan Company

For product information and technology assistance, contact us at **Cengage Learning Customer & Sales Support, 1-800-354-9706.**

For permission to use material from this text or product, submit all requests online at **www.cengage.com/permissions.** Further permissions questions can be e-mailed to **permissionrequest@cengage.com.**

Library of Congress Control Number: 2009934813

Student Edition:
ISBN-13: 978-0-495-81322-4
ISBN-10: 0-495-81322-2

**Wadsworth**
20 Davis Drive
Belmont, CA 94002-3098
USA

Cengage Learning is a leading provider of customized learning solutions with office locations around the globe, including Singapore, the United Kingdom, Australia, Mexico, Brazil, and Japan. Locate your local office at **international.cengage.com/region.**

Cengage Learning products are represented in Canada by Nelson Education, Ltd.

To learn more about Wadsworth, visit **www.cengage.com/wadsworth**

Purchase any of our products at your local college store or at our preferred online store **www.ichapters.com.**

Printed in the United States of America
1 2 3 4 5 6 7 13 12 11 10 09

# Contents

## 1 Orientation to Student Teaching

# 2   Programming

# 3   Working with Children

# 4 Communication

# 5 Interactions

# 6 Professional Concerns

# Infant/Toddler Placements

# Preface

*Student Teaching: Early Childhood Practicum Guide, 7th edition* is designed to promote the readers' smooth and successful transition from being a student of early childhood education to becoming a practicing, professional early childhood educator with recognized competencies — the kind of teacher that we would wish for all young children. This new teacher would satisfy and fulfill the goals, outcomes, standards, and ending expectations of his or her training program.

Student teachers assume teaching responsibilities under guided supervision. It involves an individual struggle to put theory into practice, and student teachers will experience a memorable journey of both personal and professional growth. It is a synthesizing experience from which each student emerges with a unique professional style.

The text will serve as a useful reference tool for teaching tips and problem-solving techniques. Chapter topics are diverse and will aid the student teacher's desire to create classroom settings where young children thrive as their teacher, or the teaching team, guides behavior and offers educational activities and opportunities that recognize each child's unique needs and individual potential. Text is accompanied with examples of practicing professionals and their skills and common problems. These are related to current and classic theories of child development and early childhood education.

As we watched student teachers struggle with wondering what to do during the initial days of student teaching—wanting ideas about classroom management and guidance strategies, seeking to understand atypical children in their classrooms, questioning assessment, and wondering how to build partnerships with families—we were inspired to provide them with an up-to-date text that serves their needs.

## ORGANIZATION OF THE TEXT

All chapters offer learning objectives, chapter summaries, suggested activities, review questions, websites to search, and lists of references. Scenarios, presenting a narrative focusing the readers' attention on chapter content, open each chapter. Each scenario deals with issues, problems, and dilemmas, and questions that others have encountered in and out of the classroom. Questions following each scenario promote contemplative and reflective thought, and can be used for class discussion. Comments of former student teachers are interspersed in chapter text where appropriate. These personal revelations give further first-hand perspectives on teaching young children.

Chapter 1, Introduction to Student Teaching Practicum, includes training guidelines, initial feelings, key participants, the currently employed student teacher, useful forms, professionalism, an orientation to first working days, and an introduction to the National Association for the Education of Young Children's (NAEYC) *Code of Ethical Conduct* and *Standards for Programs*. Descriptions of the variations that may exist in placement classrooms, cooperating teachers' and college supervisors' supervision styles are covered. Student teachers gain insight into how quickly they might assume full teaching responsibilities and duties. Maintaining records, writing in a journal, and collecting items for a professional portfolio are explained. A section of the text will increase your understanding of important classroom routines, areas, and supporting personnel. It is designed to aid your acceptance as an entering teaching team member.  This chapter prepares the reader for what is to happen, and what is expected.

Chapter 2, A Student Teacher's Values and Developing Teaching Style, introduces student teachers to the subject of how their values impact their teaching style. We firmly believe that teaching style evolves from each teacher's individual values. Thus, student teachers are presented with exercises designed to help them define their values and see how these translate into classroom activities. The acquisition of values is mentioned, as is the development of teaching style. Professional ethics are discussed in greater detail than in previous editions. An example, using sections of NAEYC's *Code of Ethical Conduct*, illustrates how the code may guide the student teacher in relating to differences in values between one culture and another. Examples of authoritative and authoritarian styles are given and other styles are introduced, along with precautions related to stereotyping and the need for flexibility.

Chapter 3, Being Observed: Discovering Your Competencies, includes the goals and methods of observation, and provides several examples of observation forms that college supervisors or cooperating teachers might use, along with a self-rating sheet that student teachers can employ to assist them in identifying strengths and weaknesses. Competency-based training, critical thinking, and reflective behaviors are discussed because we believe that self-analysis is critical to becoming an effective teacher. Standards for associate and initial licensure levels are introduced and display the recommended skills and abilities that successful candidates accomplish before graduation. The text reminds student teachers of their responsibility to guide their own growth and improvement of competencies by using the many forms of feedback and suggestions that they receive.

Chapter 4, Instructional Planning, encourages student teachers to look at child interests and needs and the ways that early childhood curricula is planned and delivered.  It emphasizes the student teacher's ability to plan activities by observing and conversing with children to ascertain what interests and engages them. Accepted standards are discussed and assessment is introduced. Activity resources and other curriculum approaches are mentioned, along with the implications of the federal, state, and local standards and legislation. How play affects learning and the need to be an adept conversational companion are covered, along with schedules that outline plans for a day or longer period. Written lesson and activity plans for early childhood  activities and instruction are presented in detail. Sample plans and forms that a student teacher might use are also included. Theme and project approaches to teaching are explained, to alert the student teacher to instructional advantages and possible drawbacks of each. Topics such as promoting children's cognitive skills, using community resources, and tips for conducting and planning group instruction are offered.

Chapter 5, Classroom Management: Beyond Discipline, includes information on conflict resolution and looks at the five areas of classroom management: the physical arrangement of the classroom, curriculum choices, time management, managing classroom routines, and the guidance or disciplinary function. New research on guidance as social and emotional development is discussed and several management techniques are suggested. The role of the family is also introduced.

Chapter 6, Understanding Behavior, highlights information related to Erikson, Maslow, and other developmental theorists. The relationship between Erikson's psychosocial theory and the observed behavior of children has been clarified and simplified in this edition. The chapter includes several observation forms, together with their applications, when looking at specific children. The forms are then analyzed to demonstrate how theories help in understanding behavior.

Chapter 7, Working with Children with Special Needs, introduces the student to federal laws that mandate special education and related services to all identified children with special needs. Ideas for how a student teacher might be involved in a preliminary diagnosis and strategies for working with children with specific disabilities have been updated. Team efforts and the role of the family have been emphasized.

Chapter 8, Common Problems of Student Teachers, starts with a focus on the relationship between stress and classroom conditions. Causes and effects of stress on student teachers are discussed, as are ideas about how to reduce stress. Conferencing, time management, when to seek help, authenticity, active listening, interpersonal communication, preparing *one-day wonders*, and conflict resolution all receive attention. Two interpersonal problem-solving strategies are explained in a step-by-step fashion with examples and exercises given for practice and mastery

Chapter 9, Student Teachers and Families, begins with the importance of school-home collaboration and the school's family-relations philosophy and goals. Student teachers are urged to recognize family strengths and resources. We include ways that student teachers may interact with families, daily exchanges at opening and pick up times, oral and written communications, planning and provide help in conducting and planning conferences, home visits, and parent-school meetings. Other topics covered in this chapter are interactions with parent volunteers, home cultures, and student teacher pitfalls and precautions.

Chapter 10, Quality Programs in Early Childhood Settings, discusses programs and whether they meet children's needs, are balanced, and meet other standards of quality. The relationship between different types of accreditation and quality is updated, along with findings of several studies that have looked at quality in preschool and elementary school programs.

Chapter 11, Professional Commitment and Employment, the educators' necessity to keep current and their commitment to lifelong learning are explained. Educators' growth in career competencies can occur by using a variety of courses of action and following various paths to excellence. Many employers and programs have an employee professional growth plan that is mandated by law or the program's sponsoring agency, and students are apprised of ways to obtain monetary support for additional education and training that promotes upward mobility. Facts and figures affecting American children and families are cited. Child abuse, family characteristics, immigrant families, Latino families, school attendance, and child care arrangements are discussed. Current factors influencing the career field of education and early education are also included. Educators searching for employment are provided with recommendations, tips, and suggestions to aid their search. The diversity of employment opportunities in the field of education are growing and reflect societal and cultural realities.

Chapter 12, Student Teaching with Infants and Toddlers, includes updated material on quality indicators and studies related to quality. Special issues such as separation from parents, infant/toddler child care and identity formation, infants born to teenage parents, toilet learning, and biting are discussed. Signing is described, as a technique to enhance infant communication, and several activities for encouraging early learning are included.

## REVISIONS TO THE SEVENTH EDITION

The seventh edition has become more compact, concise, and timely due to instructors' and students' user comments. To those familiar with the text, the former chapter on child development and learning theory has been greatly reduced and, where appropriate, combined with the chapter on case studies on behavior. Chapter 11, Professional Growth and Employment, is a combined, streamlined chapter of the former chapters on trends and professional development. Chapter 12, Student

Teaching with Infants and Toddlers, is now concise enough for student teachers to use as a quick, go-to guide for teaching the youngest of learners. You'll soon see by reading this edition that chapters have been logically combined and trimmed without sacrificing valuable material.

Suggested Activity and Review sections have also been trimmed. The overall text emphasizes the student teachers' emerging competency development and ability to display and document their growth and achievement to satisfy and fulfill their training programs standards and goals.

Scenarios now introduce chapters and promote classroom discussion. New examples of professional and accepted teaching practices were included. Further help in interpersonal problem solving has been added as well as greater depth concerning employment particulars and alternative ways for educators to use their skills and abilities in various positions in the field of education. Professionalism, ethics, advocacy, and professional growth issues are retained and are given additional attention. Websites for students' further study and research are still present.

Photographs have more clarity and reflect current practice. Current research has been cited throughout the book.

## ANCILLARIES

The following ancillaries are available to accompany the seventh edition of *Student Teaching: Early Childhood Practicum Guide*.

### Electronic Instructor's Manual

An updated *Instructor's Manual* provides general instructional activities for student teachers, suggested instructional activities by chapter, answers to chapter review questions, teaching resources, and the test bank.

### PowerLecture

The PowerLecture, is a one-stop digital library and presentation tool that includes preassembled Microsoft® PowerPoint® lecture slides by Amy Jauman, in addition to a full Instructor's Manual and Test Bank. It also includes ExamView® testing software with all the test items from the printed Test Bank in electronic format, enabling you to create customized tests in print or online.

### Companion Website

The book-specific website at www.cengage.com/education/machado offers students a variety of study tools and useful resources such as tutorial quizzes for each chapter, additional readings, activities, and downloadable forms from the text. The instructor area of the book companion website offers access to password-protected resources such as an Instructor's Manual and Microsoft PowerPoint slides.

## USING THE TEXT

Instructors are urged to select those chapters most relevant to the needs of their students. We recognize that many associate degree programs have required courses in child development, home, school, and community; these topics have been simplified or removed from the seventh edition. The chapter on student teaching in and infant/toddler center can easily be omitted by programs that do not include such placements.

Instructors in both associate and baccalaureate degree programs may want to pick and choose the trends and issues presented in Chapter 11. Some may be relevant only in certain situations, but the new employment section will be valuable to both educational levels. Instructors may find the comprehensive test questions of value and are urged to select those that they feel are most useful.

# About the Authors

Jeanne M. Machado received her MA degree from San Jose State University and a vocational life credential from the University of California, Berkeley. She has experience as an early childhood education instructor and department chairperson at San Jose City College and Evergreen Valley College. As a past president of two professional associations—Northern California Association for the Education of Young Children (Peninsula Chapter) and California Community College Early Childhood Educators—Jeanne is deeply involved in early childhood education issues.

Her book *Early Childhood Experiences in the Language Arts* is currently in its ninth edition. In 2006, she co-authored *Employment Opportunities in Education: How to Secure Your Career,* published by Delmar Learning.

Helen Meyer-Botnarescue received her Ph.D. from the University of Alabama. She also received a life credential in psychology. Currently, Helen is a professor of education emerita from the Department of Teacher Education at California State University, East Bay. In addition, she has served as graduate coordinator of the Early Childhood Education master's program. She has been an advisor to the campus Early Childhood Center. Helen is an active member of four professional organizations: Northwest Association of Early Childhood Teacher Educators, an affiliate group of the National Association of Early Childhood Teacher Educators; the Oregon Association for the Education of Young Children, a branch of the National Association for the Education of Young Children; the World Organization for Preschool Education (OMEP); and the Association for Childhood Education International (ACEI), and its state and local affiliates. She currently is chair of NAECTE's International Committee and co-chair of ACEI's Heritage Committee. In past years, she has served on the governing boards of both the National Association of Early Childhood Teacher Educators and its California affiliate. Helen has been an active member of l'Organisation Modiale pour l'Éducation Préscolaire (OMEP) and has presented at its international congresses. She is a former president of the California Association for Childhood Education and has written extensively for the ACEI journal, *Childhood Education,* and has authored columns for the newsletters *The Activist* and *Heritage Happenings.*

# Acknowledgments

The authors wish to express their appreciation to the following individuals and institutions for their contributions to this text.

## Reviewers

Carolyn Babione,
Indiana University Southeast

Alice Joey Beaudreau,
Capital Community College

Kate Cryderman Cole,
Macomb Community College

Eileen Donahue Brittain,
Jamestown Community College—
Cattaraugus County Campus

Sandra Duncan, Nova Southeastern
University

Mara Maislen,
Capital Community College

Denise McConachie,
Missouri Baptists University

Barbara Nilsen,
Broome Community College (retired)

Rhonda Steele,
Christopher Newport College

Susan Thompson,
University of Northern Colorado

## Illustrations and Photos

Mary Stieglitz, Ph.D.
Jody Boyd
The parents of photographed children

## Individual Assistance

The directors and staff of the San Jose City College and Evergreen Valley College Child Development Centers, and enrolled student teachers.

Barbara Kraybill, Director, Afterschool Programs, Livermore, California

## Preschools, Centers, and Elementary Schools

San Jose City College Child Development Center

Evergreen Valley College Child Development Center

Young Families Program, San Jose, California

California State University Associated Students' Child Care Center

Pexioto Children's Center, Hayward, California

Parent-Child Education Center, Hayward, California

Festival Children's Center, Hayward, California

Jackson Avenue School, Livermore, California

Harder School, Hayward, California

St. Elizabeth's Day Home, San Jose, California

Donnelly Head Start, Donnelly, Idaho

Cascade Elementary School, Cascade, Idaho

Redeemer Lutheran Church Child Development Center, Redwood City, California

We also wish to express our appreciation to We Care Day Treatment Center, Concord, California, for permission to photograph attending children.

## Students, Instructors, and Professors

San Jose City College

Evergreen Valley College

California State University, East Bay

# Orientation to Student Teaching

# CHAPTER 1

# Introduction to Student Teaching Practicum

**OBJECTIVES** After reading this chapter, you should be able to:

1. Identify four important goals of a student teaching experience.
2. Describe the relationships and responsibilities of student teacher, cooperating teacher, and supervisor.
3. List important skills a student teacher might use to build a sense of staff teamwork.
4. Name two characteristics of professional educators.

Student teaching—also called *practicum teaching, field experience,* or *internship*—is both a beginning and an end. It begins a training experience that offers the student a supervised laboratory in which to learn. New skills will develop, and the student will polish professional skills already acquired.

## STUDENT TEACHER SCENARIO

**Setting:** Tisha's placement classroom

Tisha, a student teacher, faced her worst fears on the first day in her placement classroom. She felt like an outsider. There wasn't one child who spoke English well. The children were friendly enough, and only a few seemed to notice that Tisha's skin color was different. Some children seemed out of control and ignored what she said to guide them. The cooperating teacher was welcoming but so busy she had little time to interact with her. Things improved as the day progressed because Mrs. Solorzano, the teacher's aide, interpreted what some of the children said and explained classroom routines and procedures when she had a question. Tisha felt this classroom would be a good learning opportunity, even if she felt uncomfortable at times.

She planned an activity for a later time that involved making a large collage of families and sharing photographs of her own family. She wanted a variety of ethnic representations, so she planned to collect pictures torn from magazines for the children to cut out. She would also urge children to bring photographs or make drawings of their own families to add to the collage. She felt a class discussion of the finished collage could highlight diversity and similarities, and decided to discuss her plan with her cooperating teacher.

## Questions for Discussion:

1. Something evidently did not prepare Tisha for her first day. What could have helped prepare her?

2. Should she consult her college supervisor right away or perhaps wait and see if things improve?

3. Could seeking her college supervisor's help make the supervisor suspect she was not prepared for student teaching?

4. What assumptions are possible concerning the skin color and language ability of Tisha, Mrs. Solorzano, and some of the children?

Practicum teaching is usually the final step in a formal training program offering a certificate, degree, license, or credential. Theory offered in prior early childhood classes will be applied and tested. It requires reflecting upon and drawing on previous coursework, training, workshops, and background experience. Congratulations! You have satisfied all the prerequisites for practicum teaching. Now you will assume the duties and responsibilities of a teacher and become a member of a professional teaching team.

One of the culminating phases of your professional preparation for teaching, your practicum experience, provides opportunities to "try your wings" if you are not presently employed. If employed, the experience will sharpen and expand already acquired competencies. Many practitioners agree their student teaching class was the most formative and valuable experience in their training program.

## TRAINING GUIDELINES

In consultation with other professional groups, the **National Association for the Education of Young Children (NAEYC)** has taken the lead in advocating training guidelines for higher education programs in early childhood education, which includes all institutions that award associate of arts degrees, 4- and 5-year baccalaureate degrees, and advanced degrees. Required student teaching coursework is usually undertaken at each training level. NAEYC (2008) has revised and updated its standards first published in 2003. They complement and support other professional standards, such as those developed by the Council for Exceptional Children (CEC), Division for Early Childhood (DEC), the **National Council for Accreditation of Teacher Education (NCATE)**, and the National Board for Professional Teaching Standards (NBPTS).

The importance of supervised, practice teaching has not been overlooked or ignored by other organizations. The **Child Development Associate (CDA)** program, sponsored by the Council for Professional Recognition (2006) also requires that time be spent in supervised fieldwork. Many states have developed their own training guidelines that outline a specific number of student teaching hours be completed at approved or suggested schools or centers. Each graduating student of a college, university, or other type of early childhood teacher training program is expected to have successfully completed a supervised, practicum experience, or alternative equivalent, during which the student assumes major responsibility for a full range of teaching duties for a group of young children. Skills, knowledge, and attitudes gained prepare the student to demonstrate the knowledge and competencies required to meet state standards and licensing requirements, or to acquire permits, certificates, or credentials.

**National Association for the Education of Young Children (NAEYC)**—largest American early childhood professional organization, which deals with issues of children from birth to age eight and those who work with young children.

**National Council for Accreditation of Teacher Education (NCATE)**—an organization that accredits colleges, schools, or departments of education in higher education programs at the baccalaureate and advanced degree levels in the United States. It is a coalition of 35 professional associations.

**Child Development Associate (CDA)**—an early childhood teacher who has been assessed and successfully judged to be competent through the use of the national CDA credentialing program.

## INITIAL FEELINGS

Students can approach student teaching with mixed feelings. If you have dreamed of becoming a teacher for a long time, that dream will now become a reality. The challenge presents risks and unknowns, as well as opportunities for growth, insight, and increased self-awareness. Student teaching will be memorable. You will cherish and share with others this growth stage in your development as a person and teacher.

## THE MECHANICS OF STUDENT TEACHING

Student teaching in an early childhood program involves three key people: the student teacher, a cooperating teacher who is responsible for a group of young children, and a supervisor who is a college instructor or teacher trainer. The cooperating teacher models teaching techniques and practices, and both the supervisor and cooperating teacher observe and analyze the development of the student teacher's skills. They also serve as collaborators, mentors, consultants, and advisors. These three key people are more fully described as follows:

*Student Teacher:* A student experiencing a period of guided teaching, during which the student takes increasing responsibility for the work with a given group of learners over a period of consecutive weeks. Other terms used include *practicum student*, *apprentice*, and *intern*.

*Cooperating Teacher:* An experienced early childhood professional who works with a class of young children while serving as a mentor who collaborates, guides, and counsels a student teacher. A cooperating teacher also consults with an early childhood college supervisor, employed by an institution of higher education or another early childhood teacher-training program. Other terms used include *mentoring teacher*, *supervising teacher*, *laboratory school teacher*, *critic and teacher*, *master teacher*, *directing teacher*, and *resident teacher*.

*College/University Supervisor:* An early childhood educator in an institution of higher learning, or an educator conducting not-for-credit training, who instructs, guides, consults, collaborates, and supervises early childhood practicum students. This educator assesses student progress in attaining professional practice and standards. Other terms used include *early childhood adult educator*, *faculty supervisor*, *off-campus supervisor*, *resident supervisor*, *clinical teacher*, and *teacher trainer*. In some college training programs, two or more educators are responsible for a student teacher group.

## KEY PARTICIPANTS IN STUDENT TEACHER DEVELOPMENT

Personality, settings, child groupings, the commitment and professionalism of individuals, and many other factors contribute and influence the quality and variety of training opportunities. Key participants (student teacher, cooperating teacher, and supervisor) each play a role in student teacher development.

Each student teacher is responsible for serious effort. We have all met people who have a knack for getting everything possible from a given situation. Their "antennae" are actively searching, receiving, and evaluating. As a student teacher, you will guide much of your own growth. Your cooperating teacher and supervisor will support and reinforce your commitment to learn, but your increasing skill will depend, in part, on you.

As their first duty, cooperating teachers must fulfill the requirements of their positions; child instruction is paramount. Student teacher collaboration and guidance are additional tasks, for which a cooperating teacher may or may not be compensated. Even in laboratory school settings, educating and caring for children supersedes the training of student teachers, which is seen as an auxiliary function.

Cooperating teachers differ. One might place mentor teachers on a degree-of-control continuum, ranging from *highly directive* (high structure) to *collaborative* (unstructured) styles. Cooperating teachers falling nearer the unstructured end believe student teachers should be given considerable latitude as emerging professionals learning to make decisions on their own. These would promote collaboration and student ownership of problem solving. Directive-style cooperating teachers may choose to adopt a more unstructured mode as their student teacher becomes more competent in handling classroom responsibilities, or this may not happen at all, depending on the mentor teacher's dedication to a directive style.

Experienced cooperating teachers are effective when they collaborate and suggest their student teachers find alternative ways to solve classroom difficulties. By explaining their actions, techniques, and strategies (what was done and why), cooperating teachers promote student teacher growth. Added skill and insight may be obtained when a student teacher both observes classroom practice and participates in mentor/student discussions.

The supervisor's role includes being encouraging, understanding, sensitive, supportive, and responsive to the student's concerns, as well as being serious and rigorous in promoting each student teacher's attention to high, professional standards of performance and timely completion of responsibilities. Supervisors also plan, schedule, and conduct meeting times when practicum students can voice evolving ideas, discoveries, and insights. They may also serve as a mentor to a cooperating teacher, meeting with them periodically as well, to give supportive assistance and suggestions. End-of-term evaluations of student teachers, recommendation letters to school districts and other employers, final reviews of portfolios, sending recommendations to state certification agencies, and providing career counseling can be additional responsibilities and tasks. Most supervising educators are aware that although they are instrumental contributors to their student teacher's professional development, the student's cooperating teacher may be more influential.

## BEFORE PLACEMENTS

College and university departments, and individual college instructors (supervisors), develop guidelines for selecting placement sites long before the practicum begins. Decisions may be influenced by college, university, state or national standards, or by the NAEYC, the National Association of Early Childhood Teacher Educators (NAECTE), or the American Associate Degree Early Childhood Teacher's (ACCESS) recommendations, or by NAEYC's *Code of Ethical Conduct* (2005). (See the Appendix for a section of text from this document.) Some colleges and universities endeavor to canvass their community preschools, elementary schools, or child care centers to identify those meeting their training standards and designate these as certified practicum placement sites. Others exclusively select NAEYC-accredited child development programs. Decisions involve selection of the best training sites for students, considering the constraints involved in each situation. Selection criteria may depend on location, staff experience and training, licensing and accreditation of the placement site, state laws and guidelines, the willingness and ability of the site administrators and staff to carry out procedures and responsibilities, as well as other factors.

The student teacher should recognize that decisions concerning the number of placements per semester, quarter, or training period have already been established. In some communities, a wide variety of child classrooms are available and possible. In other areas, placement classrooms are few or limited.

Colleges and universities may offer early childhood education training programs that include coursework for diverse teaching specialties. School-age after-school care and infant/toddler teaching are two areas commonly provided within traditional early childhood or child development training programs. Some colleges and universities make student teacher placements in these settings and both private and public kindergartens and elementary school classrooms, where students assume assistant teacher or aide duties.

Student teaching classes are offered at baccalaureate degree–granting colleges and universities, both private and public. Students enrolled in these classes are completing coursework to fulfill state credentialing or certification requirements or to acquire an advanced degree, such as a master of arts degree. Student teachers at an elementary school primary grade level usually function as practicing teachers, with full responsibility for their assigned classrooms while under the supervision of their assigned cooperating teachers. Rarely do student teachers at the preschool or preprimary school level immediately assume full teaching responsibilities. More commonly, they gradually perform an increasing number of duties, program planning, and instruction, working their way up to taking on all teacher responsibilities while still under their cooperating teachers' supervision.

## The Currently Employed Student Teacher

Currently employed student teachers may be required to student teach in one or two different child facilities or classrooms. For the currently employed student teacher, the task of putting in unpaid hours at another center may seem an undue hardship, yet many will welcome the opportunity to gain additional competencies and they benefit from the professional consultation that occurs. Increasingly, students entering early childhood work start classes after employment.

## Health Concerns

You will need all the strength you can muster during your practicum; take care to monitor your health. Make getting enough sleep a priority. Many colleges offer free or low-cost health and psychological services to their students. Eating properly, exercising, and having time for fun (even if you are enjoying your classroom experience) is important. It is wise to correct minor health problems and schedule medical, dental, and eye examinations so they will not interrupt your practicum assignment.

Careful attention to hand washing while student teaching can help eliminate some of the germs encountered while working with children. It is not unusual to be exposed to common childhood illnesses and colds while student teaching. Taking time out during the day to relax may help you maintain balance. Some universities may provide informal meetings with other student teachers, to share thoughts and voice concerns regarding the student teaching experience. Close friends, family, and peers usually offer the opportunity to clarify thoughts and voice concerns. They may provide moral support and function as a cheering section.

## Learning and Growth

Being unique individuals, each student teacher has developed a unique learning style. Life and school experiences mold how you see yourself and how you proceed toward knowing and accomplishing new knowledge or skills. Hopefully, your student teaching class will offer diverse ways to learn and will also give structured aid in the form of clear guidelines and suggestions, by both your instructor and your cooperating teacher.

A portion of your time will be spent pondering what you have read and experienced. You will closely observe other adults in child classrooms to gauge the outcomes of their behaviors, but you will also need to become an avid watcher of yourself and of the reactions of others to you. Professional teaching requires continuous analysis, adjustment, and refocusing. Growth will build and proceed on what you already know as you take tentative and then firm steps in new directions.

Part of the joy of teaching is experimenting and inventing new approaches. These innovations should take into account whether they mesh with your basic

*Student Teacher Quote*—"I worked hard to get into this final class. My college supervisor insisted I student teach at a center other than my job at a private preschool, and I resented it. I'm so glad now because I realize I needed to see how another program functioned. I'm acquiring skills, getting great ideas, and really enjoy being part of a truly professional teaching team."

**Janice Washington, Evergreen Valley College Child Development Center, San Jose, CA**

conclusions, considering what is safe and developmentally appropriate for young children.

Most cooperating teachers and college supervisors were student teachers at the beginning of their own careers. Their feelings tend to be empathetic and supportive, while at the same time they expect a serious student attempt to develop competence.

The student teaching experience can be viewed as a miniature world or a human laboratory that will be full of memorable events including the ups and downs all student teachers experience. Ideally, every student comes to a clarification of self in relation to people and environments that are designed to provide quality care for young children. New insights concerning values, goals, cultures, self-realization, and other important life issues are examined.

**Student Teacher Progress** If the student completes student teaching duties and responsibilities successfully, the student receives recognition of teaching competency. Observation and analysis of the student's performance, followed by consultation with the teaching team, is an integral part of student teaching (see Figure 1–1).

How should student teachers view their progress and learning in a student teaching class? An early childhood or primary school classroom may be seen as a growing place for everyone, not only for the student teacher. Everyone who enters the classroom can grow from each experience. It is presumed that all adults—even the cooperating teacher and supervisor—are unfinished products. Each participant is viewed as a combination of strengths and talents, with the possibility of expanding.

## ORIENTATION

Orientation meetings may take place before your first working day, and may include meeting staff, taking a facility tour, reviewing oral and written school guidelines, and completing various forms. Not all schools provide a formal orientation. Making a conscious effort to remember people's names and taking notes is advisable. Remember, first impressions are important; be aware that your body language and what you wear will send messages to others.

Introductions and tours enable the student teacher to become familiar with people and settings, and help reduce anxieties (see Figure 1–2). Anxieties may

▶ **Figure 1-1**
Consulting with your cooperating teacher happens frequently in student teaching.

© Cengage Learning

▶ **Figure 1-2**
The school receptionist/
secretary is an important
staff member.

also increase when responsibilities and requirements are described. Supervisors and cooperating teachers require the completion of various assignments; keeping each in order may be accomplished by color coding or using different folders or binders. A date book or daily appointment calendar is also recommended because many important meetings, appointments, and deadlines will occur. As always, the newness, details, and the amount of information to read and remember may temporarily produce stress.

Notice the center's surroundings; look for uniqueness, and observe special features of the neighborhood and community. Observe the diversity of the placement classroom's attending children and families.

## Forms, Forms, Forms

Various written forms and guides will be available during orientations.

Possible supervisor guides and forms follow:

◆ practicum class guide sheet

◆ personal data sheet (see Figure 1–3)

◆ listing of student teacher responsibilities (see Figure 1–4)

◆ suggested tips (see Figure 1–5)

◆ forms used for assessment

Placement center forms and written materials may include family guides, policy statements, newsletters, center handbooks, and visitor and observer rules. Cooperating teachers may provide you with a student teacher assignment sheet, a responsibilities sheet, a daily schedule, children's named photographs (with pronunciation guides, if necessary), classroom rules, observation forms, staff meeting dates and times, and suggestions for guiding child behavior.

Many forms must be on file in a placement classroom before the student's first working day; the following forms are common to student teaching:

◆ student teacher sign-in sheets, to keep track of arrivals, departures, and volunteer and assigned work hours

◆ tuberculin (TB) clearance, which is mandatory in many states

◆ personal data or background form

◆ physical examination form or physician's report

▶ Figure 1-3
Personal data sheet example.

PERSONAL DATA SHEET

NAME _____

ADDRESS _____

PHONE _____ MESSAGE PHONE #_____ EMERGENCY PHONE_____

TRANSPORTATION (Car? Public transportation? Other?)

E-MAIL _____

HEALTH (Concerns you wish to share affecting your work) _____

EXPERIENCES WITH CHILDREN (past employment, volunteer, family, etc.)

_____

_____

_____

COLLEGE      year_____ major_____

**COURSES in early childhood major not presently completed**

_____

_____

**Previous college work related to student teaching**

_____

_____

Presently Employed_____ Where (optional)_____

Hours_____ Duties (optional)_____

_____

_____

SPECIAL INTERESTS

_____

_____

WHAT WOULD YOU LIKE YOUR COOPERATING TEACHER TO KNOW ABOUT YOU? _____

_____

IF YOU COULD CHOOSE YOUR PLACEMENT CLASSROOM, IT WOULD BE . . . . . . _____

_____

HOBBIES AND SPECIAL TALENTS OR SKILLS _____

_____

CAREER GOALS _____

_____

▶ **Figure 1-4**

Sample of student teacher responsibilities.

1. Be prompt and prepared.
2. If you are ill on your assigned days, call your supervisor and cooperating teacher as early as possible.
3. If you must be absent, phone ahead and let your school know you are unable to be there that day. Preferably, let the school know ahead of time if there will be an unavoidable absence during your student teaching assignment.
4. Remember, the cooperating teacher depends on your services as a fellow teacher.
5. Sign in and out if required.
6. Consult with your supervisor on lesson planning when help is needed.
7. Make an appointment with your supervisor to discuss class-related questions or problems.
8. Remember to avoid conversations that label children or deal with confidential information.
9. Sign in the lesson plan book at least one week in advance if your cooperating teacher or supervisor requests it.
10. Complete assignments.
11. Complete your student teacher file, and take it to the director's office as soon as possible. (Included in this file are TB clearance, personal data sheet, rating sheets, return envelope.)
12. Be sure to have your fingerprint card and background check completed prior to beginning your first observation and/or student teaching assignment.
13. Please see and do what needs to be done without direction. Ask questions. Assume as much teaching responsibility as you can handle.

▶ **Figure 1-5**

Sample of trainer's tips for student teacher's first days.

1. Get your TB and criminal background clearances to your center's director as soon as possible. (Note: This is not required in some states.)
2. Leave your belongings in the place provided.
3. Sign in.
4. Enter the children's room quietly, wearing your name tag.
5. Look for emergency room evacuation plans (posted on wall).
6. Consider child safety. Watch and listen for rules and expectations.
7. Actively involve yourself helping staff and children. See what needs to be done. Ask only what is necessary of staff after saying hello or introducing yourself. (Do not interrupt an activity. Wait until the cooperating teacher is free.)
8. Let the staff handle child behaviors that are puzzling on the first days.
9. Write down any questions concerning children, programs, and routines that baffle you, and discuss them with your supervisor.
10. If you are sick on your scheduled day, call both your supervisor and your cooperating teacher.
11. Keep a brief diary of your activities, feelings, perceptions, and the like. You may want to buy a pocket-sized notebook.

◆ criminal background clearance
◆ immunization records

## Criminal History and Background Check

An increasing number of states require a criminal history and background inquiry prior to field placement. All paid and volunteer staff members may be required to comply and receive clearance, which is then placed in the school's personnel files.

# ESTABLISHNG PROFESSIONAL RELATIONSHIPS

Student teachers who have not worked previously with young children in an employed or volunteer capacity will be establishing their first working relationships with other professionals and classroom adults. They become the newest members of an instructional team and may interact with allied support staff, administrators, specialists, consultants, families, community representatives, and other adults somehow connected to young children's health and welfare or facility maintenance. As beginning teachers, they soon realize the importance of others' contributions to a smoothly running and educationally appropriate classroom.

In attempting to set up positive relationships, student teachers may want to remark on an individual's skill or dedication. Compliments need to be real and specific, if used. Trumped up ones are transparent and recognized as false flattery. Explicit compliments pinpoint exactly what behaviors or actions were noticed and appreciated. Networking well with others is an important career skill. In any field of work, many workers lose their jobs not because they don't have job skills, but because they do not have the ability to get along with coworkers. Networking and building relationships requires the ability to communicate and work effectively with others whose beliefs, values, and ideas may differ from your own. It also means showing respect, withholding judgment, and being open-minded enough to listen thoughtfully. Being able to resolve work-related problems effectively with win-win outcomes also helps. Chapter 8 provides assistance in this area.

NAEYC's *Code of Ethical Conduct* (2005) includes Principle P-1.7, which speaks to an early childhood practitioner's development of relationships with children in his or her care. (See Figure 1–6.)

The time and energy a student teacher devotes to relationship building has benefits for both children and teachers. Focus your attention on your ability to create warm, comfortable, and friendly interactions with children. Provide personal attention, and be alert to individuality. Just being near and sitting calmly reassures some children who may not approach you until they feel safe in your presence. Smiling, laughing, telling a short humorous story, or sharing a silly picture may help (Schiller and Willis, 2008). Other more outgoing children will be curious to know more about a new teacher and will quickly initiate conversation. Gallagher and Mayer (2008) recommend that teachers should feel comfortable sharing what is personally important to them in their out-of-school lives while also gently probing children's feelings, family and life experiences, and interests.

Teachers carefully model social behaviors such as caring and concern for others, and use firmly established relationships to nurture children's social and emotional growth. They also find that well-established, positive relationships with children in their care diminish behavior problems, promote children's vocabulary development, promote children's expression of ideas, break down barriers between children and adults, relieve stress, promote children's well-being, and provide teachers with more insight into children's individual learning styles.

***Student Teacher Quote***—*"I memorized all the children's names the first week, and they are learning mine. Some are calling me Miss Valentine, but that's to be expected because I've made myself a heart-shaped name tag to help them remember."*

**May Valentine, Parent-Cooperative Preschool, Santa Clara, CA**

# BECOMING A PROFESSIONAL

Continuous learning is the mark of a professional in any occupational field (Machado & Reynolds, 2006). VanderVen (1988) defines an educator's professionalism as the ability to knowledgeably and competently make a sustained difference, to diagnose and analyze situations, to select the most appropriate interventions, to apply them skillfully, and to describe why they were selected.

You learned the term *transition* during your training. A planned transition intends to move children smoothly from one activity to another. You will move from being a professional student to being a professional educator. During student teaching, you are in a transforming phase of your career. The National Association

▶ **Figure 1-6**
Selected section of
NAEYC's *Code of Ethical
Conduct (2005).*

> **The National Association for the Education of Young Children. Washington, DC.**
>
> P-1.7 We shall strive to build individual relationships with each child; make individualized adaptations in teaching strategies, learning environments, and curricula; and consult with the family so that each child benefits from the program. If after such efforts have been exhausted, the current placement does not meet a child's needs, or the child is seriously jeopardizing the ability of other children to benefit from the program, we shall collaborate with the child's family and appropriate specialists to determine the additional services needed and/or the placement option(s) most likely to ensure the child's success. (Aspects of this principle may not apply in programs that have a lawful mandate to provide services to a particular population of children.) p. xvii
>
> **SOURCE:** Feeney, S., & Freeman, N.K. (2005). Ethics and the early childhood educator. Washington, DC: National Association for the Education of Young Children.

**professional ethics—**beliefs regarding appropriate occupational behavior and conduct as defined and accepted by recognized professionals in that occupation.

**practitioner—**person engaged in the practice of a profession or occupation, in this case, early childhood education. Other terms used: educator, teacher, assistant teacher, infant educator, aide, student teacher.

for the Education of Young Children has provided help to smooth your transition with two important published guides, *The Code of Ethical Standards and Statement of Commitment* (Feeney & Freeman, 2005) and *Preparing Early Childhood Professionals: NAEYC's Standards for Programs* (Hyson, 2003), which identifies standards for associate, baccalaureate, masters, and doctoral programs leading to advanced degrees. The first book presents professional parameters for responsible and ethical educator behavior. (See a sample section of the code of conduct in Figure 1–7.) Professionals regard this as a necessary guide for professional conduct and **professional ethics** invaluable to all in the career field. If you can count on one thing during your practicum experience, it will be to face unexpected decisions, dilemmas, and situations daily, which will test your professional resolve to do the right thing. You will encounter many types of diversity and a wide variety of behaviors and conditions.

The second book is the product of NAEYC's accreditation efforts, and contains clear descriptions of what teacher training programs in institutions of higher learning attempt to accomplish with their early childhood graduates. In addition, we suggest you obtain a copy of your state's standards for early childhood teacher licensing and/or certification and study them. The volumes listed above can serve as reference books in your developing professional library.

You may become a different type of professional educator than your classmates. Your diversity, gifts, talents, career accomplishments, and training program will have produced a professional educator of a unique sort. Although standards are designed to promote quality and excellence in graduating teacher candidates, they are not used to create cookie-cutter teachers—just the outstanding ones that children deserve. Extra attention to teacher or **practitioner** conduct is required, because of the impressionable vulnerability of young children, and the influence a teacher may have with families. Bobinski (2008) notes that student teachers who view their work as an opportunity to make a difference in children's lives become result-focused professionals who are often seen as "movers and shakers."

When you reach the level of student teaching, others presume you have a certain amount of educational background and some degree of professional skill. Some families may feel you are an expert in child-rearing and may try to seek your opinion on a wide variety of developmental issues. You will need to direct these people to

## SECTION 1 ETHICAL RESPONSIBILITIES TO CHILDREN

*Ideals*

**1-1.1**—To be familiar with the knowledge base of early childhood care and education and to stay informed through continuing education and training.

**1-1.2**—To base program practices upon current knowledge and research in the field of early childhood education, child development, and related disciplines, as well as on particular knowledge of each child.

**1-1.3**—To recognize and respect the unique qualities, abilities, and potential of each child.

**1-1.4**—To appreciate the vulnerability of children and their dependence on adults.

**1-1.5**—To create and maintain safe and healthy settings that foster children's social, emotional, cognitive, and physical development and that respect their dignity and their contributions.

and

**1-1.8**—To support the right of each child to play and learn in an inclusive environment that meets the needs of children with and without disabilities.

**1-1.9**—To advocate for and ensure that all children, including those with special needs, have access to the support services needed to be successful.

**1-1.10**—To ensure that each child's culture, language, ethnicity, and family structure are recognized and valued in the program.

**1-1.11**—To provide all children with experiences in a language that they know, as well as support children in maintaining the use of their home language and in learning English.

**SOURCE:** Feeney, S., & Freeman, N.K. (2005). Ethics and the early childhood educator. Washington, DC: National Association for the Education of Young Children.

your cooperating teacher, who may refer them to the director or other staff, who in turn may refer them to professionally trained individuals or community resources.

**Confidentiality** protects children and families, and should be maintained at all times. Staff meetings and individual conferences are conducted in a spirit of mutual interest and concern for the welfare of everyone involved as well as for the center's high standards. At such conferences, student teachers are privy to personal information that should not be discussed elsewhere. This point needs to be stressed. Student teachers can become so involved with classroom happenings and individual children that they inadvertently discuss privileged information with a fellow student teacher or friend, or in earshot of a parent or another individual. One can easily see how this might happen—and cause irreparable damage. Classes of student teachers are frequently reminded by their instructors that actual child and family names cannot be used in class discussions.

The student teacher's appearance, clothing, and grooming contribute to a professional image. Take your cues from observing what other staff wear. Fortunately, comfortable and functional clothing that allows a student teacher to perform duties without worry or hindrance is relatively inexpensive (see Figure 1–8). Many supervisors suggest a pocketed smock or apron and a change of shoes.

**confidentiality**—
requirement that results in evaluations and assessments be shared with only the parents and appropriate school personnel.

▶ **Figure 1-8**
Casual clothing is acceptable in most classrooms.

© Cengage Learning

## Responsibilities

A clear picture of the responsibilities of the student teacher, cooperating teacher, and supervisor will help students make decisions about handling specific incidences as professionals. As a general rule, it is better to ask for help than to proceed in any questionable situation that goes beyond your responsibilities and duties (barring emergency situations that call for immediate action).

Your main responsibilities at the beginning of your practicum experience are:

◆ prompt arrival

◆ reliable attendance

◆ active participation

◆ completion of assigned duties

◆ decision making based on knowledge of best practices

◆ working with minimal direction, but consulting when in doubt

◆ working as a supportive and caring team member

Some college student teacher programs require their student teachers to sign a student teacher contract that lists responsibilities and expectations. High on the list is student commitment to growth, quality, excellence, and dedication to improvement of present career skills.

## Exposure to Blood–borne Pathogens

You will be instructed at your placement site about exposure to potentially infectious materials and substances, such as children's blood, as well as skin, eye, and mucous membrane secretions, and will be provided with protective gloves and equipment. If a classroom situation occurs, a mentor teacher will usually prefer to handle the incident. Discuss this with your cooperating teacher. Privacy laws protect families who decide not to disclose child conditions; therefore, it is wise to follow exposure guidelines strictly.

It is suggested that each student teacher consult his or her private physician regarding the advisability of hepatitis B vaccination.

## Distance Learning

A growing number of colleges offer teaching practica using satellite locations and electronically monitored classroom placements. Packaged course content may be provided and accessed through the Internet, by interactive television, compact discs, or some other technological vehicle. Students may conference with their college supervisors by phone, e-mail, Internet chat, periodic face-to-face meetings, or by other means and arrangements. Some distance learning classes have evolved with unique features that attempt to promote a quality student teaching experience in rural settings. Distance learning often makes study available at any hour of the day or night and at nontraditional campus locations. It is becoming commonplace to keep in touch with one's college supervisor by computer or through video conferencing.

## STUDENT TEACHING GOALS

The most important goal of student teaching is to gain professional teaching competence. The acquisition of skills allows the completion of training and new or continued employment. Specific objectives vary, but they generally are concerned with understanding children, planning and providing quality programs for children and families, acquiring technical teaching skills, and personal and professional development. Individual **goals** reflect each student teacher's idea of professional conduct and skill, and how each feels about the kind of teacher and person he or she would like to become.

You will probably begin by working to establish a collaborative and cordial relationship with your cooperating teacher and your supervisor. You will meet and exchange ideas and concerns; accept the suggestions, advice, and the supportive assistance each provides to aid your professional growth.

Becoming a reflective educator is another objective. Understanding family circumstances and discovering what families want for their children's education are others. The prime concern of many student teachers is their personal goal of developing confidence in their teaching abilities.

**goals**—overall, general overviews of what student teachers expect to gain from the practicum experience.

## Student Teacher Observational Record Keeping

Prior to your student teaching class, you completed coursework covering methods, techniques, and observational strategies. It is time to review that material now because you will be watching and listening to children closely. You will be focusing on how your behavior and actions affect individual children or the total child group. Remember that children's nonverbal messages are as important as their verbal ones; you will be constantly alert to new and repeated behaviors as well as puzzling ones.

Busy cooperating teachers are usually quite interested in daily observations and accounts of child incidents and happenings written by student teachers. It gives cooperating teachers an outside opinion of what's going on in the classroom. This may be the first perception shared by another concerning child behavior the cooperating teacher is trying to trace or evaluate. You may want to take notes and keep records concerning child behaviors. The cooperating teacher may assign more lengthy observation exercises. Anecdotes are jotted down quickly, with the date and time, unlike records of accidents, injuries, or illnesses noted during the day, which are detailed in a specific format for school records. Each site has its own specific form to use. Student notes are confidential and should be guarded closely, as one can easily understand the danger of them lying around.

## Student Journals (Logs)

Many training programs require the student teacher to begin a **journal** or log of experiences and feelings. This is sometimes called a *reflective journal* (Hillman, 2006).

Supervisors periodically monitor journal entries or student audio or video recordings to keep on top of student growth, work actions, concerns, feelings, questions, and needs. It is suggested that student teachers make at least one, 5-minute daily entry, written or typed, on participation days, while impressions are still fresh. Some college supervisors provide suggestions for recorded topics.

Other supervisors may assign journal questions that require analyzing and reflecting to be answered during the practicum period (Hillman, 2006).

In journaling, students jot down reflections and opinions that are based on their evolving knowledge. One purpose of journaling is to have student teachers focus on themselves as learners. Student teachers can wonder, question, celebrate insights, describe setbacks, generate ideas, and keep track of their growth as teachers. Supervisors may suggest that students write in their journals on the right two-thirds of the page, so supervisors or cooperating teachers can dialogue with them in the left-hand space. Journal entries can use a variety of formats; some are dated in left-hand margins, some are handwritten, while others are electronic.

Reading assignment reactions may also be recorded in journals, if supervisors so request. Time required either to write or react to journal entries may be built into training class seminars.

**journal**—a written, pictorial, or audio record of experiences, occurrences, observations, feelings, questions, work actions, reflective thoughts, and other happenings during student teaching.

When college supervisors comment in their student's journals and give supportive assistance or encouragement, a journal becomes a communication device and promotes shared understandings and intimacy. Log entries are sometimes included when student teachers develop professional career portfolios, which will be mentioned later in this chapter.

# PREPARING FOR YOUR FIRST DAY

Before your first day of student teaching, you have been given your cooperating teacher's name and the school's address, and you may have attended orientation meetings for student teaching. Your first working day is near. You have either an on-campus or off-campus child center or school assignment. If your soon-to-be students live off-campus, a stroll through the neighborhood will help you discover something about them. Observe the community, its businesses, its recreation, its uniqueness, and do not overlook the opportunity to observe resources for planning child activities. Perhaps a construction site is an interesting possibility for a field trip, or an orchard or park holds treasures to be discovered.

With an on-campus laboratory school placement, you may have previously participated in the children's program and perhaps completed observation assignments. The center and its staff and children may be familiar. Take a new look at the campus and the resources of the campus community.

If you have been asked to meet with the director or principal at an off-campus school, call to make an appointment. Plan to have the meeting at least 15 minutes to a half hour before you are scheduled to be in the classroom. Ask about available staff parking. Remember to avoid family parking spots or drop-off areas.

It is time to dust off the resource idea files and books you have collected during your training, because you may be using them to plan activities. Choose a short activity to offer on your first day, even if one has not been assigned. Brush up on finger plays or short songs that may be used as fill-ins or *transitions*. If you do not have them memorized, put them on cards that can slip into your pocket. It is important for you to be prepared to step in with an activity if you are asked to do so (see Figure 1–9).

Some good ideas for first-day activities that have worked well for other student teachers include:

- ◆ a name tag–making activity
- ◆ a puppet who tells a short story about his name, introduces the student teacher's name, and wants to know the children's names
- ◆ a favorite book or short audio recording to discuss
- ◆ an art or craft activity that uses children's names
- ◆ a collage or chart that shows interesting things about a student teacher's life
- ◆ a flannel board activity
- ◆ a game made by the student teacher that involves children's names and places in their community
- ◆ a beanbag activity that uses children's names
- ◆ a new song or movement activity
- ◆ a storytelling experience
- ◆ a tape recording of school or neighborhood sounds to guess and discuss

## Last-Minute Preparations

Activities that can be easily carried and set up quickly work best. Get the necessary materials together the night before your class. If you received a set of classroom rules and a schedule of routines and planned activities, study it beforehand.

▶**Figure 1-9**
You will want to plan an activity that captures student attention.

Think about clothing. Make sure you wear something comfortable and appropriate. A smock, shirt, or apron with a pocket will hold a small notebook, pen, tissues, and other small necessities. You should wear shoes that will protect your toes and help you maintain balance and speed on the playground.

## BECOMING PART OF THE CLASSROOM STAFF

There probably will be time for a smile and a few quick words with your cooperating teacher your first day. Your introduction to the children can wait until a planned group time. Introduce yourself briefly to other classroom adults when you are in close proximity. Your cooperating teacher may ask that you observe instead of participate. This will give you time to scan the classroom environment and play areas and become familiar with classroom rules and schedules, which are usually posted in young children's classrooms. Next, focus on child behaviors and planned child instruction. Otherwise, actively participate in supervising and interacting with the children. Pitch in with any teaching or assistant tasks. Wear a provided or self-made name tag. Don't worry about looking busy, but rather, be friendly and responsive. If time permits and you are duty-free, sit with or near children to reassure and build trust.

Ask questions when necessary, but try not to interrupt your cooperating teacher. Jot down other questions on a note pad that you carry with you. Judge where you are the most needed. Do not worry about assuming too much responsibility; your cooperating teacher will let you know if you are overstepping your duties. New student teachers tend to hold back and wait to be directed. Put yourself in the teacher's place. Where would the teacher direct you to supervise or assist children when he or she is busy with other work? Periodically scan the room to determine where you can be the most useful.

### Computers

Many classrooms have multiple computers and software available. Usually, computers in child areas have rules and require adult supervision. Prepare yourself by learning operational procedures when you have no supervision responsibilities.

Preview child programs before or after class sessions, after first consulting with your cooperating teacher.

Ask your cooperating teacher if a school password is necessary if you are asked to enter student data. Some classrooms require student teachers to do digital record keeping.

## Supplies

Familiarize yourself with storage areas to minimize the need to ask questions about the location of equipment and supplies. Make your inspection when you are free from room supervision (see Figure 1–10). Become familiar with yard storage, also. During team meetings, inquire about your use of supplies for planned activities.

## Child Records

**allergies**—physiological reactions to environmental or food substances that can affect or alter behavior.

While some early childhood centers allow student teachers access to child and family records, others do not. Knowing as much as possible about each child increases the quality of your interaction. Confidentiality is expected. If a review takes place, take note of any child **allergies**, specific interests, or special needs.

Emergency information, children's health histories, attendance data, court orders, observation records, assessments, test results, conference notes, and other information may be included in children's files.

More commonly, cooperating teachers or directors will informally alert you to the special needs or circumstances, prohibitions, health-related conditions, and the individual particulars of attending children: in other words, everything you need to know.

## Emergency Procedures

Acquaint yourself with the location and use of first aid supplies. For emergencies such as fire and earthquake, familiarize yourself with procedures and posted evacuation plans showing exit routes and evacuation areas. Most states require that plans be posted. Enforce all classroom health and safety rules. If you have any questions regarding health and safety, be sure to note them for discussion.

▶ **Figure 1–10**
Do you know where sleeping cots are stored after naptime?

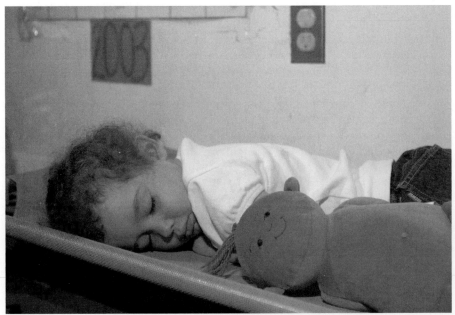

© Cengage Learning

## Opening Procedures and Activities

Become aware of how children and parents are greeted on arrival. What room activities or choices are available for child exploration at arrival time? A keen observer will notice which children separate and make the transition from family to center with ease, and which classroom adults contribute to the classroom's welcoming atmosphere or tone.

## Dismissal Procedures

Become aware that each center or school has a policy regarding adults who can remove a child from the classroom at a session's close or at any other time. You should not release children to arriving adults. Authorized adults are identified in children's records when families enroll their children. Releasing children is your cooperating teacher's responsibility. In most schools, adults coming to pick up children are directed to talk with the child's teacher before exiting. Because of security concerns, people authorized to pick up children may have to have special badges or security cards.

In today's society, some families may consist of a variety of related or unrelated individuals and children. Because of problems that exist between single or divorced parents or other family factors, court-issued restraining orders can affect who is authorized to pick up a child.

## Knowing the Program Well

Cooperating teachers overwhelmingly state that they appreciate student teachers who are watchful and learn room and program particulars quickly. This is difficult for new student teachers unless they consciously endeavor to discover the lay of the land. Figure 1–11 attempts to help you focus on aspects of the classroom, program, procedures, and interactions with children.

**▶ Figure 1-11**
Knowing Your Classroom

**Facilities**

Where are materials and supplies stored?

Are storage areas organized?

Where are exits? How do windows open, lights work, temperature controls operate? How do doors open?

What is the classroom layout? Are there recognized traffic patterns?

What school area or rooms have specific functions? House particular staff?

What is the play yard's appearance, equipment, built-ins?

Where are the safety controls, fire extinguisher, alarm, etc.?

Is any safety hazard apparent?

Are there special building features for individuals with special needs?

Where are emergency health supplies? Who is authorized to administer first aid?

**Children**

What individual physical characteristics are apparent?

What is the multicultural composition of the group?

What activities are popular?

Can all children in the room be viewed from one spot in the room? Do all children seem to lose themselves in play?

What kinds of play exist? Is it solitary, cooperative, or some other kind of play?

(continues)

▶ **Figure 1-11** (continued)

What languages are spoken?

Does any child seem uncomfortable with adults?

What seems to be the group's general interest, general behavior? Are there any children who need an abundance of teacher attention? Are there any children with special needs?

**Teaching Behaviors and Interactions**

Are children "with" teachers?

How is guidance of child behavior undertaken?

Are all children supervised?

What style of teaching seems apparent?

Are feelings of warmth and acceptance of individuality shown? If you were a child in this room, how might you feel?

Do teachers show enthusiasm?

**Program**

Does an atmosphere exist where children and teachers share decision-making and show respect for individual differences?

Are children exploring with teachers more often than being directed by them?

What are the planned activities?

Is there small group or large group instruction?

Is it a developmentally appropriate program?

How do activities begin and end?

Is the program based on child interest?

Does lots of dialogue exist among children? And among children and adults?

Are the children "tuned in" or "out"?

How are children moved from one activity to the next?

**Overall First Impressions**

What immediate questions would you like answered about the classroom? What emotions have occurred as you observed?

What were your first impressions of the classroom?

## Pitfalls

It is not unusual for the student teacher to acquire some inappropriate habits unconsciously. It helps to be aware of these pitfalls in advance. During work time, avoid having extended social conversations or small talk with other adults. This can happen when a student teacher seeks the company of other adults as a source of support. Use your breaks for this purpose if necessary.

Do not discuss children with other adults in the child's presence. Avoid the tendency to label children, and save questions for staff meetings. Realize gossip benefits no one and is unprofessional.

## THE EARLY DAYS

First impressions are important. Show initiative, be alert to the total classroom, listen closely, try to be self-directed, and, if the situation calls for it, take action. Your natural enthusiasm and life-is-an-adventure attitude will be catching. Display your caring nature and positive attitude toward child accomplishment. Smile and make eye contact with children frequently.

## After-Session Staff Conferencing

After the critical issues have been discussed at team meetings, the cooperating teacher and other staff may be interested in the questions and impressions you have gathered. Be prepared to rely on your notes or journal; they are useful in refreshing your memory. Think of team conferences as debriefings, where participants compare ideas, hypothesize, reflect, and make assumptions calling for the cognitive processing of information.

This meeting is also an appropriate time to clarify your cooperating teacher's expectations during your next few workdays. If a class calendar and weekly activity sheet are available, these will aid your activity planning. Most schools have their own systems for planning activities. You may be asked to schedule your own activities at least a week in advance, on a written plan. The cooperating teacher may want you to stay within the planned subject areas or may give you a wide choice.

## BECOMING A TEAM MEMBER

Become aware of each staff member's function and contribution to the operation of your assigned classroom. Support staff efforts may be connected to the realization of the center's goals (see Figure 1–12).

In addition to your own growth and development, one of your major goals as a team member is to add to the quality of young children's experiences. This involves teamwork. Teamwork takes understanding, dedication, and skill. Your status and acceptance as a member of the team will be gained through your own efforts.

**Team teaching** involves and includes those people employed or connected to the daily operation of an early childhood center who work to achieve the goals of that

> **team teaching**—an approach that involves co-teaching, in which status and responsibility are equal rather than having a pyramid structure of authority, with one person in charge and others subordinate.

▶ **Figure 1-12**
Checklist of nonteaching support staff.

Do the following staff members exist at your placement center?

|  | Yes | No | Names |
|---|---|---|---|
| 1. Clerical staff | _____ | _____ | _____ |
| 2. Food service personnel | _____ | _____ | _____ |
| 3. Maintenance staff | _____ | _____ | _____ |
| 4. Bus drivers | _____ | _____ | _____ |
| 5. Community liaisons | _____ | _____ | _____ |
| 6. Health or nutrition staff | _____ | _____ | _____ |
|  |  |  | _____ |
| 7. Consultants or specialists | _____ | _____ | _____ |
|  |  |  | _____ |
| 8. Classroom aides | _____ | _____ | _____ |
| 9. Volunteers | _____ | _____ | _____ |
| 10. Others | _____ | _____ | _____ |
| **In what capacity?** | _____ | _____ | _____ |

center. They include paid and volunteer staff and parents. Understanding the duties and responsibilities of each team member will help you function in your role.

## GOALS OF THE TEAM AND PROGRAM

Joint planning with your cooperating teacher is crucial to your success and competency growth. Team spirit is enhanced when your efforts reinforce or strengthen classroom program goals and aid the efforts of other members.

Inadvertently, some student teachers may tend to emphasize what they feel is the superiority of their college's training. Teaching methods, materials, staffing, and just about every school feature may differ from what was experienced in the college's training program. It may take a while for the student to realize that community programs have fewer resources, tighter budgets, and perhaps less expertise. Sensitivity is necessary, along with an open mind. It is commendable to be enthusiastic and idealistic but also to appreciate the cleverness and ingenuity many developmentally appropriate centers display while operating on limited funding and resources.

### Team Meetings

Team meetings often include only the staff members associated with child instruction. Because staff meetings are new to student teachers, they are full of learning opportunities. Attend staff meetings if your student teaching schedule permits; the extra time involved will be well spent.

To make these meetings as successful as possible, and to make them work for you, there are several things you can do before, during, and after the meeting. Before a meeting, mark your calendar and obtain an agenda, if it exists. Study it and jot down any questions or notes, and try to identify the meeting's purpose. Arrive on time for meetings, and stay for the whole thing if possible. Bring writing materials. During the meeting, record comments concerning your classroom work. At first, participate as a listener until you discern if contributing is appropriate. Watch and learn from staff interactions. Notice that team members help others reach their individual objectives. Take note if another expresses an individual preference in teaching tasks.

After the meeting, mark your calendar with future meeting dates, including times and places. Complete any tasks assigned, and be prepared to discuss these if asked.

The more understanding you possess concerning individual and group dynamics, the better prepared you will be to function as an effective team member. As you become a part of the group, it is highly likely that your initial thoughts and feelings will change.

Ask yourself the following questions:

- ◆ Do common bonds exist?
- ◆ Was satisfaction of individual needs apparent?
- ◆ Is there shared responsibility in achieving group goals?
- ◆ Was group problem solving working?
- ◆ Are members open and trusting?
- ◆ Are individual roles clear?
- ◆ Did you notice cooperation?
- ◆ Do members know each others' strengths?
- ◆ Was the meeting dominated by one or a few?

### Staff Behaviors

A number of behaviors may be exhibited during staff interactions. Some of these can be evaluated as positive team behaviors, because they move a team toward the completion of tasks and the handling of responsibilities. The following is a summary of supportive and positive staff behaviors:

- giving or seeking information; asking for or providing factual or substantiated data
- contributing new ideas, solutions, or alternatives
- seeking or offering opinions to solve the task or problem
- piggybacking, elaborating, or stretching another's idea or suggestion; combining ideas
- coordinating activities
- emphasizing or reminding the group of the task at hand
- evaluating by using professional standards
- motivating staff to reach decisions
- bringing meeting to a close and reviewing goals; making sure everyone understands the expected outcome
- recording group ideas and progress

Individual staff members sometimes exhibit attitudes and sensitivities that soothe and mediate opposing points of view. Some examples follow:

- encouraging, praising, respecting, and accepting diverse ideas or viewpoints
- reconciling disagreements and offering a light touch of humor to help relieve tension
- compromising
- establishing open lines of communication
- drawing input from silent members
- monitoring dominance of discussions

Student teachers increasingly find that teaching teams contain differing cultural viewpoints. In situations where communicating across cultures takes place, Delpit (1995) suggests careful listening to alternative viewpoints:

> To do so requires a very special kind of listening, listening that requires not only open eyes and ears, but open hearts and minds. We really do not see through our eyes or hear through our ears, but through our beliefs. To put our beliefs on hold is to cease to exist as ourselves for a moment—and that is not easy, but it is the only way to learn what it might feel like to be someone else and the only way to start the dialogue.

As a student teacher, you may have a clearer picture of the student teacher/cooperating teacher relationship than you do of your professional relationship with the assistant teacher, aide, or family. Usually, student teachers, aides, and volunteers work under the direction of a cooperating teacher who makes the ultimate decisions regarding the workings of the classroom. Moving from assistant to fellow teacher, a student teacher assumes greater responsibility as time passes. Because of the changing role and increasing responsibilities, clear communication is a necessity. When one becomes an employed teacher, one becomes legally responsible for the direction of other adults in the classroom. This is a form of protection for enrolled children.

## Continuing to Observe

Observe the unique characteristics of enrolled children, constantly monitor their behaviors, and conjecture causes for behaviors and their underlying needs (see Figure 1–13). Unconsciously or consciously, you will begin to sort children into loose groupings that may change daily, in an almost unlimited number of ways. More noticeable characteristics will be the first to be recognized, but as you gain additional experience, subtle differences and similarities will also appear.

You will experience differing emotions with each child as you observe and interact with children in the class. Many of the children will become memorable, as children in your first class, the ones who taught you something about all children, or something about yourself.

▶**Figure 1-13**
You will come to know each child as an individual.

## Family Contacts

Family members may wonder who you are or immediately accept you as another adult classroom worker. Read their faces and introduce yourself if they seem interested. Be friendly and open rather than talkative. Mention your student teacher status and your training program. Remember, in this meeting as in all others you are representing the early childhood teaching profession.

Every classroom has a *feeling tone*; that is, it projects a certain atmosphere that creates feelings and perceptions in the minds and hearts of those who enter. Your classroom, no doubt, was designed and furnished with children in mind but may include a family corner or an area designed to make visitors feel welcome.

In today's busy world, some families will look rushed and anxious to get their children out the door. Others you observe will take time to touch base with their children and teachers before leaving. All families will appreciate your knowing the location of their child's belongings and what needs to be taken home, and also your aid in promoting the child's transition back into their care. Activities planned for pick-up times should allow children to easily stop and finish.

## Professional Portfolio Development

**professional portfolio**—a representative collection of your student teacher accomplishments.

Many training programs required their student teachers to put together a representative collection of their training accomplishments, called a **professional portfolio**. Wolf and Dietz (1998) define a teaching portfolio as follows:

> A teaching portfolio is a structured collection of teacher and student work created across diverse contexts over time, framed by reflection and collaboration that has as its ultimate aim the advancement of teacher and student learning.

A student teacher portfolio is not a miscellaneous collection but rather selected items, records, and documentation of student teacher growth, progress toward goals, and attainment of professional standards. It represents a student teacher's accomplishments and teaching effectiveness. Training programs hope developing a portfolio will help student teachers become more reflective and therefore will improve their classroom practice. Other advantages can be the recognition of a student teacher's past performance compared to present skills and identified future growth areas. Input and interactions with college supervisors and cooperating teachers are sometimes included in a portfolio.

The portfolio represents who you are, what skills and competencies you possess, and what experiences occurred during your training. Often a completed portfolio is a graduation requirement.

An examination of portfolio materials should enable a supervisor, staff member, or another person to raise questions and draw inferences about the portfolio's owner. The owner's assumptions of how young children learn, what the educator values, how children should spend their time, and the ways in which the educator and children should interact should be apparent. Items selected should emphasize quality, not quantity.

Portfolio entries should reflect the desired teacher competencies your training program hopes to have promoted and produced by the end of your training program. Many associate degree training programs use the NAEYC's (2007) standards or The Council for Professional Recognition's (2006) CDA competency standards to guide their training program's desired student teacher outcomes. A comparison of these two standards is seen in Figure 1–14.

A portfolio may also include before and after features, or may display specialized student talents and abilities. It can include a vast number of diverse visual, audio, electronic, and written evidence, such as:

◆ statement of educational philosophy or mission

◆ a supervisor's comments, observations, evaluations, or ratings

◆ letters of recommendation from supervisors, instructors, mentors, fellow staff members, parents, and others

◆ thematic units of study, projects, or activities

◆ examples of child work and case studies

◆ photographs of such things as developed room centers, and so on

▶ **Figure 1-14**
A Comparison of Standards.

**NAEYC STANDARDS**

**1. Promoting child development and learning**

Well-prepared early childhood professionals understand what young children are like; understand what influences their development, and use this understanding to create great environments where all children can thrive. This standard emphasizes knowledge of the range of influences on child development—including cultural contexts, economic conditions, health status, and learning styles—and an ability to apply knowledge to improve social interaction, assessment and more.

**2. Building family and community**

Well-prepared early childhood professionals understand and value children's families and communities, create respectful, reciprocal relationships; and involve all families in their children's development and learning. This standard emphasizes that respectful relationships with all families – whatever their structure, language, ethnicity, and child's ability or disability – are the foundation of early childhood education.

**3. Observing, documenting, and assessing**

Well-prepared early childhood professionals understand the purposes of assessment; use effective assessment strategies; and use assessment responsibly to positively influence children's development and learning. Good assessment practices measure what is developmentally and educationally significant in order to guide decisions about curriculum and instruction.

**4. Teaching and learning**

Well-prepared early childhood professionals build close relationships with children and families; use developmentally effective teaching and learning strategies; understand content areas and academic subjects; and use their knowledge to give all children the experiences that promote comprehensive development and learning. Teaching and learning are at the heart of teacher preparation, and the elements of this standard reflect the highly interconnected nature of early development and learning.

(continues)

▶ **Figure 1-14** (continued)

### 5. Becoming a professional

Well-prepared early childhood professionals identify themselves with the early childhood profession; use ethical, professional standards; demonstrate self-motivated ongoing learning; collaborate; think reflectively and critically; and advocate for children, families, and the profession. Early childhood professionals provide one of the most important services to society; they must understand and cultivate their role as professionals doing critical work.

### CDA SUBJECT AREAS

**Subject Area 1: Planning a safe, healthy learning environment.** Safety, first aid, health, nutrition space planning, materials and equipment, play, etc.

**Subject Area 8: Principles of child development and learning.** Developmental milestones from birth through age 5, cultural influences on development.

**Subject Area 4: Strategies to establish productive relationships with families.** Parent involvement, home visits, conferences, referrals, etc.

**Subject Area 5: Strategies to manage an effective program operation.** Planning, record keeping, reporting, etc.

**Subject Area 7: Observing and recording children's behavior.** Tools and strategies for objective information collection, etc.

**Subject Area 2: Steps to advance children's physical and intellectual development.** Large and small muscle, language and literacy, discovery, art, music.

**Subject Area 3: Positive ways to support children's social and emotional development.** Self-esteem, independence, self-control, socialization.

**Subject Area 6: Maintaining a commitment to professionalism.** Advocacy, ethical practice, work force issues professional associations, etc.

**Council For Professional Recognition**

2460 16th Street, NW, Washington DC 20009-3575
Business 202-265-9090 800-424-4310
Fax. No. 202-265-9161

♦ sample lesson plans and outcomes

♦ examples of developing specializations

♦ certificates for CPR or first aid, awards, and other commendations

♦ examples of individualized instruction and individual learning plans

♦ conference attendance documentation or other professional activities

♦ accreditation activities

♦ examples of self-created classroom instructional materials

♦ college transcripts and certification test results

♦ evidence or documentation that displays teaching ability or competency and the fulfillment of standards

The format of portfolios differs from one institution to another, but written materials usually include *articulation of learning outcomes*, *reflections* or related experience, and *documentation*.

Some training programs review portfolios at college exit interviews, and also suggest their student graduates use them when appropriate during job interviews. Most often a portfolio is used to facilitate, highlight, and chart student teaching competency, ongoing growth, and a student's ability to use accepted, current, and professional learning theories and actually apply them in daily practice.

## Electronic Portfolios

Electronic portfolios, often referred to as e-portfolios, work the same as traditional portfolios but may contain photographs and many other types of visuals and audio besides text. This can increase portfolio readability when flow isn't interrupted. A student teacher needs diverse technological skills including computer skill and familiarity with software, a digital camera, and a scanner in order to design, create, organize and edit competency documentation. E-portfolios are space savers that can store large amounts of information that can be easily distributed and duplicated. The hyperlink feature common to e-portfolios makes navigating through them quite easy and efficient. Their nonlinear structure means support documentation can be virtually attached where appropriate, without comprising the overall continuity (Jones & Shelton, 2006). A good website to use if one is compiling an e-portfolio is *http://electronicportfolios.com/* because it includes step-by-step instructions.

## Getting Organized

Suggestions for managing the multiple tasks and projects assigned in student teaching follow:

- ◆ Plan 1 week in advance.
- ◆ Color-code project folders.
- ◆ Decide what is (1) important and urgent, (2) important but not urgent, (3) not important but necessary, and (4) not important and not urgent.
- ◆ Work on only one thing at a time.
- ◆ Narrow focus by working on parts of a task.
- ◆ Gather resources and bring tasks to closure.

## ▶ SUMMARY

The practicum teaching experience is a culminating step in a training sequence for early childhood teachers. Three key participants—the student teacher, the cooperating teacher, and the supervisor—form a team, enabling the student teacher to gain new skills and sharpen previously acquired teaching techniques.

Student teaching involves the integration of all former training and experience. The cooperating teacher and supervisor guide, model, mentor, observe, collaborate, and analyze the student teacher's progress in an assigned classroom as the student teacher assumes greater responsibilities with children. Initial orientation meetings, and written requirements and guidelines, acquaint the student teacher with expectations and requirements. The student teaching experience is unique to each training institution, yet placement in a classroom for a supervisor's analysis of professional competency is common to all.

A caring, supportive atmosphere helps each student teacher attain professional educator skills, based on accepted ethics and standards, and helps develop the student teacher's personal style and philosophy.

It is a good idea to get an understanding of the children's environment by acquainting yourself with their home neighborhood and community.

In time, you will develop smooth working relationships and earn team status and acceptance with other staff members. Meetings are important vehicles for learning, and they will be a part of your future employment.

## ▶ HELPFUL WEBSITES

**http://nccic.org**
National Child Care Information Center. This resource provides links to other sites, and information promoting high-quality care is available.

**http://ericeece.org**
ERIC Clearinghouse on Elementary and Early Childhood Education. This site is best known for its information, research, and publications.

**http://nbcdi.org**
National Black Child Development Institute. This organization's website is a resource for information that improves the quality of life for African American children.

 Additional resources for this chapter can be found by visiting the companion website at *www.cengage.com/education/machado.*

# ▶SUGGESTED ACTIVITIES

A. Read the following early childhood center's philosophy statement. Which ideas or phrases do you feel are important? Discuss with the class how this description relates to centers or schools where you have observed or have been employed.

## Philosophy for a Children's Center or Classroom

An early childhood center is an environment where professional trust exists, and adults and children grow emotionally, intellectually, socially, and physically as they interact and participate. All people involved in center operations and functions are viewed and treated as possible learners who may have diverse learning styles.

It is believed that what the young child encounters and experiences promotes his or her learning. An early childhood center is a place where both children and adults become aware of themselves through their relationships with others in the classroom environment. It is also a place full of human feelings that are accepted and valued. A center should provide opportunities to wonder, question, explore, succeed, celebrate life, and ponder meanings and discoveries. It recognizes ethnic, cultural, economic, and social similarities and differences, and believes each individual possesses talents, gifts, and abilities. It promotes the sharing of self.

In a supportive environment, each person is accorded worth, and is respected. Individuals learn and know their rights and accept the rights of others without causing harm to self or others. It is believed that growth occurs at an individual pace as individuals follow their own destinies and designs.

B. If you were to describe yourself using a self-designed logo or a popular song title, what would it be? As you enter this student teaching experience, try to describe briefly who you are and any individual unique teaching perspectives or life experiences that may affect your teaching abilities. Share with a classmate.

C. Discuss and compare ways others made you feel welcome or accepted during your first workweek with two or more classmates. Make a list to share with other groups. Put the most effective ways first. Example: Your cooperating teacher had prepared the children to sing you a welcome song.

D. Create a full morning's guide for your placement classroom daily teaching duties and responsibilities using Figure 1–15 as a model.

▶ **Figure 1-15**
Guide to daily teaching responsibilities.

> ▶ **THREE-YEAR-OLDS—MORNING PROGRAM**
>
> Note: This figure is a segment of a longer 8 A.M. to 12 P.M. session. It ends at 10 A.M.
>
> 8:30–8:45     **Arrival of Children**
> - Greet each child and parent.
> - Help children locate their lockers.
> - Help children with name tags.
> - Help children initiate an activity.
>
> 8:30–9:20     **Free-play Time Inside**—Art, block play, dramatic play, manipulative materials, science, math, housekeeping area, language arts.
> - Supervise assigned area. Proceed to another area if there is no child in your area.
> - Interact with children if you can. Be careful not to interfere in their play.
> - Encourage children to clean up after they finish playing with materials.
> - Manipulative materials, including modeling dough and scissors, stay on the table.
> - Be on the child's level. Sit on the floor or on a chair, or kneel.
> - Children wear smocks when using paint or chalk. Print children's names on their art work in upper left corner.
> - Give five-minute warning before clean-up time.

▶ **Figure 1-15**

| | |
|---|---|
| 9:20–9:30 | **Transition Time**—Clean up, wash hands, use bathrooms. Help with clean-up. Guide children to bathroom before coming to group. All children should use the bathroom to wash hands and be encouraged to use the toilet. |

  • Place soiled clothes/underpants in plastic baggies and place them in children's cubbies.
  • Children flush the toilet.
  • Let them wash hands, using soap.
  • Bathroom accidents should be treated matter-of-factly.
  • Use word "toilet."
  • Help children with their clothes, but remember to encourage self-help skills.

9:30–9:45    **Large Group**—Assist restless children. Leave to set up snack if it is your responsibility. Put cups and napkins around table. Make sure there are sufficient chairs and snack places.
  • Teacher of the week leads group time.
  • Show enthusiasm in participating with the activities.

9:45–10:00   **Snack**
  • There should be one teacher at each table.
  • Engage in conversation.
  • Encourage self-help skills. Provide assistance if needed.
  • Encourage children to taste food.
  • Demonstrate good manners such as saying please and thank you.
  • Help children observe table manners.
  • Children should throw napkins in trash can.
  • If spills occur, offer a sponge. Help only if necessary.
  • Quickly sponge down tables.

11:30–12:00  **End-of-Morning Session**—Help with clean-up. Double check that all areas are clean and all materials are in their correct places. Share any observations with teachers, and solicit their observations and feelings during your team meeting.

## ▶ REVIEW

A. Select the answer that best completes each statement.
  1. Student teaching practices and procedures are:
     a. very similar when one compares different teacher training programs
     b. as different as pebbles in a pile
     c. uniform and dictated by state law
     d. different at training institutions and agencies but always involve five key individuals
  2. The individual who is supposed to gain the most new skills through student teaching is:

  a. the student teacher, but the cooperating teacher's and supervisor's new skills may surpass the student's skills
  b. the child
  c. the supervisor, who has learned each student teacher's unique way of performing duties
  d. the reader of this text
  e. impossible to determine

B. Read "Getting the Most out of Student Teaching" (see Figure 1–16 following listed references). Write a short summary of the items that you feel will be the most difficult, and also the easiest, to follow.

## ▶ REFERENCES

Bobinski, D. (2008, June 23). Is your work an obligation or an opportunity? *Idaho Business Review, 29*(31), 17A.

Council for Professional Recognition. (2006). *Competency standards—Preschool, infant/toddler, family child care, home visitor.* Washington, DC: Author.

Delpit, L. (1995). *Other people's children: Cultural conflict in the classroom.* New York: The New Press.

Feeney, S., & Freeman, N. (2005). *Ethics and the early childhood educator: Using the NAEYC code.* Washington, DC: National Association for the Education of Young Children.

Gallagher, K. C., & Mayer, K. (2008, November). Enhancing development and learning through teacher-child relationships. *Young Children, 63*(6), 80–87.

Hillman, C. B. (2006). *Mentoring early childhood educators: A handbook for supervisors, administrators and teachers.* Portsmouth, NH: Heinemann.

Hyson, M. (Ed.). (2003). *Preparing early childhood professionals: NAEYC's standards for programs.* Washington, DC: National Association for the Education of Young Children.

Jones, M., & Shelton, M. (2006). *Developing your portfolio: Enhancing your learning and showing your stuff.* New York: Routledge.

Machado, J. M., & Reynolds, R. E. (2006). *Employment opportunities in education: How to secure your career.* Clifton Park, NY: Delmar Learning.

National Association for the Education of Young Children, National Association of Early Childhood Teacher Educators, and the American Associate Degree Early Childhood Teacher Educators. (2005). *Code of ethical conduct: Supplement for early childhood adult educators.* A joint position statement, retrieved February 6, 2005, from http://www.naeyc.org.

National Association for the Education of Young Children. (2007). *NAEYC early childhood program standards and accreditation criteria.* Washington, DC: Author.

National Association for the Education of Young Children. (2008). *Draft core. NAEYC standards for early childhood professional preparation programs.* Washington, DC: Author. Retrieved September 25, 2008, from www.naeyc.org/about/positions/draftprepstds0808.asp.

Schiller, P., & Willis, C. A. (2008, July). Using brain-based teaching strategies to create supportive early childhood environments that address learning standards. *Young Children, 63*(4), 52–55.

VanderVen, K. (1988). Pathways to professionalism, In B. Spodek, O. Saracho, & D. Peters (Eds.), *Professionalism and the early childhood educator* (37–160). New York: Columbia University Press.

Wolf, K., & Dietz, M. (1998, Winter). Teaching portfolios: Purpose and possibilities. *Teachers Education Quarterly, 25*(1).

▷ **Figure 1-16**
Getting the most out of your student teaching.

1. Examine your attitude and decide you are going to expend every effort to learn new skills. Risk trying new ways and making mistakes. Communicate your desire to be given added and more challenging responsibilities. Welcome and encourage feedback from those supervising you.

2. When in doubt, ask questions. Select the time and place most convenient for your supervisors or write questions down for them if conferencing is immediately impossible. Be willing to come early or stay late if necessary.

3. Being professional involves a timely arrival and telephone calls when you need to be late or absent. Inform your college supervisor of field trips, testing, or special events when her observation of your work would not be possible. Your dress, personal appearance, and manner represent your professional image.

4. Make decisions using your best judgment. Seek clarification if you are uncertain of rules or expectations.

5. Realize the cooperating teacher's first priority is the needs, safety, and welfare of children. You are an added responsibility. Be aware there are times when the cooperating teacher cannot focus on you or your concerns.

6. See what needs to be done and do it without waiting for directions. Observe and study the children, program, and environment. Familiarize yourself with all aspects of the situation. Know where equipment and materials are stored. Be alert to daily schedules and routines.

7. See yourself as a needed assistant being increasingly responsible and alert to where you are most necessary.

8. Be friendly, learn names, and fit into classroom life quickly by being helpful and sensitive to school staff members.

9. Watch teacher skills, techniques, and behaviors with children and parents. Try to identify the goals of instruction behind words and actions.

10. Avoid socializing with other adults during work periods and instead be watchful, observant, and ready to learn from children and classroom situations. Scan the area, develop "eyes in the back of your head." When sitting, choose positions that allow the best classroom views.

11. Remain nonjudgmental when site politics are present. Try to inwardly evaluate staff conflicts. Discuss with your college supervisor your position as a "fence sitter" who avoids taking sides if a difficult situation or power struggles between adults arise.

12. When viewing new techniques or methods, remain open-minded and reflective. If ethics are involved, ask for a college supervisor consultation quickly.

13. Receive input from supervisors with the belief that both compliments and suggestions for growth will enable you to become a more skilled and valuable early childhood educator.

# CHAPTER 2

# A Student Teacher's Values and Developing Teaching Style

**OBJECTIVES** After reading this chapter, you should be able to:

1. Define the role of personal values in teaching.
2. Describe how activities you enjoy reflect personal values and relate to what happens in the classroom.
3. Define and describe your emerging teaching style.

## STUDENT TEACHER SCENARIO

**Setting:** Nate, a student teacher, is talking to his university supervisor about student teaching in a kindergarten class for his yet-to-be-assigned student teaching placement.

Nate had always wanted to be a kindergarten teacher. His university supervisor, Mrs. Castillo, however, suggests that he might be more employable in an upper grade.

"But I really enjoy music and art, and I think I'd have more opportunity to infuse them into my lessons in a kindergarten. I can bring my guitar into the classroom, teach some songs, relate what the children are singing to art, language, reading, and even dance. I've already collected several picture and picture story books, with themes that involve music and other fine arts."

"I understand why you feel the kindergarten placement would be better than the primary grade one, but I'm still concerned about whether a school district would hire you for a kindergarten class. Think your options over, okay?"

Nate thought about what Mrs. Castillo said over the next few days. He then sought her out for further discussion.

"Mrs. Castillo, I've given a lot of thought to what you said about my student teaching placement and I still want to student teach in a kindergarten for the next assignment."

"I'll try to accommodate your desires as I check with the schools I know, to see if there is a principal and supervising teacher who will accept you," Mrs. Castillo answered.

## Questions for Discussion:

**1.** Are you as in touch with your values, as they relate to your future teaching, as Nate is?

**2.** Could Mrs. Castillo be somewhat biased regarding kindergarten teacher gender, or was she just being realistic about males being hired more for upper grades?

**3.** If you could advise your supervisor concerning a second student teaching placement, what would you request? Why?

• • • • • • • • • • • • • • • • • • • • • • • • • • • • • • • • • • • • • • • •

## KNOWING YOURSELF AND YOUR VALUES

We will begin this chapter with an exercise. On a separate sheet of folded paper, number the spaces from 1 to 20. Then list, as quickly as possible, your favorite activities. Do this spontaneously; do not pause to think.

Now go back and code your listed activities as follows:

◆ Mark those activities you do alone with an *A*.

◆ Mark those activities that involve at least one more person with a *P*.

◆ Mark with an *R* those activities that may involve risk.

◆ Mark those in which you are actively doing something with a *D*.

◆ Mark with an *S* those activities in which you are a spectator.

◆ Mark activities that cost money with an *M*.

◆ Mark activities that are free with an *F*.

◆ Mark with a *Y* any activity you have not done for one year.

Now that you have coded your activities, what have you learned about yourself? Are you more a spectator than a doer? Do you seldom take risks? Did you list more than one activity in which you have not participated for more than one year? Do you frequently spend money on your activities, or do most of your activities cost little or nothing? Were any of your answers a surprise? What do your activities say about your values? We hope you learned something new about yourself.

Let us try another exercise. Complete the following sentences as quickly as possible:

**1.** School is . . .

**2.** I like . . .

**3.** Children are . . .

**4.** Teaching is . . .

**5.** Girls are . . .

**6.** I want . . .

**7.** Children should . . .

**8.** Boys are . . .

**9.** Parents are . . .

**10.** Teachers should . . .

**11.** I am . . .

**12.** Fathers are . . .

**13.** I should . . .

**14.** Mothers are . . .

**15.** Teachers are . . .

**16.** Parents ought to . . .

**17.** School ought to . . .

**18.** Aggressive children make me . . .

**19.** Shy children make me . . .

**20.** Whiny children make me . . .

Did you find this activity easier or more difficult than the first? This exercise is less structured than the first. You had to shift your thinking from statement to statement. We hope it made you take a thoughtful pause as you were forced to shift your thinking, as verbs changed from simple or declarative to the more complex conditional or obligatory forms. Present-tense forms such as "is" or "are" encourage concrete, factual responses. With the conditional *should* or obligatory *ought*, your response may have become more a reflection of what you feel an ideal should be. In addition, with the present tense, a response is usually short whereas with the conditional or obligatory phrasing, you may have used more words to explain your response.

Look at your answers. Do you find you have different responses depending on whether the present, conditional, or obligatory form of the verb was used? What do these differences tell you about yourself? Van Leuvan (1997) believes an initial step and essential component in the development of reflective processes in teaching is the examination and clarification of one's belief about what constitutes and contributes to effective teaching. Nieto's research (2009) "has made it clear that previous experiences as well as values, dispositions, and beliefs fuel [the] determination" to teach.

## THE ACQUISITION OF VALUES

Let us reflect on how we acquire our values. Logically, many of our values reflect those of our parents. As children, we naturally absorbed our first values through observing our parents and family members and through direct parental teaching (see Figure 2–1). Few children are even aware that they are being influenced by their parents; they take in parental attitudes and values through the processes of observation and imitation. We want to be like our fathers and mothers, especially

▶ **Figure 2–1**
Family teachings and traditions influence children who absorb values through observation and imitation.

Margo Silver/Riser/Getty Images

because they appear to have the power over the rewards we receive. Smiles when we do something they approve of, hugs, and "that's right," said over and over, shape our behavior so that we begin to accept what our parents accept. Wedman, Espinosa, and Laffey (1998) point out that a person's beliefs about teaching are well established before entering college.

Why are you attracted to the profession of teaching? Is there a teacher in your family? Does your family place a value on learning? Did you enjoy school yourself? Were your parents supportive of school when you were young? The chances are that you answered positively to at least one of these questions. One reason many people teach professionally is that they truly enjoyed being a student themselves. Learning has been fun and often easy. As a result, an education is highly valued. Teachers frequently come from families in which the profession is valued, not because it pays well but, more likely, for the pleasure received in working with young children and the intangible experience of influencing young lives (see Figure 2–2).

Nieto (2009) mentions attitudes and values "such as a sense of mission; solidarity with, and empathy for, students; the courage to challenge mainstream knowledge and conventional wisdom; improvisation; and a passion for social justice" also as values of some who want to teach.

Grant and Murray (1999) suggest:

> Teachers of both genders choose teaching for the intrinsic satisfactions and joy of the work. They feel whole and connected and engaged in meaningful work in a way that many in modern society do not. The leading reasons teachers say they chose the profession are that they like to work with children (66 percent), that they like the inherent meaning and value of the job (38 percent), and that they are interested in a specific subject-matter field (36 percent).

Vartuli (2005) notes that teachers' beliefs are often implicit and unarticulated, yet, they influence the teachers' perceptions, judgments, and decisions, and direct their actions in many ways. Teachers' views of their competencies may determine the amount of effort they expend, their perseverance when confronted with obstacles, their resilience when faced with adversity, their interactions with children, and, consequently, children's educational outcomes.

▶ **Figure 2–2**
Nurturing young children is one of the appealing aspects of a teaching career.

One problem many teachers face is accepting negative attitudes from parents or caregivers who do not place similar values on education. You need to remember that some parents may come from cultures where educational opportunities were denied or limited. In addition, some parents may feel that their education systems failed them. These parents may not share your values. What can you do? Always show, through your actions—which speak louder than your words—that you care for their children and that you want to help them. Assuming that the parents want the best for their children and want them to have better opportunities, you can earn the parents' respect and cooperation.

On a separate sheet of paper, judge the following as true or false:

1. Your ethnic background was not an issue when you were a child.
2. Your neighborhood was multicultural.
3. People treated you differently because of your ethnic heritage.
4. You were financially secure most of your childhood.
5. Religion is important in your life.
6. You're proud of your racial group.
7. Life was full of hope rather than despair in childhood.
8. You have been the object of discrimination.
9. Your ethnic group is minimally understood by most Americans.
10. Your identity and sense of self are well formed.

© Cengage Learning

Many of our most enduring values were formed through contact with our family when we were too young to remember. Others were acquired through repeated experience. Let us use the example of Nate from our Student Teacher Scenario. He was raised by parents who loved music. His father was a professional musician and played in a symphony orchestra. His mother had been an opera singer but became a stay-at-home mother after the birth of Nate and his siblings. She encouraged a joy of music in all of her children by singing as she completed household tasks. Nate's father encouraged his children to try out several musical instruments he had in the house. After trying the piano, Nate tried the guitar and stayed with it.

## Krathwohl's Hierarchy

One way of looking at the acquisition of values is to look at Krathwohl's taxonomy (1984). Krathwohl and his associates were interested in looking at the *affective domain*, or the field of knowledge associated with feelings and values.

Krathwohl arranged the affective domain into a hierarchy as follows:

1. receiving (attending)
2. responding
3. valuing
4. organization
5. characterization by a value or value complex

For you, as a teacher of young children, the first three levels are the most important. Let us return to Nate. Is it not possible that Nate acquired his love for music from both of his parents? Surely he enjoyed listening to his father practice and his mother singing. *Receiving* pleasure may have encouraged Nate to *respond* by wanting to learn how to play a musical instrument. Later, after he experienced lessons on the piano, Nate became more interested specifically in playing the guitar. In fact, he *valued* the experience and wanted to share his love of music with his students.

Let us use the hierarchy in another exercise. Write your answers on a separate sheet of paper.

1. What types of awareness do you want your students to have? List those things you want the children to notice. (Examples: books, a terrarium, a piano, puzzles, blocks.)
2. What types of behaviors do you want your students to develop? Describe the behaviors you hope to see. (Examples: listening to stories, sitting quietly, showing curiosity, sharing.)
3. What do you want students to recognize about classroom procedures? (Examples: the predictability of routines, the bell schedule, when recess comes.)
4. What responses do you want to encourage? (Examples: willingness to answer questions about a story read to them, smiling and laughing at a humorous poem, showing excitement.)
5. What responses do you hope to see that may indicate a student has developed a value? (Examples: asking to take home a book read in class, sharing the book with a friend, bringing a book from home to share.)

We will not continue further with this exercise because you may not know if students have absorbed your stimulus into their value systems until after they move on from your class. For yourself, however, go back over this exercise and ask yourself the following:

1. Why did I choose that particular example as the stimulus I wanted my students to receive and respond to?
2. What does this reveal about my own value system?
3. Is this value a part of *me*, a part of my character?

If you cannot answer these questions, we suggest that you go back and repeat the exercise with another stimulus. For example, your choices may range from some facet of the curriculum, like story time and books, to some facet of behavior, such as paying attention, sharing toys, or not fighting.

## YOUR VALUES

Why is it important for you, as a student teacher, to be aware of your values? We hope you already know the answer. In many ways, the answer lies in what Rogers (1966) calls *congruence*. Self-knowledge should precede trying to impart knowledge to others. By looking closely at your values, you will be able to develop a philosophy of teaching more easily. Your particular life stories can be the starting point for reflection and dialogue (Jones, 1994).

Let us move on to another exercise. Take a sheet of 8 × 11 unlined paper. Divide in half vertically. Then divide in thirds horizontally. In the top left-hand section, draw a picture of what you believe is your best asset. Next to it in the top right-hand section, draw a picture of something you do well. In the middle left-hand section, draw a picture of something you would like to do better. In the middle right-hand section, draw a picture of something you want to change about yourself. In the bottom left-hand section, draw a picture of something that frightens you. In the bottom right-hand section, write five adjectives that you would like other people to use to describe you.

affective—caused by or expressing emotion or feeling.

Look at your drawings and think about what your **affective** responses were to this exercise. Did you find it easier to draw a picture of something that frightens you? Was it easier to draw than to list five adjectives? Did you feel more comfortable drawing or writing your responses? What does this say about you? Were you able to write the first two or three adjectives quickly and then forced to give some thought to the remaining two?

Some of us have more difficulty handling compliments than negative criticism. Some might find it easier to draw a picture of something we do well. Some of us have negative feelings about our ability to draw anything; being asked to do an exercise that asks for a drawn response is a real chore. Did you silently breathe a sigh of relief when you came to the last part of the exercise and were asked for a written response? Does this suggest that you are more comfortable with words than with nonverbal expressions?

If you are more at ease with words, what are the implications regarding any curriculum decisions you might make? Would you be inclined to place a greater emphasis on language activities than on art activities? If you can deal more easily with the negative aspects of yourself than with the positive aspects, what are the implications for your curriculum decisions? Is it possible that you would find it easier to criticize rather than compliment a student? Is it possible that you are inclined to see mistakes rather than improvements? Think about this.

How do the activities you enjoy reflect your personal values and thus influence your classroom curriculum? Go back to the first exercise you completed in this chapter. What were the first five activities you listed? List them on a separate piece of paper. Next to this column, write five related classroom activities. Does your list look something like this?

| Activity | Related Curriculum Activity |
|---|---|
| Playing the piano | Teaching simple songs with piano accompaniment |
| Jogging | Allowing active children to run around the playground |
| Skiing | Climbing, jumping, gross motor activities |

## PERSONAL VALUES AND ACTIVITIES

What is the relationship between activities and personal values? Van Leuvan (1997) believes that teachers who aim to improve their professional practice must not only recognize what they are doing but also must understand the origins and effects of their actions. In this way, they might consider alternative approaches to teaching and learning. It seems obvious that we would not become involved in an activity that did not bring us some reward or pleasure; we have to be motivated (see Figure 2–3). Usually, that motivation becomes intrinsic because significant people in our lives provided an extrinsic reward, usually a smile or compliment. Given enough **feedback** in the form of compliments, we learn to accept and even prize the activity.

Many of us want to teach young children because we genuinely like them. When did we learn this? Some teachers, as the oldest in their respective family, learned to care for and enjoy being with younger brothers and sisters. Others had positive experiences from babysitting. Raths (2001) asserts that the reasons a person chooses to teach might be a product of his upbringing, a reflection of his life experiences, and a result of the socialization processes of schooling. Nevertheless, we frequently have strong beliefs about the role education can play, about explanations for individual differences in academic performance, about right and wrong in a classroom, and many other areas. Nieto (2009) specifically notes, "Sensibilities such as love, engaging with intellectual work, the hope of changing students' lives, … and a belief in the potential of public education … are at the heart of what makes for excellent and caring teachers."

Deal and White (2006) point out that students entering a teacher preparation program come with many beliefs, based on their previous experiences. They call these entering beliefs *naïve*. They further assert that reflection, often a part of any teacher preparation program, encourages students to think about their own teaching and may encourage change.

Perhaps we want to teach young children because they are less threatening than older children. What does this say about us? In addition, young children are often more motivated to please the adults in their lives than are teenagers.

Attitudes toward or against something are often formed when we are so young that we do not know their origin. We only know that we have a tendency to like or dislike something or someone. Because these attitudes arouse a strong *affect*, or feeling for or against, they can influence our values. People of different backgrounds who do not share similar ideals often find their values being challenged.

Goffin and Washington (2008) point out that "a gap exists between one's espoused values and one's practices" and that "conflicting values may co-exist." If you find yourself struggling with these inconsistencies, we urge you to be thoughtful, open-minded, and reflective concerning your training experiences, stepping back at times to think or reflect about your conclusions and experiences in child classrooms, and to participate in discussions that clarify and enlighten. This is called **reflective teaching**.

Some college supervisors require student teachers to write personal or life histories and mission statements. They recommend including sections describing experiences as pupils, as scholars preparing for teaching, as members of ethnic and cultural groups, and as members of unique and diverse families.

One recent study (La Paro, Siepak, & Scott-Little, 2009) looked at beliefs held by students at different points in their teacher preparation programs about children, discipline and behavior management, and teaching practices. They found that regardless of where they were in their programs, all students valued children but held differing opinions regarding teaching strategies.

**feedback**—information given and deemed to be a true and accurate account of what happened. May be evaluated as positive, negative, or otherwise by the informant or listener.

**reflective teaching**—a serious effort to thoughtfully question teaching practices, perceptions, actions, feelings, values, cultural biases, and other features associated with the care and education of young children.

▶ **Figure 2-3**
Because she enjoys music, this teacher incorporates musical experiences in her program.

© Cengage Learning

They moved from a more teacher-centered belief to a more student-centered one. Beginning students also felt they could control children's behavior with praise but later acknowledged that children can learn to control their own behavior.

## DISPOSITIONS

**disposition**—a consistent inclination or tendency.

Now that you have looked at your personal values and activities, how do these define your dispositions? Katz (1993) defines **disposition** as "a tendency to exhibit frequently, consciously, and voluntarily a pattern of behavior that is directed to a broad goal."

The National Council for the Accreditation of Teacher Education (NCATE) requires that dispositions of student teacher candidates be evaluated. Da Ros-Voseles and Moss (2007) identify nine dispositions:

- ◆ empathy—seeing and accepting another person's point of view
- ◆ positive view of others—believing in the worth, ability, and potential of others
- ◆ positive view of self—believing in the worth, ability, and potential of oneself
- ◆ authenticity—feeling a sense of freedom and openness that enables one to be a unique person in honesty and genuineness
- ◆ meaningful purpose and vision—committing to purposes that are primarily person-centered, broad, deep, freeing, and long range in nature
- ◆ creating a safe learning environment
- ◆ encouraging risk taking
- ◆ modeling desired practices
- ◆ providing opportunities to plan, act, and reflect on dispositions in classroom activities and assignments

The first five dispositions were developed and expanded upon by the addition of the last four. Do you see yourself as possessing, or working toward developing, these dispositions?

Rike and Sharp (2008) identify 12 dispositions and have developed an instrument, the Early Childhood Education Behaviors & Dispositions Checklist, that purports to measure these. Colker (2008) also identifies 12 characteristics that she sees "effective early childhood teachers" as having. The numbers of dispositions may vary from one researcher to another, but all focus, in one way or another, on relationships and, ultimately, on the establishment of a learning community.

## PROFESSIONAL ETHICS

**ethics**—a set of moral principles or values that serves as the basis for conscientious, sound, professional decision making or judgment.

Katz (1992) defines *ethics* as a set of statements that helps us deal with the temptations inherent in our occupations. **Ethics** may also help us act in concert with what we believe to be right, rather than what is expedient. Making decisions in the best interests of children and their families may take courage and commitment to professional excellence. One may risk losing a job or license, or risk other serious consequences by sticking to one's ethical standards.

How do values impinge on ethics? Obviously, if we value being honest, we might do what we know is right rather than what is expedient. Likewise, if we value creativity as a process, we might object to teaching in a back-to-basics school that emphasizes children's use of photocopied worksheets to learn reading, writing, and mathematics, with few opportunities for creativity. We might, in fact, choose not to take a position in a school whose values are in opposition to ours.

Educators have considerable power over children's daily lives and general welfare and often are seen as experts by parents. This occupational situation enables teachers to influence lives and impact self-esteem. It also gives them the opportunity to cause short- and long-term damage.

Speaking of the power a teacher exerts over the children they care for, Stephens (1999) notes:

> I possess tremendous power to make a child's life miserable or joyous. I can be a tool of torture or an instrument of inspiration. I can humiliate or humor, hurt or heal. In all situations it is my response that decides whether a crisis will be escalated or de-escalated, a child humanized or de-humanized.

So many situations may test ethics in student teaching. Cecile, a student teacher, faced a situation that unfortunately may not be unique. Cecile's cooperating teacher often made comments about the occupation and community status of the children's parents. It seemed to Cecile that some children received more attentive teacher treatment if the cooperating teacher was awed by parents with perceived high status and income. Cecile thought, "Who cares if the children's parents are doctors or lawyers!" After discussing the situation with her college supervisor, she was able tactfully to approach the subject with the cooperating teacher. Cecile decided to risk a retaliatory cooperating teacher evaluation, but, as it turned out, that fear was not realized during or at the close of her placement.

Other examples of student teacher dilemmas (encountered by the author's student teachers) include student teachers who do the following:

◆ saw other student teachers cheating on exams

◆ noticed licensing law violations at their placement sites

◆ accidentally broke, damaged, or lost some type of classroom equipment

◆ saw others in an act of theft

◆ overheard a teacher lying to a parent

◆ received sexual advances from a fellow teacher

◆ heard discriminatory classroom comments

When faced with some dilemmas, you may be able to make an equally strong argument for each of the opposing sides. In other cases, your initial position may be clear, but with further explanation or new information, you may mediate or change your position.

Recognizing that ethics apply to the education of adults as well as to the relationships among teachers, children, parents, and staff, the National Association of Early Childhood Teacher Educators and the American Associate Degree Early Childhood Teacher Educators (ACCESS) jointly adopted the *Code of Ethical Conduct: Supplement for Early Childhood Adult Educators,* which is "designed to be used with the existing Code [and] addresses the particular ethical issues faced by those preparing the next generation of early childhood professionals" (Freeman & Feeney, 2004). Ward (1992) would certainly be in agreement, as she insists that "members of a profession monitor themselves."

Figure 2–4 lists a segment of NAEYC's *Code of Ethical Conduct* (revised April 2005) concerned with ethical responsibilities to colleagues. (See also a reprint of the entire code in the Appendix.)

## When Values Clash

In our diverse society, individual values are bound to clash. Some parents may advocate spanking, others may feel their daughters should not participate in active sports, and a staff member may feel it appropriate to accept an expensive personal gift from a parent. The I-2.4 section of the NAEYC code bids teachers to respect families' child-rearing values and their right to make decisions for their children. The P-1.1 code section states:

> Above all, we shall not harm children. We shall not participate in practices that are emotionally damaging, physically harmful, disrespectful, degrading, dangerous, exploitative, or intimidating to children (2005).

▶ **Figure 2-4**
Reprinted with permission
from the National Association
for the Education of Young
Children. © Copyright 2005.

### SECTION III ETHICAL RESPONSIBILITIES TO COLLEAGUES

In a caring, cooperative workplace, human dignity is respected, professional satisfaction is promoted, and positive relationships are developed and sustained. Based upon our core values, our primary responsibility to colleagues is to establish and maintain settings and relationships that support productive work and meet professional needs. The same ideals that apply to children also apply as we interact with adults in the workplace.

#### A—Responsibilities to co-workers

*Ideals*

**I-3A.1**—To establish and maintain relationships of respect, trust, confidentiality, collaboration, and cooperation with co-workers.

**I-3A.2**—To share resources with co-workers, collaborating to ensure that the best possible early childhood care and education program is provided.

**I-3A.3**—To support co-workers in meeting their professional needs and in their professional development.

**I-3A.4**—To accord co-workers due recognition of professional achievement.

*Principles*

**P-3A.1**—We shall recognize the contributions of colleagues to our program and not participate in practices that diminish their reputations or impair their effectiveness in working with children and families.

**P-3A.2**—When we have concerns about the professional behavior of a co-worker, we shall first let that person know of our concern in a way that shows respect for personal dignity and for the diversity to be found among staff members, and then attempt to resolve the matter collegially and in a confidential manner.

**P-3A.3**—We shall exercise care in expressing views regarding the personal attributes or professional conduct of co-workers. Statements should be based on firsthand knowledge, not hearsay, and relevant to the interests of children and programs.

**P-3A.4**—We shall not participate in practices that discriminate against a co-worker because of sex, race, national origin, religious beliefs or other affiliations, age, marital status/family structure, disability, or sexual orientation.

The code notes "*this principle has precedence over all others in this Code.*" It is clear that when ethical dilemmas arise, teachers are first to consider what is best for the child. If parental values are inflexible, parents can choose to terminate a child's attendance. Centers may be able to propose other, less final, solutions. The center or school has the responsibility to communicate clearly its ethical and professional position to parents and to try, *if possible*, to problem-solve difficulties. Principle 2.2 states, "We shall inform families of program philosophy, policies, curriculum, assessment system, and personnel qualifications, and explain why we teach as we do, which should be in accordance with our ethical responsibilities to children."

Yet, it is more often in the differences between a center's or school's values and those of a family where difficulties arise. Luo and Gilliard (2006) explore perceptions by Chinese graduate students of American early childhood education programs, both in preschool and elementary school. They point out some of the critical differences. Chinese students come from a society where children are raised on policies based on Confucian ideals, which emphasize obedience to parents and respect for elders. Education brings honor to the family, and there exists an expectation that children should learn at a very young age. Luo and Gilliard summarize, "Confucianism remains a part of the Chinese social fabric and way of life." So, what are teachers in the United States to do? Ideal 2.5 helps: "To respect the dignity and preferences of each family and to make an effort to learn about its structure, culture, language, customs and beliefs."

Remembering principle 2.2, we will respect our differences and explain why we teach as we do. Still, as Luo and Gilliard write, "American and Chinese early care and education philosophies are vastly different, as they shape children to be citizens in two very different societies." For example, they note that the philosophies of many programs in the United States "tend to have less structural learning and play time with more fluid boundaries between children and teachers" (Luo & Gilliard, 2006). Tan (2004) also stresses the high value Chinese families place on education. She states, "Chinese parents and Chinese society… equate children's academic achievement with parental success." This may, in part, account for the high achievement of Chinese American students throughout their school years, from preschool to graduate school.

Looking at preschool programs in China, Tang (2006) highlights the difficulties Chinese early childhood teachers experience when they attempt to utilize the project approach in kindergartens in Shanghai. The major barrier comes from the teachers' attitudes toward the children. The traditionally held view is that children are dependent on adults. To accept children as active learners challenged this view. Tang writes, "There is a gap between kindergarten teachers' knowledge about children's learning and applying that knowledge into kindergarten activities. This has led to a gulf between the concept of the child as an active learner and the practice . . . in the kindergarten."

## TEACHING STYLE

What is meant by teaching style? It is the vehicle through which a teacher contributes his or her unique quality to the **curriculum**. Much has been written about teaching style, in particular, the phenomenon of teachers modeling themselves after the teachers who influenced them in the past.

Placing a student teacher with a cooperating teacher has its advantages and disadvantages. Most college supervisors try to place student teachers with those cooperating teachers who are willing to allow the student teacher to practice and will provide a positive model. However, there are many excellent teachers who are unwilling to work with student teachers. This is because it takes much energy and time to work with student teachers; they have to be watched, referred to resources, conferenced with, and encouraged. In addition, most colleges and universities do not compensate cooperating teachers in any tangible form for their time and energy. As a result, some student teaching placements may be less than desirable.

Of course, this situation sometimes works out well. A student teacher with experience as a teacher aide may do quite well in a classroom where the cooperating teacher is less than an excellent model, providing little supervision or guidance. In some cases, the student teacher may even act as a positive role model for a mediocre cooperating teacher.

Good cooperating teachers will offer suggestions about different lessons to try. They will introduce the student teachers to all areas of the curriculum, usually one area at a time (see Figure 2–5). Most cooperating teachers will allow a certain amount of time for student teachers to observe and become acquainted with the children. Before the end of the student teaching experience, however, most strong cooperating teachers will expect a student teacher to handle the whole day, and all parts of the curriculum. All student teachers will inevitably borrow or copy their cooperating teachers' styles; this results from having worked so closely together.

*Student Teacher Quote*—"I like a well-organized, tidy classroom. My cooperating teacher likes the three-ring circus approach to classroom activity, which offers plenty of child choices. I suspect my supervisor chose to place me here to broaden my horizons, to "loosen me up" so to speak, and it's happening. I can tolerate clutter and minor confusion better."

**Bobbette Ryan, State Preschool, Hayward, CA**

**curriculum**—overall master plan of the early childhood program, reflecting its philosophy, into which specific activities are fit.

*Student Teacher Quote*—"I was intimidated watching my cooperating teacher. She was so professional. After a while, I realized I had teaching strengths she admired and appreciated. We made a great team. She 'zigged,' I 'zagged,' but we pulled together. Our different approaches to the same goals made the classroom livelier. Oh what discussions we had!"

**Maeve Critchfield, Third Grade, San Lorenzo Unified School District**

▶ **Figure 2-5**
At first, student teachers will work in areas where they are most comfortable. Later, they will be expected to handle all parts of the curriculum.

**observation**—the process of learning that comes from watching, noting the behavior of, and imitating models.

**congruent**—refers to the similarity between what a person (the *sender*) is thinking and feeling and what that person communicates; behaving in agreement with or as a reflection of inner feelings and values.

Sometimes, though, a cooperating teacher's style is so unique, so much a part of himself, that it is too difficult to copy. We are reminded of a male cooperating teacher who stood 6 feet 4 inches tall and weighed around 240 pounds. Female student teachers had problems using his behavior control techniques; the difference in their sizes precluded the use of physical presence as a guidance tool. One complaint the college supervisor heard regularly was, "Of course Mr. Smith has no problems with control! Look at him!" What many student teachers failed to recognize initially was that Mr. Smith used other techniques as well, such as close **observation** of the classroom, moving toward the source of potential trouble before it erupted, quietly removing a child from a frustrating activity, and firm and consistent application of classroom rules.

A cooperating teacher may be so gifted that a student teacher feels overwhelmed. In this situation, the student teacher should be directed to look at only one facet of the cooperating teacher's expertise at a time. For example, in focusing on how the teacher begins each day, the student teacher may find a model that is not quite as difficult as the total model appears. It may be that the cooperating teacher takes time each morning to greet each child with a smile and a personal comment.

There are also situations where the cooperating teacher is unable to explain how something is done, like the mathematician who can solve a complex problem without knowing how. Intuitive teachers and those who are very involved have this difficulty; they are unable to explain why they do one thing and not another.

Teaching styles are also an extension of the teacher's self. Rogers and Freiberg (2004) contend that teachers must know themselves before effectively teaching others. This means that you have enough self-knowledge to judge from observing your cooperating teacher what activities and techniques will work for you, which ones you may have to modify, and which ones are best not used. Techniques with which you are truly uncomfortable are best put aside until you can become comfortable with them.

Rogers and Freiberg (2004) emphasize the need for teachers to be *congruent*, *acceptant*, and *empathic*. Being **congruent** means that your actions are a reflection of who you are as a person (see Figure 2–6). Being **acceptant** means that you accept, or *prize* (to use another term Rogers and Freiberg employ), each and every one of your students. Every child deserves to be accepted, but it is important to differentiate between acceptance of a child's value as a fellow human being and his behavior, which you may or may not accept. **Empathy** means that you are able to put yourself in the child's place, to understand why he or she is acting as he or she is. The Native American expression about withholding judgment until you have walked in another's moccasins relates to having empathy.

Another way of remembering these characteristics is to use the acronym *CARE*. To congruence, acceptance, and empathy we add *reliability*; children need to know that their teachers are reliable, that boundaries exist, and that certain behaviors are acceptable and others are not. Remember, safety for your students rests in your ability to *CARE*.

Cartwright (1999) lists the following characteristics as those desirable for early childhood teachers: knowing yourself, or self-awareness; good physical health; integrity; a grounding in theory; a strong background in general knowledge; trust in children; unconditional caring; intuition; detachment; laughter; and the ability to be a model. Do some of these not remind you that *CARE*ing counts?

McNamee, Mercurio, and Peloso (2007) remind us that student teachers also need to experience *CARE*ing, and that in receiving *CARE* themselves, they become more *CARE*ing with their own children.

▶ **Figure 2-6**
This indoor obstacle course allows these toddlers to enjoy being physically active and is congruent with the student teacher's physically active lifestyle.

© Cengage Learning

## Specific Models of Teaching Style

Miss Noelle is the teacher in a small child development program of 17 children, between the ages of two and a half (toilet trained) and five. The program employs a full-time assistant teacher, Mrs. Quandt—called Mrs. Q by all—and a volunteer, part-time lunch aide, Mrs. Swanson. Mrs. Swanson and her husband are called Grandma and Grandpa by the children, and she often reads stories and he frequently helps with woodworking projects. The program is located in a small house owned by the Swansons, remodeled for use as a child development center. The front door is not used; teachers, volunteers, and families enter through a fence on the side, to a screened back porch with tables and chairs for snacks and lunch (weather permitting) and cubbies for the children along the wall to the house.

The door opens into a large room, remodeled from the former back bedroom and indoor dining area off the old kitchen. This room has shelves with all kinds of toys and puzzles. Blocks are located in a carpeted corner on the left; two double-sided easels are on the right. Cars and trucks can be found on the remaining wall area, neatly arranged on shelves. All shelves are within reach of the children, and the older ones frequently help the younger ones. This room opens into a hall that leads to the front rooms of the house, with a bathroom with child-sized toilets on the left and the kitchen on the right. The kitchen is protected from entry by a cottage door, usually left open at the top.

Miss Noelle's desk and file cabinet can be found in the kitchen. The other door from the kitchen, to what used to be a small dining room, is always closed for safety reasons. In the front, Mr. Swanson has remodeled the front bedroom with a large archway providing access into what is now the dramatic-play center. The former living room is the gathering place for circle time and quiet activities. Two large beanbag chairs can be found in the back corner beside a bookshelf with several picture and picture story books for children to peruse. The front room opens into the former dining room, now used as the discovery center. It houses shelves containing a variety of attractive junk for children to explore and the resident hamster, in his cage.

Miss Noelle has a BA in child development from a local university; Mrs. Quandt is completing her AA in early childhood education from the local community college. Mr. and Mrs. Swanson are retired—she from elementary school, he from a career as a union carpenter.

Miss Noelle's program begins with free play as children enter at irregular times, from 7:30 to 9:00 in the morning; at 9:00, she gathers the children in the front room for group time. Miss Noelle calls the children by singing a few notes or playing a few chords on her guitar. She uses music to indicate transitions and has taught the children many simple songs. After asking the children what day it is and what the weather is like, Miss Noelle usually reads a story, stopping every so often to ask the children what they think will happen next. Often, the story is a familiar one and the children enjoy shouting out familiar repetitive lines they remember well. Many times, the older children will request a book they love; at other times children will bring a book from home for Miss Noelle to read.

After group time, the children are free to go where they wish—to the dramatic-play center, currently arranged as a grocery store, or to the discovery room, to see what new materials may be there. Some are intrigued by the change in the celery stalks that were placed in colored water 2 days ago. Miss Noelle asks them what they think has happened, and asks them to draw a picture of the changes. A few will go to the back room to play with manipulatives, such as cars, trucks, and blocks. Mrs. Q oversees the activities in the back room and Miss Noelle those in the front part of the house. One or two children will choose a favorite book and settle down on one of the beanbag chairs to "read."

The rest of the day proceeds much as does any child development/preschool program. Snack time is followed by toilet time and washing hands. Free play continues. Lunch is followed by quiet/nap time. Free play outdoors follows, until children leave. Some leave as early as 3:30, and others depart at various times until the center closes at 5:30.

Miss Noelle sees herself as a model for her children. She rarely raises her voice and usually speaks softly to the children. When there are disagreements between children, she attempts to guide them to a resolution, reminding older children that they are models for their younger peers. Miss Noelle is looking forward to marriage and having children of her own.

It is easy to see that Miss Noelle values all the children in her care. It is also apparent that she is able to empathize with them. She is gentle with those who have experienced a serious loss and refuses to allow an angry child to bait her. In one case when a child tried to kick another and was out of control, Miss Noelle simply picked him up, held him gently on her lap, and spoke soothingly to him until he was calm.

If a student teacher were to ask Miss Noelle about her teaching style, she would answer that it was based on her belief in the inherent goodness of all children, and in their innate need to explore their world. She would mention that she has a parent handbook that includes a statement of her beliefs and her curriculum goals. As she prepared it, she asked families and the children themselves for their ideas. "I'm still learning and growing myself," she would confess.

Miss Noelle's teaching seems very much a part of who she is: calm and imaginative, with a desire to create a total learning environment for her children. In looking at Roger's and Freiberg's criteria, it is clear that Miss Noelle is congruent, acceptant, reliable, and empathetic, and that her children perceive these characteristics in her as well. One can tell that each child is as important as the next. She uses many nonverbal responses; touching one child on the shoulder as a reminder to settle down, giving another a sympathetic hug, and getting down on her knees to speak directly and firmly to an angry child. From her words and actions, it is obvious that Miss Noelle thoroughly enjoys teaching the children in her care. Another way to look at Miss Noelle's teaching style would be to recognize that it is child-centered.

Let us now look at another teacher, Ms. Trinh, a first grade teacher with 17 years experience and a class of 25 children. Many of the families, whose older children have been in Ms. Trinh's room previously, request that younger siblings be placed there also. They understand that Ms. Trinh expects parents to help in the classroom in some way. They may bake cookies for a party, sew costumes for a play, or read a story to their child at least once a week. One working mother with computer competencies set up a page on the Internet for Ms. Trinh. On it Ms. Trinh includes assignments, work completed by the students, requests for materials she may want, and includes a column written for and by the families. Ms. Trinh regularly e-mails those families with computer access and keeps in touch informally when children are brought to and picked up from school each day.

Ms. Trinh starts each day by having children line up outside the door, walk quietly into the classroom, sit on a carpet square at the front of the room, and form a semi-circle around her by the white board. She then takes roll and assigns jobs to various children; this is done on a rotating schedule to ensure that all children have an opportunity to perform each task. One child looks at the calendar and announces what day of the week and month it is; another places a sun sticker on the calendar to indicate sunny weather; four more share the topics they have chosen to share. Children then go to the centers to which they have been assigned. A child may protest that she would prefer to go to a different center, but Ms. Trinh would remind her, after looking at the schedule on her BlackBerry, that the child's turn would come in two more days.

Although Ms. Trinh does not like the assertive discipline policy the school uses, she reluctantly does use it when necessary. She has the classroom rules posted prominently in the front of the room next to one of the white boards; interestingly, there are only three. The first, *I have the right to express myself in the classroom*, is illustrated by a picture of a raised hand placed next to the words. *I have the right to be heard in my classroom* is portrayed with several children's heads listening to a child standing and speaking. The rule *I have the right to feel safe in my classroom* has with it a picture showing the international sign for *no* with two children fighting.

Upon entering Ms. Trinh's classroom, the visitor is impressed by how quiet it is. All of the children seem to be busy at the assignments they have been given. Two parents are busy assisting, one at the reading center and the other at the art center, where children are busy constructing papier mâché figures for a puppet show that they will present later to their peers. The bilingual teacher is assisting two Hispanic children with their Spanish language arts lesson, and Ms. Trinh is circulating throughout the room, checking on the progress of those working independently on math and science assignments.

What kind of teacher does Ms. Trinh appear to be? In talking to her, it is obvious that Ms. Trinh sees herself as a good teacher. She is proud of the fact that most of her children meet the end-of-the-year goals set by her district. Her children obey class rules and respect each other. As one listens to Ms. Trinh and observes more closely, it becomes more apparent that, in spite of the seeming flexibility of the center and the assistance of the bilingual teacher and parent volunteers, the classroom is more teacher-oriented than child-oriented. Children are assigned to the centers, albeit on a rotating basis; they do not have a choice.

Is Ms. Trinh a congruent teacher? As a child, Ms. Trinh's family emigrated from Vietnam. She is proud of her citizenship and owning her own home. She generally socializes with family and is quiet and deferential to her parents and their friends. Because Ms. Trinh expects her students to be respectful toward her and quiet in the classroom, she is a congruent teacher.

Ms. Trinh is respected by many families. They are pleased that most of her students are already reading and completing first-grade mathematics assignments. They like her use of asking the fourth-grade teacher for buddies to help her students in writing. They admire the fact that she is calm, soft-spoken, and a strict disciplinarian.

If one inquired about Ms. Trinh's philosophy of education and curriculum goals, she would respond, "I follow district guidelines and state standards. I expect students to respect each other and me; I expect them to behave; I expect them to put effort into their learning, just as I had to when I came to the United States."

**authoritative**—substantiated, supported, and accepted by most professionals in the field of early childhood education, or having an air of authority; therefore, the classroom is child oriented.

**authoritarian**—characterized by or favoring absolute obendience to authority, therefore the classroom is teacher oriented.

Another way of studying these two teachers is to look at their leadership styles. As we know, Miss Noelle runs as child-centered preschool program, with a flexible curriculum that offers much free choice and emphasizes play. We also know that the children's needs come first. What is her leadership style? One might conclude that it is **authoritative**. The children all have a say in choosing what they will do from day to day. Miss Noelle respects all opinions and ideas, and she models this to her children.

There is an obvious difference between teaching in a child development center and in an elementary school, and both teachers seem to like children. However, Ms. Trinh runs a teacher-centered classroom and seldom deviates from requirements set by district and state guidelines. In terms of leadership style, Ms. Trinh is more **authoritarian**, or teacher-centered.

Although she uses centers in her classroom, Ms. Trinh developed them when she was placed on a first-grade teaching team as a newly hired teacher. All three teachers from the school's first grades designed the centers cooperatively.

## OTHER TEACHING STYLES

We presented examples of two teaching and two leadership styles. With most teachers, however, you will find other variants of these two. Many elementary school teachers follow a more or less set schedule from day to day. Free play usually starts the day in preschool; a *sponge* activity, such as journal writing or a few simple math problems, frequently starts the day in elementary school. In preschool, quiet play alternates with active, noisy play. Rest follows lunch. In elementary school, reading and mathematics are usually taught in the mornings, and less structured activities such as art, music, or physical education, occur in the afternoon.

While observing as a student teacher, you will find there are almost as many different teaching styles as there are teachers. Teachers tend to emphasize those areas of the curriculum that they feel are more important; they also tend to emphasize those areas in which they have greater expertise. The major characteristic of all truly great teachers is their ability to empathize with their students. Look closely; does the teacher show evidence of really liking the students? Does that teacher *CARE*? *CARE*ing is the secret to good teaching.

Young (2009) mentions that teachers must be able to build relationships in the classroom. But great teachers are not all alike. When polled and asked to select a great teacher whom they remembered, half of those chose "a teacher who was harsh, demanding, and authoritative, while the other half selected a teacher who was nurturing, warm, and endearing."

Are you interested in looking at what your emerging teaching style might be? Both Indiana State University's Center for Teaching and Learning and Michigan State University have surveys you might complete to find out. Both define four teaching styles: Formal Authority, Demonstrator or Personal Model, Facilitator, and Delegator. Where do you think Miss Noelle and Ms. Trinh might fall? Where do you think you might fall?

### Stereotyping Good and Bad

To fully understand a teacher's style, one has to understand the teacher's philosophy and underlying attitude toward the students. Does this teacher accept the children? Does this teacher feel that children are inherently good? Some teachers believe that all children have to be taught to be good. Their teaching style reflects this attitude. Usually authoritarian, they have rigid classroom rules. Children are told that they will behave in a particular way; any infringement on the rules will usually bring swift punishment.

Does the teacher feel that children can be trusted? The teacher's style will reflect this belief. Classroom rules will be elicited from the children, with the teacher

> *Student Teacher Quote*—"I've learned that I am a rather biased person rather than the enlightened minority group member I thought I was. Understanding and accepting this was my first step toward change. I've had to analyze the origins of my attitudes."
>
> **Felecia Arii, Second Grade, Oakland Public Schools**

reminding them of a rule they may have overlooked. Children who misbehave are not considered bad but as needing more socialization time in which to learn. Punishment often takes the form of physical removal from the situation, and isolation until the child feels ready to rejoin the class.

A teacher may believe that most children are good and then have an experience with a psychologically damaged child who challenges this belief. At this point, the teacher may accept the fact that most, but not all, children are good. The danger is that the experience with the psychologically damaged child can lead the teacher to formulate a stereotype about all children who look like this child, who come from the same socioeconomic background, who belong to the same racial or ethnic group, or who are of the same sex. Of Miss Noelle and Ms. Trinh, who is most likely to use stereotypic thinking? Stereotypic thinking occurs more often in rigid people than in flexible people.

## Flexibility

Let us also look at another factor: curriculum planning. The amount of planning needed is often overlooked in a classroom like Miss Noelle's. The visitor does not realize how much work goes into the arrangement of the learning centers. The classroom looks open, free, and **flexible**. Indeed, it is all of these. None of it is possible, however, without a great deal of careful planning. Ask Miss Noelle how long it has taken to develop her classroom and how much work she still does during free time to maintain the atmosphere. You will find that she is continually trying new things. Evenings and weekends are often spent designing new activities Miss Noelle thinks her children will enjoy.

**flexible**—willing to yield, modify, or adapt; change or create in a positive, productive manner.

In contrast, observe Ms. Trinh. During questioning, you will discover that she is still using some of the materials she developed during her student teaching years, and those designed by the first-grade teachers with whom she worked when first hired by her district. If she makes a change, it is usually at the request of her principal or at the suggestion of one of the other first-grade teachers with whom she has established a friendship. She sometimes may make changes on her own but is quite comfortable with what she has always done.

## ▶ SUMMARY

In this chapter, we discussed the relationships between our attitudes and values, the curriculum choices that might be made as a result, and how these could reflect our developing teaching style. Several learning exercises were included to help you define more clearly some of your personal values and the curriculum choices to which these might lead.

We observed Miss Noelle, a model authoritative preschool teacher with a clearly stated, and written, curriculum philosophy and goals of education. We have also looked at what is perhaps a typical teacher, Ms. Trinh. Although more authoritarian than Miss Noelle, and perhaps less acceptant of all children, Ms. Trinh's teaching style, with its emphasis on meeting district and state standards, is admired by many parents.

We also suggested that there is a relationship between a teacher's ability to *CARE* and her philosophy of education, which leads her to establish clear curriculum goals for students. Of the two teachers described,

Miss Noelle obviously *CARE*s; Ms. Trinh would protest that she does *CARE*; however, from the visitor's observation she appeared to lack empathy for one assertive boy in her room.

What should you, as a student teacher, do? Perhaps of greatest importance is to discover your own teaching style. With what areas of the curriculum are you most comfortable? Why? Do you see yourself as a *CARE*ing person? Are you developing a philosophy of education? In our two examples, do you see the relationship between each teacher's beliefs and curriculum practices? Think about your curriculum goals; consider how your feelings about working with young children influence these goals. Remember, especially, the positive attributes of both Miss Noelle and Ms. Trinh. Think, especially, of how Miss Noelle looks at herself as a learner, how she looks at each child, how she listens to them, how flexible her curriculum is, how child-centered her curriculum style is, and how authoritative her leadership style.

# ▶HELPFUL WEBSITES

**http://www.selectsmart.com**
This website will present you with a choice of many different kinds of questionnaires and personality tests designed to help you get to know yourself; several are yes/no tests; others are multiple-choice exercises.

**http://www.zerotothree.org**
Zero to Three is an organization that publishes many books and the journal, *Zero to Three*. They wrote the infant/toddler section in the NAEYC publication *Developmentally Appropriate Practice in Early Childhood Programs*.

**http://ChildCareExchange.com**
Child Care Exchange publishes the journal *Exchange*, as well as the e-newsletter exchangeeveryday, a daily, concise review of articles from early childhood journals and inserts from books on many different topics of interest to early childhood professionals. They also sponsor the World Forum conferences.

 Additional resources for this chapter can be found by visiting the companion website at **www.cengage.com/education/machado.**

# ▶SUGGESTED ACTIVITIES

A. Complete the following exercises in small groups of three to five. Discuss the processes involved in making any decisions. What did you learn about yourself and your peers as a result?

1. Draw a picture of what you collectively believe to be an effective teacher and label each part of the drawing to indicate what characteristics are being exemplified.

     For example, a picture of an extremely large ear might indicate a willingness to listen to children; an apron with many pockets, including several labeled *objects,* might indicate the many different items an effective teacher needs at his or her fingertips. Use your collective imaginations; nothing is too extreme, but you must justify why the item is included.

2. Draw a picture of your collective vision of an ideal child/student. As in the above exercise, label each part of the drawing that exemplifies a desired characteristic.

B. Write your emerging philosophy of education. Describe it in relation to your teaching style. Discuss it with your peers and supervisor.

C. In small groups, discuss the following:

1. Following your cooperating teacher's directions, you have always placed your purse and coat in the teacher's closet. The closet is locked after the teacher, assistant, and any parent volunteers have arrived. Only the teacher and assistant have keys. One day, after you have left the center and stopped at a store to buy a few groceries before going home, you discover that $10 is missing from your wallet; only a five and a one remain. Your immediate reaction is. . . .

2. You are a student teacher in a preschool classroom for four-year-old children.

     One day, Mike arrives with a black eye, wearing a long-sleeved sweater in spite of the pleasant weather. He winces when you approach him to give him a good morning hug. When you ask him what's wrong, Mike shakes his head and doesn't answer.

     Later in the day, as the weather has turned sunny and warmer, you are able to persuade Mike to remove his sweater. Almost immediately, you notice bruises on his left arm. Quickly, you report to your cooperating teacher. "Sarah, would you come and look at Mike? I think he's been abused. What are the procedures we should follow?" Sarah replies, "Leave it to me; I'll talk to Mrs. R. (the director). She needs to know about possible child abuse and she'll take care of it." By the time the children are being picked up by their parents, no one from either Child Protective Services or from the police has arrived to look at Mike or interview anyone.

     What should you do?

3. A parent of one of the three-year-olds in the parent-participatory preschool where you are student teaching has formed a close relationship with you; you are both about the same age, and you both have experienced financial stresses, which you've shared. One day, Ms. Sharif confesses that she's just discovered she's pregnant again (she has a baby now, as well as a three-year-old in your class) and that she's thinking of having an abortion. What is your reaction?

## ▶ REVIEW

A. List five personal values.

B. Write a short essay describing how the values you listed in question A influence what you do in the classroom.

C. Read the following descriptions of classroom interaction. Identify each teaching behavior as student-centered or teacher-centered. If a behavior is neither, identify it as such.

1. Teacher A is standing to one side of the playground during outdoor free play. She is busy talking to her assistant. One child approaches another who is riding a tricycle. The first child wants to ride the tricycle and attempts to push the rider off. Teacher A quickly calls, "How many times do I have to tell you to wait until I blow the whistle? You won't get your turn until you learn to wait!"

2. Teacher B is busy assisting four children on a cooking project. The bilingual assistant teacher is working with six children on a reading worksheet. A parent volunteer is working with five others on an art project, and the student teacher is overseeing the remaining children with their unfinished reading assignments. A child with the student teacher complains in a loud voice, "This is a dumb assignment! I want to cook! Why can't I?" Teacher B looks up and signals the student teacher to try and resolve the problem alone.

3. Two boys are arguing loudly as they enter the preschool. Teacher C, who is standing by the door greeting each child, quickly takes a boy in each hand. She quietly asks, "What's the matter with you two today?" After listening to each boy and insisting that each listen to the other, she suggests a separate active play, based on the knowledge of what each enjoys doing. They comply, and minutes later they and another child are spotted playing cooperatively with the large blocks.

4. Teacher D is standing in front of her class. The children are watching as she explains the activity: making pumpkins out of orange and black paper. After the children go to their assigned tables, it is apparent that at least two children do not know what to do. They sit glumly with their hands in their laps. Teacher D comes over and says, "Don't you two ever listen to directions?"

5. During roll, one of the boys in Teacher E's room begins to cry. Another child yells, "Crybaby." Teacher E quietly speaks, "Sean, remember that we agreed we wouldn't call each other by names that can hurt. Elijah, come over here by me so we can talk. The rest of you can choose what activities you want to do. Mrs. Montoya, will you take over so I can talk to Elijah?"

6. The children are all sitting on the floor in a semi-circle facing Teacher F when he asks, "Who has something they want to share today?" Several hands go up. "Let's have George, Ana, Mike, and Jan share today." Noting a look of disappointment on Mary's face, he says, "Mary, I know you're disappointed, but remember, you shared something with us yesterday. Don't you think we ought to give someone else a chance today?" Mary nods in agreement, and George begins to speak.

7. Deerat is standing at the front of the class reading a story from the basic reader. The other children are following along, reading silently. It is obvious that Deerat is a good reader and tries to vary her tone of voice. The child fluently reads the paragraph, but something is wrong. Teacher G interrupts her. "You are reading carelessly. It's not *the* coat, it's *a* coat. Now, start over again, and read every word correctly."

8. Ron is a new child in preschool. After greeting him and walking with him to the table with crayons and paper, Teacher H goes back to the door to greet more children. When Teacher H thinks to look back at Ron, he notices Ron is busy drawing all over the top of the table. He quickly goes over to Ron, hands him another piece of paper, and says quietly, "Ron, use paper for drawing." He later comes back with a wet sponge and shows the child how to clean up the marks.

## ▶ REFERENCES

Cartwright, S. (1999, November). What makes good early childhood teachers? *Young Children, 54*(6), 4–7.

Colker, L. J. (2008, March). Twelve characteristics of effective early childhood teachers. *Young Children, 63*(2), 68–73.

Da Ros-Voseles, & Moss, L. (2007, September). The role of dispositions in the education of future teachers. *Young Children, 62*(5), 90–98.

Deal, D., & White, C. S. (2006, Summer). Voices from the classroom: Literacy beliefs and practices of two novice elementary teachers. *Journal of Research in Childhood Education, 20*(4), 313–329.

Goffin, S. G., & Washington, V. (2008, July/August). Leadership choices in early care and education. *Exchange, 20*(4), 42–45.

Freeman, N., & Feeney, S. (2004, November). The NAEYC Code is a living document. *Young Children, 59*(6), 12–17.

Grant, C., & Murray, C. (1999). *Teaching in America: The slow revolution.* Cambridge, MA: Harvard University Press.

Jones, E. (1994). Constructing professional knowledge by telling our stories. In J. Johnson & J. McCracken (Eds.). *The early childhood career lattice: Perspectives on professional development.* Washington, DC: National Association for the Education of Young Children.

Katz, L. G. (1992). Ethical issues in working with young children. In *Ethical behavior in early childhood education.* Washington, DC: National Association for the Education of Young Children.

Katz, L.G. (1993). Dispositions as educational goals. Eric Document #363454.

Krathwohl, D. R., Bloom, B. S., & Masia, B. B. (1984). *Taxonomy of educational objectives: The classification of educational goals. Handbook II: Affective domain.* New York: David McKay.

La Paro, K. M., Siepak, K., & Scott-Little, C. (2009). Assessing beliefs of preservice early childhood education teachers using Q-sort methodology. *Journal of Early Childhood Teacher Education, 30*(1), 22–36.

Luo, N., & Gilliard, J. L. (2006, April-June). Crossing the cultural divide in early childhood teacher education programs: A study of Chinese graduate students' perceptions of American early care and education. *Journal of Early Childhood Teacher Education, 27*(2), 171–184.

McNamee, A., Mercurio, M. &. Peloso, J. M. (2007). Who cares about caring in early childhood teacher education programs? *Journal of early childhood teacher education, 28*(3), 277–288.

National Association for the Education of Young Children, National Association of Early Childhood Teacher Educators, and the American Associate Degree Early Childhood Teacher Educators. (2005). *Code of ethical conduct: Supplement for early childhood adult educators.* A joint position statement, retrieved February 6, 2005, from http://www.naeyc.org.

Nieto, S. (February, 2009). From surviving to thriving. *Educational leadership, 66*(5), 8–13.

Raths, J. (Spring, 2001). Teachers' beliefs and teaching beliefs. *Early childhood research and practice, 3*(1).

Rike, C. J., & Sharp, L. K. (2008, Spring). Assessing preservice teachers' dispositions: A critical dimension of professional preparation. *Childhood Education, 84*(3), 150–153.

Rogers, C. R. (1966). To facilitate learning. In M. Provus (Ed.). *Innovations for time to teach.* Washington, DC: National Education Association.

Rogers, C. R., & Freiberg, H. J. (2004). *Freedom to learn* (4th ed.). Upper Saddle River, NJ: Pearson/Merrill/Prentice Hall.

Stephens, K. (1999, January). Bringing light to darkness: A tribute to teachers. *Young Children, 49*(2).

Tan, A. L. (2004). *Chinese American children & families: A guide for educators & service providers.* Olney, MD: Association for Childhood Education International.

Tang, F. (2006, International Focus Issue). The child as active learner: Views, practices, and barriers in Chinese early childhood education. *Childhood Education, 82*(6), 342–346.

Van Leuvan, P. (1997, Summer). Using concept maps of effective teaching as a tool in supervision. *Journal of Research and Development in Teacher Education, 30*(4).

Vartuli, S. (2005, September). Beliefs: The heart of teaching. *Young children, 60*(5), 76–86.

Ward, E. H. (1992). A code of ethics: The hallmark of a profession. In *Ethical Behavior in Early Childhood Education.* Washington, DC: National Association for the Education of Young Children.

Wedman, J. M., Espinosa, L. W., & Laffey, J. M. (1998, Winter). A process for understanding how a field-based course influences teacher's beliefs and practices. *The Teacher Educator, 34*(3), 189–214.

Young, E. (2009, February). What makes a great teacher? PDK summit offers many ideas. *Phi Delta Kappan, 90*(6), 438–439.

# CHAPTER 3

# Being Observed: Discovering Your Competencies

**OBJECTIVES** After reading this chapter, you should be able to:

1. List two important goals of student teacher observation, assessment, and evaluation process.

2. Describe five observation techniques.

3. Complete a self-assessment.

4. List four desirable dispositions or competencies of teachers.

5. Develop a plan that identifies your priorities for future competency development.

## STUDENT TEACHER SCENARIO

**Setting:** Morgan is a student teacher in a four-year-old class. Her college supervisor has just arrived to observe.

Morgan's cooperating teacher suggests she take a quick look at her activity plan, which includes collecting leaves in the play yard and returning to sort them.

Unfortunately, rain has made the plan unusable. Remembering that physical activity seemed necessary for the group at this time of day, Morgan starts a substitute activity.

She gathers the group and initiates a discussion of children's names. Morgan draws the letter B on a chart-sized piece of newsprint, and a child offers that his is a B name. "B is the first letter of your name, Brent. I see the B on your name tag."

Morgan then asks the group to watch where she puts the B chart. She quickly crosses the room, tapes the chart to a wall, and returns. She then discusses how she can go and touch the chart using baby steps, and then return and sit down. She demonstrates.

"Can anyone think of another way?" Morgan asks. A child suggests using elephant steps, which he demonstrates, followed by the rest of the children. The game proceeds with other names and other suggestions about different ways to cross the room. The activity holds the children's interest and encourages them to create clever ways to cross the room.

## Questions for Discussion:

1. What do you think of Morgan's alternate activity?

2. Do you feel the alternate activity was planned as a back-up or created on the spot? Why?

3. Acting as the college supervisor, what teaching skills would you commend? Why?

• • • • • • • • • • • • • • • • • • • • • • • • • • • • • • • • • • • • • • • • • •

As more discoveries are made about the process of human learning, and as our society changes, teachers examine existing teaching methods, try new ones, and sometimes combine elements of both new and old methods. Observation is important to this process. The student teacher begins by being watched and ends up watching herself as a practicing teacher.

Teaching competency can be viewed as a continuum—you can have a little of it, some of it, or a lot of it—and there's always room for more competency growth.

As student teachers gain experience, they may feel teaching is more of an art and craft than a science. Beginning teachers are problem solvers, who experiment by trying one action and then another. They learn from mistakes and overcome embarrassments. Many things can be taught *and learned* by practitioners of any craft, along with experiencing intuitive insights. The act of teaching involves the heart and the mind.

An early childhood practicum course offered by a college or other training program has identified course objectives and student teacher learning outcomes. One objective universal to all training programs is providing a quality "practice" classroom for its student teachers and a concurrent lecture/seminar experience. One student learning outcome common to all training programs is the development of a student teacher's ability to assess and evaluate his or her own teaching strengths and professional skills. And many training programs also expect student teachers to create and complete a standards-based professional portfolio.

**assessment**—a process that objectively collects data or information.

**evaluation**—making a *judgment* concerning a relative value, worth, usefulness, productivity, effectiveness, or another quality or element.

**observation**—the viewing and recording of a student teacher's behaviors, actions, dispositions, abilities, and other student class assignments. It also includes interactions with children, families, and professional and support staff.

To aid student growth and determine a training program's effectiveness, both **assessment** and **evaluation** will occur during the practicum class. Assessment is defined as a process that objectively collects data or information that will be used to recognize and improve student achievement. This involves systematically gathering, analyzing, and interpreting evidence of a student's performance and to determine the degree to which a student teacher's actions and behaviors match student learning outcomes and expectations. Supervisor and cooperating teacher **observation** is but one tool for data collection.

Evaluation can be a judgment of a student teacher's work, or it can be a judgment related to some other aspect of the student teaching practicum, such as a person, program, process, policy, or practice. It usually pinpoints a place on a continuum between expert, competent, adequate, barely adequate, and incompetent; or between exceeds standard, meets the standard, and does not meet the standard; or a place on a grading scale, if it is a judgment of student teacher competency.

The National Association for the Education of Young Children's (NAEYC) *Standards for Early Childhood Professional Preparation, Associate Standards Summary* for a 2-year degree (Hyson, 2003) are presented in Figure 3–1. They were also displayed in Chapter 1 but are expanded here.

## GOALS OF ASSESSMENT, EVALUATION, AND DISCUSSION

Important goals of the assessment, evaluation, and discussion process for student teachers include:

◆ making valid assessments of performance through specific, descriptive feedback

▶ **Figure 3-1**
NAEYC Associate Standards Summary.

**Standards Summary**

There are six core standards, each of which describes in a few sentences what well-prepared students should know and be able to do. It is important to note, then, that the standard is not just that students know something about child development and learning—the expectations are more specific and complex than that.

*Standard 1. Promoting Child Development and Learning*
Students prepared in early childhood degree programs are grounded in a child development knowledge base. They use their understanding of young children's characteristics and needs and of the multiple interacting influences on children's development and learning to create environments that are healthy, respectful, supportive, and challenging for each child.

*Standard 2. Building Family and Community Relationships*
Students prepared in early childhood degree programs understand that successful early childhood education depends upon partnerships with children's families and communities. They know about, understand, and value the importance and complex characteristics of children's families and communities. They use this understanding to create respectful, reciprocal relationships that support and empower families and to involve all families in their children's development and learning.

*Standard 3. Observing, Documenting, and Assessing to Support Young Children and Families*
Students prepared in early childhood degree programs understand that child observation, documentation, and other forms of assessment are central to the practice of all early childhood professionals. They know about and understand the goals, benefits, and uses of assessment. They know about and use systematic observations, documentation, and other effective assessment strategies in a responsible way, in partnership with families and other professionals, to positively influence the development of every child.

*Standard 4. Using Developmentally Effective Approaches to Connect with Children and Families*
Students prepared in early childhood degree programs understand that teaching and learning with young children is a complex enterprise, and its details vary depending on children's ages, characteristics, and the settings within which teaching and learning occur. They understand and use positive relationships and supportive interactions as the foundation for their work with young children and families. Students know, understand, and use a wide array of developmentally appropriate approaches, instructional strategies, and tools to connect with children and families and positively influence each child's development and learning.

*Standard 5. Using Content Knowledge to Build Meaningful Curriculum*
Students prepared in early childhood degree programs use their knowledge of academic disciplines to design, implement, and evaluate experiences that promote positive development and learning for each and every young child. Students understand the importance of developmental domains and academic (or content) disciplines in an early childhood curriculum. They know the essential concepts, inquiry tools, and structure of content areas, including academic subjects, and can identify resources to deepen their understanding. Students use their own knowledge and other resources to design, implement, and evaluate meaningful, challenging curricula that promote comprehensive developmental and learning outcomes for every young child.

*Standard 6. Becoming a Professional*
Students prepared in early childhood degree programs identify and conduct themselves as members of the early childhood profession. They know and use ethical guidelines and other professional standards related to early childhood practice. They are continuous, collaborative learners who demonstrate knowledgeable, reflective, and critical perspectives on their work, making informed decisions that integrate knowledge from a variety of sources. They are informed advocates for sound educational practices and policies.

**SOURCE:** Reprinted with permission from the National Association for the Education of Young Children. www.naeyc.org.

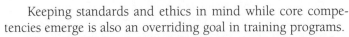

◆ collaborating in a fashion that generates helpful suggestions and ideas

◆ creating a positive student teacher attitude toward self-improvement and gaining self-knowledge

◆ establishing the student teacher's habit of self-assessing teaching performance

▶ **Figure 3-2**
Teachers look for effective ways to help children handle their strong emotions.

Keeping standards and ethics in mind while core competencies emerge is also an overriding goal in training programs.

Through observation and feedback, the student teacher receives objective data she cannot collect herself. Evaluation may sound ominous to the student teacher, because the word is usually associated with making a grade or passing a class or training program. A breakdown in trust may occur.

The quality of the feedback given to a student teacher is an important factor, and feedback needs to be consistent and constructive throughout a student teacher's placement.

Observational feedback may pinpoint behaviors the student can then examine while teaching (see Figure 3–2). Discussions following observations usually include:

◆ identifying what went well

◆ a descriptive view

◆ an examination of situational factors

◆ the creation of action plans

◆ additional analysis of written records

◆ child behavior particulars

◆ action/reaction relationships

◆ other features of the observation related to the discussion

Ideally, when a supervisor builds trust during discussions, a student teacher is able to:

◆ Develop a clear picture of the supervisor/student teacher relationship.

◆ Feel that he or she is supervised by an educator who listens well, clarifies ideas, encourages specificity, and takes time to understand the student's perspective.

◆ Frequently request value judgments.

◆ Become convinced his or her supervisor is an advocate for success.

However, time can be a limiting factor. Colleges and other training programs vary greatly, in both the expected number of visits to observe student teachers in action and the amount of time available for consultation. Whereas one supervisor may have the luxury of being assigned only a few student teachers, another may have many. College and other training program decisions are influenced by budgets, state supervision formulas, accreditation standards, politics, philosophy, and other factors.

*Student teacher quote*—"Why do I seem to do poorly when I'm being watched? Things run smoothly when I don't know I'm being observed. Fortunately, both my strong points and growth areas are talked about in daily meetings. So that anxious feeling I had when I was first observed is now a tiny knot in my stomach. Maybe I'll always have it."

**Casey Morgan, Intergenerational Program, Saratoga, CA**

## OBSERVATIONS

Observations can be categorized three ways: informal, co-educator, and formal.

An *informal* visit is best described as a casual, unfocused visit by a supervisor in which an overall picture of the classroom emerges. The student teacher's style, the cooperating teacher's style, staff interactions, room organization, children's behavior, classroom routines, and the learning environment are all observed. The supervisor may or may not pitch in. Notes may be written later and can include a supervisor's questions about room particulars, unique child behaviors, or features that are uncommon, unusual, or unexpected.

In a *co-educator* observation, the supervisor, like the cooperating teacher, is an active participant in the classroom, sharing teaching responsibilities. Together, they spend enough time in the classroom to determine its dynamics. They focus on the children, the program, and the student teacher's involvement in child learning. Supervisors gain experience with the diversities and problems that exist, and may be able to understand the classroom from the student teacher's point of view. They are also able to model techniques and step in during student teacher difficulties. Many college supervisors cannot spend this kind of time with their individual student teachers. In some placement classrooms, college supervisors may prefer formal observation.

*Formal* observation is defined as the observation of a student teacher that happens when a supervisor slips in, noticed or unnoticed, and remains unconnected to classroom action. Some type of recording takes place, in the form of a narrative, a **checklist**, a tally, or another type described in this chapter. Many training programs embrace formal observation as a more reliable and accurate method, because the observer, exempt from teaching responsibility and able to catch details, can see events unfold from beginning to end. Often, a supervisor focuses on a different dimension of students' work during subsequent observations. Some supervisors take copious notes as they try to capture the total picture, so enough data are collected to provide quality feedback. Others may use a self-created note system similar to shorthand.

Training programs collect data on student teachers' actions in many different ways. The most common collection techniques follow.

**checklist**—a method of evaluating children or teachers that consists of a list of behaviors, skills, concepts, or attributes that the observer checks off as the child or teacher is observed to have mastered the item.

**time sampling**—a quantitative measure or count of how often a specific behavior occurs within a given amount of time.

## Direct Observation

Direct observation is usually accomplished by a recorded specimen description, time sampling, and/or event sampling. This can be either *obtrusive*, where the observed individual is aware of the process, or *unobtrusive*, where data collecting occurs without the subject's knowledge, perhaps from an observation room (see Figures 3–3 and 3–4).

Supervisors who use direct observation often tell their students that they will enter the classroom quietly and sit where they can best observe. They may provide an observation schedule, or may drop in without notice. If scheduled, the student teacher will be able to alert the cooperating teacher. Your supervisor may have discussed the observation method to be used, such as **time sampling**, and whether the cooperating teacher will join the observation discussion.

Many supervisors feel one-on-one conferencing is best for a number of reasons, including not wanting to make the student teacher apprehensive about having two pros in attendance. Other supervisors may feel that two pros can give more feedback and advice, or offer different perspectives. Either way, evaluative conferencing is a professionally private matter.

During an observation, the observer may use any or all of the following observation techniques and instruments, or may develop their own personal style of viewing and recording.

*Time sampling:* An observer watches and codes a set of specific behaviors within a certain time frame.

*Specimen description or narrative: A stream of consciousness* reporting that attempts to record all that occurs. It involves recording everything that the individual does or says, with as much information about the context (people involved, circumstances that might be influencing the behavior, and so on) as possible.

*Event sampling:* A detailed record of significant incidents or events.

*Criterion-referenced instrument:* An analysis of whether the observed person can perform a given task or set of tasks (see Figure 3–5).

▶ **Figure 3–3**

You will be observed while working with children. How will you respond to, "Teacher tie my shoe?"

© Cengage Learning

▶**Figure 3-4**
You may chat with your cooperating teacher while someone else is supervising the children.

## Additional Observational Techniques

A specific set of questions can be prepared during an observation or after an observation. These questions can be used in an evaluation interview (see Figure 3–6).

The observer can also use a rating scale that sets a point value on a continuum to evaluate a characteristic or skill (see Figure 3–7). Videotaping, audio recording, or digitally recording a student teacher are other common observation techniques. These have the advantage of being replayed or stopped at certain points during conferencing.

Combinations of observational techniques are possible.

## CLINICAL SUPERVISION

Clinical supervision was initially promoted as a method to improve instructional practices by providing supervisors with a structured and cooperative approach.

The steps in clinical supervision are as follows:

1. the pre-observation conference, where the *focus* for the upcoming observation is decided
2. the observation itself
3. the analysis by the supervisor, with consideration of possible strategies for improvement
4. the post-observation conference
5. the post-conference analysis by the student teacher and the supervisor, at which time strategies for improvement are elicited from the student teacher and confirmed, or counseled for change, by the supervisor

Lacey, Guffey, and Rampp (2000) describe clinical supervision as a goal-oriented model that assumes a professional relationship exists between a student teacher and a supervisor, in an environment characterized by a high degree of mutual trust, understanding, support, and commitment.

## Reflective Supervision

Reflective supervision tries to bring the student teacher and college supervisor together in a collaborative way, to help the student teacher develop a disposition and

▶ **Figure 3-5**
Segment of a Criterion-Referenced Observation Instrument.

## SEGMENT OF A CRITERION-REFERENCED OBSERVATION INSTRUMENT

### I Field-Based Assessment of Competencies

*The 10 competency areas include:*
1. Child Development Principles
2. Program Planning and Curriculum Development
3. Program Implementation and Classroom Management
4. Program Administration
5. Family and Community Relations
6. Cultural Pluralism
7. Children with Exceptional Needs
8. Assessment of Children
9. Evaluation of Program Effectiveness
10. Professional Behavior

### II Program Planning and Curriculum Development

*Knowledge*
1. Demonstrates knowledge of child development principles in planning programs.
2. Demonstrates knowledge of factors to consider in planning an appropriate environment, indoor and outdoor, which enhances the development of children.

*Application*
1. Implements a curriculum based on child development principles, including the following areas: large and small motor activities, language arts, science and math, creative arts, social sciences, and personal development.
2. Demonstrates the ability to work as an effective member of a team in program planning.
3. Helps provide an environment that meets the needs of young children.
4. Selects and utilizes alternate teaching techniques and curriculum materials in situations that would stimulate and encourage active child participation.
5. Demonstrates the ability to interpret and use collected data in planning curriculum to meet the individual needs of the child.

▶ **Figure 3-6**
Sample section of an interview instrument used for a cooperating teacher's evaluation of a student teacher.

| Interview questions for cooperating teacher | Percentage | | | | |
|---|---|---|---|---|---|
| | Almost always | Usually | Undecided | Sometimes | Seldom |
| 1. Does the student teacher plan adequately for classroom experience? | | | | | |
| 2. Does your student teacher utilize up-to-date teaching methods effectively? | | | | | |
| 3. Does your present student teacher provide adequately for individual differences? | | | | | |
| 4. Is your student teacher able to manage the behavior of children? | | | | | |

(continues)

▶ **Figure 3-6** (continued)

| Interview questions for cooperating teacher | Percentage | | | | |
|---|---|---|---|---|---|
| | Almost always | Usually | Undecided | Sometimes | Seldom |
| 5. Does your student teacher meet class responsibilities on time? | | | | | |
| 6. Is your student teacher able to evaluate children adequately? | | | | | |
| 7. Does your student teacher cooperate with you? | | | | | |
| 8. Is your student teacher willing to do more than minimum requirements? | | | | | |
| 9. Does your student teacher attend extra classroom-related social and professional functions? | | | | | |
| 10. Does your student teacher seem ethical in his relationships with staff, children, and parents? | | | | | |
| 11. Is your student teacher able to motivate children? | | | | | |
| 12. Does your student teacher demonstrate facility in oral communication? | | | | | |
| 13. Is your student teacher able to organize? | | | | | |
| 14. Does the student teacher seem to believe in developmentally appropriate practice? | | | | | |
| 15. Does your student teacher demonstrate an adequate background in early childhood education? | | | | | |

▶ **Figure 3-7**
Sample segment of a longer student teacher rating instrument (rating scale).

Name_____

The professional qualities of each student teacher will be evaluated on the following criteria:

A four-point scale is used:
(1) needs improvement
(2) satisfactory
(3) above average
(4) outstanding

| PERSONAL QUALITIES | 1 | 2 | 3 | 4 |
|---|---|---|---|---|
| 1. Attendance and punctuality | ____ | ____ | ____ | ____ |
| 2. Dependability | ____ | ____ | ____ | ____ |
| 3. Flexibility | ____ | ____ | ____ | ____ |
| 4. Resourcefulness | ____ | ____ | ____ | ____ |
| 5. Self-direction, sees what needs to be done | ____ | ____ | ____ | ____ |
| 6. Sensitive to other people's needs and feelings | ____ | ____ | ____ | ____ |
| 7. Tact, patience, and cooperation with others | ____ | ____ | ____ | ____ |
| 8. Sense of humor | ____ | ____ | ____ | ____ |
| 9. Additional Comments: _____ | | | | |

| WORKING WITH CHILDREN | 1 | 2 | 3 | 4 |
|---|---|---|---|---|
| 1. Aware of safety factors | ____ | ____ | ____ | ____ |
| 2. Understands children at their own levels | ____ | ____ | ____ | ____ |
| 3. Finds ways to give individual help without sacrificing group needs | ____ | ____ | ____ | ____ |
| 4. Skill in group guidance | ____ | ____ | ____ | ____ |
| 5. Skill in individual guidance | ____ | ____ | ____ | ____ |
| 6. Listens to children and answers their questions | ____ | ____ | ____ | ____ |
| 7. Consistent and effective in setting and maintaining limits | ____ | ____ | ____ | ____ |
| 8. Encourages self-help and independence in children | ____ | ____ | ____ | ____ |
| 9. Sensitive to children's cues in terms of adding to their knowledge or encouraging verbal skills | ____ | ____ | ____ | ____ |
| 10. Aware of total situation, even when working with one child | ____ | ____ | ____ | ____ |
| 11. Additional Comments: _____ | | | | |

| WORKING WITH OTHER TEACHERS, PARENTS, AND VOLUNTEERS | 1 | 2 | 3 | 4 |
|---|---|---|---|---|
| 1. Willingness to accept direction and suggestions | ____ | ____ | ____ | ____ |
| 2. Is friendly and cooperative with staff members | ____ | ____ | ____ | ____ |
| 3. Respects confidential information | ____ | ____ | ____ | ____ |
| 4. Establishes good working relationships | ____ | ____ | ____ | ____ |
| 5. Shows good judgment in terms of knowing when to step into a situation | ____ | ____ | ____ | ____ |

Additional Comments: _____

ability to construct knowledge (Titone, Sherman, & Palmer, 1998). It is characterized by supervisor and student teacher interactions that practice collegiality and that demonstrate teaching as a reflective, inquiry-based, and knowledge-producing activity.

The method assumes the following to be the basic needs and rights of the student teacher:

**1.** to be treated professionally

**2.** to have an opportunity to develop self-understanding in a nonthreatening atmosphere

3. to learn to analyze curriculum

4. to learn to understand the socio-cultural dynamics present in every classroom

5. to work in an intentionally collegial relationship with an experienced teacher and full-time faculty member (Titone et al., 1998)

The ultimate goal of the relationship between the student teacher and supervisor is to enable the student teacher to develop the disposition and ability to self-assess accurately, in every context in which he or she works.

## Cognitive Coaching

Cognitive coaching is a process that involves student teachers exploring the thinking behind their practices. This type of process helps student teachers talk about their thinking and also become aware of teaching decisions.

A supervisor skilled in cognitive coaching asks probing questions. Student teachers may feel uncomfortable working out questions for themselves rather than being given immediate answers. When faced with self-analysis, teachers experiencing a cognitive coaching evaluation search their own minds, unlocking ideas that might not have presented themselves.

## RELIABILITY

Observations must serve as a reliable and accurate source of information. In student teaching, the participants understand that each observation record covers only a short space of time compared to the length of the student teacher's placement. Areas of competence that receive similar interpretations from different observers over a period of time should be of special interest to student teachers.

While all observers have different points of reference, depending upon their individual life experiences in the student teaching situation, their goals are similar. They honestly attempt to examine, interpret, and reflect on what they have seen, and possibly recorded, to improve student performance through follow-up dialogue (see Figure 3–8).

Any attempt to interpret meaning brings with it the possibility of misinterpretation, based on the limits of what one can perceive and the observer's **biases**. Observers may have a mind-set that predisposes them to look at particular teaching skills and

**biases**—particular tendencies or inclinations, especially ones that prevent impartial consideration; prejudices.

▶ **Figure 3–8**
Posted schedules help observers to see student teacher actions during transitions.

© Cengage Learning

overlook others. Using a variety of observation tools and forms can help remedy the situation.

**Reliability** refers to the extent to which observations are consistent over time and "the extent to which a test is consistent in measuring over time what it is designed to measure" (Wortham, 1995). The similarity of information in data gathered in different observations confirms the reliability of the measurement. For example, if both a videotaped observation and a time sampling seem to point to the same measurement of skill or teaching behavior, the reliability of the data is greater.

The degree of obviousness of the collection method also merits consideration. Videotaping may produce unnatural behavior. Hidden cameras and tape recorders raise ethical questions. Observation rooms and one-way screens are familiar and unobtrusive methods commonly used in laboratory training centers. Objective recording of teaching behavior is a difficult task. Observations can be subjective and reflect the observer's special point of view.

Supervisors and cooperating teachers try to keep all observations objective during student teaching. Discussions between the observer and the observed can add additional factors for consideration, before analyses and evaluations occur.

Ongoing and cumulative evaluations of students' performances are designed to verify their competencies. In student teaching, these evaluations allow students to discover, plan, and ponder. Without outside assessment and evaluation, assessment is limited to self-assessment.

> **reliability**—a measure indicating that a test is stable and consistent, to ensure that scoring variations are due to the person tested, and not the test.

## Observers and Evaluators

It is possible to be observed and assessed by many people during your student teaching experience. Some students prefer only the supervisor's and cooperating teacher's assessments. Others actively seek feedback from all possible sources.

A wide base of observational data on competency seems best. Other possible observers in most student teaching placements are:

- self (see Figures 3–9 and 3–10)
- classroom assistants, aides, and volunteers
- other student teachers
- the center or school's support staff (cooks, nurse, secretary)
- children
- parents
- community liaison staff
- administrative staff or consulting specialists

Student teachers can develop their own rating systems based on teaching characteristics that are important to them. Simple tallies are helpful in recording changes in behavior.

**Student teacher quote**

"I believe being observed is a necessary evil. How else could I improve what I don't know needs to be improved?"

**B.K. Sutton, Kindergarten Placement, Private School**

## Discussion

Discussions held after data and evidence are collected are keys to growth. The meeting's tone, format, location, time of day, and degree of comfort can be critical. The communication skills of both participants contribute to success in promoting student teacher skill development.

Two types of discussions, *formative* and *summative*, occur during student teaching. An initial, *formative* discussion sets the stage for later discussions. Goals, time lines, and evaluative procedures are explained. Additional formative discussions will follow placement observations. A *summative* conference finalizes your total placement experience and scrutinizes both the placement site and your competencies.

▶**Figure 3-9**
Student teaching self-evaluation form.

**Instructions:**

Evaluate your own performance on this form. To the left of each characteristic listed below, write a W if you are working on it, M if it happens most of the time, or an A if it happens always.

**Relationships**

____ 1. I arrive on time with an appropriate attitude.

____ 2. I greet children, parents, and staff in a friendly and pleasant manner.

____ 3. I accept suggestions and criticism gracefully from my coworkers.

____ 4. I can handle tense situations and retain my composure.

____ 5. I make an effort to be sensitive to the needs of the children and their parents.

____ 6. I am willing to share my ideas and plans so that I can contribute to the total program.

**Goals**

____ 1. The classroom is organized to promote a quality child development program.

____ 2. I constantly review the developmental stage of each child so that my expectations are reasonable.

____ 3. I set classroom and individual goals and then evaluate regularly.

____ 4. I have fostered independence and responsibility in children.

**Classroom Skills**

____ 1. I arrive prepared.

____ 2. I face each day as a new experience.

____ 3. I can plan a balanced program for the children in all skill areas.

____ 4. I am organized and have a plan for the day.

____ 5. I help each child recognize the role of being part of a group.

____ 6. I help children develop friendships.

____ 7. I maintain a child-oriented classroom, and the bulletin boards enhance the program.

**Professionalism**

____ 1. I understand the school mission and philosophy.

____ 2. I'm professional in my demeanor and in my personal relationships while on the job.

____ 3. I assume my share of joint responsibility.

**Personal Qualities**

____ 1. I have emotional stability.

____ 2. My general health is good and does not interfere with my responsibilities.

____ 3. My personal appearance is suitable for my job.

____ 4. I would evaluate my effectiveness as a member of my teaching team using the following scale:

$$- \quad 0 \quad 1 \quad 2 \quad 3 \quad 4 \quad 5 \quad +$$
$$\text{[Low]} \qquad \qquad \text{[High]}$$

**My Teaching Team**

____ 1. I've earned the respect and acceptance of team members and families. Use yes or no.

During discussions, you will examine the collected data, add comments about extenuating circumstances, form plans to collect additional information, and consider initiating new actions that could strengthen your existing skills through change or modification. Don't be afraid to ask for clarification. Restate what you think you heard to check on meaning. Try to attend closely and reflect rather than formulate an answer or quick response. Keep calm even if inner emotions are strong. Suggestions for improvement are self-discovered and formed jointly with the cooperating teacher or supervisor.

▶ **Figure 3-10**
Rate yourself.

## STUDENT SELF-EVALUATION

Put a check on the number in each line that best describes your behavior or performance.

| 1 | 2 | 3 | 4 | 5 | REFLECTION |
|---|---|---|---|---|---|
| I often think critically about how my behavior affects children and other adults. | Sometimes I try to analyze classroom interactions. | From time to time I think about how I affect others in the classroom. | I rarely rehash what happened during the day in the classroom. | I give little thought to classroom interactions. | |
| I have a clear idea of important goals with children and work daily to accomplish them. | Some of my goals are clear; others are still being formed. | My goals are not always clear, but at times I think about them. | I use my center's goals for planning and have a few of my own. | I mainly handle each day by providing activities that teach specific concepts and note which children engage. | CLARITY OF GOALS |
| I'm always responsible for what I do and say. | Most of the time I take responsibility for what happens. | At times I feel responsible for my actions. | I can't control all that happens—that's my attitude. | What goes wrong is mostly others' fault. | RESPONSIBILITY |
| I do what's assigned and needed before deadlines, and check to see it's completed on time. | I usually complete jobs in a timely manner. | I finish jobs that I choose to finish mostly on time. | I start, but often something happens before I finish assignments. | I'm late, and often don't finish what's expected of me. | DEPENDABILITY |
| I always find what I need and create when necessary in activity planning. | I'm pretty good at getting what needs to be secured. | I sometimes can find or create what is necessary. | I rarely know how to go about getting things I need for the classroom. | I expend little effort at locating hard-to-find items or materials for child instruction. | RESOURCEFULNESS |
| I rarely need others to direct my work. | Most of the time I don't need the help of my supervisor. | I ask for help when the going gets rough and that's not often. | I need advice frequently and depend on others to solve my problem. | Lots of help and supervision are necessary. | INDEPENDENCE |
| I'm active in teacher associations and attend nearby conferences. | Sometimes I attend professional association meetings and training opportunities. | I go to the library occasionally to consult the experts. | I haven't the time now to join or attend professional group doings but plan to in the near future. | I don't wish to become a member of a professional group. | PROFESSIONAL GROWTH |

(continues)

▶ **Figure 3-10** (continued)

| | | | | | |
|---|---|---|---|---|---|
| I change and create new happenings in my classroom and try new ways joyfully. | I will try some new ways and strategies. | If it is suggested, I try new ways to do things. | I'm pretty stressed about trying something I've not done before. | The old routines and ways are comfortable. Why change anything? | CREATIVITY |
| I respect and enjoy being a helpful team player. | I do help others on my team. | I will share ideas and give time to other team members. | I don't really function well with others; I'd rather do it myself. | Teams don't accomplish much and waste time. Not helpful at all. | TEAM MEMBERSHIP |
| I'm aware of children's cultural backgrounds. | I'm sensitive to the cultural learning styles of attending children. | I've developed the skill to promote multicultural respect and dignity. | My students' cultural diversity is reflected in classroom displays and materials. | I've expended time and effort to become knowledgeable concerning the culture of attending children. | CULTURAL SENSITIVITY |

Child behavior resulting from student teacher behavior is a focal point for discussions. Influencing factors such as room settings, routines, child uniqueness, and the student teacher's techniques, methods, and behaviors are examined closely.

Discussions that are descriptive and interpretative and involve value statements or standards are common.

Giving criticism is as much a skill as receiving it. Instructional criticism is given with the intent to improve, and usually specific ideas are offered for the listener's consideration. Discussions need to be viewed by student teachers as opportunities for growth, and met with a determination to get as much as possible from the supervisor. It is a time to listen and understand, rather than a time to defend one's actions.

Ideally, when you know and value yourself, and have a strong sense of your individual identity and self-worth, criticism can be taken at face value, in stride, and can be seen as providing helpful suggestions that can lead to reflection concerning new ideas, changes, and professional growth possibilities. You may hear yourself saying, "I'll take that into consideration. Thanks for sharing it with me."

Teachers are committed to lifelong learning, and student teachers begin to gauge the complexities inherent in working in the career field during their practicum experience. During discussions, student teachers can discover career skills they want to investigate, try out, or polish.

We have met student teachers who become angry, even aggressive, taking suggestions as personal attacks and others who have melted in tears, and still others skilled enough to walk away when strong emotions overcome them, saying, "I need to think about what you've said, and I'll get back to you." Asking questions to better understand, paraphrasing to clarify points, taking notes, and adding unknown information about a viewed situation were also common student techniques to help us—their college supervisors—see things in a more complete light.

### Pre- and Post-Conference Supervisor Meetings

More and more supervisors are conducting pre-observation conferences, so student teachers can brief them about classroom details and the activities or lesson plan the supervisor will observe. Post-conferences, after supervisor observation, are a standard procedure, and the review of observation notes helps student teachers reflect on their skills. Tips, resource ideas, and possible areas for growth are discussed.

## Dealing with Evaluations

Student teachers should try to develop a positive attitude about what may appear to be an emphasis on their weaknesses. However, this attitude may come slowly for some student teachers. Conferencing covers student teachers' strengths but sometimes brings with it that lingering feeling of having just received a report card.

SkillPath Seminars (1997) offers additional pointers in Figure 3–11.

When handling evaluator comments, one strategy a student teacher will find useful is saying, "Yes, I understand your concern. I was concerned as well. Let me tell you about the circumstances that occurred. Tell me what you would have suggested in that case." Discussions can describe a wide range of student and teacher behaviors. Clarification of terms can be helpful to student teachers. Keeping records of discussions will aid your planning; they can be reviewed prior to follow-up conferences. Action plans resulting from previous discussions are usually the primary focus of later talks.

College supervisors have the ultimate and final burden of approving a candidate for graduation from training programs. If one questions a gathering of supervisors, one hears both anguish and elation; elation that they have had a small part in an individual teacher's development, and anguish because they are forced to make tough decisions.

Their goal as supervisors is to assure that each candidate possesses the knowledge, skill, and competency necessary to interact sensitively, creatively, and successfully with both children and adults, and that student work has satisfied training standards. The task of assessing individual students involves observing human relations. Some student teachers of diverse cultural and language backgrounds may be tremendously talented and insightful with children, but they may find readings and academic testing particularly difficult, and may need tutoring assistance. With a language barrier, they may be unable to establish and maintain professional relationships with children and adults.

## Accepting Credit and Compliments

Student teachers may have a tendency to struggle when responding to complimentary comments instead of accepting credit in a humble and modest way. They deflect or let compliments pass without acknowledgement. It should not be too difficult to say, "Thank you for noticing the work necessary to set up my planned activity," or "I've been working on my ability to give children more time to work out answers to their own problems; I'm happy you noticed," or "I didn't give up on that problem though and it was a good solution, too."

> ***Student teacher quote***—*"My peer observation was valuable and eye-opening. The peer, I observed, had designed a unique science display on butterflies and her planned activity gave me ideas I used in my placement classroom."*
>
> **Joan Chang, Elementary School, San Jose, CA**

- Be your own best critic.
- Know your strengths and weaknesses.
- Assume the best intentions.
- Recognize that everyone needs feedback to grow.
- It's OK to dislike your behavior and still like yourself.
- Think about improving, not labeling yourself.
- Deal with the issue, forget personalities.
- You are the only person responsible for your behavior, not others.
- When the intention to learn from our mistakes overcomes our fear of failure, we're less likely to view criticism as a personal put-down.

▶ **Figure 3–11**
Receiving criticism. Used by permission of SkillPath Seminars.

# PEER OBSERVATIONS

It is wise to follow college instructor guidelines closely, if peer observations are assigned. Often, peer evaluators are asked to stick to the positive aspects of a peer's behavior, and suggest growth areas carefully or not at all unless requested. A rating form used by a peer can focus on a variety of teaching skills (see Figure 3–12).

Post-evaluation discussions center on the observed explaining to the observer what was happening during the observation, and what student teacher intentions

▶ **Figure 3-12**
Partial segment of a peer rating sheet.

Student teacher's name _____ Peer's name _____

Date _____

### STUDENT TEACHER EFFECTIVENESS SCALE

Excellent, Above Average, Average or Adequate, Needs Improvement, Unacceptable, Unable to Determine

   1         2         3         4         5         6

Place rating on continuum line.

A. Feeling Tone

  Warm _____ Cool
  Friendly _____ Withdrawn
  Supportive _____ Authoritarian
  Interacts often _____ Interacts rarely
  Accepts dependency behavior _____ Does not accept dependency behavior
  Physical contact often _____ Rare physical contact
  Open to suggestion _____ Rigid

B. Quality of Presentation and/or Interactions

  Organized _____ Seems disorganized
  Enthusiastic _____ Neutral
  Flexible _____ Rigid
  Clear _____ Vague
  Reasonable age level _____ Unreasonable age level
  Appropriate child expectations _____ Inappropriate expectations
  Promotes problem solving _____ Furnishes all answers
  Motivates _____ Turns off
  Rewards attention to tasks _____ Ignores or negatively reinforces attending behaviors
  Sensitive to cultural diversity _____ Ignores
  Expands interests _____ Ignores opportunities
  Provides developmentally appropriate activities _____ Activities limited by understanding
  Manages time well _____ Poor time management
  Discovery centers planned and prepared _____ Poor or little planning/preparation
  Child-initiated activities _____ Teacher-dominated activities
  Plans outdoor activities _____ Ignores outdoor planning
  Activity smoothness _____ Poorly sequenced
  Activity cleanup _____ Little or no cleanup

Greatest Strengths:

Areas for Future Growth:

Additional Comments:

_____
_____
_____

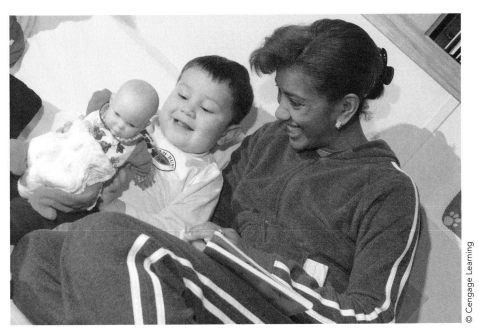

"Am I able to develop close, intimate relationships with children?"

© Cengage Learning

were present. The assignment may involve turning in both peers' notes of the after-observation discussion.

Increasingly, peer evaluations are seen as aiding student teachers' reflective thinking and their success in analyzing skills. Student teachers observing others often ask themselves important questions about their own teaching styles (see Figure 3–13).

## COMPETENCY-BASED TRAINING

Federal funds have provided for the identification of the Child Development Associate (CDA) **competencies**. A CDA is a person who is able to meet the physical, social, emotional, and intellectual growth needs of a group of children in a child development setting. These needs are met by establishing and maintaining a proper child care environment and by promoting good relations between parents and staff.

> **competencies**—the knowledge and skills desired in education professionals in various staffing positions in early childhood care.

CDA competencies are a widely distributed and accepted listing of early childhood teacher competency goals (see Figure 3–14). Your training program may use CDA competency guidelines in your training; if not, you may wish to view them for your own purposes.

### National Association for the Education of Young Children's Developmentally Appropriate Practice

NAEYC's **Developmentally Appropriate Practice in Early Childhood Education (DAP)** (Bredekamp & Copple, 1997; Copple & Bredekamp, 2009) is a tremendous accomplishment. Identifying competent teacher behaviors in a detailed fashion, it serves as a guidebook for many early childhood educators and teacher training programs. (Excerpts from the volume are found in the Appendix.) We suggest student teachers become familiar with the entire volume.

NAEYC's accredited early childhood centers and schools are considered to be "high quality programs." Saluja, Early, and Clifford (2002) report accredited programs employed teachers aware of developmentally appropriate practice who have as a group completed more years of education that do lower quality schools. Many of the characteristics of teachers in NAEYC accredited programs are listed in Figure 3–15.

▶ **Figure 3-14**

CDA competency goals and functional areas. Reproduced from *Essentials for Child Development Associates Working with Young Children* by permission of Carol Brunson Day, Ph.D.

| | CDA Competency Goals | Functional Areas | Definitions |
|---|---|---|---|
| I | To establish and maintain a safe, healthy learning environment | 1. Safe | Candidate provides a safe environment to prevent and reduce injuries. |
| | | 2. Healthy | Candidate promotes good health and nutrition and provides an environment that contributes to the prevention of illness. |
| | | 3. Learning Environment | Candidate uses space, relationships, materials, and routines as resources for constructing an interesting, secure, and enjoyable environment that encourages play, exploration, and learning. |
| II | To advance physical and intellectual competence | 4. Physical | Candidate provides a variety of equipment, and intellectual competence activities, and opportunities to promote the physical development of children. |
| | | 5. Cognitive | Candidate provides activities and opportunities that encourage curiosity, exploration, and problem solving appropriate to the developmental levels and learning styles of children. |
| | | 6. Communication | Candidate actively communicates with children and provides opportunities and support for children to understand, acquire, and use verbal and nonverbal means of communicating thoughts and feelings. |
| | | 7. Creative | Candidate provides opportunities that stimulate children to play with sound, rhythm, language, materials, space, and ideas in individual ways and to express their creative abilities. |
| III | To support social and emotional development and provide positive guidance | 8. Self | Candidate provides physical and emotional security for each child and helps each child to know, accept, and take pride in himself or herself and to develop a sense of independence. |
| | | 9. Social | Candidate helps each child feel accepted in the group, helps children learn to communicate and get along with others, and encourages feelings of empathy and mutual respect among children and adults. |
| | | 10. Guidance | Candidate provides a supportive environment in which children can begin to learn and practice appropriate and acceptable behaviors as individuals and as a group member. |
| IV | To establish positive and productive relationships with families | 11. Families | Candidate maintains an open, friendly, and cooperative relationship with each child's family, encourages their involvement in the program, and supports the child's relationship with his or her family. |
| V | To ensure a well-run, purposeful program responsive to participant needs | 12. Program Management | Candidate is a manager who uses all available resources to ensure an effective operation. The Candidate is a competent organizer, planner, record keeper, communicator, and a cooperative co-worker. |

| CDA Competency Goals | | Functional Areas | Definitions |
|---|---|---|---|
| VI | To maintain a commitment to professionalism | 13. Professionalism | Candidate makes decisions based on knowledge of early childhood theories and practices, promotes quality in child care services, and takes advantage of opportunities to improve competence, both for personal and professional growth and for the benefit of children and families. |

▶ **Figure 3-15**

Teacher characteristics*.

The teacher is able to
- form positive partnerships with families.
- establish and maintain teacher-family communication.
- communicate with families about individual child needs.
- establish a positive home-school working relationship.
- ascertain information concerning a family's definition of their own identity, including race, religion, home language, culture, and family structure.
- exhibit sensitivity concerning family's feelings about non-family child care.
- share information with families concerning program rules, expectations, and routines throughout the length of child attendance.
- foster children's well-being through showing respect and maintaining the classrooms' positive emotional climate and by participating in child-teacher conversation that displays caring, affection, and joy.
- express warmth to children through physical attention, eye contact, voice tone, and smiles.
- encourage and recognize children's achievements and accomplishments.
- respond appropriately, promptly, with developmentally appropriate reactions to children's negative and positive emotions, feelings, hurt and fear by providing comfort and supportive assistance.
- encourage children's appropriate expression of positive and negative emotions.
- evaluate and change the way they respond to children's individual needs.
- display a sensitivity to diverse child temperaments, abilities, activity levels, and cognitive and social development levels.
- promote and support child competence, self-reliance, exploration, and classroom materials use.
- display profession guidance and class management techniques and strategies.
- converse frequently and listen with attention and respect.
- encourage child-to-child interactions.
- support and encourage child friendships and play.
- help children practice social skills.
- help children resolve conflicts by promoting their expression of feelings, encouraging them to describing problems, and by creating and trying alternative solutions.
- guide children to learn and follow classroom rules.
- facilitate shy, withdrawn, bullied or excluded children's movement towards positive peer interaction.
- counter potential bias and discrimination by using a variety of teaching techniques including treating all children with equal respect and consideration.
- share classroom decision making through joint decisions about rules, plans, and activities.
- prevent behaviour problems by anticipating and preventive planning.
- promote dialogue about his/her own and other's emotions.

*(continues)*

▶ **Figure 3-15** (continued)

- model pro-social and respectful behavior with all children and staff.
- work with others to develop and implement children's individual learning plans as needed.
- observe and identify children's challenging behaviors and contextual factors that are influential.
- respond to children's challenging behaviors with attention to the child's and others safety, in a calm and respectful manner that provides information on acceptable behavior.
- actively teach appropriate social communication and the skill of self-regulation of emotions.
- guide and support child behaviors such as persistance when frustrated, playing cooperatively, using language to communicate needs, turn taking, gaining control of physical impulses, expressing negative emotions without harming others or self, using problem-solving techniques, and gaining self awareness.
- promote children's self confidence and positive attitudes toward learning such as persistence, engagement, curiosity, and mastery.
- offer activities with children that help children learn to understand empathize with, and consider another's perspective.
- offer print awareness activities.
- offer varied experience with books.
- provide children with varied and multiple activities involving writing.
- offer activities and experiences promoting children's phonological awareness.
- support child's self-initiated writing efforts.
- provide books and writing materials.
- plan activities and materials in the domain of mathematics.
- provide a curriculum with varied opportunities for children to learn key science concepts and principles.
- offer drawing and graphing activities.
- provide children with access to technology.
- use technology to extend class learning.
- present activities and opportunity to children to gain an appreciation of art, music, drama, and dance in ways that reflect cultural diversity.
- offer a curriculum to encourage good health practices.
- offer a curriculum to build an understanding of diversity.
- offer activities concerning the community in which children live.
- promote and maintain a classroom learning environment in which diverse children can progress and increase their autonomy, responsibility, and empathy.
- recognize socially appropriate behavior.
- work with families to help children participate successfully in the early childhood setting.
- support the development and maintenance of the child's home language.
- use a variety of teaching strategies.
- use of a conversational manner in teaching, and an informal easygoing teaching style.

*NOTE: This is not a complete or comprehensive listing but rather the authors attempt to paint a picture of the many abilities and competencies teachers in high quality programs display.

## THE WHOLE TEACHER

Teaching competency growth can be compared to child growth. Teachers develop intellectually, socially-emotionally, physically, and creatively, as do children. Skills often omitted on competency listings, yet ones becoming more and more important to early childhood teachers in our society, are stress management techniques, holistic health awareness and practice, moral and ethical strength, researching skill, parenting education and family guidance counseling, public relations, and political know-how. Job situations can create the need for skills not covered in your teacher training. As society changes, a teacher's role as a partner to families may change also.

## Personal Abilities

What personal characteristics, dispositions, traits, abilities, or gifts are described in early childhood teachers? Many writers in the field of education believe effective teachers have few problems with child guidance, possess a sense of humor, are fair and empathetic, are more democratic than autocratic, and are able to relate easily and naturally to pupils on any basis, in groups or one to one. Teacher behaviors that exemplify the effective teacher include:

- a willingness to be flexible, and to be direct or indirect as the situation demands
- an ability to perceive the world from the child's point of view
- the ability to personalize their teaching
- a willingness to experiment, and try new things
- skill in asking questions, to draw answers from the child, as opposed to seeing themselves as a kind of answering service
- knowledge of subject matter and related areas
- the ability to assess child growth and development
- the ability to reflect back an appreciative attitude, as evidenced by nods, comments, smiles, and the like
- use of conversational matter in teaching, and informal, easygoing teaching styles

Effective teachers are a unique combination of skills and abilities. They are similar in dedication to excellence but achieve their goals in diverse and dissimilar ways.

## REFLECTIVE BEHAVIORS

Not all educators agree on what constitutes reflective teaching, as it is still under study, but Schoonmaker (1998) has identified three possible elements:

1. cognitive functioning, which includes information processing and teaching decisions
2. background, which includes individual past experiences, goals, values, and social interactions
3. individual perceptions, feelings, and interpretations of classroom events and happenings

Teacher training programs that emphasize reflective teaching are based on a desire to help student teachers move toward serious and thoughtful questioning, and to provide an understanding of their own and others' teaching practices, perceptions, actions, feelings, values, and cultural biases.

A myth among some student teachers promotes the idea that teaching success can happen if someone will only tell them how to attain it, or point them to a book containing all the answers. Reflective teaching behaviors, on the other hand, lead student teachers to construct their own, personal theory of teaching and learning, through hands-on classroom experiences, careful and keen observation, and social interaction with children and other adults. Loranger (1997) lists and describes these reflective teacher behaviors (see Figure 3–16).

## Emotional Intelligence

Schoonmaker (1998) believes that learning to deal with the wide range of emotions that children can evoke in student teachers and the thought of being in charge are so overwhelming that "it colors almost everything they do." *High emotional intelligence,* a term used by Kremenitzer and Miller (2008), is believed to be displayed

▶ Figure 3-16

List of reflective behaviors with descriptors. Originally published in Ann L. Loranger's article titled "Exploring Reflective Behaviors with Pre-service Teachers" in the fall 1997 issue of *Teaching and Learning: The Journal of Natural Inquiry*, Vol. 12, No. 1. It is reprinted here with permission from the publisher.

| Behaviors | Descriptors |
|---|---|
| Risk-taker. | Open to change; willingness to try new approaches to learning; willing to change direction in the middle of a lesson; willing to consider new evidence; invites evaluation of teaching. |
| Flexible/thinks on feet. | Knows when to change direction during a lesson; seizes "teachable moments." |
| Willingness to confront. | Willing to explore conceptions of self as a teacher, not so secure as to not want to learn and grow; willing to confront conceptions of self squarely and openly. |
| Considers context when making decisions. | Carefully examines context when making decisions; understands that contexts either enable or limit educational activity. |
| Accepts multiple perspectives. | Views an issue simultaneously from the perspective of several people (teacher, student, researcher, family). |
| Accepts responsibility for success/failure of lesson. | Recognizes decisions she makes; looks to herself for explanations when things go awry; accepts responsibility for choices. |
| Ability to recognize dilemmas and make rational choices. | Ability to use practical, pedagogical, and ethical criteria when making choices; ability to assess consequence of choices. |
| Links theory and practice/ makes connections. | Knows how to use research and integrate it into instruction; comes to value theory as a means for expanding understanding. |

when teachers cope with job stresses successfully and are able to, when emotional themselves, model positive behaviors and attitudes for children. These authors suggest that a strong correlation exists between reflective thinking and good classroom management skills, especially when (1) teachers are able to accurately perceive and express emotions, (2) they are able to use and generate coping behaviors that help them better handle emotionally charged situations or suggest coping strategies to children, (3) they are able to understand and label a wide range of emotions and/or help children do so, and (4) they are able to reflect upon, manage, and regulate their emotions while promoting children's emotional growth and ability to think about courses of action before taking action.

## Dispositions

*Dispositions* are associated with the writings of Katz (1993) and are used to describe desirable teaching behaviors. Various attempts to define the term include words like *inclinations, traits, tendencies, propensities, proclivities,* and *predilections.* Katz believes usage of the term *dispositions* is ambiguous and inconsistent. She believes dispositions are habits of mind, or tendencies to act or react to events, people, situations, or happenings in ways unique to the individual. Descriptors such as kind, friendly, assertive, thoughtful, curious, and so on, might apply, rather than descriptors associated with skill or specific knowledge.

A student teacher can have a goal to strengthen certain desirable teaching dispositions and weaken undesirable ones. Having skill and knowledge of professional practices may not mean one actually uses them. Katz uses the example of a children's curriculum that presents early, formal instruction in reading skills during preschool that may undermine children's dispositions to be readers.

## Critical Thinking

College and university educators have designed courses of study and subsequent class activities to help college students majoring in education become aware of and use critical thinking skills. Many concluded that identifying critical thinking skills and using them can be increased through training exercises. Ennis (1985) identified thirteen dispositions, which were defined as attitudes and motivations, of critical thinkers. These include the ability to:

1. Adopt an open-minded approach.
2. Take a position, and change it when the evidence and reasons are sufficient to do so.
3. Take into account the total situation.
4. Try to be well informed.
5. Seek as much precision as the subject permits.
6. Deal in an orderly manner with the parts of a complex whole.
7. Look for alternatives.
8. Seek reasons.
9. Seek a clear statement of the issue.
10. Keep in mind the original or basic concern.
11. Use credible sources and mention them.
12. Remain relevant to the main point.
13. Display sensitivity when faced with the feelings, level of knowledge, and degree of sophistication of others.

Let's look at a couple of classroom situations and decide what critical thinking skills could be modeled by this teacher.

*Situation 1:* A posted chart keeps slipping off the wall. Children bring it to the teacher's attention, and Jamie asks, "Why won't it stay? What can we do to fix it?"

*Situation 2:* Large wooden blocks are being carried outside for play on a cement patio. Children are busily making structures. Teacher knows these blocks were donated by the parent group and now are being scratched and damaged. She decides to discuss the problem with the class.

*Situation 3:* Everyone wants a turn looking at a new book read at story time. The waiting list is long, and some children are anxious that they won't have a turn before having to leave for home.

Many classroom environments may encourage teacher action prior to thinking or taking the time to process a decision. As a student teacher, you will take on an increasing number of daily decisions. Would you use the thoughtful, reflective approach of a critical thinker in the situations above?

In the first situation, a critical thinking approach to the falling chart problem would begin with the teacher recognizing the alertness and helpfulness of the children. Jamie might be answered, "Let's find that out, Jamie. Why might the chart keep slipping?" If nothing is offered by the children, the teacher could think out loud, giving a few possible reasons using disposition #8 above—such as, "Is there wind blowing in our window?"—and also perhaps involving #3, #5, and #12 above.

The teacher's behavior would suggest the teacher enjoys the quest for answers. If children offer ideas such as "The tacks fell out," "The glue came off," or "Johnny did it," each idea is accepted and investigated. Analyze the last two situations to determine how many critical thinking skills might be modeled by the teacher.

How does a student teacher become proficient in critical thinking skills? Many times teachers learn through conscious effort, practice, experimenting, making mistakes, and by using reflective thinking and of course, seeing or hearing other teachers using them.

## Self-Perception

Researchers have attempted to probe how effective teachers view their abilities and the abilities of others. If a teacher likes and trusts himself, that teacher is more likely to perceive others the same way. An excerpt from Hamachek (1992), whose writings are dated but still valuable, follows:

> They seem to have generally more positive views of others—students, colleagues, and administrators. They do not seem to be as prone to view others as critical, attacking people with ulterior motives: rather they are seen as potentially friendly and worthy in their own right. They have a more favorable view of democratic classroom procedures. They seem to have the ability to see things as they seem to others—from the other's point of view. They do not seem to see students as children "you do things to" but rather as individuals capable of doing for themselves once they feel trusted, respected, and valued.

Students entering the field of teaching have their own ideas regarding qualities important for success.

You will receive feedback from your cooperating teacher, your supervisor, and perhaps others. This input is the basis of your understanding of how your competencies are viewed by others. Your perception of your teaching competencies is formed based on your own self-analysis and others' feedback.

## Self-Analysis

Self-analysis will increase your awareness of discrepancies and inconsistencies between your competency goals and your present teaching behavior. As you become more accurate in self-perception, your professional identity and confidence will grow. You may even be able to predict how others will react to your teaching behaviors. You will resolve the tendency to center on yourself (a common tendency of beginning teachers) and will develop the ability to focus more on children's learning and teacher and child interactions. You will come to realize teachers wear many "hats" on any given day. This can include negotiator, nurse, record keeper, companion, confidant, co-explorer, keen observer, traffic supervisor, translator, instructional planner, guidance counselor, maintenance person, supply clerk, and timekeeper, to name but a few.

After self-assessment, you can decide what additional skills you would like to acquire. Put these skills in the order of their importance to you. They are your goals. You are the director of your learning and the designer of your plan for future accomplishment.

## THE LAST STEP

All is for nothing if, armed with the information you have received as feedback concerning your competencies, you don't take action to increase and strengthen your growth. Should your supervisor or cooperating teacher ask, "What skills and abilities are you working on?" or "What are your short range goals?" You should be able to describe them and perhaps match them to some list of standards. Let's look at an example of a long-range goal that practicing teachers hold dear. When asked about the goal of attaining the teaching skill/ability/competency to develop and instill in each child in their care a love of books, early childhood educators could describe what plans and actions they have made or are taking to reach this goal. This might include an attempt to become more knowledgeable and familiar with a wide range of children's literature that is appropriate to the children they serve, presenting books and using a new strategy that engages children or that they have seen other teachers use, examining a classroom library collection to ascertain whether existing books suit children's backgrounds and interests, trying a new approach with nonfiction books based upon their own creativity or their research, or some other plan or action that increases their teaching skill or ability. They also might describe and evaluate the success and effectiveness, or lack of it, in what they have attempted.

## ▶ SUMMARY

Observation, assessment, evaluation, and discussion are integral parts of student teaching. Different methods are used to observe the student's progress. The realization of professional growth through the use of observational tools and subsequent discussion depends on a number of different factors.

It is important for the student teacher to maintain a positive attitude and consider self-evaluation as a vehicle for improvement. Planning to enhance strengths and overcome weaknesses takes place during discussions and is a growth-promoting part of student teaching.

The complete teacher emerges from of a vast array of possible teaching skills and abilities. Teaching competencies, or student performance objectives, have been identified by individuals and groups, based on value judgments concerning appropriate or desirable teaching behaviors. There are many teaching competency lists in circulation.

Examples of different types of rating and self-rating forms were presented to aid the student's development of a plan of priorities for future competency growth.

## ▶ HELPFUL WEBSITES

http://www.cdacouncil.org
Council for Professional Recognition. This site provides information about Child Development Associate (CDA) credentialing.

http://www.ncate.org
National Council for Accreditation of Teacher Education. Search for information concerning national standards and accreditation.

 Additional resources for this chapter can be found by visiting the companion website at *www.cengage.com/education/machado.*

## ▶ SUGGESTED ACTIVITIES

A. Form groups of four. On slips of paper, write down your fears about being observed and evaluated. Put the slips in a container. Each student takes a turn drawing a slip of paper and describing the fear and the possible cause.

B. On the continuum between each extreme, where do you belong? After moving the columns farther apart and drawing a line between the words, draw a stick person on the spot representing you

| | |
|---|---|
| Talkative | Quiet |
| Eager to please | Self-assured |
| Outgoing | Shy |
| Punctual | Late |
| Accepting | Rejecting |
| Leader | Follower |
| Flexible | Rigid |
| Sense of humor | Serious |
| Organized | Disorganized |
| Studious | Unstudious |
| Patient | Impatient |
| Warm | Cold |

| | |
|---|---|
| Enthusiastic | Apathetic |
| Active | Passive |
| Open | Secretive |
| Direct | Indirect |
| Good communicator | Poor communicator |
| Autonomous | Conformist |
| Creative | Conservative |
| Animated | Reserved |
| Talented | Average |
| Sexist | Nonsexist |
| Specialist | Generalist |

C. As a class, try voting on the validity of the following statements. Use a thumbs-up signal if the statement is true. Remain still if you believe the statement is false, or if you cannot decide. When voting on the more controversial statements, ask your instructor to turn away from the class and elect a student to count the votes and record the final tally.

1. It is unfair to compare one student teacher to another.
2. It is wise to let one student teacher tutor another.

3. Peer observations should be part of everyone's student teaching experience.
4. Confidentiality in rating student teachers is imperative.
5. Sharing discussion notes with another student teacher may be helpful to both students.
6. Evaluations by supervisors or cooperating teachers should not be shared with employers of student teachers.
7. A student teacher's placement could inhibit the growth of professional teaching competencies.
8. One can experience considerable growth without evaluative feedback.
9. Criticism is threatening.
10. Being observed and evaluated is really a game. Self-discovery and being motivated to do your best are more important.
11. An individual's manner of dress, hairstyle, and the like should not be included in an assessment, because these have nothing to do with effective teaching.
12. Observation and evaluation can increase professional excellence.
13. Every student should receive a copy of all written performance evaluations.
14. There is no such thing as constructive criticism.
15. Observers often more easily see their own teaching weaknesses and inadequacies in the student teachers they observe.

# ▶ REVIEW

A. Name three tools used in observational data collection. Give examples.

B. Complete the following statement:

The five individuals who could probably provide the most reliable and valid data concerning my teaching competency are . . .

C. Five individuals observed the same traffic accident. Match the person in Column I to the feature in Column II that he or she would be most likely to have observed.

| I | II |
|---|---|
| 1. car salesperson | a. driver's license and/or license plate numbers |
| 2. police officer | b. children involved in the accident |
| 3. doctor | c. damage to the automobiles |
| 4. teacher | d. make and model of the automobiles involved |
| 5. insurance adjuster | e. injuries of those involved |

D. Write three pieces of advice to student teachers to help them accept constructive criticism.

# ▶ REFERENCES

Bredekamp, S., & Copple, C. (Eds.). (1997). *Developmentally appropriate practice in early childhood programs* (Rev. ed.). Washington, DC: National Association for the Education of Young Children.

Copple, C., & Bredekamp, S. (Eds.). (2009). *Developmentally appropriate practice in early childhood programs: Serving children from birth through age 8.* Washington, DC: National Association for the Education of Young Children.

Ennis, R. H. (1985). A logical basis for measuring critical thinking skills. *Educational Leadership, 43*(2), 56–64.

Hamachek, D. (1992). *Encounters with the self* (4th ed.). New York: Harcourt Brace.

Hyson, M. (Ed.). (2003). *Preparing early childhood professionals: NAEYC's standards for programs.* Washington, DC: National Association for the Education of Young Children.

Katz, L. C. (1993). *Dispositions, definitions, and implications for early childhood practice.* Champaign, IL: ERIC Clearinghouse on Elementary and Early Childhood Education.

Kremenitzer, J. P., & Miller, R. (2008, July). Are you a highly, qualified, emotionally intelligent early childhood educator? *Young Children, 63*(4) 106–112.

Lacey, C. H., Guffey, J. S., & Rampp, L. C. (2000, Spring). Clinical supervision using interactive compressed television. *The Teacher Educator, 35*(4), 97–107.

Loranger, A. (1997, Fall). Exploring reflective behaviors with pre-service teachers. *Teaching and Learning, 12*(13), 45.

Saluja, G., Early, D. M., & Clifford, R. (2002). Demographic characteristics of early childhood teachers and structural elements of early care and education in the United States. *Early Childhood Research and Practice, 4*(1), 132–141.

Schoonmaker, F. (1998, Spring). Promise and possibility: Learn to teach. *Teacher's College Record, 99*(3), 27–32.

SkillPath Seminars. (1997). *Conflict management skills for women.* Mission, KS: SkillPath.

Titone, C., Sherman, S., & Palmer, R. (1998, Winter). Cultivating student teachers' disposition and ability to construct knowledge. *Action in Teacher Education, XIX*(4), 43–49.

Wortham, S. C. (1995). *Measurement and evaluation in early childhood education* (2nd ed.). Englewood Cliffs, NJ: Prentice-Hall.

© Cengage Learning

# Programming

# CHAPTER 4

# Instructional Planning

OBJECTIVES **After reading this chapter, you should be able to:**

1. Complete a written activity plan or lesson plan form.
2. Describe three different approaches to curriculum development.
3. Plan a group activity.
4. Describe a teaching unit (theme) approach to early childhood instruction.
5. Outline preparation steps in theme construction.

## STUDENT TEACHER SCENARIO

**Setting:** Outdoor play area. Inge, a student teacher in an urban public school preschool, is about to present an outdoor science activity.

Inge has planned an exciting outdoor science activity. After turning in her lesson plan, securing her cooperating teacher's approval, and collecting her visuals at a local creek, she takes a group of three-and-a-half-year-olds to a shaded, grassy area outdoors.

She has prepared a small table and a covered tub with air holes. Children's paint aprons are waiting on a chair. At this time of day, other mixed-age classes are using the play yard. Inge gathers her group of seven children and tells them she has a surprise in the tub, but they are to put on paint aprons first. The group stands around the tub. Inge has children guess what is in the tub. Then with a flourishing "Ta Da," she removes the cover. Small creek frogs start to jump from the tub. Pandemonium and panic break out immediately. Some children run away screaming. Other children in the yard approach and crowd around the tub, delighted with the frogs. Inge tries to assure the children left in her group that the small frogs will not hurt them. Other teachers in the yard come to help.

### Questions for Discussion:

1. What step or steps on Inge's activity plan guide were poorly conceived (see Figure 4–9)?

2. Think about Inge's educational intent. What would you say to Inge if you were her cooperating teacher?

3. Can anything positive be found from Inge's failed plan?

4. Does Inge's cooperating teacher share some responsibility for the lesson's outcome?

# LOOKING AT ACCEPTED CURRICULUM STANDARDS AND PRACTICES

All professional early childhood teachers face the task of designing daily activities for young children. They will, no doubt, plan based on their own philosophy, or a teaching team's philosophy, concerning what is best and right. They will consider recognized professional standards. Early childhood learning standards can cover a wide range of developmental areas, including health and physical well-being, social and emotional well-being, language development, symbol systems knowledge, academic or intellectual knowledge, and general knowledge of the world around them, or some other human growth and development area. Such standards are defined here as statements that describe learning outcomes as the result of educational experiences. Just as some families expect young children to clear dishes after eating or make their beds upon rising, other do not. Preschools and centers also differ. Well-known standards are found in the following publications, but some programs create their own or use other sources not listed:

◆ *Developmentally Appropriate Practice in Early Childhood Programs* (Bredekamp & Copple, 1997; Copple & Bredekamp, 2009), a publication of the National Association for the Education of Young Children.

◆ *Head Start Performance Standards* (The Head Start Bureau, Administration for Children and Families, Department of Health and Human Services, 1975).

◆ *Early Childhood Program Standards and Accreditation Performance Criteria* (National Association for the Education of Young Children, 2007).

◆ *Early Childhood Curriculum, Assessment, and Program Evaluation* (National Association for the Education of Young Children and the National Association of Early Childhood Specialists in State Departments of Education [joint position statement], 2003).

◆ *Early Learning Standards: Creating the Conditions for Success* (National Association for the Education of Young Children and the National Association of Early Childhood Specialists in State Departments of Education [joint position statement], 2002).

In addition to those listed above, early childhood standards have also been established by state legislatures and Congress. State standards may exceed a state's licensing regulations in an effort to improve the quality of that state's early childhood programs. Figure 4–1 displays a page from California Department of Education's 2008 standards publication, *California Preschool Learning Foundations* (2008). The No Child Left Behind Act, an education reform act passed by Congress in 2001, and a federal administration initiative, *Good Start, Grow Smart* (2002), were both designed to help children achieve the goal of reading at grade level by the end of the third grade. Both of these, and other factors, have promoted the planning or development of early learning guidelines or standards in one-fourth of the states in the United States.

▶ **Figure 4-1**
California Preschool Learning Foundations—Selected segment of mathematics domain.

| At around 48 months of age | At around 60 months of age |
|---|---|
| 2.0 Children begin to understand number relationships and operations in their everyday environment. | 2.0 Children expand their understanding of number relationships and operations in their everyday environment. |
| 2.1 Compare visually (with or without counting) two groups of objects that are obviously equal or nonequal and communicate, "more" or "same."* | 2.1 Compare, by counting or matching, two groups of up to five objects and communicate, "more," "same as," or "fewer" (or "less").* |

(continues)

▶ **Figure 4-1** (continued)

| At around 48 months of age | At around 60 months of age |
|---|---|
| **Examples** | **Examples** |
| • Examines two groups of counting bears, one with two bears and the other with six bears, and indicates or points to the group of six bears when asked which group has more.<br>• Communicates, "I want more—she's got more stamps than me" during a small group activity.<br>• Communicates, "We have the same," when referring to appie slices during snack time. | • Counts the number of rocks he has and the number a friend has and communicates, "Five and five, you have the same as me."<br>• Compares a group of four bears to a group of five bears and communicates, "This one has less."<br>• Counts her own sand toys, then counts a friend's and communicates, "You have more." |
| 2.2  Understand that adding to (or taking away) one or more objects from a group will increase (or decrease) the number of object in the group. | 2.2  Understand that adding one or taking away one changes the number in a small group of object by exactly one. |
| **Examples** | **Examples** |
| • Has three beads, takes another, and communicates, "Now I have more beads."<br>• When the teacher adds more cats on the flannel board, indicates that there are now more cats.<br>• While playing bakery, communicates that after selling some bagels there are now fewer bagels in the bakery shop.<br>• Gives away two dolls and communicates that now she have fewer. | • Adds another car to a pile of five to have six, just like his friend.<br>• Removes one animal from a collection of eight animals and communicates, "She has seven now."<br>• Correctly predicts that if one more car is added to a group of four cars, there will be five. |

\* Comparison may be done visually, tactilely, or auditorily.
From California Department of Education (2008). California Preschool Learning Foundations (Vo. 1) Sacramento, CA: Author.

Geist and Baum (2005) point out standards do not dictate how goals should be met but give schools and teachers the freedom to create their own curriculum and implement it. Helpful websites, which contain links to both national and state standards in all content areas, are http://www.educationworld.com and http://www.edstandards.org.

You may have worked at a facility using local, state, national, or independently created standards during your training. If the school was publicly funded, you may have been required to cite what standard was used to create a lesson or activity plan.

The dilemma facing educators creating program curricula is to put philosophy and standards to work in curriculum design and daily lessons and/or activities and to weigh or insert parental and perhaps community concerns and input into that curriculum. An additional task is to decide *what to teach* and *how to teach*. *What* can be defined as the scope of information, experiences, and skills to be presented, offered, and promoted. The *how* is defined as the teaching techniques and teaching vehicles to be used.

## IDENTIFYING CHILD INTERESTS AND NEEDS

You will plan, prepare, and present classroom activities. The teaching day may contain structured (teacher-planned) and unstructured (child-initiated) activities. The cooperating teacher's philosophy, the school's philosophy, the identified program goals, and the classroom setting determine the balance between child-initiated activities and teacher-planned activities. In activity-centered classrooms, student teachers arrange room centers to invite and promote child discovery and learning.

Many experts suggest young children's attitudes and learning behaviors are the foundation of children's success. Hyson (2005) states that children's positive approaches to learning include at least four dimensions. These are (1) initiative, engagement, and persistence; (2) reasoning, planning, and problem solving; (3) curiosity, and eagerness to learn; and (4) invention and imagination.

Hyson believes adults can encourage and discourage these positive approaches, and teacher observation can discern children's needs for special support and assistance. Observation is complex because children have many ways of displaying competencies, which may be influenced by their unique temperaments, cultural conditioning, innate characteristics, and individual family beliefs and values.

Burman (2009) cautions an educator to avoid a curriculum that does not interest or excite, or one that does not support children's thinking or learning styles. Boring activities and passive participation can or may encourage disengagement and possible disruptive child behavior. Instead, Burman urges teachers to use child–teacher *conversations* to discover interests and concerns. She posits doing so can lead to a more suitable curriculum. How can teachers become skilled conversationalists? She believes by listening intently to children's agendas, passions, feelings, logic, and intelligent thinking, and by probing for information. And by asking questions that clarify and check if the educator has understood accurately while also enjoying the intimacy of the child's conversational sharing behavior.

The authors remember the challenge and effort it takes to have meaningful conversations with every child every day, especially those high-energy dynamos who rarely sit still long enough to chat or the cautious children who aren't quite sure they trust adults.

## Using Child Interest and Improvising

Teaching is a complex task requiring continual, on-the-spot decision making (Carter & Curtis, 1994). Carter and Curtis believe master teachers have certain qualities that distinguish them from teachers who depend on curriculum activity books, follow the same theme plans year after year, or struggle daily to get the children involved in anything productive. Master teachers possess a set of attitudes and habits of mind to respond to classroom dynamics and multiple needs of children with the readiness of an improvisational artist.

An example of the master teacher mind-set can be seen in the actions of one student teacher, Fredrica, in the following:

> A book about cats was brought to school by a child. After being previewed, Fredrica shared the book with a group of the child's friends. Susan, a four-year-old, went to the scrap paper and craft table later in the afternoon and cut long paper claws for one hand. She then asked Fredrica for tape to secure them to her fingers. They again looked at the book's illustrations to look for cats with long claws. Susan enjoyed meowing, pretending to scratch a tree trunk, and climbing on the outdoor structure. Other children wanted to cut and color cat claws of their own. Fredrica supplied the materials and soon a number of children were pretending to be cats! Fredrica was prepared to intervene if claws were used aggressively.

*Student Teacher Quote*—"My supervisor suggested I plan activities in areas of my own personal interests or hobbies. Since I'm a needlework enthusiast, I planned an activity that taught simple embroidery skills. The children (even the boys) loved working with the blunt needles and colorful thread. Some children completed longer term sewing projects the next day."

**Amanda St. Clair, Evergreen Valley College, San Jose, CA**

The following day Fredrica set up a discovery area, which included domestic animal sounds, cat figures to manipulate, and pictures of different house cat varieties. Poems about cats were part of story times, a cat visited the school, and cat-care particulars were listed by the children on a wall chart, printed with child ideas. Fredrica and the children explored how the cats' sharp claws helped them climb trees in one activity, and how cats use their claws to protect themselves in another. Larger cats were named and their similarities compared in a book Fredrica found at the public library.

You will be searching for activity ideas that will interest and challenge the group of children to which you are assigned. Observing children's play choices and favorite activities will give you ideas (see Figure 4–2). Children's conversations provide clues as to what has captured their attention. Watch for excitement among the children and make comments in your pocket notebook concerning individual and group curiosity and play selections. What are they eager to try? How much time is spent exploring or concentrating on an experience (see Figure 4–3)?

▶ **Figure 4-2**
Children discuss ways to use classroom materials.

© Cengage Learning

▶ **Figure 4-3**
Discovering together is an enjoyable aspect of teaching "The flower's name is peony."

© Cengage Learning

Effective teaching includes being observant of children's interest in their environment, and using your own interests and enthusiasm to motivate them. After the children's interests are identified, you can use the three-W strategy to discover *what is known*, *what is unknown but can be known*, and *what has been learned*. This format provides an easy way to engage children in learning.

Many times, a teacher piques children's interests by focusing their attention on a new feature, event, or object. The unknown serves as the basis for teacher activity planning, and the teacher's supportive assistance. The spontaneous or creative planning ability of an educator striving to adjust classroom circumstances, to lead children to answers with or without teacher's help, is part of the joy of teaching. The third *W* aims to promote putting what is learned into words, acts, or representations. It is a kind of recap, or solidifying activity that reinforces what has been discovered or experienced.

## CONSTRUCTIVISM AND DEVELOPMENTALLY APPROPRIATE PRACTICE

It is difficult to find material dealing with early childhood curriculum development pedagogy that does not mention the terms *child-centered, child-initiated, active learning, constructivist,* and *developmentally appropriate practice.*

The first three terms are self-explanatory. **Constructivism**, as a cognitive-developmental notion, has direct roots within the structuralism that underlies Piaget's theory of intellectual development (O'Loughlin, 1991). A *constructivist* takes the position that learners must have experiences with hypothesizing and predicting, manipulating objects, posing questions, researching answers, imagining, investigating, and inventing for *new constructions* to be developed (Fosnot, 1989).

What distinguishes the constructivist approach is the mental action that takes place as children infer from what they are experiencing and create a system of knowledge from the activity. A secure, rather than coercive, classroom environment is believed to allow children to cooperate, develop respect for one another, exercise their curiosity, and gain confidence in their ability to figure things out on their own and become autonomous.

**constructivism**—a term relating to constructivist theory based on the belief that children construct knowledge for themselves rather than having it conveyed to them by some external source. This theory is often attributed to the work of Jean Piaget.

### Developmentally Appropriate Practice (DAP)

The National Association for the Education of Young Children's (NAEYC's) *Developmentally Appropriate Practice* (DAP) in Early Childhood Programs (Bredekamp & Copple, 1997, Copple & Bredekamp, 2009) has been highly praised and acclaimed as one of the field's most respected guide to activity planning. Regarded by some educators as a curriculum model and by others a guide, it has been revised and expanded. It is a must-read-*and-study* for educators who plan curriculums for young children. Figure 4–4 presents a subsection of the guide's 2009 revision and outlines a wide range of developmentally appropriate teacher strategies.

▶ **Figure 4-4**
The excellent teacher.

> **To be an excellent teacher means...**
>
> **teaching to enhance development and learning**
>
> Good teachers continually use their knowledge and judgment to make intentional decisions about which materials, interactions, and learning experiences are likely to be most effective for the group and for each individual child in it. Many different teaching approaches and strategies have value in the early childhood classroom.
>
> ***Excellent teachers use a wide range of teaching strategies***
> An effective teacher makes use of the strategy that fits a particular situation and the purpose or purposes she has in mind. She considers what the child or children already know and can do and the

(continues)

▶ **Figure 4-4** (continued)

learning goals for the specific situation. Often she may try one strategy, see that it doesn't work, and then try something else. She has a variety of strategies at the ready and remains flexible and observant so that she can determine which to use. Here are some of the strategies excellent teachers have at their disposal:

- Teachers **acknowledge** what children do or say. They let children know that they have noticed by giving children positive attention, sometimes through comments, sometimes through just sitting nearby and observing (*"Thanks for your help, Kavi" "You found another way to show 5"*).

- Teachers **encourage** persistence and effort rather than just praising and evaluating what the child has done (*"You're thinking of lots of words to describe the dog in the story—let's keep going!"*).

- Teachers **give specific feedback** rather than general comments (*"The beanbag didn't get all the way to the hoop, James, so you might try throwing it harder"*).

- Teachers **model** attitudes, ways of approaching problems, and behavior toward others, showing children rather than just telling them (*"Hmm, that didn't work and I need to think about why" "I'm sorry, Ben, I missed part of what you said. Please tell me again"*).

- Teachers **demonstrate** when they show the correct way to do something. This usually applies to a procedure that needs to be done in a certain way (e.g., using a wire whisk, writing a letter P).

- Teachers **create or add challenge** so that a task goes a bit beyond what the children can already do. (For example, when the teacher removes several chips from a set, asks how many are left, and finds the children can count the remaining chips accurately, he may then add difficult by *hiding* the remaining chips. Figuring out how many are left just from knowing the number that were removed is more challenging.) In other cases, teachers **reduce challenge** to meet children where they are (e.g., by simplifying the task).

- Teachers **ask questions** that provoke children's thinking (*"If you couldn't talk to your partner, how else could you let him know what to do?"*).

- Teachers **give assistance** (e.g., a cue or hint) to help children work on the edge of their current competence (*"Can you think of a word that rhymes with your name, Matt? How about bat … Matt/bat? What else rhymes with Matt and bat?"*).

- Teachers **provide information**, directly giving children facts, verbal labels, and other information (*"This one that looks like a big mouse with a short tail is called a vole"*).

- Teachers **give directions** for children's action or behavior (*"Touch each block only once as you count them" "You want to move that icon over here? OK, click on it and keep holding down, then drag the icon to wherever you want"*).

Some of these strategies involve less action and direction on the part of the adult and more on the part of the child; in others, the adult is more proactive or directive.

From: Copple, C. & Bredekamp, S. (Eds) (2009) Developmentally appropriate practice in early childhood programs: Serving children from birth through age 8. Washington, D.C.: National Association for the Education of Young Children.

## A CURRICULUM CONTINUUM

Educators tend to envision curriculum approaches and practice along a continuum between child-centered or child-based to traditional, teacher-decided activities (see Figure 4–5). There is disagreement concerning which curriculum style is best suited for children. Copple and Bredekamp (2009) believe the early childhood field has become polarized and is in heated debate over direct instruction models of curriculum versus child-guided models. They offer educators planning curriculum examples of how a school or center can draw on both styles. Figure 4–6 is a list of their statements.

▷ **Figure 4-5**
Instructional approach continuum.

| Teacher Controlled Curriculum | Instruction (including theme instruction or other approaches) | Child-Initiated Curriculum |
| --- | --- | --- |
| Activity plans primarily grow out of teacher decisions concerning the appropriate content of activities based on the teacher's idea of children's educational, social, and physical needs and interests. | Activity plans usually grow from child interests and needs. Teacher both instructs and plans child-choice opportunities around a central topic, content area, theme, or learning center. | Children follow their own search for answers while teacher plans to support children's investigation and discussion. Teacher provides materials and settings to aid discovery and further child research and discussion. |

▷ **Figure 4-6**
Example of ways practice can draw on two approaches.

The following statements are offered as a few examples of the many ways that early childhood practice draws on *both/and* thinking and to convey some of the complexity and interrelationship among the principles that guide our practice.

- Teachers *both* need to have high expectations for all children's learning *and* need to recognize that some children require additional assistance and resources to meet those expectations.
- Children *both* construct their own understanding of concepts *and* benefit from instruction by more competent peers and adults.
- Children benefit *both* from engaging in self-initiated, spontaneous play *and* from teacher planned and –structured activities, projects, and experiences.
- Children benefit from *both* opportunities to see connections across disciplines through integration of curriculum *and* opportunities to engage in focused, in-depth study in a content area.
- Children benefit *both* from predictable structure and orderly routine in the learning environment *and* from the teacher's flexibility responsiveness to children's emerging ideas, need, and interests.
- Children benefit *both* from opportunities to make meaningful choices *and* from having a clear understanding of the boundaries within which choices are permissible.
- Children benefit *both* from situations that challenge them to work at the edge of their developing capacities *and* from ample opportunities to practice newly acquired skills.
- Children benefit *both* from opportunities to collaborate with peers and acquire a sense of being part of a community *and* from being treated as individuals with their own strengths, interests, and needs.
- Children need to develop *both* a positive sense of their own self-identity *and* respect for other people whose perspectives and experiences may be different from their own.
- Children *both* have enormous capacities to learn and almost boundless curiosity about the world *and* have recognized, age-related limits on their cognitive and linguistic capacities.
- Children who are English language learners *both* need to acquire proficiency in English *and* need to maintain and further develop their home language.
- Teachers must commit themselves *both* to closing the achievement gap that exists between children of various socioeconomic cultural, and linguistic groups *and* to viewing every child as capable of achieving.

From Copple, C. & Bredekamp, S. (2009). Developmentally appropriate practice in early childhood programs. Washington, DC: National Association for the Education of Young Children

## ACTIVITY RESOURCES

The curriculum files, resource books, and activity ideas you collected during training may now come in handy. You will have to discern whether the ideas fit your situation. Teachers' and children's magazines often have timely, seasonal activity planning ideas.

Draw on your own creative abilities. All too often, student teachers feel that tried-and-true ideas are superior to what they invent. The new and novel activities you create will add sparkle and uniqueness to your teaching. Do not be afraid to draw from or improve upon a good idea, or to change successful activities your children have already enjoyed. Some classroom activities are designed because of an overabundance of scrap or donated material. Take another look at materials in storage that are not receiving much attention or have been forgotten. Perhaps these can be reintroduced in a clever, new way to promote a curriculum goal.

## CURRICULUM

When curriculums are designed, planned daily activities follow. Curriculum design groups usually go through a series of steps. First, discussion takes place with all concerned individuals. Discussion can include philosophies of education, theories, standards, principles, values, research, views on how children learn best, and many other topics. Usually the group considers social, emotional, intellectual, physical, and, in faith-based programs, even spiritual growth. Next, goals and objectives are written and attention is given to how these will be recognized, assessed, and realized. A plan for inside and outside environment comes next, along with the creation of activities. At this point, many programs plan a periodic review procedure, so all steps can be revisited if goals and objectives are not being accomplished.

Most pre-kindergarten curricula include arts and creativity, music and movement, language, science, large and small motor skill development, cooking and nutrition activities, numbers and measurement, perceptual motor activities, health and safety activities, social understandings, multicultural awareness activities, and plant and animal studies. Snow (2006) reports that despite the National Research Council's study *Adding It Up: Helping Children Learn Mathematics*, early mathematics has been and continues to be largely absent from some early childhood programs.

Schickedanz (2008) suggests that teachers purposefully increase the integration of children's learning activities within multiple content areas and instructional contexts. Fredrica, the student teacher cited earlier in this chapter, did so in her planned follow-up activities on the study of cats. With cat sounds (auditory discrimination), discussions of cat varieties (vocabulary development visual discrimination), tree-climbing skill (science and physical development), and cat care chart (language arts), multiple content and instructional areas came into play. Fredrica could also have easily encouraged counting cat claws, suggested imitating cat's walking motion, or promoted children's authorship of cat stories.

Areas of preschool study with different degrees of acceptance include gardening, social justice, economics and consumer awareness, ecology and energy study, moral and ethical values, changing family patterns, introduction to photography, introduction to technology, structure games, and tolerance, nonviolence, and peaceful solution training. These may or may not be considered developmentally appropriate, but they are found in the curriculum of some schools and centers.

In planning activities, you will be striving to provide for active exploration integrated with children's previous out-of-the-classroom experiences. You will attempt to offer age-appropriate activities that suit the needs and characteristics of the group. Children will be encouraged to explore, manipulate, converse, move about, play, and freely talk about what is happening and what it means to them. Activities will provide for children with different levels of ability when possible.

Your previous early childhood education training courses have promoted your sensitivity to and awareness of cultural pluralism. Activities and interactions with children are also designed to eliminate practices and materials that discriminate on the basis of race, gender, age, ethnic origin, language, religion, sexual orientation, or special needs.

The social-emotional emphasis in activity planning has gained additional status. Social skills involve cooperation, assertion, responsibility, empathy, and self-control and are viewed as key, both to acceptable behavior and academic success. Gamel-McCormick (2000) surveyed kindergarten teachers regarding what they felt were the most important skills entering kindergartners could possess and found teachers' top skill choices were:

◆ exhibits self-control

◆ interacts cooperatively

◆ communicates needs and preferences

◆ cares for own bathroom needs

◆ attends to peer or adult talking

Gamel-McCormick also noted a significant number of the teachers surveyed included pre-academic and academic skills in their definitions of readiness.

## Preparation for Kindergarten

Spotting readiness and early literacy problems is being given top priority in many kindergartens. A number of elementary school districts test incoming kindergarteners for pre-reading skills. Early childhood educators have also increased their efforts to prepare children in their care to be successful when instruction in reading begins. The challenge for early educators is first to realize children are language learners from birth onward and that the language arts encompass the areas of listening, speaking, viewing, writing, and reading. Then, educators must also realize what constitutes developmentally appropriate instruction in these areas. Many educators fear this new curriculum emphasis in early childhood has lead to skill-and-drill lessons or the use of workbook pages with very young, uninterested children.

In developing activities, remember that each class is unique and that each child is an individual. What is or is not learned depends on classroom materials and interactions between adults and children, or between children, as they attempt to understand what is experienced and how it relates to them and to others.

## Assessment and Curriculum Planning

The major functions of assessment in the early years involve assessment to inform instruction, assessment for diagnostic and selection purposes, and assessment for accountability and program evaluation. When child assessment is used carefully and appropriately, it is used to adjust instruction and promote educational benefits.

With increased state and federal legislation affecting the early childhood years, there appears to be more pressure on educators to use standardized tests. The issue of using standardized testing is a controversial one. Advocates believe this type of assessment identifies atypical developmental patterns, determines whether children are reaching program goals, and makes instructional programs accountable.

Others with opposing views suggest young children are rarely able to communicate their understanding when standardized assessments are used, and that testing often creates stress. Wesson (2001) notes that children whose English is limited invariably score lower in language fluency areas when testing is conducted in English. Most educators acknowledge that the younger the child, the more likely he or she is to be incorrectly labeled.

In early childhood, strategies other than standardized testing are often preferred, professionally accepted, and widely used. These include observation, child portfolio development, and the documentation of children's accomplishments. These approaches can allow instruction planners to tailor the curricula to individual children's needs, and to do so without labeling children unfairly.

## Being Aware

Classroom events evolve naturally, as children react to the weather, the setting, the choices set out, activities, people encountered, and so on. The dynamics and personalities present influence children. Student teachers need to be curious, watchful, and ready to support child discoveries, rather than closely focusing on planned, teacher-directed efforts.

Some early childhood programs identify locations in their community that offer possible learning opportunities for young children, such as a dairy farm, museum, or sports arena. These programs secure community guest speakers and/ or plan school field trips to local and community sites.

# GOAL STATEMENTS

When the proposed outcomes (goals) of a center's planned instruction are stated in written form such as in a center's handbook, they may identify fields of study and also mention the cultivation of children's talents and dispositions, such as perseverance in tasks, responsibility, self-control, self-esteem, empathy, honesty, problem solving, cooperation, inventiveness, kindness, friendliness, social connectedness, creativity, and so on. The procedures to assess how well a center's instruction has attained its goals may also be specified, along with the timelines in which to do so.

## Monthly, Weekly, and Daily Schedules

Schedules alert teachers to planned events. Children's needs dictate what takes place so food, rest, and toileting times are inserted in time slots. Active periods alternate with quiet ones. Group times include announcements of that day's events and activities, and also recognize and welcome each child.

With a schedule, teachers and children can anticipate what comes next. Teachers plan in advance for necessary room settings, materials, equipment, furniture, and staffing needs. Each center and school decides on the flexibility of its daily schedule, and most deviate often when the unexpected occurs so children can benefit from a newly created activity. Schools are rarely slaves to schedules, but rather capitalize on unplanned learning opportunities, or immediately revise a schedule when planned activities in some way fizzle or fail to capture interest. Figure 4–7 displays one school's morning schedule. It includes transition statements that help move children from one activity to another to maintain a smoothly flowing program. Koralek (2008) reminds teachers that planned transitions are opportunities for child learning.

## Play and Learning

Children often use play to translate experience into understanding. Teachers frequently see in child's play the reenactment of behaviors the child has viewed in others. Behaviors that may be puzzling or significant in their lives are tried on for size. They step inside the other person's shoes and seemingly gain insight through the reliving.

In children's random and investigative play, discoveries are made. Happenings are tested, retested, varied, and extended. Focus may be keen, and at times children are eager to talk about what they understand and experience.

▶ Figure 4-7

A school's schedule of morning activities with transition tips.

| Arrival/hand washing/ table toys | • Have children move their picture or name from "home" to "school" on an Arrival Chart.<br>• Make a feelings poster with pictures of faces showing different emotions (happy, shy, sleepy, excited, frustrated, sad, and so on). When they arrive, children place clothespins labeled with their names on the "feeling faces" that best represent their emotional state at that time. |
|---|---|
| Large group | • Ask children to come to circle as if they were moving through peanut butter, wiggling through jello, in a marching band, a plane flying to the airport, a car driving on a road, a bird flying to its nest, and so on. |
| Center time/hand washing/snack | • Hang a chart on the wall. Children write their name under "Yes, I ate snack today" or "No, thank you, I'm not eating snack today."<br>• Make a snack menu providing visual directions of what to eat ("Take two apple slices and three pieces of cheese, please").<br>• Have one child wear a hard hat and inspect each center during cleanup to see if it is picked up. If it is, the child makes an X over a picture list of all the centers. If not, he recruits some helpers! |
| Book time and music | • Sing the expectations of the transition: "If you're finished cleaning up, please choose a book" (tune: "If You're Happy and You Know It").<br>• Create a basket of easily accessible (class-made, repetitive text) favorite books that wok well for independent reading. |
| Gross motor | • Draw pairs of different colored shapes on the end of wooden craft sticks. Give each child a stick and then call a shape. Matching pairs line up together. Collect the sticks as a ticket to the next activity.<br>• Tape cardboard cutouts of feet (or other shapes) on the floor to indicate where children will line up. Change these to introduce new vocabulary (ladybug, butterfly, cricket) or work on concepts (patterns, emotion faces, colors, shapes, letters).<br>• Use a fun, simple song to remind children about the expectations for walking in the hallway: "We're walking in a line. . . . one in front and one behind, we're walking in a line" (tune: "Farmer in the Dell"). |
| Dismissal | • Take turns creating body patterns (for example, clap, touch head, clap, touch head).<br>• Hide an item in a bag and give clues to help children identify it. |

From Hemmeter, M. L., Ostrosky, M. M., Artman, K. M., & Kinder, K. A. (2008, May). Moving right along: Planning transitions to prevent challenging behavior. *Young Children, 63*(3): 18–22.

Peers often function as tutors or providers of information. During play, adults observe, supply, talk about, encourage, and appreciate without interfering, except when safety is a factor. Adults do ask provocative questions and give suggestions, but they guard against inflicting their own directions or intentions concerning the child's choice of play.

## Planning for Play

You will most likely be asked to plan and set up varied play opportunities, including providing well-equipped play areas with abundant materials for props. The importance of child make-believe play is not overlooked in child-appropriate curricula. At times, you will join child play with small groups or individual children and make-believe yourself, carefully avoiding directing, overpowering, or stifling child initiative and control. Most often, you will zip in and out, providing additional materials, redirecting damage or aggression, and asking leading questions that might add depth, while still being interested, enthusiastic, supportive, communicative, responsive, warm, and understanding. Not an easy teaching task!

## HOW LANGUAGE INSTRUCTION FITS INTO ALL ACTIVITY PLANNING

Federal legislation has proposed teacher retraining, to facilitate explicit, early reading instruction involving alphabet knowledge, letter sounds, early emergent writing experiences, and carefully designed group projects (Kantrowitz & Wingert, 2002). Early childhood educators have mixed feelings about how to incorporate literacy activities into diverse curriculums and developmentally appropriate practice. Some educators fear children will be pushed into early reading exercises. Others fear not enough will be done for preschoolers living in poverty, those just learning English, and those with special needs. But most educators would agree that teacher–child verbal exchanges should be warm, engaged, and responsive.

Student teachers should focus on their ability to be conversational partners, who promote children's oral speech development, increase children's vocabulary, increase the understandings behind words, promote more complex grammar, and recognize when language development or social integration is not proceeding as expected. They value extended conversations that are cognitively challenging, and realize some children may need explicit phonics instruction to succeed when reading instruction begins.

Federal funds have supported Title 1 preschool programs since 1965. These programs are designed to prevent skill deficiencies and the need for remediation by offering an intensive, high-quality literacy curricula to eligible children living in lower-income families. To see what educational activities Title 1 preschool programs offer to increase literacy see Figure 4–8.

▶ **Figure 4-8**
Title 1 Literacy goals and ways to reach them.

**Title 1 literacy goals include the children's:**

- learning the letters of the alphabet;
- learning to hear individual sounds in words;
- learning new words and how to use them;
- learning early writing skills;
- learning to use language to ask and answer questions;
- learning about written language by looking at books; and
- becoming familiar with math and science.

**In what ways do Title 1 teacher daily work to reach literacy goals? They:**

- Promote growth in children's listening and speaking skills.
- Read aloud with children and emphasize meaning while involving children's active participation.
- Promote print-recognition and children's understanding that it has meaning and many purposes.

- Offer activities to experience print through writing.
- Teach about books—how to handle, recognize book features, recognize authorship and created illustrations, left to right reading progression of letters and words across page plus top to bottom reading direction.
- Teach about letters—recognizing, naming, capitals and lowercase, knowing letters in own name, and relating some letters to their sounds.
- Build background knowledge and thinking skills by introducing new concepts and words.
- Have engaging conversations that promote discussions. Plan and present activities that help children rhyme, and break words apart into their separate sounds (segmenting).
- Plan and present activities that put sounds together to make words (blending).
- Read to children every day.
- Offer listening opportunities with stories.
- Teach about numbers and counting.

Source: U.S. Dept of Education (2004).

## Instructing Non–English-Speaking Children

Census figures predict that by the year 2025 more than half of the children enrolled in U.S. schools will be members of minority groups not of European American origin (U.S. Bureau of the Census, 1995). The new immigrants arriving are expected to be primarily from Asia and Latin America. Language learning is an especially important issue for many of more than 12.5 million young Latino children in the United States. The greatest growth of this population is of immigrant children with limited English (Eggers-Pierola, 2005). Other new immigrant families have arrived from Asia. Many of these immigrant families may not have the education or amenities other families enjoy and have a high incidence of poverty (U.S. Department of Education, 2003).

Early childhood teachers, regardless of their preparation or background, will have the task of helping these children learn English and making it a successful experience (Genishi, 2002).

Plutro (2000), noting a study of the diversity of Head Start families, found that enrolled families spoke more than 150 languages and dialects. In nearly 20 percent of children's homes, a language other than English was spoken, the most common being Spanish, followed by Chinese, Hmong, and Vietnamese.

## Working with Hispanic Families

In the United States, the largest group of children with limited English is Hispanic. Eggers-Pierola (2005) advises teachers to involve Hispanic children's extended family, along with parents, in early childhood program activities and operations. Collaborating with families includes meeting to define goals and program planning. Familiarity with families, she believes, can result in an educator's increased ability to refer to and portray family routines, activities, environments, traditions, and so on, in center learning activities. Padron, Waxman, and Rivera (2002) define *culturally responsive teaching* as teaching that incorporates the day-to-day concerns of attending children, such as important family and community issues, into classroom learning opportunities.

## Diversity and Citizenship

Educators work in classrooms where children's ethnic, cultural, and economic living situations are diverse. Children's homes may or may not have displayed acceptance or respect for others, whom they judge to be different. To deal with this common situation, acceptance and respect are accorded at school and the teacher becomes a model of behaviors, some of which her students may not have experienced previously. Some programs give attention to displaying America's founding strengths in the classroom. This approach used to be called *teaching citizenship and building civic pride*.

Might this approach be applicable to preschool classrooms? Part of it is already there, but it is not called *civics*. Pre-kindergarten classes emphasize children's individual rights and responsibilities. They promote free speech but not hurtful speech. Voting activities take place, and children's ideas and diverse opinions are given dignity. Most classrooms solve problems with a *together-we-can-fix-this* attitude. Each child is felt to be a valued individual. Diverse faith-based and cultural events happen, and American citizenship and culture is considered preeminent. Delpit (1995) suggests teachers appreciate the "wonders of the cultures" represented in their classrooms.

## Written Activity or Lesson Plans

Activity plans are useful devices that encourage student teachers to think thoroughly through the different parts of their planned activities. Beginning teachers try to foresee possible problems and find solutions. With adequate preparation through written planning, the student teacher can approach each planned activity with a degree of confidence and security. Cooperating teachers and supervisors often contribute ideas on the student's written plans, or collaborate with the student, sometimes making plans a team effort. Written plans are a starting point from which actual activity flows, depending on the children's reception and feedback. Monitoring the children's interest is a teaching task, and will often result in improvising and revising the activities to suit their needs. Written **lesson plans** move one step further and isolate a teacher's or student teacher's plan for what will happen during a specific time block, in a specific location.

**lesson plans**—the working documents from which the daily program is run, specifying directions for activities.

**schedule**—a planned series of happenings for a specific time period, to accommodate needs and goals.

A weekly classroom plan, or **schedule**, is usually developed to pinpoint specially planned activities that will take place in different learning centers or room areas. The plan includes which classroom adult has responsibility for preparation, providing necessary materials and equipment, supervision, and cleanup.

The activity plan guide in Figure 4–9 is one of many possible forms that can be used by student teachers. It is appropriate for most, but not all, planned activities. Story times, finger plays, flannel board stories, songs, and short-duration activities usually are not written in activity-plan form. Activity plan titles are descriptive, such as "Sink and Float," "Make Farmers' Cheese," or "Tie Dyeing." They quickly clarify the subject of the planned experience.

▶ **Figure 4-9**
Activity plan guide.

1. Activity title _____
2. Curriculum area _____
3. Materials needed _____
   _____
   _____
4. Location and setup of activity _____
5. Number of children and adults _____

▶ **Figure 4-9** (continued)

6. Preparation _____
   _____
   _____
   _____

7. Specific behavioral objective _____
   _____
   _____
   _____
   _____

8. Developmental skills necessary for success _____
   _____

9. Getting started _____
   _____
   _____

10. Procedure (step by step) _____
    _____

11. Discussion (key concepts, attitudes, facts, skills, vocabulary, etc.) _____
    _____
    _____
    _____
    _____
    _____
    _____

12. Apply (or additional practice of skill or learning) _____
    _____

13. Cleanup _____

14. Terminating statement _____

15. Transition _____

16. Evaluation: activity, teacher, child _____
    _____
    _____
    _____
    _____
    _____
    _____

Filling in the *curriculum area space on a lesson plan form* sometimes leads to indecision. Many early childhood activities are hard to categorize. Subjects seem to fall into more than one area. Use your own judgment and designation; it is your plan.

Identification of materials, supplies, and tools comes next. Some activities require visual aids and equipment for teachers, as well as those materials used by children. Make sure you, as the student teacher, know how to use the visual aids and operate the equipment. Estimating exact amounts of necessary materials helps calculate expenses and aids preparation. You will simply count out the desired quantities. Student teachers generally know what classroom supplies are available to them and what they will have to supply themselves.

The *location* of a planned activity has much to do with its success. The following questions can help decide the best locations:

◆ What amount of space will children need? Are special needs accommodated?

◆ What room or outdoor features (for example, windows, water, flat floor, storage or drying areas, rug, lighting, grass, shade) are necessary?

◆ Will electrical outlets be necessary?

▶ **Figure 4-10**

Some art activities are more successful with just a few children at a time under close supervision.

© Cengage Learning

**objectives**—aims; specific interpretation of general goals, providing practical and directive tools for day-to-day program planning.

◆ Will noise or traffic from adjacent areas cause interference?

◆ Will one adult be able to supervise the location?

Self-help and child participation in *cleanup* are necessary considerations. Cleanup might involve a sorting game, with teacher and children working together, or a teacher might provide containers, strategically placed for small item storage or throw away. Adjacent soapy water and sponges help take care of messes. Cleanup often will not proceed smoothly if a student teacher does not prepare beforehand. Seeing cleanup as an integral part of the ending of any planned activity is the key.

Activities that actively engage children and invite exploration suit young children's needs. *Random setups* can lead to confusion and conflict over work space and supply use. A good setup helps a child work without help; it also promotes proper respect for classroom supplies and equipment, and facilitates consideration for the work of others. Each setup reflects a teacher's goals and philosophy of how children learn best.

Student teachers usually begin planning for small groups before tackling larger groups and the total-room activity plans. A number of fascinating early childhood activities call for close adult supervision and can happen safely and successfully only with a few children at a time (see Figure 4–10). Instant replays or ongoing activities may be necessary to accommodate all interested children. Waiting lists are useful in these cases, and children quickly realize they will be called when it is their turn. The number of children on activity plan forms could read "Two groups of four children," for example.

*Preparation* sections on lesson plans alert the student teacher to tasks to be completed prior to actual presentation. This could include making a number of individual portions of paste, moving furniture, mixing paint, making a recipe chart, or a number of other, similar teacher activities. Preparation includes attention to features that minimize child waiting and decrease the need for help from the teacher (see Figures 4–11 and 4–12).

## LESSON PLAN GOALS AND OBJECTIVES

Planned and unplanned activities and experiences have some type of outcome. Written student teaching plans include a section where **objectives** are identified, and this serves as the basis for planning, presentation, and all other form sections.

▶ **Figure 4-11**
The trays used in this activity set up invite exploration and delineate child space.

▶ **Figure 4-12**
This student teacher of toddlers has prepared for easy clean up and is deciding on the best arrangement of materials to promote self-help.

Cooperating teachers and supervisors differ in requiring activity plans with specific behavioral or instructional objectives. **Instructional objectives (IO)** are more general in nature and may defy measurement. Examples of **specific behavioral objectives (SBO)** and instructional objectives follow:

**SBO:** When given four cubes of different colors (red, blue, green, and purple), the child will point to each color correctly on the first try when asked.

**IO:** The child will know four colors: red, blue, green, and purple.

**SBO:** When given a cut potato, paper, and three small trays of paint, the child will make at least one mark on the paper using a printing motion.

**IO:** The child will explore a printing process.

**instructional objectives (IO)**—aims or goals, usually set for an individual child, that describe in very specific and observable terms what the child is expected to master.

**specific behavioral objectives (SBO)**—clearly describes observable behavior, the situation in which it will occur, and the exact outcome or the criteria of successful performance.

▶ **Figure 4-13**
Verbs used in writing specific behavioral objectives.

| | | | | | |
|---|---|---|---|---|---|
| ask | count | hold | paint | return | take |
| attempt to | cut | jump | paste | say | tell |
| choose | dry | look at | pick | select | touch |
| close | empty | make motions | point to | sequence | turn |
| collect | explore | mark | pour | show | use |
| color | find | mix | put hand on | sing | use two hands |
| comment | finish | nail | put in order | solve | wait |
| complete | follow two directions | name | remove | sponge off | wash |
| contribute | guess | open | replace | state a favorite. . . | weigh |

**SBO:** After seeing the teacher demonstrate cutting on a penciled line and being helped to hold scissors with the thumb and index finger, the child will cut apart a two-inch strip of pencil-lined paper, in two out of five attempts.

**IO:** The child will learn how to cut on a line.

**observable behavior—** actions that can be seen rather than those that are inferred.

Note: Written specific behavioral objectives use verbs that clearly describe **observable behavior** (see Figure 4–13). They consist of three parts:

1. conditions and circumstances in which learning takes place
2. the child's observable behavior
3. acceptable performance or criteria for success

It is best for beginning teachers to accomplish one objective per activity, do it thoroughly and well, and keep the activity short and lively. Student teachers tend to plan activities involving multiple concepts or skills. Usually, none of these skills is accomplished because of the amount and diversity of learning. Objectives of any kind may or may not always be realized. Evaluation sections analyze whether the student teacher achieved what he set out to do. Centers with clearly defined objectives, combining their teaching team's efforts, have a greater chance of realizing their objectives.

## DEVELOPMENTAL SKILLS

Each activity builds on another. A child's skill and knowledge expands through increased opportunity and experience. Knowing the children's developmental skills makes student teachers aware of their capacities and levels. The ability to sit and focus for a period of minutes can be the requirement in a planned preschool activity, and having the ability to pick up small objects can be part of another. Planning beyond children's capacities may occur because of the student teacher's eagerness to enrich the children's lives and try out different ideas. A close look at the children's achievements and abilities will help the student teacher plan activities that are successful for both the children and the student teacher.

### Planning for Skill Attainment

Petersen (1996) discusses skill-focused activities as follows:

There are certain skills that every teacher wants children to master before they leave the program. These are skills agreed on in the early childhood field as appropriate to the development, limitations, and capabilities of children with whom the teacher is working. They are probably skills that the early childhood program and the children's parents believe are important for teachers to teach. These skill-focused activities should consistently appear in daily lesson plans.

*Skills* can be divided into intellectual, social-emotional, and motor skills, and some skills seem to overlap and fit more than one category. Intellectual skills are skills such as memory, problem solving, sorting, ordering, categorizing, predicting, and making hypotheses. Motor skills may deal with eye-hand coordination, balance, and strength in both small and large body muscles. There is an individual timetable and a natural sequence in the appearance of children's motor skills. Muscle systems develop and become controllable with use, practice, proper nutrition, and, at times, adult guidance. Take riding a tricycle as an example. It is a definite motor skill that many but not all children master during preschool years, depending on their life circumstances and their individual physical developmental capability.

As mentioned previously, social-emotional skills deal with interaction with others, sharing, group living, playing, impulse control, negotiation, self-regulation, cultural and accepted manners, and so on, and cannot be ignored when lesson planning.

## Suggestions to Start Student Teacher Planned Activities

Some student teachers find that a lesson plan outlined on a 3 × 5 card, kept on the lap or in a pocket, acts as a cue card reminding them step by step how the activity unfolds. Planning a first statement that creates a desire to know or act can focus child attention. Motivational statements need to be studied for appropriateness. Statements that create competition ("The first one who . . .") or are threatening ("If you don't try it, then . . .") cause unnecessary tensions. Appropriate motivational statements strike a child's curiosity, and often stimulate the child to action or exploration. They capture attention, and, hopefully, engage the child's mind, like the examples that follow:

"John brought a special pet. I think you'll want to see him."
"There are some new items in the collage box for pasting today. Where have you seen a shiny paper like this?"
"Today you'll be cooking your own snack. Raise your hand if you've seen someone make pancakes."
"Do you remember the sound our coffee-can drums made yesterday? There's a bigger drum with a different sound here today. Let's listen."

Focusing activities such as finger plays, body movement actions, or songs are often used as a getting-started routine. When planned, this is written in the "getting started" section of the lesson plan. Many teachers find helpful the practice of pausing briefly for silence that signals that children are ready to find out what will happen next. The following types of statements are frequently used:

"When I hear the clock ticking, I'll know you're listening."
"If I see your eyes, I can tell you're ready to find out what we're going to do in the art center today. Martin is ready, Sherry is ready. . ."

Lowering the volume of your voice can motivate children to change their behaviors so they can hear. This creates a hushed silence, which is successful for some teachers. Enthusiasm in a teacher's voice and manner is a great attention-getter. Children are quick to notice the sparkle in the teacher's eyes or the excitement reflected in her voice's tone, stress, or pitch.

During an activity's first few minutes, expectations, safety precautions, and reminders concerning class or activity rules should be covered if necessary. Doing so will avoid potential activity problems.

## Procedure

When an initial demonstration or specific instruction needs expressing, this can be noted and written briefly in a step-by-step fashion. Because active involvement is such an important aspect for the young child's learning, participation is part of most planned activities.

This section of the plan outlines sequential happenings during the activity. Student teachers identify important subcomponents chronologically. The student teacher mentally visualizes each step and its particular needs and actions.

## Discussion

Teacher discussion and questioning is appropriate for many child activities, it can be intrusive in others. When deeply involved, children do not usually benefit from a break in their concentration. Other activities lead to a vigorous give-and-take, question-and-feedback format that helps children's discovery and understanding.

The following three questions clarify the written comments that might be included in the *discussion* section of a lesson plan form:

1. What key points, concepts, ideas, or words do you intend to cover during conversation?
2. What types of questions, inquiries, or voluntary comments might come from the children?
3. Are you going to relate new material to that which was learned previously?

## Apply Section of a Lesson Plan Form

Sometimes, an activity leads to an immediate application of a new knowledge or skill. If the idea of a circle was introduced or discovered, finding circular images or objects in the classroom can immediately reinforce the learning. Repetition and practice are key instruments in learning.

## Evaluation after Presentation

Hindsight is a valuable teaching skill. One can evaluate many aspects of a planned and conducted activity. Goal realization, a close look at instructional techniques or methods, and student teacher actions usually come under scrutiny. The following questions can aid both activity- and self-evaluation:

1. Was the activity location and setup appropriate?
2. Would you rate the activity as high, middle, or low in interest value and goal realization?
3. What could improve this plan?
4. Should a follow-up activity be planned?
5. Was enough attention given to small details?
6. Did the activity attempt to reach the instructional objectives?
7. Was the activity too long or too short?
8. If you planned to repeat the activity, how would you change it?
9. Were you prepared?
10. Which teacher–child interactions went well? Which ones went poorly?
11. Was the size of the group appropriate?
12. Was the activity a success with the children?
13. Were my reactions to boys and girls nonsexist and unbiased?
14. Was the activity above, at, or below the group's developmental level?
15. What did I learn from the experience?
16. What seemed to be the best parts of the activity?
17. Did I learn anything about myself?
18. How good was I at helping children put into words what they experienced or discovered?
19. In what ways do I now know more about the children involved in the activity?

Evaluation and comments from others will add another dimension. Team meetings usually concentrate on a total day's happenings but may zero in on the student teacher's supervision and planned activities.

## OTHER ACTIVITY PLAN AREAS

Many activity plans pay close attention to cleanup. Usually, both children and adults clean up their shared environment. Drying areas, housecleaning equipment, and hand washing can be important features of a plan.

In a **terminating statement**, a teacher may summarize what has been discovered and enjoyed, and tie loose activity ends together, bringing activities to a satisfying group conclusion:

> When we watched Roddie, the hamster, eating celery and lettuce today, Leticia noticed Roddie's two large teeth. Leticia wonders what other foods he might like. Sam plans to bring some peanut butter on toast for Roddie tomorrow, to see if he likes it. Ting wants to telephone the pet store to ask the storekeeper what hamsters eat. Shawn thinks a library book would tell.

**terminating statement**—an ending summary or recap of what has been discovered, discussed, experienced, enjoyed, and so on, after a learning activity.

### Unforeseen Distractions

Even the best-prepared activities can go awry because of events beyond the teacher's control. Although the true-to-life example given below is humorous, the educator's quick thinking and open-ended questioning is to be commended.

> A kindergarten teacher thought it a good idea to have a live mouse visit the classroom. The children's favorite storybook that year involved a small boy's pet mouse and the reactions of family members. The teacher secured a mouse from the sixth grade science teacher. He assured her the mouse was tame and friendly. She introduced the mouse to her class by gathering the children in a circle with children's legs outstretched, touching the feet of a peer. The mouse was in a cage at the circle's center. She unlatched the cage door and the mouse immediately ran up her leg. She stifled a scream, clamped down, and caught the mouse through her pant's leg about knee high. In a barely controlled voice she asked, "Can anyone think of a way we can get the mouse back in the cage?"

(Compliments of Thelma Fracolli, elementary school kindergarten teacher, Fremont, CA)

### Promoting Cognitive Skills

You will remember from child development classes that young children often rely heavily on what they see.

When you interact, you can expect some children will begin to pause, reflect, think about and try out more than one idea or attend to more than one factor. Children are problem-solvers by nature and display curiosity, generate questions, and pursue answers. They attempt to solve problems and also seek novel challenges, and they persist because success and understanding are motivating in their own right (National Research Council, 2000). Many tasks or experiences presented to young children are purposely open-ended, with different ways available to proceed. Many activities promote diverse and individual courses of action, or ways of using, thinking about, or creating things. These types of activities promote reflective thinking and child planning.

The dialogues teachers have with young children often involve imagining, observing, predicting, brainstorming, and creative problem solving. Discussions can be lively. Child answers are accepted and further discussions welcomed and promoted. Child comments are based on child experience and are consequently correct in light of what the child knows.

Educators intent on promoting children's thinking should listen closely and interact with pertinent comments, acknowledgments, and questions that follow children's line of thinking and focus. Questions that only test the children's memories rarely ask for higher thought processes. Thought-provoking teacher questions call for children's conjecture, mental choices, opinions, judgments, cause-and-effect identification, predictions, solutions, reasoning, hypothesizing, and creative expression. These types of questions require effort to formulate, and teachers must learn restraint, resisting urges to jump ahead in conversations, rather than allowing conversational silences and pauses as the child mulls over mentally, cogitates, and processes the question toward a response. Rephrasing or paraphrasing by the teacher may help clarify child meanings, or alert one child to another child's ideas on a given subject, perhaps encouraging interaction between children.

## Using Community Resources

The whole community is a learning resource for young children. Each neighborhood has unique features and people with special talents and collections. Industries, businesses, and job sites may provide field trip opportunities, speakers, or activity material giveaways. Cultural events and celebrations, ethnic holidays, buildings, and parks and recreation areas easily integrate into the school's activities to promote a reality-based children's program.

## Pitfalls with Lesson Plans

The biggest pitfall for the student teacher is the tendency to stick to the plan when children's feedback during the activity does not warrant it. Teachers should take their cues from the children's behavior; expanding their interests may mean spending additional time providing additional opportunities and materials. In some cases, it can mean just talking if the children want to know more.

If children's avid interest cuts into another planned activity that follows, it might be postponed or revised to fit into the schedule. The unforeseen frequently happens. Getting the children to refocus on a new planned activity may mean having to clear the children's minds of something more important to them.

Teachers usually try to relate unexpected occurrences to the planned activity. For example, "That was a loud booming noise. We can listen for another while we finish shaping our bread before it goes into the oven." If efforts to refocus fail, a teacher knows the written plan has been preempted.

A real teaching skill involves using unplanned events to promote specific, identified curriculum objectives, or objectives that were not even considered but are timely and important.

## Teaching Tips

We mentioned before, your enthusiasm while presenting the lesson plan must be considered. When your eyes sparkle and your voice sounds excited when you talk about what your class is accomplishing, the children will likely remain interested and focused. Your level of enthusiasm needs to be genuine and appropriate.

You will be eager to start the activities you have designed, anxious to see whether you have captured the children's attention and stimulated their developmental growth. When you feel that the group joins in your excitement and discovery, no other reward is necessary.

Children see things that you do not, ask unexpected questions, and make statements you will be challenged to understand. Listen closely to children's responses; if you cannot understand them, probe further. More often than not, you will understand the wisdom of their thoughts, which are based on their unique past experiences.

Do not panic when a child corrects you or when you do not have an answer. Develop a together-we-will-find-out attitude. A teacher who has all the answers often fails to notice the brilliance, charm, and honesty of children.

Planning back-up activities, for situations when interest lags or an activity finishes before expected, is another great idea. Many students have devised an emergency bag with fill-in activities that can be easily introduced and set up, such as a favorite book or art activity.

## Room Environments

Looking closely at room environments will be a challenging aspect of student teaching. You may be asked to take over a particular area, redesign or restructure it, or create a new interest or discovery area. In other classrooms, the cooperating teacher may not want anything moved or improved. In this case, you cannot help but evaluate its arrangement.

You will be looking at child behaviors affected by physical surroundings and you will notice popular and unpopular room areas. Problem room areas may be immediately apparent. Some room spaces will appear designed for special purposes, accommodating the needs of one or many children.

Experimentation in placement of furniture, equipment, and supplies is an ongoing teacher task in most classrooms (see Figure 4–14). Pre-kindergarten classrooms may change dramatically from week to week, depending on the course of study. Many pieces of preschool furniture have been designed for multi-use flexibility and utmost mobility.

Effective classroom arrangements do not just happen. They are a result of hard work and planning. Considerable thought and observation of child play pursuits is involved. Because of budget (usually for lack of it), creative solutions to classroom environments abound.

▶ **Figure 4-14**
Bookcases are angled to create an instructional corner with an element of privacy.

© Cengage Learning

Student teachers will find that some room areas need their constant attention. Analyzing the possible provoking factors may lead to one reason or many, including the room arrangement itself, furnishings, activities, *setups* (the way individual activity materials are arranged), storage, supplies or a lack of them, and cleanup provisions.

In some placement classrooms, student teachers may notice and recognize the cooperating teacher's priorities and individuality. A musically inclined teacher's room might have considerable space devoted to children's experiences and exploration of music-related activities; another child center or classroom may emphasize gardening activities, indoors and outdoors; and so on. You are probably already aware of your own favorite instructional areas and envision your own future classroom, which will incorporate your own creative ideas.

## WORKING WITH GROUPS

**Group times** are covered in detail in this chapter because student teachers frequently need help planning and conducting them. We do not intend to suggest that planned group gatherings are the best or most efficient vehicles for child learning. Play and spontaneous child activity offer equally excellent opportunities.

**group times**—also called circle or story times; time blocks during the day when all of the children and teachers join together in a common activity.

## Group Size

More early childhood teachers prefer planning and working with small groups of young children within their classrooms. Consequently, large gatherings consisting of the entire class may only happen when a group is formed early in the morning or at closing. These larger groups tend to facilitate information passing rather than instruction. Think about your former training classes and classroom discussions, and your feelings about group meetings and consultations in your own training classes. Most teachers admit they were comfortable offering their ideas and felt listened to when groups were kept small.

## Successful Group Times

Think about and analyze elements that promote success. Student teachers will tend to imitate their cooperating teachers' group times and will carry techniques learned there into their own future classrooms.

Identifying the purpose of group times precedes their planning. During such times, children not only learn but draw conclusions about themselves as learners.

## Child Characteristics and Group Times

Can group time become what you would like it to be? Go back in your memory to age and stage characteristics. Group times are based on what a teacher knows about the children for whom activities are planned. The children's endurance, need for movement, need to touch, enjoyment of singing or chanting, ability to attend, and other factors are all taken into consideration. The dynamics of the group setting and the children affect outcomes. Two friends seated together could mean horsing around. Maybe some children have sight or hearing problems. Perhaps there is a child who talks on and on at group times. All situations of this nature should be given planning consideration.

## Planning

Following are questions you might ask yourself when planning a small-group activity:

- ◆ Is this the best format for the lesson?
- ◆ How will I promote child self-help and independence?
- ◆ Why or how will children be motivated to want to know or find out about planned group subject matter?
- ◆ How will I minimize waiting?
- ◆ Will my materials attract them?
- ◆ Are materials or tools to be shared? How will children know?
- ◆ If a demonstration is necessary before children proceed, will materials distract them during a teacher demonstration and should be introduced one at a time?
- ◆ How does my setting provide for active participation?
- ◆ Who will clean up? How?
- ◆ How will children know what will happen next or where to go?

Student teachers often plan their group times with other adults. The following planning decisions are usually discussed:

- ◆ Which adults will lead? Which adults will be aides?
- ◆ When, where, and how long is the activity? How will the children be seated?
- ◆ What will be the instructional topics, activities, and goals?
- ◆ How many adults and children will attend?
- ◆ Will there be one presentation or instant replays?
- ◆ What materials or audiovisuals will be needed?

- ◆ Who will prepare needed materials?
- ◆ How will children be gathered?
- ◆ Will children be asked to raise hands before contributing?
- ◆ In what order will events happen?
- ◆ Can the children actively participate?
- ◆ Will a vigorous activity be followed with a slow one?
- ◆ Will children share in leading?
- ◆ How will the results of group time be reviewed?
- ◆ How will children leave at the conclusion?

There seem to be distinct stages in group times. For example, there is the gathering of children and adults. This then leads to a focusing of the children's attention. There is a joint recognition of the persons present at group time. At that point, someone begins to lead and present the activity. This is followed by the children participating. In the final stage of group time, there can be a brief summary and then a teacher transition statement.

## Building Attention and Interest

Teachers use various methods to gather the children and get their attention. A signal, like a bell or cleanup song, helps to build anticipation: "When you hear the xylophone, it's time to . . ." A verbal reminder to individual children lets them know that group time is starting soon: "In 5 minutes we'll be starting group time in the loft, Tina. You need to finish your block building."

In order to help the children focus, the teacher might initiate a song, finger play, chant, or dance in which all perform a similar act. Many group leaders then build a sense of enthusiasm by recognizing each child and adult. An interesting roll call, a name tag selection activity, or a simple question like "Who is with us today?" are good techniques. Children enjoy being identified. Using a playful approach makes things interesting: "Bill is wearing his red shirt, red shirt; red shirt . . . Bill is wearing his red shirt at group time today. Katrina has her hair cut, hair cut . . ."

To build motivation or enthusiasm, some teachers drop their voice volume to a whisper. Others light up, expressing enthusiasm with their faces or bodies. The object is to capture interest and build a desire in the children to want to know or find out something. Statements like "We're now going to read a story about . . ." or "You're going to learn to count to six today" do not excite children much. In contrast, statements like "There's something in my pocket I brought to show you . . ." or "Raise your hand if you can hear this tiny bell . . ." build children's interest and curiosity. Manner and tone of voice will be a dead giveaway as to whether wonder and discovery are alive in the teacher. Teachers use natural conversation. Presenting age-appropriate materials or topics close to the heart of the presenter is a key element. Experiences from one's own love of life can be a necessary ingredient. New teachers and student teachers should rely on their own creativity and use group times to share themselves.

Sheinman (2000) describes one elementary school teacher's method of gaining attention, so directions are clear and better understood:

> Sometimes I need to gain children's attention, I ask them to stop and give me "five." They have to do five things for me to give out my directions: (1) look at me, (2) close their mouths, (3) stop what they are doing, (4) open their ears, and (5) raise their hands. They are to indicate they have done all five by raising all five fingers showing that they completed what they are expected to do. When all hands are up, I give my directions.

▶ Figure 4-15
This student teacher considered the activity's necessary preparation and then enjoyed it with enthusiasm.

## Practice

Memorized songs, finger plays, or chants can be a part of the group time. Practice is necessary. Time spent preparing and practicing makes for a relaxed presenter (see Figure 4–15). Lap cards may be used as insurance if the student teacher forgets under pressure.

## Feedback

Feedback from children needs to be monitored while presenting. For example, seeing a child hesitate may cue the presenter to repeat and emphasize words. It is worthwhile to see what really interests the children and spend additional time with that part of the activity. Sometimes, even the best group time plans are discarded, revised, and another created based on feedback.

## Recognition

One technique that helps recognize individuality is giving credit to each child's idea. "LeGrand says he saw a fox in the woods, Ryan thinks it was a wolf, and Emma says it looked like a cat." Bringing a child back to focus by naming him or asking a question is common. "Todd, this dog looks like your dog, Ranger," or "Todd, can you show us . . . ?"

## Guidance

Handling child behaviors during group time can distract a student teacher and upset the sequence of thought. Quick statements, like "If everyone is sitting down, you will be able to see" or "Mei-Lee and Josh are waiting for a turn," help curb distracting behaviors. A student teacher can be very grateful when an alert aide or assistant teacher handles behaviors by moving nearer to a child so group time can proceed without interruption.

## Evaluation

With time and supervision responsibilities over, you should analyze your group activity after you have relaxed and reflected on its particulars. Hindsight is valuable now. If possible, you might consider videotaping your group time. This offers tremendous growth opportunities. Listen closely to the supervisor's and cooperating teacher's objective comments and suggested improvements.

# THEMATIC TEACHING

The **theme approach** to child program planning is popular in many early childhood centers and classrooms. A theme includes a written collection of activity ideas on one subject, idea, or skill, such as a picture book, butterflies, homes, neighborhood, kindness, friendship, biking, swimming, or animals. Activities within the theme encompass a wide range of curriculum areas, including art, music, numbers, science, small and large motor development, and so on. A theme's course of study involves a day, week, or longer period; 1 week is typical but not always appropriate because this may not allow in depth study of a topic.

Though usually preplanned, themes can be developed after a child's or group's interest is recognized. Curtis and Carter (1996) make a clear distinction between traditional and developmental themes. *Traditional theme* topics are teacher-chosen, rather than those selected by a teacher *after* uncovering topics of interest by observing child play and exploration. In *developmental theme* planning, the teacher bases her approach on inquiry and learning, which focuses on the realities of children's lives, relationships, and issues. Materials and planned activities are designed to elicit curiosity, promote the exploration of the new ideas, and pursue the questions children generate. Themes differ from teacher to teacher and school to school; each offers a unique collection and presentation of activities.

> **theme approach**—a popular child program planning approach that involves a course of study with identified child activities focused on one subject, idea, or skill such as butterflies, friendship, biking, or a picture book.

## Possible Instructional Benefits

Reasons for using the theme approach in young children's instruction vary. Some major ideas follow:

- ◆ A theme tackles instruction through a wide variety of activities that reinforce child learning as the same new ideas, facts, skills, and attitudes are encountered through different routes. Discovery and deductions happen in varied activities, keeping classrooms enthusiastic and alive.
- ◆ The classroom environment can be saturated with activities and materials on the same subject, reinforcing learning. Curriculum areas can be integrated.
- ◆ A theme approach lets children gather, explore, and experience the theme at their own pace and level of understanding, because of the number of choices in room activities and materials.
- ◆ Planned group times offer shared experiences and knowledge. Small group work can promote collaboration and cooperation.
- ◆ Teachers can identify and gather theme materials for future use, saving time and energy.
- ◆ Teachers can best guide child discovery through knowledge gained from their research during theme preparation and construction.
- ◆ Community resources become classroom materials, and community uniqueness is incorporated into instruction.
- ◆ The teacher can collect real objects and develop visual aids and audiovisuals.
- ◆ A theme can evolve from the unplanned and unexpected, giving curriculum flexibility.
- ◆ The teacher's and children's creativity and resourcefulness are encouraged and challenged.
- ◆ Once the environment is set, the teacher is free to help uninvolved individuals and interact intimately with the highly focused children.

◆ The classroom environment becomes a dynamic, changing, exciting place for both children and adults.

◆ A theme can provide a security blanket for new teachers outlining a plan for one week's activities or longer.

## Webbing

One way of planning a thematic unit is to use a process called *webbing*. Figure 4–16 presents a web based on an unplanned event that evoked considerable child interest. A seagull banged into the classroom's sliding glass patio door. The noise attracted children and teacher, and they watched the groggy, disoriented bird recover for a few minutes before it flew away. A discussion of the event took place, and the teacher then developed a web based upon children's queries and comments. This "stunned bird" web may be used in the planning of a theme on birds, or perhaps no additional activities on the subject will be planned.

In making a web, a teacher is laying out the central theme of the plan and illustrating how parts of the topic fit together in a diagram that resembles a spider web, thus the name. Webbing may provide a teacher with a picture of how one topic integrates across curricular areas. Early childhood educators frequently use the same webbing techniques with a picture book (See Figure 4–17).

## Possible Limitations or Weaknesses of Themes

Critics of thematic teaching mention several limitations of this type of programming, for both preschool and elementary school instruction.

▶ **Figure 4-16**
Unplanned event web—initial planning.

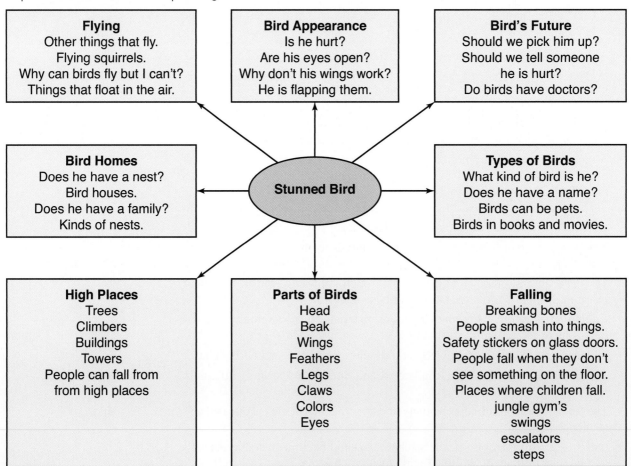

▶ **Figure 4-17**
This webbing example suits a theme based on a picture book about trains such as Donald Crew's book *Freight Train.*

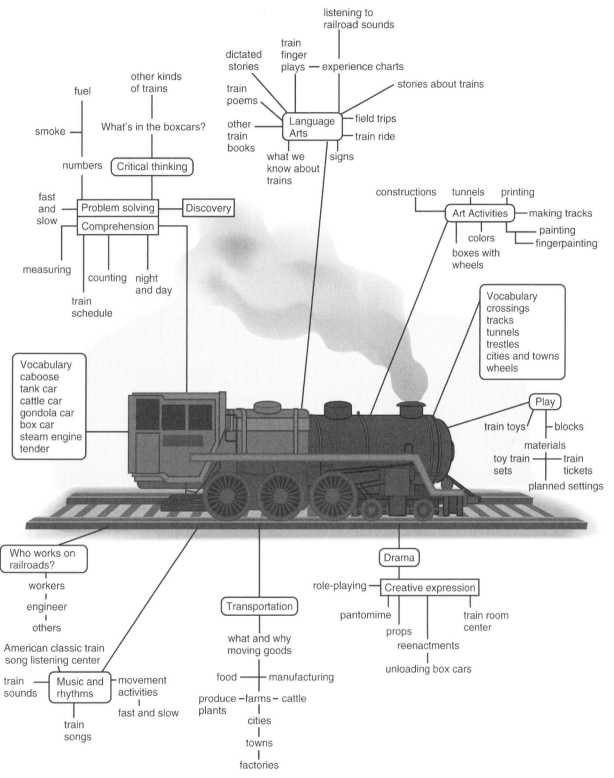

◆ Once developed, thematic units tend to become a teacher-dictated curriculum.

◆ A complete reliance on already-developed themes ignores a new group's uniqueness and needs.

◆ Themes may not be critically analyzed for appropriateness during construction.

◆ Thematic unit teaching promotes the idea that preplanned units are a preferred way to teach.

◆ Themes can overlook geographic, socioeconomic, and cultural factors.

## Thematic Subsections

This analysis of a thematic unit is provided for student teachers who may need to compile a written unit. Some of you will not be required to do so, and your preparation for unit or thematic teaching will not be this detailed. Nevertheless, what follows will be helpful to those intending to try this type of instructional approach.

Thematic units may have many subsections. Based on teaching preferences and teacher decisions, each section is either present or absent. Subsection listings contain a description of the contents.

◆ *Title page* includes theme identification, writer's credit line, ages of children, classroom location, and descriptive and/or decorative art.

◆ *Table of contents* lists subsections and beginning pages.

◆ *Instructional goals description* contains writer's identification of concepts, ideas, factual data, vocabulary, attitudes, and skills in the unit.

◆ *Background data* are researched background information, with theme particulars useful in updating adults on the subject. Technical drawings and photos can be included.

◆ *Resource list* includes teacher-made and commercially available materials and supplies, with names and addresses of where to get them. It also contains audiovisuals, community resources, consultants, speakers, field trip possibilities, and inexpensive sources of materials.

◆ *Weekly time schedule* pinpoints times and activities, supervising adults, and duration of activity.

◆ *Suggested activities* include activity plans, procedure descriptions, and plans for room settings, centers, and environments.

◆ *Children's book lists* identify children's books related to the theme.

◆ *Activity aids* describe patterns, finger plays, poems, storytelling ideas, recipes, chart ideas, teacher-made aids and equipment, ideas and directions, and bulletin board diagrams.

◆ *Culminating activities* offer suggestions for final celebrations or events that have summarizing, unifying, and reviewing features.

◆ *Bibliography* lists adult resource books on theme.

◆ *Evaluation* contains comments concerning instructional value, unit conduct, and revision needs.

## How to Construct a Thematic Unit

Initial work begins by choosing a subject and possibly webbing it. Staff considers how the theme's study can mesh with the standards used to guide instructional decisions. Then information and real materials related to the topic are researched. Next, brainstorming to generate ideas and envisioning saturated classroom environments occurs. Instructional decisions concerning the scope of the proposed course of study are made. The search for materials and resources starts, instructional goals and objectives are identified, and activities are created. A tentative plan of activities is compiled and analyzed. After materials, supplies, and visual aids have been made or obtained, a final written plan is completed. The theme is presented to children and evaluated. Each aspect of instruction is assessed. Notes concerning unit particulars are reviewed, and unit revisions, additions, or omissions are recorded. The unit's written materials are stored in a binder for protection. Other items may be boxed.

Units can be an individual, team, or group effort. Developing a unit during student teaching creates a desired job skill and may aid in preparing for the first job interview. A written theme, finished during student teaching, can display competency and become a valuable visual aid for prospective employers along with a professional portfolio.

## Saturated Environment

When thinking of ways to incorporate a unit's theme into the routine, room, yard, food service, wall space, and so on, means using your creativity. Background music, room color, the teacher's clothing, and lighting can reflect a theme. The environment becomes transformed. Butterfly-shaped crackers, green cream of wheat, special teacher-made theme puzzles, face painting, and countless other possibilities exist. Do not forget child motor involvement and child and adult enactment of theme-related concepts and skills.

A moderate number of activity choices on a theme at any given hour are deemed best, rather than a large or overwhelming array of activities at the same time. Because themes are spread out over time, this can be decided, depending on the teacher's logical sequencing of activities, on children's continued interest in the topic, or what activities complement each other.

## Project Approach

Katz and Chard's (1993) text, *Engaging Children's Minds: The Project Approach*, sensitized teachers to the idea that children in most early childhood classrooms had no active role in deciding what they wanted to learn. The project approach is popular with elementary school teachers, but Katz and others have promoted its use in early child programs.

A *project* is an in-depth investigation of a topic. The investigation is usually undertaken by a small group of children within a class, sometimes by a whole class, and occasionally by an individual child. The key feature of a project is that it is a research effort deliberately focused on finding answers to questions about a topic posed, either by the children, the teacher, or the teacher working with the children. The goal of a project is to learn more about the topic rather than to seek right answers to questions posed by the teacher. Projects evolve out of child curiosity and questions. The teacher supports the children's activities and helps children proceed in their investigations and problem solving while keeping them safe. Answers are not supplied by the teacher; the teacher only suggests avenues toward answers. Children's hypotheses may not turn out as expected, and they may learn from their mistakes. In discussing the topic pets or any other topic of interest with preschoolers and probing what children are curious about or what they may want to find out, many possible child investigative projects might be discovered.

Teachers who strongly believe in young children's innate ability to pursue information, solutions, and answers, given adult assistance, will find this educational approach attractive.

## Planning Outdoor Activities

Student teachers are expected to use all existing space for children's play, discovery, and learning opportunities. Each yard area has a number of givens, which could include boundaries, traffic patterns, and many other features.

One can think of each given as an instructional asset. Mentally list ways that fences or walls could be used for a child activity. Did you include child water painting? Displaying child work, or using a fence as a base for child easels? Using it as a base to tie on ropes that could, with old blankets, enclose an area for a playhouse, stage, or special activity area?

Your creativity in using givens for the children's activities must always consider child safety and supervision first.

Think about what play areas add beauty, and create a state of relaxed alertness, or else can be classified as warm, cozy, child-friendly places. Look at what yard features have a significant effect on the children's behavior. Movable and mobile furnishings and equipment will have many possible uses. Adding tires, boxes, signs, and donated items to the yard should be explored. Animal and insect study takes place in many centers. A great number of science discoveries can happen that are not possible in indoor settings.

Griffin and Rinn (1998) encourage teachers to add obstacle courses to play yards for variety, developmental value, spatial awareness, adventure, cooperative and gross-motor skill development, creative expression, dramatic play, self-esteem, and challenge. Make sure you consult with your cooperating teacher about outdoor plans for child activities.

## Work Ethic Activities

Remember the status that went along with being selected as the wastebasket-dumper or chalkboard-eraser? Cleaning, cooking, room maintenance, material repair, and similar activities are planned regularly in some classrooms. These work-related activities can offer opportunities for children to develop work skills and attitudes, a sense of accomplishment, independence, and feelings of competency. Working alone or in groups is possible. Polishing shoes, cleaning silverware, and shelling peas belong in this work category. Often, these activities are a popular choice.

# ▶ SUMMARY

Planning, presenting, and assessing activities are a part of student teaching. Written activity plans are usually required and encourage student teachers to examine closely all aspects of their planned activities. Guidelines and criteria for planning activities promote overall success. Consultation with cooperating teachers and college supervisors often aids in the development of written plans. Learning objectives can be written as instructional objectives or in measurable, specific behavioral objective terms.

A lesson plan form was provided in this chapter. Preparing a written plan increases student teacher confidence and reduces stress, and often it averts potential problems. A lesson plan is only a starting point and has the flexibility to change or be discontinued during its presentation, depending on interest and children's needs.

Each classroom's group times differ in intent and purpose. Student teachers plan and present group instruction and carefully analyze goals and the group's particular dynamics, needs, and learning levels.

Thematic unit teaching is a popular instructional approach. However, there are different views regarding the benefits and limitations of unit teaching. Each thematic unit is a unique collection of activities planned for a specific group of young children, and their particular geographic, socioeconomic, and cultural setting should be taken into consideration. After a thematic unit is presented, it is evaluated by the writer for possible improvement.

This chapter started with the identification of standards that have served as the basis for curriculum development in early childhood programs. It alerted the reader to the steps curricula developers follow.

## ▶ HELPFUL WEBSITES

**http://www.naeyc.org**
NAEYC/SDE. Explore the many activities NAEYC undertakes.

**http://www.teacher.scholastic.com**
Scholastic Magazine is a resource for lesson planning ideas and links to other professional sites.

**http://www.headstartinfo.org**
Head Start: Search publications for performance standards available in English and Spanish.

 Additional resources for this chapter can be found by visiting the companion website at *www.cengage.com/education/machado.*

## ▶ SUGGESTED ACTIVITIES

A. In groups of two to four, identify which activity plan section needs greater attention by the student teacher in the following situations.

1. Danielle is presenting an activity with her collection of seashells. She has repeatedly requested that children look while she explains the details of the shells. Most of the children who started the activity are showing signs of disinterest.

2. Francisco introduced a boat-floating activity that has children excited to try it. The children start pushing, shoving, and crowding.

3. Dean prepared an activity with paper airplanes landing on a tabletop landing strip. Children are zooming loudly and running about the room, interfering with the work of others. The situation is getting out of hand.

4. Claire's activity involves making a greeting card. Many children are disappointed because Claire has run out of the metallic paper used for her sample card. Others are requesting help because their fingers are sticky with glue.

5. Kate's activity making cinnamon toast works well until Joey burns his finger on the toaster oven.

6. Sanjay has given a detailed verbal explanation of how the children should finish the weaving project he has introduced. However, the children seem to have lost interest.

7. During Jackie Ann's project, paint gets on the door handles and the children are unable to turn on the faucets because of slippery hands.

B. After the class has been divided in half, select either the *pro* or *con* views on theme teaching as an instructional approach. Use 20 minutes to plan for a debate in a future class.

C. Develop a web or outline on the topic of houses, or on a subject of your own choosing.

## ▶ REVIEW

A. List two ways to identify children's interests.

B. Write three examples of motivational statements for activities you plan to present or could present.

C. Match items in Column I with those in Column II.

| I | II |
|---|---|
| 1. a curriculum area | a. ethnic dance group |
| 2. a specific behavioral objective | b. "Those with red socks may wash their hands." |
| 3. a transitional statement | c. four out of five times |
| 4. a motivational statement | d. "Snails have one foot and excrete a slippery liquid." |
| 5. an activity plan criterion | e. nutrition |
| 6. a setup | f. has three parts |
| 7. a community resource | g. "Have you ever touched a feather?" |
| 8. a performance criterion | h. too many concepts attempted |
| 9. a summary statement | i. paper left, then patterns, crayons, and scissors at the far right |
| 10. a pitfall in student teacher lesson planning | j. child safety |

## ▶REFERENCES

Bredekamp, S., & Copple, C. (Eds.). (1997). *Developmentally appropriate practice in early childhood programs* (Rev. ed.). Washington, DC: National Association for the Education of Young Children.

Burman, L. (2009). *Are you listening? Fostering conversations that help young children learn.* St. Paul, MN: Redleaf Press.

California Department of Education. (2008). *California preschool learning foundations* Vol. 1, Sacramento, CA: Author

Carter, M., & Curtis, D. (1994). *Training teachers: A harvest of theory and practice.* St. Paul, MN: Redleaf Press.

Child Care Bureau. (2002). *Good start, grow smart.* Retrieved September 19, 2005 from http://www. nccic.acf.hhs.gov/pubs/ stateplan/execsum.html.

Curtis, D., & Carter, M. (1996). *Reflecting children's lives: A handbook for planning a child-centered curriculum.* St. Paul, MN: Redleaf Press

Copple, C., & Bredekamp, S. (Eds.). (2009). *Developmentally appropriate practice in early childhood programs: Serving children from birth through age 8.* Washington, DC: National Association for the Education of Young Children.

Delpit, L. (1995). *Other people's children: Cultural conflict in the classroom.* New York: The New Press.

Eggers-Pierola, C. (2005). *Connections and commitments: reflecting Latino values in early childhood programs.* Portsmouth, NH: Heinemann.

Fosnot, C. T. (1989). *Inquiring teachers, inquiring learners: A constructive approach for teaching.* New York: Teachers College Press.

Gamel-McCormick, M. (2000). *Exploring teachers' expectations for children entering kindergarten and procedures for sharing information between Pre-K and K programs.* Conference presentation, the National Association for the Education of Young Children, Atlanta, GA.

Geist, E., & Baum, A. C. (2005, July). Yeah, buts that keep teachers from embracing an active curriculum: Overcoming resistance. *Young Children 60*(4), 28–36.

Genishi, C. (2002, July). Young English language learners: Resourceful in the classroom. *Young Children. 57*(4), 66–72.

*Good Start, Grow Smart.* (2002, April). Washington, DC: The White House.

Griffin, C., & Rinn, B. (1998, May). Enhancing outdoor play with an obstacle course. *Young Children 53*(3), 43–51.

Head Start Bureau, Administration for Children and Families, Department of Health and Human Services. (1975). *Head Start performance standards.* Washington, DC: U. S. Department of Human Services.

Hyson, M. (2005, November). Enthusiastic and engaged: Strengthening young children's positive approaches to learning. *Young Children, 60*(6), 68–70.

Kantrowitz, B., & Wingert, P. (2002, April 29). The right way to read. *Newsweek, CXXXIX*(17), 6–66.

Katz, L., & Chard, S. (1993). *Engaging children's minds: The project approach.* Norwood, NJ: Ablex.

Koralek, D. (2008, May). Teaching and learning through routines and transitions, *Young Children 63*(3), 10–11.

National Association for the Education of Young Children. (2007). *NAEYC early program standards and accreditation criteria.* Washington, DC: Author.

NAEYC Code of Ethical Conduct. (2005). In S. Feeney & N. Freeman (Eds.), *Ethics and the early childhood educator: Using the NAEYC code.* Washington, DC: National Association for the Education of Young Children.

National Association for the Education of Young Children and the National Association of Early Childhood Specialists in State Departments of Education (NAECS/SDE) (2003). *Early childhood curriculum, assessment, and program evaluation.* (joint position statement). Washington, DC: Authors.

National Research Council. (2000). *How people learn: Brain, mind, experience and school.* Washington, DC: National Academy Press.

O'Loughlin, M. (1991, April 3–7). *Beyond constructivism: Toward a dialectical model of the problematics of teacher socialization.* Paper presented at the Annual Meeting of the American Educational Research Association, Chicago.

Padron, Y. N., Waxman, H. C., & Rivera, H. H. (2002, August). Educating Hispanic students: Effective instructional practices. *Practitioners Brief 5.* Santa Cruz, CA: Center for Research on Education, Diversity and Excellence, University of California.

Petersen, E. (1996). *A practical guide to early childhood planning and methods and materials.* Boston: Allyn and Bacon.

Plutro, M. (2000, March). Planning for linguistic and cultural diversity: We must continue to respond. *Head Start Bulletin, 67,* 19.

Schickedanz, J. A. (2008). *Increasing the power of instruction: Integration of language, literacy, and math across the preschool day.* Washington, DC: National Association for the Education of Young Children.

Sheinman, A. J. (2000, August). Six behavior tips that really work. *Instructor, 110*(1), 24.

Snow, K. (2006). Connecting the early child care worker professional development with child outcomes. In M. Zaslow & I. Martinez-Beck (Eds.), *Critical issues in early childhood professional development* (pp. 137–140). Baltimore, MD: Paul Brookes Publishing Co.

United States Bureau of the Census. (1995). *The foreign-born population: 1994.* Current Population Reports. Washington, DC: Government Printing Office.

U. S. Department of Education, National Center for Educational Statistics (2003). *States and trends in the Education of Hispanics* (NCES 2003-008). Washington, DC: 12.

U. S. Department of Education, [1998, 2004]. *Federal Reading Excellence Act – Title One.* Washington, DC: U. S. Government Printing Office.

Wesson, K. A. (2001, March). The "Volvo effect": Questioning standardized tests. *Young Children, 56*(2), 16–18.

# Working with Children

# CHAPTER 5

# Classroom Management: Beyond Discipline

**OBJECTIVES**  After reading this chapter, you should be able to:

1. List the five major management areas.
2. Discuss the effects of the classroom environment on children's behaviors.
3. Define the role of the guidance function, commonly called *discipline*, in the management of the classroom.
4. List and describe five common guidance/disciplinary techniques.
5. Identify the different behaviors children display when resisting adult authority.

## STUDENT TEACHER SCENARIO

**Setting:** A child care program for two-year-olds. Marcia is the student teacher, Mrs. Rice is the cooperating teacher, and Christina is the aide. It is late afternoon; most of the children have been picked up by their parents and Christina is watching the few who remain. Mrs. Rice is talking to Marcia about an incident that happened during the morning activity period.

"Marcia, did you notice what Ramón and David were doing while you were working with the children at the crafts table?" asks Mrs. Rice.

"I'm not sure I'm following you," Marcia responds.

"Did you notice that David and Ramón were arguing about who was going to use the large red truck over by the block center and that David was biting Ramón?"

"Oh, yes, I turned to look when I heard Ramón scream," Marcia says, "but I have to admit that I didn't see what was happening because I was so busy at the crafts table. Besides, I had my back to the block and truck area. Of course, I thought David was at fault; I missed Ramón's hitting him first, and I didn't see the two of them tugging at the same truck."

"You know, we teachers have to place ourselves so we can get an overview of the entire classroom every time we plan an activity that has to be supervised. I don't mean this in a negative way, Marcia. Part of the reason you are a student teacher is to learn. Always place yourself so you can see the whole classroom, or ask Christina or me to supervise where you can't see," Mrs. Rice says gently.

"Had you seen the two boys pulling at the same truck, you might have been able to leave the crafts table and quickly intervene."

"I understand, Mrs. Rice. I know I'm here to learn, but it seems so hard at times," Marcia sighs. "I remember our college supervisor saying that we had to develop eyes in the backs of our heads; now I understand why!"

## Questions for Discussion:

1. How do you feel about what happened to Marcia? Has anything similar happened to you?

2. How might Marcia feel after her talk with Mrs. Rice? How might you feel in her place?

3. Do you think Mrs. Rice could have handled the situation differently? Why or why not?

• • • • • • • • • • • • • • • • • • • • • • • • • • • • • • • • • • • •

## CLASSROOM MANAGEMENT

What comes to your mind when you hear the words **classroom management**? Many student teachers, and many teachers themselves, associate the phrase with another word: *discipline*. Classroom management goes far beyond discipline, although the guidance function is certainly a part of what is involved in managing the classroom. Classroom management, in the fullest sense of the meaning, involves five separate parts:

1. the physical arrangement of a classroom
2. curriculum choices
3. time management
4. classroom routine management
5. the guidance, or disciplinary, function

> **classroom management**—consists of supervising, planning, and directing classroom activities and the room environment. It also involves making time-length decisions, providing appropriate direction, and guiding child behavior to enable children to live and work effectively with others.

Guidance, in turn, has two facets: managing routine behavior problems and managing serious behavior problems.

Although McLeod, Fisher, and Hoover (2003) use different words, they include the same five components in the subtitle to their text: Managing Time and Space (components 1 and 3), Student Behavior (components 4 and 5), and Instructional Strategies (component 2).

Flicker and Hoffman (2002) believe that although teachers and child educators come to work, in some cases with years of training and experience, classroom management continues to be daunting. One major difficulty lies in the fact that in our multicultural, multilinguistic, multiethnic society, the disciplinary function is viewed differently by different families. Although state laws forbid spanking as a disciplinary technique, there are families who typically use spanking to control their children's negative behaviors. As early childhood professionals, our task then becomes a delicate one to explain center or school policies and state laws.

## The Physical Arrangement of the Classroom

What is the *best* arrangement for a preschool classroom? McLeod (in McLeod et al., 2003) reminds teachers that environments have a great influence on how people

▶ **Figure 5-1**

Notice the abundant pillows for children to sit on in this book corner.

feel and behave. Put yourself at children's eye level when evaluating a classroom. Questions such as the following should be considered:

◆ Where should blocks be located? Are they easy to reach?

◆ Where should the art area be located? On an easy-to-clean floor area? Near a water supply?

◆ Should there be a clothesline on which to hang paintings?

◆ Is the dramatic-play area attractive? Are there enough changes of clothing and other props to stimulate a variety of roles?

◆ Is there a quiet corner where children can look at books (see Figure 5–1)?

◆ Is there plenty of space, especially outside, for active play?

◆ Do children have an opportunity to climb, run, and ride wheeled toys without endangering each other's safety?

◆ Are children's physical needs and safety considered?

◆ Is there a sense of order?

◆ Would the room promote child curiosity, wonder, and intrigue, or beg to be physically explored (see Figure 5–2)?

◆ Is the room aesthetically pleasing and does it offer elements of natural beauty?

◆ Are room retreats designed to offer feelings of soft, cuddly, calming textures, seating, and privacy?

◆ Is the room set up for child self-help?

◆ Do thought-out storage areas exist?

◆ Are creative materials and toys open-ended?

◆ Is there a secluded area where a child can be alone?

◆ Are room arrangements and areas flexible? Can they expand if need be?

◆ Are there smooth, flowing pathways in and out of room areas?

◆ Do visual displays reflect children's lives, interests, and cultural experiences?

Room features sometimes overlooked include background noise level, smells, temperature, and lighting.

Look at Figure 5–3. Is this the best possible arrangement this first-grade teacher could have made? What flaws can you see? Was the teacher wise in placing the reading area next to the water fountain? Where should the math manipulatives be stored? Given the configuration of the desks, what circulation problems might you anticipate? Might the way the room is currently arranged lead to guidance problems? Can you think of what you might do if this classroom were yours to rearrange?

McLeod, Fisher, and Hoover (2003) point out that teachers must consider not only the grouping of student tables or desks and chairs but also where to position their own desks and locations for interest/learning centers. They remind us further that computer stations need to be positioned in quiet areas and that bulletin boards should be colorful. Traffic patterns, storage areas, and closets must also be taken into consideration for maximum flow and minimal clutter. McLeod, Fisher, and Hoover indicate that there is a need to plan for regular classroom routines, such as taking attendance, collecting lunch money, allowing for use of the pencil sharpener, and going to the rest rooms.

Now look at Figure 5–4. Is this the best possible arrangement for this preschool play yard for three- and four-year-olds? Can you point out any possible areas of difficulty related to the placement of the play equipment in the yard? Was it wise of the person who

▶ **Figure 5-2**

Does your classroom promote child curiosity, wonder, and intrigue?

▶ **Figure 5-3**

Why might the arrangement of this first-grade classroom lead to management problems?

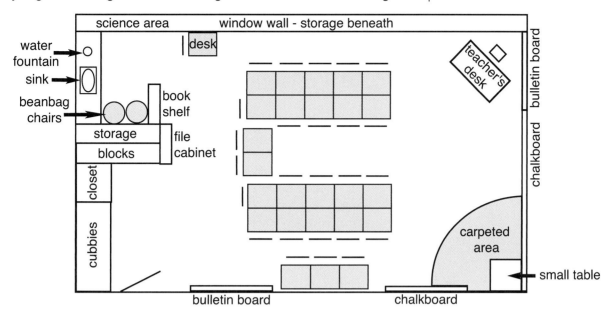

▶ **Figure 5-4**

What might be the possible problems with the arrangement of this preschool play yard?

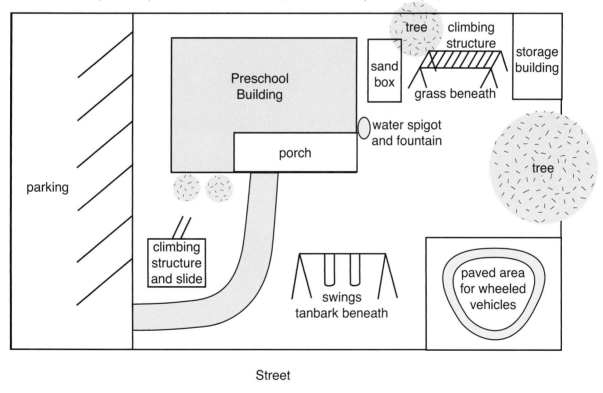

designed the yard to have placed the sand area by the water spigot and fountain? Should the storage shed be located where it is? Is the paved area for wheeled vehicles large enough and stimulating enough? Might the current configuration lead to any guidance difficulties?

## Curriculum Choices/Instructional Strategies

Each choice you make regarding curriculum is another part of classroom management.

- ◆ What materials would you set out for children to explore?
- ◆ Which materials, such as scissors and glue sticks, can be used only under direct supervision?
- ◆ How might you equip the dramatic-play and discovery centers?
- ◆ How would you develop colorful bulletin board displays that are informative and attractive?
- ◆ Which materials would be used every day and which would change after children have had ample opportunity to explore them?
- ◆ Is there a bell schedule for recess or outdoor play?
- ◆ Does your principal or director expect that certain instructional areas are to be explored in the morning or afternoon?
- ◆ Are you somewhat limited by expectations of the school board or by state standards?

Keeping children adequately motivated with new curricular choices, while retaining those materials children clearly love, contributes to effective classroom management.

> The National Association for the Education of Young Children's position statement on developmentally appropriate practices stresses the importance of child-initiated or child-centered learning . . . . [T]he importance of involving children in curricular decisions and allowing them to be responsible for their own learning is vital across all age groups. (Vartuli, 2005)

It goes without saying that motivated children, exploring curricular areas of their own choice, rarely display problem behaviors.

## Time Management

Time is a limited resource. Time management involves more than simply following a schedule; it includes observing each child closely, to recognize when a child may need to use the toilet or when he may need to be redirected from playing with a child with whom he has had altercations. Time management means knowing how long children in your care can sustain interest, so you can choose books for story time that not only pique their curiosity but are also short enough to sustain their attention. Time management means planning activities that are neither too long nor too short and giving all children enough opportunities to engage in their chosen activities. Sometimes, there never seems to be enough time to accomplish everything we would like to do.

At the elementary school level, time management also means acknowledging *time on task*. How much time is actually spent on learning? Some of the time is allotted to preparing and distributing materials. Some of the time is spent in introducing the lesson. More time is spent in delivering instruction, assigning work, and closing the lesson (McLeod et al., 2003). Then there are the times that students have to be reminded to get to work and stop visiting. So the question becomes: How much time is actually spent on task? Possibly more than it appears. Students may use part of the time, when they appear to be off-task or even day dreaming, to *think*: a critical part of problem solving and unlocking their creative potential. Can you remember times when you might have taken time to withdraw, in a sense, from active participation in a classroom, just to think? Your children or students do likewise.

Recent research on the activities of the brain, together with the burgeoning influence of schools that have implemented brain-based learning, has shown what happens in the brains of people when they think. When the material to learn is new, children and adults both need more time to reflect or think about what it is they are learning. Young children need to be taught how to talk about what they are doing because that helps them develop the capacity to reflect. Later, they can be encouraged to speak silently to themselves as a part of developing the ability to think about thinking, or *metacognition* (Abbott, 1997; Jensen, 1998).

Jensen (1998) cautions us to remember that "[a] typical classroom narrows our thinking strategies and answer options. Educators who insist on singular approaches and the 'right answer' are ignoring...[t]hat humans have survived... by trying out new things. Not always getting the right answer."

Time management also implies the wise use of your own time; try to balance your work, preparation, home and family, relaxation, and recreation times. Set priorities and try not to become so overwhelmed with preparation for school that you have no time for other things.

## Managing Classroom Routines

For student teachers, it is essential to your success that you carefully observe your cooperating teacher's routines. Should you want to introduce a change in routine, clear it with your college supervisor first; then check with your cooperating teacher. One may say no, but another may suggest that you try, but be aware of what a change in the routine may do to some of the children. Always remember that for some children, especially younger ones and those new to the classroom, routines offer predictability and, therefore, safety.

# THE GUIDANCE OR DISCIPLINARY FUNCTION IN CLASSROOM MANAGEMENT

When we think of the guidance function and its role in classroom management, what do we mean? **Guidance** can mean leadership, as in directing someone to a destination or goal. In the classroom, guidance is the teacher's function, to provide leadership, but more often it is defined as discipline. How do the terms *guidance* and *discipline* differ? *Guidance* is a less specific, more generic word; *discipline* derives from the Latin word for *pupil* and is defined as *training designed to produce a specific character or pattern of behavior*. In particular, discipline is the act of assisting the child to grow toward maturity. This is the major goal.

Gartrell (2004) makes the point of stressing that guidance can also be looked at as trying to figure out why a child may behave as she does and how to teach so that she'll behave differently.

Flicker and Hoffman (2002) advocate taking a positive approach to discipline "through discussion, explanation, limit setting, and enforcement of consequences."

Kaiser and Rasminsky (2007) insist that preventing what they call *challenging behavior*, while not an exciting topic, can be extremely important. Included in their concept of prevention are the following:

◆ making transitions fun
◆ controlling the number of children in a play space
◆ allowing for flexibility

## Conflicts Arise

Conflict among preschoolers is an expected part of social development. When children's different needs and wishes collide, feelings erupt. Play partner selection can be a factor. Transitions from one activity to another may provoke problems if

**guidance**—ongoing process of directing children's behavior based on the types of adults children are expected to become.

transitions are abrupt. Anger, frustration, and disappointment may trigger child outbreaks, and violence may have become a learned behavior. Browning, Davis, and Resta (2000) remind teachers that children may frequently witness verbal and physical aggression in their homes or neighborhoods, and emulate that model.

**Outcomes** Educators who study children's conflicts observe four common outcomes:

1. *lack of resolution*, which happens if the issue is dropped, children leave the area, select different toys or different activities, or seek other play partners
2. *mutual solution*, which is achieved through discussion, bargaining, compromising, settling on a creative alternative, or making the conflict into a game
3. *submission*, which happens if a child yields or children give in willingly or unwillingly
4. *adult intervention*, which may impose or suggest a solution or otherwise settle the conflict

As Gillespie and Chick (2001) point out, submission is an undesirable outcome because a clear winner or loser is established, creating or promoting bullying and victimization. Adult intervention, though sometimes necessary, is not the educators' primary goal, which is to minimize the need for adult intervention. When adult intervention is minimized, children negotiate and resolve conflicts themselves. Gartrell (2004) urges teachers to use the term *mistaken behavior* instead of *misbehavior*. He believes that the latter is a judgment call, the former a call that indicates the child needs to learn a different response. Childen may need practice in learning problem-solving skills, and teachers may have to take time to offer practice opportunities by providing supportive assistance. Froschl, Sprung, and Hinitz (2005) also advocate training children in techniques designed to avert conflict and prevent bullying.

Levin (2008) believes that teachers need to reassure the children in their care that they are safe. The guiding principle is to help every child feel that "'I am safe here. My body is safe; my feelings are safe; my thoughts, ideas, and words are safe; my work (the things I make and the materials I use) is safe.'"

## Managing Routine Behavior Problems

What is meant by "routine behavior problems"? Can any misbehavior be considered routine? Obviously, two-year-old children may present several routine behavior problems as they struggle with trying to establish their autonomy. But it is not just two-year-olds who struggle with autonomy. To a certain extent, all children struggle with it. What do you see then? You see children who push against limits and test boundaries. When you first take over the class from your cooperating teacher, you will often see children who seem to misbehave deliberately. You ask them to come to the circle-time area and some children say, "No." You ask others to pick up the blocks and replace them on the shelves prior to snack time and again you hear, "No" or, "Why should I?" or, "I don't want any snack today."

So, what is the student teacher to do? One set of guidelines is called the *four Cs: consistency, consideration, confidence,* and *candor*. What is meant by *consistency*? It means that you understand yourself well enough to respond to children in a fair and impartial manner. It means consistency of adult behavior, expectations, limits, and rules, which means reliability; your behavior does not change from day to day and remains reasonably predictable to the children. For children, there is safety in knowing that the adults in their lives are predictable. Such reliability gives children feelings of security and safety. This becomes especially important when you, as a student teacher, are responsible for children who may be inconsistent and unpredictable.

The second *C* is *consideration*. This means that you are considerate of the children you teach and of the adults with whom you work. You respect the children and are aware of their needs, their likes, and dislikes. You are considerate by taking time to listen, even to the child who talks constantly. It means watching all of the children closely and noting which child needs an extra hug and which one needs to be removed from a group before a temper tantrum erupts. These actions show children that you care and help you establish a warm relationship with them. Consideration helps to build rapport.

The third *C* is *confidence*. You need confidence to make decisions that reflect careful thought on your part, decisions that are free of bias and based on all evidence. Confidence implies that you realize you like some children better than others, and you know why you react differently to identical actions involving different children. Confidence is knowing when to stand up for your opinions and decisions and when to compromise. It means understanding when to be silent, and knowing that waiting may be the more mature action to take.

*Candor*, the fourth *C*, means that you are open and honest in your actions with children, fellow workers, and yourself. It means being frank and fair; you may inevitably put your foot in your mouth, but you will gain a reputation for being honest in your relations with others. Candor is the ability to admit a mistake and the courage to apologize.

Like the four *Cs*, the acronym *CARE* can also spell success in guiding children. As Rogers and Freiberg (1994) wrote, good teachers possess three qualities: congruence, acceptance of others, and empathy. As mentioned in Chapter 2, these can easily be expanded to four: *congruence*, *acceptance*, *reliability*, and *empathy*, or *CARE* (see Figure 5–5).

*Congruence*, as Chapter 2 states, is Rogers' term for understanding yourself. Always remember that with truly great teachers, their teaching is such an extension of themselves that you see the same person regardless of where they might be seen. It is sometimes difficult for a student teacher to emulate the truly congruent teacher, because the methods she uses are so much a part of her. What you as a student teacher must learn is what methods are congruent with your inner self. The best methods are always those that seem natural to use, those that are an extension of how you see yourself.

Remember that *acceptance*, as Rogers uses it, means truly caring about each child you teach. It means that all children deserve your respect regardless of how they act. The aggressive child, who acts-out, is just as deserving of your acceptance as the star pupil of the class.

As mentioned before, *reliability* means that your children know you and they know the routine for the class. Being reliable also implies fairness.

According to Rogers, *empathy* implies being able to place yourself in the child's shoes, to see from that perspective. It is the ability to see that the hostile, aggressive child may need love and acceptance more than the happy, easygoing child. Empathy also means knowing that the happy child needs attention, too, even though attention is not demanded. Learn to be empathetic; it is worth the effort.

Let's assume that you have learned how to *CARE*. Does that mean you will not have any behavior problems? Does that mean you will automatically have rapport with all your children? Of course not. It means only that you can, perhaps, understand children's behavior more easily and can plan to teach self-control to those who need to learn it.

> ▶ **Figure 5–5**
> Student teaching offers many opportunities to show children you CARE.

© Cengage Learning

## CHILD EMPOWERMENT

Your previous classes have no doubt dealt with the issue of child choice and responsibility for behavioral actions. **Empowering** children in classrooms can mean giving them the opportunity to think about and guide their own actions, thereby allowing them to choose between possible actions in any given situation.

**empowering**—helping parents and children gain a sense of control over events in their lives.

Naturally, all child group arrangements have rules to guard the safety of children and limit behaviors unpleasant to others.

It may be all too easy for a student teacher to do everything for children. It makes the student teacher appear busy and productive, in control, and active rather than passive. Giving choices within limits takes time and is usually more work, and sometimes it creates disorder. Is it easier for you to hand out the paper needed to each child or to assign a "materials manager" to distribute the paper at each table group? Is it easier to write names on the children's papers than to ask children if they want to write their own names on their work? Is it easier to promote children's taking turns as group leaders or helpers or to do the task yourself? Most teachers answer that it is *easier* to do it themselves, but sharing tasks to provide children with more experiences and to build self-esteem is the preferred, more educative, practice.

Unfortunately, when discipline or guidance is concerned, there is no magic formula. This text aims to provide you the techniques used successfully by effective early childhood teachers.

## Character Guidance

Schools and teachers consciously and unconsciously attempt to educate children (McLeod et al., 2003):

- ◆ to be concerned about the weak and those who need help
- ◆ to help others
- ◆ to work hard and to complete tasks promptly and as well as they are able
- ◆ to control violent tempers
- ◆ to work cooperatively
- ◆ to practice good manners
- ◆ to respect authority
- ◆ to respect the rights of others
- ◆ to help resolve conflict
- ◆ to understand honesty, responsibility, and friendship
- ◆ to balance pleasure and responsibility
- ◆ to ask themselves and decide what is the right thing to do

Student teachers may experience many learning situations in the classroom that are also guidance situations and may be concerned with one or more of the above-listed goals of the guidance function in classroom management.

## Guidance as Social Development

Social behaviors are sometimes seen as difficult to teach, because so often they involve the *absence* of doing, rather than doing. In other words, we teach prosocial behavior by *not* doing. We choose *not* to grab; we choose *not* to spank; we try to model in our own behaviors how we would like children to behave. But what can we do actively? Fisher (in McLeod et al., 2003) suggests the following:

- ◆ Establish a positive relationship with your students.
- ◆ Build caring relationships through modeling the behavior we want and be open to student concerns and feelings.
- ◆ Arrange classroom spaces and play materials to facilitate cooperative play.
- ◆ Use **bibliotherapy**: incorporate children's literature to enhance empathy and caring in daily reading activities.
- ◆ Actively lead group discussions on prosocial interactions.

**bibliotherapy**—the use of books that deal with emotionally sensitive topics, in a developmentally appropriate way, to help children gain accurate information and learn coping strategies.

◆ Encourage social interaction between normally developing children and children with special needs.

◆ Develop class and school projects that foster altruism.

◆ Move very young children with peers to the next age group.

◆ Arrange regular viewing of prosocial media and video games.

◆ Work closely with families for prosocial programming.

◆ Establish a bias-free curriculum.

◆ Require responsibility: encourage children to care for younger children and classmates who need extra help.

◆ Train older children as peer mediators.

◆ Cherish children: create an atmosphere of affirmation through family, classroom, and community rituals.

According to Gartrell (2006a):

> The objective is to teach children to solve problems rather than to punish children for having problems they cannot solve. The outcomes of guidance—the ability to get along with others, solve problems using words, express strong feelings in acceptable ways—are the goals for citizens of a democratic society.

To achieve this objective, Gartrell reminds teachers that:

◆ Social skills are complex and may take a lifetime to learn.

◆ Teachers should try to reduce children's needs for *mistaken behavior*.

◆ Teachers themselves must cultivate positive teacher-child and teacher-adult relationships. We are role models of behavior for children. How we handle anger, frustration, fear, sadness, and other emotions has an effect on the children in our charge.

◆ Any intervention method chosen should be solution-oriented.

◆ Teachers need to build partnerships with parents.

◆ Teachers should use teamwork with adults. Gartrell states that it is a myth to think we can handle all situations alone.

## The Role of Families

Gartrell (2004) maintains that building partnerships with children's families produces the best results. When conflicts arise, as they inevitably do, nurturing mutual respect, listening actively (more about active listening in Chapter 8), being patient, modeling reflective listening, inviting continued involvement, and collaboration are the critical ways in which conflicts may be resolved. Gartrell suggests that discipline policies should be in any handbook prepared for families and should be part of any family orientation or initial meeting.

The best resolutions to any behavior problems experienced by children are those wherein families and schools have established mutual goals. School-family partnerships work smoothly when communication channels have been established, mutual respect is evident, and families are welcome in the classroom.

### Helping Children Understand and Express Emotions and Feelings
Researchers have attempted to identify the stages in children's understandings of their own emotions, as well as the language and actions children use to express emotions. One major conclusion derived from these studies is that conversations about feelings provide an important context for learning about emotions and how to manage them (Butterfield, Martin, & Prairie, 2004). In everyday interactions, teachers have the opportunity to help children gain

insight into emotions—their own and those of others—and develop socially acceptable expressions.

Butterfield, Martin, and Prairie (2004) suggest:

◆ Establish a responsive environment for staff acceptance of children's expressions of feelings and for the appropriate adult responses.

◆ Foster a positive sense of self and consider classroom features and settings where emotions and children's reflections on feelings can be experienced. Keep a well-stocked dramatic play center.

◆ Understand children's behavior; it's the first step to managing it.

◆ Promote language skills and problem-solving abilities and child reflection concerning emotional happenings.

◆ Use storybooks dealing with emotions; ask children how they would feel in a similar situation, and discuss causes and consequences.

◆ Use audiovisual equipment. Children can recreate emotions they have seen and then dramatize a situation for themselves; discuss choices children have made in responding to their own and others' emotions.

◆ Deal with children's quarrels and disputes in a way that develops their understanding; give children time to tell their respective sides without interruption. Teachers can reflect back and ask for clarification while also urging each child to examine his personal contribution to the conflict. Talking about how they feel and what could be done differently next time helps children manage feelings rather than suppressing or denying them.

Student teachers may play a special preventive and interactional role in social-emotional development, supplementing the cooperating teacher's efforts.

## Rules

Wherever you work with children, there will be rules. Some will be unique because schools and centers vary immensely in physical structures and staffing patterns. Some rules are defined by state law, such as the no-spanking rule. Check with the laws of your own state to ascertain what they are. Economics, too, can influence rules for children. In an earlier chapter, you were asked to read the written rule statements in existence at your placement site. By now, you have probably discovered rule revisions and other rules unique to your classroom that were not included, so-called *unwritten* rules. Rules are not secret, but for them to be effective, each child needs a clear picture of the teacher's expectations of classroom behavior. Any changes in existing rules or the addition of new rules need to be discussed with the children.

All rules in an early childhood center, kindergarten, or primary classroom are related to four basic categories of actions:

1. Children will not be allowed to hurt themselves.
2. Children will not be allowed to hurt others.
3. Children will not be allowed to destroy the environment.
4. Everyone helps with the cleanup tasks.
   Another category enters the picture when group instruction begins, and that is:
5. Children will not be allowed to impact other children's access to instruction.

In other words, children cannot interrupt, hamper, impede, or delay the smoothness or flow of the educational program with disruptive actions.

Student teachers need to examine rules closely (see Figure 5–6). If rules become picky or ultra-specific, it often indicates an overuse of teacher power. One student

© Cengage Learning

▶ **Figure 5-6**
The status and procedures folders help the many adults who work there know what is expected.

teacher shared with her student teaching seminar an incident where children were admonished for eating just the frosting off their cupcakes. You will need to keep tabs on whether rules are reasonable or too numerous as you student teach.

A student teacher is an authority figure, one who assures rules are followed for the safety and welfare of all concerned. Authority figures expect that there may be occasions of child anger because the teacher's actions can block a child from her desire or goal. It is not realistic to expect children to always be happy with you.

## Age of Child

Some loose guidelines will be discussed next concerning guidance techniques for children of different ages. Teachers of infants and toddlers find that techniques requiring the physical removal of objects or the child from a given situation are used more frequently, although words always accompany teacher action. To help preschoolers with rule compliance, teachers often focus on changing environmental settings, their planned instructional program, or the way they interact or speak. It is common in preschool, kindergarten, and lower elementary school grades to have teacher–child and teacher–group discussions about classroom rules and the reasons behind them, so difficulties may be solved together. Teachers are still the ultimate authority, but children have a greater feeling and understanding that rules protect everyone. Rules become "our rules" rather than "the teacher's rules."

## Ethnic, Racial, Family, and Gender Differences

Children taught to be assertive in their own culture may be viewed as aggressive by a child of another culture (Gonzalez-Mena & Shareef, 2005). The outgoing boy who grasps another playfully around the neck as an invitation to play—a behavior appropriate at home with his brothers—may be perceived as aggressive by some teachers and peers. Gonzalez-Mena and Shareef suggest that differences among racial or ethnic families and teachers can best be worked through by setting aside judgments and challenging ourselves to be open to explore the possibilities our differences offer.

Walker-Dalhouse (2005), in her review of literature on the discipline of children from minority and low-income backgrounds, points out the discrepancy of expectations held and management techniques used by teachers. One well-documented explanation is that teachers perceive the behavior of African-American and Hispanic males as more aggressive than the same behavior among their white peers, and their treatment is more likely to be harsher, resulting in suspensions and expulsions. Aggressive behaviors by white children are often handled by conferencing with them and/or isolating them in a time-out area of the classroom. Walker-Dalhouse calls for teachers to be aware of their own prejudices and biases, pointing out how "critical it is for the teacher to establish a caring and supportive relationship with African-American [and other racial and ethnic minority] children." Does this not sound like *CARE*ing? She concludes, "We must challenge ourselves to make cultural diversity an integral part of our discussions about classroom management as we strive to become multiculturally competent."

Gartrell (2006b), in discussing problems experienced by boys, cautions us that "boys' slower developmental rates [in comparison to that of girls], physical response styles, and kinetic learning behaviors are seen as deficits." These characteristics often lead teachers, mostly female, to see them as faults to be quickly and firmly "corrected."

Carlson (2005), in citing the works of previous researchers, notes that American children may be touched by their teachers to be restrained or corrected, whereas caring and playful teacher touches may be less frequent. Carlson urges teachers to reflect on acceptable forms of touching, consider the context of any given situation, decide what touching is developmentally appropriate, determine individual children's sensitivity and preferences regarding touch, and understand that a child's permission is necessary. Carlson believes that adults do not have the right to touch children at will, but if a child's immediate safety is involved, a teacher must act, with or without consent from the child.

Teachers understand that some children may have been raised by parents or caregivers who have been overly lenient or inconsistent when it came to setting limits. Family rules might have been stated but not enforced. Other children might have received little guidance and might have been allowed to do whatever they wished. These children frequently may display inappropriate behaviors in preschool centers, elementary schools, and after-school programs.

## CLASSROOM MANAGEMENT OR DISCIPLINARY TECHNIQUES

Now let us look at specific techniques you might use to manage some of the problems you may encounter in a typical classroom.

In its narrower sense of classroom discipline or **behavior management**, discipline refers to those things you do to teach or persuade children to behave in a manner of which you approve. There are many ways to manage behavior, but there are six that have proven to be more effective than others:

1. **behavior modification**, achieved by applying principles of reinforcement to change a child's behavior
2. setting limits and insisting they be kept
3. labeling the behavior instead of the child
4. using the concept of logical consequences
5. teacher anticipation and intervention
6. conflict resolution

**behavior management**—behavioral approach to guidance, holding that the child's behavior is under the control of the environment, which includes space, objects, and people.

**behavior modification**—the systematic application of principles of reinforcement to modify behavior.

### Behavior Modification

With behavior modification, it is important to be objective. The term has acquired a negative connotation that is unfounded. Everyone uses behavior modification, whether recognized or not, from turning off the lights when children are to be quiet to planning and implementing a behavior modification plan. (See the Appendix for an example of a behavior modification plan.)

## Setting Limits

Rules must be stated, repeated, and applied consistently (see Figure 5–7). The aggressive, acting-out child must often be reminded of these rules, over and over again. You may have to repeatedly remove the acting-out child from the room or to a quiet area in the room. You may have to insist firmly and caringly that the child change the negative behavior. A technique that works one day, such as removing the child to a quiet corner, may not work the next. A technique that works with one child may not work on another.

There are several difficulties facing the student teacher regarding behavior management. One is the problem of developing a repertoire of techniques with which you are comfortable. A second difficulty is developing an awareness of and sensitivity to children, so that you can almost instinctively know what technique to use on which child. The third difficulty is recognizing, usually through the process of trial and error, what techniques are congruent with your self-image. If you see yourself as a warm and loving person, do not pretend to be a strict disciplinarian. The children will sense your pretense and will not behave.

Perhaps the most critical error made by many student teachers is putting the need to be liked by the children ahead of their need for limits. As a result, the student teacher may fail to set limits or fail to intervene in situations, often allowing things to get out of hand. When the student teacher must finally intercede, he may forget to *CARE*, or fail to accept the child causing the problem. The student teacher may not be consistent from day to day or child to child and may not take the time to develop empathy.

The children, in contrast, know perfectly well the student teacher's need to be liked, but they do not know whether the student teacher can be trusted. Trust is acquired only when the children discover that the student teacher *CARE*s. It is more important that the children respect, rather than love, the student teacher. In fact, no child can begin to love without having respect first.

It is easier to explain your limits at the beginning of your student teaching experience than to make any assumptions that the children know them. They know what limits your cooperating teacher has established, but they do not know that you expect the same. To reassure themselves that the limits are the same, they test

© Cengage Learning

▶ **Figure 5–7**
These children know that helmets are required if they ride the bikes.

*Student Teacher Quote*—"I once heard in a beginning class what one teacher tried when a child picked up a large tree branch and brandished it threateningly at other children. The teacher went to the child and said, "What a marvelous branch, could I hold it?" That led into a discussion about the branch hurting someone, and the child's deciding it needed to be given to the custodian. The teacher later had the custodian carry it in at a small group time for discussion. The child received attention and status for considering the safety of others.

*I tried this technique with a child who'd picked up a playground rock. It worked well for me, too. I'm sure it won't always work, but it might work most of the time."*

**Peter Mills, First grade, East Palo Alto Elementary School District**

them. This is when you must insist that your rules are the same as the cooperating teacher's. You will have to repeat them often. Most children will learn rapidly that your expectations are the same. Others will have to be reminded constantly before they accept the rules.

## Labeling the Behavior

What is meant by the phrase "labeling the behavior, not the child"? Essentially, we are referring to what Gordon (1974) calls *I messages,* in contrast to *you messages.* In an *I* message, you recognize that it is *your* problem rather than the child's. For example, if one of your three-year-olds accidentally spills the paint, you are angry—not because the child spilled the paint, but because you do not want to clean up the mess. Unfortunately, you may lash out at the child and say something like, "Don't you ever look at what you're doing?" or "Why are you so clumsy?" The result is that the child feels that spilling the paint is his fault when it is possible that you could have foreseen and prevented it. The paint may have been placed too close to the child's elbow. The spilled paint is your problem, not the child's. How much better to say something like, "I really hate to clean up spilled paint!" This is what is truly annoying you, not the child. Even children can understand a reluctance to clean up a spill. And we can see how much better it is to label the behavior, not the child.

There are times, of course, when you will honestly feel you do not like a child. Then, it is especially important to let the child know that it is the behavior you do not like, rather than the child. Continue to look for other times when you can give an honest compliment. Do not try to use positive reinforcement unless the child's behavior warrants it. All children know whether they deserve a compliment; do not try to fool them.

Sending *I* messages is a technique that even young children can learn. As the teacher, you can ask children to say, "I don't like it when you do that!" to other children instead of shouting, "I don't like you!" By labeling the action that is disliked, the child who is being corrected learns what is acceptable behavior without being made to feel bad. The children who are doing the correcting also learn what is acceptable. Eventually, they also learn how to differentiate between who a child is and how the child behaves. It is a lesson even adults need to practice.

## Logical Consequences

**logical consequences—** Rudolf Dreikurs's technique of specific outcomes that follow certain behaviors and are mutually agreed upon by teacher and children/ students.

Developed by psychiatrist Rudolf Dreikurs, the concept of **logical consequences** is based on his long association with family and child counseling. Eventually he related his theories of family–child discipline to the classroom and introduced teachers and administrators to his concepts of natural and logical consequences (Dreikurs, Grunewald, & Pepper, 1982).

For example, a natural consequence of not coming to dinner when called might be the possibility of eating a cold meal. In the classroom setting, however, natural consequences are not easily derived, so logical consequences are generally used instead. With older preschoolers and primary school children, this can be done effectively in the group. For example, if children forget to replace puzzles on the rack after playing with them and pieces are lost, they may decide that the logical consequence should be that no puzzles should be used for a week.

Dreikurs' key ideas relate to his beliefs that all students want recognition, and if unable to attain it in ways teachers would consider socially acceptable, children will resort to four possible *mistaken goals: attention getting, power seeking, revenge seeking,* and *displaying inadequacy.* To change the behavior, teachers need first to identify the student's mistaken goal. This is accomplished by recognizing the student's reaction to being corrected.

If the student is seeking attention, she may stop the behavior for a short time but then repeat it until she receives the desired attention. If seeking power, she may refuse to stop or may even escalate the behavior. In this case, a teacher may want to ignore the behavior, as long as possible, to avoid provoking a power struggle with the student. Or the teacher may want to provide the student with clear-cut choices: "You may choose to go to the **time-out** area until you feel able to rejoin the group, or you may go to the math center and work on the tangrams." A student wanting revenge may become hostile or even violent; a teacher may have no recourse but to isolate the student or send her to the office. A student displaying inadequacy may refuse to cooperate, participate, or interact unless working one-to-one with the teacher.

To change student behavior, Dreikurs has several suggestions, some which reinforce what has already been said:

> Provide clear-cut directions of your expectations of the students . . . [and] develop classroom rules cooperatively with students, especially those [rules] related to the logical consequences for inappropriate behaviors.

Logical consequences should relate as closely as possible to the misbehavior, so the students can see the connection between them (Charles & Senter, 2004).

Demond, a second-grade student, just sits in class when it is time for math. Given a set of problems to finish after a demonstration at the board, he lowers his head, refusing to look at you when you suggest that he should begin working. Fifteen minutes later, he still has not begun to respond. What does Demond's mistaken goal appear to be? If you identify it as inadequacy, you might say, "Demond, I know you can do this lesson. Take a look at the first problem. What does it ask you to do?"

One way to avoid the problem altogether might be to ask your cooperating teacher if you might pair the students for learning tasks, or group them in blocks of four where the primary rule is *three-before-me*, a technique that means students are responsible for teaching each other, before they raise their hands for help from you.

As Miller (2004) points out, "Each of the mistaken goals is directed toward getting an emotional need met: the need for recognition (attention getting), the need for a sense of control over one's life (power seeking), the need for fairness (revenge seeking), and the need to avoid stressful and frightening situations (displaying inadequacy)."

She warns that teachers too often react in ways that are opposite to what the child needs. We are tempted to ignore the attention-seeking child and to be stern with the child struggling with control.

Miller (2004) also states that adult follow-through is another essential step in what she calls *positive guidance*. She cautions teachers to remember that guiding a child's behavior "is a challenging task."

Marion (2007) stresses four points for the use of logical consequences to be successful:

1. The adult has delivered an I message.

2. The consequence is logically related to the unsafe or inappropriate behavior.

3. The consequence is one the adult can readily accept and that the child would likely view as fair.

4. The consequence is well timed.

Marion illustrates each point with concrete examples that are easy to follow and understand. For example, if a child has repeatedly left toys and a bicycle in the driveway, and the parent has had to move them to park or to bring the car into the garage, the parent first would state an *I* message, followed by the logical consequence should the behavior repeat. "I can't park the car with all the toys lying around. So I'll put them in the shed if you decide not to pick them up tomorrow." In this situation, the parent has stated her point of view and a logical consequence; the child would probably view the consequence as fair, certainly more fair than if

**time-out**—technique in which the child is removed from the rein-forcement and stimulation of the classroom.

the parent had said, "If you can't pick up your toys from the driveway, I may run over them another time."

Gartrell (2006a) suggests three levels of mistaken behavior, instead of Dreikurs's four. Gartrell urges teachers to drop ideas about *misbehavior,* which connotes willful wrongdoing, and to look instead at inappropriate child behavior as *mistaken.* In the process of learning such complex life skills as cooperation, conflict resolution, and acceptable expression of strong feelings, children, like all of us, make mistakes. Taking this view helps teachers see their role as mediators, problem solvers, and guides.

In Gartrell's three levels of mistaken behavior (see Figure 5–8), level-three behavior, or *survival behavior,* is difficult for the teacher to accept because of its nonsocial and, at times, antisocial aspects. Strong needs result from psychological and/or physical pain beyond the child's ability to cope, so survival behavior should be interpreted as a cry for help. At level three would be the one or two or three children who misbehave because they have a need to exert power or to express hostility; these children typically would be misbehaving with the cooperating teacher as well as with you as their student teacher.

Suggested level-three techniques include:

◆ nonpunitive intervention

◆ building a positive child-teacher relationship

◆ gathering more information by observing

◆ seeking additional information through conversations with the child, families, and caregivers

◆ creating a coordinated individual guidance plan with other adults through consultation

◆ implementing, reviewing, and modifying guidance plans as necessary

Gartrell (2006a) believes that level two, *socially influenced mistaken behavior,* is based on pleasing peers, adults, or others. Children exhibiting this behavior seek high levels of teacher or peer approval; they seem to lack self-esteem and the strength to use their own judgment. The teacher's task is to nudge the child toward autonomy and observe whether one child or a group is involved in the mistaken behavior. At level two, then, the behavior becomes intentional.

▶ **Figure 5-8**

Common sources of motivation, relational patterns, and levels of mistaken behavior (Gartrell, 2006a).

| Motivational Source | Relational Pattern | Level of Mistaken Behavior |
| --- | --- | --- |
| Desire to explore the environment and engage in relationships | Encountering | One: Experimentation |
| Desire to please and identify with significant others | Adjustment | Two: Socially influenced |
| Inability to cope with problems resulting from health conditions or the school or home environment | Survival | Three: Strong needs |

At the elementary school level, Gartrell (2004) suggests that class meetings are an effective technique in handling level-two behaviors. Students are asked for their suggestions about how any given problem might be resolved. The teacher then monitors progress and, if needed, calls additional meetings. Teacher follow-up is necessary to acknowledge progress and new appropriate behavior and to provide reminders concerning agreed-upon guidelines.

At level one, Gartrell suggests that young children may misbehave simply to experiment. The children who unintentionally test the limits of classroom rules when the student teacher takes over from the cooperating teacher are displaying level-one mistaken behaviors; they are experimenting to see whether the student teacher has the same rules as the cooperating teacher. Disagreements over toys also fall into this category. Gartrell (2004) states:

> The teacher responds in different ways to different situations. Sometimes he may step back and allow a child to learn from experience; other times he will reiterate a guideline and, in a friendly tone, teach a more appropriate alternative behavior.

Depending on the situation, Gartrell (2006a) offers the following suggestions to teachers:

◆ Increased levels of teacher firmness are necessary with level-two and three mistaken behaviors, with the element of friendliness retained. Always remember to CARE.
◆ Serious mistaken behaviors occur when life circumstances make children victims.
◆ Aggression is a nonverbal request for help.
◆ In guidance situations, the victim (wronged child) gets attention first and the teacher's assistance in calming down.
◆ Empathy-building is done by pointing out the victim's hurt.
◆ Stating that the teacher won't let anyone be hurt at school is necessary.
◆ Child–teacher discussions about how the problem could be avoided in the future take place.
◆ Asking how the aggressor could help the hurt child feel better is an appropriate technique.
◆ Assisting the aggressor to choose a positive activity is another teacher endeavor.

See Figure 5–9 for additional information showing how similar behaviors could be classified at different levels.

It is important to remember that the goal of discipline is to help children learn to assume greater responsibility for their own behavior. This is best accomplished by:

◆ treating them with respect
◆ distinguishing between what students do and who they are
◆ setting limits from the very beginning and consistently applying them
◆ keeping demands simple
◆ responding to any problems quickly
◆ letting students know that mistakes, once corrected, are forgotten
◆ *CARE*ing

It is also important to remember that "[w]hen there is serious mistaken behavior, the teacher meets with parents and other adults to develop and use a coordinated plan. Through coordinated assistance, children can be helped to overcome serious problems and build self-esteem and social skills" (Gartrell, 2004).

▶ **Figure 5-9**

Classifying similar mistaken behaviors by level (Gartrell, 2006a).

| Incident of Mistake Behavior | Motivational | Level of Mistaken Source Behavior |
|---|---|---|
| Child uses expletive | Wants to see the teacher's reaction | One |
| | Wants to emulate important others | Two |
| | Expresses deeply felt hostility | Three |
| Child pushes another off the trike | Wants trike; has not learned to ask in words | One |
| | Follows aggrandizement practices modeled by other children | Two |
| | Feels the need to act out against the world by asserting power | Three |
| Child refuses to join in group activity | Does not understand teacher's expectations | One |
| | Has "gotten away" with not joining in | Two |
| | Is not feeling well or feels strong anxiety about participating | Three |

## Anticipating Behavior, or "With-It-Ness"

The technique that takes time and experience to learn is anticipating aggressive behavior, intervening before the situation erupts (see Figure 5–10). By studying patterns in the child's behavior, you can learn to anticipate certain situations. Many children are quite predictable. Some children can be in a social atmosphere for only a short time before being overwhelmed by the amount of stimuli (sights, sounds, and actions) and may react in a negative way. If you conclude, from observing a child, that he can play with only one other child before becoming aggressive, you can take care to allow him to play with only one child at a time. If you know that another child really needs time alone before lunch, you can arrange it. Likewise, if you know a third child becomes tired and cross just before it is time to go home, you can provide some extra quiet time for that child.

Learning to anticipate behavior is not easy and requires much practice. Keep trying; it is worth the effort and the children will be happier.

## Conflict Resolution

As Marion (2007) points out, in child–child conflict and confrontation, the teacher might intervene or use preventive measures. She suggests that growth in social skill is acquired when conflict-resolution strategies are learned. Eventually, they enable children to solve problems without adult help. Now used in many public and private elementary schools, conflict resolution techniques are taught by school counselors to older students, typically in grades five and six. They then monitor play yards when the primary grade students have recess. Having older students monitor the behavior of younger students has proved beneficial to both.

▶ **Figure 5-10**
Learning to take turns is not easy. This child does not like to wait.

© Cengage Learning

**Conflict resolution** involves teaching children positive alternative and socially acceptable ways to solve problems. It may include the physical act of separating the two arguing children and asking them to take a slow, deep breath. Then the teacher describes the situation as she sees it and asks the children how they think they might resolve the conflict. The teacher might suggest negotiation and more mature and complex reasoning ideas to solve the problem.

A student teacher will also notice that a teacher still needs to monitor and step in to encourage and support conflict resolution, especially with preschoolers who use physical **aggression** in disagreements. Teacher-generated solutions may be to wait, to give children the opportunity to gain skill in using verbal, conciliatory behavior that can lead to nonviolent, satisfying, cooperative play and peaceful conflict resolution.

Marion (2007) offers these suggestions to teachers:

◆ Teachers need to think about conflict as an opportunity to teach a skill to children. Teachers should help children make clear their own understanding of the conflict.

◆ Teachers must recognize signs of stress, anxiety, or strong emotions. Children's ability to resolve conflicts increases as their verbal competence and ability to take other perspectives grows.

◆ Teachers' decisions to intervene should be made after they observe the issues of children's conflicts. Possession issues and name-calling generate less discussion than issues about facts or play decisions.

◆ Children who explain their actions to each other are likely to create their own solutions. In conflicts characterized by physical strategies and simple verbal oppositions, teachers should help children find more words to use.

◆ Teachers should note whether the children were playing together before the conflict. Prior interaction and friendship motivate children to resolve disputes on their own.

◆ Teachers should give children time to develop their own resolutions and allow them the choice of negotiating, changing the activity, dropping the issue, or creating new rules.

◆ Many conflicts do not involve aggression, and children are frequently able to resolve their disputes. Teachers should provide appropriate guidance, yet allow children to manage their own conflicts and resolutions.

**conflict resolution—** promoting child-child or child-adult problem solving through verbal interactions, negotiation, compromise, and use of acceptable physical tactics. It may include teacher support and assistance.

**aggression—**behavior deliberately intended to hurt others.

Gartrell (2006a) also urges early childhood teachers to use conflict resolution as a guidance technique. Many of the suggestions he mentions are covered in the previous discussion of Gartrell's views on logical consequences and need not be repeated here.

# ADDITIONAL MANAGEMENT AND DISCIPLINE STRATEGIES

Child behavior may always remain a puzzling challenge; yet, you need to help each child learn socially acceptable behaviors. A review of common strategies used by many teachers may be helpful. Naming strategies, describing them, and discussing when they are most appropriate and effective will sharpen your professional guidance skills.

We have looked at goals and techniques, the origins of behavior, and ways to promote self-control in children. One goal in guiding child behavior is the idea that the child will learn to act appropriately in similar situations in the future. This can be a slow process with some behaviors, speedy with others. There is a change from external "handling" of the child, to the child monitoring her own progress and acting on what is the right thing to do.

## Environmental Factors

Where misbehavior is concerned, it is easy to conclude that it is the child who needs changing. A number of classroom environmental factors can promote inappropriate child behaviors in group situations. A limited variety of activities, an above-comprehension program, meager or frustrating equipment, and a defensive-acting teacher elicit behavior reactions to unmet needs. Close examination of the classroom environment may lead to changing causative factors rather than changing child behavior. School programs, room environments, and teaching methods can fail children, rather than children failing a program.

As a student teacher, you should carefully examine the relationship between the classroom environment, the daily program, your teaching style, and children's reactions. Fortunately, your training program will have developed your teaching skill as well as an understanding of quality environments. An analysis of your placement may lead you to discover that child appeal is minimal. Rearranging or creating new learning centers may add interest. Remember, however, that any changes need the cooperating teacher's approval.

## Rapport

Rapport is an important element of guidance. Trying to develop rapport, trust, or a feeling relationship with each child can be tricky. Mitchell, the active, vigorous explorer, may be hard to keep up with, or even to talk with; he may prefer the company of his peers. So, how can one establish rapport? When it does happen, you will be aware of the "you're okay, I'm okay" feeling, and experience pleasure when he says, "I enjoy being with you" with his eyes. Children respond to straightforward, genuine teachers in a positive way.

How important is child–teacher rapport during the prekindergarten years? Data collected from Howes (2000) suggest that children with close child–teacher relationships are also socially competent with their peers. Children perceived as difficult four-year-olds tended to build child–teacher relationships that were high in conflict through the second grade in elementary school. They also tended to be less able to establish social closeness. Academic content mastery, through the use of a close child–teacher relationship, was also more difficult for these children.

## Same Behavior, Different Strategy

Child individuality can still result in unexpected reactions. The boy who finally swings at another child after letting others grab his toys and the child who hits at every opportunity are performing the same act. You will need to treat each incident differently. The ages of children, their stages of growth, and the particulars of the situations will have to be considered. You have already learned that what works with one child will not necessarily work with another. In time you will develop a variety of strategies, focus often on the child's intent, and hypothesize underlying causes.

You will be able to live with child rejection, come to expect it, and realize it is short-lived. Act you will; the child will react. Sometimes, you will choose to ignore behavior and hope it goes away. You will find ignoring is appropriate under certain conditions.

## Using Proximity

Many times, the teacher's physical presence will change a child's behavior. When the teacher becomes interested in a child's activity and asks questions concerning what the child is trying to accomplish, it may head off undesirable child behavior. Often, moving toward a group of children as you hear voices escalate in volume prevents what might become a more dangerous conflict.

## Other Common Strategies

*Stating* rules, in a positive way, serves two purposes. It is a helpful reminder and states what is appropriate and expected. "Feet walk inside, run outside" is a common, positive rule statement. Statements such as "Remember, after snack you place your cup on the tray and any garbage in the waste basket" and "Books are stored in your desk before we go to lunch" clearly indicate the students' tasks.

*Cause-and-effect* and *factual statements* are common ways to promote behavior change. "If you pick off all the leaves, the plant will die." "Sand thrown in the eyes hurts." "Here's the waiting list; you'll have a turn soon, Mark." Each of these statements gives information and helps children decide the appropriateness, or realize the consequences, of their current actions.

Using **modeling** to change behavior entails pointing out a child or teacher example of desired behavior: "The paint stays on the paper. That's the way, Kolima." "See how slowly I'm pouring the milk so it doesn't spill?" "Nicholas is ready, his eyes are open, and he is listening." These are all modeling statements (see Figure 5–11).

**modeling**—in social learning theory, the process of imitating a model.

Always using the same child as a model can create a "teacher's pet." Most teachers try to use every child as a model. When children hear a modeling statement, they may chime in "me, too," which opens the opportunity for recognition and reinforcement of another positive model. "Yes, Carrie Ann, you are showing me you know how to put the blocks in their place on the shelf."

*Redirection* is a behavioral strategy that works by redirecting a child to another activity, object, or area. Some examples of redirecting statements follow:

"Here's a big, blue truck for you to ride, Sherilyn."

"While you're waiting for your turn, Avraham, you can choose the puzzle with the airplane landing at the airport or the puzzle with the tow truck."

"Mieko, while you're waiting for Tina and Maria to finish the *Spill 'n Spell* game, why don't you and Jennifer look at some of the other games we have on the shelf and choose another one?"

Statements like "Let's take giant steps to the door" and "We're tiptoeing into snack today; we won't hear anyone's footsteps" may capture the imagination and help overcome resistance. The key to redirection is to make the substitute activity or object desirable. A possible pitfall is that every time the child cannot have her

▶ **Figure 5–11**
When lunching with children, this teacher models appropriate behavior.

© Cengage Learning

way, she may get the idea that something better will be offered. Offering a pleasurable alternative each time a difficulty arises may teach the child that being difficult and uncooperative leads to teacher attention and the provision of a desirable activity or object.

Younger preschoolers (two- and three-year-olds) intent on possessing toys and objects usually accept substitutions, and their classrooms are equipped with duplicate toys to accommodate their *I-want-what-he-has* tendencies.

In kindergarten and the primary grades, however, the use of redirection can indicate to children that they have an opportunity to make a second or third choice when blocked on their first.

*Giving a choice* of things you would like the child to do appeals to the child's sense of independence. Some examples are:

"Are you going to put your used napkin in the trash or on the tray?"

"You can choose to rest quietly next to your friend or on a cot somewhere else in the room."

"Remember, Mateo, we agreed that class would line up promptly when the bell rang. You have a choice now either to line up quickly or to be the last student to leave for recess."

*Setting up direct communication* between two arguing children works as shown in the following:

"Use your words, Xochil: 'Please pass the crackers.'"

"Look at his face; he's very unhappy. It hurts to be hit with a flying hoop. Listen, he wants to tell you."

Taking a child by the hand and helping him confront another, expressing the child's wishes or feelings, lets the child know you will defend his rights. It also lets the child know that you care that rules are observed by all.

Be careful in praising children. Kohn (2001) explains the unfortunate outcome that may occur when teachers overuse praise:

In short, "Good job" doesn't reassure children; ultimately, it makes them feel less secure. It may even create a vicious circle such that the more we slather on the praise, the more kids seem to need it, so we praise them some more. Sadly, some of these kids will grow into adults who continue to need someone else to pat them on the head and tell them that what they did was okay . . . . The most notable feature of a positive judgment isn't that it's positive, but that it's a judgment.

It is sometimes difficult to change "good job" to something more specific because it may have been used extensively in one's own upbringing. Saying "Look at how that table shines! You scrubbed every spot. Now it is clean and ready for the next person, Erlinda!" gives the child specific knowledge concerning her well-done job.

*Self-fulfilling statements,* such as "You can share, Lily. Megan is waiting for a turn" and "In two minutes, it will be Richard's turn," imply something will happen. Hopefully, you will be nearby with positive reinforcement and statements that help the child decide the right behavior and feel good about it. Positive reinforcement of newly evolving behavior is an important part of guidance. It strengthens the chances that a child will repeat the behavior. Most adults will admit that as children they knew when they were doing wrong, but the right and good went unnoticed. The positive reinforcement step in the behavior-change process cannot be ignored if new behavior is to last. Positive attention can be a look of appreciation, words, a touch, or a smile. Often, a message such as "You did it!" or "I know it wasn't easy" is sent.

*Calming-down periods* for an out-of-control child may be necessary before communication is possible. Rocking and holding help after a violent outburst or tantrum. When the child is not angry anymore, you will want to stay close until the child is able to become totally involved in play or a task.

**Ignoring** is a usable technique with new behaviors that are annoying or irritating but of minor consequence. Catching the adult's attention or testing the adult's reaction may motivate the behavior. One can ignore a child who sticks out his tongue or says, "You're ugly." Treating the action or comment matter-of-factly is ignoring. Answering "I look ugly first thing in the morning" usually ends the conversation. You are attempting to withhold any reaction that might reinforce the behavior. If there is definite emotion in the child's comment, you will want to talk about it rather than ignore it. Children can be taught the ignoring technique as well when they find someone annoying them.

> **ignoring**—a principle of behavior management that involves removing all reinforcement for a given behavior to eliminate that behavior.

When all else fails, the use of *negative consequences* may be appropriate. Habit behavior can be most stubborn and may have been reinforced over a long period. Taking away a privilege or physically removing a child from the group is professionally recognized as a last-resort strategy.

*Isolation* involves the common practice of benching an aggressive elementary-age student, sending her to a desk segregated from the rest of the class, at the extreme front or back of the classroom, or short periods of supervised chair-sitting for a preschooler. Many educators use this technique only when a child is wildly out of control or is an imminent threat to others.

Teachers refer to this practice as *time-out.* Fields and Boesser (2002) note that if applied immediately and consistently, time-out has been determined to be useful in the reduction of both verbal and physical aggressive behavior. However, as a variant on the old "stand-in-the-corner" punishment, providing a "privacy space" to which any child might go is to be preferred. Critics of the practice acknowledge it can reduce undesirable behavior but fails to teach desirable behavior (Miller, 2004). Because of its effectiveness, the technique may be overused when relatively trivial child behaviors occur. Some children, in a study by Readdick and Chapman (2000), who perceived themselves to be in time-out often, felt isolated, sad, scared, and thought they were disliked by their peers. Fewer than half of the preschoolers questioned could accurately recall what they had done before time-out occurred.

Teachers need to be careful not to shame or humiliate the child in the process. Statements such as "You need to sit for a few minutes until you're ready to . . ." allow the child an open invitation to rejoin the group and live up to rules and expectations. The isolation area needs to be supervised, safe, and unrewarding.

Teachers quickly reinforce the returning child's positive, socially acceptable new actions.

Your goal is promoting each child's self-controlled behavior, which satisfies his unique personal needs and yet allows membership and inclusion into today's society. Encourage the development of the child's self-concept as a valued, worthwhile, capable, and responsible person.

## Out-of-Control Children

Student teachers often say that the worst part of any day happens when a child loses control and has a tantrum. Bakley (2000) suggests the following techniques:

◆ *Resist telling an upset child to calm down.* Because the lack of control occurs below the level of consciousness, the child cannot willingly calm himself down.

◆ *Redirect an escalating child to a sensory activity,* such as play dough, water play, or bins of sensory materials. More vigorous physical activities, such as digging, jumping, and running, can also help. Some children will naturally gravitate to the calming motion of a swing or rocking chair. Others may want to retreat to a safe, "privacy space," away from busy activities.

◆ *Offer a firm hug or a lap to curl up in.* When a child is agitated, the external control provided by your enveloping physical presence can help restore inner control. Some experts believe a firm hug reaches deeply into the subcortical level of the brain, overriding reactions of rage and aggression.

◆ *Wait for the child to calm down before talking about what happened.* When a child is agitated, your physical approach may trigger a fight-or-flight reaction, with him striking out or running away. Wait for the child to regain composure. The more calm he is, the more likely the child will learn from the experience.

◆ *Maintain a calm demeanor when discussing misbehaviors.* Avoid no-win confrontations. Your composure sets the tone for the child's success in learning from his mistakes. Remember, although this is a child who will test your patience, she desperately needs your help to learn acceptable behaviors.

◆ *Allow children to avert their gaze when you talk about their behavior.* Because so much effort is required to make and sustain eye contact, there is little energy left for listening. Children with sensory integration problems are likely to listen better if allowed to avert their gaze.

◆ *Use simple, direct language.* Give brief, specific directions. Say "Put your hands in your lap" instead of "Keep your hands to yourself." Help the child remember what you've said by asking him to repeat it.

◆ *Keep the family informed and involved.* If a collaborative relationship with the family has been established, encourage them to implement similar discipline techniques at home.

## Violent Play

Television, current events, young children's observations of older children, and community occurrences often influence the initiation of violent, aggressive play actions. The student teacher is faced with an immediate decision, concerning children's safety and the prudence of allowing—which may be seen as approving—this type of play. Most teachers feel deeply about peaceful solutions to individual and world problems. New curriculums have been purposely designed by some early childhood professionals to promote peace and acquaint young children with the concept of the brotherhood of humanity.

Experienced teachers know that even if play weapons are not allowed at school, some children will still fashion play guns from blocks or other objects and engage in mock battles or confrontations.

Schools and centers make individual decisions concerning gun, superhero, and war play. It is best for student teachers to question their cooperating teachers if such play develops. Of course, an unsafe situation is stopped immediately and discussed later.

Froschl, Sprung, and Hinitz (2005) presented a review of the research on violence in early education environments. They insist that it is essential to establish a classroom environment based on cooperation, and one that supports children with diverse abilities, to avoid possible violent reactions from children making comparisons about or competing with one another, and drawing inaccurate conclusions.

Greenspan (2006) insists that children dramatize what they see happening in their world. If what they experience is violence, reliving it in their play may help them understand these violent events. Connolly and Hayden (2007), in looking at children from around the world exposed to wars, remind us that the children often fear for their own safety and may experience post-traumatic stress syndrome, which can affect their social and emotional development. Some may be resilient; others may have nightmares; some may be aggressive; others lack concentration; some may withdraw; many may show hyper-vigilance; some experience loss of memory, even speech; and others may experience psychosomatic disorders. As always, teachers must *CARE* and be patient. Building trust takes time, a lot of time.

## Managing Serious Behavior Problems

Many of the techniques and strategies already described may help you with children who display serious behavior problems. What do we mean by the phrase *serious behavior problems*? Depending on the age of the child, serious problems range from biting and hitting (by a two-year-old) to play that is physically aggressive, or from destroying another child's work to fighting on the play yard (by four- to eight-year-olds). And please do not overlook the overly quiet child, who tries to disappear into the background of the classroom or play yard. She may need as much help as the overly aggressive child.

What should you try to do? First of all, you want to defer to your cooperating teacher; she may have already developed plans to help the child acquire more socially appropriate behaviors. Additionally, the cooperating teacher may ask you to speak to the school psychologist, who may be seeing the child once or twice a week; or talk to the PIP (*Primary Intervention Program*) consultant working with the child; or even sit in on a parent conference with the school's student-study team. All of these resources may give you some more ideas of how to work more effectively with the child in question. With an increasing number of special needs children present in regular classrooms, more and more schools provide intervention programs.

Consider how you might handle the following situation:

Sandor, a student teacher in a third grade classroom, was faced with a male child, Rory, who was getting into fights during the first recess of every day. Upon his return to the classroom, the principal would call over the intercom, "Rory, please come to the office at once!" The result of this behavior was that Rory inevitably missed at least half of the mathematics lessons that were taking place after the first recess. Sandor discussed the problem with Ms. Olivados, his cooperating teacher. She reassured him that Rory's behavior was not new and suggested that Sandor might observe Rory during the next morning's recess and try to determine why Rory got into fights with the other children.

Following Ms. Olivados' suggestion, Sandor accompanied the class to the first recess the next day. Rory went with two or three other boys from his class to a corner of the play yard; Sandor discretely followed. Suddenly, Rory yelled, "You can't call my mother that!" and hit Derek, the boy standing next to him.

Sandor intervened by placing himself between the two and asked, "What did you say, Derek?" The boy answered, "Oh, we were just playing the dozens; Rory knows that! And besides his mother is a _____!"

"How do you know that?" Sandor asked Derek. "Oh, everybody knows," replied Derek, who attempted to kick Rory from under Sandor's arm. "What do you think you might do instead of calling each other names or calling your mothers names?" Sandor asked both boys.

Neither boy replied, and the bell announcing the end of recess sounded before Sandor was able to take the discussion any further. Both Derek and Rory continued to yell at each other as they lined up to go back to the classroom.

Sandor again placed himself between the two boys in the line to prevent any further hitting or kicking. Upon entering the classroom, Ms. Olivados noticed the angry faces of Rory and Derek, and Sandor's distraught one. Before she could ask what had happened, the intercom clicked on and the principal said, "I want Rory and Derek in my office immediately!"

What might Ms. Olivados and Sandor try the next day to prevent further altercations between Rory and Derek? How might we look at Rory's misbehavior? What might be his mistaken goal, according to Dreikurs? Does Rory seem to be vying for attention? For power? For revenge? It seems clear that he's not acting from a sense of inadequacy. Looking at Gartrell's levels of mistaken behavior, at what level of mistaken behavior does Rory's behavior appear to be? Can you think of any other possible reasons for Rory's behavior?

Should you conclude that Rory's mistaken goal is revenge or power in his relationship with Derek, what intervention might be the best one to try? Should Sandor keep the boys separated during recess? Should Rory and Derek be involved in a role-reversal exercise? Should Mrs. Olivados involve the principal? The school's PIP professionals? What might be most appropriate?

## Introducing Harmony Models in Literary Activities

Many children's books offer peaceful solutions to human conflict. Kara-Soteriou and Rose (2008) suggest using the following techniques:

◆ Excite the children's curiosity with a colorful display on a bulletin board.

◆ Introduce the concepts you want children to look for.

◆ Read the book paragraph by paragraph, pausing to ask for concepts stressed in the story.

◆ Ask children how they think the book's main character is feeling.

◆ Read the rest of the story. Discuss the character's solution to the conflict. Ask children, "Was it a good solution? Why? How does the character feel now?"

For ideas about what books to choose, contact your local children's librarian. These professionals are of infinite value in recommending books for children to hear and read. Another excellent source is found in the journals *Young Children* and *Childhood Education*. In each issue you will find reviews of children's books in each issue.

Using pictures, problem-solving steps (see Figure 5–12), and acting out make-believe role-plays in which children practice conflict resolution, is suggested by Adams and Wittmer (2001).

# GUIDANCE TECHNIQUES USED IN ELEMENTARY SCHOOLS

## Assertive Discipline

Many elementary schools use a form of behavior management called **assertive discipline** (Canter, 1976; Davidman & Davidman, 1994). While an inappropriate technique for preschools, assertive discipline has been widely used in elementary school settings. Assertive discipline has been shown to work best when an entire school staff is committed to using the technique. In assertive discipline, teachers must initially set their classroom rules—best done at the beginning of the year, elicited from the children themselves, and posted prominently in the classroom. Teachers must then consistently apply the rules and learn to use *I* messages indicating their displeasure or pleasure. "I don't like it when someone interrupts another student, Aisha." "Most of your classmates are all listening politely to Mustafa."

Consequences of misbehavior must be clearly understood and consistently applied. At the first incidence, the teacher places the child's initials on the board in a place reserved and consistently used for assertive discipline markings. At the second incidence of misbehavior, a check mark goes by the child's name, and a specific and reasonable consequence is related to it. The consequence may be to remain in the room during a recess, or to move to an isolated area of the classroom. After a second check, the consequence may be a phone call to the student's family and a request for a conference. After the third check, the child is generally sent to the office, and the family is called and notified that the child must serve detention the next day or that the child must serve an in-house suspension. (This may involve assigning the child to another classroom, attended only by other in-school suspension students. The students are expected to complete assignments their teachers send with them, and the classroom is monitored by either another teacher or a teacher assistant.) The child is usually assigned to the in-house suspension class until the family makes an appointment for a conference with the teacher and principal.

Crucial to the success of assertive discipline is following through with the predetermined consequences; empty threats cannot be allowed.

Although assertive discipline has been highly successful, it has also been criticized. Canter, however, maintains that the "assertive teacher is one who clearly and firmly communicates needs and requirements to students, follows those words with appropriate actions, responds to students in ways that maximize compliance, but in no way violates the best interests of the students" (Charles & Senter, 2004).

## Glasser's Model

Another classroom management model commonly used in elementary schools is the Glasser model (Glasser, 1985). Glasser strongly believes that students have unmet needs that lead to their behavior difficulties, and that if teachers can arrange their classes in such a way that these needs are met, there will be fewer control problems. Student needs are identified as (1) the need to belong, (2) the need for power, (3) the need for freedom, and (4) the need for fun.

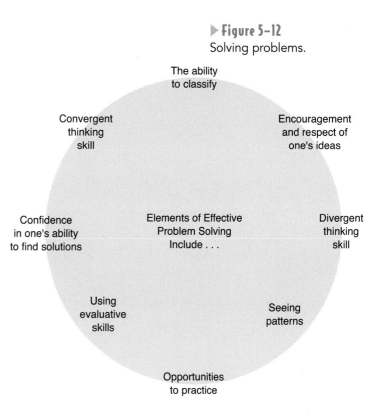

▶ **Figure 5-12**
Solving problems.

> **assertive discipline**—a form of behavior management used primarily in elementary schools. The consequences of behavior are clearly stated, understood by children, and consistently applied.

By breaking the class into small learning teams, the teacher is able to provide students with a sense of belonging, with motivation to work on behalf of the group, with power to have stronger students help weaker ones, with freedom from over-reliance on the teacher for both weaker and stronger ones, and with friends for all students, shy and outspoken. Two precautions: groups should be heterogeneously arranged, and groups should be changed at regular or irregular intervals. Changes might occur as units or themes change, or they might change every 6 weeks. Teachers should decide for themselves which tactic works best in their respective classrooms.

# ▶ SUMMARY

Throughout this chapter, you have been able to formulate an idea of the scope of the classroom management or disciplinary function. Remember that everything you do—planning activities, arranging the environment, planning the length of activities, planning how much direction you will provide—is part of the management function.

Another part of management is managing behavior. In this chapter, you were given two guidelines to use in managing behavior: the *four Cs* (consistency, consideration, confidence, and candor) and *CARE* (be congruent, acceptant, reliable, and empathetic). In addition, six specific techniques were explained: behavior modification, limit setting, *I* messages, logical consequences, anticipating behavior, and conflict resolution. Try them; experiment with others of your own. Discover which disciplinary techniques work best for you and analyze why.

The involvement of the family in establishing disciplinary goals was stressed. Collaboration with families and the teaching team was mentioned.

Helping children satisfy needs in a socially acceptable way and helping them feel good about doing so is a disciplinary goal. Classroom environments can promote self-control, especially when rapport, caring, and trust

are present. Examination of behavior, its intent, and circumstances may lead student teachers to different plans of action with different children. There is no "recipe" for handling guidance problems, but a review of common disciplinary strategies was covered in this chapter.

They are as follows:

◆ positive rule statements

◆ cause-and-effect and factual statements

◆ modeling

◆ redirection

◆ giving a choice

◆ setting up direct communication

◆ self-fulfilling statements

◆ positive reinforcement

◆ calming-down periods

◆ ignoring

◆ negative consequences

Children may try to circumvent rules and limits; yet, obedience to rules and sensitivity to others are present most of the time. Check your responses to Figure 5–13, and you will be doing fine.

▶ **Figure 5–13**
Analysis checklist in establishing a well-managed elementary school classroom.

| Students' Aptitudes | Instructional Treatments | Learning Outcomes |
| --- | --- | --- |
| What do I know about the general developmental characteristics of the students I am teaching? | In what varieties of ways can I present instruction on a topic? | Do I consider both cognitive and affective learning outcomes for my students? |
| What cognitive development abilities can I expect them to exhibit? | What types of learning tactics and strategies can I teach? | Do the cognitive outcomes include higher-level thinking skills as well as basic knowledge? |
| Which learning style does each student seem to prefer? | What is the best way to organize and sequence the presentation of a lesson? | Do I explicitly share these learning outcomes and their purpose with students? |

▶ **Figure 5-13**

| | | |
|---|---|---|
| What social/emotional characteristics must I consider? | How can I present instruction at an appropriate ability level for students to achieve success with effort? | Do I connect these outcomes to students in meaningful ways? |
| What are the social behaviors that each student exhibits? | How can I present instruction that will be interesting and motivate students? | Do I specify how students will be assessed on their mastery of the outcomes? |
| What are the academic strengths and weaknesses that each student possesses? | What textbooks and other instructional materials best engage students in active learning? | Is my system of grading a valid evaluation of the content students have learned? |
| What are the special needs of students that I must take into account? | How can I help students better understand the connections between topics? | Do I provide nongraded formative evaluation to students to monitor their progress? |
| Who has influence on the students? Their peers? Their parents? Their teachers? | How can I help students develop problem-solving skills? | Do I allow multiple opportunities for students to achieve the learning outcomes? |
| What ethnic and cultural factors influence the way students communicate with others? | How can I instruct students at higher levels of cognition? | |
| What are the interests of each student? | How can I plan instruction that fosters creativity? | |
| What level or degree of prior knowledge does each student possess of a subject? | How can I maintain high expectations for all students? | |
| | How can I help students attribute their success to their abilities and efforts? | |

# ▶ HELPFUL WEBSITES

**http://www.acei.org**

Association for Childhood Education. Check for readings. ACEI publishes the journal *Childhood Education* and several newsletters and books. In each issue of *Childhood Education*, ACEI publishes reviews of children's books, citing ages for whom the book is written and a brief synopsis of the plot.

**http://www.naeyc.org**

National Association for the Education of Young Children. Search for readings. NAEYC publishes the journals *Young Children* and *Teaching Young Children*, and many other brochures, books, CDs, and videos. Like ACEI, NAEYC periodically publishes reviews of children's books in the column, "The Reading Chair."

**http://www.fpg.unc.edu**

Frank Porter Graham Center at the University of North Carolina. Look for publications related to your interests. The quarterly journal *Early Developments* (Spring 2007) includes an article about an early intervention system used in the preschool.

**http://www.ascd.org**

Association for Supervision and Curriculum Development (ASCD). This source publishes the journal, *Educational Leadership*, which offers many readings on social and emotional growth as well as others related to several different aspects of schooling. Click "reading room."

 Additional resources for this chapter can be found by visiting the companion website at *www.cengage.com/education/machado.*

## ▶ SUGGESTED ACTIVITIES

A. Analyze your placement classroom's rules. Do many rules fall into the four basic areas mentioned in this chapter? Are there any rules that need a new category?

B. Plan a discussion with a small group of four-year-olds. Have a picture of a child who might want to join the children's classroom handy. Start your discussion with the following: "We have a rule in our classroom. The rule is we ask for a turn if we want a toy someone else has chosen to use. Here's a picture of Suzy. She wants to come to school with us. What will Suzy need to know about our classroom?"

Ask students questions like "If Suzy plays in the block center, what should we tell her?" and "If Suzy wants to join us at snack time, what should we tell her?" Share the results of your discussion group with classmates.

C. Role-play the following situations with a small group of classmates. After each situation, have the students playing children explain any insights or feelings they discovered when stepping into the child's shoes. Critique the role-playing reaction according to the child's behavior and the guidance techniques used.

1. Tonette says Renata pushed her down. You had observed the incident, and Renata accidentally tripped Tonette as she ran to pick up the ball.

2. Connor is large and muscular. He delights in terrifying other children by standing directly in their paths. He rarely physically hits, pushes, or touches the children he is frightening. You see Connor standing in front of the outside water faucet intimidating children who wish to drink.

3. Scott cries every time he is not chosen to be first in line, or when some other child gets a job he wants. You asked Geoff to go to the aquarium to feed the fish and now Scott is crying because Geoff got the job. Geoff turns to Scott and says, "Okay, stop crying. You can do it."

4. Sierra is on a painting binge. It's time to clean up. You've told her it's cleanup time. "No way," says Sierra, as she threatens you with a wet paintbrush.

D. Go back to situations one through four in the previous exercise, but think about the child's needs, feelings, and point of view. Is there any way for the child to solve the inherent difficulty in the situation? Are there setting or time factors teachers could manipulate, so the same problems will not happen again? What are *your* feelings in each situation? Discuss these with your group.

## ▶ REVIEW

A. List four classroom factors that might promote inappropriate child behaviors.

B. List four positive rule statements.

C. List four redirection statements.

D. List four modeling statements.

E. List the steps in conflict resolution.

## ▶ REFERENCES

Adams, S. K., & Wittmer, D. S. (2001, Fall). "I had it first": Teaching young children to solve problems peacefully. *Childhood Education, 77*(5), 10–15.

Abbott, J. (1997, March). To be intelligent. *Educational Leadership, 54*(6).

Bakley, S. (2000, November). Through the lens of sensory integration: A different way of analyzing challenging behavior. *Young Children, 56*(6), 70–76.

Browning, L., Davis, B., & Resta, V. (2000, Summer). What do you mean "Think before I act?" Conflict resolution with choices. *Childhood Education, 76*(2), 232–238.

Butterfield, P. M., Martin, C. A., & Prairie, A. P. (2004). *Emotional connections. How relationships guide early learning.* Washington, DC: Zero to Three Press.

Canter, L. (1976). *Assertive discipline: A take-charge approach for today's educator.* Seal Beach, CA: Canter & Associates.

Carlson, F. M. (2005). *Essential touch: Meeting the needs of young children.* Washington, DC: National Association for the Education of Young Children.

Charles, C. M., & Senter, G. W. (2004). *Building classroom discipline* (8th ed.). Boston: Allyn and Bacon.

Connolly, P. & Hayden, J. with Levin, D. (2007). *From conflict to peace building: The power of early childhood initiatives. Lessons from around the world.* Redmond, WA: World Forum Foundation, Publisher.

Davidman, L., & Davidman, P. (1994). *Teaching with a multicultural perspective: A practical guide.* New York: Longman.

Dreikurs, R., Grunewald, B., & Pepper, F. (1982). *Maintaining sanity in the classroom.* New York: Harper & Row.

Fields, M. V. & Boesser, C. (2002). *Constructive guidance and discipline. Preschool and primary education* (3rd ed.). Upper Saddle River, NJ: Merrill Prentice Hall.

Flicker, E. S., & Hoffman, J.A. (2002, September). Developmental discipline in the early childhood classroom. *Young Children, 57*(5), 82–89.

Froschl, M., Sprung, B., & Hinitz, B. (2005, June 8). Start early to stop violence: Turning critical theory research on diversity into practical action. Presentation at NAEYC's National Institute for Early Childhood Professional Development, Miami, FL.

Gartrell, D. (2004). *The power of guidance: Teaching social-emotional skills in early childhood classrooms.* Washington, DC: National Association for the Education of Young Children and Delmar Learning.

Gartrell, D. (2006a). *A guidance approach for the encouraging classroom* (4th ed.). Clifton Park, NY: Delmar Learning.

Gartrell, D. (2006b, May). Guidance matters: boys and men teachers, *Young Children, 61*(3), 92–93.

Gillespie, C. W., & Chick, A. (2001, Summer). Fussbusters: Using peers to mediate conflict resolution in a Head Start classroom. *Childhood Education, 77*(4), 192–195.

Glasser, W. (1985). *Control theory in the classroom.* New York: Perennial Library.

Gonzalez-Mena, J., & Shareef, I. (2005, November). Discussing diverse perspectives on guidance. *Young Children, 60*(6), 68–70.

Gordon, T. (1974). *T.E.T.: Teacher effectiveness training.* New York: David McKay.

Greenspan, S. I. (2006, November/December). When a child's play schemes are violent, *Early Childhood Today, 21*(3), 24–25.

Howes, C. (2000, Spring). Relationships: Child, and teacher. *Early Development, 4*(1), 12–13.

Jensen, E. (1998). *Teaching with the brain in mind.* Alexandria, VA, Association for Supervision and Curriculum Development.

Kaiser, B., & Rasminsky, J. S. (2007). *Challenging behavior in young children. Understanding, preventing, and responding effectively* (3rd ed.). Boston: Pearson Allyn & Bacon.

Kara-Soteriou, J., & Rose, H. (2008, July). A bat, a snake, and a fuzzhead: Using children's literature to teach about positive character traits. *Young Children, 63*(4), 30–36.

Kohn, A. (2001, September). Five reasons to stop saying "Good job!" *Young Children, 56*(5), 24–28.

Levin, D. E. (2008, September/October). Building peaceable classroom communities: Counteracting the impact of violence on young children. *Exchange, 30*(5), 57–60.

Marion, M. (2007). *Guidance of young children* (7th ed.). Upper Saddle River, NJ: Pearson/Merrill/Prentice Hall.

McLeod, J., Fisher, J., & Hoover, G. (2003). *The key elements of classroom management: Managing time and space, student behavior, and instructional strategies.* Alexandria, VA: Association for Supervision and Curriculum Development.

Miller, D. F. (2004). *Positive child guidance* (4th ed.). Clifton Park, NY: Thomson Delmar Learning.

Readdick, C. A., & Chapman, P. L. (2000, Fall/Winter). Young children's perception of time-out. *Childhood Education, 15*(1), 81–87.

Rogers, C., & Freiberg, H. (1994). *Freedom to learn* (3rd ed.). New York: Merrill/Macmillan.

Vartuli, S. (2005, September). Beliefs: The heart of teaching. *Young Children, 60*(5), 76–86.

Walker-Dalhouse, D. (2005, Fall). Discipline: Responding to socioeconomic and racial differences. *Childhood Education, 82*(1), 24–30.

# CHAPTER 6

# Understanding Behavior

**OBJECTIVES**

After reading this chapter, you should be able to:

1. Identify what motivates children to act as they do.
2. Describe how children learn.
3. Analyze behavior using theories of child development.
4. Recognize the similarities, as well as the differences, among children of differing cultural backgrounds and how these relate to differences observed in their behaviors.

**STUDENT TEACHER SCENARIO**

**Setting:** In a first-grade classroom the student teacher, Leah, observes the children during the first week of her spring semester assignment. After the children are dismissed, she talks with her cooperating teacher, Ms. Hails.

Leah wonders about the behavior of the little boy who was sitting under the table when children were doing table work and whether he should be allowed to sit there while the other children were doing their assigned work.

Ms. Hails explains that Carlos is new to the classroom and comes from a Spanish-speaking family. She is not sure if his grasp of English is strong enough for the planned activities. She suggests that Carlos might be a good choice for Leah's case study assignment.

A week later, Ms. Hails asks Leah what she has learned from observing Carlos. Leah responds, "I think that Carlos knows very little English; yet, when I spoke to him in Spanish, Carlos simply ducked his head and gave me a shy smile. I really don't know if he understood me or not."

"What else have you observed, Leah?" asks Ms. Hails.

"Well, I noticed that he hasn't connected with any of the other Spanish-language-dominant children in the class or at recess, and he always goes under the table when he's faced with some task I think he doesn't understand," replies Leah.

Ms. Hails responds, "I've asked our bilingual specialist to visit the classroom and see what her conclusions might be regarding Carlos' behavior. In the meantime, I'm going to ask you to spend more one-on-one time with Carlos whenever it's possible. What does he do during recess?"

"Most of the time," Leah answers, "he kicks the soccer ball around or, when the climbing structure is empty, Carlos climbs to the top and looks around at the rest of the children."

"It sounds like he enjoys physical activities," says Ms. Hails. "Does he show other signs of Gardner's bodily-kinesthetic learning?"

"Actually he does," Leah replies. "I've noticed that he'll play with the pattern blocks and likes to build with the unit blocks. And he also exhibits spatial abilities when climbing and when kicking the soccer ball."

## Questions for Discussion:

1. Do you think Carlos might be experiencing some other difficulties?

2. If you were his student teacher, what activities might you try?

3. Does language appear to be Carlos' principal difficulty? Are there any indications in the scenario that would suggest other possibilities?

To understand the behavior of any child, as the student teacher you need to remember two important concepts:

1. All behavior is meaningful to the child, even that which an adult might call negative.
2. All behavior is reinforced by the environment (people, places, and things).

Then the questions arise: Why does the child act as he does? What motivates her to repeat behaviors? How is he learning?

Let's begin this chapter by looking at some of the typical motivators or reinforcements of behavior. Perhaps the easiest ones to understand are physiological in nature: the need to eat when hungry, drink when thirsty, sleep when tired, dress warmly when cold, stay out of the sun when hot, and so forth. It is less easy to understand the psychological and emotional ones, although they control more of our actions. Figueroa-Sanchez (2008) suggests, "It is time …to consider that a foundation in literacy must include the construct of 'emotional literacy.'" She further states, "Children are more likely to learn important cognitive skills when they are confident and engage in interactions with other children as well as with adults." Another way to look at this is to recognize that all learning is emotional. Copple and Bredekamp (2009), in discussing developmentally appropriate practice, interestingly enough place both physical and social and emotional development before cognitive development:

> Feelings of interest, pleasure, curiosity encourage children to explore their world and motivate them to solve problems. Similarly, strong feelings of sadness, fear, or anger may cause children to avoid certain kinds of learning situations or relationships.

There are even those who would posit that all learning is emotional.

However, there are several theorists who can help us understand the behavior of the children in our care, for example, Erikson, Maslow, Piaget, and Vygotsky.

# ERIKSON'S THEORY OF PSYCHOSOCIAL DEVELOPMENT

Erikson's (1993) theory of psychosocial development is relevant to our understanding of behavior. According to Erikson, there are eight developmental stages people go through during a lifetime. The child goes through the first four from birth until approximately age 12. These are: the resolution of basic trust, autonomy, initiative, and industry (see Figure 6–1). The remaining four, usually resolved from approximately age 12 and continuing through the adult years, are: identity, intimacy, generativity, and integrity. Each stage has its developmental task to achieve.

## First Stage of Development

Look at Figure 6–1. For the infant (birth to approximately one-and-one-half to two years), the task is to develop basic **trust**. If the infant is fed when hungry, changed when wet, dressed to suit the weather, and given much love and attention, the infant will learn that adults can be trusted. The infant who is not fed regularly and feels rejected or neglected may learn that adults cannot be trusted.

Look at the child in Figure 6–2. What do you see? She uses all of her senses as she looks at the flowers in her environment: eyes (sight), hands (touch), nose (smell), and ears (hearing) all come into action. Perhaps she would even like to taste the flower petals.

**trust**—the first stage of development described by Erik Erikson, occurring during infancy, in which the child's needs should be met consistently and predictably.

▶ **Figure 6–1**
Erikson's developmental stages.

| Age | Task | Outcome ("Good Me") | Outcome ("Bad Me") |
|---|---|---|---|
| 0–1 year | Acquiring a sense of BASIC TRUST | Child develops the ability to TRUST the significant adults in her life | Child develops a sense of MISTRUST in all adults and a sense of HOPELESSNESS |
| | PARENTAL/CAREGIVER ROLE: | Meeting physical needs, nurturing emotional and social needs; providing stimulation of intellectual and language needs; providing unconditional LOVE | |
| 1–3 years | Acquiring a sense of AUTONOMY | Child develops SELF-CONTROL and willpower; learns give-and-take (leadership-follower roles) | Child develops SELF-DOUBT and a sense of SHAME |
| | PARENTAL/CAREGIVER ROLE: | Emotional support; firm, but gentle, limit setting; gradual granting of freedom; consistency in expectations and in establishing boundaries; providing simple choices | |
| 3–5 years | Acquiring a sense of INITIATIVE | Child develops a sense of direction and purpose; is unafraid to explore new or changed settings | Child feels a sense of GUILT; becomes uneasy with new settings; only involves self in activities he knows well |
| | PARENTAL/TEACHER ROLE: | Communication; joint problem-solving; sharing of values and ideals; continued emotional support | |
| 6–12 years | Acquiring a sense of INDUSTRY | Child learns that he is competent; experiments with methods to become competent; fully develops leadership-follower roles | Child develops feelings of incompetence and INFERIORITY; lacks understanding of leadership-follower roles |
| | PARENTAL/TEACHER ROLE: | Encouraging realistic goals; helping child become open to criticism; accepting criticism from child; answering child's questions; being open to all kinds of questions from child | |

In learning about her environment, the child feels safe and learns that she can choose to touch the flowers, smell them, and, perhaps, even pick up the box. In this way she realizes that she has some control over her environment. It is this feeling of influence or control that is important to the child's eventual learning self-control.

Think about what can happen if the child feels no control over the environment. Suppose the significant adult in the infant's life holds out a new toy toward the child, shakes it in front of his eyes, and, as the infant reaches for it, takes it away? Suppose the infant reaches for an object over and over, only to have it always withdrawn? How long do you think the child will continue to reach? Ultimately he will stop trying. The child will also learn to feel helpless. This is the child who later becomes either under-disciplined or over-disciplined.

Experiencing some influence on the environment leads the child to understand that he can affect the environment. An awareness of cause-and-effect relationships develops in this manner.

## Second Stage of Development

As the child becomes mobile and begins to talk, he enters the second stage of development. Erikson calls this the **autonomy** stage. (Its contrasts are shame and self-doubt.) Two-year-old children are motor individuals; they love to run, climb, ride, move, move, and move (see Figure 6–3). They are so active—they almost seem like perpetual motion machines! The developmental task of the two-year-old toddler is learning autonomy and self-discipline. It is this age in particular that is so trying for both parents and preschool teachers.

This stage coincides with two physiological events in the toddler's life: the ability to crawl and walk and learning how to use the toilet. Much has been written about the problems of training a child to use the toilet. (The subject is covered in more detail in Chapter 12.) Many parents, child care workers, and family child care providers do not understand that most children will essentially train themselves, especially if given an appropriate model, such as an older sibling who is toilet trained or a loving, caring parent or caregiver who anticipates the child's need to

▶ **Figure 6–2**
The toddler "scientist" yearns to feel things firsthand.

**autonomy**—the second stage of development described by Erik Erikson, occurring during the second year of life, in which toddlers assert their growing motor, language, and cognitive abilities by trying to become more independent.

▶ **Figure 6–3**
These children have become autonomous bike riders.

use the toilet and, in an unthreatening way, sits the child on the seat and compliments the child on success. Many parents who try to toilet train what appears to be a stubborn, willful child fail to understand that the child is simply attempting to develop control, over the parent, in part, but over herself as well.

At this time, the child reinforces the sense of having an effect on the environment. Assume that the toddler, as an infant, was allowed some degree of freedom, in which to crawl and explore safely. Assume that within this safe environment the infant had a variety of toys and objects with which to play and manipulate, and a loving adult to supervise. This infant then becomes an active, curious toddler, ready to expand her environment. Assume also that the parents, early childhood caregivers, and family child care providers with whom this toddler comes into contact continue to provide a safe environment in which the child can explore. What is he then learning? He is continuing to learn that he has some control over his immediate environment. This helps him learn and practice self-control. To allow for practice, the environment must be physically safe, stimulating, and offer choices.

It is this third factor—offering choices—that is critical in helping a child acquire self-control. Even an infant crawling around in a playroom can make choices about which toys he will play with and when (see Figure 6–4). As she begins to feed herself, the child can make a choice between slices of apple or orange for a snack. In the center setting, a toddler can easily make a choice between playing with clay or climbing on an indoor play structure. But always remember the young child cannot handle a choice of six different activities; this is overwhelming. Too much choice is as bad as no choice at all. In either case, one child may become confused, anxious, and angry, whereas another child will withdraw and do nothing.

But one concern that family, caregivers, and teachers share is that toddlers often seem to be breaking limits deliberately. We fail to understand that one of the ways the child can be reassured that we care is to test the limits repeatedly to see if we really mean what we say. What sometimes happens is that on days when we are rested and time is plentiful, we tolerate behavior that would not be tolerated under different circumstances.

For some parents, caregivers, and teachers, the two-year-old child becomes too difficult to handle in a caring way. Two courses of action are frequently taken. Some parents confine the child rather than tolerate the need to explore. As a result, the child's basic motor needs are squelched, and she becomes fearful and distrustful of her motor abilities. She develops self-doubt rather than self-confidence. The child also learns to feel ashamed about the anger felt toward the adults. Because

▶ **Figure 6-4**
Toddlers become autonomous as they explore in this brightly equipped activity room.

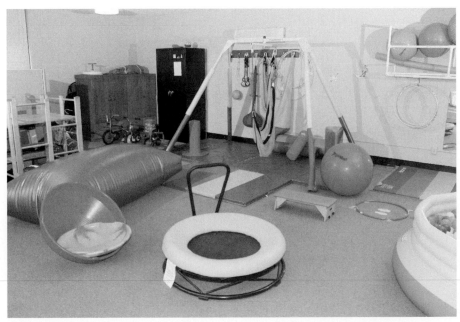

© Cengage Learning

these adults are still responsible for her primary needs, for food, water, and love, the child feels there must be something wrong with her if the adults inhibit her natural desire to explore. In the classroom, this child is the timid, shy, fearful one, with poor motor abilities due to a lack of opportunities to practice them.

Other families may allow the child to do anything. As a result, the child's behavior becomes progressively worse until the parents finally have had enough and resort to punishment. Then, we may see a child who fights against any kind of limits and becomes shameless in attempting to do the opposite of what adults expect or want. Just as the physically restrained child learns to feel ashamed, so does the unrestrained child. This child really wants to have reasonable limits set but cannot accept them without a struggle. This struggle of wills makes the unrestrained child feel just as ashamed as the overly restrained child. Both children lack the inner controls that the emotionally healthy child has developed. Both lack self-discipline: the overly restrained child through a lack of opportunities to practice, the under-restrained child through a lack of learning any limits.

In the primary school setting, difficulties with autonomy can be seen in two very different types of behavior. One is overconfidence, a willingness to try anything, and is characterized by frequent, unrealistic expectations of physical prowess. Overconfident students appear to have leadership qualities but become angry if thwarted in their attempts to lead. The opposite is the child who lacks self-confidence, a student who continually asks if he is completing an assignment the way you want him to, one who seems to need additional cues before starting a creative writing or art project; often this child will check what his peers are doing before beginning his own work.

## Third Stage of Development

The next stage roughly approximates the usual preschool years, from three to five. Erikson believes that the developmental task of the preschooler is to develop initiative, to learn when to do something by himself and when to ask for help. The result of practice in asserting his **initiative** results in a self-confident, cheerful child.

In most homes, child care centers, or preschools, the trusting, autonomous child has no difficulty. He knows what adults in his environment expect, and is usually amenable to following directions. He enjoys making decisions about what toys to play with, what choices to make in the play yard, and when to ask for help if a task becomes frustrating (see Figure 6-5).

**initiative**—the desire to do something by oneself. Identified as the third developmental stage of three- to five-year-old children by Erik Erikson.

▶ **Figure 6-5**
Learning to wait for a turn is not easy.

© Cengage Learning

On the other hand, the over-restrained four-year-old who has been denied a chance to exert initiative learns instead to develop feelings of guilt. The child learns that any self-made decisions are of no importance; adults make any decision. For example, if the child attempts to dress without help, the parents are likely to criticize the result. "Your shirt's on backwards. Don't you know front from back?" This child learns that he does not know how to dress and eventually may stop trying altogether. As the teacher, you then may see a child of four or five who cannot put on a jacket without help, who mixes left and right shoes, and who often asks, "Is this the way you want me to . . . ?" Because such children have little self-confidence, they frequently look to peers, or come to you, for ideas.

The under-restrained toddler grows to be an under-restrained preschool child and becomes your most obvious classroom problem. This child enters preschool like a small hurricane, spilling blocks, scattering puzzles, and tearing up a classmate's drawing. The under-restrained child is the one who pushes another child off the tricycle so she can ride it, or who grabs the hammer out of the hand of another child when she wants it for herself.

The under-restrained child is also under-socialized. This child has never learned the normal give-and-take of interpersonal relationships and does not know how to share or take turns (see Figure 6–6). This child has had few restrictions regarding what to do, when to do it, and where. At the same time, she often *wanted* the adults in her family, caregivers, and teachers to tell her what to do and what not to do. A word of caution: some perfectly normal children who have little or no preschool experience will act like the under-socialized child simply because they lack social experience. They learn rapidly, however, and some quickly become acclimated to classroom procedures and rules.

Remember, the child who appears unlovable is the one most in need of your love. What are some of the ways you can help this child? Use the four *Cs* and *CARE*. Although it is difficult to accept this child, all children deserve your respect and acceptance, regardless of how unlikable they may be. Remember to be firm. The under-restrained child needs the security of exact limits. Rules need to be stated repeatedly and enforced.

Children with this type of behavior test every resource you have. Again, remember to use the four *Cs* and to *CARE*, even though it may be difficult. Repeat the limits and expectations over and over. Physically remove the child whenever necessary; isolation sometimes works best.

▶ **Figure 6-6**
Choosing their own books shows initiative.

© Cengage Learning

One technique that sometimes works with the aggressive, under-disciplined child is to call the child on the behavior. What is meant by *call*? This involves saying what the child is thinking. "You want me to tell you that I hate you, but I'm not going to." Sometimes, the shock of hearing you put into words what she is thinking is enough to change the behavior.

Some children are motivated by a desire to control, because they have learned that their own safety lies in their ability to control their environment. This can provoke a tug-of-war between the child's need to control and yours. At this point, there is no sense in trying to reason, especially verbally. Simply isolate the child, repeat the rules or limits, and leave. As you leave say something like the following to the child: "I'm not going to argue with you," or "Sit here until you feel ready to rejoin us."

Be prepared to understand that you will not be successful with every child. There will always be one or two children who will relate better to another teacher.

As the teacher, your job is to provide the kind of environment where the child is able to resolve these early developmental tasks, especially if the child has not yet done so. It is never too late to learn to trust, or to develop autonomy and initiative; it is never too late to undo earlier, negative outcomes, even while working toward resolution of a different stage's positive outcome.

## Fourth Stage of Development

For school-age children, there is probably no more important task than to learn that they are capable of learning. Erikson called this stage **industry**. (Its negative outcome is inferiority.) Unfortunately, even children who have progressed smoothly through the earlier stages of development may stumble when they reach kindergarten and first grade (see Figure 6–7).

For some children in kindergarten and the primary grades of elementary school, the fine motor tasks, such as writing manuscript, shaping numerals, and coloring within specified lines, are difficult. These children may have already learned that they do not have abilities that are rewarded by their teachers.

School, instead of being a place of joy and learning, may become a place where children fail. Inferiority is the obvious result. A secondary result can be that the child develops feelings of helplessness. Successful students generally believe that

**industry**—the fourth stage of development described by Erik Erikson, starting at the end of the preschool years and lasting until puberty, during which the child focuses on the development of competence.

▶ **Figure 6–7**
These children are working on resolving Erikson's task of industry.

© Cengage Learning

they are responsible for their successes and attribute any failures to lack of effort. Unsuccessful students, however, often attribute successes to luck and failures to factors beyond their control, or to lack of ability. The unfortunate consequence in students who feel helpless is that they often give up and stop trying.

In a classroom that offers developmentally appropriate materials for children to interact with actively, there is little difficulty with industry. A developmentally appropriate classroom is likely to have centers to allow for active exploration, and enough physical space to allow for movement opportunities, at different times.

For example, a school may have a carpeted reading area, with pillows where children can go to look at and read books; a science area, with attractive junk to explore; floor space, for the children who may wish to work on the floor; a math center, with Cuisenaire rods, unifix cubes, tangrams, and other manipulatives; a writing area, managed by an student teacher, or a parent or other volunteer, where children can dictate stores or write and illustrate their own; and so on. In the classroom with many options for working alone, in pairs, or in cooperative groups, children discover that learning is enjoyable; and industry is the result.

## Emotional Development of Children

Butterfield, Martin, and Prairie (2004) suggest that there are certain key concepts that teachers should be familiar with for children at different ages. With infants, for example, one key concept is that *early experiences shape our ability to communicate through emotional signals*.

Epstein (2009) uses the terms *emotional learning* and *social learning*, the first referring to the knowledge and skills needed to self-regulate, and the latter referring to the strategies for interacting successfully with others. She considers them interdependent and links them together as *social-emotional learning* (or development or competence). According to Epstein, there are four components of social-emotional learning:

1. Emotional self-regulation and awareness, "defined as responding to experiences with an appropriate range of immediate or delayed emotions. In preschool it is characterized by a growing ability to focus and organize actions; greater forethought and less impulsivity; and an enhanced awareness of and ability to follow rules…and common procedures."

2. Social knowledge and understanding, "defined as knowledge of social norms and customs."

3. Acquisition of social skills. This "comprises the range of strategies for interacting with others. Cognitive development, especially perspective-taking and empathy, assists the development of social skills."

4. Social dispositions refer "to enduring character traits, including valued behaviors such as curiosity, humor, and generosity and unpopular ones, such as closed-mindedness, argumentativeness, and selfishness."

Epstein considers social-emotional learning as an essential aspect of early development.

Goleman (1995, 1997) and Mayer and Salovey (1995) address what they call *emotional intelligence* and the skills associated with it. The key skills include:

◆ *self-awareness:* being able to recognize and name emotions, and understand why the child feels as she does

◆ *self-regulation of emotion:* being able to verbalize and cope with emotions

◆ *self-monitoring and performance:* being able to focus on the task at hand, set goals, modify performance after feedback, and mobilize positive motivation to work toward optimal performance states

◆ *empathy and perspective taking:* becoming a good listener (see Figure 6–8), being able to empathize with others and understand another child's perspective, point of view, or feelings

© Cengage Learning

▶ **Figure 6-8**
As friends, these girls enjoy being together.

◆ *social skills in handling relationships:* the ability to express emotions in relationships and work as a member of a team or cooperative learning group, exercise sensitivity to social cues, and respond constructively to interpersonal obstacles. (Elias et al., 1997)

Elias et al. (1997) emphasize that "acquiring an integrated set of skills such as these often occurs in an experiential context, where the skills are learned through practice and role modeling." They further stress the developmental nature of the acquisition of emotional skills, and the fact that emotional skills are best learned through experience and repetition during early childhood.

*Emotional skills* (Goleman, 1995, 1997) include the following:

◆ identifying and labeling feelings
◆ expressing feelings
◆ assessing the intensity of feelings
◆ managing feelings
◆ delaying gratification
◆ controlling impulses
◆ reducing stress
◆ knowing the difference between feelings and actions

And *behavioral skills* (Goleman, 1995, 1997) include these:

◆ nonverbal communication, through eye contact, facial expressions, tone of voice, gestures, and so on
◆ verbal communication, making clear requests, responding effectively to criticism, resisting negative influences, listening to and helping others, participating in positive peer groups

In agreement with Goleman, Hyson (2004) lists the following five components of emotional intelligence:

**1.** self-awareness
**2.** adaptive coping
**3.** an ability to discern others' emotions

**4.** an ability to use words to express emotions

**5.** empathy

## Teacher Priorities

Teachers realize that emotions and cognitive development are intertwined and inseparable. In an earlier article, Hyson (2002) listed ways in which teachers can help every child develop emotional maturity. She identifies six *priorities* in promoting emotional competence:

1. *Creating a secure emotional environment.* If teachers build close relationships and an emotionally secure climate, children are able to explore and learn.

2. *Helping children understand emotions.* If teachers promote emotional understanding, children have insight into their own and others' feelings, thereby becoming more empathic and socially competent.

3. *Modeling genuine, appropriate emotional responses.* If teachers themselves show real emotions, and, if they are effective models, children are likely to adopt appropriate ways of showing their feelings.

4. *Supporting children's regulation of emotions.* If teachers gradually guide children toward expressing and regulating their emotions in appropriate ways, children will gain powerful tools that lead to healthy development in social, emotional, and academic areas.

5. *Recognizing and honoring children's expressive styles.* If teachers respect individual and cultural differences in how children express their feelings, while promoting appropriate expressions, children feel affirmed and supported.

6. *Uniting children's learning with positive emotions.* If teachers give children many opportunities to experience the joys and overcome the frustrations of new learning experiences, children become able to tackle hard work, persist at tasks, and seek out challenges.

Why is there this emphasis on emotional and social development? Epstein (2009) relates it to the pressure for accountability but cautions us "to recognize that social-emotional learning is a content area on a par with literacy, mathematics, and other disciplines." Goleman (2006) posits that "the effects on the brain of positive social and emotional experiences can actually improve attention and working memory, which are key factors in learning."

Young children, progressing toward the emotional growth and control needed in kindergarten, often display secure and trusting feelings for their teachers and peers. They are able to control, express, regulate, and understand a wide spectrum of their own feelings. They display problem-solving abilities, persistence, positive relationships with others, and an eagerness to experience classroom activities. They are headed toward academic success.

## Self-Esteem and Self-Control

Although much of the research on self-esteem was completed in the late 1960s and throughout the 1970s, the new millennium has brought a renewed interest. With the noticeable changes that have occurred in families in the past 20 years—due to the problems of divorce and subsequent single-parenthood, mobility, the rise in the incidence of substance abuse, remarriage and blended families, teenage parenthood, smaller family size, homelessness, the two-working-parent family, and difficulties with child care or after-school care—child caregivers and teachers are seeing more and more stressed and even "damaged" children. Characteristic of such children is low self-esteem. Children of divorced parents typically blame themselves for the divorce, a phenomenon that exists even in the most amicable of divorce cases.

What you see in the classroom then is the damage to these children's self-esteem: families too stressed, and parents too busy and, too often suffering from low self-esteem themselves, to parent their children properly or nourish their children's self-esteem. One word of caution: not all single parents are overstressed. Some children are less stressed after the divorce of parents who constantly argued; some single parents do earn substantial salaries, are emotionally and psychologically healthy, and are able to build their children's self-esteem. As always, be wary of applying stereotypes.

In his landmark research, Coopersmith (1967) cited three factors in the home that contribute to children's feelings of self-esteem:

1. unconditional acceptance of the child, although not necessarily accepting all of the child's behaviors
2. setting clear expectations for behavior and consistently reinforcing the need for adherence to them
3. respecting the child's need for initiative within the set limits

Some children you see in child care and school may have a parent's acceptance only when they do exactly what is demanded of them. Parents tired from working may abandon their job as parents and allow children to essentially raise themselves, or may allow the TV to raise them. Other parents may feel threatened by their children's desires for autonomy and initiative, and may not respect the need children have to exert their wills.

For the caregiver and teacher working with children with low self esteem, the task is to attempt to provide the missing elements of acceptance, clearly defined limits, and respect for the child's need to assert autonomy and practice initiative within those limits. If this sounds like *CARE*ing, it should. **Self-control** can be defined as *the ability to resist the inappropriate and act responsibly*. Acting responsibly includes respecting the rights of others, showing compassion, being honest, and at times exhibiting courage. It entails dealing effectively with anger and other strong emotions, and having patience.

**self-control**—restraint exercised over one's own impulses, emotions, or desires.

## MASLOW'S HIERARCHY OF NEEDS

Maslow (1968) attempted to develop a hierarchy of needs, by which people are motivated (see Figure 6–9). He grouped these needs according to whether they were

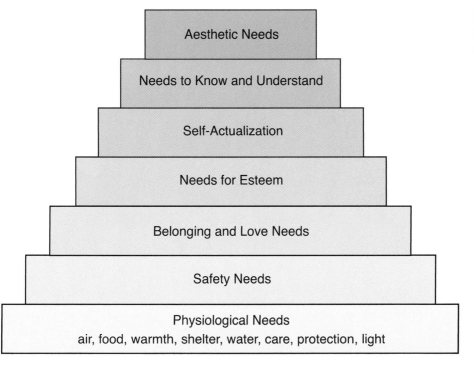

▶ **Figure 6–9**
Maslow's hierarchy of needs.

*deficiency* needs or *growth* needs, based on whether the individual was growing in a positive direction. For anyone to grow positively, Maslow felt that the deficiency needs must be filled for the growth needs to be met.

The implications for the children you teach are manifold. The child who is hungry, cold, and—more importantly—unloved may not be able to grow and learn as we would wish him to. Such a child may be afraid to grow, for fear of losing the security of what is already known. For this child, growth comes with anxiety.

Just as children are different, anxiety and fear in the child may be expressed differently. One fearful, anxious child will withdraw physically from the environment. The child may cling to the mother or the teacher, refuse to try a new activity, and limit participation to what he knows and can do best. Another fearful, anxious child will lash out verbally or physically, sometimes both.

**Maslow's hierarchy of needs** presents another way of looking at what motivates behavior. The child who is hungry, poorly clothed, and unloved may have difficulty in becoming *self-actualized*, a term Maslow uses to describe the attainment of a certain potential. The same child may have difficulty in developing the natural desire to explore and understand the environment. As stated before, both the overtly aggressive child and the fearful child are under-disciplined.

In studying Maslow's hierarchy, we find that if the goal is to help the child become self-actualized, the child's deficiency needs must first be met. The child's belongingness, love, and esteem needs must be met. Belongingness carries the implication of *family identity*, of belonging to a particular adult or group, and feeling that one is a part of this group. There is psychological safety in having a group to belong to; witness the popularity of cliques and gangs among older students in elementary schools. The group is the one that takes care of the physiological needs and makes sure that the environment is safe. The group also allows the growing child to develop self-esteem.

How is self-esteem developed? According to Maslow, it is developed in interaction with the important people in the environment. Self-esteem is developed through the continual interaction between the family, caregivers, and the child. Every time you give positive attention to a child, smile, and notice achievements, you are helping to build the child's self-esteem (see Figure 6–10).

A child from this type of environment will have no difficulty in becoming self-actualized. In contrast, the child whose home environment has not provided for these deficiency needs may have difficulty. For this child, you will need to provide those

**Maslow's hierarchy of needs**—a theoretical position that attempts to identify human needs and motivations. It describes the consequences of need fulfillment and the consequences of unmet needs on growth.

▶ **Figure 6-10**

A large part of teaching is giving attention to individual children.

© Cengage Learning

experiences that the child has missed: attention to physiological needs, safety needs, and the need to belong. The loving early childhood teacher or family child care provider can do much to help the child whose own family group has been unable to help.

## Resiliency

Children are remarkably resilient; they can survive situations that seem almost impossible. Even given a poor beginning, if a child comes into contact with a warm, loving, accepting adult, the child will be able to self-actualize. Children who seem invulnerable or untouched by negative family environments (alcoholism, criminality, poverty, and/or mental illness) are also those children who, during their first year, had at least one significant adult in their lives who cared (Werner & Smith, 1992). This adult could be trusted, thus enabling the children to resolve the question of basic trust. According to Werner and Smith, these children are able to find other adults to whom they can relate in terms of resolving the other tasks of early childhood.

Today's world is full of change, uncertainty, and challenge for everyone, and Breslin (2005) maintains that resiliency must be a primary concern. She states, "Resiliency is not a fixed attribute. Rather it is a set of protective mechanisms that modify a person's response to risk situations." She identifies four factors for teachers to examine in resilient children:

1. a heightened sensory awareness
2. high, positive expectations for themselves
3. a clear and developing understanding of their strengths relating to any accomplishment
4. a heightened, developing sense of humor

## Implications for Teachers

To summarize theorists' suggestions regarding the promotion of self-control, let's briefly look at each. Erikson relates self-control with resolving the question of autonomy, the task of toddlers. According to Maslow, self-control relates to the resolution of deficiency needs and the beginnings of self-actualization. Goleman, along with Mayer and Salovey, would suggest that the child with emotional intelligence, who can self-regulate, has self-awareness and self-control. Furthermore, empathy for others and the ability to monitor behavior are also components of self-control. Gillespie and Seibel (2006) would agree.

Self-esteem theory would suggest that self-control is related to self-worth. When provided with acceptance, respect, and clearly stated classroom rules, children who feel good about themselves will also exhibit self-control. Often, families of these children have shown interest in encouraging self-control and instilled self-esteem in their children.

Sometimes words like *empower* and *belonging* are used to indicate that teachers who empower their students and provide them with a sense of belonging are also teaching them self-control. Empowerment means allowing children control over certain aspects of classroom life. Choices such as deciding at which learning center they want to study, or what the logical consequences might be for breaking certain classroom rules empower children. For a child, being given the opportunity to feel like a part of the classroom community satisfies the universal need to belong, a point emphasized by Copple and Bredekamp (2009) when they stress, "To be an excellent teacher . . . means creating a community of learners [and] . . . teaching to enhance development and learning."

## Self-Respect

Young children often want to share accomplishments with peers and caregivers. Requests to "Look at me!" pervade daily teacher–child interactions and help children respect themselves if given teacher attention. Many children take satisfaction in their appropriate behavior and accomplishments and notice the inappropriate behavior of peers. When classrooms model respect, compassion, and concern for others, children gain self-control and self-respect with greater ease. Teachers genuinely try to model the sort of person they hope children will become.

Talking through complications or problem situations with children is one way to help them understand the consequences of different choices. Story discussions also bring to light what choices and consequences occurred for story characters. Most teachers attempt to draw from children what choices exist in life situations and what consequences might follow. This promotes the child's own ability to reflect.

## CULTURAL DIFFERENCES

**stereotype**—a simplified conception or image of a person or group based on race, ethnicity, religion, gender, or sexual orientation.

In analyzing student behavior, how do you see cultural differences reflected? The most important factor to remember is to avoid using **stereotypes**. All Asians are not quiet, nor are they all straight-A students, nor are all Asians from a single cultural group. All African Americans are not inner-city dwellers, nor do they all speak nonstandard English. All Hispanics are not Mexican or Puerto Rican or Cuban; they come from as many different, separate Hispanic cultures as do Africans, Asians, and Europeans. Among Native Americans, you will note the same great variations, depending on individual cultural backgrounds.

As a teacher, it will be important for you to remain as open-minded as possible, to avoid being tempted to ascribe to culturally diverse students behaviors that may not apply to them as individuals; being open-minded is also the most important factor in establishing a good relationship with the families of culturally diverse children. Listen carefully to what a parent may say. Even if you initially disagree, try to place yourself in the parents' shoes, to see from their perspective. Cultural differences are often immediately apparent. Even an offer to shake hands may not be appropriate. Some parents from India typically greet another person with clasped hands and a bow of the head. A parent from Japan may often bow to his child's teacher as a sign of respect. A Latina mother may not look you in the eye, as she may feel that to do so is disrespectful. Parents from Vietnam may, although legally married, have different names (Berger, 2008).

One reason for the existence of stereotypes is that when we do not have information, we rely on the news media, typically television, for the "facts." However, bad news sells better than good news, so stories of homicides, robberies, and assaults abound. Because many more of these occur in inner cities than in suburbs, the stereotype develops that because the inner city or barrio or wherever the violence is happening has more people of color living within its confines, all people of that particular race or ethnic group must be prone to violence.

We need to remember that the first African Americans to come to what is now the United States came with Columbus and Coronado, and many more arrived, as did many European Americans, as indentured servants. It was only later that they were brought as slaves (Banks, 2002). We also need to remember that Latinos had settled in the southwestern parts of the United States before the first Puritans settled in Massachusetts. If there is any one thing you should always remember about children from minority families in your classroom, it is to recognize their diversity (Berger, 2008).

## HOW DO CHILDREN LEARN?

We've looked at how psychosocial development and emotions influence how children behave, and how positive outcomes in the development of self-esteem are related to learning. Let's look briefly now at cognitive theorists, Piaget and Vygotsky.

## Piaget's Theory of Cognitive Development

According to Piaget's theory, children go through four stages of cognitive development. Gonzalez-Mena (2005) reviewed these stages in her textbook *Foundations: Early Childhood Education in a Diverse Society* (3rd ed.). Piaget posited the four stages as follows:

1. **Sensorimotor stage.** From birth to age two or three. Starting at birth, infants and toddlers learn primarily through their senses, seeing, hearing, touching (manipulating), smelling, and tasting everything.

2. **Preoperational stage.** From age two or three to eight or nine. At this stage, beginning with the development of language approximately at age two, the preschooler develops what Piaget terms *pre-concepts,* and learns by using intuition. Thus, a three-year-old child makes typical mistakes in conceptual learning and may call a cow, seen for the first time, by the name of the only large animal with which he has any experience: "horsie."

   Adults can see children's intuition at work, as they make grammatical errors in over-generalizing plurals. For example, *mouse* becomes *mouses,* just as *house* becomes *houses. Foot* becomes *foots* or *feets.* "I don't got no more cookies" becomes standard emphasis for the three-year-old, with the use of the double negative considered normal.

   Piaget often called children in the preoperational stage *perception bound,* meaning that they are limited by what they can see, hear, touch, manipulate, and so on, and that they have difficulty seeing comparisons when differences are dramatic. A child at this stage may not understand that a Chihuahua and a Great Dane are both dogs. One two-year-old, for example, called a Scottie dog a "funny cat" because her only acquaintance with small, furry black animals had been her own large, female Persian cat.

3. **Concrete operational stage.** From ages six to eight, to age eleven and even in to adulthood. At this stage, the child begins to be able to form classifications and to see the similarities among categories despite their differences. All dogs and all cats, for example, become "animals." Birds that fly, such as sparrows and cardinals, can be grouped with chickens, and sometimes with difficulty, ducks and geese.

   Also during the concrete operational stage, the child begins to understand the principle of **conservation**, which is essential to the understanding of mathematics. This includes examples such as understanding that the mass of clay does not change when it is rolled from a ball into an elongated shape; that the amount of liquid in a tall, thin glass may be the same as that in a short, fat glass; that area does not change where there are the same number of objects placed on a field, even though one field looks more crowded because the objects are scattered and the other field *seems* to have more area, because the objects are aligned along one side.

   **conservation**—the ability, usually acquired during the concrete operational stage, to recognize that objects remain the same in terms of size, volume, and area despite perceptual changes.

4. **Formal operational stage.** From age eleven to adulthood. According to Piaget, during this final stage in intellectual development, the child begins to be capable of abstract thinking. At this stage, the child can formulate hypotheses and learns to monitor his own thinking, called *metacognition.*

## The Importance of Speech and Language (Vygotsky's Theory)

Considered a sociocultural theorist, Vygotsky saw learning as taking place through social contact and the development of what he termed *private speech.* Children talk to themselves, either silently or vocally, in the attempt to internalize learning, monitor themselves, and solve problems. Vygotsky emphasized the importance of language in the development of socially shared cognition, in which adults or peers

**zone of proximal development (ZPD)—** in Vygotsky's theory, this zone comprises tasks a child cannot yet do by herself but that she can accomplish with the support of an older child or adult.

**scaffolding—**a teaching technique helpful in promoting language, understanding, and child solutions, that may include supportive and responsive teacher conversation and actions following child-initiated behavior.

assisted the child to move ahead in development by noticing what the next logical step might be. The term **zone of proximal development (ZPD)** was applied to the adult's or peer's recognition of when the child needed assistance and when the child did not. This assisted learning is called **scaffolding**.

Understanding Vygotsky's theory in teaching has led to the emphasis on cooperative learning, scaffolding (assisted learning), and teaching children to use private speech to help in their problem solving. A teacher might notice that a child is having difficulty placing one piece of a puzzle in the right place and suggests that the piece be rotated. A peer familiar with the same puzzle might do the same.

Let's move now to the application of these theories in your understanding of a child's behavior. The first step always involved your observations.

# APPLYING THEORIES TO UNDERSTAND BEHAVIOR

## Case Studies

As a student teacher, you may be asked to complete a case study on a child. The assignment frequently requires an in-depth analysis and recording of the child's achievements, development, and learning. Data collection can involve:

- ◆ systematic observations
- ◆ work samples
- ◆ assessments and test results
- ◆ samples of creative artwork
- ◆ videos, photographs, or tape recordings
- ◆ dictations
- ◆ anecdotal records (factual notes recording spontaneous events and happenings)
- ◆ checklists, inventories, or rating scales
- ◆ interviews with the child or others
- ◆ home visits and other activities

The kinds of data collected may depend on both your college instructor's assignment criteria and the purpose of the child study. A strict code of confidentiality and anonymity concerning the child's identity is observed whenever student teachers collect data or share evaluations. A family's presence in the school or classroom makes confidentiality crucial. The temptation for student teachers to discuss their case studies with other adults has led to a few unfortunate and emotionally charged discussions.

Assignments may require a view of the child as a whole, or narrower aspects of the child's development or behavior may be considered. Most training programs assign in-depth case studies, so student teachers can begin to realize the benefits accrued from watching one child intently, and attempting to satisfy curiosity about the *hows* and *whys* of that one child's actions. Student teachers, then, become researchers who reserve judgment, interpret carefully, hypothesize, explore many possible reasons for the observed behavior, and begin to see child development theories in the flesh.

# OBSERVATION FORMS

You may have already had a course on observing children, and you may have learned how to use a variety of observation forms. We are going to focus on three: the *narrative* (or *anecdotal*), *event sampling*, and *fixed interval* (or *time sampling*) *forms*. Then, more importantly, we will return to the scenario with which this chapter opened and demonstrate how to use the information to ask yourself questions and analyze the child's behavior.

## Narrative

This is one of the simplest forms to use when observing a child. A narrative describes the child's behavior as it occurs. As an observer, you can sit to one side of the room or yard with a small notebook (see Figure 6–11). After consulting with your cooperating teacher, pick a child to observe and simply record what you see. Look again at the scenario that begins this chapter. A narrative description might look like this:

▶ **Figure 6–11**
Observation can take place inside the classroom.

### *Case Study 1: Carlos*

#### Background

Carlos is a six-year-old child whose mother enrolled him in the school where you are student teaching. Subsequently, he was placed in your cooperating teacher's first-grade class room.

#### Narrative Observation

Carlos enters the classroom and holds his older sister's hand. She brings him to the seat assigned to him at one of the six tables in the room. She hands his lunch money to your teacher, give Carlos a hug, and leaves for her own classroom. Carlos sits in his seat and, ducking his head, nods to his table mates as they sit down. Ms. Hails calls the students to the carpeted circle for opening procedures. Attendance is taken; the date on the calendar is marked with a sun to indicate sunny weather today; two children share; and work assignments are given.

Children go to the various centers to which they have been assigned. Carlos remains seated on the carpet. Speaking in Spanish, the teacher tells him to go to the table where the bilingual teacher, Ms. Chavez, is stationed. He stands and moves to the table. Three other Spanish-language-dominant children are already there. Carlos sits down. When the bilingual teacher begins to hand out Spanish-language books, Carlos gets up and goes under the table. Ms. Chavez asks him to sit by her. He comes out and does as she asks. Ms. Chavez speaks one-to-one with Carlos and demonstrates what she wants completed. Carlos does as she asks until one of the other students distracts her. Ms. Chavez goes to help the other child; Carlos ducks under the table again.

Ms. Hails approaches and asks you to go to the writing center and help one of the parent volunteers with a story another child is dictating. With four children at the center, it is clear that an extra person is needed.

Obviously, the difficulty of a narrative observation is that it either must be reconstructed after the event, or the student teacher must remove himself from the action and sit on the side while writing down what he sees. The narrative can be abbreviated somewhat, through the use of an *anecdotal form*. (For an illustration of this narrative in anecdotal form, see Figure 6–12.)

## Event Sampling

Assuming Carlos is one of the regular students in your class, you might want to prepare an event sampling of his daily behavior. The narrative/anecdotal forms presented only a brief sampling of Carlos' total behavior. Perhaps completing an event sampling of under-the-table versus sitting behavior would give you a clearer picture of Carlos' typical behavior.

▶ **Figure 6-12**

An anecdotal record form of Carlos's behavior.

| Name of school: <u>ABC School</u><br>Date: <u>May 14</u> | | Student Teacher: <u>MK</u><br>Class: <u>First Grade</u> |
|---|---|---|
| Description of behavior | Time | Comments |
| C enters w/sister (S) | 8:55 | |
| S greets tchr (T); hands her C's lunch money; leads C to his table | 8:57 | |
| C sits at table; ignores other children as they come and sit at table | 9:03 | |
| T calls children to circle. | 9:05 | |
| C sits at outside of circle even when T asks him to come closer. | 9:10 | What gives w/ C? |
| T dismisses children to their assigned centers; C remains at circle rug. | 9:30 | Doesn't C understand what he's supposed to do? |
| T leads to table where bilingual assistant teacher (AT) is waiting with three other children. | 9:33 | C joins others; I follow |
| Talking in Spanish, AT hands Spanish language books to children. C takes his and goes under the table. | 9:35 | I really wonder what's wrong w/ C...does he not even understand Spanish? |

Take a 3 × 5 card and divide it into two columns; label one "Under the table" and the other "Sitting." The recording is simple; throughout the day you simply note each time Carlos sits or goes under the table. At the end of the day, you can add the number of times each kind of behavior is observed. You do this for a week. Your purpose in doing this series of event samplings is to determine a baseline of Carlos' typical behavior. Once the baseline is determined, you can develop a behavior modification plan to change the behavior. (See the Appendix for a sample behavior modification plan.) At the end of the week, you can make a chart that summarizes the event samples taken. It might look something like Figure 6–13.

**Analysis of Carlos' Behavior** What do the observations of Carlos' behavior about him? Questions you may want to ask:

- ◆ Is this typical behavior?
- ◆ What is Carlos like at home?
- ◆ Did Carlos attend kindergarten? If so, where?

  Let's assume that the answers are as follows:

- ◆ Yes, Carlos typically goes quietly to tables where he has been assigned to work. He also typically heads under the table when worksheets are introduced.

▶ **Figure 6-13**

Summary of event sampling of Carlos's under-table behavior.

| Monday | Tuesday | Wednesday | Thursday | Friday | Average. |
|---|---|---|---|---|---|
| 4 | 5 | 5 | 4 | 5 | 4.6 |

◆ According to his sister when at home, Carlos generally is quiet and plays with his next younger brother. They both like soccer and play with the family's soccer ball when the older brothers allow the younger ones to do so. He also watches soccer games on Spanish language television.

◆ When asked, his sister says that she does not know if Carlos attended kindergarten or not. The family had moved so frequently during the last year that she had difficulty doing her own work.

In considering the different theories introduced, what hypotheses come to mind?

## Analysis of Carlos' Behavior

**Erikson**. In looking at the developmental milestones Erikson proposes, it seems reasonably clear that Carlos may be over-restrained. He has not resolved the task of initiative. It is also likely that he has not resolved the earlier task of autonomy. In seeing his behavior with his sister, it does appear that basic trust has been resolved. It is possible that given the fact that he's a middle child in a large family, Carlos has learned that being quiet and obedient to his parents and older siblings brings approval. Caution: It is important to remember that family is important in Hispanic cultures; being quiet and obedient may be a family value.

**Goleman/Mayer/Salovey**. Concerning emotional intelligence, Carlos may have difficulty. It is difficult to judge his level of emotional development. He does seem to have self-awareness but is so quiet around his peers that whether he can empathize is unknown. A home visit might reveal that Carlos can empathize well with his younger siblings.

**Maslow**. Carlos has had his physiological and safety needs met, and it seems that his belongingness and esteem needs have been met at least partially. He talks so little that most of what you have learned about him has come through conversations with his sister.

**Implications for the teacher**. The number one need for Carlos is continued instruction in Spanish and much *CARE*ing. He needs to feel comfortable in the classroom. Ms. Hails will follow through on scheduling a conference with Carlos' parents to ascertain whether or not he attended either preschool or kindergarten. Your cooperating teacher may ask you to sit in on a conference with the school psychologist should any special needs be suspected.

## Fixed Interval (Time Sampling)

### Case Study 2: Maya

#### Background

Maya is a bright-eyed, eight-year-old student in the third grade. She is slightly taller than many of her age peers and enjoys excellent health. Her parents are supportive of her schooling, and both attend family-teacher conferences. Her father is a computer engineer; her mother is an accountant. She has a brother in the first grade at the same school. The two children usually walk to and from school together and appear to have a close relationship.

#### Fixed-Interval (Time Sampling) Observation Form

Look at Figure 6–14. Note that the student teacher made an observation—with few exceptions—every 5 minutes, and tried to describe what was happening. However, she does insert her assumptions more than once but places her comments in parentheses. Based on these observations, what might you conclude about Maya? Has she resolved the tasks appropriate to her age?

#### Analysis of Maya's Behavior

**Erikson**. Given her desire to compose her own tangram patterns, it would seem that Maya is clearly working to resolve the task of industry. This also reveals

▷ **Figure 6-14**

Fixed interval or time sampling model.

| Child: Maya | |
|---|---|
| T = teacher | Grade: 3rd |
| St = Student; Ss = students | Date: 12 October |

| | |
|---|---|
| 8:30 A.M.: | Enters classroom, places lunch box & jacket in cubby |
| 8:30 A.M.: | Sits at desk, talks to J. (a student in her group), ignores math "sponge" activity on board |
| 8:40 A.M.: | Still talks to J. |
| 8:45 A.M.: | (Bell rings) |
| | (I was busy taking roll & lunch count; didn't note what M. was doing) |
| 8:50 A.M.: | Talks to G. (another St. in her group) |
| | (Should be saying Pledge of Allegiance and completing math "sponge" activity on chalkboard) |
| 8:55 A.M.: | (T. reminds children that 1st activity of the A.M. will begin at 9:00 & that "sponge" problems are to be placed in her "in-basket") |
| | Maya quickly completes problems & turns in paper |
| 9:00 A.M.: | All Ss sitting quietly on carpet squares, choosing centers; Maya waves hand excitedly; "Writing center! Writing center!" |
| | T reminds her that she has been in the writing center for the past two days and that others like the writing center, too |
| | "Why not try the math center, Maya?" T. suggests |
| 9:05 A.M.: | Maya pouts, "But, I want to go to the writing center" |
| 9:10 A.M.: | Still pouting but goes to math center where tangram puzzles and pieces are arranged to stimulate problem-solving |
| 9:15 A.M.: | M. complains, "These tangrams are too easy! Can I make some of my own?" T. says "Of course, Maya; maybe you'd like to have B. work with you?" "No!" . . . emphatically said |
| 9:25 A.M.: | M. working very carefully |
| 9:30 A.M.: | M. still working carefully |
| 9:45 A.M.: | (I'm too busy; unable to check on M.) |
| 9:50 A.M.: | M. looks intent on creating a new design |
| 9:55 A.M.: | T. rings a bell & warns Ss they have five min to finish their center work; reminds those who haven't that they can finish after recess |
| 10:00 A.M.: | M. says, "I'm nearly finished with my design; may I stay in for recess and work on it?" T. suggests to M. that she should get some fresh air and exercise, too; M. groans but agrees |

(I have yard duty this A.M. recess and I notice that Maya is off by herself drawing in the dirt. I wonder if she's still working on her new tangram design or dreaming up a new one. As I approach her, she quickly erases what she's been working on.)

some degree of initiative. Maya also appears to have resolved the task of autonomy. Maya's supportive family and good relationships with her brother would seem to reveal basic trust. Trust can also be seen in Maya's relationships with her teacher and her peers. Her social exchanges with peers in her group may indicate follower and leadership abilities, but this particular set of observations does not.

**Goleman/Mayer/Salovey.** If we look at what researchers have proposed regarding emotional intelligence, Maya reveals a high degree of self-awareness and the ability to modulate her emotional responses. She can focus on a task for an extended period of time and has a sunny and positive outlook on life. If she has areas that still need to be developed, they are not obvious. We did not note much give and take with her peers except during the sponge activity, but she plays on a youth softball team; you plan to attend one of her upcoming games to observe more fully her interactions with peers.

**Maslow**. Maya is well cared for; she looks well fed and you have noticed that the lunches she brings from home are nutritious. She is always clean and dressed well but not ostentatiously. Her deficiency needs are strongly met: she has no physiological, safety, belongingness and love, or esteem difficulties. Her desire to work by herself in the classroom would suggest a need to know and understand, an example of self-actualization.

**Implications for the teacher**. Maya is one of those students who could easily become the teacher's pet, and the major problem for you as her teacher is to avoid letting this happen. You enjoy her quick mind, her eagerness to learn, her supportive family, and good relationships with both peers and adults. Maya displays a great amount of curiosity and especially enjoys challenges such as math puzzles and experiments in science. More than once her parents have mentioned that Maya has wanted to try at home an experiment completed at school. Maya enthusiastically told you about trying out spraying her mother's perfume atomizer to explore the diffusion of smell in the air and of placing food color in water to see how it diffused. The best advice for a student like Maya is to enjoy her!

## *Case Study 3: Stevie*

### Background

Stevie is a late-admit, five-year-old child at ABC School's child care center. He has difficulty separating from his mother, and the teacher is sensitive to this. As the student teacher in the room, you note that your cooperating teacher frequently kneels by Stevie and directs his attention to the block center, where Hiroku is playing. The teacher has mentioned that having Stevie play by Hiroku might help Stevie adjust more smoothly, as Hiroku is one of the more mature children at the center. The cooperating teacher has asked you to prepare an event sampling of Stevie's play behaviors, to provide additional information about the boy and to help understand his behavior at the center. A *two-dimensional play model*, combining event and time sampling, may be found in Figure 6–15.

In looking at play behavior, two theorists come to mind: Parten (1932) and Piaget (1962). Parten divided play behaviors into the following categories:

◆ *onlooking play* (observing the play of others, without reference to another child)

◆ *solitary play* (play by oneself)

◆ *parallel play* (play in which two or more children may be using similar materials but without personal interaction)

◆ *associative play* (play with objects in which two or more children are using the same materials, but each child is doing a separate activity; for example, each child is using some of the blocks but building separate structures)

◆ *cooperative play* (play in which there is a common goal toward which two or more children are working; for example, the children are using the blocks to build one house)

Piaget suggested that there are three types of play common among preschoolers:

◆ *symbolic play* (play in which the objects with which the child is playing become something else; for example, blocks become a garage or a house)

▶ **Figure 6–15**
Two-dimensional play model, combining event and time sampling.

| Child: Stevie | Symbolic | Practice | Date: 16 September Games |
|---|---|---|---|
| Onlooking: | Watching H. & J. in play-house (9:45 A.M.) | | |
| Solitary: | Pretending to be Superman on jungle gym (10:23 A.M.) | Putting puzzles together (8:35 A.M.) | |
| | | On swg. Trying to pump self (10:40 A.M.) | |
| Parallel: | Bldg rd for car in sandbox (3:20 P.M.) | Dumping $H_2O$ fr 1 container to another at $H_2O$ table (2:57 P.M.) | |
| Associative: | | Bldg towers w/sm blks next to H. (8:30 A.M.) | |
| Cooperative: | Bldg garage w/lrg blks w/H. (8:12 A.M.) | | Following H.'s directions for card game, "War" (2:10 P.M.) |

- *practice play* (play in which the child continuously repeats an activity as though to master it; for example, repeatedly going down a slide)
- *games* (play in which children follow a set of agreed-upon rules)

The resulting observation form, Figure 6–15, shows how the play activities of Stevie may be recorded. To provide more information, the time of each play activity has been noted. In looking at Figure 6–15, you can see that on Parten's dimensions Stevie uses solitary and parallel play more than associative or cooperative. Using Piaget's dimensions, we see that Stevie uses symbolic and practice play more frequently than play with games. For a new child in the center, these behaviors may not be unusual.

## Analysis of Stevie

The question now is whether Stevie has resolved the developmental tasks appropriate for his age. Let's take a look.

**Erikson.** It may be difficult to determine whether the observation of Stevie allows for any hypothesis that he has resolved the Erikson tasks of trust, autonomy, and initiative. Eventually, he does separate from his mother and seems to enjoy the activities. It suggests some resolution of trust, autonomy, and initiative. Further time in the center and additional observations could suggest more.

**Emotional intelligence.** Stevie appears to have some self-awareness and awareness of others. He seems to be able to articulate and modulate his feelings; you have rarely seen him lose his temper or cry, and you have observed him tell Hiroku that he wanted to build a garage for the red truck, not the yellow one Hiroku had chosen. In a compromise, Hiroku suggested that they each build a separate garage for their trucks, and Stevie agreed.

**Maslow.** Because Stevie appears to be well-cared for and is well-dressed, it is easy to assume that his physiological and safety needs have been met. As he becomes more comfortable in the child care center, his belongingness needs will be met easily. His esteem needs may be partially met; it may be difficult to determine at this point in time. Certainly, he will need to have opportunities to self-actualize.

**Implications for the teacher.** As the student teacher in the center, your cooperating teacher may ask you to be a special friend to Stevie. After she greets him each morning, she may ask you to plan an activity with Stevie and another child, Hiroku perhaps initially, adding another child later. Whatever activity is planned, it should be one calculated to stimulate the interests of both. Block play might be a place to start, as you've noticed that both boys enjoy playing and building with them. Later, as Stevie's interests broaden, you can plan something else. In becoming a special friend with Stevie, you may help him feel more a part of the group. And as you introduce him to activities with some of the other children, again, Stevie's needs to belong will be met. As his deficiency needs are met, Stevie will have opportunities to self-actualize.

## THE ROLES OF A STUDENT TEACHER

One role, already defined, is that of an observer. During your first days of placement, you will often be given opportunities to observe. This is an especially valuable time for both the student teacher and the cooperating teacher. Take advantage of this period. Observe several children carefully; confer with your cooperating teacher, supervisor, and peers. It is fascinating to listen to someone else's perceptions of your observations. Often, we become emotionally involved with the children whom we observe; thus, we may receive a different perspective from those who do not know them as well, or who know them better, as might our cooperating teacher. This situation may be reversed. Some cooperating teachers know that their judgments of children may be obscured by the knowledge of the children's backgrounds. A student teacher's judgment, in contrast, may not be affected by this factor.

A second role student teachers frequently play is that of being a friend to a child who, according to your cooperating teacher, needs one. This friendship role may help a newly enrolled child feel more comfortable in the classroom, and may help a shy child become more outgoing.

A third role is obviously to plan activities or lessons and to teach. As do young children, student teachers also learn best by doing.

## ▶ SUMMARY

In this chapter, we have presented several different theories to help you understand children's behaviors, together with suggestions to implement as you work with them. Among theorists mentioned were Erikson, Maslow, Goleman, Mayer, Salovey, and Vygotsky.

In terms of the Erikson tasks, the one most closely related to self-control is autonomy. If resolved during toddlerhood, teachers see a child who knows how to play and work within the prescribed limits of any classroom, who understands both leadership and follower roles, and who knows when to ask for help and when he can do a task by himself. Ideas for teachers to implement in the classroom for children who have incompletely resolved autonomy were also given: allowing choices and reminding children of limits and rules are two.

Maslow believed that self-control evolved out of self-esteem (as do the self-concept theorists) and self-actualization. Thus, everything a teacher can do to build self-esteem and a feeling of belongingness in the classroom, and, again, to allow choices, all will lead to children with good self-control.

Theorists, looking at emotional intelligence, would suggest that self-control grows out of the child's self-awareness and ability to self-modulate feelings. Afterwards, the child develops awareness of others and gains empathy for others.

Finally, we presented you with the case studies of three children, Carlos, Maya, and Stevie, and gave some suggestions, related to the different theories, designed to help you understand their behaviors. Implications for the teacher and your role as a student teacher were also presented.

# ▶ HELPFUL WEBSITES

**http://www.aecf.org**

Annie E. Casey Foundation serves children and families and helps to build supportive communities. They publish *Kids Count* Census Data Online; among the data presented are state profiles of child well-being.

**http://www.nccic.org**

National Child Care Information and Technical Assistance Center (NCCIC). The NCCIC is a service of the Child Care Bureau, and is a clearinghouse that provides comprehensive child care information, lists resources, and offers technical assistance to child care administrators and others.

**http://eric.ed.gov**

This is the main page for ERIC. Go to the Thesaurus and then click on the topic that interests you. Many topics are available, such as Speech and Language and Disabilities. Other topics related to early childhood and elementary education can also be found

here, such as strategies to enhance the achievement of gifted minority children.

**http://ncedl.org**

The National Center for Early Development and Learning is a national research program supported by the US Department of Education's Institute for Educational Sciences (IES) (formerly the Office of Educational Research and Improvement). You can access different topics from their face page; Research, for example, will list current and completed studies. If you click on any one of them, you will be given a summary of the study's purpose, who's directing it, and, if completed, the principal findings.

 Additional resources for this chapter can be found by visiting the companion website at *www.cengage.com/education/machado.*

# ▶ SUGGESTED ACTIVITIES

A.  With your cooperating teacher's approval, select a child to observe. Try some of the observation forms presented. Discuss the results of data gathered with your peers, cooperating teacher, and supervisor.

B.  Read the following Case Study of Maria (see Figure 6–16, an anecdotal observation). Discuss the case with your peers and supervisor.

*Background*: It is the beginning of the school year. As the student teacher, you have just been placed in a bilingual kindergarten at Adelante School. Many parents choose this school because of its attention to providing lessons in both languages. One student intrigues you. Maria arrives each morning accompanied by her mother and a younger sibling in a stroller. She appears to be in good health; her hair is always carefully brushed and she usually wears a bow in her ponytail. Her clothes are always clean. She generally joins in music and art lessons enthusiastically but is reluctant to participate in reading and math activities. You often have had to persuade her to come to the carpeted circle for story time. During recesses she doesn't interact with the other children, choosing instead to go to the swings or stand to one side by herself, watching the others.

What questions come to mind about Maria? Do you think she has resolved the Erikson tasks appropriate for her age? Have her deficiency needs been met (Maslow)? Does she show emotional intelligence

in her behavior, or do you need to observe her more closely? Does she show self-awareness? Has she established any relationship with the cooperating teacher, you, or any of her peers?

(Note: There are no absolute answers to the above questions. They are meant solely to direct your thoughts.)

C.  Critique the following observations in a small group of three or four peers.

1.  The following chart, Figure 6–17, was developed by Dmitri, a student teacher in a preschool classroom for four-year-olds. He was interested in Anthony's attending behavior during the morning activity time. He developed a simple form to check off observations as he noticed them, throughout the 9:30 A.M. to 10:15 A.M. activity hour. On a 3 × 5 card, which he could hold in his hand, Dmitri drew a vertical line, dividing the card in half lengthwise. Then he wrote "Attending" on one side, "Nonattending" on the other. Question: How much attending behavior should a teacher expect of a four-year-old child during a free-choice center activity?

2.  Michaela is a three-and-a-half-year-old attending a morning preschool. Look at the two-dimensional play model, combining event and time sampling, which was used to gather data in Figure 6–18. Questions: Do three-year-olds

do as much onlooking and solitary play as Michaela? Should the teacher be concerned?

3. Adam is a four-year-old at a private child care center. Figure 6–19 is a time sample of his behavior during outside free play. Questions: Is

Adam's poor gross motor coordination something that should concern his teacher? Was there any theorist in this chapter whose theory might explain anything about motor development?

▶ **Figure 6-16**
Anecdotal record on Maria.

| Name of School: _____ | | Student Teacher: _____ Date: _____ | |
|---|---|---|---|
| Identity Key (do NOT use real name) | Description of What Child Is Doing | Time | Comments |
| M. — Maria<br>T. — Teacher<br>ST. — Student Teacher<br>S. — Susie<br>J. — Janine<br>B. — Bobby<br>Sv. — Stevie | M. arrives at school. Clings to mother's hand, hides behind her skirt. Thumb in mouth. | 9:05 | Ask T. how long M. has been coming. I bet she's new. |
| | M. goes over to puzzle rack, chooses a puzzle, goes to table. Dumps out, and works puzzle quickly and quietly. B. & Sv. come over to work puzzles they've chosen. M. looks at them, says nothing, goes to easels, watches S. paint. S. asks M. if she wants to paint. M. doesn't answer. | 9:22<br><br><br>9:30 | Her eye/hand coordination seems good.<br><br>I wonder why M. doesn't respond. Ask T. if M. has hearing problem. |
| | M. comes to snack table, sits down where T. indicates she should. Does not interact with other children at the table. | 10:15 | Is M. ever a quiet child? |
| | M. stands outside of playhouse, watches S. & J. They don't ask her to join them. | 10:47 | She looks like she'd like to play. |
| | M. goes right to swings, knows how to pump. | 10:55 | Nothing wrong with her coordination. |
| | During Hap Palmer record M. watches others, does not follow directions. | 11:17 | Hearing? Maybe limited English? (She looks of Spanish background.) |

▶ **Figure 6-17**
Attending/nonattending chart.

| | | Attending | Nonattending | |
|---|---|---|---|---|
| Mon. | 9:05 | yes (t.i.)* | | |
| | 9:16 | | no | (looking out the windows) |
| | 9:27 | | no | |
| | 9:40 | | no | |
| | 9:48 | yes (t.i.) | | |

(continues)

▶ **Figure 6-17** (continued)

| | | | | |
|---|---|---|---|---|
| Tues. | 9:07 | | no | |
| | 9:18 | | no | |
| | 9:25 | yes (t.i.) | | |
| | 9:34 | yes | | |
| | 9:40 | | no | (looking out windows again) |
| | 9:47 | | no | |
| | 9:55 | | no | |
| Wed. | 9:02 | | no | |
| | 9:12 | yes (t.i.) | | |
| | 9:20 | yes (t.i.) | | |
| | 9:35 | | no | |
| | 9:42 | | no | |
| | 9:58 | | no | |
| Thurs. | 9:05 | | no | |
| | 9:15 | yes (t.i.) | | |
| | 9:33 | yes | | |
| | 9:48 | | no | (staring off into space; eyes closed) |
| | 9:55 | | no | |
| Fri. | Anthony was absent | | | |

*t.i. = teacher initiated

▶ **Figure 6-18**
Observation sample.

| Child: Michaela | | | Date: 17 Nov. |
|---|---|---|---|
| | Symbolic | Practice | Games |
| Onlooking: | Watches three girls in playhouse, when asked to join, shakes head no. (9:35 A.M.)<br><br>Watches M. & A. at easels. T. asks, "Do you want to paint, M.?" "No." (11:05 A.M.) | Watches children go up & down slide. (10:22 A.M.)<br><br>Watches children in sandbox, filling cups & pails over & over. (10:35 A.M.)<br><br>Watches children on swing. (10:45 A.M.) | |
| Solitary: | "See my cracker? It's a plane!" Zooms cracker thru air; makes plane sounds. (10:03 A.M.) | Sits on swing while teacher's aide pushes. (10:50 A.M.) | |
| Parallel: | Picks up egg beater at H$_2$O table. Beats H$_2$O. Says, "I'm making eggs for breakfast." (11:12 A.M.) | Picks up paintbrush at easel; lets paint drip. Picks up next brush. Repeats with remaining brushes. (11:35 A.M.) | |

▶ **Figure 6–19**
Observation time sample.

|  |  |
|---|---|
| 10:05 a.m.: | A. runs stiffly toward two of his friends on tricycles. "Let me ride!" he shouts. |
| 10:10 a.m.: | A. is happily riding on the back of E.'s tricycle. E. has to stop to let A. climb on. A. first placed his left foot on, lifted it off, placed the same foot on again, took it off; finally he put his right foot on and then successfully put his left foot on. |
| 10:15 a.m.: | A. is still riding on the back of E.'s tricycle. |
| 10:20 a.m.: | A. and E. have switched places. A. had difficulty pedaling up the slight grade. E. pushed from behind. |
| 10:25 a.m.: | E. has suggested that he, A., and S. go to the workbench. A. picks up the hammer and a nail. He hits the nail awkwardly into a block of wood. E. says, "Hey, watch me! Hold the nail like this!" |
| 10:30 a.m.: | E. is holding A.'s hands with his, showing him how to drive the nail into the block of wood. |
| 10:35 a.m.: | A. is sitting in the sandbox, shoveling sand into a bucket. E. is still at the work bench. |
| 10:40 a.m.: | A. is putting sand into another bucket. He looks surprised when the bucket overflows. He reaches for the first bucket. S. says, "I'm using it now," and pushes a third pail toward A. |
| 10:45 a.m.: | A. and S. are smoothing down the sand, calling it a road. They go and get a couple of cars to run on their road. E. joins them, having completed his project at the workbench. |
| 10:50 a.m.: | When called to clean up for activity time, A. climbs out of the sandbox. As he does this, his foot catches on the edge and he falls down. He gives the sandbox a kick and joins the others to come inside. |

# ▶ REVIEW

**A.** According to Erikson, what are the first four stages of psychosocial development? What are the tasks associated with each?

**B.** Read the following description of behavior and answer the questions at the end.

Cindy, an only child, is a small, assertive three-and-a-half-year-old attending your child center for the first time. Her family recently moved to your community. Her mother and father are both teachers in local school districts. Her mother reported that Cindy's birth was normal, and she has had no major health problems. Coming to your child center will be her first experience with children her own age, except for religious instruction school.

Cindy appears to like child care very much. She is a dominant child despite her small size, and rapidly becomes one of the leaders. She plays with just about all of the toys and materials supplied at the center. Her favorite activities, however, appear to be the dramatic-play center and easel painting when inside, and either the sandbox or swings when outside. She occasionally gets into arguments with her peers when they no longer accept her leadership. Cindy has difficulty resolving these conflicts and frequently has a tantrum when she is unable to have her own way.

1. Would you suggest that Cindy has basic trust? What evidence suggests this?
2. Do you think Cindy has resolved the task of autonomy? What evidence suggests that?
3. Erikson would suggest that Cindy's task at age three-and-a-half is to learn to use initiative. What evidence is there in the brief description of her behavior that suggests she is going through this phase of development in a positive or negative way?
4. Using Maslow's hierarchy of needs, at which level would you place Cindy? Why?

**C.** List five characteristics of an autonomous, six-year-old child with positive self-esteem.

## ▶ REFERENCES

Banks, J. A. (2002). *Teaching strategies for ethnic studies* (7th ed..). Boston: Allyn & Bacon.

Berger, E. H. (2008). *Parents as partners in education: The school and home working together* (7th ed.). Upper Saddle River, NJ: Pearson/Merrill/Prentice Hall.

Breslin, D. (2005). Children's capacity to develop resiliency: How to nurture it. *Young Children, 60*(1), 47–52.

Butterfield, P., Martin, C. A., & Prairie, A. P. (2004). *Emotional connections: how relationships guide early learning.* Washington, DC: Zero to Three Press.

Copple, C., & Bredekamp, S. (Eds.). (2009). *Developmentally appropriate practice in early childhood programs serving children from birth through age 8.* Washington, DC: National Association for the Education of Young Children.

Coopersmith, S. (1967). *The antecedents of self-esteem.* New York: W. H. Freeman.

Elias M. J., Zins, J. E., Weissberg, R. P., Frey, K. S., Greenberg, M. T., Haynes, N. M., Kessler, R., Schwab-Stone, M. E., & Shriver, T. P. (1997). *Promoting social and emotional learning: Guidelines for educators.* Alexandria, VA: Association for Supervision and Curriculum Development.

Epstein, A. S. (2009). *Me, you, us: Social-emotional learning in preschool.* Ypsilanti, MI: High Scope Press; Washington, DC: National Association for the Education of Young Children.

Erikson, E. H. (1993). *Childhood and society* (reprint of 2nd ed.). New York: Norton.

Figueroa-Sanchez, M. (Annual Theme, 2008). Building emotional literacy: Groundwork to early learning. *Childhood Education, 84*(5), 301–304.

Gillespie, L. G., & Seibel, N. L. (2006). Self-regulation: A cornerstone of early childhood development. *Young Children, 61*(4), 34–39.

Goleman, D. (1995, 1997). *Emotional intelligence: Why it can matter more than IQ.* New York: Bantam Books.

Goleman, D. (2006). *Social intelligence: The new science of human relationships.* NY: Random House.

Gonzalez-Mena, J. (2005) *Foundations: Early childhood education in a diverse society* (3rd ed.), Mountain View, CA: Mayfield Publishing.

Hyson, M. (2002, November). Emotional development and school readiness. *Young Children, 57*(6), 76–78.

Hyson, M. (2004). *The emotional development of the young child: Building an emotion-centered curriculum.* New York: Teachers' College, Columbia University.

Maslow, A. H. (1968). *Toward a psychology of being* (2nd ed.). Princeton, NJ: Van Nostrand Reinhold.

Mayer, J., & Salovey, P. (1995). Emotional intelligence and the construction and regulation of feelings. *Applied and Preventive Psychology, 4*(2).

Parten, M. B. (1932). Social participation among pre-school children. *Journal of Abnormal and Social Psychology, 27*(3), 243–269.

Piaget, J. (1962). *Play, dreams, and imitation in childhood.* New York: W. W. Norton.

Werner, E., & Smith, R. S. (1992). *Overcoming the odds.* New York: Cornell University Press.

# CHAPTER 7

# Working with Children with Special Needs

**OBJECTIVES**

After reading this chapter, you should be able to:

1. List at least five characteristics of *special* children.
2. Discuss the concept of inclusion (least restrictive environment).
3. Discuss how inclusion has impacted early childhood programs.

## STUDENT TEACHER SCENARIO

**Setting:** A first-grade classroom in a public school.

Matt is the newly assigned student teacher. Mrs. Levinson is his cooperating teacher, and Dr. Canalas, the university supervisor. After Matt's first week in the room, Dr. Canalas and Mrs. Levinson meet after school with him.

"Well, Matt, how do you like the class?" asks Mrs. Levinson.

Matt answers, "The children sure are little! And what is happening with Carl? He's constantly moving: tapping his foot, rapping his fingers, sharpening his pencil, asking to go to the boy's room. I've noticed he has difficulty writing; his handwriting is almost illegible, and he moves awkwardly at recess."

"You've observed some of the same behaviors we have," Mrs. Levinson states. "Dr. Canalas, what have you noticed? You've only come once, but I know you're pretty observant. Any hypotheses?"

"I'd like Matt to tell us what he thinks might be behind Carl's behavior. Matt, what hypotheses come to you?" Dr. Canalas turns toward Matt.

"Well, I've only been here a week but I can't help but think Carl might be hyperactive. In fact, could he be AD/HD? Then again, could he be somewhat slow intellectually? I don't think he has a problem hearing, but I'd want that checked, too. Do you think I'm on the right track?" Matt asks.

## Questions for Discussion:

1. Does Matt seem to understand what might be causing Carl's behavior in the classroom?

2. What are some of the symptoms of a child who has AD/HD?

3. Are there other background factors that might cause the same observed behavior displayed by Carl?

4. In a week's time, does a student teacher really have the time to observe an individual child sufficiently? What might you say to your cooperating teacher and college supervisor if you were put in Matt's situation?

# LAWS RELATING TO THE EDUCATION OF YOUNG CHILDREN WITH SPECIAL NEEDS

We know that most of you think all children are special; so do we. However, it is important to recognize that some children have needs beyond those of the average child; some have needs that can be met only by a team of specialists, working together for the welfare of the children. To meet the needs of special children, the federal government has passed several laws related to people with special needs (see Figure 7–1). Although the first law was passed over 40 years ago (PL 89–313, 1965), the primary law that currently defines how preschools, child care centers, and public schools are to serve special needs children is PL 101–476 and its subsequent amendments.

▶ **Figure 7–1**
Public laws related to special education for young children.

| PL 89–313 | (1965) | Provided federal funds to establish early intervention programs for "children with disabilities," birth to age five. (Voluntary.) |
|---|---|---|
| PL 90–538 | (1968) | Established the Handicapped Children's Early Education Program (HCEEP), now the Early Education Program for Children with Disabilities (EEPCD). (Voluntary initially.) |
| PL 91–230 | (1969) | Provided funds to states for the education of "young children with disabilities." (Voluntary.) |
| PL 93–644 | (1974) | Amended Head Start legislation and required that 10 percent of children served must be those with disabilities. |
| PL 94–142 | (1975) | The Education for All Handicapped Children Act; discussed in detail in this chapter. |
| PL 98–199 | (1983) | Provided grants to states to plan, develop, and implement a service delivery system for handicapped children, birth through age five. (Mandatory for states receiving federal funds.) |
| PL 99–457 | (1986) | Again provided funds to states to plan services for children, birth through age five, as a condition to receiving further federal funds. (Essentially, then, became mandatory.) Also discussed in this chapter. |
| PL 101–336 | (1990) | Americans with Disabilities Act: Required that individuals with disabilities, including children, have equal access to public and private services. |
| PL 101–476 | (1990) | The Individuals with Disabilities Act (IDEA); discussed in this chapter.* |
| PL 102–119 | (1991) | Allowed states up to two years to implement PL 101-476 (IDEA), because of differences between fiscal years of some states and federal government. |

*This act has been evaluated and refunded. The act (IDEA) has emphasized the inclusion of children with special needs (Lewis & Doorlag, 2006).

# Individuals with Disabilities Act, PL 101–476

The key provisions of this law are:

- ◆ Free and appropriate public education must be made available for all children with special needs (included are special education and related services, the use of the term "children with disabilities," and the stipulation of age restrictions of 3 to 21 years; states with programs for children from birth to age three are also covered).

- ◆ Each child identified as needing special education or related services must have an **Individual Education Program (IEP)** written by the multidisciplinary team working with the child and with the parents' approval. For children under three, and in recognition of the importance of the family, each identified child must have an **Individual Family Services Plan (IFSP)**.

- ◆ Parents are to be involved at every step in the process, from identification, assessment, and educational placement, to evaluation of that placement. Furthermore, parents must agree to the assessment procedures used to identify the need for services, and must approve the IEP, and the evaluation.

- ◆ Each child is to be placed in the **least restrictive environment (LRE)** (see Figures 7–2, 7–3, and 7–4).

- ◆ Due process is guaranteed for every child and family. The parents have the right to sue a district if they feel that the best interests of their child are not being met.

- ◆ Any assessment of a child must be done with instruments that are nondiscriminatory in terms of race and ethnicity. Assessment must also be in the child's dominant language or in the child's preferred mode of communication (sign language, for example).

- ◆ All children and youth between the ages of 3 and 21 (under IDEA) receive the same free services as those guaranteed in the earlier law (PL 94–142).

- ◆ State grants for infant and toddler programs are also funded, so that states may develop comprehensive, coordinated, multidisciplinary, interagency programs. With infants and toddlers an IFSP is prepared and monitored.

**Individual Education Program (IEP)**—with children with special needs, an individual education program states the short-term and long-term learning objectives, how they will be accomplished and by whom, and provides the applicable dates. It must be approved by both parents and school.

**Individual Family Services Plan (IFSP)**—required initially by the 1986 Education of the Handicapped Act Amendments and reaffirmed by IDEA; the IFSP is often developed by a transdisciplinary team that includes the family, any needed specialists, such as a physical therapist, a language therapist, an educator, who cooperatively determine goals and objectives that build on the strengths of the child and family.

**least restrictive environment (LRE)**—a provision of Public Law 101–476 that children with disabilities be placed in a program as close as possible to a setting designed for children without disabilities, while being able to meet each child's special needs.

▶ **Figure 7-2**

The "least restrictive environment" may be having the child sit in a special chair . . .

▶ **Figure 7-3**

. . . or it may be having the physical therapist position the child's head while the child uses his arms . . .

. . . or it may be letting the child roll free on a mat.

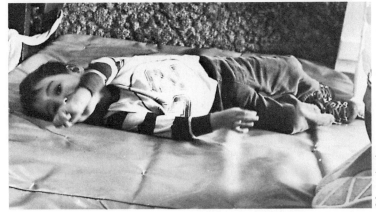

Recognizing the difficulty of being able to pinpoint specific diagnoses with the very young, under IDEA a child does not have to be specifically labeled to receive services. Recent amendments to PL 101–476 have added as special needs categories: children with persuasive developmental disorders, including autism spectrum disorder, and children with traumatic brain injuries. Three additional services are also included: rehabilitation counseling, social work services, and spoken descriptions of on-screen video productions (through descriptive video service (DVS), provided over the second of two audio channels on stereo television sets). Subsequent reauthorizations in PL 105–17 (IDEA '97) and PL 108–446 (Individuals with Disabilities Education Improvement Act of 2004) placed a major focus on maximizing student participation in the general education curriculum (Lewis & Doorlag, 2006).

Both the "special" and "typical" child profit from association with each other. One private preschool has long had a policy to integrate special and typical children. The director allows four, identified special children in a class of 24. In the 40 years since this policy was put into effect, the school has enrolled cognitively impaired children, children with orthopedic problems, a blind child as well as a few who were partially sighted, and a hard-of-hearing child, together with several children with behavior disorders and those with speech and health difficulties. With family permission, other children have learned to help the special children with bathroom visits and other activities, and both children have benefited.

## Implications of Special Education Laws

The major shift mentioned above in providing services in the general education curriculum is better known as **inclusion**. Inclusion has led to having various kinds of children with special needs, even those with severe disabilities, included in regular classrooms, both at the preschool and public school level. What it means for you, as a student teacher, is that you may be asked by your cooperating teacher to work with a child with special needs.

**inclusion**—a term that has widely replaced the term "mainstreaming" that emphasizes placement of the child with special needs in the regular classroom with, perhaps, greater assistance from special education services.

## Student Teaching with Children with Special Needs

Student teachers in 2-year degree or other shorter training programs may feel inadequate, because few of their academic classes go into any depth or detail on teaching strategies, goals, specific disabilities, program modifications, and so forth, to prepare them to work with children with special needs. Because many states now require a class on working with children with special needs for certification or licensing, baccalaureate-level student teachers may have encountered at least one specific special education course. Whether this one course sufficiently prepares student teachers for the complexities they may encounter with a special needs student varies.

An understanding of the positive aspects of including young children with special needs in regular classrooms helps (see Figure 7–5).

Advocates of inclusion usually cite the following benefits:

◆ All attending children, both those with and those without disabilities, make gains.

◆ Social and play skills of children with disabilities grow and develop.

◆ Children's sensitivity to and acceptance of disabled peers results.

The higher the quality of the child development program, the more likely individualized intervention occurs. Severe disabilities require intensive, professional support systems.

What is a student teacher to do? First, accept the disabilities you find. They may range from mild to moderate to severe. Become a team player in helping each child reach his or her potential. Know that your cooperating teacher may have already:

◆ assessed the classroom environment and staff requirements

◆ developed a routine or schedule for each identified child with special needs

◆ developed individual learning objectives and plans

◆ made curriculum modifications or adaptations to enhance child participation, which may include special equipment, room arrangement, classroom materials, activity simplification, peer mentoring, or other adjustments, giving attention to child preferences and needs

◆ assessed individual children's progress

Most cooperating teachers will expect student teachers to be instrumental in helping them both observe children with special needs and work toward helping the children reach the goals of their IFSP or IEP. Student teachers also must be made aware of any individual adaptations that may be necessary, as well as the teaching team's efforts.

Ask for specifics on each child if you have questions. Be alert and inquisitive about child behaviors or teaching practices you may find questionable. Teacher behaviors that might seem unfeeling might instead, on asking for explanations, be planned to encourage independence and self-help skills.

Using book or Internet resources will increase your knowledge of specific disabilities to discover resources for families and teachers. A second list of websites is found at the end of this chapter. Most communities have local, state, and federal agencies, school districts, and other entities that have been created to help children with special needs, and their families. Investigate. The administrator or director of the school where you are student teaching is responsible, after considerable collaboration with the teaching team and family, to make child or family referrals if necessary.

▶ **Figure 7–5**

This child is attending an inclusive classroom with the aid of her walker.

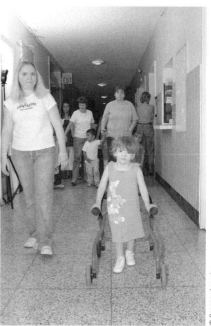

© Cengage Learning

## CHILDREN WITH SPECIAL NEEDS

"Special children" are as different from each other as are typical children, but not all children with special needs are easily recognizable (see Figure 7–6). There are signs that can help you identify a special child. Does Johnny hold his head to one side constantly? Does he squint? (He may need glasses.) Does he ignore directions, unless you are close to him and facing him? Is his speech unclear? Does he have frequent bouts of middle ear infections? (He may have a hearing problem.)

Is Sally not learning to talk at the same rate as her peers? (She may have a language delay problem.) Is she still using baby talk when most of her peers have outgrown it? (She may have a speech problem.) Is she frequently out of breath? Does she sneeze often? (She may have an allergy that should be properly diagnosed by a doctor.)

▶**Figure 7-6**
Not all children with special needs are easily recognizable.

Fortunately, most health problems are diagnosed by family doctors. Children taking medication often have to be observed, to ascertain if the dosage is appropriate; doctors often must know if a child's behavior changes in any way, such as with increasing drowsiness or irritability. It is probable that the cooperating teacher or a school nurse, if there is one, would monitor medication reactions. However, your cooperating teacher might ask you to help her monitor the child's behavior if she is taking medication.

Is the child extremely aggressive or withdrawn? (He may have a behavior disorder.) Is the child extremely active? Does he have a short attention span? Is he easily distracted? Does he have problems with cause-and-effect relationships? Does he have difficulty putting thoughts into words? (He may have a learning disability.)

Is the child much slower than her peers in talking and completing cognitive work, such as classifying objects? (She may be cognitively impaired.) Does the child have difficulty with social relationships? Does he have problems looking you in the eye when you talk with him? (He may have Asperger's syndrome, a form of autism.) It is important to note that these characteristics are only indications of a problem, not solid evidence that the problem does exist. Only a qualified person can make the actual determination.

In your child care center, do you have a child talking in sentences, at age two or two-and-a-half? Is this child larger and taller than other children of the same age? Does this child enjoy excellent health? Does he already know the names of the primary and secondary colors? Does the child already know the letters in his name? Does this child see relationships between seemingly unrelated objects? This child may be special in the sense of being gifted or talented.

## Working with the Special Child in Inclusive Settings

There are few concepts that have been as misunderstood as inclusion. Nowhere in any special needs law does the word appear. As mentioned before, PL 101–476 refers only to LRE. However, the LRE phrase does state that the focus is on maximizing the student's participation in the general education curriculum (Batshaw, Pellegrino, & Roizen, 2008).

As Grisham-Brown, Hemmeter, and Pretti-Frontczak (2005) state, inclusive settings are those settings that are designed to address the needs of children who are developing normally, children who are at risk, and children with disabilities. The range of inclusive programs includes child care programs, public school, preschool, and school-age programs, Head Start, and other center-based programs.

What does this mean for you as a student teacher? Can children with special needs be integrated smoothly, all day, into regular programs? Does the mandate mean that you will have to work with disruptive children in a regular classroom (preschool or elementary) or a child care center? If, after you finish your teacher training, you decide to open your own family child care home or preschool, will you have to enroll children with special needs? According to a question and answer bulletin from the U.S. Department of Justice, Civil Rights division, Disability Rights section (October 1997), the answer, clearly, is "yes."

Whether you realize it or not, many preschools and child care centers always have had children with special needs, especially those with less obvious disabilities. Many preschool and primary age children do not have obvious special needs and are enrolled before any diagnosis is completed. Typically, children with less severe disabilities, or those with "hidden" disabilities, are frequently diagnosed in preschool and elementary school. You yourself may have had a vision impairment, mild to moderate hearing loss, a learning disability, scoliosis (spinal curvature), or **attention deficit disorder (ADD)** diagnosed in elementary school. Also, children of all ages experience bouts of depression that go undiagnosed.

The implications for teachers and caregivers of young children involve, first of all, the need for collaboration. As Mastropieri and Scruggs (2007) suggest, families, caregivers, and teachers all need to be involved. Existing routines, in both at-home and out-of-home settings, need to be considered, as must the goals in each setting. For the greatest chance of success, all adults in the child's life should plan together for the ultimate good of the child. Building positive, collaborative relationships among team members (families, regular and special education teachers, and other specialists) "can substantially improve the school and life functioning of students with disabilities" (Mastropieri & Scruggs, 2007).

In agreement, Lewis and Doorlag (2006) propose that teachers look at their instructional methods to see how these might be adjusted to meet the needs of special students. Furthermore, they suggest that the children themselves be involved in any implementation of integration (they use the concept of a "friends helping friends" approach). Lewis and Doorlag also state that inclusion must be planned carefully, and that teachers need to model appropriate behavior. In addition, any appropriate behaviors, such as positive interaction between children with special needs and other children, should be encouraged and praised. Finally, cooperative learning activities have proven to be most successful in integration. Turnbull, Turnbull, and Wehmeyer (2007) caution, however, that successful inclusion requires support from administration and support personnel as well as from the families of the children with special needs.

The research on inclusion does not describe the quality of inclusive practices, nor does it allow for the amount of time spent in inclusive settings, or the extent to which students from culturally and linguistically diverse backgrounds receive appropriate respect, support, and accommodations (Turnbull, Turnbull, & Wehmeyer, 2007).

If you have the opportunity to work and teach in an inclusive setting, you may also find it a fulfilling experience and, in the process, learn more about yourself.

In general, working with the special child is not much different than working with the typical child. Your cooperating teacher will, in most instances, give you clues for teaching a special child.

## Children with Speech Impairments

The child with a speech or language impairment may need one-to-one tutoring (see Figure 7–7). Two early indications of hearing impairment are lack of language skills and unclear speech. If you suspect a child has a hearing loss, you should discuss your perceptions with your cooperating teacher. She may suggest to the family that the hearing be checked. If the child is experiencing language delay, it

**attention deficit disorder (ADD)**—a disorder that causes children to have difficulty sustaining attention in the classroom and concentrating on an assigned task for any length of time.

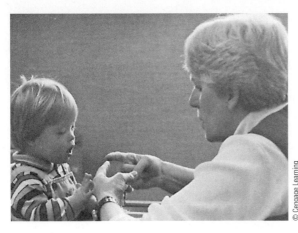

▶ **Figure 7-7**

It is common to work one to one with a child with special needs.

may be because the family has not spent much time talking to the child. Indeed, some children speak in what sounds like television language. Typically, the child will use words verbatim from his preferred television program. For example, he might talk like his favorite action figure or mimic Bart Simpson. You should provide these children with opportunities to use verbal language. You may need to name objects for them and provide them with descriptive adjectives. You may engage in a variety of language activities with these children, such as feelie-box games and guessing games in which they use descriptive language.

## Children with Cognitive Impairment

The child with cognitive impairment may need no special attention beyond your being attuned to activities that may prove frustrating to the child. Your teacher may ask you to assist the child in activities known to be more difficult. For example, during a finger play, you may be asked to hold the child on your lap and to manipulate the child's fingers. The child with cognitive impairment might also need some extra help with language; slow language development is often characteristic.

Children with mild cognitive impairment often integrate well into the preschool setting. They frequently have good social development, and their physical development may appear normal. Their language may be simpler than that of peers, but they often make their needs known through gestures and body language. They may not be able to do some of the cognitive tasks well, but they can derive as much pleasure from painting, role-playing, and playing with clay, blocks, and trucks as any other child. Knowing that this child is less able cognitively than some of the other children, you can work with activities the child *can* do successfully, and reduce the amount of stress associated with goals set too high.

## Children with Orthopedic or Health Disabilities

There are many different types of physical disabilities and health problems. In working with children who have orthopedic or health disabilities, the only difficulty you may encounter is whether your setting is wheelchair accessible, and whether you need to be more attentive to health problems on days when air quality is poor. Asthma and allergies are the most common health problems for young children, and affected children are more sensitive to smog and seasonal pollens.

Your cooperating teacher may want you to help a child in a wheelchair go to the bathroom, or may ask you to assist a child with leg braces as he sits at, or rises from, a table or the floor.

Some other specific strategies include:

◆ acquainting yourself with any special equipment needed by the child

◆ being alert to medication the child may be taking

◆ remembering to tell your cooperating teacher about any changes you may have noticed in the child's behavior that may have been missed

◆ being aware of the fact that a chronically ill child may be absent frequently, and that close contact must be kept among families, the school, and specialists

## Children Who Are Deaf and Hard-of-Hearing

Children who are hearing-impaired may wear hearing aids or, if profoundly deaf, may use sign language. Another child may even wear cochlear implants. These children will vary in their competencies just as typical children do. Their language may be somewhat delayed, and your cooperating teacher may ask you to work with them on language games. You are not expected to learn sign, but you may find it helpful to learn a few simple signs from the sign language specialist or classroom assistant.

Strategies for working with a child who is hearing-impaired include:

◆ speaking directly to him using normal, well-articulated speech and normal gestures

◆ seating the child where she can see you if you are reading a story, doing a finger play, or some other verbal activity

◆ encouraging others to include the hearing-impaired child in their activities

◆ encouraging the other children to follow your examples above

◆ being alert to the need for your cooperating teacher to change the batteries in a child's hearing aid if the child seems confused, is rubbing her ears, or uses any other signal to indicate she is not hearing (your cooperating teacher or the specialist may show you how to do this, to save her attention and time)

In one case with which your author has familiarity that involves a child who was hard of hearing, all of the children learned sign language to better communicate with the child. In fact, the children learned sign language faster than the teacher.

## Children Who Are Blind and Partially Sighted

As with deaf and hard-of-hearing children, those with visual problems vary widely in their abilities. Children so affected have often been in regular classrooms for years.

The following strategies can be employed with such children:

◆ Be alert to the child who may not see well, who may be holding books close to his face, placing his head close to the picture he is drawing, or complaining of headaches or nausea after trying to concentrate on a visual work activity (see Figure 7–8).

◆ Remember that the partially sighted or blind child needs to have a room where furniture and equipment are kept in predictable arrangements. If you bring in a newly designed activity center, be sure to orient the visually impaired child to its placement and use.

◆ Set the television to a channel that provides a verbal description of what is happening for viewers with visual limitations.

Commercial and public television programs are sometimes closed-captioned (CC) for the hearing impaired, or may employ DVS for the blind and partially sighted. Your school may also have a special computerized television that enlarges the page of any book and provides either black print on a white background or the reverse, white print on black. The child chooses the degree of enlargement and the print and background that works best for her.

## Children with Behavior Disorders

There is probably no area more controversial than behavioral difficulties affecting children. Many teachers may think a child is emotionally disturbed but do not know how to approach the family. The term "behavior disorders" is now commonly used to indicate children who have problems with behavior but who may not, in terms of a psychiatric definition, be truly "emotionally disturbed."

Often, when you see a young child with behavior problems, you may see a family with problems. The

▶ **Figure 7-8**
If this boy consistently holds his head this close to the pages of books, he may need to wear glasses.

© Cengage Learning

term "dysfunctional" is sometimes used to describe families with problems (substance abuse, poverty, homelessness, for example) that affect their children. To many families, even the suggestion of a behavior problem with their child brings about a defensive reaction, such as "Are you telling me I'm a bad parent? That I don't know how to raise my own child?" Teachers and administrators attempt to avoid value-laden terms that may arouse a defensive reaction in families. Instead, they will substitute terminology such as "acts out," "has no friends," "daydreams," "fights," or "tries to hide in the back of the room." We have to understand how difficult it is for families to accept the possibility that something may be "wrong" with their child. If the family has no idea that their child is not perfectly normal, it becomes extremely difficult to convince them that there may be a problem.

Facing the possibility that their child may not be perfect, some families actually grieve for the lost image of what their child was to have been. They grieve much the same as they would if the child had died. They become angry and often accuse teachers of prejudice and of not really knowing their child. Some families verbally attack teacher skills and any suggested diagnosis; others deny that anything is wrong. Most go through a phase in which they blame themselves for causing the child's problems.

The child with a behavior disorder may or may not present a problem in the classroom. In one example, a child with a (depressive) behavior disorder was placed in a regular preschool. The children quickly learned to tolerate his temper tantrums and screaming. To a visiting stranger, they would explain, "Don't worry about George. He just needs to be alone now." In many ways, the children were more tolerant than some of the adults.

Certainly, the child who shows aggression presents a challenge and must be watched closely. For this reason, it is not uncommon for the teacher to assign an assistant or student teacher to work on a one-to-one basis with the child to try to control the child's outbursts. Some good techniques are holding the child on your lap, allowing the child to hit a heavy chair cushion instead of another child or adult, removing a child to the back of a classroom or "benching" them on the playground, allowing the child to punch clay or pound nails into scrap wood instead of hurting others, having the child bite on a leather strap or chew a wad of sugarless bubblegum instead of biting, or having the child run around the playground when it might serve to calm him. Remember that behavior modification works well with children who have behavior disorders.

Be aware that as the withdrawn, depressed child becomes better, he is likely to become aggressive. This is known as the **pendulum effect**. When a depressed child reaches this stage and begins to act out, some families become angry and fearful and stop therapy. They may not understand that it takes time for a child to learn how to deal with anger in socially acceptable ways. We can reassure the family that this phase is normal. Whatever technique is used, you may be asked to remain with the child for safety purposes. At the same time, you can acknowledge the child's anger, and suggest better ways to channel his energy.

Burgess and Younger (2006) looked at the self-perceptions of students in middle school with behavior disorders. They found that in comparison to a control group of typical students, shy and withdrawn students tended to internalize problems and chose more negative than positive self-descriptors. Aggressive students tended to externalize problems, but differences were not significant. For teachers of younger children, the findings suggest that attempts should be made to integrate shy and withdrawn students into classroom activities and to build their self-confidence whenever possible.

## Children with Learning Disabilities

The child suspected of having learning disabilities presents a challenge. Although some families are willing to accept a diagnosis of possible learning disabilities, others are not. What is a **learning disability**? According to PL 94–142, and reaffirmed by PL 101–476, a "specific learning disability" means a disorder in one or more of

**pendulum effect**—a phenomenon observed especially with children in therapy for the treatment of depressive disorders. Children swing from non-expression of emotions to explosive outbreaks.

**learning disability**—a condition thought to be associated with neurological dysfunction and characterized by difficulty in mastering a skill such as reading or numerical calculation.

the basic psychological processes involved in understanding or in using language, spoken or written, which may manifest itself in an imperfect ability to listen, think, speak, read, write, spell, or do mathematical calculations (Federal Register, 1977).

School districts commonly define learning disabilities in terms of a child's actual achievement in relation to the achievement of his age peers. The unfortunate result of this practice has been postponing the identification of a problem until the achievement is 2 or more years behind, a practice that has meant, in too many cases, 3 and even 4 years of failure for the child. The damage to the child's self-esteem can be almost irreparable.

Another commonly used definition is that a learning disability is reflected as a significant discrepancy between the child's potential ability and her actual achievement in learning to read, write, or figure. The curriculum areas of reading, language arts, and mathematics are most typically involved.

Does this mean that a preschooler does not have a learning disability? Many preschool teachers, families, and educational psychologists who are capable diagnosticians would disagree.

What are some of the characteristics you might see in a preschooler that could signal the possibility of a learning disability? Typically, you see a child who appears immature; who frequently has difficulties with language, both receptive and expressive; who acts impulsively; and who may seem to be "hyperactive." (Be careful about calling a child hyperactive; be aware that high energy is not necessarily hyperactivity.)

Ask yourself the following questions:

◆ Does the child in your preschool have difficulty using language?

◆ Does he use unreferenced pronouns because he can't remember an object's name?

◆ Is this the child who cannot think of more than one word to describe an object in a feelie box, or repeats a word a playmate has just used, instead of coming up with her own?

◆ Does this child display poor coordination for her age?

◆ Does he dislike changes in the routines of the preschool?

◆ Does the four-year-old child prefer interacting with the three-year-olds more than with children her own age?

◆ Do you have to constantly remind the child of the rules?

None of these characteristics by itself would be symptomatic of a possible learning disability; taken together, and being seen daily, they might be cause for suggesting a more formal evaluation by a qualified expert in learning disabilities. In the meantime, the child's family may ask your cooperating teacher to arrange for some one-to-one learning for their child. In turn, the cooperating teacher may ask them to attend a conference, involving everyone who works with the child, to develop an individual learning plan that will involve them all (see Figure 7–9). (See the Appendix for checklists that can be used to determine modality strengths and weaknesses.)

## Dyslexia

Many children with a specific learning disability have a condition known as dyslexia, a problem "manifested by difficulty in learning to read, write, or spell, despite conventional instruction, adequate intelligence, and socio-cultural opportunity" (Orton Dyslexia Society, 1988). As a student teacher in an elementary school, you may be asked to work one-to-one with a dyslexic student, to allow the student extra time to finish a written assignment, or to have the student present an oral report instead of a written one. You may be asked to write a story the student dictates. Allowing the student to record his responses to test questions is another possibility.

*Student Teacher Quote*—"I was asked to work with one of the children who had a learning disability. I really got involved in what was happening in the child's home. I became interested in the child's life."

**Deanna Miller, First-Grade Classroom, San Lorenzo Unified School District, CA**

▷ **Figure 7-9**
Part of an individual family services plan.

SCHOOL: ABC Preschool        STUDENT'S NAME: Tommy        C.A.: 43        DATE: 14 Oct

LONG-RANGE GOAL: Tommy will expand his vocabulary both at school and at home.

FUNCTIONAL DESCRIPTION OF THE PROBLEM: Tommy speaks in telegraphic sentences; his language is frequently unintelligible, which has led to interpersonal problems with peers. Assessments by School District DEF show that Tommy is developmentally normal on all criteria except language. His pediatrician's report shows no difficulty with hearing but a severe case of pneumonia when Tommy was 8 mo., followed by a relapse at 9 mo. Tommy's mother admits overprotecting him and worrying about his frequent bouts with upper respiratory infections. Tommy's attention span appears short relative to peers at ABC Preschool.

BEHAVIORAL STRENGTHS: Tommy is agile and well coordinated.

| SHORT-TERM OBJECTIVES | INTERVENTION ACTIVITIES AND MATERIALS | PERSON(S) RESPONSIBLE |
|---|---|---|
| (Section 3153, Title V Regulations) (Specify time, specific behavior, evaluation conditions & criteria) | | |
| 1. Tommy will use 3–4 word sentences when talking in the classroom. (6 mo.) | ST or aide will model speaking in complete sentences & ask child to repeat model; "Feelie Box" will be used on 1:1 | Teacher, with assistance of ST or aide |
| 4. Tommy will retell stories using complete sentences of 3–4 words. (8 mo.) | Mother or father will read to boy each evening before bed, model complete sentence construction & have him repeat or construct his own sentences | Parents |
| 6. Tommy will practice using sentences under guidance of District DEF's speech therapist. Word lotto games, etc., will also be used. (6 mo.) | Peabody Early Experiences Kit | Speech & language therapist |
| 9. Mr. & Mrs. Fabian will be offered an opportunity to participate in LDA (Learning Disabilities Association) support group & to receive counseling. (on-going) | District DEF psychologist gives parents information regarding County LDA support group; may ask LDA to call parents | DEF School Dist. psychologist |

CRITERION MEASURE without modeling or prompting. Tommy will be speaking in 3–4 word complete sentences.

Reviewed: _____

_____
Speech Therapist

_____
Teacher

Revision(s) Recommended:

_____
School Psychologist

_____
Date: _____

(Parent 1)                    (Parent 2)

Interventions used by Wadlington, Jacob, and Bailey (1996) involve helping dyslexic students with organizational and study skills, which, of course, are of value to all the students. They also advocate using a multisensory approach to reading tasks, providing books on audiotape or CD for students to use, together with the standard readers. In spelling, they concentrate on having students learn words that are phonetically regular before introducing any that are not. They accept handwriting that is not perfect, as long as it is legible, and encourage the use of computer word-processing programs. Extra time is allowed for all language arts activities and for test-taking. Children might be encouraged to record test responses on tape or disc. You may want to talk to your cooperating teacher about some of these ideas.

## Children with Attention Deficit/Hyperactivity Disorder (AD/HD)

One category in special education often seen in child care and schools today is **attention deficit with hyperactivity disorder (AD/HD)**. The *Diagnostic and Statistical Manual of Mental Disorders (DSM-IV-TR)* (American Psychiatric Association, 2000), recognizes three kinds of attention disorders: the predominantly inattentive type, the predominantly hyperactive-impulsive type, and the combined type (American Psychiatric Association, 2000).

Children with AD/HD typically have difficulty concentrating for prolonged periods of time, some even for 5 or 10 minutes. For some of these children, taking a stimulant drug such as Ritalin or Dextroamphetamine appears to help. For others, especially those allergic to drug therapy, specially designed computer games appear to help.

If you have children with AD/HD in your classroom, one proven way to work with them is to keep them busy. Allowing them the freedom to move from one center to another is another way. On the other hand, a room with many choices may be difficult for AD/HD children; in many ways, they need less stimulation rather than more. You may have to suggest gently to the child that he choose one of two options. "I notice no one is painting at one of the easels, and I also notice that your friend Jean Pierre is the only child playing with the blocks. Why don't you paint a picture or join Jean Pierre?" Your room may have a sheltered corner or area where these children may go when over-stimulated.

Like all children, those with AD/HD need *CARE*ing and the freedom to grow and learn. To that end, you first need to learn as much as you can about AD/HD. Then, in cooperation with the interdisciplinary team working with the child, you and your cooperating teacher can set attention goals for your students. There may be a need to modify assignments and to tailor academic materials to individual learning styles and abilities. The need to be flexible is paramount (for example, allowing a student to lie on the floor to read or work while "hiding" under a desk). If an assignment is completed, there may not be a need for a student to sit at a desk. In fact, one of the authors once taught in an L-shaped third-grade classroom, where there was a study carrel off to the side, where any student could go. Although originally planned for an AD/HD student, many of the so-called typical students would move to the study carrel, where they found it easier to concentrate.

One interesting finding about AD/HD students is their ability to hyperfocus; that is, they demonstrate intense levels of concentration and attention in completing tasks in which they are totally absorbed. This has been discovered to be one of the "key descriptors in biographies of creative individuals" (Cramond, 1995, quoted by Turnbull, Turnbull, & Wehmeyer, 2007).

## Autism Spectrum Disorders and Asperger's Syndrome

Children diagnosed as autistic represent a wide range of abilities, as do all children; some are high-functioning and succeed in inclusive settings, and some are low-functioning and may be in inclusive settings only for short periods of time, for activities such as art, music, lunch, and recess. **Autism spectrum disorder (ASD)** is defined by the American Psychiatric Association as a category of pervasive

**attention deficit with hyperactivity disorder (AD/HD)**—like ADD, it causes attention problems and an inability to sit still and concentrate for very long. Children with AD/HD are said to "bounce off the walls."

**autism spectrum disorder (ASD)**—a pervasive developmental disorder usually seen with qualitative impairments in communication, social interactions, and restrictive or repetitive patterns of behavior that first occur before the age of three.

***Student Teacher Quote***—*"When I started student teaching in Ms. Hessler's first-grade class, I wondered who Jessica was. She always had an aide who seemed to work only with her. She wouldn't always look at me when I spoke to her. What a surprise to learn she was supposedly autistic! I never would have guessed!"*

**Brianna Fitzgerald, Kindergarten Classroom, Redwood City Elementary School District, CA**

**Asperger's syndrome**—one of the autism spectra but generally seen at less severe levels. Children with Asperger's often remain in regular classrooms with a sensitive teacher who recognizes the frequently seen delay in the child's social development and subsequent difficulties with peers.

**gifted children**—children who perform significantly above average in intellectual and creative areas.

developmental disorders. The primary characteristics include "social aloofness and a desire for preservation of sameness" (Hyman & Tobin, in Batshaw, Pellegrino, & Roizen, 2008).

**Asperger's syndrome** is a term often applied to those children who usually are able to remain in inclusive settings. You will notice their uniqueness by their failure to develop peer relationships and their use of nonverbal behaviors, such as a reluctance to look eye-to-eye with a peer or an adult, awkward facial expression, body posture, and gestures to regulate social interactions. They may have no problem with spoken language or with cognitive development but may have difficulty in sustaining a conversation. They adhere to strict routines and often demonstrate narrowly defined interests (American Psychiatric Association, 2000).

In a classroom setting, you may notice few differences between children with Asperger's and other children other than the difficulty of the child with Asperger's to develop friendships and his desire to regale you with details about his specific interests. One boy we know is totally fascinated with severe weather phenomena. He thoroughly enjoys telling about the latest earthquake or hurricane, and what damage it caused, yet he has problems relating to the interests of his peers and has not established any friendships.

Willis (2009) presents an excellent definition of autism spectrum disorder and makes concrete suggestions for teachers, complete with strategies to use in the classroom. She concludes that just as all children can learn and want to so do children with ASD. In the classroom, they function best with:

◆ structure and a predictable routine

◆ environments that do not distract

◆ verbal reminders of what will happen next

◆ picture schedules to give them clues about what to do

◆ a quiet place to go where they can be alone for a few minutes, and

◆ nothing to overwhelm their senses with too much light or noise

Most children, regardless of an autism spectrum disorder diagnosis, respond better with these same cues and environments.

## The Gifted Child

Teachers are considering new ways to think about and observe **gifted children**. Very young children, culturally and linguistically diverse children, and economically disadvantaged children may escape detection as gifted children, particularly if standardized assessments are used. Smutny (2001) urges educators to consider factors fundamental to a fair assessment of children's abilities, as follows:

◆ *Look for giftedness in domains other than academic* (creative imagination, wit, improvisation, kinesthetic abilities, and hands-on problem solving). Become aware of your own ideas about what giftedness looks like, or what behaviors indicate high potential. Don't assume that gifted children are early readers or even high achievers. Don't assume that an athletic child with little interest in academics or a bilingual student struggling with English is unlikely to be gifted.

◆ *Look beyond "good" or "bad" behavior.* Consider the role that good behavior plays in the assessment of a child's ability. Do children who please the teacher get more opportunity as a reward for their good behavior? While problem behavior needs to be addressed, always remember that some gifted kids act up out of frustration or boredom.

◆ *Create activities that demand higher-level thinking and creative solutions.* It is obvious that a child who needs hands-on activities to process information and analyze problems will not show these abilities if no such activities occur in the classroom. Be willing to incorporate different learning styles and materials, so that more students can demonstrate their strengths.

◆ *Allow students to express their ideas in different ways.* For example, a child from another culture may have a novel solution to a problem but may express this better through diagrams and drawings than through verbal or written expression. Offer students a variety of ways to show what they are learning.

◆ *Ask children about their work.* Do not assume that you know what a student is trying to do, or whether or not it works. It may be that their ideas are more interesting or sophisticated than are their abilities to express them. Uneven development is common in young children, and cultural differences may enhance this phenomenon.

If some of these suggestions sound appropriate for all children, they are. Many techniques used for children with special needs are indeed appropriate for all. Remember also: when assessing the behavior of young children, teachers need to be sensitive to differences in learning style, development, and cultural background, which influence the way they process information and respond to activities in the classroom (Smutny, 2001).

## English Language Learners

Children of immigrant families are increasingly represented in classrooms. Their numbers have grown dramatically during the past decade and include Hispanics, Asians, Pacific Islanders, Haitians, Africans, and others. According to Garcia, Jensen, and Scribner (2009) there are approximately 14 million English Language Learners (ELLs) in schools in the United States today. They come not only from immigrant families but also from families of U.S. citizens who do not speak English at home. In border states, such as California, Arizona, New Mexico, Texas, and Florida, ELLs represent one out of every four students.

Student teachers may face the immediate task of communicating acceptance and respect to children with varying degrees of English proficiency. No single description fits these children; they are as widely diverse as native-born children. Teachers must strive to decrease children's feelings of alienation and isolation, if they exist (Lewis & Doorlag, 2006; Mastropieri & Scruggs, 2007). Many of these children and their families have backgrounds and cultural understandings that can be tapped as classroom resources.

Student teachers need to become familiar with planning and implementing programs for students who do not understand and/or speak English. Agirdag (2009) recommends that the following five practices be used when teaching ELLs:

◆ Welcome the languages in your classroom.

◆ Ask students to share their languages.

◆ Have students help their peers.

◆ Expand the school's cultural repertoire.

◆ Involve the parents.

Garcia, Jensen, and Scribner (2009) caution you to remember that children of immigrant families may have a degree of proficiency in their home language and/ or in English. Thus, you need to ask the following questions:

◆ How proficient is the child in the language spoken in the home?

◆ What English words does the child seem to know, if any?

◆ Is the child's language and speech appropriate for his age?

◆ What degree of comfort or discomfort is present at school?

◆ What experiences are developmentally appropriate for this child?

## Children Born to Mothers Who Were Substance Abusers

Children born to mothers who have been substance abusers are often born addicted to the drugs the mother abused during pregnancy. These children may appear to be hyperactive, have an attention deficit, or be learning disabled. Caregivers working with these children have noted that they often overreact to stimuli; thus, they need environments that contain fewer, rather than more, curriculum possibilities, and fewer children with whom to interact. They may strike out at anyone nearby—child or adult—and their behavior may be unpredictable. Obviously, this leads to difficulties in establishing friendships with the other children. Children born to substance-abusing mothers have been shown to work better in a small group and in rooms with minimal stimuli.

## WORKING WITH CHILDREN WITH SPECIAL NEEDS

Some techniques proven effective for teaching children with special needs are:

◆ Providing structure. A well-planned classroom is essential. Classroom rules are posted for older children, and repeated often to younger ones, so everyone understands the limits.

◆ Consistent discipline.

◆ Behavior modification.

◆ *CARE*: Be *congruent*, *acceptant*, *reliable*, and *empathetic*. It works with all children, especially those with special needs.

◆ Alternating quiet time with activities. Provide for enough physical exercise to tire the active child and allow the child the freedom to move around often.

◆ Being openly loving. One parent and educator, Armstrong (1996), questions whether AD/HD exists or whether children so labeled simply need *CARE*ing and love.

Armstrong decried the tendency of parents and educators to ask medical doctors to place the seemingly inattentive, overactive child on drug therapy. He advocates instead that we use diet, physical exercise, relaxation exercises, and proven educational techniques, such as those previously mentioned. We urge you to do the same.

### Vulnerable Children

Which children are considered "vulnerable"? Initially, these were children who had a parent or parents who had psychiatric problems or were substance abusers. Children living in poverty, with inadequate housing, clothing, or insufficient food, are also considered vulnerable. Weissbourd (1996) lists the attributes of teachers who work with vulnerable children in Figure 7–10. These attributes, in fact, are important characteristics for any and all teachers.

### At-Risk Children

Today, we can look at a broader definition of vulnerable children and include any child living in an environment that is not optimal for the child's positive growth. Look again at the attributes listed in Figure 7–10. If you can internalize them, you will have no difficulty with **at-risk children** or any others.

Breslin (2005) suggests that these children not be labeled, as that tends to focus on deficits rather than on the strengths and competencies the children have. She stresses how often these children possess a heightened sensory awareness and

**at-risk children**—because of exposure to adverse environmental factors (e.g., poverty or low birth weight), children are considered at risk for developmental delay and/or for doing poorly in school.

▶ **Figure 7-10**

Attributes of effective teachers working with vulnerable children. From *The Vulnerable Child* by Richard Weissbourd. Copyright 1996 by Richard Weissbourd. Reprinted by permission of Perseus Books Publishers, a member of Perseus Books, L.L.C.

**Attributes of Effective Teachers Working with Vulnerable Children**

1. Effective teachers operationalize high expectations for every child.
2. Effective teachers attribute failure to aspects of a child or classroom that can be positively influenced, rather than to intractable aspects of a child, family, or community.
3. Effective teachers provide every student with the elements from which real and durable self-esteem is built, including specific, tangible skills and achievements, progressively increased responsibilities, and opportunities to give to others.
4. Effective teachers view children as having complex constellations of strengths and weaknesses and communicate this understanding to parents.
5. Effective teachers work to develop children's adaptive capacities, their ability to manage disappointment and conflict.
6. Effective teachers pick up on the quiet troubles that undermine children in school, such as mild hunger or wearing the same clothes day after day and respond aggressively to these problems.
7. Effective teachers view the classroom and school as a complex culture and system and seek to understand the difficulties of a child in terms of the interactions between a particular child and a particular culture and system.
8. Effective teachers engage parents proactively and have the skills to work with parents when a child is in crisis.
9. Effective teachers are self-observing and are responsive to feedback and ideas from both other school staff and children—they see children as active partners in their education.
10. Effective teachers know when to respond to a child's problem themselves and when a child needs to see another professional who has specialized training.
11. Effective teachers innovate, take risks, and reshape their activities based on close attention to results.

emphasizes the need for teachers to have high, positive expectations for these children. Furthermore, Breslin stresses the need for teachers to help the children develop a clear understanding of their strengths and how these strengths relate to their respective accomplishments, reminding us to help the child develop a sense of play. "Humor is not an innate gift, but it can and should be cultivated. It is a frame that can keep things in perspective" (Breslin, 2005).

## Children Who Fall Through the Cracks

Many children you are likely to see in your rooms may have some of the characteristics of a child with special needs but on such a mild basis that they do not qualify under the law for any supportive help. Others may be special because of some recent trauma, like losing a beloved grandparent, having a sibling with cancer, or witnessing an accident that caused injury or death to someone. Our best advice: remember that all children are unique, and that all, at one time or another in their lives, are likely to need special love and care.

## Working with Parents of Children with Special Needs

Research (Chinn, Winn, & Walters, 1985) has shown that families of children with special needs go through a process similar to the grief reactions described by Kubler-Ross in *On Death and Dying* (1969). In interactions with parents, you may see a father denying that his son has a problem, while the mother, wracked with

▶ **Figure 7-11**
A wheelchair-bound child has access to sand play on this specially designed playground equipment.

guilt, is blaming herself. Families often project feelings of blame on the elementary or preschool. One reason for the high divorce rate among families of children with special needs is that two parents are seldom at the same step in the grief process at the same time, a fact that obviously can lead to dissension at home.

In cases where the child has a clear disability, diagnosed by a medical doctor at an early age, families have had to adjust, and learn to accept the child and any concomitant problems, earlier than families of children who have what are often called "invisible handicaps," like learning disabilities, mild retardation, Asperger's syndrome, and behavior disorders. What this means to teachers in both preschool and elementary school settings is that they may have to be especially sensitive to what stage of grieving a child's family is in. Working with these families may require all of a teacher's communication skills, and a teacher still may not be successful in persuading a family that their child needs special attention. This is one reason why elementary schools may assign a child, whose family is "income eligible," to work with a "Chapter 1" teacher. (Chapter 1 of PL 95–581, the Education Consolidation Act of 1981, provides federal funds for compensatory education of children from low-income families.) Another child may receive help from a reading specialist, student teacher, teacher assistant, or volunteer.

## Commonly Used Tests

Retardation or cognitive impairment is easily measured with any well-known, standard intelligence test. Intelligence testing, often called *IQ testing* (for *Intelligence Quotient*), uses a figure based on standard deviation from the norm with 100 as the mean or average. Despite the fact that it has come under fire over the past 40 to 50 years, its use is still widespread. As a tool for understanding the child's intellectual development, in regard to predicting possible success in school, the IQ test provides valuable information. Combined with other measures of a child's development, such as the checklist found in the Appendix, the IQ test can provide a differential picture of the child's school-related abilities.

One major drawback to any IQ test is that it may discriminate against children from racial or cultural minorities. Even if translated into other languages, there is still the question of appropriateness. For most preschools, a developmental checklist provides as good or better information than an IQ test. The major advantage to the IQ test, of course, is in diagnosing cognitive impairments and giftedness. However, tests seldom provide clues about how to work with the child once diagnosed.

If we use a developmental checklist that relies on our observation of the child, we can develop a learning plan based on what we see. Noting that a three-year-old child can walk upstairs alternating feet, but walks downstairs one step at a time, we might have the child hold our hand at first. Then, we can have the child hold onto a railing. Finally, we can urge the child to try without any support. If we note that a child is still speaking two-word sentences, we can provide for more language experiences on a one-to-one basis. In every case, we should not urge the child to accomplish tasks that are not appropriate to her developmental level. The child who cannot gallop will not learn to skip, but perhaps the child is ready to learn how to slide one foot after the other sideways.

Head Start has developed a screening and assessment process that occurs throughout the program year, on a periodic schedule, rather than only on the child's entrance into a Head Start program. This allows analysis and, it is hoped, reassurance that the child is on track for achieving the expected developmental outcomes, as outlined in the child's IEP developed by staff and family. The Head Start screening assessment process is called *Early and Periodic Screen, Diagnosis, and Treatment Program* (EPSDT) (O'Brien, 2001).

## The Individual Family Services Plan

Look back at Figure 7–9. You should note that it represents only selected items that might be listed on Tommy Fabian's IFSP. (Remember, at the elementary school level the IFSP becomes, as required by law, an IEP.) As stipulated by law, a multidisciplinary approach is taken that involves the preschool, local school district, and a local community resource group. The student teacher, under the direction of the cooperating teacher, has an important role in modeling language and listening to responses; the school district speech therapist and psychologist each have their roles in working both with Tommy and with the family. Finally, a community organization, the local county chapter of the Learning Disability Association (LDA), has been enlisted for family support. It is important to remember that having a child with special needs often leaves families feeling disbelief, anger, and helplessness; a support group can be invaluable in alleviating these feelings.

## Unique Challenges in Early Childhood Inclusion

A common myth is that inclusion in early childhood programs is easy, because of the playful nature of many of the programs. However, Cook, Klein, and Tessier, with Daley (2004) point out that in K–12 programs the general education teacher is credentialed at the same level as the special educator, but the same is not always true at the preschool level. The level of education and experience among preschool teachers varies widely. The early childhood special education specialist may have to take on an unfamiliar role; for, even when the early childhood staff is highly trained, there may be philosophical differences between the regular staff and the specialist.

## ▶ SUMMARY

In this brief introduction to the special child, we presented an overview of current thinking regarding the integration of the child with special needs into the regular classroom. In many instances, the child with special needs functions very well there and such integration has almost always been successful. Of course, there may be awkward moments initially, but other children often prove more tolerant than adults in accepting the special child. Children with special needs are no different than any other child; if you meet them with kindness and *CARE*, they will respond.

We provided an overview of the public laws, especially PL 101–476, and listed some of the major provisions. We discussed the concept of least restrictive environment, or inclusion, and emphasized that what is least restrictive for one child may not be so for another.

We presented a sample of short-term objectives, from an IFSP for a family with a preschool child who may have a possible learning disability. We have also explained why working with families who have children with special needs can present difficulties.

Finally, we offered some practical suggestions for working with the special child. We agree that these techniques seem appropriate for all children. Methods that work well with one population are often applicable to another.

## ▶HELPFUL WEBSITES

http://www.ncela.gwu.edu/
The National Clearinghouse for English Language. This site provides information on acquisition and language instruction for linguistically and culturally diverse learners.

http://www.naeyc.org
National Association for the Education of Young Children. You will find many different topics related to children between the ages of birth and eight years. Investigate those related to special needs and inclusion.

http://eric.ed.gov
ERIC Clearinghouse on Education. Go to the Thesaurus and click on the topic you wish to research. Behavior disorders and learning disabilities can be researched on this database, where information on special and gifted education is maintained.

http://www.cec.sped.org
The Council for Exceptional Children is the primary group for parents, professionals, and others interested in any type of special needs. The website contains a directory to maneuver through to the particular site you want to investigate. Much valuable information.

## Additional Websites for Student Teachers Working with Children with Special Needs

http://www.niccyd.org
National Information Center for Children and Youth with Disabilities. NICCYD provides free, online publications, case studies, and information on several different types of special needs, such as visual and hearing impairments, cerebral palsy, mental retardation, and assessing programs for infants and toddlers.

http://www.aaidd.org
American Association on Intellectual and Developmental Disabilities. The AAIDD produces much information of value to parents and professionals working with children and adults with developmental disabilities. You will find that articles and fact sheets are available here.

http://www.autism.com
Autism Research Institute. This organization conducts research and disseminates the results to parents and professionals interested in all types of autism spectrum disorders.

http://www.asperger.org/index_asc.html
This site is the primary one for those with interests in Asperger's syndrome, one of the autism spectra. It contains articles and suggestions for working with children with Asperger's.

http://www.ccbd.net
Council for Children with Behavior Disorders. This is an international organization that is dedicated to improving educational practices for children with emotional and behavior disorders.

http://www.ici.umn.edu
The Institute on Community Integration at the University of Minnesota is a federally designated University Center for Excellence in Developmental Disabilities and is part of a national network of similar programs.

http://www.nabe.org
The National Association for Bilingual Education sponsors an annual conference and posts articles of interest to those teaching children who are English language learners.

http://www.fpg.unc.edu
FPG Child Development Institute. Click publications dealing with disabilities.

http://www.chadd.org
Children and Adults with Attention Deficit/Hyperactivity Disorder. The title tells exactly what you might find at this website.

http://ldanatl/.org
Learning Disabilities Association of America (LDA). This is an excellent resource for educators and parents.

http://www.gtworld.org
Gifted and Talented World is an online support community for gifted and talented individuals and those who support and work with them.

http://interdys.org
Formerly the Orton Dyslexia Society, now the International Dyslexia Association (IDA). This site provides information and resources for people coping with dyslexia.

 Additional resources for this chapter can be found by visiting the companion website at *www.cengage.com/education/machado*.

# ▶ SUGGESTED ACTIVITIES

**A.** Visit a preschool or elementary school that has children with special needs in attendance. Spend at least one morning watching the special children, if identified, and take notes as you observe. What similarities or differences do you find between the special children and the others? Discuss your answers with your peers and supervisor.

**B.** Read the following profile of a child. Then read the statement made by the parent. What would you consider to be an appropriate response? Discuss possible responses with your peers, cooperating teacher, and supervisor.

1. Kathy caught your attention for two reasons. First, she is always cocking her head to one side and holding it close to the paper when she draws or writes. You notice that she frequently squints when she tries to read material on the chalkboard and has, more than once, copied a math problem incorrectly. One day, she asks to switch seats with Alicia, so she can see the side chalkboard more easily. You have to repeat directions for Kathy, and have noticed that she sometimes asks her seatmate to explain the directions to her again. You do not have the services of a school nurse to check sight and hearing, but your cooperating teacher has called Kathy's mother, scheduled a conference, and has asked you to sit in.

   When her mother arrives, your cooperating teacher asks about Kathy's behavior at home. The mother admits that Kathy does sit close to the television and seems inattentive at times. "I thought Kathy might have a problem hearing but her father put an end to that! You know what he did? He sat in the kitchen while she was in the family room and whispered, 'Kathy, do you want some ice cream, honey?' Well, Kathy answered right away! Her father and I both think Kathy just gets too involved in things. She's not deaf!"

2. Josip is one of those children who never sits still for a minute. He moves around constantly from the moment he enters the child care center until nap time, when he must be urged strongly to lie down. Nap time is agony for Josip: he twists and turns, grumbles, sighs, and disturbs everyone around him. Yet, when he does fall asleep, he is difficult to awaken. Sometimes your cooperating teacher has allowed him to continue to sleep. You talk to your cooperating teacher and hypothesize that you think Josip does not get enough sleep at night. She suggests that you call Mrs. Milutin and ask her to come in for a short conference. "Mrs. Milutin," you ask, "when does Josip go to bed? Sometimes he really takes a long nap at school."

   Mrs. Milutin responds, "Well, of course he sleeps at school! That is why his father and I cannot get him to sleep at home! Maybe if you do not allow Josip to sleep at school, he will sleep better at home!"

**C.** Visit a residential center for children with special needs. Discuss your observations with your peers and supervisor.

# ▶ REVIEW

**A.** List five characteristics of a child with special needs.

**B.** Read the following descriptions of behavior. Identify the child in each situation who may be special. Discuss your answers with your peers and supervisor.

1. Ladan is a new child in your room of four-year-olds. Her mother says that the family speaks English in the home, but you have doubts. In the classroom, Ladan seems to be more of a spectator than a participant. You note that when playing "Simon Says," Ladan does not appear to know what to do but copies her neighbor.

2. Richie is an abused two-year-old who has recently been placed in a foster home. He enters preschool every morning like a small whirlwind, running around the room, kicking at block structures other children have built, knocking over puzzles others are making, and screaming at the top of his lungs.

3. Even though Kosuke has been in your kindergarten class for nearly the entire year, his behavior has not changed noticeably from the first day. He still clings to his mother's hand when she brings him to school, and he cries for 3 to 5 minutes after she leaves. He has only one friend in the room, and efforts to persuade him to play or work with another child are met with tears. He appears totally absorbed by cars and plays with the toy cars or the large trucks in the play center to the exclusion of other activities. This absorption continues in his drawings—always of cars.

4. Elena, a pretty, dark-haired seven-year-old in your after-school child care center, complains every day after lunch about her headaches and her queasy stomach. You wonder if she is coming down with the flu (it had been going

around), but Elena has no fever, and the complaints are a chronic occurrence.

5. Jorge is a student in a bilingual first grade but seldom talks, in either Spanish or English. When he does speak, he usually speaks so softly that only the students next to him can hear. When you urge him to speak up, Jorge often lowers his head and says nothing. He does appear to understand when given directions, but you are concerned about his noncommunicative behavior. When his mother is questioned, she's not concerned because Jorge's older brother, Sergio, had displayed similar behavior when he first entered school.

# ▶ REFERENCES

Agirdag, O. (2009, April). All languages welcome here. *Educational Leadership, 66*(7), 20–25.

American Psychiatric Association. (2000). *Diagnostic and statistical manual of mental disorders* (4th ed.). Washington, DC: Author.

Armstrong, T. (1996, February). ADD: Does it really exist? *Phi Delta Kappan, 77*(6), 396–401.

Batshaw, M. L., Pellegrino, M. D. & Roizen, N. J. (2008). *Children with disabilities* (6th ed.). Baltimore, MD: Paul H. Brookes Publishing.

Breslin, D. (January, 2005). Children's capacity to develop resiliency: How to nurture it. *Young Children, 60*(1), 47–51.

Burgess, K. B., & Younger, A. J. (2006, Spring). Self-schemas, anxiety, somatic and depressive symptoms in socially withdrawn children and adolescents. *Journal of Research in Childhood Education, 20*(3), 175–187.

Chinn, P. C., Winn, J., & Walters, R. H. (1985). *Two-way talking with parents of special children: A process of positive communication.* St. Louis, MO: C. V. Mosby.

Cook, R. E., Klein, M. D., & Tessier, A., in collaboration with Daley, S. E. (2004). *Adapting early childhood curricula for children in inclusive settings* (6th ed.). Upper Saddle River, NJ: Pearson/Merrill/Prentice Hall.

Federal Register. (1977). PL 94–142, 300.5.

Garcia, E. E. Jensen, B. T., & Scribner, K. P. (2009, April). The demographic imperative, *Educational Leadership, 66*(7), 8–13.

Grisham-Brown, J., Hemmeter, M. L., & Pretti-Frontczak, K. (2005). *Blended practices for teaching young children in inclusive settings.* Baltimore, MD: Paul H. Brookes Publishing.

Hyman, S. L. & Towbin, K. E. (2008) "Autism spectrum disorders" in Batshaw, Pellegrino, & Roizen, *Children with Disabilities* (6th ed.), Baltimore, MD: Paul H. Brookes Publishing.

Kubler-Ross, E. (1969). *On death and dying.* New York: Macmillan.

Lewis, R. B., & Doorlag, D. H. (2006). *Teaching special students in general education classrooms* (7th ed.). Upper Saddle River, NJ: Pearson/Merrill/Prentice Hall.

Mastropieri, M. A. & Scruggs, T. E. (2007). *The inclusive classroom: strategies for effective instruction* (3rd ed.). Upper Saddle River, NJ: Pearson/Merrill/Prentice Hall.

O'Brien, J. (2001, April). How screening and assessment practices support quality disabilities services in Head Start. *Head Start Bulletin, 70*(8), 20–23.

Orton Dyslexia Society. (1988). *Definition. Perspectives.* Baltimore: Author.

Smutny, J. F. (2001, Winter). Identifying young gifted disadvantaged children in the K–3 classroom. *Gifted Education Communicator, 32*(4), 35–36.

Turnbull, A., Turnbull, R., & Wehmeyer, M. L. (2007). *Exceptional lives: special education in today's schools.* (5th ed.). Upper Saddle River, NJ: Pearson/Merrill/Prentice Hall.

U.S. Department of Justice, Civil Rights Division, Disability Rights Section. (1997, October). *Commonly asked questions about child care centers and the Americans with Disabilities Act.* Washington, DC: Author.

Wadlington, E., Jacob, S., & Bailey, S. (1996, Fall). Teaching students with dyslexia in the regular classroom. *Childhood Education, 73*(1), 33–38.

Weissbourd, R. (1996). *The vulnerable child.* Reading, MA: Addison-Wesley.

Willis, C. (2009, January). Young children with autism spectrum disorder: Strategies that work. *Young Children, 64*(1), 81–89.

# Communication

# CHAPTER 8

# Common Problems of Student Teachers

**OBJECTIVES**

After reading this chapter, you should be able to:

1. Describe the goals of interpersonal communication during the student teaching experience.
2. Identify communication skills that aid in sending and receiving verbal and nonverbal messages.
3. Define "authenticity" of communication.
4. Identify a sequential approach to interpersonal problem solving.

## STUDENT TEACHER SCENARIO

Sumi, a student teacher, was working at a private early childhood center part time while student teaching. The center was located near a shopping mall. In addition to regularly enrolled students, it allowed children on a drop-in basis. Sumi had worked at the center a short while and had some serious concerns over some of the head teacher's practices. What troubled her most was that the center rules had gotten out of control and that many rules were picky and overly precise. For example, at line-up time children were expected to stand up straight and put both hands on top of their heads. This was difficult for some children because it was hard for them to hold this arm position for an extended period. At first, she thought perhaps the teacher was teaching body part vocabulary this way, but no other requests asked children to put their hands on another body part during line-up. Then there was a rule about children drinking all their milk at snack time before selecting a cracker from a basket. When she asked the head teacher about the rules, the head teacher explained it was done so drop-in parents could readily see she had control over the children, and the "milk first" rule was necessary because drop-in parents paid an additional fee for any food served to their children.

### Questions for Discussion

1. If Sumi consulted her college supervisor concerning practices at her workplace, how might her supervisor respond?
2. If Sumi were to discuss her concerns about line-up and snack time again with her head teacher at her place of employment, what would you suggest her first statement should be?
3. Because this center was not her student teaching placement classroom, should Sumi just forget about her concerns? If yes, explain your reasoning.

This chapter is not intended to solve all problems encountered during student teaching, nor is it meant to minimize the many successful and creative solutions student teachers achieve. It will probe possible reasons for difficulties, especially those related to communication, and help alert the student teacher to possible courses of action. Knowing that problems occur and knowing there are ways to avoid and handle them will be helpful. You will relate more strongly to some ideas in this chapter than to others. Knowledge may help you escape some problems, confront others, and cope with ones that cannot be changed. Open communication with others, such as cooperating teachers, college supervisors, and children, is often the key.

# KINDS OF PROBLEMS

Do you know of any human relationship that is problem-free and always smooth sailing? Student teaching, involving close human interaction and communication, is no exception. Pressures, feelings, desires, needs, risks, and possible failures are inherent.

## Stress and Anxiety

During the first days and weeks of student teaching, **stress** may increase, usually from student teachers desiring to become good practicing teachers, confounded by feelings of self-doubt and lack of confidence. As you grasp the challenges through watching your cooperating teacher and attempt to put your own theory into practice, the task seems monumental. Three sequential stages in teacher training are commonplace:

**stress**—internal or external demand on a person's ability to adapt.

1. focus on self, or self-protection
2. focus on children
3. focus on outcomes of teaching

Initial focus on self appears to be a necessary and crucial element in the first stage of teacher development.

A research study probing student teacher anxieties suggests supervisors' and cooperating teachers' observations, assessments, and evaluations of student teacher competency were the most frequently mentioned contributing factors. Program planning, child behavior, class management, and staff relationships were other anxiety producing areas (Morton, Vesco, Williams, & Awender, 1997).

Student teachers without past child care employment experience can feel overwhelmed by a beginning realization concerning teacher workloads. Teaching is hard work, requiring intelligence, preparation, creativity, determination, and perseverance. This reality is quickly understood. Other sources of stress can be too much work to do in too little time, lack of recognition of efforts, noise and activity level in classrooms, children's challenging behaviors, tension between staff members or other classroom adults, or other factors.

The symptoms of stress can include, but are not limited to, tense muscles, difficulty concentrating, upset stomach, headaches, fatigue, sleep difficulty, low morale, and irritability.

An early focus on oneself may produce **anxiety**. A student teacher can feel uncomfortable until there is a clear feeling of exactly what is expected, and may react in a number of ways. These can include becoming defensive, avoiding necessary child guidance, missing class, becoming critical of the placement classroom, looking for faults in others, withdrawing into busy work such as classroom maintenance, or other behaviors.

**anxiety**—a general sense of uneasiness that cannot be traced to a specific cause.

More positive courses of action are:

◆ seeking additional written or oral guidelines (see Figure 8–1)
◆ organizing tasks into time blocks
◆ clearly outlining assignments on a calendar, file, or using a binder system
◆ seeking the supervisor to communicate anxieties
◆ using stress-reduction techniques

Both stress and anxiety are often alleviated when a student teacher remains "socially connected" and can talk concerns out with friends or other student teachers. Many training programs promote a buddy system during student teaching so confidential feelings, worries, stresses, and anxieties can be shared and discussed but remain confidential. This does not aim to replace discussion with cooperating teachers or supervisors but rather acts as a supplement to those discussions.

Looking at the first three recommended courses of action above suggest a student teacher's lack of information or lack of organization may be causing stress. The next actions either express or confront the stress, and may possibly reduce tension.

What other stress-reduction techniques are helpful? SkillPath Seminars (1997) suggests the following:

◆ Talk to yourself, emphasizing positive thinking.
◆ Visualize your success.
◆ Reward yourself for a job or task well done.
◆ Take on the responsibility to change situations that cause stress.
◆ Exercise.
◆ Learn to play as hard as you work.
◆ Take care of health concerns.
◆ Reject perfectionism, yet strive for excellence.
◆ Maintain optimism.
◆ Develop a sense of humor.
◆ Interject fun into your work.
◆ Seek counseling if necessary.

▶ **Figure 8-1**
Ask for more information when you need it.

It will be helpful if you continue to pay attention to healthful living, use your sense of humor about the student teaching situation, develop or rely on a support system, obtain an upbeat outlook, exercise, and learn relaxation techniques. It's best to stay away from gossiping if it exists at your workplace, and eliminate destructive self-talk.

Canter (1998) suggests that stressed teachers should look for opportunities to:

◆ Take a walk around the room or yard.

◆ Do some deep breathing exercises to relax.

◆ Identify the source of stress.

◆ Talk to a colleague about it.

◆ Surround themselves with positive-thinking people, who appreciate the challenges of the teaching profession and the significance of a teacher's role in society.

The negative comments of staff at a placement site, and their complaining about lack of administrative support, work overload, families, and so on, may affect a student teacher's stress level (Canter, 1998). Stress promotes a chemical change in the body, creating tenseness and nervousness that gears the body for action.

## Feelings

Clear, authentic communication of feelings, done with skill and sensitivity, may have not been modeled or taught at home or during schooling. To be effective when expressing feelings, it should be clear that the speaker takes responsibility for the feelings. Feelings should not be confused with thoughts, evaluations, or solutions, but stated with clarity and directness. The speaker avoids implying others are to be blamed or judged for causing the feelings. Using the words "angry," "pleased," "happy," "annoyed," "frustrated," "hurt," "upset," or similar descriptors adds clarity for the listener, who will not have to rely on tone of voice, sarcasm, or other implied body messages. The student teaching experience puts student teachers, children, and other adults in close contact, and adds the anxiety-producing element of observing and assessing the student teacher's competency development. If you have already acquired the abilities of speaking openly and frankly without alienating people, being a skillful listener, and receiving and accepting suggestions, this chapter will serve as a review, perhaps providing additional insights and communication techniques.

Keirsey and Bates (1984) offer the following advice for individuals seeking to understand and communicate with others:

> If I do not want what you want, please try not to tell me that my want is wrong.
> Or if I believe other than you, at least pause before you correct my view.
> Or if my emotion is less than yours, or more, given the same circumstances, try not to ask me to feel more strongly or weakly.
> If you will allow me any of my own wants, or emotions, or beliefs, or actions, then you open yourself, so that some day these ways of mine might not seem so wrong, and might finally appear to you as right—for me.

People are different in fundamental ways. They want different things. The importance of relating and communicating with others in early childhood work cannot be overestimated. Many early childhood teachers face cultural diversity daily, which necessitates increased awareness, sensitivity, and skillful communication.

Very strong feelings can be accepted as natural, normal, and to be expected. Once accepted, there is the chance to move on and get past them, or at least cope.

You will find it is possible to be excited, even eager, to try your ideas and activities, ready to develop your own teaching style, and still be somewhat apprehensive. The caring and involvement student teachers bring to their work are commendable. These will further their success in student teaching.

A contrast to the anxious approach to student teaching is the relaxed, confident one. This happens after a few successes. Self-confidence and self-esteem are important primary goals of student teaching. They evolve in student teachers as they do in children, through actions resulting in success and through the feedback received from others. A strong feeling of success through child interactions is described by Read and Patterson (1980):

> A child's face lights up when he sees us come into the room, and we know that our relationship with him is a source of strength. He is seeing us as someone who cares, who can be depended on, and who has something significant to give him. It makes us feel good inside to be this kind of person for a child. It gives us confidence. (see Figure 8–2)

Hints for dealing with anxiety suggest trying not to worry about being the teacher; instead, reflect on teachers you liked when you were a child. Another method is to relax and treat children your own way, the way you really think about them. This will give you the confidence required to give more, try more, and be more effective. One of your authors still meets with some of her elementary school classmates who all had Mrs. Bertulli as their teacher in fourth grade. They agree they share a liking of opera music. Mrs. Bertulli, an opera buff, used it frequently to calm her class during rest periods. Because our beloved teacher offered what she enjoyed, which were arias from *Aida*, we grew to love them, too.

## Time Management

For some student teachers, time management is a continuous problem. A date book, file, or pocket and desk calendar help. Organization is a key element. Devise a system that puts what you need within reach; it will save time. Plan ahead and break large tasks into small, specific pieces. Use daily lists and give tasks priorities. Think of "must do first," medium priority, and "can wait" categories. Do not waste time feeling guilty. Working with a colleague or friend is a strategy that often gets difficult tasks accomplished.

▶ **Figure 8-2**
Building trusting and caring relationships aids communication.

Cooperating teachers sometimes complain that students are not prepared, are tardy, or are unreliable. Assignments should involve planning ahead and analyzing task time lengths. Last-minute desperation increases tension, destroys composure, and creates stress. Only the student teacher can make adjustments to provide enough time and rest necessary for student teaching. Von Bergen (2003) believes disorganization sends out "ripples of difficulties." Every time you can't find what you need, stress mounts and time is wasted. One can miss deadlines, feel frustration, and become less comfortable and less confident. With organization one becomes more productive, efficient, and usually maintains a more positive work/life balance. It pays to not only organize available time but also schoolwork, materials, schedules, and so on, using your own system of organization.

If you have not discussed with your family and friends how your practicum may affect your relationship and time with them, do so. Solicit their supportive understanding, so they will be aware of the possible mental and physical stress you may experience because of your workload. Fortunately, you can assure them that student teaching is a temporary experience.

## Worry

Practicing teachers, and some student teachers, tend to mull over their teaching day, worrying about particular children or some other feature of their classroom. Von Bergen (2003) suggests that on-the-job stress may be replayed during sleep. This, she feels, allows thoughts and emotions to rise and fall in different parts of the brain, perhaps to produce solutions to problems that might not emerge any other way. Though not a research-proven theory, we mention it here because rarely is there mention of any positive effects of worrying. We, in fact, would urge you not to worry, but rather have faith in your ability.

## Seeking Help

It can be difficult for some student teachers to ask for help or suggestions. The risk involves having either the cooperating teacher or supervisor feel you have limited ability to solve your own problems. Therefore, student teachers sometimes turn to other student teachers. Trust is an important element in this dilemma. Fortunately, one builds trust through human interactions, and seeking help usually becomes easier as time passes. Self-doubt may cause a student teacher to resist asking questions, for fear of looking dense, needy, or vulnerable. Leeds (2001) suggests asking "smart questions." She believes the following types of questions are effective problem solvers:

◆ *Pose a question that lets the other person answer what you want to know.* "Would you like me to plan another physical development activity or branch out to another area?"

◆ *Begin conversations with open-ended questions.* "What kinds of words or actions might I use to calm Rocky?"

◆ *End conversations with closed-ended questions.* "Am I making sense? Have I addressed everything?"

◆ *If you are dealing with a problem, explain what you have done so far, and pose your question.* "I read the label on the powdered paint can and mixed in more powder, but I'm wondering if the paint is still too runny. What do you think?"

◆ *Ask questions at a neutral time, when the problem can be separated from strong emotions.*

◆ *Avoid asking negative questions.* For instance, instead of saying, "You didn't like the way my lesson went, did you?" ask questions such as, "How could I have improved my planned activity?"

It is important to seek help quickly in many instances, and to use consultation times and meetings to pick the brains of others and seek assistance.

▶ **Figure 8-3**
Mentoring is an important part of a supervisor's job.

The role of both the supervisor and cooperating teacher includes on-site mentoring and advice (see Figure 8–3). A beginning teacher needs encouragement, reassurance, comfort, guidance, instruction in specific skills, and insight into the complex causes of behavior. In the British primary school system, it is customary for a beginning teacher to receive advice and supportive assistance on a daily basis throughout the first full year of teaching. Some school districts in the United States provide mentor teachers to newly hired teachers or develop other strategies to assist them.

## The Half-a-Teacher Feeling

During their experiences, many student teachers are led to feel, either by the children, cooperating teachers, or other staff members, that because of their position, they are not quite students and not quite teachers. Because of this neither-here-nor-there attitude, student teachers are not always treated as figures of authority. Read the poem in Figure 8–4. It may bring a knowing smile. Children at first, may not recognize you as a teacher, and may feel you are an adult who has no authority. This can lead to testing behavior, and your cooperating teacher may wish to reintroduce the idea that you are, indeed, a "real" teacher who knows and enforces classroom rules.

Sometimes early in student teaching, a strong team feeling has not been established, yet its development is critical, for all involved. It may be best to consult with your supervisor first; cooperating teachers have a number of factors to consider in relinquishing control of their classroom.

Often they feel uneasy when their routines, or classroom behavior standards, are threatened. They may also feel like they are asking too much too soon of their student teachers, and may be unclear of their roles in giving assignments. It may be difficult for cooperating teachers to interchange their roles and become co-teachers instead of lead teachers. They can also be worried about child safety.

Most cooperating teachers get a real sense of teaming with student teachers as time passes and they observe student competencies increase. For example, a cooperating teacher in a recreation department–affiliated preschool in Santa Clara, California, related, that one of her student teachers was so perceptive that she would anticipate what she, the teacher, wanted or needed without her having to ask. As a result, the cooperating teacher felt they worked as a team and the children really accomplished a great deal.

Student teachers may feel frightened about taking risks, and torn between being eager to try new things but afraid of observer feedback if they differ significantly from their cooperating teacher's style. They may decide to play it safe, not realizing they are losing opportunities for growth in doing so. New and beginning teachers are usually enthusiastic and optimistic, with a passion for teaching. Many hope to change children's lives, and existing practice, for the better.

## Guidance

Student teachers often find that the children will obey the rules when the cooperating teacher is present. Children test and question the authority of a new adult. Student teachers may tend to force issues, or completely ignore children when classroom rules are broken. These situations may be temporarily troublesome. In time, the children will realize that the student teacher means what he says, and consistency and firmness will win out or the student teacher learns to foresee and prevent behaviors before they appear by adjusting or changing a causative factor.

When student teachers feel they cannot deal with these situations, they tend to stay close to self-controlled or affectionate children. This type of behavior indicates a possible withdrawal from the total room responsibility. If you are

▶ **Figure 8-4**
"Not Quite."

**Not Quite**

Her classroom
Her rules
Her kids
And ——
She's "the teacher" here.
I'm just an almost, a
    "not quite"
Who's working hard to
    get it right.
But wait and see
A real teacher I'm
    beginning to be!

experiencing difficulty, look back at the ideas in chapters dealing with classroom management, and consult with both your cooperating teacher and supervisor for suggestions.

## Attachments

At times, a child may form a strong bond or attachment with a particular student teacher and prefer her company instead of the cooperating teacher. The child may be inconsolable for some time after the student teacher's departure. Most student teachers worry about this behavior, and their supervisor's and cooperating teacher's reactions to it. It is an important topic for team meetings.

Male student teachers often have a unique experience while student teaching, based on children's lack of experience with males as teachers. Some children seek physical contact and tend to lean on, follow, and want to hold a teacher's hand as they do with some female teachers. After a short period, the children will view the male student teacher as just another teacher, with his own individuality. If this does not happen, further study of the situation is in order. In our society many young children do not have a father figure in their homes.

Male student teachers may experience family bias and suspicion concerning their choice of a career with young children. This may be voiced and is a difficult issue to deal with. Highly publicized cases that have been in the media can lead to family fears. Most center directors face the issue of new, male student teachers head on, and as early in the placement as possible, with family meetings that focus on father figures and parenting skills that relate to men.

## Philosophic Differences

Sometimes the cooperating teacher's view of child education and how children learn is quite similar to the student teacher's; in other placements, it is not. Gaining an understanding of methods, techniques, curriculums, goals, and objectives of classrooms is the task of the student teacher. When conflicting views are present in a supportive atmosphere, they are respected. Student teachers can see this as a chance to clarify their own philosophies.

It is disconcerting and uncomfortable for both student and cooperating teachers when their teaching styles clash. Open discussion, particularly when done in a caring way that preserves the dignity of each teacher's opinions, is the best course of action.

Student teachers should not surrender their philosophical values, but tenaciously retain what they feel is best for children. Every wave of newly trained preschool and primary school teachers has its own contribution to make. The old or established way is always subject to questions in education. Practicing teachers continue to try innovative approaches; some are used in a complete or modified form, others are tried and discarded. Thoughtfulness and open-mindedness help student teachers, as does a "win-win" attitude.

## Talk, Talk, Talk

Student teachers during their own years of schooling may have experienced teachers who talked constantly at them rather than with them. With this memory, they may have a mistaken image of teacher conduct. Skilled teachers have the ability to focus, listen, and learn. They realize they are participants in, rather than leaders of, most teacher–child conversations. In the classroom, they feel their main role is not telling children what to do but rather imparting knowledge for child growth and development. In their planned activities, they do give information, but view this as only part of their job.

Burman (2009) gives teachers a number of suggestions regarding listening:

◆ Listen carefully includes listening for intent, for children's thinking, giving up control of the conversation, and honoring children's ideas.

- ◆ Try to make sense of what the child is saying.
- ◆ Give the child the power to take the conversation to places and directions she chooses.
- ◆ Ask children for their opinions and ideas.
- ◆ Respond to children's conversational agenda by becoming attuned and by not feeling you always have to teach something.
- ◆ Choose the time and place for conversations carefully so talking is not pressured and one can concentrate instead of listening haphazardly or half–heartedly.
- ◆ Embrace silence. "It takes time to reach a level of comfort with someone when moments of silence do not make us squirm" (p. 88).
- ◆ Ask good questions, such as open-ended ones, questions that involve higher-thinking-level skills, questions that clarify or focus ideas, and questions that connect experiences and ideas.
- ◆ Model thinking out loud.
- ◆ Build vocabulary. Tie words to real-life experience. Connect words to ones already known. Use correct and precise terms. Introduce new words.

Student teachers may find it difficult to give total attention to child conversations because they are aware of the need to supervise every child in a room. Without a second adult in the classroom, this can be nearly impossible, but student teachers can sit or stand in places that allow for seeing as much of the room as possible, instead of turning their backs to most classroom action while talking to one child. Teachers laugh at the expression concerning teachers with "eyes in the backs of their heads," but they realize that at all times they have total responsibility for the safety and welfare of all children in their care.

## Personality Conflicts

Whether or not you believe everyone has their own "vibe," you probably readily admit that you work much better with some people than with others.

Communication skill is critical in working relationships. Most difficult situations can at least become bearable through open communication.

## Being Held Back

Very often, student teachers are not given the opportunity to work with children as much as they would like. As a result, they can become frustrated and feel that their potential for growth as teachers is being stifled. This can also happen when a cooperating teacher steps in during an activity or incident and assumes the student cannot handle the situation. These occurrences reduce the student's opportunity to work out of tight or uncomfortable spots. In the first example, the student is not allowed to start; in the second, to finish.

The student needs to know the thinking behind the cooperating teacher's behavior; the cooperating teacher needs to grasp the student's feeling. Neither can happen without communicating.

> Your master teacher is not able to read your mind. The only way he is going to know the things you are worried about, any feeling of inadequacy or uncertainty you may have, as well as your positive feelings, is to tell him. (Gordon-Nourok, 1979)

A special, agreed-upon signal can be used by the student teacher to alert the cooperating teacher to her need for help, in the form of immediate consultation, or suggestion.

## Sensing a Need for Child Activities and Using One-Day Wonders

One way to avoid misunderstandings and difficulties with your cooperating teacher is to come prepared with a number of short activities that could be called **one-day wonders**. These preplanned activities are a sort of insurance policy, and relieve the panic of possibly being asked to do a last-minute activity or when sensing the need for children's engagement in an activity at certain times of the day (see Figure 8–5). One can fit a number of preplanned activities, stored separately, in a large tote bag or cardboard file that can be stowed somewhere in the classroom.

A simple lesson, appropriate for fall, might be to come to class with the following materials for each child: a 2-inch ball of clay (carefully wrapped in plastic so the clay won't dry out), paper plates to define work space, and lunch bags for gathering leaves and seeds lying on the ground. This lesson has been successfully used with preschoolers and primary-age children. During free play or recess, children can be asked to pick up and place in the bags items from the play yard that remind them of fall. Typically, students will gather all kinds of leaves, twigs, seed pods, dry weeds, and even stones and pebbles.

On returning to the classroom, the following directions can be given: "At the science (or discovery) center, you will find a stack of paper plates and a large plastic bag with balls of clay. You may choose the science center as one of your options to explore this afternoon. Place one of the paper plates on the table; take one of the balls of clay from the plastic bag and place it on your plate. Shape the ball of clay into any form you wish, and use any of the materials you brought in from the play yard as decoration. When you finish, leave your sculpture on its paper plate and place it on the shelf by the window." You may want to demonstrate the process as you give the directions.

Other one-day wonders designed by former student teachers follow:

◆ Provide colored, gummed paper worker hats (precut chef, cowboy, firefighter, nurse, sailor, farmer, cab driver, etc.), art paper, and crayons. Children lick and stick, add a face if they wish, and possibly share a story about their hat, or give their created person a name.

◆ Provide tongs, blunt tweezers, chopsticks, three colors or more of colored cotton balls (shake powdered tempera and balls in *closed* plastic, zippered bags), small containers. For this activity, children sort colors by picking up the cotton balls with the variety of tools provided.

**one-day wonders—** preplanned and often prepackaged collections of materials that student teachers can easily set up or use on the spur of the moment to engage young children.

▶ **Figure 8-5** Observers and assistant teacher may be unable to discern whether the lead teacher is using a "one-day wonder." Courtesy of Iowa State University Child Development Laboratory School.

◆ Provide mounted photos of children, snapped in action in the classroom. This causes lots of discussion and excitement. Say, "Tell me about the photograph you've chosen." This works especially well if children can stand in front of the group of photos, giving all a good look before commencing.

◆ Provide small plastic cars and roads, drawn on shelf paper by the student teacher beforehand, with other features such as houses, stop signs, trees, dead-ends, railroad tracks, parking spots, and the like. Use your imagination. A roll of masking tape secures the road to table tops or floors. This wonder is good for outside as well as inside, as shelf paper can be rolled and ready. Many children will want to talk about what they are doing and where they are going.

One-day wonders for math can relate to graphing months in which children have birthdays. Stars or small sticky notes can be pasted on a prepared calendar chart. Favorite foods, numbers of brothers and sisters, which student is wearing what colors: all of these lend themselves to graphing.

Science activities can be as simple as having magnets available. Probing magnetism can extend to having children discover which items around the classroom will hold magnets and which will not.

Other science activities can relate to classifying a variety of leaves and flowers and discussing their similarities and differences. A teacher is only limited by her imagination and ability to predict what developmentally appropriate activity will interest children.

## Site Politics

One of the most difficult placement situations is one that is consumed with conflict. Power struggles between teachers, the director or principal, parents, the community, or any other group can cause the student to feel as if he is being pressured to take sides. The student teacher is usually afraid to join either faction and tries to be a friend to all. This situation should be discussed with your supervisor—quickly. Make sure to convey that you are willing to work through a difficult situation but that you want your supervisor aware of your placement site's tensions.

**role model**—a person whose behavior is imitated by others.

**collaboration**—parents and teachers working together for the ultimate good of the children or students.

## Developing Supportive Staff Relationships

Just as you **role model** behaviors for children, you will consciously or unconsciously model behaviors for colleagues. These behaviors may include empathy, friendliness, kindness, concern, and **collaboration**.

Professional conduct encompasses valuing staff diversity, in special abilities, talents, and educative ideas and approaches. Working together to accomplish goals may require acceptance of differences, careful listening and observation, the ability to communicate effectively and honestly, and the elimination of any need to change others, or to defend any position on issues (see Figure 8–6). These attributes, along with the use of reflective thinking to find the many avenues to reach goals, skillful collaboration, and the development of team spirit, give staff an edge in goal realization.

▶ **Figure 8-6**
The teaching team can be small or have many members.

© Cengage Learning

# THE ROLE OF COMMUNICATION AND CONFLICT RESOLUTION

**communication**—giving or receiving information, signals, and/or messages.

**Communication** is a broad term that we define as giving and/or receiving information, signals, or messages. Human interactions are full of nonverbal signals, accounting for 60 to 80 percent of most human encounters. Some of the more easily recognized nonverbal communications are facial expressions, body position, breathing tempo, and voice pitch, volume, and inflection (see Figure 8–7).

A two-way process of sending and receiving information occurs in true communication, and communication skill can be learned. Many experts agree a large percentage of what is communicated in any conversational exchange is influenced by the tone of voice and body language of the sender.

Being conscious of what messages people are conveying as they speak with body gestures and tone of voice is important. The whole climate of interpersonal relationships in an educational setting can be affected by an individual's ability to read nonverbal cues.

▶ **Figure 8–7**
Clint loves to make faces that cause peers and teachers to laugh.

## Conflict Resolution

**Conflict resolution** usually refers to strategies that enable individuals to handle conflicts cooperatively, possibly attaining win-win situations. Mediation by a neutral third party can be part of the process. Skills enlisted by conflict resolution participants can include, among others, communication, cooperation, tolerance, and positive expression of emotions (see Figure 8–8).

All conflicts may not be resolvable using this text's recommended conflict resolution techniques. Some problems do not have immediate fixes or short-term solutions, and it is unfortunate if student teachers hold that expectation. Teacher training programs are introducing full semester conflict resolution classes because the coursework is viewed as essential.

Student teacher growth and self-realization can depend on the communication skill of the student teacher and others. According to Rogers and Freiberg (1994), it is through a mutually supportive, helping relationship that each individual can become better integrated and more able to function effectively. Student teachers can model appropriate communication behaviors, increasing effectiveness for other adults and children.

No doubt your student teaching group contains people with diverse opinions and backgrounds. Your placement site may also reflect our multiethnic and multicultural society. Delpit (1995) believes we all carry worlds in our heads, and those worlds are decidedly different. She feels it is the responsibility of a dominant group member to attempt to hear the other side of an issue, and after hearing, to speak in a modified voice that does not exclude the concerns of minority colleagues. When a conflict exists, all participants in a discussion should state their perspective so that all the individual perspectives held can be understood. This affords an opportunity to gain a broader view before jumping into a solution.

Working productively with other staff members requires a mutual exchange that takes place in an atmosphere of openness, respect, and honesty.

**conflict resolution**—a process to resolve disputes between people with different interests. This resolution process can have constructive consequences if the participants air their different interests, make trade-offs, and reach a settlement that satisfies the essential needs of each.

## Communication: Reacting to Bias

Functioning and working in a multicultural society, a teacher may encounter bias. What one adult deems appropriate and worthwhile, another may see as inappropriate. Carter and Curtis (1994) suggest teachers have seven choices when responding to adults who express bias. These are attacking, defending, empathizing, investigating, reframing, excusing, and ignoring. Some of these responding teacher's choices can come as an assault to others, whereas others may foster awareness and sensitivity (Carter & Curtis, 1994). Analyze the following teacher responses and decide which promote the early childhood goal of working as a supportive partner with families.

▶ **Figure 8–8**
Possible positive outcomes in conflict resolution attempts.

**WHAT MAY RESULT IN CONFLICT RESOLUTION EFFORTS IS:**

• the *recognition* that a problem exists, which focuses attention and motivates individuals to take action
• a *clarification* of one's values, points of view, goals, wants, and ethics, and to what degree and intensity one cares
• an *understanding* of others' goals, wants, values, and ethics
• a *focus* on change
• a *confidence* in oneself and the conflict resolution process when resolution is successful
• a *feeling* that personal relationships with other staff can weather problems and disagreements
• a *clearing of the air* and *reduction of stress*
• an *emotional release*
• a *new outlook* about conflict being a part of many working group situations
• a *wake-up call* regarding how one's actions and ideas can create problems with others
• a *realization* that confrontational techniques can be scary, yet may lead to positive outcomes
• a *realization* that boredom or staleness may be a problem in itself and a "ho-hum" attitude changes nothing

*Situation:* Alfredo's mom tells you most of the activities planned at school, and much of the equipment, does not allow Alfredo to be a real boy, and are more suited for girls. A teacher's seven choices of statements might be:

1. "Alfredo chooses his own activities, Mrs. Santos. You don't want us to force him to play more vigorous games, do you?"
2. "We're an accredited school; we've been approved by experts."
3. "You are distressed over Alfredo's behavior at school."
4. "You are concerned that Alfredo will not learn to play like a real boy."
5. "Alfredo chooses many sedentary activities over more vigorous play right now. He is really enjoying books and exploring writing tools. Your feeling is that this behavior might not allow him to develop the physical skill necessary for play with other boys his age. Our program offers vigorous outdoor play, but at the moment, Alfredo is following his own interests."
6. "Well, Alfredo is just being Alfredo."
7. "Mrs. Santos, has this been a good day for you?"

Which choices may identify the problem appropriately? What bias is present? Could the family's cultural expectations cause the expressed feelings and conclusions?

## Caring and Sharing: A First Step in Communicating

What makes a person interesting or easy to talk with? Why do we discuss problems with some individuals and not with others? Perhaps it is because the person with whom we can talk freely loves and accepts us as we are at that moment. Love and acceptance (and respect for a colleague) can be demonstrated a number of ways. Saying it may be the easiest way; showing it through actions may be the toughest. With children, giving attention and honoring with their freedom of choice helps develop their feelings of self-worth and value. Touching also usually reinforces rapport; a pat, hug, or open lap for young children expresses love and acceptance. A wink, a notice of accomplishment, or a sincere recognition of a special uniqueness in an individual helps feelings of caring and sharing grow.

Setting the stage for easy approaching and trust also helps. NAEYC's *Early Childhood Program Standards* (2005, 2007) state that warm, sensitive, and responsive teacher–child relationships help children develop a secure, positive sense of self, and encourages them to respect and cooperate with others. It also notes children who see themselves as highly valued are more likely to feel secure, thrive physically, get along with others, learn well, and feel part of a community.

Student teachers plan ways to establish rapport with children and adults (see Figure 8–9). Being an upbeat person and making sincere, appropriate remarks is recommended.

Children's communication skill and degree of cooperation may affect how a student teacher relates to and views them. Student teachers tend to gravitate toward conversation with children who respond, use the student teacher's name, and establish eye contact, as well as to those children who are most like them. They also interact with the child who gains their attention. Popular, well-liked children usually fit this description. Seeing the challenge in developing trust and open communication with each child, student teachers will notice some children who may ignore their conversational overtures or otherwise reject them. They sometimes find that approaching a small group of children or a child in solitary play works best to initiate conversation. Children who feel good about themselves and experience caring teachers usually communicate successfully with newcomers such as student teachers.

## Authenticity

Much has been written about being "*real*" with children and adults. This means honestly sharing your feelings without putting down or destroying anyone's feelings of competency and self-worth. The term "congruent sending" was coined by Gordon (1972), well known for his work in human communication. His definition follows:

> Congruence refers to the similarity of what a person (the sender) is thinking or feeling inside, and what he communicates to the outside. When a person is being congruent, we experience him as "open," "direct," or "genuine." When we sense that a person's communication is incongruent, we judge him as "not ringing true," "insincere," "affected," or just plain "phony."

The resulting risk in sending real messages without skill is that we may experience rejection. Student teachers can learn to express a wide range of real feelings in a skillful way. Anger is perhaps the hardest to handle skillfully. Ginott (1972) has advice for dealing with anger:

> The realities of teaching make anger inevitable. Teachers need not apologize for their angry feelings. An effective teacher is neither a masochist nor a martyr. He does not play the role of a saint or act the part of an angel. He is aware of his human feelings and respects them. Though he cannot be patient, he is always authentic. His response is genuine. His words fit his feeling. He does not hide his annoyance. He does not pretend patience. He does not demonstrate hypocrisy by acting nice when feeling nasty.

▶ **Figure 8-9**
Student teachers establish rapport on their first working days. Bending to the children's level helps do so.

© Cengage Learning

> An enlightened teacher is not afraid of his anger because he has learned to express it without doing damage. He has mastered the secret of expressing anger without insult.
>
> . . . When angry, an enlightened teacher remains real. He describes what he sees, what he feels, and what he expects. He attacks the problem, not the person.

Remember that not all situations or conflicts can be solved; anger and strong emotions directed toward you may be displaced. Your function may be that of a "listening board" who suggests the conflict would be best resolved if the speaker were to address the problem with the person with whom the problem exists.

A student teacher's idea that the perfect teacher is always calm and cool may inhibit communicating and produce feelings of guilt. A multitude of emotions will be present during student teaching days; a daily journal helps students pinpoint feelings in early stages, and written expression is often easier than speaking with a supervisor. Usually, pleasant feelings are the ones most easily described and discussed. Recognizing the buildup of angry feelings may take a special tuning-in to the self. Common tension signals include:

- shrill, harsh, or louder voice tone
- inability to see humor in a situation
- withdrawal or silence
- continual mental rehashing of an emotionally trying encounter

Sharing feelings, including those you consider negative, may help develop a close feeling with others.

## Stating Common Goals and "I" Messages

The first words spoken when one wants to confront and solve a problem or difficulty in the workplace needs thoughtful consideration. This text presents two techniques. The first is to simply state the situation as the speaker sees it and at the same time include how the situation results in a consequence that impedes a jointly held program goal. It does not blame or judge but states the reality of the situation. It calmly outlines a problem the speaker wants to solve. You can probably picture the incident or behavior that initiated the following first statements.

"When student teachers take their breaks together, it leaves just one teacher in the classroom. Some areas are difficult to supervise and children's safety can be compromised. Let's work on a schedule of breaks or some other way to fix the problem."

"I've noticed parents sometimes are frustrated at pick-up time because they can't find papers their child wants to take home. They don't seem to know where to look. I think we want a smooth and less stressful pick-up time, any ideas?"

"Every morning at circle (circle time), the day of the week and the name of the month are discussed, but children seem uninterested and have not been able to learn them. I'm wondering why we are giving this learning a priority and if it is developmentally appropriate for three-and-a-half-year-olds. What do you think? I think is this something we should investigate."

The second strategy to use in opening statements is starting out with an *I* message, which communicates the sender's feelings without blaming or judging another person. It is a widely recognized and accepted technique. Consequently, it is sometimes recognized and receives a here-we-go-again response in adults who recognize it is the beginning of a problem-solving strategy. Still, it has frequently been used successfully and should be considered. Examples of *I* messages follow:

"I'm sad that these pages in our book about horses are torn and crumpled. Book pages need to be turned with care, like this."

*I* messages—Thomas Gordon's term for a response to a child's (or adult's) behavior that focuses on how the sender feels rather than on the child's (or adult's) character.

"I get upset when materials I had planned to use with the children disappear."

"Wait a minute. If all the student teachers take a break together, there will be only one adult in the classroom. I'm frustrated; I thought there was a clear statement about taking separate breaks."

"I'm confused about this assignment. I feel like I missed an explanation. Can we talk about it sometime today?"

"I'm feeling insecure right now. I thought I sensed your disapproval when you asked the children to stop the activity planned for them."

One should guard against *I* messages that are destructive; they sometimes send solutions or involve blaming and judgmental phrases. Often they deal with saying you did this or that. These are false *I* messages:

"I feel frustrated when you behave so stupidly."

"I am angry when you don't keep your promises. No one will be able to trust you."

The ability to send *I* messages is a communication skill that follows recognition of feelings and an effort to communicate directly with the individuals concerned. At times, we provoke strong feelings within ourselves, and an inner dialogue ensues. *I* messages do not tend to build defensiveness, as do **you messages**. With *I* messages, the communication starts on the right foot.

Exercising integrity during moments of choice is an important consideration. Moral dilemmas are frequently faced by student teachers who may or may not weigh decisions before responding to stimuli. It is sometimes so easy to give defensive responses during periods of growth, like student teaching. This type of response may stretch or cloud the truth.

**you messages**—Thomas Gordon's term for a response to a child's (or adult's) behavior that focuses on the child's (or adult's) character (usually in negative terms) rather than on how the adult feels.

## LISTENING: THE ABILITY TO RECEIVE

> We listen with our ears, of course,
>> but surely it is true
>> That eyes, the lips, and hands, and feet
>> will help us listen, too.

Though commonly used with children, this poem may aid student teachers' communicative listening skills. The poem is describing **active listening**, a term also attributed to Gordon (1972), who notes:

> In recent years psychotherapists have called our attention to "active listening." More than passively attending to the message of the sender, it is a process of putting your understanding of that message to its severest of tests—namely, forcing yourself to put into your own words to the sender for verification or for subsequent correction.

We encounter four basic types of verbal communication from other adults:

1. communication, for *building relationships*
2. *cathartic* communication, for releasing emotions and relating our troubles
3. *informational* communication, for sharing ideas, information, and data
4. *persuasive* communication, for reinforcing and changing attitudes or producing a desired action

People who listen well interact with others more effectively and make fewer mistakes.

To practice good listening, try the following tips:

◆ Focus on content and ideas.

◆ Do not prejudge or second-guess.

◆ Listen for feelings.

◆ Jot down facts when appropriate.

**active listening**—the process of putting into your own words a message you received from another based on your understanding of what you thought you heard.

◆ Make eye contact; watch nonverbal cues.

◆ Avoid emotional rebuttals by keeping an open mind. Realize there are emotionally laden words.

◆ Give signs to the sender that you are actively receiving.

◆ Try to identify main and supportive ideas. Store key words; they'll make messages easier to remember.

◆ Rephrase, ask, and/or answer questions, whether explicit or implied.

◆ Understand that there are times when not responding is best.

The active listening process is probably more difficult to learn than *I* message sending. Most individuals have developed listening habits that block true listening (see Figure 8–10). Lundsteen (1976) has labeled four chief listening distortions:

1. *Attitude cutoff* blocks the reception of information at the spoken source because expectation acts on selection. For example, if a student has a strong negative reaction every time he hears the word "test," he might not hear the rest of this message: "The test of any man lies in action."

2. *Motive attributing* is illustrated by the person who says of a speaker, "He is just saying that for public relations," and by the child who thinks, "Teachers just like to talk; they don't really expect me to listen the first time because they are going to repeat the directions 10 times anyway."

3. *Organizational mix-up* happens as one is trying to put someone else's message together: "Did he say 'turn left, then right, then right, then left,' or. . . ?" or "Did he say 'tired' or 'tried'?"

4. *Self-preoccupation* causes distortion because the listener is busy formulating his reply and never hears the message: "I'll get him for that; as soon as he stops talking, I'll make a crack about how short he is, then . . ."

Preoccupation with one's own message is a frequent distortion for young listeners. Hanging on to their own thoughts during communication takes a great deal of their attention and energy.

▷ **Figure 8-10**

Hearing others. From Communications Briefings, (1997) Vol. XVI, NO. IV, Alexandria, VA: Capitol Publications. Reprinted with permission from Communication Briefings. All rights reserved.

## WHY WE DON'T HEAR OTHERS

If you want to listen so you really hear what others say, make sure you're not a:

- Mind reader. You'll hear little or nothing as you think "What is this person really thinking or feeling?"
- A person who rehearses. Your mental tryouts for "Here's what I'll say next" can tune out the speaker.
- Filterer. Some call this selective listening—hearing only what you want to hear.
- Dreamer. Drifting off during a face-to-face conversation can lead to an embarrassing "What did you say?" or "Could you repeat that?"
- Identifier. If you refer everything you hear to your experience, you probably didn't really hear what was said.
- Comparer. When you get side-tracked assessing the messenger, you're sure to miss the message.
- A person who derails. Changing the subject too quickly tells others you're not interested in anything they have to say.
- A person who spars. You hear what's said but quickly belittle it or discount it. That puts you in the same class as the person who derails.
- A person who placates. Agreeing with everything you hear just to be nice or to avoid conflict does not mean you're a good listener.

Source: *The Writing Lab*, Department of English, Purdue University, West Lafayette, IN 47907.

The student teacher hopes others recognize her teaching competencies. Being anxious to display your knowledge can focus communication on sending messages that concentrate on self rather than really listening to others. New listening skills will take conscious practice. To gain skill in reflective listening, an exercise called *mirroring* is often used. The following examples mirror back to the child the feeling the listener believes he received:

1. *Child, pleading:* "I don't want to eat these baked potatoes. I hate them."
   *Listener:* "You don't like baked potatoes."

2. *Child, pleading and forlorn:* "I don't have anything to do today. What can I do? I wish there was something to do!"
   *Listener:* "You're bored and lonely."

3. *Child, angry and confused:* "I hate Julie. She always cries and tries to get her way. If I don't do what she wants, she goes home."
   *Listener:* "You're angry and confused."

4. *Child, stubborn and indignant:* "I don't want to take a bath. I'm not even dirty. I hate baths anyway. Why do I have to take a bath every day?"
   *Listener:* "You don't want to take a bath."

5. *Child, crying:* "Kiyoko won't let me play with her dolls. She's mean. Make her give me some of them to play with."
   *Listener:* "You're angry with Kiyoko."

6. *Child, crying because of a hurt finger:* "Ow! Ow! It hurts! Ow!"
   Listener: "It sure hurts."

Adults often find mirroring and reflecting back feeling statements easier with children than adults. With use, mirroring statements feel more comfortable, and the sender, whether a child or an adult, feels he has been heard. With adults, clarifying mirroring-type *questions* seems more natural. This is done as follows:

"Am I hearing you correctly, that you're really angry right now?" "Is frustration what you're feeling?" "You're saying you don't want to be told what to do?"

## Communication Tips

Harris (1995) suggests the following tips to improve staff communication:

◆ Beware of kicking and stroking at the same time. When we tell someone something positive, then reprimand, then end with a positive, we call that sandwiching. Some workshops teach this as a soft technique, but it does send conflicting messages.

◆ Whenever possible, plan the message. Think of what the message is, along with how, where, and when you want to send it.

◆ For communication to be effective, spend as much time listening as talking. Be attentive.

◆ Do not imply a choice if there is not one. Tentative language and manner are fine in some circumstances, but they often suggest an option that may not exist.

◆ Record an hour or so of routine, day-to-day conversations on a tape or digital recorder. Look for hidden agendas, soft or padded language, and other indicators that you are not sending clear messages.

◆ Say what you mean; mean what you say.

◆ Feedback is a continuous process, not just a one-time action. Learn to give and elicit feedback on a regular basis.

◆ Look at the person you are talking to and establish eye contact throughout the conversation. (But do be aware that in some cultures this may be considered rude.)

◆ If it appears that no one is listening, the problem may be exactly that; no one *is* listening.

Additional suggestions follow:

◆ Try to think of two possible ways to resolve the problem at hand before speaking to a colleague or supervisor.
◆ When weighing possible solutions, identify possible joint benefits.
◆ Paraphrase differing opinions to clarify ideas.
◆ Admit to changing your mind, and view it as appropriate and mature.
◆ Admit doubt and error. Be seen as a collaborator.

Warner (1995) notes there is not much that can be done about negative or unprofessional teachers except to smile, be pleasant, minimize contact, and seek out professional, positive-minded colleagues.

Copeland (1997) outlines three choices in dealing with problems important to staff members. (This chapter concentrates on choice 2.)

*Choice 1:* I am satisfied with things the way they are. I can live with what's going on, so I won't worry about it.
*Choice 2:* I am unhappy with my situation, and I am on a path of trying to resolve the conflict. If my first effort doesn't succeed, I will try something else.
*Choice 3:* I will quit my job.

## A PROBLEM-SOLVING PROCESS

Most problems can be faced in a sequential manner. This text suggests problem solving in a rational manner, when emotions are under control. Take some time alone to cool down or physically burn off excessive tension before you try to use it. Substituting new behaviors into your problem-solving style takes time and effort. Practice is necessary.

Sending *I* messages and active listening will avert conflict buildup. However, you do have the choice of living with a problem and not working on it. This can work for short periods, but it usually erodes the quality of your relationship with others or with yourself. Alienation occurs in most instances, but you may prefer this course of action and be prepared for its consequences. Most often, you will choose to confront others or yourself and work toward solutions that eliminate the problem. Familiarize yourself with the following steps, which suit many different situations.

*Step 1.* The recognition of facts, tensions, emotions, or an expression of a problem occurs.
*Step 2.* Analysis takes place. (Who and what are involved? When and where is the problem happening? Whose problem is it?)
*Step 3.* *I* messages or state the facts and consequences (as they relate to joint goals) messages are sent. (This step can include active listening *and* reflecting skills.)
*Step 4.* Discussion takes place. (This involves probing for more data. Who owns the problem?)
*Step 5.* Both sides of the problem are clearly stated.
*Step 6.* Possible solutions are proposed.
*Step 7.* An agreement is secured to try one of these solutions, and if the solution does not work, an agreement is made to meet again.
*Step 8.* Individual respect for willingness, time, and effort to solve the problem is expressed, in an attempt to reinforce positive behaviors.

This process can be attempted, but it will not work if one party refuses to talk, mediate, or look for courses of action that will satisfy everyone involved. Refusing to act on solutions also hinders the process. Problem solving can be two-sided, even when only one person is involved.

At step 2, you may realize the problem belongs to another, and the best course of action is to help that person communicate with someone else. It may be that only one person can own the problem, such as when the issue is with using inappropriate language. Often a problem may disappear at step 3.

The discussion in step 4 can include "I'm really interested in talking about it" or "Let's talk; we'll examine just what's happening to us." However, there is a tendency to blame rather than identify contributing causes. Getting stuck and not moving past step 4 stalls resolution of the problem. Statements like "You're right; I really avoid cleaning that sink" or "I'm really bothered by interruptions during planned group times" all involve owning the problem.

Before possible solutions are mentioned, a clear statement of conflicting views in step 5, adds clarification.

*With a child:* "You'd like to paint next, and I told Carlos it's his turn."
*With a fellow student teacher:* "You feel the way I handle Peter is increasing his shyness, and I feel it is helping him."
*With a cooperating teacher:* "I think my activity was suitable for the group, but you believe it didn't challenge them."
*With a supervisor:* "You feel I tend to avoid planning outdoor activities; I think I've planned quite a few."

Your confrontation might start at step 6. ("Let's figure out some way to make the noisy time right before nap a little calmer and quieter.") Finding alternate solutions admits there are probably a number of possibilities. "Together we'll figure a way" or "That's one way; here's another idea." A do-it-my-way attitude inhibits joint agreement. Thinking alternatives over and then getting back together is helpful at times. Seeking a consultant who offers ideas can help solve problems that participants see as hopeless.

When all parties decide to try one solution, as in step 7, consideration should be given to meeting again if that particular alternative does not work. ("We'll try it this week and discuss whether it's working next Monday.")

Step 8 reinforces both sides. "We figured it out." "Thanks for taking the time to solve this." "I appreciated your efforts in effecting a solution." This process is not to be used as a panacea, but it does provide helpful guidelines.

Classroom problems can involve any aspect of the student teaching situation (see Figure 8–11). Interpersonal conflicts will take courage to resolve, as well as consideration of the proper time and place to confront the issues.

▶ **Figure 8-11**
This teacher is attempting to redirect a group of children's "rowdy" behavior in the play yard.

© Cengage Learning

The teacher is sometimes afraid to confront a child who is hostile, caustic, or vengeful. Such a teacher avoids and avoids until the accumulation of feelings becomes so unbearable an explosion occurs, and the teacher loses control. Once out of control, there is no possibility of bringing about a positive resolution. But when the hateful, rejection emotions subside, there is always hope that the teacher can come to terms with the child and reach a depth of relatedness and mutuality. (Moustakas, 1966)

Arrange to problem-solve when participants have no classroom responsibilities, and where there will not be any interruptions or noninvolved observers.

## Using Problem Solving with Children

Gartrell (2006) defines conflict mediation in early childhood classrooms as happening when a third person assists others to resolve conflicts. This usually happens when two children work with a mediator who is most often the teacher or a student teacher. It falls in the curriculum area of *social-emotional learning*, and it involves learned skills and behaviors that work successfully when conflict takes place.

When faced with children in disagreement, student teachers often hesitate if the children are showing signs of working toward resolution or negotiation, or if tempers are calming rather than escalating. They monitor whether bullying is involved, and notice if a particular child is having trouble sticking up for her rights. They watch before deciding to become the neutral, third party who attempts mediation, unless harm is eminent. When they do attempt to intervene, they realize volatile and strong emotions may be present. A good first step can be for the teacher to bend to eye level and circle the children with her arms at their waists. This act in itself may assuage children's feelings somewhat, and other techniques are used such as counting to three slowly before they take turns telling what happened or breathing in and out a few times may help them calm down and listen. Another technique is to ask children to sit down together with the teacher, and then say, "Please wait until I count to 10 before you tell me what happened. Then both of you will have a turn to tell me."

Then the teacher plugs in step 1, by recognizing child emotions and saying, "Looks like we have a problem." She then gives one child a chance to state his case while she reminds the other to listen and he will be next. ("It is your turn to speak, and your time to listen.") Both sides of the problem are then stated by the mediator. Step 4, active listening, has occurred, and the mediator moves on to steps 5 and 6, during which she promotes negotiation and ideas for solutions by saying something like, "Can you think of a way to ask for a turn?" The mediator then works toward a solution that satisfies both children. In a stalemate, she suggests a solution, but chances are the children will think of something. When children agree, she verbally applauds their problem solving and reinforces the behavior with, "That is a fine idea; both of you were able to talk about ways that felt right to both of you and you solved your problem. If this idea does not work, we will come back together and try another idea."

It may take many mediated sessions for some children to resolve differences, and some may have a hard time breaking behavior habits that have been successful in getting them their way in the past. The process is offered here because it depends a great deal on a teacher's ability to communicate.

## Negotiation Skills

It has been said that we do not get what we deserve in life, but rather what we negotiate, and that negotiation is not about fairness.

After an individual or staff conflict is apparent, one usually decides if it is worth resolving and then identifies who has the power to make a resolution decision. The goal in negotiation is to uncover a solution that contending participants feel comfortable with: in other words, win-win or get-give resolutions.

Negotiating a series of steps can aid progress and create an attitude of "How are we going to work together on this?" It is important to clarify your position, know what is desired, what options could be considered, and what you might settle for. Many times, options that are acceptable to both parties depend on the creative brainstorming that ensues during the negotiation process. Active listening is mandatory. Thinking about settings conducive to negotiating and the comfort of participants can enhance outcomes. Taking a walk together in a secluded area or finding a comfortable meeting room when a group of people is involved may work.

Written materials by negotiation experts suggest opposing sides speak in tune with the other side's interests, mentioning why options offered might benefit one or both sides. Face-saving solutions are seen as important considerations.

Negotiations end with a commitment, an agreed-upon plan, or a follow-up date to try again for an amicable solution.

It is easy to see that staffs with a sense of community, who respect diversity and diverse opinions, have an advantage in the negotiation process. Groups that believe conflict is natural and healthy may more effectively handle problems.

Unfortunately, negotiation breaks down when attitudes include an unwillingness to confront conflict or even admit it exists, or when an unwillingness to listen or accept others' ideas characterizes behavior. Delpit (1995) suggests teachers must learn to be vulnerable enough in their thinking to turn upside down to allow others' ideas to enter consciousness.

## Resistance

Resistance to rules and not conforming to what is expected can be seen both in children and adults. It is usually viewed as negative behavior. Moustakas (1966) believes it is healthy:

> Resistance is a way for the child to maintain his own sense of self in the light of external pressures to manipulate and change him. It is a healthy response, an effort of the individual to sustain the integrity of the self.

Resistance and controversy can become challenges that develop our understanding and let us know others at a deeper level. Though confrontations may frighten student teachers in early days, later they are seen as opportunities to know more about children and adults and promote conflict resolution skill.

## ▶ SUMMARY

Student teaching is a miniature slice of life and living. Problems arise and are common to all. Some situations change with time; others need extended communication to be resolved.

Growth and change are experienced sometimes easily, sometimes painfully. It is helpful to maintain a caring and sharing feeling, open communication, and a sense of humor. Time and successful experience take care of most initial difficulties. The supervisor's and cooperating teacher's roles are to provide supportive assistance. Team status may evolve slowly and depends on student effort.

Sending and receiving oral and written messages effectively is a necessary skill for student teachers. The whole climate of the student teaching experience depends in part on communication. Developing rapport with adults and children during the early days helps student teachers become relaxed and comfortable.

Love and acceptance are established in a variety of ways. Authenticity in communication is deemed highly desirable and effective. Skill in sending *I* messages, being able to state the facts and consequences of problem situations, and active listening are communication techniques that student teachers can practice and use with both adults and children.

Problem-solving skills are important. There seem to be definite styles of relating to others during problem-solving situations. Students are urged to practice new techniques in negotiation. Early fears of confronting tend to disappear as communicative problem solving becomes a way to know and understand others.

## ▶ HELPFUL WEBSITES

http://www.peace-ed.org
Peace Education Foundation. Take a look at classroom-tested curricula.

http://www.clas.uiuc.edu
Early Childhood Research Institute. This is a good source for those working with culturally and linguistically diverse children and families.

http://www.vanderbilt.edu/csefel/
The Center on Social and Emotional Foundations for Early Learning. Use "social outcomes" and "emotional outcomes" as search phrases; also "communication techniques."

 Additional resources for this chapter can be found by visiting the companion website at www.cengage.com/education/machado.

## ▶ SUGGESTED ACTIVITIES

A. Form groups of six for the following role-playing activity. Select two members to role-play; others will be observers. Switch between role-playing and observing until all group members have had a turn in both roles.

   *Directions:* Dramatize each of the following role-played statements or situations. Then observers will decide whether the role-players used active listening; if not, they will make suggestions for active listening responses.

1. *Student teacher to cooperating teacher:* "Your room needs more organization."
2. *Cooperating teacher to student teacher:* "Jennifer, have you been having problems at home lately?"
3. *Irritated cooperating teacher to student teacher:* "Taylor, you've been ill too often. We rely on our student teachers to be here every day."
4. *Critical parent to student teacher:* "My daughter needs her sweater on when she goes out of doors."
5. *One student teacher to another:* "Mrs. Nguyen, the director, only sees what I do wrong, not what I do right."
6. *One student teacher to another:* "You always leave the sink a mess."
7. John, a preschooler, is dumping paint on the floor.
8. *Student teacher to child who is not going to the wash area:* "It's time to wash hands."
9. Mary, a four-year-old, hit you because you insisted that she share a toy.
10. *College supervisor to student teacher:* "Filomena, I'm confused. Your assignments are always late. Weren't my directions clear?"
11. *Cooperating teacher to student teacher:* "When you were doing your activity, I had a difficult time not stepping in. The boys were destroying the girls' work."
12. *First child:* "Give me back my paint brush." *Second child:* "You can't have it."

B. In the following situations, state as clearly as possible what you think are both sides of the problem. Then describe two possible alternate solutions that both parties might accept because they satisfy both participants.

1. Cecelia has been assigned to student teach from 9:00 AM to 2:30 PM on Tuesdays. Her cooperating teacher, Mr. Kifer, notices she has been leaving early. Cecelia has been arriving 10 to 15 minutes early each day. Her cooperating teacher confronts Cecelia one day before she departs. "Leaving early, Cecelia?"
2. Henri, a four-year-old, has been told repeatedly by the student teacher that he must put the blocks he used back on the shelf. Henri has ignored the request continually. The student teacher requests that the cooperating teacher ask Henri to replace the blocks because he does not respond to the student teacher.
3. The cooperating teacher has been silent most of the morning. The student teacher can feel tension mounting and says, "I'm really feeling uncomfortable because I sense there is something wrong." The cooperating teacher ignores the remark, and walks off as she has done on other days. At the end of week, the student discusses the situation with the supervisor.
4. Christopher, a student teacher, is fuming. "After all the work I put into the activity, she didn't even mention it," he says to Charlotte, another student teacher.
5. "I'd really like to present this new song to the children," says Robin, a student teacher. "You didn't put it in the plan book, Robin, and I have a full day planned," the cooperating teacher says. "Let's talk about it; I can see the disappointment on your face." Robin replies, "It's not disappointment. I can't see why the schedule is so inflexible." "Let's talk about that after the morning session, Robin."

6. "I sure needed your help at circle today," the cooperating teacher says. "I was in the bathroom with Anthony; he's got those pants that button at the shoulders," the student teacher answers.

7. "I'm really tired today, Mrs. Cuffaro," the student teacher answers, when asked why she stayed in the housekeeping area most of the morning. Mrs. Cuffaro says, "There were lots of children who could have used your assistance, Annette. Will you have time to talk when the children are napping?" "Sure," Annette replies.

8. Miriam, an attractive student teacher, is assigned to an on-campus laboratory school. Male friends often hang around the lobby or ask the secretary to give her messages and notes. The secretary has told Miriam this is bothersome. Miriam tells the secretary that the notes often concern getting a ride home because she does not have a car.

## ▶ REVIEW

A. Briefly describe what you feel are prime areas or issues of conflict in student teaching.

B. Arrange the following problem-solving steps in order, based on the eight-step sequence found in the text. You may find that more than one applies to the same step.

1. *Cooperating teacher:* "We'll put paintings without names in this box this week and see what happens." *Student teacher:* "Okay."

2. *Student teacher:* "You feel children's artwork should always have the child's name printed in the upper left corner."

3. *Cooperating teacher:* "You could put names on the artwork when you're the adult in the art area."

4. *Student teacher:* "I feel the child's name should be put on the artwork only when the child gives permission to do so. If the children don't ask to have their names put on, they will learn the consequences when it's time to take the art home."

5. *Student teacher:* "I could tell each child what will happen if there is no name on a painting."

6. *Cooperating teacher:* "There's been quite a bottleneck when parents try to find their child's artwork at departure time. Sometimes, there are no names printed in the upper left corner."

7. *Student teacher:* "You would like to put each child's name on his artwork, and I think each child can learn something if I don't print his name when he does not give me permission to do so."

8. *Student teacher:* "I appreciate your understanding my point of view."

9. *Cooperating teacher:* "You could write the child's name lightly if that child said no."

10. *Cooperating teacher:* "I think the lesson to be learned isn't worth the commotion at closing."

11. *Student teacher:* "This is the way I feel about names on artwork."

C. List as many possible alternative solutions as you can for the following problem.

Winona has been placed with a cooperating teacher who, in her opinion, has created a classroom environment that offers the children few play choices. She has communicated this to her cooperating teacher, who then asks Winona for suggestions.

## ▶ REFERENCES

Burman, L. (2009). *Are you listening? Fostering conversations that help young children learn.* St. Paul, MN: Redleaf Press.

Canter, T. (1998). *First-class teacher: Successful strategies for new teachers.* Santa Monica, CA: Canter and Associates, Inc.

Carter, M., & Curtis, D. (1994). *Training teachers: A harvest of theory and practice.* St. Paul, MN: Redleaf Press.

Copeland, T. (1997, January/February). How to help your staff cope with conflict. *Child Care Information Exchange,* 182.

Delpit, L. (1995). *Other people's children: Cultural conflict in the classroom.* New York: The New Press.

Gartrell, D. (2006, March). Guidance matters, *Young Children,* 61(2), 88–89.

Ginott, H. (1972). I'm angry! I'm appalled! I am furious! *Teacher and child.* New York: Macmillan. Reprinted in *Today's Education Magazine,* NEA Journal (Nov. 19, 1972).

Gordon, T. (1972). The risks of effective communication. *Parent Notebook.* New York: Effectiveness Training Associates.

Gordon-Nourok, E. (1979). *You're a student teacher!* Sierra Madre, CA: SCAEYC.

Harris, J. (1995, July/August). Is anybody out there listening? *Child Care Information Exchange,* 104.

Keirsey, D., & Bates, M. (1984). *Please understand me* (5th Ed.). Del Mar, CA: Gnosology Books.

Leeds, D. (2001, September). Good things come to those who ask: The power of questions. *Bottom Line,* 22(18), 6–8.

Lundsteen, S. W. (1976). *Children learn to communicate.* Englewood Cliffs, NJ: Prentice-Hall.

Morton, L. L., Vesco, R., Williams, N. H., & Awender. M. A. (1997). Student teacher anxieties related to class management, pedagogy, evaluation, and staff relation, British Journal of Educational Psychology 67, 33–39,

Moustakas, C. (1966). *The Authentic Teacher*. Cambridge: Howard A. Doyle.

National Association for the Education of Young Children. (2005, Spring). Governing board approves new standards and criteria. NAEYC's *Accreditation Update, 6*(2), 1–5.

National Association for the Education of Young Children. (2007). *NAEYC early childhood program standards and accreditation criteria*. Washington, DC: Author.

Read, K., & Patterson, J. (1980). *The nursery school and kindergarten* (7th ed.). New York: Holt, Rinehart & Winston.

Rogers, C., & Freiberg, H. (1994). *Freedom to learn* (3rd ed.). New York: Merrill/Macmillan.

SkillPath Seminars. (1997). *Conflict management skills for women*. Mission, KS: SkillPath Publications.

Von Bergen, J. M. (2003, September 7). Dreams can reveal job anxiety and sometimes produce solutions, *Idaho Statesman* 1CB.

Warner, J. (1995). *The unauthorized TEACHER'S survival guide*. Indianapolis, IN: Park Avenue Publications.

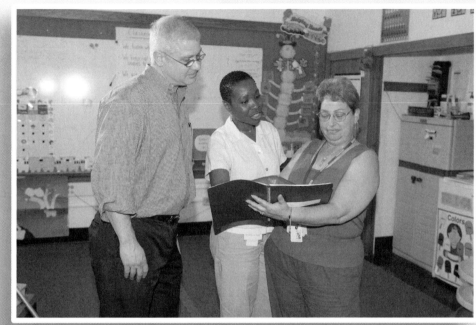

© Cengage Learning

# Interactions

# CHAPTER 9

# Student Teachers and Families

**After reading this chapter, you should be able to:**

1. List five or more common home or school involvement activities.
2. List three possible goals of home visits.
3. Discuss four student teacher skills or behaviors that build or strengthen family-friendly relationships.

## Student Teacher Scenario

**Setting:** A community college laboratory school.

Mark, a four-year-old, has been enrolled since age three in the child development center attached to an older community college in a large city.

Observing Mark was a joyful experience for those enrolled as early childhood majors who chose him as a subject of study. He was energetic, with his own pack of special buddies who were willing to investigate or participate in any classroom or outdoor adventure. Physically strong, of average height, and well coordinated, he possessed obvious good health. Mark was often described as a sweet dynamo, quick to offer his ideas in classroom discussions. Mark was also the kind of child his teachers described as progressing above average in all developmental areas.

His single mother, a community college sophomore, expected to transfer to a local university in the fall. She often picked up Mark's older, elementary school–aged brother first, so both came into the center at pick-up time. Mark would excitedly show his brother his school projects, or demonstrate how he could maneuver a new piece of outdoor equipment. It was easy to see that Mark idolized his brother, and a close relationship was apparent with his mom. His professionally employed father had custody on some weekends but never attended school functions. Mark talked, at times, about camping trips and ball games with dad.

Without warning, Mark's behavior changed. He appeared sleepy, withdrawn, uninterested in the activities around him. He sat in one spot for long periods and sought to be alone in the play yard. His friends approached him, but he would either not talk or say he didn't want to play when they offered ideas. The staff alerted Mark's mom to his bad day and suggested monitoring his health. Teachers had talked to Mark, asking if he felt sick, but he indicated he didn't hurt anywhere. The staff's plan was to record Mark's behavior the next day and engage him by delicately probing and offering as much close, physical contact as he seemed willing to accept.

A meeting with Mark's mother was set as soon as possible. His behavior led teachers to suspect depression. When the meeting took place, Mark's mother immediately broke down and was extremely distraught. She explained that Mark's father, who had remarried about 6 months earlier, had begun a suit for full custody of Mark's older brother but not for Mark. The father believed that Mark was the result of a relationship that Mark's mother had while they were legally separated.

## Questions for Discussion:

1. Was the center's handling of Mark's changed behavior appropriate?

2. Is documenting Mark's daily behavior important? Why or why not?

3. Is parent–center communication working effectively here? If yes, what brings you to that conclusion? If no, explain.

# DISCOVERING A CENTER'S FAMILY RELATIONS PHILOSOPHY

Centers and schools differ widely in their philosophy and attitudes toward parents and families. All programs have beliefs and values that guide staff behaviors. Program handbooks usually articulate family relations specifics, and most programs invite, plan, and require family involvement. As a student teacher interested in high-quality care, working with families cooperatively as a team member is a primary goal. This supports the best interest of children.

The National Association for the Education of Young Children's *Code of Ethical Conduct* (2005) has many sections that deal with family–school relationships and ethical responsibilities to families. See a few of these in Figure 9–1.

Stephens (2005) suggests that building authentic partnerships with families goes farther than occasional school–home meetings, visits, and joint holiday celebrations; it requires putting a high priority on family needs. Staff, Stephens believes, should be provided with training in *family engagement* and family-friendly

▶ **Figure 9-1**
Ethical Responsiblities to Families

I-1.12—To work with families to provide a safe and smooth transition as children and families move from one program to the next.                                                          p.xvi

P-1.2—We shall care for and educate children in positive emotional and social environments that are cognitively stimulating and that support each child's culture, language, ethnicity, and family structure.

P-1.3—We shall not participate in practices that discriminate against children by denying benefits, giving special advantages, or excluding them from programs or activities on the basis of their sex, race, national origin, religious beliefs, medical condition, disability, or the marital status/family structure, sexual orientation, or religious beliefs or other affiliations of their families. (Aspects of this principle do not apply in programs that have a lawful mandate to provide services to a particular population of children.)

P-1.4—We shall involve all those with relevent knowledge (including families and staff) in decisions concerning a child, as appropriate, ensuring confidentiality of sensitive information.                p.xvii

**SOURCE:** From Feeney, S., Freeman, N.R. (2005). Ethics and the early childhood educator: Using the NAEYC Code. Washington, DC: National Association for the Education of Young Children.

human relations and interactions. Training would encompass skill in rapport building, using a variety of methods to communicate, developing anti-biased communication, planning engaging family meetings or events, using constructive problem solving that avoids casting blame, conducting family–teacher conferencing, practicing professional confidentiality, and gathering accurate, relevant, and timely data for family referrals when called for.

Epstein (2000) identifies six major types of home/school family partnership activities programs can include. These are:

1. providing information on child development and helping parents strengthen parenting skills
2. increasing and encouraging school-to-home and home-to-school communications
3. involving families in school activities as volunteers at school, home, or other locations.
4. assisting families in setting up home conditions to support learning
5. involving families in decision making through participation in advisory or other school operations
6. collaborating with the community and other local resources

As a student teacher, your first step is to identify your placement classroom's family relations philosophy and policy. Ask questions if written materials do not articulate it sufficiently.

Most centers adhere to a nondiscrimination policy. Children are cared for and belong to unique types of families, and teachers are obligated to facilitate and ensure individual families, no matter how diverse, are accepted and included in center–family interactions. Many centers officially welcome diversity and alert all families to their nondiscrimination policy that asserts the center's goal of accepting and validating family uniqueness, and also building a sense of classroom community, to benefit each child's pride in family and learning potential. Figure 9–2 lists possible heads of families, who care for and parent young children. It is not intended to be a complete listing. Harlan (2007) points out that couples with

▶ **Figure 9–2**
Possible heads of families.

- grandparents
- adoptive parents
- foster parents
- step parents
- gay/lesbian parents
- single parents
- teen parents
- AIDS/HIV parents
- parents in rehabilitation
- incarcerated parents
- drug-dependent parents
- immigrant parents
- non–English-speaking parents
- divorced parents
- migrant parents
- relative guardians
- non-relative guardians

*This is not a complete list, and combinations of categories do exist.

children now occupy less than one in every four households. The lowest percentage ever recorded by the U.S. Census.

> As marriage with children becomes an exception rather than the norm, social scientists say it also is becoming the self-selected province of college-educated and the affluent. The working class and the poor, meanwhile, increasingly steer away from marriage, while living together and bearing children out of wedlock. (P. 9A)

## INTERACTING WITH FAMILIES

Most interactions with parents or family members are informal. The most frequent interaction occurs when people bring and pick up children from the center or school (see Figure 9–3). The entering person may pause at the doorway before entering before saying something to the teacher, who then smiles or nods; these constitute interactions. Stonehouse (2003) emphasizes how crucial a teacher's words and actions are whenever they work with family. She asks preschool staff members to put themselves in their shoes and see things from their perspectives. She asserts that the relationship between the teaching staff and families, perhaps more so than the activities and experiences offered to children, are likely to be a major determinant of the long-term impact on participating children (p. 2). Stonehouse believes teachers should consider how it would feel if no one in their child's classroom acknowledges their presence and waiting or if the staff is always too busy to talk. Or consider a family member who takes time off from work to volunteer in the classroom and then feels his or her effort has been wasted.

When teachers note an important development during the day, they will mention it at pick-up time. In preschool and infant/toddler centers, daily written notes are sometimes used to share child activities and behaviors, such as food consumption, diaper changes, and a child's general mood, if significant. If there has been an issue, teachers take the time to explain what has happened. Communications such as these are typical of the informal kind. In elementary school classrooms, face-to-face contact with parents and family members may be infrequent; it is different in early childhood programs.

More formal communication consists of scheduled parent-teacher conferences and home visits. During a parent–teacher conference, a teacher might discuss the

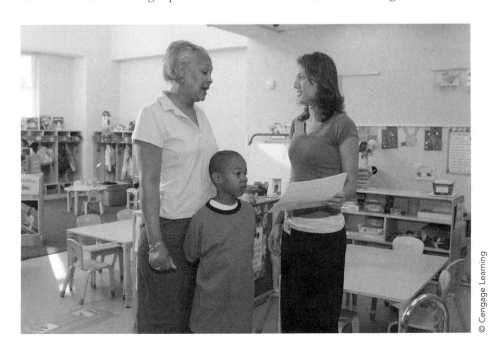

▶ **Figure 9–3**
LeShan lives with his grandmother.

© Cengage Learning

▶ **Figure 9-4**
Teachers gather the
necessary material to
conference effectively
with parents.

developing friendship between two children (see Figure 9–4). In each case, the families will have prior notice about the conference or home visit. They can then plan ahead and anticipate questions they may want to ask on topics of concern or interest.

Kyle and McIntyre (2000) believe that to educate effectively, teachers must reach out to students' families in ways not traditionally imagined, and bridge the ever-widening gap between home and school, so that children realize they are important, cared about, and expected to achieve. Research suggests one of the keys to successful teaching is creating personal connections with children, inside and outside of school. Kaczmarek (2007) notes specialized centers with families who have children with special needs are currently making efforts to effectively collaborate. Early childhood centers offer families with children with disabilities the routine support it gives to all families, and they may have to obtain additional help if these families needs go further than a center's staff can provide. Collaboration can involve coordinated planning and communication between families, teachers, and early intervention professionals—a planned family orientation meeting at the center allows families to meet all individuals involved with their child. This includes classroom staff and other enrolled families. The classroom and its layout, equipment, and material, as well as the center's curriculum, routines, activities, procedures, and policies are explained. This is accomplished before a child's first day. The center also makes sure ongoing communication happens and families are linked to community resources when necessary.

## THE IMPORTANCE OF HOME-TEACHER PARTNERSHIPS

Although educators agree that relationships between schools and families are important, pre-service teachers and student teachers may have received little training or experience working with families. Teachers are the most influential link in school-home collaboration. Communication seems the biggest barrier. Without providing teachers with strategies and techniques, partnerships may not happen.

While teachers may feel completely at home with children and fellow teachers, Winkleman (1999) suggests that collaborating with families can be a frightening and sometimes difficult challenge.

Winkleman surveyed student teachers who soon would become new elementary school teachers. He found their anxieties about families centered in four general areas:

1. defending curriculum and teaching practices
2. involving families in their child's education
3. deciding how much family participation they want in their classroom
4. communicating children's problems and weaknesses

Family surveys and interviews with families or volunteers can gather information that assesses the need for improved relationships. Most families want to be informed about their child's program, educational progress, and what happens at school. Many families are eager to learn how to support their child's growing skills, knowledge, and ability. Validating and celebrating what parents and families do for children, and what teachers endeavor to do, help partnerships thrive.

There are a vast number of levels of family involvement that aid center goal realization. All sorts of discussion groups, workshops, socials, volunteer projects, work parties, and so on, between families and schools are possible. Many schools now alert families during their child's enrollment interview to the expected level of family participation in school activities. With changing family life patterns, teachers may feel that it is becoming harder and harder to involve the many diverse and work-consumed families.

Student teachers can observe their cooperating teacher's attention to teacher–family relationships, noting the effectiveness of communications and actions.

First impressions of a child center or school facility form as parents and family members observe the outside area, enter, and notice lobby areas. The upkeep and maintenance of the school, grounds, and equipment catch parents' eyes. Sounds and smells are noted. The people and conversations encountered, and staff manner and demeanor, create distinct impressions. Family member phone inquiries also allow callers to assess the warmth, knowledge, and careful attention to detail provided by the answering staff member. Each center is felt to have a unique personality, as judged by each new family. In elementary schools, student teachers may be asked to send a letter or card to families, to introduce themselves and share information about the student teacher's background, goals as a student teacher, and experience or training.

Most cooperating teachers will introduce student teachers to parents, family members, volunteers, and professionals visiting the classroom. If you are meeting a person for the first time, and your cooperating teacher is busy and unable to introduce you, introduce yourself and remain friendly and professional.

As the student teacher becomes acquainted and skilled, some cooperating teachers may feel that family contact can be handled by the student. It is wise to discuss this with your college supervisor if you feel this is difficult for you. Helping people feel at ease is an art.

## Home Cultures

Teachers attempt to gain insight by studying children's home cultures, their histories, and the culture's impact on families and children. In California and many other states, this can be a monumental task because of the variety of cultures present and the differences in social class, economic circumstance, and family values. Many centers and schools base their partnership efforts on the following assumptions:

◆ Parents are children's first and primary teachers.

◆ Regardless of diversity, a family's support of their child's education is influential.

◆ To promote children's school success, congruence between home and school is essential.

◆ A center should take the initiative in eliminating barriers to partnership formation and maintenance.

*Student Teacher Quote*—"I was placed in a parent-cooperative preschool whose play yard was full of some of the most interesting and creative play structures and play areas I've ever seen. They were all designed, constructed, and maintained by a crew of father volunteers who had weekend work parties. These men were very involved and one asked me whether the children really liked the latest addition and what features of it seemed the most fun for the children."

**Nana Ghukar, Student Teacher Placement Classroom, Campbell, CA**

◆ Clear messages are necessary in both oral and written communication.

◆ Classrooms are examples of democratic principles and freedoms in action.

In order to be better informed, early childhood educators purposefully acquaint themselves with the cultures of attending children. Centers want to understand family uniqueness and diversity. They do not gather information for purposes other than to be able to sensitively and intelligently interact with families without alienating them and to increase their ability to offer appropriate and individualized learning experiences for children. In knowing families better, they gain the ability to understand each child's learning style, special needs, abilities, and individual characteristics.

In all learning, new learning is built on what children already know. If Father's Day activities are planned, they celebrate fathers and/or other primary care providers in the child's family. Cards made at school might read "Happy Father's Day Mom," or list some other primary care provider. Teachers investigate whether school library collections contain some familiar family images and check bulletin boards and other wall displays to see if they mirror children's families and communities.

What family information is of importance and of primary interest to early childhood educators? Most educators when asked will mention the following.

◆ educational desires for their children

◆ family stress factors

◆ interest in school involvement and ability to participate

◆ pride in their culture or subculture

◆ family strengths and advantages

◆ family legal issues, court orders, etc.

◆ size and connectedness to supportive others, and/or support services

◆ engagement in neighborhood and community happenings

◆ past experiences with educational institutions

◆ home languages

◆ health and care availability

◆ availability and use of public funds or services

◆ home literacy activities

◆ ability to converse or read English

Figure 9–5 displays Bradley and Kibera's (2007) four dimensions of family cultures, and lists questions for reflection and discussion. It also lists questions that probe areas of interest not mentioned above.

What happens if partnerships are successful? Families become involved, take action, and feel instrumental in their child's learning, and feel respected, capable, and accepted. They have gained insight into their child's growth and development. Families know their child's teacher has a sincere interest in children's school success. They understand that the school offers an individualized program that takes into consideration parents' wishes and values. Parents and families come to see themselves as important teachers, and believe teachers describe their child's educational accomplishments accurately. They recognize the classroom as an example of democratic practice.

Some educational writers, such as Igoa (1995), have alerted educators to a cultural divide that families new to the United States may experience as they struggle to be accepted as insiders, rather than outsiders, at schools and in communities. Other writers warn that family relationships can be stressed or strained when young children do become insiders. Historically in America, this has been a concern with each wave of new families. Most children have been able to separate fairly easily

▶ **Figure 9-5**

Cultural dimensions of families.

Four dimensions of culture are listed here with questions that encourage further exploration of the influences of culture in your work. The questions can be modified for individual self-assessment, for use as a tool to explore differences among staff, or as the basis for discussing cultural issues with families.

| Dimensions | Questions for reflection and/or discussion |
|---|---|
| Values and beliefs | How is *family* defined? What roles do adults and children play? How does the family make sense of a child's behavioral difficulties? How does culture inform the family's view of appropriate/inappropriate ways of dealing with problem behavior and guiding children? What is most important to the family? |
| Historical and social influences | What strengths and stressors does the family identify? What barriers do they experience? |
| Communication | What is the family's primary language? What support is required to enable communication? How are needs and wants expressed? How is unhappiness, dissatisfaction, or distress experienced and expressed? |
| Attitude toward seeking help | How does the family seek help and from whom? How do members view professionals, and how do professionals view them? |

**SOURCE:** From Bradley, J. & Kibera, P., Closing the gap: Culture and the promotion of inclusion in child care. In Koralek, D. (Ed.) (2007) Spotlight on Young Children and families (pp. 38–42). Washington, DC: National Association for the Education of Young Children.

between what is expected and rewarded at school from what goes on at home. In the past, the majority of new families in the United States wanted to join the American mainstream and intended to become citizens. They viewed education as the key to future family success and employment. Many families held on to traditions and religious practices, and congregated in groups of like-speaking others. They anticipated their children's adoption of English, and many learned English from their children.

Today, this supportive attitude and desire to become Americanized as soon as possible may or may not be present, for a number of reasons. Families may wish to return to their homeland, or they may believe that the American way is not a model to emulate. This can be a controversial discussion, particularly at a time when immigration issues are debated. It is suggested that you reflect, investigate, and consider your own family background.

Eggers-Pierola (2005) has suggestions for student teachers who wish to become culturally and linguistically responsive teachers when working with Latino children. She suggests that teachers open their hearts and recognize the community that surrounds children, to establish lasting and supportive partnerships. She notes that extended family and family friends may be key players in a child's upbringing, and she feels that committed teachers engender committed families. Consequently, a culturally and linguistically sensitive educator should:

◆ Know that to understand the child, she must know the community.

◆ Extend her work to the child's family circle and neighborhood.

◆ Welcome the child's extended family members as co-teachers, co-planners, and initiators of activities.

◆ Prepare to work with parents when there are disagreements.

◆ Provide opportunities for intergenerational engagement that mirror *la familia*.

## Working with Families Learning English

Nearly one of every five people in the United States spoke a foreign language at home in 2007 (Sharpe, 2008). Over 34.5 million spoke Spanish, and 8.3 million Chinese or another Asian language. Teachers do not believe a language deficit exists for children living in these families, or feel these children have experienced shallow or limited home literacy opportunities or that learning English will be difficult for some of them. Experts suggest a family-by-family approach that builds on a home language and the possible literacy experiences that a child may have encountered. Teachers build on child strengths to promote school language success. Many children may be like four-year-old Dominic, an immigrant, Portuguese-speaking child, who though speaking but a few English words, amazed his preschool teachers with the speed and ease of his English learning. In a short time, he became the interpreter for the two other Portuguese-speaking children in the class. As his teachers became more familiar with his family, they found Dominic had wide and varied home language experiences, including listening to his two older brothers teach their parents English. Living in a large extended family in a rural community, the family frequently participated in local events and celebrations. His grandmother read Dominic letters from the "old country" or read from the Bible, and his father entertained the family frequently in the evening by playing an eight-string guitar and singing native songs.

Dominic's preschool program, which his teachers felt was based on the best practice for diverse second language children, offered many activities where teachers and children collaborated as "peers" to create a tangible product or outcome, such as constructing a large packing box playhouse. They solved problems, applied learning, analyzed situations, explored patterns, and talked about likenesses and differences. Teachers promoted higher-level thinking skills and children's language development using all curriculum areas. When possible, school activities were connected to child experience, and dialogue between children and teaching staff was accorded a high priority. Teachers provided English models just above what children could grasp and activities that challenged child abilities. Is it any wonder that Dominic thrived in his home and school environment?

## Boards, Committees, and Councils

Family members may serve on advisory committees, boards, or councils, and may have active administrative involvement, including teacher hiring and dismissal. They may exercise budgetary control and assume legal responsibilities. Each center differs uniquely, with greater parent involvement mandated in publicly funded programs. Church-associated, parent-cooperative, and nonprofit programs also frequently use parent advisors. For-profit centers, on the other hand, may rarely seek or depend on family input in administrative decisions, but exceptions do exist.

## Establishing a Professional Image and Rapport

The student teacher's professionalism is displayed by her actions, appearance, and demeanor. Student teachers' friendly, supportive behaviors and conversational skills help families who want to know more about the student teacher's role in the classroom. It is best to explain your position as a *learner*, and a fledgling novice, hopeful of working toward ever greater classroom responsibility and competencies.

## Understanding the Cooperating Teacher's Role

A cooperating teacher may have communicated to enrolled families information about her role as a mentor, guide, collaborator, and consultant in the student teacher's growth. The visits of the college supervisor may also have been discussed. The aim was to give families a clear picture of the student teacher's roles and responsibilities, and her role as a work supervisor. Family fears concerning the student teacher's handling of behavior, degree of confidentiality, and lack of experience, among other concerns, can be allayed through discussion. Most families see student teachers as a classroom asset, able to offer their children additional attention and educational opportunity.

## Daily Classroom Interactions with Adult Staff and Volunteers

In many classrooms, outside observers may have difficulty distinguishing the different roles of teachers, teaching aides, volunteers, and student teachers. Each may possess uniquely individual skills and style. A hierarchy of responsibility may not be readily apparent. The student teacher understands that the cooperating teacher has ultimate responsibility for children, classroom, other adults, and the planned program—no easy task in most busy classrooms.

## Pitfalls

Unfortunately, some families may view student teachers as experts, to be quizzed on child development issues, their child's intelligence, talents, educational progress, and so on. This may feel complimentary, but student teachers should refer all such queries to their cooperating teachers.

Unfortunate is the student teacher placed in a program where political or other issues have developed. Most supervisors visit and evaluate placements sites, but occasionally an undercurrent of tension escapes detection. The roles of fence-sitter and cooperating teacher's defender are both difficult ones. Our advice is to direct complaints or criticisms to the person or persons involved, and to broach the matter quickly with the cooperating teacher and college supervisor.

Student teachers in campus laboratory schools may have children's parents or family members as classmates and friends. Parents can view student teachers as inside information resources. Student teachers need to guard their comments closely, avoid gossip, and emphasize the confidentiality expected of them. It can be a difficult situation when the child of one's best friend or one's college instructor becomes part of the student teacher's child group. Our advice is, again, to direct the friend or instructor to the cooperating teacher if questions exist.

## Children's Separation from Parents

Student teachers will observe daily how individual children enter and separate from their adult caregiver at arrival. Separating from family can be painful, even though a child sees preschool as an interesting place. Some children need time to adjust to group care, and experience **separation anxiety**. Student teachers are often asked to aid entering children by providing attentive, patient support and comfort or by trying to interest the child in a center activity. This type of child behavior is usually a preschool teacher's problem, but kindergarten teachers sometimes also encounter separation anxiety, in both children and an occasional parent. Words that help could be: "You want your mom, but she needs to go to work. After nap time, she'll come to get you. Let's go see what Lorie and Wong are making at the center table."

**separation anxiety**—
emotional difficulty experienced by some young children when leaving their parents or other primary caregivers.

## Problems with Reunion at Pick-Up Time

Many systems and ideas have been used to make pick-up time easier for children, teachers, and the person picking up the child. You should know that only certain individuals can leave the classroom with a child, and that a list or file exists specifying which adults have clearance to do so. This should have been discussed during your beginning days; if not, talk to the cooperating teacher before you release a child to someone you do not know, or to anyone questionable.

Children's belongings, including projects and artwork, are collected before-hand. Children are made ready to be picked up, and at times, are partially or fully dressed for outdoors. Teachers usually step in to help parents with dawdling or obstinate child behavior. The teacher's goal is to have a smooth transition. Schools adopt a variety of procedures to make departure times successful and as stress-free as possible.

## Conferencing: Communication Techniques

In two-year college training programs, student teachers may be invited to sit in on conferences or home visits, playing the role of observer. They may be asked to study child behaviors or actions, but conclusions are confidential and discussed only with cooperating teachers. Four- and five-year college training programs may or may not offer student teachers opportunities to conduct parent conferences and home visits.

The following are guidelines that practicing teachers use to plan and conduct teacher–parent conferences:

◆ Families and teachers both have time constraints, so time planning is important.

◆ In working with others, the first rule is to put them at ease. Seat people comfortably. Offer something to eat or drink, especially if the conference is at the end of a workday.

◆ Try to begin the conference in a positive manner. Even if one needs to report a child's negative behavior or ask a difficult question, comment on the child's positive behaviors or actions before stating other concerns or behaviors.

◆ Try to elicit a description of the child's behavior noticed in school from the family. This is especially appropriate in a parent-cooperative center or a center setting that encourages families to observe and then consult with staff (see Figure 9–6). If a child has not been seen in action at school, ask about the child's observed behavior at home or in other social settings. This will allow you to study the degree of parent perceptivity regarding the child's behavior.

◆ Be specific when describing child's behavior. Avoid generalities. Use descriptive, preferably written accounts, taken over a period of at least 3 consecutive days, with several samplings per day.

◆ Keep samples of the child's work in a folder, with the child's name and the date the sampling was taken. Actual samples of work can speak louder and more eloquently than words.

◆ Avoid comparisons with other children. Each child is unique. Most develop in unique ways that make comparisons unfair.

◆ When presenting negative aspects of behavior, avoid making any evaluation about the goodness or badness of the child.

◆ Remember that attitude is important. One must choose to care.

◆ Keep conferences focused. Remember that most parents are busy and their time is valuable; do not waste it. Discuss whatever is supposed to be discussed and do not stray off course.

◆ Be cheerful, friendly, and tactful.

◆ Act cordially. The last thing you want is to appear argumentative.

◆ Be honest. Do not say "Tony is certainly a creative child" when you mean "Tony often finds ways to avoid listening to directions."

◆ Be businesslike. In this situation, a teacher is a professional, not a close friend.

◆ Know facts and the program so well that you can discuss them without defensive statements.

▶ **Figure 9–6**

"Have you noticed Ceceil's interest in books?"

© Cengage Learning

◆ Be enthusiastic about being able to consult with the family.

◆ Do not discuss another child unless it is appropriate.

◆ Do not make judgments before all the evidence is in.

◆ Do not betray confidences. Children will sometimes tell something that should not be repeated and is best overlooked. If, however, an educator thinks the disclosure is important to the child's welfare, do discuss it.

◆ Observe body language; it will often tell you more about how people are really feeling than the words they say.

In the rest of this chapter, we will present some ground rules for home visits, as well as some ideas for other family involvement.

## PLANNING THE HOME VISIT

Some schools have a policy that the family of each enrolled child must be visited at least once during the school year. Other schools, both public and private, have a policy that teachers should visit the families of every enrolled child during the latter part of the summer, prior to the opening of school. If you are student teaching in a school where home visits are an accepted feature, planning a home visit usually involves the cooperating teacher's selection of which home. The cooperating teacher may ask you to accompany her on a visit to the home of a child with whom you are having difficulty establishing rapport. Other times, you may be asked to visit the home of a child with whom you have had considerable interaction.

In planning a home visit, teachers and student teachers should familiarize themselves with the neighborhoods in which the home visit will take place. Some educators believe a home visit can be the single most effective act that can be performed for developing harmonious relationships between a child and teacher.

Successful home visits have brief agendas but are flexible and responsive to issues the families might raise (Kyle & McIntyre, 2000). Questions a teacher prepares beforehand help guide discussions. Questions can probe child interests, favorite activities, how the child learns best, interactions with other children out of school, what the child talks about having done at school, or other features of the child's school and home life.

Another point that should be made concerns planning home visits at homes of families from diverse ethnic or social groups. Families may be suspicious of the motive behind teachers wanting to visit because the practice is new to them.

Most teachers visiting homes consider what the child or siblings will be doing while adults talk. They select child materials to carry with them, such as small objects to manipulate, coloring and other books, crayons, puzzles, and puppets that a child can use without adult help. If other children are to be home, other safe items can also be planned. Teachers can introduce play items as teacher's *traveling toys*, which will go back in the bag at the end of the visit, or if the budget permits, as gifts to remain with the child.

## OTHER SCHOOL–HOME INTERACTIONS

A center may conduct regular parenting education programs, and may send home frequent information concerning school happenings and planned events (see Figure 9–7). Modes of communication to keep families informed include family visits to the classroom to observe or participate, sending videotapes home or making them available for family viewing in a room at the school, audio recordings, newsletters or bulletins, a notebook that travels back-and forth so both family and teacher comments are exchanged, phone calls, and e-mail.

Some preschools, especially those associated with adult education classes offering child development theory, include parent education as a mandatory part of

▶ **Figure 9-7**

Example of a teacher's newsletter to families.

---

**Kindergarten News**

October 24

Language Arts: Reviewing M, F, R, S, N, T, and learning the short sound of the vowel a.

Working on colors, especially purple.

Math: Continue counting, sorting, and patterning, and working with the numbers 2 and 3.

Social Studies: This week is Red Ribbon Week when we talk about keeping our bodies healthy.

Science: The sense of touch and taste.

Music: We will be studying the opera Lucia Di Lammermoor.

Art: Halloween art.

P.E.: Working with balls.

We will have a Halloween Party Friday morning. There is a 12:00 dismissal. We will be making a costume, so do not send one.

Progress reports will be given out Friday. Attached to this newsletter is your scheduled time for a conference, either Friday afternoon or sometime Monday. If the time scheduled doesn't work out for you, please let me know and we can reschedule.

Next Tuesday, Nov. 2, we will be privileged to have the San Francisco Opera Guild come to our school and perform a preview of Lucia Di Lammermoor.

Regards.

M. Andreozzi

---

their program. Topics may range from child guidance, to problems specific to areas of the curriculum, to planning for emergencies, and a countless number of other topics (see Figure 9–8). Kieff and Wellhousen (2000) caution educators about making assumptions when planning family meetings, such as assuming the following about family members:

- That they can read take-home announcements.
- That they are available for the times scheduled.
- That they have transportation.
- That they can understand English.
- That they can bring foods, snacks, and so on.
- That they are children's biological parents.
- That they have circumstances, lifestyles, and cultures that are the same as the teaching staff.
- That they will communicate the barriers they face in attending school meetings.

Family planning worksheets may prove helpful as you plan your own strategies to engage families in the learning experiences (see Figures 9–9 and 9–10).

Typically, the September meeting is called *Back-to-School Night,* and offers explanations of the class curriculum. Generally, teachers arrange displays of the children's work on bulletin boards and explain curriculum goals for the year. Many teachers have sign-up sheets posted for volunteer help, and all teachers attempt to establish rapport with their respective family groups. Student teachers are traditionally introduced at this time also.

Most public school districts and private schools send newsletters home. These typically include a calendar of upcoming school events and informative articles for families on specific parts of the curriculum and ideas to try at home. They frequently include news about topics taught in class that week, children's illustrations, and requests for family volunteers if necessary. Newsletters frequently include a question-and-answer section. They may also contain a swap column, or notices of toys to exchange, and may

▶ **Figure 9-8**
Building child skill and promoting children's self-help can be the topic of a school–family meeting.

▶ **Figure 9-9**
Family involvement planning worksheet.

**Family Involvement Planning Worksheet**

Name of activity/event _____

Proposed date and time _____

Location _____

Targeted participants _____

Consider the descriptors below to identify family-related factors that could create barriers, and prevent or limit the participation of families. After identifying possible barriers, adapt the activity or event to incude all families.

**Family structures**

Consider who are the primary caregivers for the children. Consider the presence of younger and older siblings living at home.

| | | |
|---|---|---|
| ❏ divorced parents | ❏ split families | ❏ same-sex parents |
| ❏ single parent | ❏ foster parents | ❏ family member with disability |
| ❏ grandparent(s) | ❏ legal guardian | ❏ teen parents |
| ❏ blended family | ❏ widowed parent | ❏ other_____ |

Possible barriers include _____

**Family lifestyles**

Consider the daily challenges or routines affecting the children and each family.

| | | |
|---|---|---|
| ❏ income level | ❏ unemployment | |
| ❏ employment hours and time of day, number of jobs | ❏ caring for an elderly or a disabled family member | ❏ incarcerated parent |
| | | ❏ community |
| | | ❏ education level |
| ❏ risks or dangers involved in work | ❏ latch-key child care | ❏ housing |
| | ❏ transportation | ❏ access to telephone |
| ❏ travel distance | ❏ reading ability | ❏ resources |
| ❏ migrant status | ❏ number of family members or siblings | ❏ other_____ |

Possible barriers include _____

(continues)

▶ **Figure 9-9** (continued)

**Family cultures**

Consider the cultural aspects of each family. Avoid stereotypes.

❑ religious backgrounds          ❑ nonverbal communication styles
❑ holiday celebrations               eye contact
❑ dietary restrictions                  gestures
❑ views on child-rearing           touching
❑ languages                                proximity during conversations
                                                 ❑ other_____

Possible barriers include _____

How the activity or event can be adapted to include all families represented in the class or

school _____

Note. This is for teacher use only and is confidential material.

_____

**SOURCE:** Reprinted with permission from the National Association for the Education of Young Children.

▶ **Figure 9-10**

Common barriers and possible modifications checklist.

**Common Barriers and Possible Modifications Checklist**

| Barriers | ❑ Modifications |
|---|---|
| Time | ❑ breakfast meetings |
| | ❑ weekend events |
| | ❑ one event scheduled over a number of days |
| | ❑ open invitations |
| Transportation | ❑ school bus or van |
| | ❑ car pool arranged by teacher or parent volunteer |
| | ❑ buddy system among families |
| Child care | ❑ school-provided child care |
| | ❑ chid care provided by parent organization |
| | ❑ buddy system among families |
| | ❑ artwork created by children in the art center |
| | ❑ artwork generated during a theme/project study |
| | ❑ opportunities for children to make multiple gifts and cards, and to pick their recipients |
| | ❑ family members share expertise and culture |
| | ❑ bias-free curriculum |
| Food | ❑ multiple menus available |
| | ❑ buffets |
| | ❑ picnics |
| Printed material | ❑ translate copies |
| | ❑ make audiotapes |
| | ❑ make telephone calls |
| | ❑ use voice mail or e-mail |
| Special guest | ❑ guest not specified by role |
| | ❑ a pal or friend |
| | ❑ open invitations to extended family members or a noncustodial parent |
| Expense | ❑ support provided by community businesses underwriting the event or materials needed |

▶ **Figure 9-10** (continued)

| Misunderstanding the role as parent volunteer in the classroom | ❏ volunteer training sessions<br>❏ specific routines created<br>❏ recorded or printed instructions |
| Misunderstanding the parental role in home-extension learning activities | ❏ specific routines created for home-extension learning activities<br>❏ parent workshops to explain activities<br>❏ demonstration tapes<br>❏ demonstrations during home visits |
| Discomfort in school situations | ❏ alternative home visits or neighborhood meetings<br>❏ buddy systems among families<br>❏ small-group meetings |

**SOURCE:** Reprinted with permission from the National Association for the Education of Young Children.

even contain a column written by the family members of enrolled children. Most school newsletters remind families of planned study sessions or education meetings.

## Parenting Education Meetings

The following ideas are suggested by Foster (1994):

◆ Plan together with families and include the children—they have ideas, too. You may want to have a committee of family members, teachers, and a few children do some parts of the planning.

◆ Assess family needs and interests.

◆ If the school, center, or child care facility is not close to where families live, ask them for help in locating an alternative meeting place.

◆ If you have families who do not have cars or do not drive, the meeting place should be accessible by public transportation, or carpools should be arranged.

◆ During the meeting, arrange activities for children, so families do not have to worry about caring for them or keeping them occupied.

◆ Plan refreshments and activities.

◆ Plan for a meeting that will last no more than an hour and 15 minutes.

◆ Open with a short introduction.

◆ Decide whether the presentation will be a lecture, a video, a panel discussion, or something else.

◆ Keep in mind the families' abilities to process English if it is not their primary language.

◆ If this is the first meeting of the year, think about having an icebreaker so families can get to know each other.

◆ Remember that people talk more frequently in small groups, so you might want to plan a short presentation, followed with small discussion groups, and ending with sharing from each small group.

◆ People enjoy handouts and activities that involve making something they can take home.

◆ Always be sure to thank the people for coming, and have fliers with information about the next meeting—topic, date, and time—available to hand out.

Eggers-Pierola (2005) describes one teacher's observation of the diversity found in parents' and family members' greeting styles at one parenting night meeting:

With the families we have here—from seven different cultures—I make a point to learn about cultural differences in communication, like eye contact, touching behavior, tone, and the distance people use when talking with each other. One day, at a parents' night, I watched as parents greeted each other when they arrived, and noticed for the first time what amazingly different conventions they had for greeting each other or greeting someone from a culture not their own. Some gave each other three kisses on alternate cheeks, intoning the same greeting words; the same families simply nodded and said "Hello" when greeting someone from another culture. Others kissed on two cheeks, another pair of mothers by one kiss and a hug. The men in two of the cultures hugged and patted each other's backs. When they greeted children, I saw even more differences in style, although many bent down to the level of the children. When I brought this up at circle time and asked children to play act how they greet and what they say to the different people they meet in and outside of their families, even more differences became apparent, such as the fascinating subtleties of rhythm of speech, words, and actions as the children role-played the greetings.

## Teacher Presentation Skills at Parent/Family Meetings

When conducting a presentation to families, you will use many of the same strategies you use with children. Although many of your child activity presentations concentrate on discovery and exploration, with parents and families you relay clearly stated facts. Depending on the topic, or to further illustrate some learning, hands-on and active audience participation may, at times, add insight and create interest.

You will want to show enthusiasm for teaching, and look straight in the eyes of your audience, panning the whole room while using expressive but natural gestures and varying your tone of voice. This will clarify your main points and express your emotions. As with children, use examples, anecdotes, and stories of classroom happenings. Creating curiosity and excitement in your subject matter is well worth the effort. Help your audience visualize how the school's curriculum creates child learning opportunities, and either suggest home activities or prepare a helpful handout, if the presentation's topic calls for it. Teachers plan time for family questions and comments at the end of presentations or they may encourage audience members to ask questions as they arise.

At any meeting, family may want to discuss their attending child. Many teachers develop the habit of jotting down each day at least one significant observation of each child; this, they believe, helps them identify children who may have escaped their attention. This may seem a near impossible task to suggest to a student teacher, but many practicing teachers do it. As a professional student teacher, you will stress again that you are in training, and questions addressed to you should be directed to the cooperating teacher if they concern children's progress and abilities. If comments were to be made by a student teacher, they would concern positive aspects of a child's individuality. Some families alarm easily, as you will be sure to find when you have full classroom responsibility. It can be hard to overcome the notion in some families' thinking that parents only hear from teachers and schools when there is something wrong.

## PRECAUTIONS

Be aware that some single or isolated parents may need a support group, especially if they have no family members or friends living close by. A number of centers help parents or primary care providers form support groups such as babysitting co-ops or used clothing exchanges that encouraged connectedness. At one Head Start center, the number one request by families who were asked about preferences for family meeting topics was meeting with other single parents and planning discussions of *stress and the single parent.*

Unfortunately, many families cannot exist without the income from two working family members. Be sensitive to ways in which people can involve themselves in the life of the center. Educational meetings are fine, but not if people on limited incomes must hire a babysitter to attend. Knowing this, some school directors make arrangements for children to be cared for on-site at the school's expense. Many families may not have a car and must rely on public transportation. Find out about bus schedules and what routes are available. Make sure the meetings end on time.

Parenting education may not seem valuable to every family. Many will choose to attend when the topic presented meets their needs but be absent when it does not. Others may find it too hectic to try to attend a meeting held in the evening, so schools sometimes plan weekend ones.

## Collaboration

The NAEYC revised statement on developmentally appropriate practice, and other newer guidelines and standards, recommend that preschool program goals be developed in collaboration with families (Bredekamp & Copple, 1997, Copple & Bredekamp, 2009). This focus on **collaboration** is a departure from older ideas, which emphasized early childhood educators as supportive assistants, rescuers, or compensators for families with less than ideal home environments, and it recognizes the importance of working with families' expressed educational wishes and desires as planning and goal-setting partners. Collaboration strengthens home involvement in school activities and family–teacher bonds.

## Families Seeking Help

Because of the increasing focus on early literacy and pre-reading skills, brain growth, development during early childhood, and ordinary child-rearing concerns, an increasing number of questions are directed to early childhood personnel. Many families seek direct help concerning what home literacy activities they can provide. (Practical, home literacy-developing activities are found in Figure 9–11.)

Early childhood educators can promote each family's confidence in their ability to influence children's literacy. Through center outreach and involvement activities, centers may change reluctant care providers into very active and resourceful ones, who promote children's educational opportunities.

Your student teaching assignments and experiences may involve a higher level of school–home interaction than in previous years, as colleges and training programs give greater emphasis to involvement. Competencies in this area of teaching are increasingly important as teachers assume a leadership role and develop creative strategies to involve families and other community members in the life of the school or center.

**collaboration**—a desire or need to create or discover something new, while thinking and working with others. It is a process of joint decision making. It involves discussion, different views and perspectives, shared goals, building new shared understandings, and perhaps the creation of a new outlook or course of action.

▶ **Figure 9–11**
Home language and literacy promoting activities.

**HOME LANGUAGE AND LITERACY–PROMOTING ACTIVITIES**

Families and teachers working together to identify language and literacy-developing home activities frequently include the following activity suggestions:

- Give each child—no matter how young—*daily* individualized attention that includes talking about what has captured his interest at the moment or describes what the instructing adult is doing. Become a focused listener who tries to understand.
- Be responsive and open to the child's verbal and nonverbal communicative attempts, by answering with positive comments, suggestions, and recognition of each child's efforts.
- Model an interest in books and reading materials in daily life, including the daily mail, magazines, and so on.
- Read aloud and share such things as labels, instructions, shopping lists, recipe cards, words on objects, phone messages, coupons, notes, signs, calendars, alphabet letters, advertisements, directions, and other printing you find in the home or community environment.

(continues)

▶ **Figure 9-11** (continued)

- Be creative in obtaining reading material for the home by investigating yard sales, library sales, used book stores, inexpensive children's book clubs (like Scholastic), and free book offers.

- Make your local library a frequent destination for family outings, encouraging its further use and investigation by children. Check on all available library services and resources. Make books part of family life for all members, infants and elders included.

- Write notes and postcards to your children and be an avid sharer of personal, daily happenings and stories.

- Create meal times that are full of informative conversation, stories, and sharing.

- Play all sorts of games where rules are read and discussed, including board and card games. Check resale and thrift store offerings. Investigate and create spelling and alphabet games as part of daily life.

- Encourage scribbling, printing, drawing, and art. Use child-created products as starting places for discussion, rather than correcting beginning attempts at learning or child-created spellings.

- Probe gently for more information or details when speech or writing seems incorrect to you, knowing that age, time, and experience will correct usage. Focus on keeping child communication attempts coming, rather than focusing on perfection. Correct with subtlety and gentleness, just as you accepted immature speech forms such as "baba" for bottle when the child was learning to talk.

- Keep in touch with your children's teachers to find out new and evolving school interests and accomplishments. Request the teacher's suggestions on how to expand these interests at home.

- Explore the community and home neighborhood for opportunities to experience and explore. Record and relive these away-from-home activities, along with children's reactions to them.

- Make family scrapbooks with labels or stories attached.

- Encourage children's efforts to initiate conversation, read words or letters, print, use writing tools or computers, or record their ideas by providing attention and approval.

- Have fun with words. Try playful rhyming, riddles, new captions for pictures, silly naming or spelling, emphasizing certain syllables in words, rhythmic chanting, and so on.

**SOURCE:** Adapted from Machado, J. M. (2007, 2010) *Early childhood experiences in language arts.* Belmont, CA: Wadsworth, Cengage Learning

# ▶ SUMMARY

In this chapter, we discussed a school's family-relations philosophy and described interactions between families, cooperating teachers, and student teachers. We mentioned again the importance of communication skill and nonverbal communication. Specific techniques and recommendations for conferencing with people, conducting a home visit, and presenting family education programs were included.

Much of family–teacher communication is informal. Therefore, it is important to be aware that the impression you make in informal interactions may often set the stage for how people view and accept you.

Awareness of communities can be obtained in various ways, some as simple as a driving through the neighborhood or as complex as a formal, written survey. Such knowledge helps teachers become more sensitive to a child's needs and interests. An important goal of a school's involvement efforts is to promote family collaboration and engagement with what is going on at the school, and to gain active support for the educational opportunities offered at school and those that can be reinforced at home.

# ▶ HELPFUL WEBSITES

**http://www.parentoutreach.org**
Parent Outreach California. Resources for families are available.

**http://www.npin.org**
National Parent Information Network. Select information concerning the process of parenting and family involvement.

**http://www.asha.org**
American Speech-Language-Hearing Association. Activities to stimulate language growth are offered.

 Additional resources for this chapter can be found by visiting the companion website at **www.cengage.com/education/machado.**

## ▶ SUGGESTED ACTIVITIES

A. With your cooperating teacher's permission, interview some of the families at your center. What kinds of support systems are present in their lives that aid their abilities to parent? What type of school-planned involvement activities do they enjoy or choose not to attend? Why?

B. How are local schools or other public or private agencies in the community helping new immigrants? What kinds of specialized materials are being used, if any? What kinds of specialized services are offered? Discuss your findings with your peers and supervisor.

C. Role-play the following parent–teacher confrontational exchanges. In groups of six peers, select members to role-play the teacher and the parent. Discuss scenarios, and share with the entire training group when finished.
   1. Mrs. G. decides to have her class of three-year-olds celebrate the birthday of Dr. Martin Luther King, Jr. Mr. L. complains, emphasizing this is beyond his child's understanding.
   2. Miss R., Joshua's mom, feels his teacher takes far too many field trips with the children.
   3. Mrs. T. tells her child's teacher that in 6 months her child hasn't learned one new thing.
   4. Mrs. S., a parent, says, "Don't ever call me at home!" with considerable anger in her voice.
   5. Mr. N., a teacher, asks Mardell's mother to find objects at home that begin with the letter *B*. She glares at him and says, "I'm paying you to educate my daughter. Preschool homework is ridiculous."
   6. A parent volunteer, Mrs. P., says, "After watching Raoul today, I can see he is bored in your classroom."

D. Examine Figure 9–12. In speaking to this child's family, what might be one of the family's concerns?

E. Discuss the following child statements with peers and formulate a teacher response. Analyze responses for teacher attempts to give equal status to nontraditional families.
   1. Megan says, "I have two mommies, and they are both called Mary."
   2. Vladimir says, "My mom's boyfriend takes me home from school. He lives at our house."
   3. Ana says, "My sister is my momma, and grandpa takes care of me, too."
   4. Madison says longingly, "I wish you 'was' my momma."
   5. Ryan says, "I don't have a daddy."

▶ **Figure 9–12**
Seeing individuality.

© Cengage Learning

## ▶ REVIEW

A. If you were to write a nondiscrimination policy statement or a school–home relations philosophy for a pre-kindergarten, what would it include?

B. Rate your knowledge and effectiveness in teacher-family working relationships using the following rating scale:
   1 = Very knowledgeable; 2 = Knowledgeable;
   3 = Some general knowledge; 4 = Meager knowledge;
   5 = No knowledge

   1. I am able to conduct professional conferences and interviews with parents. _____
   2. I could design and develop an adequate parenting education and involvement program for an early childhood center. _____
   3. I feel comfortable planning and conducting meetings and workshops. _____
   4. I possess the ability to successfully involve people in classroom activities. _____

5. I am aware of a wide range of family involvement possibilities and strategies. _____
6. I possess professional communication skills and abilities useful in family contacts. _____
7. I can develop positive relationships with the families of attending children. _____

8. I understand the importance of school-home partnerships concerned with children's growth and education. _____

C. Name five tips for planning a parent-teacher conference, or five suggestions for techniques useful in a student teacher presentation at a parenting meeting.

# REFERENCES

Bradley, J., & Kibera, P. (2007). Closing the gap: Culture and the promotion of inclusion in child care. In Koralek, D. (Ed.), *Spotlight on young children and families* (pp.34–42). Washington, DC: National Association for the Education of Young Children.

Bredekamp, S., & Copple, C. (Eds.). (1997), Copple & Bredekamp (Eds.) (2009). *Developmentally appropriate practice in early childhood programs* (rev. ed.). Washington, DC: National Association for the Education of Young Children.

Copple, C., & Bredekamp, S. (Eds.). (2009). *Developmentally appropriate practice in early childhood programs: Serving children from birth through age 8*. Washington, DC: National Association for the Education of Young Children.

Eggers-Pierola, C. (2005). *Connections and commitments: Reflecting Latino values in early childhood programs*. Portsmouth, NH: Heinemann.

Epstein, J. (2000, July 21). The national view of school, family, community partnerships: Current status and future view. Conference presentation, Northwest Regional Laboratory Invitational Conference, Improving student success through school, family, and community partnerships. Portland, OR.

Feeney S., & Freeman, N. K. (2005). *Ethics and the early childhood educator: Using the NAEYC code*. Washington, DC: National Association for the Education of Young Children.

Foster, S. M. (1994, November). Success parent meetings. *Young Children 50*(1), 37–39.

Harlan, B. (2007, March 7). Marriage with kids now exception in U.S., *San Jose Mercury News*, 9A.

Igoa, C. (1995). *The inner world of the immigrant child*. New York: St. Martin's Press.

Kaczmarek, L. A. (2007). A team approach. In Koralek, D. (Ed.), *Spotlight on young children and families* (pp. 28–37).

Washington, DC: National Association for the Education of Young Children.

Kieff, J., & Wellhousen, K. (2000, May). Planning family involvement in early childhood programs. *Young Children, 55*(3), 18–25.

Kyle, D., & McIntyre, E. (2000, October). Family visits benefit teachers and families—and students most of all. *Practitioner Brief #1*. Santa Cruz, CA: Center for Research on Education, Diversity and Excellence, University of California Brochure.

Machado, J. M. (2010). *Early childhood experiences in the language arts: Early Literacy*. Clifton Park, NY: Thomson Delmar Learning

National Association for the Education of Young Children, National Association of Early Childhood Teacher Educators, and the American Associate Degree Early Childhood Teacher Educators. (2005). *Code of ethical conduct: Supplement for early childhood adult educators*. A joint position statement, retrieved February 6, 2005, from http://www.naeyc.org.

Sharpe, R. (2008, November 14). English loses ground. *USA Today*, 12.

Stephens, K. (2005, May/June). Meaningful family engagement. *Exchange, 163*, 18–24.

Stonehouse, A. (1995, 2003). *How does it feel? Child care from a parent's perspective*. Redmond, WA: Child Care Information Exchange.

Winkleman, P. H. (1999). Family involvement in education: The apprehensions of student teachers. In M. S. Ammon (Ed.), *Joining hands: Preparing teachers to make meaningful home-school connections* (pp. 79–100). Sacramento, CA: California Department of Education, California Commission on Teacher Credentialing.

# SECTION 6

© Cengage Learning

# Professional Concerns

# Quality Programs in Early Childhood Settings

**After reading this chapter, you should be able to:**

1. Discuss the relationship between a program's philosophy and its quality.
2. Discuss the importance of the teacher and director/principal in a quality program.
3. List the program standards evaluated under NAEYC accreditation criteria.
4. Discuss the relationship between accreditation and other forms of program evaluation and quality.

## STUDENT TEACHER SCENARIO

**Setting:** You are a student teacher at Little Pals Preschool. Mrs. Kumar, the director, is interviewing Ms. Perez, mother of four-year-old Andrea. Ms. Perez is considering enrolling her daughter in the school.

"Here's our brochure, Ms. Perez. We have an excellent program. Our local community college frequently places student teachers in our classrooms. You are quite lucky because we actually will have an opening next week in the four-year-olds' room. Please follow me; I'm sure you would like to see the classroom."

As they approach a classroom door, Ms. Perez notices that the school's interior is freshly painted and spotlessly clean. As they enter the classroom for four-year-old children, Ms. Perez notes that the room is quiet and tidy. All the children are seated, working on what look to be photocopies. Mrs. Kumar whispers that the children all know their ABCs and can count to 50. Mrs. Kumar approaches the cooperating teacher, who is applying smiley face stickers on some of the children's papers, and introduces her. As the student teacher, you are helping children at one of the tables. Many elaborate pieces of child art decorate the walls, along with alphabet letters, numerals, word charts, and crayoned pages of coloring books. A world globe and a collection of library books are available. A computer and television set sit along one wall. The center of the room features a large, colorful round rug that Mrs. Kumar says is used for group instruction.

Mrs. Kumar enthusiastically describes extra lessons in dance that take place 1 day a week. These lessons are available if parents so choose. Mrs. Kumar shows Ms. Perez the play yard. It is full of expensive, commercially designed, large climbing structures, swinging bridges, and slides. It looks like an elaborate, well-tended city park.

Before Ms. Perez leaves, Mrs. Kumar asks if she has any questions. She says, "No," and leaves after thanking Mrs. Kumar for the tour and her time.

## Questions for Discussion:

1. As a student teacher in this classroom, what questions do you think Ms. Perez should have asked?

2. Would this type of school impress a parent favorably? Why?

3. As a student teacher at Little Pals, do you have any reservations concerning the quality of the school? Why or why not?

In looking at the concept of quality, what comes to mind? High quality always suggests something that goes beyond the ordinary. In a program for young children, then, quality suggests that it exceeds minimal standards. We might also want to include the fact that a high-quality program, in general, seeks to employ well-trained teachers, who more than meet the minimal education requirements of their respective states, and usually pays a higher salary and offers more benefits than lower-quality programs. As have many states, California has moved toward requiring all teachers in publicly funded preschools to have BA/BS degrees in early childhood education (ECE), child development, or related fields. With funding from the state's *First Five Initiative* and other funding sources, representatives from community colleges and 4-year universities have met and planned a seamless transition, from the 2-year to 4-year institutions, with three goals to consider:

1. Increase, retain, and maximize resources to support students' professional development, tuition, tutoring, mentoring, and book expenses as they transition from high school to Ph.D. in the field of ECE.

2. Promote and develop academic programs in ECE at institutions of higher education that address the current and future needs of the ECE profession.

3. Ensure that the early childhood workforce reflects the racial, ethnic, and linguistic diversity of the population they serve (Thompson, 2006).

In June 2008 the first cohort groups of early childhood professionals graduated with their BA degrees. Success was strongly related to the support the students had been given and the sense of community they experienced in the program (Chavez, 2008).

Why do we see this move to requiring teachers in preschool settings to have bachelor degrees? One thrust has come from the requirement by the federal government that all teachers in Head Start programs should hold bachelor's degrees. Supporting influences come from researchers like Whitebook (1995). She points out that high-quality centers are those that meet standards higher than the minimum set by the state. They are also the programs "that have access to extra resources beyond parent fees." In one quality, nonprofit, parent-participation preschool with which we are familiar, the director has a master's degree in ECE, and every teacher but one with a master's has a bachelor's degree in ECE, child development, or a related field. Child development researchers have identified continuity of care from consistent, sensitive, well-trained, and well-compensated caregivers as key ingredients of good quality care (Groginsky, Robison, & Smith, 1999).

In addressing what she calls *quality teaching* in K–12 schools, Kennedy (2006) writes that most states adhere to the hypothesis that teachers are made in "carefully constructed higher education programs where [students] acquire both content and pedagogical knowledge." But then she questions whether this is true. Kennedy concludes that there are many factors that affect the quality of teaching, such as unreliable circumstances like the failure of props to support a science lesson, or unresolved discipline problems in the classroom. In the end, the important lesson is to think not just about *teacher* quality but to think about *teaching* quality. We must always remember that teaching is inherently an unpredictable, complex enterprise.

A study by Early, Bryant, Pianta, Clifford, Burchinal, Ritchie, Howes, and Barbarin (2006) indicates that "education and credentials by themselves are not sufficient" to ensure quality. However, these authors caution that it could be harmful to children to cut costs by lowering teacher or educational standards. The key is to properly compensate teachers according to the degrees they hold. Similarly, Pianta, Howes, Burchinal, Bryant, Clifford, Early, and Barbarin (2005) completed a study that failed to show any relationship between program quality and staff-child ratio or length of day. One difficulty lies in the variability among programs and preparation, especially at the preschool level. For example, regulations are more demanding in state-funded programs and the ranges of both quality and education are more limited, making associations harder to detect (Early et al., 2006).

A study by Hestenes, Cassidy, Hedge, and Lower (2007) that looked at the quality in inclusive and non-inclusive infant/toddler programs in North Carolina found that "teacher education and staff/child ratios are key predictors of quality programs." In a report, *Preschool Matters*, disseminated by the National Institute for Early Education Research, the principal conclusion was "quality costs money." Principal researcher, Barbara Gault, drew the following conclusion:

> The estimated costs of a six-hours-per-day program range from $5.17 per child hour at the lowest quality level to $8.18 per child hour at the highest level. (For the full report, check the website of the Institute for Women's Policy Research at www.iwpr.org.)

## MEETING CHILDREN'S NEEDS

Among the factors to consider in evaluating the quality of an early childhood program is whether the program meets each child's developmental needs. There must be an awareness of and attention to the needs of the children.

What are the needs of children during their early years? Accepting the validity of theories discussed in previous chapters, we know that their needs are to self-actualize, to know and understand, and to develop aesthetically. Children need to trust the significant people in their environment, resolve the questions of autonomy and initiative, and learn to become industrious.

### Implications According to Maslow's and Erikson's Theories

Let us briefly return to the theories of Maslow and Erikson. The implications, and the factors to consider, for a quality program include:

◆ The assurance of an environment that considers the child's physical safety. Quality programs for young children have the physical environment arranged so that children can explore without encountering physical dangers, such as electric cords or unprotected outlets, tables with sharp edges, and so on.

◆ Attention is given to the child's need for psychological safety. Essentially, quality programs provide for predictability, decision-making opportunities, and reasonable limits. With predictability comes the safety of knowing that certain activities will happen at certain times with consistency, such as snack time, group time, indoor and outdoor play, and the like (see Figures 10–1 and 10–2).

◆ Children have little control over their lives, and in our modern society, they have little opportunity to contribute to the family welfare. If, however, they have freedom of choice within the limits set, they can and do exert control over this part of their lives and thus learn how to make decisions. They also learn to accept the consequences of their decisions. Limits allow the child the safety of knowing which behaviors are acceptable and which are not. Limits teach children the concepts of right versus wrong and help the child develop inner control over behavior.

◆ Attention is paid to belongingness and love needs. A quality program will provide for these. All children need to feel that they are a part of a community: a preschool, child care center, elementary classroom, and family can provide the sense of group identity that is so important for the young child's positive growth.

◆ Meeting esteem needs is considered. Care is taken by all staff members to ensure that the children's **self-concepts** are enhanced. Look to see how the workers in a program relate to the children. Do they CARE? Do they take time to listen to the children? Do they compliment children when they have accomplished goals? Do they make a conscious effort to bolster the children's self-esteem?

◆ Helping children self-actualize is also a factor. Quality programs have enough equipment and materials with which the children can interact (see Figure 10–3). Are there enough art materials, books, and cut-and-paste opportunities? Is there a climbing apparatus? Are there plenty of tricycles and swings, so that no child has to wait too long? Are there enough puzzles? Are they challenging? Is the dramatic-play center well furnished? Are there enough props to stimulate sociodramatic play? Are there both large and small blocks? Is there a water table, a sand area, a terrarium, an aquarium, and several hand magnifying glasses? Are there enough small manipulatives? Are the play areas and yard clean and well kept? Do the children look happy?

◆ A physically attractive classroom is essential. Is it uncrowded? Is there a schedule of activities? Are rules and consequences decided in part by the children themselves? Is there a sufficiently large play yard to encourage active play? Are there structures that encourage climbing and jumping and in a safe way?

▶ **Figure 10–1**
This climbing structure allows room for these four girls to play on it at the same time.

**self-concepts—**
perceptions and feelings that children may have about themselves, gathered largely from how the important people in their world respond to them.

▶ **Figure 10–2**
The indoor water table is large enough to accommodate several children together.

▶ **Figure 10-3**

Exploring what to build with the blocks requires cooperation.

© Cengage Learning

**syntax**—involves the grammatical rules that govern the structure of sentences.

▶ **Figure 10-4**

A wall chart with each child's contribution promotes language use and understanding.

Where Went On Our Train Ride

(Katie) I went to Disneyland. (Ryan) I think were in jail. (Fatima) thinks she went to Disneyland. (Brandon) I went to here. (Angel) to my casa (Joe) Jail (Gabriel) To Disneyland. (Christine) We go to school. (Angel) hey, I go to school too (Tara) To Disneyland (Joe) would play (Fatima) would see the firework (Gabriel) I would eat pizza.

(Joe) Pizza Pizza

The End

© Cengage Learning

## A Balanced Program

A quality preschool or elementary school program will have a balanced curriculum that includes language, mathematics, motor activities, arts and crafts, music, creative movement, and science opportunities; none of these is neglected. Because of its importance, language will be emphasized across curricular areas in a quality preschool program. Look at and listen to how language is used and encouraged. It is during the preschool years, from age two-and-a-half to five, that the child makes the most progress in language. At the same time, the child is learning the **syntax** rules of language, such as present, past, and future tenses and the use of the negative, interrogatory, and conditional forms of speech. All of this language ability is, for the most part, acquired without formal teaching. A quality preschool program, however, recognizes this growth of language in the young child and provides opportunities for the child to hear language being used in proper context, to listen to models of language, and to practice growing language competencies. In addition, a quality program affords many opportunities for language enrichment (see Figure 10–4).

A quality program for both preschool centers and elementary schools will have a quiet corner or private space for the children, so that any child can be alone when necessary. Children, especially those who spend long hours in a center or school every day, need time and space to be alone. Some children live in homes that afford them little or no privacy; the center or school may be the only place where they can experience privacy.

## Personnel and Philosophies

Perhaps the most important factor in quality programs is the personality of the teacher and director or principal. As thoroughly as students entering a teacher preparation program or teachers being considered for a position may be screened, it is not always apparent what their personal characteristics or dispositions might be. Cartwright (1999) lists good physical health, integrity, a grounding in theory, general knowledge, unconditional caring, intuition, and laughter as needed characteristics for early childhood educators.

As reported in Chapter 2, Feeney, Christensen, & Moravcik (2006) describe a number of *dispositions* (relatively stable habits of mind or tendencies to respond to experiences in certain ways) that they believe are crucial—such as curiosity, openness to new ideas, a sincere liking for children, and so forth. We might want to add that a teacher needs to *CARE*.

Pratt (2008) writes about his daughter Lina's letters to him about her experiences in school. In one of the first letters he received, she refers to how her class is a community with caring teachers and a student-centered curriculum dominated by cooperative learning and where listening is fun.

The second-most-important factor is the underlying philosophy of the program, or the basic principles by which the program is guided. Are there stated objectives? Is there a written statement of philosophy? Is the curriculum based on background knowledge of child development principles? Are there printed materials describing the program in terms of what the teacher, director, principal, district, and state standards want for the children? Or does the program assume that you know all you need to based on the program label (for example, Montessori, Christian, Reggio Emilia)?

## STANDARDS OF QUALITY PROGRAMS

The U.S. Department of Education (2005) includes the following as components of high-quality preschool programs:

1. The program contains a clear statement of goals and philosophy that is comprehensive and addresses all areas of child development, including how the program will develop children's cognitive, language, and early reading skills, the cornerstones of later school success.

2. Children are engaged in purposeful learning activities and play, and are taught by teachers who work from lesson and activity plans (see Figure 10–5).

3. Instruction is guided by a coherent curriculum that includes meaningful content (such as science) and has a strong and systematic focus on cognitive skills, including the language, early reading, writing, and math skills children need to develop before they enter kindergarten (see Figure 10–6).

> **Student Teacher Quote**—"I'll never forget the time I watched my cooperating teacher's enthusiasm at reading group time. She looked as if she enjoyed the story as much as the group of children. At recess I asked if it was a new reading series. She told me the book had been used for three years at her grade level. I marveled at her ability to make reading the story new, alive, and interesting to yet another group of children."
>
> **Marie Ota, First Grade, New Haven Unified School District, Union City, CA**

▶ **Figure 10–5**

Lesson and activity plan preparation is all part of the student teaching experience.

© Cengage Learning

▶ **Figure 10-6**
Art activities play an important part in a well-balanced preschool curriculum.

© Cengage Learning

4. Instruction is always intentional and frequently is direct and explicit. There is a balance between individual, small-group, and large-group activities.

5. The classroom environment is one where children feel well cared for and safe. It also stimulates children's cognitive growth and provides multiple and varied opportunities for language and literacy experiences.

6. Teachers frequently check children's progress. Ongoing assessment allows teachers to tailor their instruction to the needs of individual children, as well as identify children who may need special help.

7. The preschool staff regularly communicates with parents and caregivers so that they are active participants in their children's education.

8. Services are sufficiently intensive to allow more time for children to benefit from cognitive experiences. Preschools that operate for a full day, on a year-round basis, or have provided children with 2 years of preschool, show better results than those that offer less intensive services.

(To access or order the complete report, go to http://www.edpubs.org.)

Although intended for preschool programs, the above-listed characteristics can be applied just as easily to elementary programs.

The NAEYC is widely recognized for its leadership role in the development of standards for preschool center accreditation (see Figure 10–7). Standards vary somewhat between organizations and agencies, but in studying the above list, it is easy to see that Maslow's hierarchy of needs and Erikson's developmental tasks are considered, although not specifically stated. NAEYC's list, however, goes beyond simply relating conditions to developmental theory. It also introduces the importance of looking at minimum standards, as set by governmental authorities, and suggesting that a quality program exceeds such minimal standards. For example, federal or state standards may propose that a ratio of 12 children (two- and three-year-olds) to 1 adult is sufficient. A quality program may have 8 to 10 children for every adult.

Although a child care center cannot become licensed without meeting minimum state standards regarding the number of children per square foot of indoor and outdoor space, there are programs that *average* the number of children throughout the day and so exceed the maximum recommended number during hours of prime use. For example, a center may be licensed for 28 children and may have as few as

10 present at 8 A.M. and eight at 5 P.M.; yet, they may have as many as 34 present between 10 A.M. and 3 P.M. The total number of children present throughout the day may be averaged so that a parent may never be aware of the overcrowding at midday. Some centers will employ a nutrition aide at lunchtime to assist in meal preparation. Although this person may not work directly with the children, she may be counted as an adult when figuring the ratio of children to adults. Many parents are unaware of these types of practices, none of which would be present in a quality program.

## Has the No Child Left Behind Act Made a Difference in Quality?

There has been a degree of controversy about the efficacy of the No Child Left Behind Act (NCLB) in relation to quality schooling. The NCLB has its proponents and detractors. There are many who decry the emphasis on end-of-year testing; others praise the rating of schools by their Adequate Yearly Progress (AYP). NCLB clearly has impacted education in the United States. "There is more testing and more accountability. . . . Yet, some provisions of the act. . . are causing persistent problems," especially when it concerns testing students with special needs and English language learners (Jennings & Rentner, 2006). As these authors conclude, "The key question is whether the strengths of the legislation can be retained (if it is re-authorized) while its weaknesses are addressed."

Certainly the alignment of state standards to curriculum goals and assessment is one positive outcome of NCLB. But Kagan, Carroll, Comer, and Scott-Little (2006) decry the absence of alignment in the transition between preschools and K–12 education. They find that horizontal alignment to standards at the prekindergarten level can be seen as positive in a variety of programs—public, private, or federally funded and regulated.

All five domains of early learning and development (approaches to learning, cognition, language development, physical/motor, and socio-emotional) show close alignment, from standards to curriculums to assessments. At the kindergarten level, however, there is a lack of horizontal alignment among standards, curriculums, and assessments. Kagan et al. (2006) conclude that early learning standards, curriculums, and assessments need to be age-appropriate and include all areas of development. Furthermore these standards, curriculums, and assessments must be aligned both vertically and horizontally. The authors see alignment as a key to accountability and one way to ensure the quality of services and outcomes for children.

© Cengage Learning

▶ **Figure 10-7**
Programs often display their licenses, awards, and accreditation certificates if they have received them.

## Quality in Family Child Care

A recent study by Doherty, Forer, Lero, Goelman, and LaGrange (2006), of 231 licensed family child care homes in Canada, explored the factors they hypothesized affected quality care: level of provider general education, intentionality (providers are looking for opportunities to learn about child development, for example), training and experience in child care, use of support services, and the work environment. Using the Family Day Care Rating Scale, they found that intentionality was predictive of higher quality, as was a college/university degree in early childhood education or a related discipline. The authors maintain that "quality child care is a skilled occupation requiring specific knowledge and skills." However, most family child care providers enter the profession without having any child care–related training. Training can be provided in a variety of ways, including evening and Saturday offerings, distance learning, and via the Internet.

A study by the Institute for Women's Policy Research (2005) recommended, among other suggestions, the development of community mentoring programs, conducting needs assessments to determine gaps in service, the creation of a single entry point from which providers can access services and resources, and the development of high standards for licensure. (For more information, go to http://www.iwpr.org).

## TYPES OF QUALITY PROGRAMS

It is important to recognize that there are many different types of early childhood programs (see Figure 10–8). There are child care centers, state-funded child care programs, Head Start and Montessori programs, **parent cooperatives**, and private, nonprofit, and for-profit preschools and primary schools. In each of these, a student teacher or family can find programs with varying amounts of quality, some good, some mediocre, and some even poor. "[T]here is no precise 'cookie-cutter' model, and parents should have a role in deciding what their child's early education program looks like" (U.S. Department of Education, 2005).

A preschool program reflects the underlying philosophy of its director, head teacher, or proprietor. It takes time to interview and observe carefully to determine quality. It is also easy to be deceived by a verbally persuasive director, head teacher, or proprietor. Smooth talk and right answers do not make a quality program.

In elementary schools, a building principal is one of the key factors in assuring a quality program. As Biddle and Saha (2006) indicate, school principals in both the United States and Canada value, know about, and use education research. They strive to keep themselves informed and work to improve their respective schools. Lipsitz and West (2006) looked at what makes a good school. Although they considered criteria for middle schools, the findings are appropriate for the primary grades as well. High-performing schools are academically excellent in that they challenge all of their students to do well; they are developmentally responsive in being sensitive to the developmental levels of their students; they respect student needs and interests; and they are "socially equitable, democratic, and fair—they provide every student with high-quality teachers, resources, learning opportunities, and support and make positive options available to all students."

**parent cooperatives—** programs staffed by one professional teacher and a rotating staff of parents.

▶ **Figure 10–8**
One usually cannot judge quality from a school's exterior.

© Cengage Learning

# WHO DECIDES THE QUALITY OF A PROGRAM?

As we suggested, the director has the responsibility for the quality of a preschool program. Indirectly, families also have a say in a program's quality. Obviously, there would be no program without client families. Thus, if a client buys an inferior service, in this case child care or a preschool, he has the choice to stop using it. The solution is, however, not always so simple.

Shlay, Tran, Weinraub, and Harmon (2005) looked at low-income African-American parents and their perception of quality in a child care program and their willingness to pay. The researchers found that the African-American parents' definition of quality "focuses squarely on the caregiving environment, specifically the qualifications, experience, training, and behavior associated with the child care provider." It was clear that these low-income parents understood what quality is and that they would be willing to pay for it if they could.

In a recent study of family satisfaction with the educational experience of their children, Fantuzzo, Perry, and Childs (2006) showed that families with children in Head Start or kindergarten were more satisfied than were families with children in child care or first grade. The writers believe that the study has "important implications for educational policy and practice" and that it "substantiates that there are distinct dimensions of parent satisfaction," and they urge district administrators to "gather information about satisfaction levels. . .across grades." It is clear that families do recognize whether their children are enrolled in a satisfactory program.

Quality is also dependent on the type of program. For example, in a program sponsored by a public school district, quality is determined not only by the principal in whose school the program is located but also by the local board of education and its policies, and ultimately by district, state, and federal government regulations and standards. However, in most public schools, ultimate quality depends on the individual teacher and the supervising principal.

In a private program, quality may depend on several people. In a proprietary preschool, quality is related to the personality and training of the proprietor. Is this person a loving, caring human being? Does this person have formal training in early childhood education? Does the proprietor hire people who are loving and caring, who have formal training? In any proprietary school, you will find the same range of quality as in a public program.

Who determines quality in a Montessori program, for example? Does the name promise that all its programs will have the same standards and quality? In the United States, there are *two* main approaches to Montessori education, both using the Montessori name. One branch includes schools under the sponsorship of the Associatione Montessori Internationale (AMI), with headquarters in Switzerland and headed by Maria Montessori's family. AMI schools adhere closely to Maria Montessori's original curriculum. Its teachers are trained in the philosophy and the **didactic** (teaching) materials designed by Dr. Montessori herself. In AMI schools, you will generally find the same **Montessori equipment** used, regardless of where the school is located. You will also find that the teachers have basically the same training in philosophy and methodology. Still, there will be differences in quality. Does the teacher really *like* children? Does that person *CARE*? Look carefully.

The other type of Montessori program is sponsored by the American Montessori Society (AMS), headquartered in New York. AMS schools are less like the original Montessori schools in that, although they use the didactic materials developed by Dr. Montessori, they make use of modern trends toward a greater emphasis on gross motor and social development. AMS programs vary widely, so again the personalities of the directors and teachers are the important factors.

Another determining factor for the quality of a program is who or what organization sponsors the school. Many churches sponsor schools and child care programs. In this case, quality depends not only on the personality of the director and teachers but also on the philosophy of the sponsoring church. Church-sponsored schools can also be excellent, mediocre, or poor. The teachers or child care workers always make the difference.

**didactic**—often applied to teaching materials, indicating a built-in intent to provide specific instruction.

**Montessori equipment**—early childhood learning materials derived from and part of the Montessori approach.

## Studies of Quality

The *Cost, Quality and Child Outcomes in Child Care Centers* Study (National Center for the Early Childhood Work Force, 1995b) is described as a landmark study linking data on program costs and quality to child outcomes. Four hundred randomly selected centers in California, Colorado, Connecticut, and North Carolina were assessed. Half the centers were nonprofit and half were for-profit.

The following study conclusions were highlighted by researchers:

◆ Child care at most centers in the United States is poor to mediocre.

◆ Children's cognitive and social development are positively related to the quality of their child care experience, across all levels of maternal education, child gender, and ethnicity.

◆ Consistent with previous research, the quality of child care is related to specific variables:
—staff-child ratios
—staff education
—administrators' prior experience
—teacher wages
—teacher education
—specialized training

◆ States with more stringent licensing standards have fewer poor-quality centers. Centers that comply with additional standards beyond those required for licensing provide higher-quality services.

◆ Centers provide higher-than-average overall quality when they have access to extra resources that are used to improve quality.

◆ Center child care, even mediocre-quality care, is costly to provide.

◆ Good-quality services cost more than those of mediocre quality but not a lot more.

◆ Center enrollment affects costs.

Bryant, Maxwell, and Burchinal (1999) stated findings from a study involving 508 children in North Carolina's *Smart Start*. "Overall, only 14 percent of the preschool classes in 1994 were providing good quality care. In 1996, 25 percent of the preschool classes were providing it."

Wiechel (2001) describes *Smart Start's* quality improvement efforts:

North Carolina's *Smart Start* is a comprehensive public/private initiative to help children enter school healthy and ready to succeed. The North Carolina Partnership for Children provides state-level leadership for the initiative, sets statewide benchmarks for young children and families, and makes grants to county or multi-county collaboratives. These collaboratives assess community early childhood needs and design comprehensive plans to improve and integrate services.

Most professionals agree with NAEYC's National Institute for Early Childhood Professional Development, which holds that "the most important determinant of the quality of children's experiences is the adults who are responsible for children's care and education" (NAEYC, 1994). Freeman and Feeney (2006) note that while more and more early childhood educators are entering the field better prepared, there is great variability between one state and another regarding licensing criteria. Even with the emphasis on having better-qualified teachers—that is, more holding bachelor's degrees—the Center for the Child Care Workforce in 2004 found that "salaries of many early childhood educators fell well below those earned by similarly qualified workers in other professions."

Working with experts, Kagan, Brandon, Ripple, Maher, and Joesch (2002) developed four guiding principles as the basis for implementing adequate compensation:

1. Teachers with comparable qualifications and experience should receive the same salary and benefits, whether teaching in a public elementary school or in early childhood education.

**2.** Staff compensation should vary by qualifications and by degree of responsibility.

**3.** Staff should have a range of formal qualifications, with a portion of center teachers and family child care teachers holding bachelor's degrees and administrators holding advanced degrees.

**4.** Entry-level positions should be maintained so that pre-service qualifications do not become a barrier to individuals from low socioeconomic backgrounds or minority groups seeking to enter the field.

Kagan, Brandon, Ripple, Maher, and Joesch (2002) note that many of the experts they consulted in developing their recommended guiding principles as the basis for implementing adequate compensation cited the same principles as those that many early childhood professionals have advocated for decades: that early childhood staff should earn wages linked to those earned by public elementary school teachers, with salaries varying depending on the locale, experience, degrees held, levels of training, work responsibilities, and professional behavior and skill. Health, retirement, and vacation benefits should also be provided to all staff positions.

A study by the National Center for the Early Childhood Work Force (1995b), *Cost, Quality and Child Outcomes in Child Care Centers (CQ&O)*, reinforces what was found in the 1993 National Child Care Staffing Study: overall quality of care in center-based child care programs is poor to mediocre (Whitebook, Phillips, & Howes, 1993).

Many factors contribute to poor quality, including strong price competition in the marketplace, lack of consumer demand for quality, poor licensing standards, staff–child ratios, staff education, administrator experience, and center revenue and resources, to name but a few.

One promising finding about the CQ&O study team programs was that those accredited by the NAEYC (25 of 390 preschools and 14 of 222 infant/toddler classrooms) consistently received higher scores on the Early Childhood Environment Rating Scale (ECERS-R) and the Infant/Toddler Environment Rating Scale (ITERS-R) (Cryer & Phillipsen, 1997). As accreditation has become more popular, we do find more quality programs.

The ECERS-R is a 43-item scale with seven categories: space and furnishings, personal care routines, language-reasoning, activities (fine motor, art, music/movement, blocks, and the like), interaction (supervision of gross motor activities, for example), program structure, parents and staff, with attention to cultural diversity and the inclusion of special needs children subsumed within the first seven categories (Clifford, 1998). The ITERS-R includes 35 items, including adult personal area, meals/snacks, personal grooming, furnishings for relaxation, art, dramatic play, space to be alone, and others. As with the ECERS-R, attention to cultural diversity and inclusion of special needs infants and toddlers are subsumed under the other items.

Greenberg and Springen (2000) report that an ongoing study of early child care by the National Institute of Child Health and Human Development found that children in high-quality, center-based care outperformed children in other kinds of high-quality care (for example, family child care homes, relatives, and so on) in language development and cognitive skills like problem solving and reasoning. They also tended to have fewer behavioral problems.

Most experts and researchers believe that a high-quality program has a recommended low child–adult ratio, a relatively small group size, age-appropriate activities, a safe environment, and access to comprehensive services as needed, such as health and nutrition and parent involvement.

Head Start's Family and Child Experiences Survey (FACES) is a longitudinal study of a nationally representative sample of Head Start programs. Its purpose is to examine the overall quality and outcomes of Head Start using specific program performance measures (see Figure 10–9) (Tarullo & Doan, 1999).

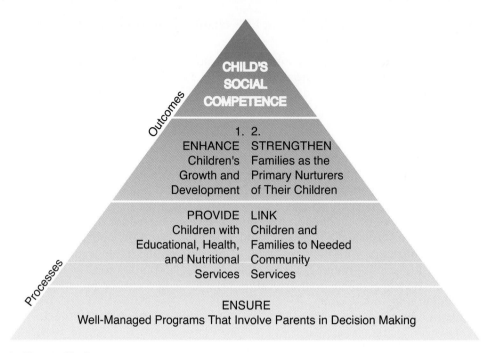

▶ **Figure 10-9**

Quality ratings in preschool and infant classrooms. From Cost, quality, and child outcomes in child care centers. (1995, May). *Young Children, 50*(4). Reprinted with permission from the National Association for the Education of Young Children, NAEYC, ©1995.

In 1997 and 1998, children and families in 40 national Head Start programs were observed and assessed by teachers and parents in the areas of emergent literacy, numeracy, general cognitive skills, gross and fine motor skills, social behavior and attitudes, positive learning attitudes, emotional well-being, and physical health. Classrooms were assessed on scheduling, the early learning environment, and teacher behavior. Tarullo and Doan (1999) reviewed the preliminary findings and report the following:

> Research has consistently linked aspects of classroom quality such as low child–adult ratio, small group size, responsiveness of teacher–child interaction, and richness of learning environments to better child outcomes. For the first time, using a national sample, FACES tests the same linkages in Head Start. Preliminary data show that the higher the quality of a Head Start classroom, the more likely that children will show higher levels of skills, and over time, display greater gains in developmental outcomes.

Additional study data is available at the Head Start Bureau web page, at http://www.acf.dhhs.gov.

## The Quality 2000 Initiative

The *Quality 2000: Advancing Early Care and Education Initiative* proposes that its "primary goal. . .is that by the year 2010, high-quality early care and education programs will be available and accessible to all children from birth to age five whose parents choose to enroll them" (Kagan & Neuman, 1997).

The recommendations made by the people involved in writing the initiative are not simple: each is comprehensive and broad; each is a vision of what might be. Each includes several examples of strategies that, if followed, are designed to achieve the goal of the recommendation.

The first recommendation concerns program quality; the second, children; the third, parents and family; the fourth, staff credentialing; the fifth, staff training and preparation; the sixth, program licensing; the seventh, funding and financing; and the eighth, governance structures.

A related Canadian study replicated and extended the CQ&O study of the United States and looked at quality in seven of Canada's provinces. Goelman, Forer, Kershaw, Doherty, Lero, and LaGrange (2006) found many of the same phenomena as the U.S. study: staff education levels were significant predictors of child care center quality, as were child-to-adult ratios and staff wages. Goelman and his associates extended the study to include other variables and found that the number of staff or adults was a significant direct predictor of quality, just as the presence of a student teacher was a significant indirect predictor.

## Legislative Efforts

The National Institute for Early Childhood Education Research (2006) notes that many states have explored ways to look at the issue of quality. Among these are Pennsylvania, Vermont, North Carolina, Montana, Maryland, Colorado, Tennessee, and the District of Columbia. These states have developed *quality rating systems* (QRS) to support their early care and education communities in assessing, improving, and communicating the quality of their programs. Rhode Island completed 2 years of work in developing their QRS and began implementing it in 2007. In all of the states, staff qualifications is one of the criteria. To check on QRS in your state, go to the National Child Care Information Center website at http://www.nccic.org and click on *Popular Topics* and then *Quality Rating Systems.*

Neugebauer (2009a) reports that 18 states currently use a QRS or a quality rating and improvement system QRIS to evaluate all of the early child care programs in their states; 26 are either exploring or designing one, and 9 of the 26 are piloting systems. In fact there are only 5 states that have not. All 18 states using QRS/QRIS consider professional development, staff qualifications, and training in their respective scales. Sixteen rate the learning environment and curriculum; 15 rate parent and family involvement; and 12 rate administrative policies and procedures. Neugebauer concludes that early research results seem to indicate that using a quality rating system can make a difference.

Most QRS or QRIS contain five common elements (Jacobson, 2008):

◆ standards

◆ accountability (assessment and monitoring)

◆ program and practitioner outreach and support

◆ financial incentives specifically linked to compliance with quality standards

◆ family/consumer education

Jacobson raises the question as to whether "quality rating systems improve children's learning" and suggests that preschool rating systems need fine-tuning if they are to improve programs.

Mitchell (2008) advises that any QRS should be simple, dynamic, aligned with child outcomes, and begun when funding is available. Perhaps it is the term "dynamic" that is the important piece in fine-tuning rating systems. But without adequate funding quality rating systems might not be implemented.

In her paper Mitchell answers the question regarding the efficacy of QRS. Yes, they do work; the quality is improving, and there are better child outcomes in higher-quality centers (based on evaluations in North Carolina, Oklahoma, Pennsylvania, and Tennessee).

Many states award stars on the basis of quality. In Montana, for example, three stars are awarded to any center accredited by the National Association for the Education of Young Children, the National Association of Family Child Care, or the National School-Age Care Alliance.

How have states financed legislative and other state efforts to improve quality? The National Institute for Early Education Research (2009) cites the following facts in its latest newsletter:

◆ After almost 50 years of increasing support for early education, the General Assembly of North Carolina is on the brink of cutting what taxpayers do for the state's youngest. Like many other states, North Carolina has been hurt by the current recession.

◆ A Texas measure would pay for full-day preschool. Texas currently pays for half-day preschool, widely thought to boost student performance in later years, for qualifying children. But under a bill winding through the legislature, the state would pay for schools to offer full-day programs.

◆ The Florida Department of Education recently released the latest scores for centers that participate in the Voluntary Pre-kindergarten program. State leaders hope a scoring system will promote the importance of quality preschool and help parents choose the right programs. The program offers free preschool for any four-year-old through state-approved providers.

◆ Child advocates in Oregon want the state to invest more in early childhood education, namely Head Start. They recognize a massive expansion isn't realistic, so they're lobbying for modest growth.

◆ For every dollar that Hawaii invests in early childhood education, $4.20 can be saved in the form of reduced spending on remedial education, crime, and health and welfare, according to a new study released by the Good Beginnings Alliance. The findings are included in the report "The Economic Benefits of Investment in Early Childhood for Hawaii."

◆ In Phoenix, AZ, the cigarette tax provides $30 million to help preschool-age children with health care and early education. The money comes from a "First Things First" initiative, passed in 2006, that imposed an 80-cent tax on a pack of cigarettes, with the money earmarked for early education.

Many studies have associated quality child care with positive outcomes for children, including better language, cognitive, and social skills, fewer behavioral problems, and stronger mother–child relationships (Groginsky, Robison, & Smith, 1999). The High/Scope Perry Preschool project found low-income children's attendance in a quality early education program led to children's greater academic success, better adult job achievement, and half as many arrests in later life (Schweinhart, Barnes, & Weikart, 1993; Schweinhart & Weikart, 1997).

## The True Cost of Quality Child Care

Family budgets are strained in many households because of child care costs. If child care fees were increased and parents assumed the true costs for quality care, experts estimate the cost for parents would leave little left for other family living expenses. Political platforms often include promises to enhance child care quality and access, but child care advocates do not expect an infusion of federal, state, or private monies in amounts necessary to alleviate the present situation in the United States.

Research has just begun to undercover the true costs of operating a quality early childhood program. Hidden costs have been borne by early childhood workers through foregone wages and benefits. The CQ&O study team (Helburn, 1995), after studying 401 child care centers, estimates that 25 percent of the full cost of care and education of enrolled children was covered by some form of subsidy, primarily through low staff wages, but also building, rent, or occupancy aid, volunteers, donated goods, and in-kind contributions.

Conclusions cited in the *Cost, Quality and Child Outcomes in Child Care Centers* public report (Helburn, 1995) estimated as much as 19 percent of the center's full costs were borne by workers, who earned less than workers in other fields with similar educational backgrounds and comparable skills.

# ACCREDITATION AND ITS RELATIONSHIP TO QUALITY

**Accreditation** of preschool programs and child development centers is more recent, than is accreditation in K–12 schools. Now we see after-school and family child care homes being accredited also.

Best known of the many accrediting organizations in the United States are the National Association for the Education of Young Children (NAEYC), the National After-School Association (NAA), and the National Association for Family Child Care (NAFCC). The Catholic Education Association (CEA), the Lutheran Schools Accreditation (LSA), the Association of Christian Schools International (ACSI), and the American Montessori Society (AMS) also accredit their respective schools as do several other organizations.

## Elementary School Evaluation

Many states have instituted their own versions of accreditation, commonly referred to as a *coordinated compliance review* (CCR) or a *contract monitoring review* (CMR). In California and other states, the state board of education requires that all schools in the state undergo periodic CCRs. These involve a self-study and review by a team of evaluators, who look to see how closely the school meets standards set in the Desired Results Developmental Profile for each student. "In this way, California's standards must come alive in its early childhood programs" (Grondlund, 2006). Included on the review team are teachers, administrators, and state board of education representatives who have all received training in how to conduct a CCR. The reviewers prepare a report for the state superintendent of instruction, and the state board of education members, who have the final authority to accept the report, ask that the school undergo further review or reject the report. Reviews are conducted every 3 years, so it is a continuing process.

Nationwide, both the Catholic Education Association and the Lutheran Schools Accreditation accredit their respective parochial schools. Christian and private schools may also be accredited by their sponsoring associations. Families interested in placing their children in these schools should ask whether the school is accredited. It does not automatically verify quality, but it does suggest that certain standards are maintained. Families might be wise to ask for a copy of the last accreditation report to review.

## NAEYC Accreditation

In 1985, the NAEYC, concerned with how to ensure quality programs for young children, especially as they relate to developmentally appropriate practices, established the National Academy of Early Childhood Programs to administer accreditation procedures. Any program wishing to be accredited must write the NAEYC and request that it be placed on the calendar for an accreditation visit.

Once the date of the visit is confirmed, the program conducts a self-study, involving formal reports by the administrator, staff, and families. The result is a program description that includes a center or school profile, the results of classroom observations (completed by both the teacher and the director), and the results of the administrator report that ties together the results of the ratings of the program by staff and parents. After completion of the self-study and its subsequent reception at NAEYC, a trained validator visits the center or school to verify the self-study much in the same manner as the Visiting Committee or the CCR reviewers. The validator's report is then read by at least three commissioners who make the final accreditation decision.

NAEYC's revised Early Childhood Program Standards and Accreditation Performance Criteria (2005a) were approved by its governing board in April of 2005. The criteria are believed to be a major step forward and include the following focus areas:

1. children
2. teaching staff

**3.** family and community partnerships

**4.** leadership and administration

In each of the areas, program standards are listed, together with their rationales and an example of each criterion. There are five criteria in the focus area for children: relationships, curriculum, teaching, assessment of child progress, and health. Under focus area 2, teaching staff, there is only one criterion, and two criteria each are in the family and community partnerships and leadership and administration focus areas.

It is believed that with implementation of the new criteria in September 2006, "NAEYC-accredited programs will help families, educators, and many others in our communities recognize the value of setting high standards for all programs for young children" (NAEYC, 2005b).

As more and more programs implement developmentally appropriate practices, and especially as families begin to demand accredited programs for their children, the number of approved programs has risen. In 2002, there were 8,192 NAEYC-accredited early childhood programs, serving more than 720,000 young children (NAEYC, 2002). Today, there are more than 10,000 (Neugebauer, 2009b).

Does accreditation assure quality? In many ways, yes. The self-study alerts teachers, directors, principals, and others involved in the process to any areas of needed improvement, especially those impinging directly on standards required for accreditation. Often, then, when validators arrive, changes have already been instituted to improve an area likely to cause concern. National Academy validators observe to see how closely school goals and objectives match the program standards of the National Academy.

In an attempt to understand why quality remains low, with soaring investment in early care and education, and with so many accredited centers, Kagan, Brandon, et al. (2002) suggest:

> The answer is twofold. Most important, the resources to do the job are simply inadequate. . . .While inadequate resources are absolutely the first and major problem, they are not the only issue. *How resources are spent* is also important.

State lawmakers have turned their attention toward accreditation by promoting voluntary accreditation. The National Conference of State Legislatures' publication *Making Child Care Better: State Initiatives* notes that accreditation legislation in some states often includes language that is broad enough for programs to acquire accreditation by a range of organizations, but other states specify NAEYC accreditation (Groginsky, Robison, & Smith, 1999).

A number of states have chosen to develop differential subsidy rates, to more closely match the cost of providing accredited care, improve quality, and to increase family availability to accredited programs (Warman, 1998). In northern California, funds from Contra Costa County's *First Five* and Alameda County's *Every Child Counts* programs provides, as previously stated, subsidies for preschool teachers to further their education, and currently are funding articulation programs between 2- and 4-year institutions (Thompson, 2006).

Also in California, the California Association for the Education of Young Children (CAEYC) established a program in 2004, the Professional Development Academy, to support the training of early childhood education professionals, caregivers, and parents. The Academy has three major focus areas:

◆ professional staff development

◆ leadership training

◆ on-site consultation

A variety of delivery options are used, such as a series of 1-day seminars, offered at different locations throughout the state, and on-site training for centers and homes that choose to subscribe to the service. Currently, some of the training modules are available though the Internet with follow-up contact by e-mail and telephone (Phipps, 2004).

Believing that quality education begins with preparing quality faculty, the Frank Porter Graham Child Development Institute of the University of North Carolina–Chapel Hill (FPG) has established relationships with several colleges and states, to promote the development and well-being of young children and families. "The institute regularly hosts special conferences and training events that further the knowledge and skills of faculty and in institutions across the state and nation" (FPG, 2003). One model developed by FPG, *Walking the Walk*, seeks to address the nationwide shortage of a culturally and linguistically diverse pool of early childhood teachers.

A highly trained teaching staff is the strongest predictor of program quality, along with the levels of staff compensation. Teacher and administrator turnover is a problem, and a staffing crisis exists in most areas of the country. *La Ristra*, New Mexico's publication, concludes that ignoring factors that contribute to lack of quality is a poor course of action:

> An acute problem left unattended eventually becomes status quo, yet is no less in need of urgent action. So it is with the child care staffing crisis. For three decades advocates and researchers have sounded warnings that without massive sustained effort to improve child care employment, turnover will continue unabated and children, families, and caregivers will suffer the consequences. . . . At the heart of the crisis lie the insufficient resources to attract and retain a workforce able to sustain developmentally appropriate environments for children. (Turner, 2002)

Whitebook and Sakai (2002) point out that centers receiving intensive support—like on-site technical assistance from an early childhood professional, custom-designed training for staff and directors, funds to cover release time for staff participating in training, and an ongoing, facilitated support group for directors—achieved accreditation at more than twice the rate of centers receiving moderate support, or seeking accreditation independently, and at nearly 10 times the rate of centers with only limited support.

## THE COMER PROJECT FOR CHANGE IN EDUCATION

Dr. James P. Comer's work in the public schools of New Haven, Connecticut, shows us that change can take years (Goldberg, 1997). The original School Development Project started in the 1968–1969 school year, with two elementary schools in low-income, predominantly African-American areas. Test scores were 19 months below grade level and did not reach grade level until 1979—10 years later. By 1984, scores were 12 months *above* grade level. What had happened?

Learning obstacles were identified and remedied. The project focused on what might be called *the ecology of the total school*: children, parents, administrators, custodial staff, and the community in which the school was located. Changes were made: schools were painted and cleaned; staff became a part of the decision-making process; teachers and administrators were retrained or transferred.

Today, the *Comer Project for Change in Education* is now operating in more than 600 schools, in 82 school districts, in 26 states. The results continue to be good, but experience has taught those involved that change, although slow, "can yield to good will and hard work" (Goldberg, 1997). Comer, Ben-Avie, Haynes, and Joyner (1999) state that there are six points that need to be considered if change is to occur:

1. To reform schools we must understand the complex dynamics that affect them.
2. To reform schools we must start where the children are.

**3.** To reform schools we must keep pace with our changing society.

**4.** To reform schools we must focus on relationships and child development.

**5.** To reform schools we must develop group goals, trust, and accountability to standards.

**6.** To reform schools we must make financial commitments and policy changes.

Comer concludes with the following plea:

> The Agricultural Extension Service helped make America the breadbasket of the world. Today's economy needs to have educated workers, but our schools can't change even when they want to. Rather than turning to radical and unproven formats of schooling, we should create an Education Extension Service that helps all involved in the education enterprise to put child development front and center, and move toward a system of education that will keep the nation in the economic and democratic forefront in the twenty-first century. (Comer et al.,1999)

How well Dr. Comer's vision for schools in the United States might flower, we can only trust that educators, the public, you, and especially the federal government take heed. If it took 10 years to accomplish a turnaround in the two public schools in New Haven, where the Comer project started, it might be wise not to expect immediate changes under the No Child Left Behind Act.

## MENTORING PROGRAMS

The more experienced worker, tutoring and serving as an example to the new worker, has always been a way of training (see Figure 10–10). Mentoring programs have emerged as one of the most promising ways to stabilize and support the child care workforce to guarantee more reliable and high-quality care for young children (National Center for the Early Childhood Work Force, 1995a). Some states—including Arkansas, California, Florida, Maine, Maryland, Minnesota, Montana, Ohio, Rhode Island, South Dakota, Utah, West Virginia, and Wisconsin—operate mentoring and apprenticeship programs for early childhood teachers (Groginsky, Robison, & Smith, 1999).

*Student Teacher Quote*—"My cooperating teacher and I became good friends. We still see one another at district meetings. I was privileged to have apprenticed under such an excellent model."

**Rich Bacon, Third Grade, Hayward Unified School District, CA**

▶ **Figure 10–10**
A new teacher confers with her mentor.

© Cengage Learning

The National Center for the Early Childhood Work Force (1995a) describes the **mentoring** effort:

> Throughout the country, mentoring programs have emerged as one of the most promising strategies to retain experienced teachers and providers and thereby guarantee more reliable, high quality care for young children. Experienced teachers and providers participate in programs designed to give them the skills necessary to teach other adults how to care for and educate infants and young children. Upon taking on the role of mentor teacher, most teachers and providers receive additional compensation for training protégés; gain new respect from their co-workers and parents, and renew their own commitment to working with children in the classroom or home. As dozens of programs develop, the need to share information grows.
>
> The Early Childhood Mentoring Alliance, a newly emerging group, intends to provide a forum for sharing information and providing technical assistance. The alliance is supported by a consortium of foundations.

## Teacher-Support Programs for Public School Teachers

Beginning and newly credentialed elementary school teachers are finding that many public school districts are not letting them "sink or swim" in their first teaching year. Many districts realize teacher quality is the single most important factor in improving student achievement (Haycock, 1998). These districts are investing in and designing teacher-induction programs that focus on supportive assistance (see Figure 10–11). American schools expect to hire more than 2 million teachers in the next decade (Moir, Gless, & Baron, 1999).

California's *Beginning Teacher Support and Assessment (BTSA)* program is a state-wide initiative, jointly administered by the California Department of Education and the California Commission on Teacher Credentialing. This program allots $3,000 for each beginning teacher, and some local districts augment that with additional funding. Funds are being used in a number of ways, including on-site collaboration, classroom supplies, aids, technical assistance, and so on. Beginning teachers

**mentoring**—guidance by an experienced and trusted teacher, who is frequently paired with a new, inexperienced teacher or aide, and who assists the new teacher with ideas and advice.

▶ Figure 10–11
These experienced teachers are collaborating with a new teacher at their school.

are assigned mentor teachers, who consult with them on a regular basis, and are given released time to visit their mentors' or other classrooms. Unfortunately, given California's current budget difficulties, it is doubtful that this program will be funded for the next budget year.

Most new teachers see themselves as agents of change and are inspired and committed to the idea that they will make a difference in children's educational lives. Teacher-induction programs hope to sustain and nurture that idealism.

# ▶ SUMMARY

In this chapter, we attempted to provide guidelines by which you can evaluate the quality of an early childhood education program. We have suggested that a quality program is one that takes into consideration the developmental needs of the children and that exceeds, rather than meets, minimum standards for state licensing. We have also suggested that quality programs may be found in many different settings, ranging from federally funded programs to parent cooperatives to proprietary, for-profit centers.

We also presented a review of the accreditation process sponsored by states' boards of education coordinated compliance reviews, as these apply to the provision of quality elementary school programs. NAEYC's National Academy of Early Childhood Programs and its accreditation process were briefly explained, as was the impact on quality programs for children from birth through age eight. (Most accredited programs are for children from birth through age five, with public schools not applying for accreditation through NAEYC but, instead, undergoing coordinated compliance or other quality reviews, such as CMR.)

Quality programs depend on you as student teachers. You need to strive to preserve and improve programs when you enter the field. Quality programs can exist only if quality people fight for them.

# ▶ HELPFUL WEBSITES

**http://www.naeyc.org**
National Association for the Education of Young Children. Proceed to *Academy* for NAEYC accreditation information.

**http://www.ecs.org**
Education Commission of the States. On this website you will find information about education in every state, K–12 issues, and publications available. Included are readings on state funding, teacher qualifications, program standards, legislation, and other early childhood issues.

**http://www.fpg.unc.edu**
Frank Porter Graham Child Development Institute, University of North Carolina-Chapel Hill. This site offers, among other choices, readings on quality care. The institute is involved in many different projects such as Walking the Walk and studies of program quality.

**http://www.ed.gov/offices/OERI/ECI**
National Institute on Early Childhood Development. It is a division of the Office of Educational Research and Improvement (OERI) of the U.S. Department of Education and sponsors comprehensive and challenging research to help ensure that America's children are successful in school and beyond. OERI is changing its name to the Institute for Educational

Sciences (IES); you may find either or both websites being used.

**http://www.edpubs.ed.gov/**
Publications of the U.S. Department of Education. This is a helpful resource, containing much valuable information. Many of the publications are free.

**http://www.acf.hhs.gov/programs**
The Administration for Children and Families is a division of the Department of Health and Human Services. Its main page will take you to Head Start. The site provides general information and lists of its publications.

**http://www.eric.ed.gov**
ERIC clearinghouse main page. Go to the Thesaurus and look for any topic on quality.

**http://nieer.org**
National Institute for Early Education Research, a unit of Rutgers University, publishes the newsletter *Preschool Matters*; NIEER supports early education initiatives by providing objective, nonpartisan information based on research. Check for information on quality rating systems (QRS).

**http://www.cde.ca.gov/sp/ed/ci/drdppinstructions.asp**
State of California, Child Development Education. Follow instructions to find a listing of Desired Results Developmental Profiles.

**http://www.mcrel.org**
Mid-Continent Research for Education and Learning (MCREL). The mission of this group is to make a difference in the quality of education.

**http://www.ChildCareExchange.com**
Child Care Information Exchange. If you want to receive the daily newsletter, *Exchange Every Day*, it

is free. Readings are short and helpful websites are frequently listed, especially when a synopsis of a longer article or book is given.

 Additional resources for this chapter can be found by visiting the companion website at *www.cengage.com/education/machado.*

## ▶ SUGGESTED ACTIVITIES

A. Visit at least three of these different types of early childhood programs: a Montessori school, a Head Start program, an NAEYC-accredited program, a proprietary child care center, or a public school kindergarten, first-, second-, or third-grade classroom. Evaluate them on the standards of a good program from NAEYC. Interview the teachers and/or the principal of the school you visit and ask them about their self-study.

B. Discuss the following in a small group. Report your group's reactions.

The growth in child care and preschool education, along with the need for families to be more informed about quality has spurred the adoption in several states of systems for rating program quality through the assignment of stars or other quality indicators that consumers are used to seeing for other services like hotels and restaurants. . . .Eighteen states are now using some sort of quality rating system (QRS) and 26 others are considering them. With numbers like that, it's safe to say the move to QRS is a trend (Neugebauer, 2009b).

## ▶ REVIEW

A. List five features of a quality early childhood program, according to the Federal government, and six of the program standards listed in the NAEYC accreditation procedures.

B. Read each of the following descriptions of different early childhood programs. Decide whether each paragraph is describing a quality program, a mediocre program, or a poor program. Indicate if you do not have sufficient data to make a decision. Discuss your answers and opinions with peers and your college supervisor.

1. This private preschool/child care center is located in a former public school. Each morning, the director greets every child as they enter. Each child has a wide choice of activities. Clay containers are placed on one table; crayon boxes and paper on another; scissors, old magazines, and scraps of construction paper are on a third, with sheets of blank paper and glue sticks. Some children prefer to go to the block area, the book corner, or dramatic-play corner. The outside play area beckons those who wish to climb, ride, swing, or play at the water table or in the sandbox.

   The director has a degree in early childhood education, as does the only paid aide. Parents are seen often; both fathers and mothers stay with their

children for a few minutes. The director speaks to each parent and sends home a monthly newsletter to inform parents of special activities and to solicit help for special projects (both the indoor and outdoor climbing structures were built by parents).

2. This after-school program is sponsored by a franchised nonprofit organization. The director of the program has an AA degree in early childhood education. Certified teachers, with the state-required 24 units of early childhood or holding a Child Development Associate certificate, work with the children (aged 5 to 9). In addition, there are many volunteers, recruited from the local community college and high school. The program is located in unused classrooms in four elementary schools, and in the nonprofit organization's main facility.

   Because the main facility does not meet state standards, children are asked to join the organization. As a result, the organization is exempt from having to meet standards. For example, although there is ample outside play area at the school sites, there is little other than a paved basketball court at the main facility site.

   This after-school program has a written statement of purpose and goals, a conceptual outline covering such items as safety, self-image, adult role models, a stimulating environment, and so on; a parent advisory group; and a daily schedule listing curriculum factors. The child-to-adult ratio is listed as 15:1 but has been known to exceed 25:1 when volunteers have been absent.

The program schedules free time for the first 30 minutes so that the children can unwind from their school day. This is followed by snack time, activity time (arts and crafts, gymnastics, swimming in the facility's pool, field trips), cleanup time, and free time during which quiet activities such as games, reading, homework, and drawing can be done.

## ▶ REFERENCES

Biddle, B. J., & Saha, L. J. (2006, March). How principals use research. *Educational Leadership, 63*(6), 72–77.

Bryant, D. M., Maxwell, K. L., & Burchinal, M. (1999). Effects of a community initiative on the quality of child care. *Early Childhood Research Quarterly, 14,* 449–464.

Cartwright, S. (1999, November). What makes good early childhood teachers? *Young Children, 54*(6), 4–7.

Chavez, J. (June 12, 2008). Personal communication.

Clifford, R. M. (1998, November 20). *Measuring quality in preschool settings: The development of the revised early childhood environment rating scale.* Paper presented at the National Association for the Education of Young Children Conference, Toronto, Canada.

Comer, J. P., Ben-Avie, M., Haynes, N. M., & Joyner, E. T. (1999). *Child by child: the Comer process for change in education.* New York: Teachers College Press.

Cryer, D., & Phillipsen, L. (1997, July). A close-up look at child care program strengths and weaknesses. *Young Children, 52*(5), 23–29.

Doherty, G., Forer, B., Lero, D. S., Goelman, H., & LaGrange, A. (2006). Predictors of quality in family child care. *Early Childhood Research Quarterly, 21*(3), 296–312.

Early, D. M., Bryant, D. M., Pianta R. C., Clifford, R. M., Burchinal, M. R., Ritchie, S., Howes, C., & Barbarin, O. (2006). Are teachers' education, majors, and credentials related to classroom quality and children's academic gains in prekindergarten? *Early Childhood Research Quarterly, 21*(2), 174–195.

FPG Child Development Institute, University of North Carolina at Chapel Hill. (2003, Spring). Elevating the educators: the quest for quality begins with effective faculty. *Early Developments, 7*(1), 14–15.

Fantuzzo, J., Perry, M. A., & Childs, S. (2006). Parent satisfaction with educational experiences scale: A multivariate examination of parent satisfaction with early childhood education programs. *Early Childhood Research Quarterly, 21*(2), 142–152.

Feeney, S., Christensen, D., & Moravcik, E. (2006). *Who am I in the lives of children?* (7th ed.). Upper Saddle River, NJ: Pearson/Merrill/Prentice Hall.

Freeman, N. K. & Feeney, S. (2006, September). The new face of early care and education: Who are we? Where are we going? *Young Children, 61*(5), 10–16.

Goelman, H., Forer, B., Kershaw, P., Doherty, G., Lero, D., LaGrange, A. (2006). Towards a predictive model of quality in Canadian child care centers. *Early Childhood Research Quarterly, 21*(3), 280–295.

Goldberg, M. F. (1997, March). Maintaining a focus on child development: An interview with Dr. James P. Comer. *Phi Delta Kappan, 78*(7), 479–483.

Greenberg, S. H., & Springen, K. (2000, October 16). Back to day care. *Newsweek,* 61–62.

Groginsky, S., Robison, S., & Smith, S. (1999). *Making child care better: State initiatives.* Washington, DC: National Conference of State Legislatures.

Grondlund, G. (2006). *Make early learning standards come alive: connecting your practice and curriculum to state guidelines.* St. Paul, MN: Redleaf Press; Washington, DC: National Association for the Education of Young Children.

Haycock, K. (1998, Summer). Good teaching matters: How well-qualified teachers can close the gap. *Thinking K–16, 3*(2), 1–2.

Helburn, S. (Ed.). (1995). *Cost, quality and child outcomes in child care.* Center for Research in Economics and Social Policy, Department of Economics, University of Colorado.

Hestenes, L. L., Cassidy, D. J., Hegde, A. V., & Lower, J. K. (2007, Fall). Quality in inclusive and noninclusive infant and toddler classrooms. *Journal of Research in Childhood Education, 22*(1), 69–84.

Institute for Women's Policy Research. (2005). Retrieved August 16, 2009, from http://www.iwpr.org.

Jacobson, L. (2008, October 28). Eye on research. *Education Week, 7,* 18–19.

Jennings, J. & Rentner, D. S. (2006, October). Ten big effects of the No Child Left Behind Act on public schools. *Phi Delta Kappan, 88*(2), 110–113.

Kagan, S. L., Brandon, R. N., Ripple, C. H., Maher, E. J., & Joesch, J. M. (2002, May). Supporting quality early childhood care and education. *Young Children, 57*(3), 58–65.

Kagan, S. L., Carroll, J., Comer, J. P., & Scott-Little, C. (2006, September). Alignment: A missing link in early childhood transitions? *Young Children, 61*(5), 26–32.

Kagan, S. L., & Neuman, M. J. (1997, September). Highlights of the *Quality 2000 Initiative:* Not by chance. *Young Children, 52*(6), 14–18.

Kennedy, M. M. (2006, March). From teacher quality to quality teaching. *Educational Leadership, 63*(6), 14–19.

Lipsitz, J., & West, T. (2006, September). What makes a good school? Identifying excellent middle schools. *Phi Delta Kappan, 88*(1), 57–66.

Mitchell, A. (July 29, 2008). Quality rating and improvement systems. Retrieved on March 3, 2009, from http://www.eec.state.ma.us/docs/Anne%20Mitchell%20QRIS20presentation.ppt.

Moir, E., Gless, J., & Baron, W. (1999). A support program with heart: The Santa Cruz project. In M. Scherer (Ed.). *A better beginning: Supporting and mentoring new teachers* (pp. 106–113). Alexandria, VA: Association for Supervision and Curriculum Development.

National Association for the Education of Young Children. (2005a, July). NAEYC accreditation: governing board approves new NAEYC early childhood program standards and accreditation performance criteria. *Young Children, 60*(4), 50–54.

National Association for the Education of Young Children. (2005b, September). NAEYC accreditation: facts about the new NAEYC accreditation system. *Young Children, 60*(5), 74–75.

National Association for the Education of Young Children. (NAEYC). (2002). Our mission. *Young Children, 57*(6), 98–99.

National Association for the Education of Young Children. (1994, March). Professional development. *Young Children, 49*(3), 32–37.

National Center for the Early Childhood Work Force. (1995a, January). Mentoring programs: An emerging child care career path. *Compensation Initiatives Bulletin, 1*(3).

National Center for the Early Childhood Work Force. (1995b). *Cost, quality, and child outcomes in child care centers.* Washington, DC: Author.

National Institute for Early Education Research. (December/January 2007). It's in the stars: More states are using quality rating systems for Pre-K, *Preschool Matters, 5*(1) 4, 11. New Brunswick, NJ.

National Institute for Early Education Research. (2009, March 25). Early news roundup, *NIEER Online News, 8*(7), 3–4. Retrieved March 25, 2009, from info@nierr.org.

Neugebauer, R. (2009a, July/August). Quality rating and improvement systems: A strategic movement for defining quality. *Exchange, 31*(4), 66–68.

Neugebauer. R. (2009b, March/April). Where are we headed with center accreditation? Trends in quality assurance. *Exchange, 31*(2), 14–17.

Phipps, P. (2004, Winter). CAEYC launches new professional development academy. *Connections, 32*(2), 17.

Pianta, R. C., Howes, C., Burchinal, M. R., Bryant, D. M., Clifford, R. M., Early, D. M., & Barbarin, O. (2005). Features of pre-kindergarten programs, classrooms, and teachers: predictions of observed classroom quality and teacher-child interactions. *Applied Developmental Science, 9*(3), 144–159.

Pratt, D. (March 2008). Lina's letters: A nine-year-old perspective on what matters most in the classroom. *Phi Delta Kappan, 89*(7), 515–518.

Schweinhart, L. J., Barnes, H. V., & Weikart, D. P. (1993). *Significant benefits: The High/Scope Perry preschool study through age* 27. Ypsilanti, MI: High/Scope Press.

Schweinhart, L. J., & Weikart, D. P. (1997). Evidence that good early childhood programs work. *Phi Delta Kappan, 66,* 545–551.

Shlay, A. B., Tran, H., Weinraub, M., & Harmon, M. (2005). Teasing apart the child care conundrum: A factorial survey analysis of perceptions of child care quality, fair market price, and willingness to pay by low-income African American parents. *Early Childhood Research Quarterly, 20*(4), 393–416.

Tarullo, L. B., & Doan, H. M. (1999, March). Linking Head Start quality to child outcomes: The *FACES* study. *Head Start Bulletin, 65,* 18–19.

Thompson, S. (2006). Revised Mission Statement and Goals, Early Childhood Education Workgroup. E-mail received June 27, 2006.

Turner, P. (Ed.). (2002). *La Ristra: New Mexico's comprehensive professional development system in early care, education, and family support.* Santa Fe, NM: Office of Child Development, Youth and Families Department.

U.S. Department of Education, Office of Elementary and Secondary Education. (2005, July). ABC serving children under Title 1: Non-regulatory guidance. Washington, DC: U.S. Government Printing Office.

Warman, B. (1998, September). Trends in state accreditation policies. *Young Children, 53*(5), 45–48.

Wiechel, J. (2001, Summer). Eliminating the "non-system" of governance. *State Education Leader, 19*(2), 13–15.

Whitebook, M. (1995, May). What's good for child care teachers is good for our country's children. *Young Children, 50*(4), 40–45.

Whitebook, M., Phillips, D., & Howes, C. (1993). *The national child care staffing study revisited.* Oakland, CA: Child Care Employee Project.

Whitebook, M., & Sakai, L. (2002, November). Readers write. *Young Children, 57*(6), 7.

# CHAPTER 11

# Professional Commitment and Employment

After reading this chapter, you should be able to:

1. Describe the professional growth of early childhood educators.
2. List four different activities that promote individual professional growth.
3. Discuss why advocacy efforts are important to student teachers.
4. Describe three sectors of early childhood employment where an AA degree graduate might find work.
5. List five societal factors that are influencing young children's care and education programs.

## STUDENT TEACHER SCENARIO

**Setting:** Elena was enrolled in a small, private preschool in a suburban neighborhood, with about 18 children.

Elena, a four-and-a-half-year-old, had attended the preschool for over a year. She enjoyed music and art, and books were a favorite choice. She was often found in the book loft with friends, pretending to read, laughing, and pointing to illustrations. Able to read a few words, she delighted in sharing these with her teachers. Active in the play yard, she was a popular playmate, easily enticing others with her creative play games. Elena's mother asked for a teacher conference and described a troubling behavior Elena had displayed at home. Elena had been stung by a bee a few months earlier, and since had become hysterical at times, screaming, "It's on me! Get it off!" while flailing and flapping her arms as if to remove a bee.

The staff developed a plan of action, contingent on Elena experiencing an episode at school. Teachers would remain calm and protect Elena and others from harm or distress by gently moving her to a quiet area if possible. When Elena quieted, staff planned to say something calming, like "I don't see any bees around you, Elena," or "There are no bees near you," or something similar.

Elena was alone with a student teacher when she became highly agitated, trying to slap imaginary bees from her body. The student teacher waited, showing no excitement, and acted as a calm observer. As Elena quieted, the student teacher said, "There really aren't any bees. This is a game, isn't it?" Elena answered, "My mother thinks there are bees." Elena then walked off to play with others.

## Questions for Discussion:

1. Do you feel the staff and student teacher have a trusting relationship with this parent? Why or why not?

2. If you had been this student teacher, in what ways might you have added to your professional growth through this incident?

3. How would you describe the student teacher's skill in calming Elena?

4. What might have happened if the student teacher had not had prior knowledge of Elena's home behavior?

- - - - - - - - - - - - - - - - - - - - - - - - - - - - - - - - - - - - - - - - - -

As a student teacher, you may already be considered a professional. **Professionals** are those individuals whose work is predominantly intellectual in character. They make constant decisions that call for a substantial degree of discretion and judgment. Some of your skills are new, emerging, and wobbly, whereas others are definitely observable, and you are currently being measured—against standards established by those in your profession.

> **professionals**—individuals engaged in occupations considered learned endeavors, such as law, medicine, or as in this text, education.

The No Child Left Behind Act of 2001 and its complementary early childhood presidential initiative, *Good Start, Grow Smart* (2002), have put a new emphasis on early childhood educators' professional development. The act was an effort that assumes that well-prepared early childhood teachers handling young children in pre-kindergarten programs are critical to children's healthy development, school readiness, and eventual responsible citizenship. Many schools that are publicly funded are now accountable for showing children's progress, and their teachers are accountable for offering the necessary research-based experiences to do so.

*Good Start, Grow Smart* calls for federally funded early childhood programs to formulate early learning guidelines—goals for the skills and competencies that preschool age children should accomplish before starting kindergarten—and to identify how these should be measured. It also requires pre-kindergarten staff members to have the necessary qualifications. This includes training, certification or degree, and vocational experience. Programs were structured to include written professional staff development plans.

If you are employed in an early childhood public program and have been given a professional development plan, you can follow that plan and also develop your own personal growth plan for career skill improvement. You will most likely do this because you have probably decided on a long-range career goal. If you are working in another type of program, particularly a private one, you may develop your own self-created plan. Hopefully, you believe, as do other teaching professionals, that you will need to become a lifelong learner.

## DEFINITIONS

Farstrup (2007) defines what it means to be a professional in the following:

> Being a professional means continually updating and increasing one's knowledge and skill. It means knowing how to identify and apply proven principles and methods of instruction. Being a professional means having the ability to make well-informed judgments and decisions in the best interests of students who we serve and apply relevant research. Professionals are willing to be accountable for the quality and results of their work and act in an ethical, positive, and civil manner at all times.

Maxwell, Field, and Clifford (2006) reviewed studies on the topic of professional growth and found no common definition of the term. They created their own definition, which includes three components: *education*, *training*, and a *credential/certificate/license*. A simpler definition of professional development is *getting better*—more competent and skilled—in one's chosen profession. Those who attempt to become early childhood professionals develop a conscious commitment, intentionality, and concern for excellence. They achieve and maintain the career capabilities that ensure quality, developmental care, and educational opportunity for the young children they serve. In doing so, professional identity develops, and as professionals, there is collaborations with others of like purpose. Professionals devote energy to group efforts that strive to attain goal realization. They realize the value of their contributions to the lives of children, families, and society. They are well informed and aware of current research, ethics, and standards. They sometimes become the "movers and shakers," the leaders, advocates, organizers, innovators, and reflective thinkers, who apply their talents and knowledge and are vocal about problems facing career professionals, children, and families.

Professional growth takes time and effort, and has its own reward. Improving children's school lives and educational future means living a career that matters.

## PROFESSIONAL CONCERNS

Your teaching day includes tasks that may appear custodial in nature, such as helping at cleanup time, supervising the children as they wash their hands, serving snacks, and encouraging them to rest (see Figure 11–1). Each of these is a learning time for children, and your professional skill is at work. Helping a child who is struggling to slip on a sweater is done in a professional way and is an opportunity to help the child become more independent.

Professional status, educators agree, is a problem for this career field. Societies award status to trained, educated individuals, who provide valuable services to society. People can easily tick off on one hand the high-status professions, and possibly what they consider middle-status professions. Early childhood workers may not be among them.

Increased status is happening in a growing number of places, and it is often the result of an increase in the qualifications necessary to hold such positions. What are the possible reasons for educators not receiving the recognition and status they

▶ **Figure 11–1**
Serving at snack time may appear custodial.

deserve? There are no simple answers but rather many conjectures by many writers. Included among those frequently cited reasons are the following:

- a blurred image between parenting and paid child care practitioners in the public's mind
- public attitudes and perceptions that almost anyone can watch children, and that child care requires little or no specific knowledge, education, or skill
- practitioners' attitudes toward themselves, particularly feelings of personal or collective lack of power
- lack of early childhood teacher self-esteem or assertiveness
- a public perception that children's teachers provide dedicated service, rather than a service for personal gain
- the turnover rate of pre-kindergarten teachers, as opposed to the lifelong careers of other recognized professionals
- a lack of collective political clout for the career group
- lack of employee bargaining power
- low entry-level requirements, minimum qualifications or degrees

Public elementary school professionals may find some of the above listed reasons applicable to their situations. There often is a general public concern about the quality of public school education and the lack of uniformity from one state to another.

In addition, public school professionals may notice a general acceptance that public education has failed and private schooling is superior. Another widely held and expressed view is that teacher unions, such as the National Education Association and the American Federation of Teachers, have become too politically powerful and protect incompetent teachers.

Many early childhood staffers' reticence to accept themselves as professionals may be partly responsible for low salaries. The babysitter image, in the public's view, has been difficult to escape. Advocacy training is now a recommended part of pre-service training for early childhood educators.

A teacher's pride in the profession is justified. By participating in student teaching, you now realize that the job of an early childhood or public elementary school teacher is demanding, challenging, and complex. It involves constant decisions, and can be physically and emotionally taxing, as well as being highly satisfying and rewarding. Heather Robinson (2008), a practicing public school teacher, notes people have said that the teaching profession creates all other professions. She tackles the myth that all teachers have the summer off:

> Summers off? Think again. Teachers who truly aspire to make their mark and contribute only their best to our nation's future enroll in summer training courses and continue their education in constant pursuit to perfect their craft. We are a profession of lifelong learners. In a continually changing world, it's not only advised but imperative that we never cease to improve and devour each new piece of research that reveals to us another small piece of the educational puzzle.

## PROFESSIONAL BEHAVIOR AND COMMITMENT

Professionalism entails understanding children and yourself, and practicing your craft diligently. Some of the demands that professionals make on themselves follow:

1. A professional gives a full measure of devotion to the job.
2. A professional follows professional ethics and standards.
3. Professionals accept responsibilities assigned to them, with as much grace as they can muster, and then work in a positive way to change those duties that deter their teaching.

4. A professional joins with others in professional organizations that exchange research and ideas. They act and advocate to the benefit of all children and families in areas related to children's well-being and education.

5. A professional understands and is aware of prejudices, and makes a concerted effort to get rid of them.

6. A professional treats children and others as people with feelings.

7. A professional speaks up for the child when the child needs somebody to speak out on their behalf.

8. A professional is an educator who is informed about research, issues, and trends in education.

Katz (1972) has proposed that teachers go through three stages of professional development. During the first year, they focus on *survival*. During the next 2 to 5 years, they begin to *consolidate* what they know and begin to feel a deeper understanding of what they are doing and why they are doing it. Finally, they reach the *maturity* level and function as a true professional.

Severe tests of a student teacher's professional commitment may happen if a placement site models attitudes that downgrade the value and worth of the profession. A good grasp of professional conduct and commitment helps the student teacher sort out less than professional behavior. Improved and continued high standards in the profession depend in part on the newly trained professionals' enthusiasm, idealism, knowledge, and skills, and the experienced professionals' leadership. Newly trained professionals can strengthen the field through their identification with practicing, committed professionals (see Figure 11–2).

## Advocacy

You should view advocacy as a career responsibility that goes beyond improving conditions at your job site, because advocacy concerns all job sites and educational opportunities, for all children. Gathering more support by identifying, enlisting, and convincing policy makers, the business world, and the general public to give a higher priority to early childhood education, or the education of older children, is a common and ongoing advocacy activity. Advocacy efforts include the search for successful solutions to problems. In the past, what has contributed to successful advocacy?

▶ **Figure 11-2**
Professional teachers are "with" children rather than "over" them.

© Cengage Learning

- ◆ advocacy by individual educators
- ◆ increased understanding of the process by those advocating
- ◆ communicating clear messages
- ◆ studying ways others have successfully advocated
- ◆ organizing and forming liaisons with other concerned individuals and groups
- ◆ not giving up, but rather, searching for better solutions

Most experts agree that child and family advocating takes time, practice, and skill. By speaking out with substantiated facts, passion, and personal concern, and expressing concerns with clarity, one has a better chance of influencing listeners. Besides becoming proactive you need to become a well-informed advocate. Your listeners can include family, friends, other educators, the general public, business leaders, manufacturers, developers, legislators, board of education members, and community leaders.

One needs to become knowledgeable and skilled by joining an advocacy group. Advocacy usually involves one or more of the following areas: quality, delivery systems, funding, standards, and research.

Unfortunately, educators can become stale and silent. This may happen if they are not engaged in changes and developments in their professional field, feel overwhelmed with their teaching tasks, feel there is no place to share their concerns and questions, feel isolated and work in facilities full of apathy, or if program administrators withhold support and believe advocacy activities are threatening or out of character for staff members. Well-trained professionals entering the workforce can bring new advocacy energy and dedication to the field and renewed hope and support to other professionals' advocacy efforts.

Meyer (2005) notes advocacy action can be simple and private or more bold and public. It can start with a question, a problem, a concern, or something witnessed that doesn't seem right. Migrant programs for field workers' children have come into being because an educator or another individual observed unsupervised young children in a field with adult workers, who were unable to watch children while working. High school child centers for teen parents have been established because someone noticed teenage parents struggling to stay in school and parent adequately. Many college child centers and training facilities came into existence because concerned faculty noticed that college students, often unable to afford child care, were bringing their young children to campus. In many cases, the entire faculty of a college advocated for change, and may have had a difficult time convincing their school board that on-campus child care—or preschool teacher training—should be a college function.

## How Student Teacher Advocacy Can Begin

Advocacy usually begins when teaching colleagues meet socially and talk about concerns and conditions in their school, community, or beyond. Cunniff and Risley (2006) point out most colleges have education clubs, often referred to as Teachers of Tomorrow Clubs. Many of these are affiliated with larger groups that sponsor state-wide Future Teacher Conferences and advocacy activities. If there is a campus education major group or club, *join it*. If the club is planning *Week of the Young Child* or other activities, join them and gain experience. Advocacy groups can exist anywhere a like-minded group of educators gathers for a safe forum with a sense of purpose. Professional associations are mentioned later in this chapter and many have ongoing advocacy activities.

Advocacy activities can be diverse and involve letter writing, marches, celebrations, fund-raising, T-shirt slogans, bumper stickers, and many other strategies. To become familiar with advocacy groups who advocate on child and family issues and worker issues, see Figure 11–3.

▶ **Figure 11-3**
Groups that advocate.

**GROUPS THAT ADVOCATE**

- American Associate Degree Early Childhood Educators {http://www.accessece.org}
- International Reading Association {http://www.reading.org}
- National Association for Bilingual Education {http://www.nabe.org}
- National Association for Early Childhood Teacher Education {http://www.naecte.org}
- National Council of Teachers of Mathematics {http://www.nctm.org}
- Program for Infant/Toddler Caregivers {http://www.pitc.org}
- Zero to Three {http://www.zerotothree.org}
- Council for Exceptional Children {http://www.cec.sped.org}
- Association for Childhood Education International {http://www.acei.org}
- American Federation of Teachers {http://www.aft.org}
- National Black Child Development Institute {http://www.nbcdi.org}

(Note: This is not a comprehensive list.)

## How Has Past Advocacy Affected You?

Your course of study, your instructor's credentials and background, your on-campus child center experience, your placement in an actual, functioning classroom for student teaching, and many other aspects of your educational experience have been influenced by someone's, or some group's, past advocacy. Many community colleges with early childhood AA degree programs are in the process of examining their programs, to gain recognition of their excellence by participating in an accreditation process that examines all or most aspects of their training programs. Advocacy groups in the recent past have been instrumental in the development of national AA degree training standards, accreditation procedures, and the transferability of your credits to institutions of higher education granting BA degrees.

When you enter the workforce, even more of your work life will be impacted by past and current advocacy efforts, including the amount and kind of funding your center or school receives, your working conditions, compensation, the standards to be followed, the curriculum that was adopted, the factors that protect child safety, the college training and degree you must hold, and much, much more. In San Jose, California, a local newspaper reported that a newly hired pre-kindergarten teacher was told by her site director that the director would supervise her class at break time so the new teacher could clean, sweep, vacuum, and mop the classroom and the adjoining children's bathroom. The new teacher asked if her break time would follow the cleaning, and was informed that *was* her break time (Rockstroh, 2005). Fortunately, California law sets a duty-free break time, and licensing law prohibits any teacher activity unrelated to the teaching function. Advocacy was instrumental in the creation of both laws.

Student teachers may feel it is hard to find the time to pursue advocacy activities. In your daily contacts in and out of school, you can still be instrumental in developing others' opinions of child development and early childhood education. You are, right now, a representative of the profession. What you say and do can influence others' priorities and voting behaviors.

## Becoming Aware

Advocacy means being aware of legislation, the legislative process, and individuals who support child and family issues. Another step in understanding advocacy is identifying groups or individuals who monitor and help author legislation and are politically active. The National Association for the Education of Young Children is well known for its advocacy efforts, as are many other associations, and has set goals, one of which is to make all members politically effective. Politically effective members can be described as aware, knowledgeable, having the ability to competently discuss and debate issues, and possessing the capacity to act in ways that influence decisions. NAEYC's public-policy efforts include influencing national, state, and local legislators.

Student teachers can view the National Association for the Education of Young Children's position statements online at http://www.naeyc.org/about/positions.asp, and journal articles and other useful resources can be found at NAEYC's "Beyond the Journal" page, at http://www.journal.naeyc.org. NAEYC student members can sign up for NAEYC's "Children's Champion" e-mail alerts that help advocates become informed on major issues. Go to www.naeyc.org/policy.

Students sometimes feel advocacy for compensation is a self-serving activity. But many research studies have found that a positive relationship exists between better quality care and teacher compensation (Ghazvini & Mullis, 2002; Phillips et al., 2000; Sachs, 2000).

The National Black Child Development Institute (NBCDI) has developed a unique program, *The Parent Empowerment Project*, which seeks to educate, motivate, and inspire parents to excellence as their child's first teacher. Since 1970, the Institute has worked to improve and protect the well-being of African-American children through a variety of innovative programs, advocacy, educational publications, and dynamic training conferences.

## PROFESSIONAL GROWTH AND DEVELOPMENT

The goal of professional growth includes the unfolding of abilities and the achievement of greater self-actualization. True self-actualization leads to an increasing sense of responsibility and a deepening desire to serve humanity.

When your future job includes promotional advantages or rewarding incentives, it may add impetus. Your attitude toward your profession should include giving a high priority to activities that contribute to your skill development. Your efforts to grow professionally will become part of your life's pattern. You will experience the tugs and pulls of finding the time and energy to follow your commitment and still have a balance in your life.

### Professional Growth Plans

Many public agencies, state governments, and school districts are giving new attention to the development of written professional growth plans for school employees, knowing that staff-development efforts impact the quality of services. Research has repeatedly emphasized that the educational background of staff members is a critical component of high-quality child care and staff turnover (Honig & Hirallal, 1998; Burchinal et al., 2000).

The majority of early childhood educators, especially those in the private sector, will plan individual courses of action to attain professional growth. They may not have the inducements—like stipends, release time, transportation provisions, or salary schedules—that reward their efforts, as do many public employees.

Many growth plans recommend using local resources, referral agencies, conferences, continuing education classes, and professional readings as vehicles of growth, in addition to seeking new information in other ways. Teachers will have a variety of choices, and they learn daily from experiences with children in their care. Working toward a goal is suggested, and if taking college coursework is planned, one should get advice from college counselors as well as other knowledgeable professionals. If you are employed at a NAEYC-accredited school or program, these centers must have an implementation plan for staff member's professional development. When possible, these plans suggest credit-bearing coursework that improves staff credentials and competencies (NAEYC, 2007).

***Student teacher quote***—"I will be advocating for children and myself as soon as I can. My cooperating teacher is a strong advocacy model and so aware of what needs to be done to influence quality child care and education policy. She takes the time to meet and work with professional groups. She is truly a dedicated individual."

**Dale Wildeagle, Student Teacher Placement Classroom, San Jose, CA**

## Individual Learning Cycles

Just as you have watched children take enormous steps in learning one day and just mark time another, your professional growth may not be constant and steady. Harrison (1978) observed the phenomenon of *risk and retreat* in self-directed learning:

> The learning cycle is our name for the natural process of advance and retreat in learning. We observed early in our experiments with self-directed learning that individuals would move out and take personal risks and then would move back to reflect and integrate the experience.

Such risk and retreat relates to what Piaget described as the process of equilibration. You, as a learner, assimilate new material first as an accommodation with past learning (the risk); then, the assimilation becomes play (the retreat). Such a retreat is important to the process of equilibration as you seek to establish connections between old and new learning.

Reflection, or standing still at times, may give ideas time to hatch. Being aware of your own creative thinking can make you more aware of this creative process in children.

Career ladders in early child education picture steps leading to advanced certificates, credentials, and degrees. Vertical steps depict how completing professional preparation and training can lead to increased responsibility. Figure 11–4 displays NAEYC's professional categories. These are used in a number of state plans. Each state's specific definition of what constitutes completion of each level may differ. Many large centers have career ladders that show up, down, and lateral job positions, and necessary qualifications. Salary schedules also may be attached. Horizontal growth that leads to expertise rather than upward mobility takes place when study leads to learning a second language or learning to play a piano.

## Standards and Compensation

The rising demand for high-quality child care and education, new standards, and stiffer educational staff qualifications has begun to increase salaries, benefits, and improve working conditions. Bright spots occur in some areas of

▶ **Figure 11-4**
Career ladder citing certificates, credentials, and degrees.

> ▶ **CAREER LADDER CITING CERTIFICATES, CREDENTIALS, AND DEGREES**
> ▶ Doctorate
> ▶ Master's Degree* awarded after a number of college credits are accumulated in an approved associate degree program
> ▶ Bachelor's Degree in Early Childhood/Child Development**
> ▶ Associate Degree in Early Childhood Education**
> ▶ A certificate* awarded after a number of college credits are accumulated in an approved associate degree program
> ▶ Completion of a Child Development Associate (CDA) credential at an institution of higher education that articulates into a certificate program or an associate degree program.
> ▶ Certificate of completion of an entry level early childhood training course with specified hour or unit credit.
>
> *Certification in some states may be undertaken by state departments, associations, training agencies, or private entities.
>
> **Degree granting institutions have different department names, such as Family Studies, Human Services, Early Childhood, Child and Family Studies, and so on.

the career field, particularly publicly funded programs, including Head Start, military child care, and state-funded preschool or universal pre-kindergarten programs. There is still a long way to go before equitable compensation becomes a reality for many early childhood educators. While professional groups strive for excellence, taxpayers and other funding sources are requiring accountability.

NAEYC (2009) has increased its professional preparation standards from five standards to six based upon current professional knowledge and research. These new standards are found in Chapter 3, Figure 3-1, on page 53. The key elements of each of the six standards can be found below and on the next page in Figure 11-5. It is prudent here to clarify terms used in typical standard's statements. You will find these in early childhood education professional literature. *Standards* usually define widely held expectations for young children, programs, teachers, future teachers, and institutions of higher education (Zaslow & Martinez-Beck, 2006). *Professional preparation standards* are widely held expectations for candidates (students in training) like you. *Early learning standards* encompass expected learning and development outcomes for young children, and *benchmarks* refer to child accomplishments at certain points in an offered program of study. *Program standards* and *guidelines* promote the quality of a child curriculum and environment by identifying expected characteristics. And *content standards* refer to what a student (child) should know and be able to do within a particular discipline, such as recognizing 20 alphabet letters before kindergarten, or counting to 10 by age four. Notice content standards mention a particular point in time and they differ from school to school, and many schools may not identify them at all.

▶ **Figure 11-5**
Key elements of the new NAEYC standards.

**KEY ELEMENTS OF STANDARD 1**

**1a:** Knowing and understanding young children's characteristics and needs

**1b:** Knowing and understanding the multiple influences on development and learning

**1c:** Using developmental knowledge to create healthy, respectful, supportive, and challenging learning environments

**SOURCE:** Reprinted with permission from the National Association for the Education of Young Children. www.naeyc.org.

**KEY ELEMENTS OF STANDARD 2**

**2a:** Knowing about and understanding diverse family and community characteristics

**2b:** Supporting and engaging families and communities through respectful, reciprocal relationships

**2c:** Involving families and communities in their children's development and learning

**KEY ELEMENTS OF STANDARD 3**

**3a:** Understanding the goals, benefits, and uses of assessment

**3b:** Knowing about assessment partnerships with families and with professional colleagues

**3c:** Knowing about and using observation, documentation, and other appropriate assessment tools and approaches

**3d:** Understanding and practicing responsible assessment to promote positive outcomes for each child

(continues)

▶ **Figure 11–5** (continued)

| KEY ELEMENTS OF STANDARD 4 | KEY ELEMENTS OF STANDARD 5 | KEY ELEMENTS OF STANDARD 6 |
|---|---|---|
| **4a:** Understanding positive relationships and supportive interactions as the foundation of their work with children | **5a:** Understanding content knowledge and resources in academic disciplines | **6a:** Identifying and involving oneself with the early childhood field |
| **4b:** Knowing and understanding effective strategies and tools for early education | **5b:** Knowing and using the central concepts, inquiry tools, and structures of content areas or academic disciplines | **6b:** Knowing about and upholding ethical standards and other professional guidelines |
| **4c:** Using a broad repertoire of developmentally appropriate teaching/learning approaches | **5c:** Using their own knowledge, appropriate early learning standards, and other resources to design, implement, and evaluate meaningful, challenging curricula for each child | **6c:** Engaging in continuous, collaborative learning to inform practice |
| **4d:** Reflecting on their own practice to promote positive outcomes for each child | | **6d:** Integrating knowledgeable, reflective, and critical perspectives on early education |
| | | **6e:** Engaging in informed advocacy for children and the profession |

## PROFESSIONAL GROWTH OPPORTUNITIES

Early childhood teachers have a wide range of alternative routes to professional growth. These include additional credit coursework leading to a degree, training without college credit, apprenticeships and exchanging teaching, independent study, visitation and travel, professional group membership (see Figure 11–6), mentoring by other professionals, attending conferences and workshops, in-service training, and skill and study sessions.

## Financial Support for Schooling

Financial aid can be a determining factor in an early childhood education student's ability to attend higher education institutions. One common way to obtain financial support is to borrow money. *Loans* may be obtained from state, federal, or private sources. The loans must be repaid, typically with interest, but are sometimes forgiven in exchange for teaching or other services. *Grants,* requiring no repayment, are available from state, federal sources, and institutions of higher education. *Work-study* programs require part-time work in exchange for college expenses. *Scholarships* are generally based on merit, and recognize grades, test scores, special talents, heritage, leadership ability, and/or community service work. The first step in securing financial aid involves filling out an application at a Financial Aid Office at a campus location. Another way is obtaining an online application at http://www.fafsa.ed.gov./index.htm. States such as California have special early childhood education scholarships for practitioners including First 5 and the CARES (Cooperative Agencies Resources for Education) programs. One of the most available and widespread scholarship programs is the T.E.A.C.H. (Teacher Education and Compensation Helps) program that functions in 20 states and has aided the professional growth of employed early childhood educators and directors. This scholarship program involves the educator's employer

▶ **Figure 11-6**
Sampling of possible association member services and benefits.

**SAMPLING OF POSSIBLE ASSOCIATION MEMBERSHIP SERVICES AND BENEFITS**

- association website may disperse early childhood education news and information
- exclusive access to members-only services
- online shopping with member discounts for the latest resources
- online registration for events, conferences, institutes, workshops, and training opportunities
- listing of accredited programs
- association position statements available on current topics and issues
- networking with colleagues at an online community website
- listing of career openings and members seeking employment at an early childhood career forum
- association news delivered to your e-mail address monthly
- affiliate member groups may have local chapters
- association advocacy activities conducted at national, state, and local levels, including legislative alerts and lobbying information
- discounts on conference registrations, books, and other publications
- interest forums that promote collaboration on topics of interest
- online discussion groups
- a member service center
- association recommended insurance information
- student discount membership fees

who makes a financial contribution and offers supportive assistance. In 2008, 28.3 million in public and private funds sustained the T.E.A.C.H. program. California's Berkeley-based Institute for College Access and Success is an organization working to make higher education more available and affordable to students of all backgrounds.

**Teach for America** Teach for America (TFA), founded by Wendy Kopp, is a national teaching corps that recruits high-performing college graduates to teach in low-performing public schools after they have participated in summer or crash-training courses. In fiscal 2008, a year with a less than vibrant economy, 25,000 college seniors competed for the privilege of taking on one of the toughest jobs in teaching (Foote, 2008). After training, corps candidates are placed in problem schools with declining student achievement and impoverished students. Foote points out that the United States' high school graduation rate is nineteenth among the world's top developing countries. Many education theorists suggest this figure is the result of secondary school teachers who have lost teaching dedication because they have experienced a lack of supplies and materials, worked with inadequate staffing and support services, taught in poor working conditions and facilities, received inequitable compensation, and endured administrator apathy. Kopp believes the transformation of teaching into a financially rewarding profession with high standards of admission and accountability could limit teacher turnover and establish school staff stability. She notes a good number of TFA alumni are now school leaders, school developers, administrators, and elected school officials dedicated to educational improvements and excellence. A recent TFA survey indicates that one-third of former TFA alumni are still teaching at the K–12 level.

## Continuing Education Classes

Local college career placement and counseling centers can offer a review of college catalogs and bulletins that list night and weekend classes at off-campus locations. Coursework descriptions and particulars can be examined. Additional college services often include career guidance, financial aid information, housing particulars, job placement boards, and tutoring assistance.

## Articulation Agreements

It is wise to examine the transferability of community college or other training coursework credits to baccalaureate degree programs at degree-granting institutions. Although agreements have been developed in many geographic locations, it pays to check. If articulation agreements exist, usually both institutions have had representatives meet and tailor coursework so a smooth transition is possible. Credits can be accepted as elective units or as equivalent units. Because institutions differ, it is prudent to consult with college counselors and early childhood department chairpersons at both institutions.

## Distance Learning via the Internet

A number of colleges offer distance learning opportunities, offered online, on television, by satellite, by correspondence, and a few by conference call. Questions to ask regarding such programs should concern the institution's qualifications, instructor's credentials, accredited units, the availability of financial assistance, transferability of credits, necessary computer skills, and associated costs.

## Computer Expertise

Many colleges are now insisting students display computer literacy and skill before graduation. Teacher training programs—already full of requirements and electives—have been slow to require testing or coursework. Most student teachers in community college programs pursue an independent course of study to acquire computer expertise. Many public libraries have developed computer centers where Internet access and help are available. The increasing computer skills children exhibit surprise most new early childhood teachers (see Figure 11–7). Commercial

▶ **Figure 11-7**
Are you as much at home with computers as the children in your class?

© Cengage Learning

early childhood program software is abundant and entering young children's lives at an amazing rate.

The teacher with **computer literacy** is able to guide children through computer-based learning and discovery opportunities. The computer is a valuable adult communication, recording, and researching tool.

**computer literacy**—
familiarity with and knowledge about computers.

# DEMONSTRATION-TEACHING AND MENTORING

You may know a teacher with whom you would like to study, whose direction and tutelage could be growth producing. Volunteering in that teacher's classroom offers opportunities for closer examination of techniques. It may be possible to earn college credit through enrolling in a cooperative work experience program or independent study course; check with your college.

In a demonstration-teaching arrangement, you watch and discuss methods with practicing teachers. Hearing explanations and asking questions give insight into different ways to accomplish teaching goals. Most professionals will provide this type of short-term arrangement.

## Mentoring

Mentoring programs are an established and increasingly available vehicle to enhance staff professional development and retention. Mentoring for teachers offers an approach to teacher training within the context of the teaching environment and emphasizes excellence in daily practice. Merrill (2002) notes mentoring programs differ, and range from informal buddy-system arrangements to structured meetings with a trained mentor, who may be a fellow employee or a mentor provided through a partnership with another local program or agency. Many mentors have received training in mentoring skills, adult development, observation, and communication. Funding may be provided for both the mentor and the one mentored. Most mentors are chosen for their expertise and are considered master teachers. Increased collaboration in the mentoring process often leads to sharing ideas, reflective thinking, research and implementation, enthusiasm, and improved overall program quality. In other words, it is a dynamic professional growth opportunity for both participants.

## Internships

Internships are employed positions, for a designated period of time. Teacher interns work under the direction of experienced practitioners and assume a variety of teaching responsibilities (see Figure 11–8).

## Independent Study

Self-planned study allows one to choose the subject, sequence, depth, and breadth of professional growth. Your home library will grow yearly, funds permitting. You will spend much time reading books and other professional materials; these resources will be a tribute to your professional commitment. Professional journals and magazines provide research articles and practical activity suggestions. Organization and association publications carry timely information. A starting point for independent study may be the bibliographies and book titles you collected during your training.

## Visits and Travel

Other teachers' classrooms will always be a valuable resource and study possibility. Observing other classrooms offers good ideas, clever solutions, and provocative discoveries. It is amazing how many early childhood programs extend professional

▶**Figure 11–8**
Internships can couple pay with learning.

courtesy to visiting early childhood contemporaries if approached. Travelers, contacting administrators and directors beforehand, often are able to tour facilities, interview staff, and observe program activities. A written letter of introduction from a supervisor, to include in a request-to-visit letter along with your email address, is a good idea. For tax purposes, keep records of visits, including notes on conversations, photographs, happenings, and ideas that might help your professional growth. Professional groups' conferences often schedule tours of outstanding local programs.

Almost every country in the world has group child care, and you have probably developed a list of programs in your own community you would like to observe. The professional courtesy of allowing observers is widespread. Directors and staff members frequently provide guided tours that include explanations and discussions of goals, program components, and teaching philosophies.

A fascinating experience awaits the student teacher on first attending an early childhood education conference sponsored by an early child professional association such as NAEYC. There will be so much to see and sample and so many inspiring ideas that it is a virtual overdose of stimuli that wholesomely feeds your attempt to grow.

## Workshops, Meetings, and Skill and Study Sessions

Workshops, skill sessions, and meetings are smaller versions of state and national conferences. Diverse and varied, they cover topics related to early childhood. Practical and theoretical presentations are popular.

Identification with the spirit of professionalism—which can be defined as *striving for excellence*—motivates many of the attending participants. Most communities schedule many professional growth meetings each year and encourage student teacher attendance.

## In-Service Training

In-service training sessions are designed to suit the training needs of a particular group of teachers or caregivers. They are arranged by sponsoring agencies or employers. Typically, consultants and specialists lead, guide, plan, and present skill-development sessions and/or assessments of program components at the sponsoring school's location. There is usually no fee and attendance is mandatory. Often, staffs decided the nature and scope of the in-service training, and paid substitutes free up staff members from child supervision duties.

## LEADERSHIP

Leadership is an outgrowth of professionalism and can take multiple and various directions. One can lead the career field in discovery through research and its application, lead an association's or organization's efforts to increase recognition and compensation, lead by encouraging teachers-in-training to create developmentally appropriate classrooms, lead by becoming an effective liaison with legislators, or lead through advocacy actions or involvement in many other possible areas that promote career excellence.

Leadership often begins with achieving expertise recognized by other professionals. The saying "Leaders are born, not made" may not be true for early childhood career professionals. Many leaders have worked diligently, taken opportunities offered them, or sought out opportunity themselves, through advanced training, coursework, apprenticeships, scholarships, and other leadership-training vehicles. Formal leadership training opportunities for promising individuals have been funded by professional associations, private individuals, foundations, and other entities interested in the welfare of children and families. The funding sources may have recognized potential, or may have put faith in the recipient because of certain criteria, such as a high grade point average or past recognition or awards. Professional associations, along with college and university professors and counselors, are good sources of information concerning leadership training.

Professional excellence entails mastery. Professional mastery affects recognition, position, status, and compensation.

## EMPLOYMENT

This section will present important facts and figures regarding current happenings in the lives of American children and families. Most of these items will affect your work life and future. Following this is a section that concerns educators searching for employment now and in the future. Tips and suggestions about securing the employment are covered.

### Families and Children: Facts and Figures

Family characteristics and the lives of children in the United States are changing, and will continue to do so. As this book is written, America faces a dramatic economic downturn, with many families worried about their jobs, health care, savings, the environment, and the families' survival in difficult times. The following collection of facts and figures highlight trends affecting not only children and families but also the field of education and consequently teachers:

- ◆ In the past 10 years, the United States has seen a dramatic increase in the number of children who live without their parents, in a household headed by a relative (Birckmayer, Cohen, Jensen, & Variano, 2005).

- ◆ Child-rearing occupies a smaller share of a person's adult life, because there are longer periods before and after raising children, compared to previous generations.

- ◆ One in ten women in their forties remained childless in 1979; in 2004, it was one in five.

◆ In California, more than half of the state's newborns are Latinos, as were the *majority* of children entering California kindergartens in the fall of 2006 (Figure 11–9).

◆ Percentages of grandparents caring for grandchildren living in their homes have increased. In Antioch, California, a city in the metropolitan Bay Area, the figure is 41.6 percent of the city's children. In Pittsburg, California, the figure is 37.2 percent, according to the U.S. Census Bureau's *American Communities Survey, 2005–2007* (San Jose Mercury News, 2008).

◆ More unmarried mothers are choosing to remain single, a rise of over 18 percent since the 1930s.

◆ Preschoolers from white families with an income exceeding $60,000 per year were the most likely preschoolers to attend some kind of preschool program (San Jose Mercury News, 2006).

◆ The majority of children under the age of six receive some type of child care or education each week. Out-of-home care averages 31 hours a week (U.S. Department of Education, National Center for Educational Statistics, 2005a).

◆ Minority students will comprise over 49 percent of American students in the next decade but just five percent of their teachers.

◆ An estimated one-quarter of all children aged three to nine have parents who were born outside of the United States (Gadsden & Ray, 2002).

◆ The fastest-growing segment of the U.S. population is the children of immigrants (Sadowski, 2004).

◆ Immigrant family populations have been rising in virtually every state. Many areas have little infrastructure to accommodate them (Sadowski, 2004).

◆ Children from immigrant families are more likely than their peers to live in poverty, to be behind in grade level, and to live in overcrowded housing (Sadowski, 2004).

◆ More than 70 percent of children from immigrant families speak languages other than English at home.

▶ **Figure 11-9**
Ethnic diversity in classrooms is here to stay.

© Cengage Learning

◆ According to a report by Farley (2007) on a 2007 UNICEF study of 21 wealthy nations' investment in child welfare programs UNICEF released in 2007, the United States was ranked as number 20 of the nations studied.

◆ Racially segregated residential areas are increasing in many areas of the United States, especially in California, and Latinos have fewer white classmates in schools (Krieger, 2006).

◆ A record number of babies were born in the United States in 2007—4.3 million (Jayson, 2008). The last time this number was this high was 1957. Professional women are delaying childbearing and waiting to have their babies until their 20s and 30s.

Facts and figures for school districts and teachers:

◆ School districts are recruiting elementary school teachers from overseas to fill shortages in math, science, and special education, especially in poor urban and rural school districts.

◆ The American Federation of Teachers Union estimates at least 18,000 of the nation's 3.7 million teachers were hired from out of the country (Bazar, 2008).

◆ In Illinois, early childhood teachers are leaving jobs in community-based programs because compensation and benefits are better in public schools (McCormick Tribune Center for Early Childhood Leadership, 2009).

◆ Some school districts offer higher teacher salaries and bonuses when student test scores improve, or if teachers work in hard-to-staff schools (Toppo, 2008).

◆ Scott-Little, Brown, Hooks, & Marshall (2008) report 14 states and some local school districts have implemented quality rating systems that include visiting classroom observers who rate classroom quality and teaching practices. Thirty additional states are considering or developing likewise systems (National Child Care Information Center, 2007).

## Child Poverty

Poverty is defined in terms of a family income failing to meet a federally established threshold, living at or below which signifies that the family lacks basic financial resources and, consequently, adequate access to food, health care, and shelter (Leventhal & Brooks-Gunn, 2002). In 2001, almost 12 million children (16 percent) lived in families where the income was at or below poverty level (U.S. Census Bureau, 2002). These figures are climbing because of current unemployment figures. Poverty during early childhood often affects children's academic achievement, literacy development, and cognitive abilities to a greater degree than poverty experienced in late childhood.

Not all social scientists conclude that family income is of prime importance to child outcomes. Some consider other factors to be most important, such as a strong family work ethic, a mother's educational attainment, a mother's literacy skills, family modeling of reading and writing, authentic family uses of literacy, family beliefs and attitudes toward literacy, parents' conversational styles, family educational goals for children, and a home literacy environment that includes availability and exposure to print (Britto, Fuligni, & Brooks-Gunn, 2006). All of these influence young children's educational outcomes.

Scientists agree that children's basic physical and emotional needs must first be satisfied (see Figure 11–10). Unfortunately, this is often not the case for economically disadvantaged children, who experience more hearing problems, ear infections, dental problems, lead exposure, poor nutrition, asthma, and poor housing arrangements than other children (Rothstein, 2004).

▶ **Figure 11-10**

Equipment to promote children's physical developmental needs is important.

© Cengage Learning

## Where Are the Children?

Quinn (2005) notes that the U.S. Census Department report *Who's Minding the Kids?* reported that over 22 percent of working mothers had multiple child care arrangements, sometimes called *hybrid care* (see Figure 11–11). Non-parental care includes babysitters, nannies, grandparents, center-based care, preschools, pre-kindergartens, relatives, friends, and family care providers.

Every week in the United States nearly 5 million individuals other than parents care for and educate young children between birth and age five (Lowenstein, Ochshorn, Kagan, & Fuller, 2004).

## Factors Influencing a Family's Choice of Care

Many factors seem to influence family selection of child care, including availability. Over 35 percent of all public schools in the United States offered pre-kindergarten classes. Many of these are half-day programs, so many of the working families choosing them needed additional arrangement for afternoon care. Kirp (2005) points out middle-class families are insisting on quality child care and publicly supported pre-kindergartens.

Family income, race, and the mother's educational attainment level are believed to also influence child care selection. Children with more highly educated mothers are more likely to participate in center-based early childhood programs (U.S. Department of Education, 2002).

## Other Trends and Issues Affecting the Field

With increased public investment, accountability has become an increasingly voiced issue. Head Start has adopted *outcome accountability assessments*. Standardized assessments and the use of *benchmarks* to identify child performance in publicly funded pre-kindergartens are commonplace, because many parents are interested in knowing if pre-kindergarten enrollment has actually helped their child succeed. Teachers whose classes do not live up to identified outcomes are under pressure to change.

▶ **Figure 11-11**

Britney and La Neta go to a family day-home after school.

© Cengage Learning

Most educators realize that test reliability and validity at the preschool age has its limitations and dangers, particularly when children are labeled. Test results may be situation dependent and based on English language skills. Research strongly suggests the quality of instruction and adult-child interactions in early education affect child achievement and social skills.

**Curriculum Content Standards** Roskos, Rosemary, and Varner (2006) observe:

> With title wave force, the standards movement swept into the early childhood education field at the start of the 21st century with the promise of a seamless PreK–12 continuum of cognitive development and learning linked to academic achievement.

This standards movement also includes the push for content standards, which are appearing in state plans. Because teachers will have to adjust their instruction to the needs of diverse children to a greater degree than before, a larger number of individual learning plans will be necessary to meet content standards. If high teacher/student ratios exist, or if teachers are without the necessary resources to provide individualized instruction, teachers may find content standards hard to achieve.

**State-Administered and Universal Pre-K** About 86 percent of teachers in state-funded programs held a bachelor's degree or higher in 2004 (U.S. Department of Education, National Center for Educational Statistics, 2005a). What does all this mean for student teachers who continue their education and obtain BA degrees? More job opportunities, better compensation (in some cases the same pay as public school teachers), a chance for increased benefits, possible stipends for future training, a better public image, and a hope that the inequities that exist for early childhood educators will, at least partially, disappear.

**School-Age Programs** Before- and after-school child care programs are a viable and growing phenomenon, and many hire community college early childhood graduates or majors. The demand has grown in proportion to the number of employed family members. School-age child care is seen as a regular program, designed for children ages five to twelve, during the times when school is not in session and families are working.

School-age programs are often good employment choices for teachers-in-training who wish to eventually work in elementary school, or for part-time work. If attached to a public school system, higher than average hourly compensation and some benefits may be available.

**Homeschooling** Over 850,000 children nationwide are homeschooled. About one-fifth of these children were also enrolled in public or private schools part time. Of all American students, 2.25 percent were homeschooled in the spring of 2003 (U.S. Department of Education, 2005b). About 75 percent of these children were white, and their parents had higher levels of educational attainment than did parents of children enrolled in other types of schools.

The most common reasons families choose to home school are beliefs that a better education could be provided at home, faith-based education would not take place in schools, character and morality development is questionable, and local schools are not able to deliver quality experiences.

Homeschooling families sometimes hire others to provide educational lessons and activities. This includes tutors and specialists in subject matter and study areas such as music, art, mathematics, science, and sports.

**Second Language Teaching** A future teacher has a good chance of being a second language instructor at some point in his or her career. If you speak a second language, this will be an advantage when teaching children with that native language. Your school district or other employers will be searching for teachers with cultural knowledge and linguistic skill. A greater volume and variety of positions will be offered, especially if you obtain specialist credentials.

**Asian Students** Researchers are looking closely at figures that show a steady climb in the enrollment of Asian students from immigrant families in institutions of higher education. In 2006, Asian students accounted for 36 percent of entering freshmen in California's public universities (Krieger & Fernandez, 2006). For the first time, Asian students outnumbered other ethnic groups at the University of California at Berkeley. A factor promoting this trend is Asian students' strong performance in high school. Another factor believed to influence Asian students' academic achievement is the fact that Asian students are more likely to have a college-educated parent, and books and computers are usually found in their homes. Asian families tend to expect their children to attend college, as do many other parents from all ethnic backgrounds. Asian families seem to be more knowledgeable about both preparing and applying for college admission.

## EARLY CHILDHOOD EMPLOYMENT

Is it a good time to be job hunting? After an examination of the field of education, Feller (2005) reported that 40 percent of America's teachers plan to leave teaching by 2010, and 42 percent of teachers currently practicing their craft are 50 or older. Teachers who entered the field during the baby boom years are now retiring. Simon (2005) estimated that a half million teachers will be needed before 2010 (see Figure 11–12). Some teachers in urban school districts have become disillusioned and have left teaching. Still others, especially in the shortage areas of mathematics and science, never take teaching jobs because private industry and other businesses pay substantially more than teaching.

Stout (2009) reports President Obama has called for sweeping changes in U.S. education. He proposes lifting limits on **charter schools**, improving early childhood education quality, linking teacher pay to performance, and the president envisions a "new culture" of accountability in America's schools. A recently enacted stimulus package calls for spending 5 billion dollars on Early Head Start and Head Start programs (Stout, 2009). All of these proposals will create new jobs for educators.

**charter school**—schools exempt from some local and state regulations. They can be charted by a school district, a state board of education, a post-secondary institution, or a chartering agency. Some charter schools are publicly funded while others are privately funded by businesses and corporations.

▶ **Figure 11–12**
Many more teachers will be needed as older teachers retire.

© Cengage Learning

## Employment for Elementary and Higher Level School Teachers

To meet what is already a shortage in many districts, some districts encourage paraprofessionals to acquire their teaching credential, and some districts help with financing and adjusted work hours. Other districts have attracted retiring military personnel, especially those trained in one of the sciences or in mathematics.

A few of the well-known programs involved in recruiting and training teachers are Teach for America (mentioned earlier), Troops to Teachers, Recruiting New Teachers, and Pathways to Teaching Careers. At the high school level, Phi Delta Kappa sponsors the Future Educators of America (FEA), which conducts an annual summer camp and offers scholarships.

School districts are hiring overseas teachers because their recruitment efforts in the United States have failed. The Philippines, Canada, and some European countries have supplied teachers with specialties in mathematics, music, special education, science, bilingual Spanish, middle school French, Japanese, and Mandarin. Simon (2005) noted that 500,000 new teachers have been hired in elementary and secondary school classrooms in the past five years. Career changers—post baccalaureate degree and mid-career job switchers—are the biggest trend in education employment, with 70,000 entering teaching in the last few years. These "second-act" educators are filling teacher positions. Some states have created many alternative routes to teacher certification.

Fredix (2006) researched the U.S. Bureau of Labor Statistics, which listed occupations with the largest projected job growth in the United States for 2004 to 2014. Post-secondary teachers, Fredix found, placed third, following registered nurses. An early childhood educator with a long-range goal of becoming a college educator would be interested in this prediction.

From the information provided so far it is easy to see that certain specialties and teaching skills are in short supply for educators at multiple levels, especially in certain geographic locations. Do not overlook using library references to investigate an area's economic growth, housing, and quality of life when considering employment options.

Relocating to areas of high population growth, or to areas in the path of progress, will afford more opportunity and more job openings, but one must investigate to discern credential requirements. The Internet will aid your search, but it is beneficial to first become familiar with your college's career center. At all educational levels school and campus career centers differ in the services they provide, but most will provide search help and suggestions, resume development, counseling, a website for posting and upgrading your resume, and a search library. Many career centers hold job fairs, and some have staff members who work exclusively with alumni and have the ability to put you in touch with alumni living in the geographic area where you are searching. Career centers may also schedule meetings with school recruiters.

## Early Childhood Education Majors and Graduates Employment

When vying for positions, educators with specialties and those who can convince employers of their competencies will have an edge. Males and bilingual speakers are in demand. Centers are searching for those who have completed or are working on college degrees, the higher the better.

**Where to Look** There are many ways to classify early childhood places of employment because programs are diverse. Two broad categories of program types will be explored first. These are programs that provide *direct services to children* *and families* (see Figure 11–13), and those providing *indirect services to children, families, and educators* (see Figure 11–14). You will notice these figures also provide possible job titles in each category. Figure 11–15 will examine the sponsors, owners, and administrators of public and private early childhood programs. The figure also describes some program characteristics. Notice a program may be either non-profit or for-profit, and that families may receive free services or pay fees on a sliding fee scale. Programs in the public sector use federal, state, county, city, or other public taxpayer funds to operate.

Many programs are unique and may fit into more than one category. In the category of specialized and unique programs, we should mentioned cooperative preschools, community and church-sponsored programs, industry-sponsored and worksite centers, Montessori schools, residential treatment programs, military child centers, hospital child centers, campus child care and development centers, special education programs, license-exempt centers, neighborhood play groups, and mall care programs that may or may not be licensed. Non-accredited programs are not discussed here. The authors strongly suggest accredited center employment if it is offered and available.

We have not discussed job titles. A short examination of job titles in early childhood education on the Internet will produce at least 50 different job titles for early childhood educators. One often has to read a job description to find if it is really early childhood employment or one in some related field.

We also have not discussed self-employment. Figure 11–16 list business enterprises other early childhood or education majors have created. Many early childhood education students prefer to work for themselves and become entrepreneurs. Some have discovered special abilities that make their businesses successful or have seen an unfilled child, family, or program need and then worked to fill it. The largest group of self-employed educators is family day-home operators and private preschool owners.

## Finding Job Announcements

The most common places to find job announcements are the websites of professional early childhood associations, such as the Association for Childhood Education International (ACEI), and their journals or publications, for example, NAEYC's *Young Children*. A personal visit is always best, but Internet contact can also be successful. Your best leads may come from family members or friends and the other professionals and students with whom you have developed a networking relationship. Job fairs held in many cities are sponsored by a variety of groups and organizations and well worth attending.

## Prepare Before Filling Applications

You will want to list and examine your skills and abilities thoroughly before submitting an application or creating a cover letter or resume. What you submit needs to be perfect or near perfect to gain the attention you wish. "The better the job, the more the competition" is a general rule of thumb. When you are really in touch with your skills, abilities, talents, accomplishments, qualifications, and experience, the more effectively and convincingly you will be able to describe them in person or on paper. If you have a professional portfolio and letters of reference, these will aid you. If you are making phone calls to unearth job openings or get an interview, practice what you will say beforehand. Your goals are to sound professional while speaking with a friendly ease as you make your first impression.

Many times you will be able find out specific hiring information about the employer, such as whether they will keep your application on file when there are no openings. If applying in person, carry along everything you will need to fill an application. In most cases, you should ask to take the application with you, so you have time to study it, figure out what the employer is looking for, and tailor both

*Student teacher quote*—*"My dream is to have a school of my own among evergreen trees in a small mountain town. I'll call it 'Tiny Pine-y' or 'Evergreen Academy' or such."*

**Nomsa Ncube, Student Teacher Placement Classroom, San Jose City College, CA**

▶**Figure 11-13**
Direct Services to Children and Families.

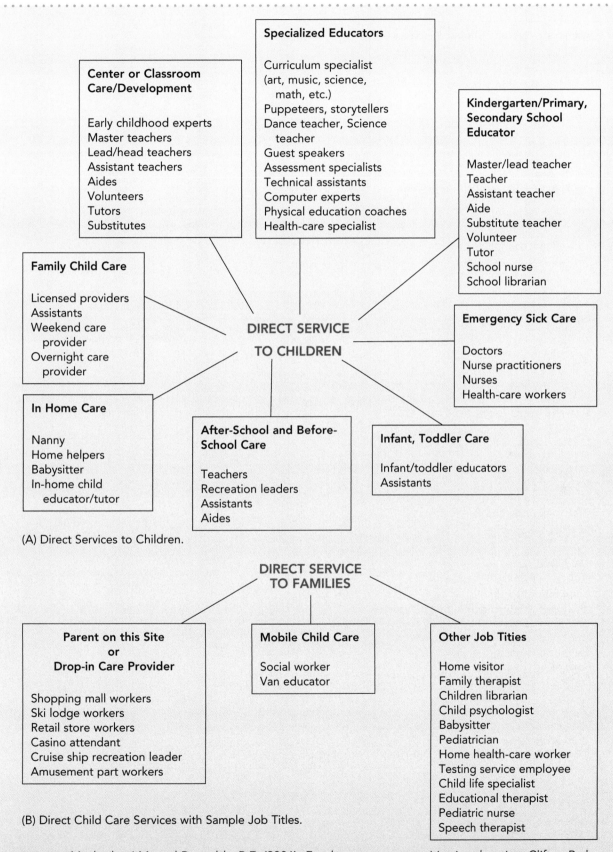

(A) Direct Services to Children.

(B) Direct Child Care Services with Sample Job Titles.

**SOURCE:** Machado, J.M. and Reynolds, R.E. (2006). *Employment opportunities in education.* Clifton Park, NY: Thomson/Delmar Learning, p. 28.

▶ **Figure 11-14**
Indirect Services to Children, Families, and Educators, with Sample Job Titles

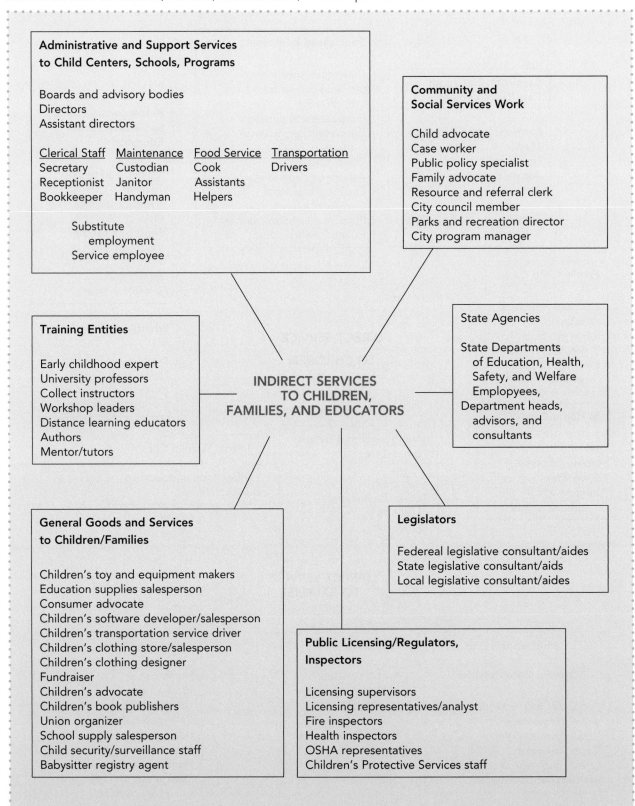

**Administrative and Support Services
to Child Centers, Schools, Programs**

Boards and advisory bodies
Directors
Assistant directors

Clerical Staff | Maintenance | Food Service | Transportation
Secretary | Custodian | Cook | Drivers
Receptionist | Janitor | Assistants
Bookkeeper | Handyman | Helpers

Substitute
  employment
Service employee

**Community and
Social Services Work**

Child advocate
Case worker
Public policy specialist
Family advocate
Resource and referral clerk
City council member
Parks and recreation director
City program manager

**Training Entities**

Early childhood expert
University professors
Collect instructors
Workshop leaders
Distance learning educators
Authors
Mentor/tutors

**INDIRECT SERVICES
TO CHILDREN,
FAMILIES, AND EDUCATORS**

**State Agencies**

State Departments
  of Education, Health,
  Safety, and Welfare
  Employees,
Department heads,
  advisors, and
  consultants

**General Goods and Services
to Children/Families**

Children's toy and equipment makers
Education supplies salesperson
Consumer advocate
Children's software developer/salesperson
Children's transportation service driver
Children's clothing store/salesperson
Children's clothing designer
Fundraiser
Children's advocate
Children's book publishers
Union organizer
School supply salesperson
Child security/surveillance staff
Babysitter registry agent

**Legislators**

Federeal legislative consultant/aides
State legislative consultant/aids
Local legislative consultant/aides

**Public Licensing/Regulators,
Inspectors**

Licensing supervisors
Licensing representatives/analyst
Fire inspectors
Health inspectors
OSHA representatives
Children's Protective Services staff

**SOURCE:** Machado, J.M. and Reynolds, R.E. (2006). *Employment opportunities in education.* Clifton Park, NY: Delmar Learning, p. 29.

▶**Figure 11-15**
Features of Private and Public Early Childhood Programs.

| Sponsor, Owner/Administrator | Characteristics |
|---|---|
| **Public** | |
| Federal, state or county agency such as Office of Economic Opportunity, Department of Health and Human Services, U.S. Military, State Department of Education, Social Services, school districts, college districts | Funds allocated by Congress, state legislatures, or county government or agencies |
| | Program developers and supervisors may be quite remote from schools themselves, in off-site offices |
| | Programs exceedingly varied |
| | May also include schools providing services to special groups such as developmentally delayed or challenged, speech impaired, bilingual, after-school care, etc |
| Other agencies such as a neighborhood council, community service organization, welfare agency, or community action programs | Often a parent or community board serves an advisory function |
| | Program standards and guidelines are available and may be mandatory |
| | Program may be accredited |
| | Universal pre-kindergarten and some state pre-K programs are open to all interested parents and exist in some states. |
| | Nonprofit |
| | Enroll greater numbers of English as a second language children |
| | Programs may be affected by *No Child Left Behind Act* legislation requiring child testing. |
| | Parent fees may be on a sliding scale reflecting parent income |
| | Centers may be located in low-income and rural communities |
| | Facilities located on public property |
| | May be unionized |
| **Private** | Profit making |
| Individual or group business | Higher parent fees |
| | A small or large school operated by a single owner or a large chain with absentee owners, run by a paid director and a staff |
| | May be accredited |
| Religious group (faith based) | May use church personnel for staffing and have secular emphasis or may simply permit use of church facilities |
| | May be accredited |
| Parent cooperative | Parents hire a professional director and serve as assistants on a rotating basis, with regularly scheduled meetings for families, which usually include parenting education |
| **Private nonprofit** | An incorporated entity that has been granted nonprofit status through legal application to a federal, state, or local agency |
| | A wide variation of programs |
| | May be accredited |

**SOURCE:** Machado, J.M. and Reynolds, R.E. (2006). *Employment opportunities in education.* Clifton Park, NY: Delmar Learning, pp. 30–31.

▶ Figure 11-16

Samples of Self-Employment Businesses and Services.

- emergency care provider
- ski lodge child care
- tennis or health club provider
- weekend and overnight provider
- parent magazine or newsletter publisher
- teacher identity item manufacturer (apron, jewelry, etc.)
- children's film and audiovisual rental service
- children's photography service
- advertising/promotion, fundrasing service
- bulk food service supplier
- food service
- scrap item supplier (teacher's warehouse)
- teaching aid manufacturer (puppets, toys, equipment, etc.)
- curriculum idea book publisher
- private school tax consultant
- field trip coordinator
- visiting teacher, speaker service
- industry child care consultant/specialist
- testing service
- substitute teacher service
- child and family lobbyist
- workshop and in-service training service
- specialty teacher (dance, foreign language, gymnastics, science etc.)
- family day care respite service
- child home safety consultant
- nanny service provider
- Saturday fathers activity service
- preschool backpack manufacturer
- surveillance services to parents wishing to monitor sitters in their own home
- parent educator service
- school auditor, accountant, payroll, or collection service
- online parent advisor
- overnight preschool care service
- soccer camp for preschoolers
- children's song writer
- children's stamp set manufacturer
- princess party organizer
- ethnic storyteller
- nature docent
- flannel board set designer and manufacturer
- gingerbread "create and decorate your own cookie or house" bakery
- paint-and-take ceramics center
- toy store owner
- children's hairdresser on wheels
- toy exchange store
- nanny and au pair agency

**SOURCE:** Machado, J.M. and Reynolds, R.E. (2006). *Employment opportunities in education*. Clifton Park, NY: Delmar Learning, pp. 182–183.

application and resume to highlight how you match what the employer needs and desires. This involves fact finding, and a smart job applicant takes the time and makes the effort to know as much as possible about the employer's operation. Fact finding includes looking at the job site, neighborhood, and community. Some schools will allow school tours.

All materials submitted need to be attractive, neat, businesslike, and honest—no truth-stretching or omissions—printed in an easy-to-read font, on appropriate paper stock, in an acceptable format, using current educational and occupational terms. It is crucial that any submissions be grammatically correct with no misspellings. Libraries, bookstores, and the Internet are the best resources for books on resume writing, and computer programs are plentiful. Our Online Companion website (www.cengage.com/education/machado) has a few cover letters and resumes for you to examine and offers additional tips. Most resources will tell you to adapt your resume to the specific job you seek.

## Pre-Interview Activities

There is definitely an art to interviewing, and practice interviewing is recommended. Interview questions can be direct or situational, and many will be asked by a committee of diverse individuals connected to the school's operation. It pays to do whatever you can to feel relaxed and confident; whether that means a new haircut or new shoes, it is worth the investment. Dress to fit in, rather than catering to the latest style. Appearing well groomed, articulate, professionally skilled, and personable is your objective; being likeable is a real plus. The Online Companion website (www.cengage.com/education/machado) has a list of suggested interview questions to practice.

If you are male, you may occasionally encounter interviewers who are suspicious and/or feel that men are less able to care for and educate young children. During job interviews, male applicants may ask about policies concerning teacher–child physical contact and bathroom supervision, to probe employer's attitudes and policies. Sometimes a double standard exists in these areas. As with other applicants, qualifications are what matter most.

## Family Home Providers

Some early childhood majors start their training with job experience working in a family provider's home, and are well aware of this type of employment. Other students are relatively unaware of this type of child care.

Most students do not realize that two-thirds of all workers in the early education field are self-employed, and that the majority of these are family child care providers (Krantz, 2002). Many make a good living, and their business is profitable. Unfortunately, a good number of people think these providers have no formal training, but this is not the case: about 13 percent of these providers have college degrees; an estimated 11 percent have not graduated from high school, and the remaining 76 percent fall somewhere between these two figures in educational attainment. Family day-home providers often suffer from an image problem, and unfortunately and undeservedly, may be the least respected of all educators.

## QUESTIONS MANY GRADUATES ASK FOLLOW. ANSWERS ARE IN PARENTHESES.

- Should I bring a portfolio to an interview? (It is best if the employer has a chance to see it before-hand. Ask about this when you are invited to interview. Those using electronic portfolios [mentioned in Chapter 1] and carrying a laptop to interviews may be able to pinpoint portfolio sections that display competencies or answer interviewer's questions visually. If they haven't already done so, an interviewee can also provide a URL address for his portfolio for interviewer further investigation. Be sure to inquire when an interview is planned if one can bring a laptop. You should review it before submitting it because interviewers may ask questions about portfolio contents during the interview.)

- When should I ask about salary? (You can ask if a salary schedule is available once you have been asked to interview, or ask when a job has been offered. Many employers tend to probe what salaries have previously been received. Have in mind a range rather than a fixed figure.)

- Can I ask questions during an interview? (Of course, but ask only what you really want to know.)

- Should I negotiate salary when a job offer is made? (Most professionals do this, and it is easier to raise your salary at this time than it will be later. Negotiating rarely jeopardizes the job, as the employer has usually already decided that they want you.)

- What is the worst error I can make during an interview? (Making negative comments about a former employer is a big one. This can make interviewers uneasy. Most interviewers, who know the early childhood field, know there are many valid reasons for leaving past employment, including unethical employers.)

## ▶ SUMMARY

The commitment to update continually and gain additional skills begins in training and continues for a lifetime. Each professional teacher is responsible for her own unique growth-planning schedule and career goal setting. Many activity choices leading to advanced skills are available, and most professionals engage in a wide variety. Additional coursework and training, professional group membership, conference and workshop attendance, in-service training, school visits, and other experiences leading to increased knowledge and the discovery of new techniques and instructional strategies. Social interactions in educative settings reinforce individual teacher's commitment to professionalism.

The solitary pursuit of a true professional, bent on increasing excellence, includes self-directed study, reflection, and analysis. Going online and reading professional journals, magazines, and books that present new and classic strategies, practices, techniques, ideas, issues, trends, and research is both never-ending and personally rewarding.

Many factors affect American families. Current information concerning trends in society were discussed, especially those that are related to children, family life, and schools. Diverse child care arrangements were described, including state and federally funded pre-kindergartens, school-age programs, and family child care.

An attempt was made to inform readers about career opportunities in the many types of programs serving young children and families. Tips and suggestions of how to begin an employment search, recognize job titles, find and fill out job applications, and secure interviews were provided

## ▶ HELPFUL WEBSITES

**www.naeyc.org/toolbox.asp**
Advocacy tips are provided.

**http://wwwcareerforum.naeyc.org/post/cfm**
This NAEYC website posts job openings.

**http://www.nccp.org**
National Center for Children in Poverty. Search for publications and policy information.

**http://www.emurse.com**
This site provides help for student teachers in preparing and distributing resumes.

**http://www.craigslist.org**
Craigslist. Check jobs listed by city and state.

**http://www.teachforamerica.org**
Teach for America provides information on improving outcomes for children living in poverty.

 Additional resources for this chapter can be found by visiting the companion website at **www.cengage.com/education/machado.**

## ▶ SUGGESTED READING

Machado, J. M., & Reynolds, R. E. (2006). *Employment opportunities in education: How to* *secure your career*. Clifton Park, NY: Delmar Learning.

## ▶ SUGGESTED ACTIVITIES

**A.** In groups of four to six, develop a chart that lists factors that promote professionalism, and those that impede professionalism, in early childhood teachers.

**B.** Rate each statement based on the scale below. Discuss your results with the class.

Strongly agree = 1; agree = 2; cannot decide = 3; mildly disagree = 4; strongly disagree = 5

1. Being professional includes proper makeup and clothing at work.
2. It is unprofessional to keep using the same techniques over and over.
3. Professional commitment is more important than professional growth.
4. Professional growth can involve course work that does not pertain to children and/or families.
5. A teacher can grow professionally by studying children in the classroom.
6. Professional association fees are so expensive that student teachers can rarely afford to join.
7. One of the real causes for the lack of status of early childhood teachers is their own attitude toward professional growth.
8. It is difficult to feel like a professional when salaries are so low.
9. Most teachers who pursue professional skills receive little recognition for their efforts.
10. One can learn all one needs to know about handling children's behavior by watching a master teacher.
11. Sweatpants, T-shirts, and sneakers are very comfortable, but they are not very professional looking (Franquet, 1997).
12. The community should see child care as not just a social service but as an income-generating, job-creating industry that is vital to the economic infrastructure of any city (Petersen, 2002).

**C.** Make your own list of current issues in early childhood teaching. In groups of three to five, arrange your lists in order of their importance for young children's education and well-being in the United States or do a web search of charter schools and list five facts you uncover. Share and compare results with your training group.

## ▶ REVIEW

**A.** List five current trends or issues affecting families or children.

**B.** Describe briefly what you feel should be public policy on child care for young children in the United States. Include children living in poverty and immigrant children.

**C.** Why might it be a good time to graduate and enter a career in early childhood education? List your main ideas (at least four).

## ▶ REFERENCES

Bazar, E. (2008, October 23). Schools in need employ teachers from overseas. *USA Today*, 2A.

Birckmayer, J., Cohen, J., Jensen, I. D., & Variano, D. A. (2005, May). Supporting grandparents who raise grandchildren. *Young Children, 69*(3), 100–104.

Britto, P. R., Fuligni, A. S., & Brooks-Gunn, J. (2006). Reading ahead: Effective interventions for young children's early literacy development. In D. K. Dickinson and S. B. Neuman (Eds.), *Handbook of early literacy research*, 2, (pp. 311–322). New York: The Guilford Press.

Burchinal, M. R., Roberts, J. E., Riggins, R., Zeisel, S. A., Neebe, E., & Bryant, D. (2000). Relating quality of center-based child care to early cognitive and language development longitudinally. *Child Development, 71*(2), 339–357.

Cunniff, P. A., & Risley, R. A. (2006) *Best practices in teacher preparation programs: Focus on students*, Jackson, MS: Phi theta Kappa International Honor Society, Center for Excellence

Farley, M. (2007, February, 15). Study: U.S. not the best for kids. *San Jose Mercury News*, 1A.

Farstrup, A. E. (2007, June/July). What does it mean to be a professional? *Reading Today*, 24(6), 17.

Feller, B. (2005, August 18). 40% of teachers plan to quit by 2010. *Chicago Sun Times*, P12. Retrieved September 6, 2005, from http://www.suntimes. com/output/education/cst-nws-teach.html.

Foote, D. (2008). *Relentless pursuit: A year in the trenches with Teach for America*. New York: Knopf.

Franquet, M. (1997, July). R-E-S-P-E-C-T: Can I have some? Please! *Young Children*, 52(2), 36–41.

Fredix, E. (2006, September 7). Firms look to avoid labor shortage. *Idaho Statesman*, 3B.

Gadsden, V., & Ray, A. (2002, November). Engaging fathers: Issues and considerations for early childhood educators. *Young Children*, 57(6), 32–45.

Ghazvini, A., & Mullis, R. L. (2002). Center-based care for young children: Examining predictors of quality. *The Journal of Genetic Psychology*, (163), 112–124.

*Good Smart, Grow Smart*. (2002, April). Washington, DC: The White House.

Harrison, R. (1978). *Self-directed learning: Human growth games*. Beverly Hills, CA: Sage Publications.

Honig, A. S., & Hirallal, A. (1998). Which counts more for excellence in childcare staff: Years of service, education level or ECE coursework? *Early Child Development and Care, 145*, 32–46.

Jayson, S. (2008, July 17). Is this the next baby boom? *USA Today*, 1D

Katz, L. (1972, February). Developmental stages of preschool teachers. *The Elementary School Journal*, 24–30.

Kirp, D. L. (2005, July 31). All my children. *The New York Times*, E7.

Krantz, L. (2002). *Jobs rated almanac* (5th Ed.). New York: St. Martin's Press.

Krieger, L. M. (2006, January, 17). School segregation growing in California, study finds. *San Jose Mercury News*, 1A, 13A.

Krieger, L. M. & Fernandez, L. (2006, April 20). Asians surpass mark at UC. *San Jose Mercury News*, 1A, 17A.

Leventhal, T., & Brooks-Gunn, J. (2002). Poverty and child development, *International encyclopedia of social and behavioral sciences*, 3(14), 11889–11893.

Lowenstein, A. E., Ochshorn, S., Kagan, S. L., & Fuller, B. (2004, March). Report #2: The effects of professional development efforts and compensation on the quality of early care and education services. *Child Care and Early Education, National Conference of State Legislature*, #6164–0002.

Maxwell, K. L., Field, C. C., & Clifford, R. M. (2006). In M. Zaslow and I. Martinez-Beck (Eds.), *Critical issues in early childhood professional development* (pp. 21–44). Baltimore, MD: Paul Brookes Publishing Co.

McCormick Tribune Center for Early Childhood Leadership (2009, Winter). The status of the early childhood workforce in Illinois, *The Director's Link*. Wheeling, IL: National-Louis University.

Merrill, S. (2002). Mentoring in Head Start programs. *The Head Start Bulletin*, 72, 32–33.

Meyer, R. J. (2005, May). Taking a stand: Strategies for activism. *Young Children*, 60(5), 80–92.

National Association for the Education of Young Children. (2007). *NAEYC early childhood program standards and accreditation criteria*. Washington, DC: Author.

National Child Care Information Center. (2007, Winter/Spring). Systematic approaches to improving quality of care: QRS gain ground across the nation, *Child Care Bulletin*, 32, 26–34.

Petersen, D. (Quoted in Corcoran, K.). (2002, November 12). Report: Child care is cog in economy. *San Jose Mercury News*, 1–2B.

Phillips, D. A., Mekow, D., Scarr S., McCartney, K., & Abbot-Shinn, M. (2000). Within and beyond the classroom door: Assessing quality in child care centers. *Early Childhood Research Quarterly*, 15, 475–496.

Quinn, M. (2005, November 10). Juggling child care providers. *San Jose Mercury News*, 1–2B.

Robinson, H. (2008, October, 20). I am not a babysitter. *Newsweek*, 19.

Rockstroh, D. (2005, December 7). Teacher ordered to use breaks to play janitor. *San Jose Mercury News, C9*.

Roskos, K., Rosemary, C. A., & Varner, M. H. (2006). Alignment in educator preparation for early and beginning literacy instruction. In M Zaslow and I. Martinez-Beck (Eds.), *Critical issues in early childhood professional development* (pp. 255–279). Baltimore, MD: Paul Brookes Publishing Co.

Rothstein, R. (2004). *Class and school*. New York: Teacher's College Press.

Sachs, J. (2000). Inequities in early care and education: What is America buying? *Journal of Education for Students Placed at Risk*, 5, 383–395.

Sadowski, M. (Ed.). (2004). *Teaching immigrant and second-language students: Strategies for success*. Cambridge, MA: Harvard Education Press.

*San Jose Mercury News*. (2006, February 12). Analysis of data from the 2000 Census. *San Jose Mercury News*, 1A, 12–13A.

*San Jose Mercury News*. (2008, October 19). Grandparents caring for grandchildren: A closer look at communities using the 2005–2007 U.S. Census Bureau, American Community Survey. *San Jose Mercury News* 1A.

Scott-Little, C., Brown, G. E., Hooks, L. M., & Marshall, B. J. (2008, November). Classroom quality rating systems: How do teachers prepare and what do they think about the process? *Young Children*, 63(6), 40–45.

Simon, C. C. (2005, July 31). Those who can, and can't. *New York Times*. Retrieved July 31, 2005, from http://www.nytimes.com/2005/07/31.html?ex=1126152000Ben=816c1c82bcab7086Bei=5070.

Stout, D. (2009, Wednesday March 11). Obama opens door to charter schools. *San Jose Mercury News*. 1–2A.

Toppo, G. (2008, 8 October 22). Teachers take test scores to bank. *USA Today*, 1.

U.S. Census Bureau, (2002, March). Current population surveys, 1976–2002. Retrieved May 16, 2002 from http://census.gov/prod/2003pubs/p60-222.pdf

U.S. Department of Education, National Center for Education Statistics. (2002). *The condition of education 2002*. NCES 2002-025. Washington, DC: U.S. Government Printing Office.

U.S. Department of Education, National Center for Educational Statistics. (2005a). *Child care and early education arrangements of infants, toddlers, and preschoolers:* 2001. Washington, DC: U. S. Government Printing Office.

U.S. Department of Education, National Center for Educational Statistics. (2005b). The condition of education 2005. *Education Statistics Quarterly*, 7(1&2), 281–297.

Zaslow, M. & Martinez-Beck, I (2006). *Critical Issues in early childhood professional development*. Baltimore, MD: Paul Brookes Publishing. Co.

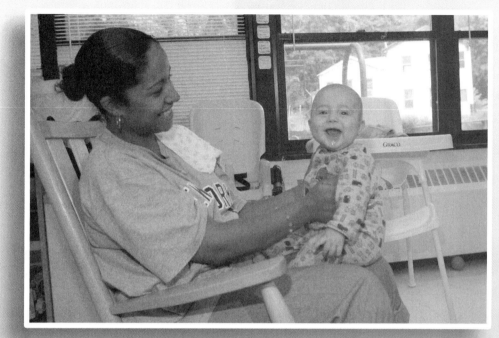

© Cengage Learning

# Infant/Toddler
# Placements

# CHAPTER 12

# Student Teaching with Infants and Toddlers

**OBJECTIVES** After reading this chapter, you should be able to:

1. List at least three characteristics of a quality infant/toddler center.
2. Describe caregiving as a teaching activity.
3. Cite five techniques for approaching and working with children.
4. Identify 10 activities for infants and toddlers.

## Student Teacher Scenario

**Setting:** A family child care home. The caregiver, Robin, and her husband, Tom, recently bought a new split-level home so that the lower level could be devoted to her child care. Downstairs, there are two reasonably large rooms, a bathroom, and an ample storage area under the stairs for a lot of the children's toys.

The infant room is the smaller of the two rooms. Currently, Robin has seven children in her care: two babies (a one-month-old girl and a four-month-old boy), 2 four-year-old girls, and 1 five-year-old boy, Gordon, who attends an afternoon kindergarten program.

The infant room is furnished with a crib, a playpen, a carpeted area for crawling, a wind-up swing, and a mirror placed low on the wall, so infants can see themselves. The room for older children is well furnished with a low table and chairs for crafts, puzzles, snacks, and so on. There is a low couch, which is perfect for Robin to sit on for reading to the older children when the infants are sleeping. Robin has decorated the walls with the letters of the alphabet and numbers from 1 to 10. She also had a local artist paint a mural of teddy bears playing on the wall by the couch. The window wall is opposite, with built-in shelves below for puzzles, toy cars, and other play objects.

Outside, Robin has a large, grassy, fenced area with a climbing structure, a swing set, and a paved area for wheeled toys such as tricycles, wagons, and large trucks. Tom has built a playhouse and a cave-like structure, which the children enjoy.

Five-year-old Gordon's mother has asked Robin whether or not Robin will be able to take care of her newborn when she arrives. She is anxious about the care for the new baby because she'll be student teaching during the spring semester of the next year.

"I'm really hoping you'll be able to take the new baby. Any chance one of your current children won't be here next fall? You've been so good with Gordon so I know how good you'd be with my new baby."

"I'm not sure," Robin answers, "but Gordon will be in first grade next year, so he'll not be here until 3:00 PM after school closes."

"The doctor says that the baby is due in December. Hey, did you decide to follow through on applying for accreditation?" Gordon's mother queries.

"I don't think it's worth the effort for me," replies Robin. "I'm always fully enrolled. For me, taking all that time and completing all that paperwork is almost too overwhelming to even think about!"

## Questions for Discussion:

1. Would you want to place your own baby or toddler in Robin's family child care home?

2. Does Robin's family child care program seem like a quality one? (Check the criteria listed in this chapter to guide your response.)

3. What are the licensing recommendations in your state concerning adult–child ratios in family day homes?

## STANDARDS

Most infants and toddlers today are cared for by relatives or in family child care homes. Many parents feel, rightly or wrongly, that the infant thrives better in an environment most like the home. State licensing in most states mandates adult–infant and adult–toddler ratios in licensed family child care homes. The National Association for the Education of Young Children (NAEYC) has been urging a ratio of 1:4 as a national standard. A quality center may deliberately choose to keep its ratio at 1:3.

One of the reasons for the lack of national standards lies in the belief that all young children, especially infants and toddlers, belong at home with their mothers. This attitude, however, does not reflect what is happening in the workplace. The fastest growing group of new workers is women with children under the age of six.

## CHARACTERISTICS OF A QUALITY INFANT/TODDLER CENTER

Many of the quality characteristics mentioned in our discussions of child care centers for preschool and school-aged children also apply to infant/toddler centers. A study by the National Institute of Child Health and Human Development (1996) highlighted the following as critical to the provision of sensitive, warm, responsive care:

◆ A low caregiver-to-infant/toddler ratio was the number one indicator of quality. The closer the ratio came to 1:1, the higher the quality. Thus, high-quality care was frequently found in home settings with relatives and sitters.

◆ A smaller group size provided for higher-quality care.

◆ Caregivers who were less authoritarian were more likely to provide positive interactions with infants.

◆ A safe, uncluttered physical environment with age-appropriate materials was an important quality indicator.

*Student Teacher Quote*—"I asked to be placed in an infant/toddler center. Student teaching there pointed out caregiver skills I hadn't dreamed of. Thank heavens I've a strong back. That's really necessary!"

**Michaela Grossman, Center for Infants and Toddlers, Pleasanton, CA**

Reinsberg (1995) lists *security* as the most important factor, so infants can develop a sense of trust. To accomplish this, "primary caregivers and other consistent staff are the single most important factor." At Reinsberg's college center, student teachers were assigned for longer periods of time, to provide for greater consistency and to reduce the caregiver–infant/toddler ratio to 1:2 on most days.

To respond to the NICHD finding about group size, the center kept the group size in the infant/toddler room lower than the number for which it was licensed. To guarantee greater safety for rapidly growing infants, a partition was installed to separate the very young infants from the older, more mobile ones.

Diapering routines were changed to become more responsive to the needs of the children. Rather than adhering to a strict schedule, caregivers began to wait until they noticed that an infant appeared uncomfortable, or that a toddler was ready for a change. Then, adhering to the principles outlined by Magda Gerber (trained by Dr. Pikler in Hungary prior to her immigration to the United States), caregivers slow down the process of changing diapers. They talk to the child about what they are doing and involve the child in the process (see Figure 12–1). In this the caregivers are modeling similar behaviors as those observed by Gonzalez-Mena (2004) in Hungary when she visited the Pikler Institute. (Gonzalez-Mena was familiar with the work of Gerber, who founded the organization Resources for Infant Educarers.) The same process—going slowly, talking to the child about what was happening, involving them—was followed when feeding the infants and toddlers.

The emphasis must be on responsive caregiving in daily activities, such as feeding, grooming, diapering, and bathing, where the focus is on close, one-to-one interactions with infants and toddlers (Gonzalez-Mena, 2004; Petersen & Wittmer, 2008). Infants essentially need and desire one-on-one interaction with caregivers—physical contact, attention, and sensitive recognition of their attempts to communicate. Relevant, tailor-made caregiver actions and responses lead to early conversation skills, which promote social, intellectual, and emotional development as well as language growth. This happens when adults listen and observe closely and truly believe that infants are constantly communicating. This happens as they share intimate moments, verbalize, maintain eye contact, smile, and enjoy mutual, playful episodes. The key points at Pikler's Institute include:

◆ Valuing independent activity. Caregivers do not interfere with a baby's ability to discover pleasure in free movement, and they constantly reinforce the activity generated by the child.

▶ **Figure 12-1**
The curriculum in an infant center includes changing diapers.

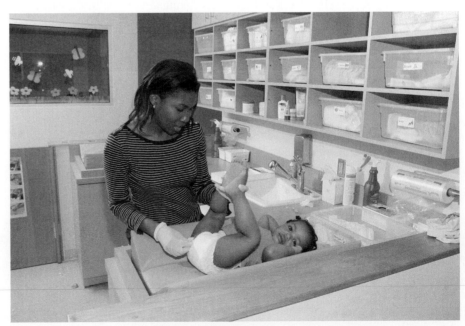

◆ Developing a special caring relationship between the adult and the child. Caregivers take a consistent, gentle approach, in which they show respect for each child's personality, and understand his or her needs.

◆ Treating the child like a partner. Caregivers foster children's self-awareness by encouraging them to be active participants in whatever is happening. This helps them to know, express, and assert themselves as individuals. Children become active partners in every interaction. (Gonzalez-Mena & Chahin, 2004)

In agreement with the concept of responsive interactions with infants, Wingert and Brandt (2005) state:

> Science is now giving us a much different picture of what goes on inside [infants'] hearts and heads. Long before they form their first words or attempt the feat of sitting up, they are already mastering complex emotions—jealousy, empathy, frustration—that were once thought to be learned much later in toddlerhood.

The concerns of Wingert and Brandt are seconded by Lally and Mangione (2006), who insist that infancy demands responsive care. Learning by infants begins in the womb, and from conception infants follow developmental paths that are genetically programmed and genetically wired:

> Babies have their own learning agenda . . . to learn language, to become more skillful in their . . . muscle functioning, to construct knowledge about . . . people and things in the world about them, to seek out significant relationships . . . and to use relationships to learn appropriate and inappropriate ways of relating to others (Lally & Mangione, 2006).

Petersen and Wittmer (2008) further affirm the need for responsive caregiving of infants. They emphasize the need for what they call "on-demand" caregiving with the very young as each infant maintains his own unique schedule. Although much of a day may be spent in the routines of care, such as eating, diapering, and napping, each "moment of care can be filled with rich and affectionate interactions between the baby and the teacher."

Another aspect of responsive care is touching the child. Carlson (2005) reminds us about how much touch matters:

> Humans need nurturing touch for optimum emotional, physical, and cognitive development and health—especially in infancy. Daily touch plays a significant role in early brain development.

Close communication with parents and the need to reevaluate what teachers do at an infant center is essential to assure continuing quality care. Many centers chart feeding times and amounts, sleeping times, and diapering times in a notebook that goes home with the parent every day. The parent then enters the feeding, sleeping, and diapering times in the same notebook and brings it back to the center each day. What procedures does your center use?

The following characteristics are needed in an infant/toddler center:

◆ Kind, leisurely physical and emotional care from one primary caregiver comes first.

◆ Encouragement for parents to stay and play as much as they can. (This may be one reason for the growing number of businesses with child care facilities on site or located nearby.)

◆ Caregivers that take time to provide the emotional support a baby needs.

◆ Caregivers that have one primary goal: each baby should have a happy day.

## Quality Family Child Care

In the home of one of our former students, three large, sunny rooms in the bottom level of her split-level house serve as a family child care center. A fourth room, the downstairs bathroom, houses the changing table and potty chairs for the preschoolers. A door from the room used by the preschoolers opens to a large fenced backyard, with a climbing structure and covered sandbox. In the infant room, a large playpen serves to separate the older, crawling babies from the very small ones.

Our former student and her daughter are licensed for a total of 12 infants, toddlers, and preschoolers. Although she could take more infants, she will only enroll two, and no more than four toddlers, together with six preschoolers. Of the two infants for whom she cares, one is more mobile than the other and is allowed to roam safely in the carpeted room. A mirror is attached to the wall at floor level, as infants thoroughly enjoy looking at themselves. Electrical outlets are covered and no electrical cords are evident. A rocking chair is in one corner of the room. A bookshelf loaded with appropriate toys for the crawler to reach is along the wall. A second bookshelf contains small board books with brightly colored pictures and minimal stories.

The four toddlers have a second room, separated from the infant room by a gate. In the toddler room are more age-appropriate toys: books, blocks, cars, trucks, trains, puzzles, and other stimulating things lined on shelves within reach of toddlers and preschoolers (see Figure 12–2). A small table with four chairs is along the window wall and a soft couch is on the opposite one. The walls are brightly painted with cartoon characters, compliments of a friend who is a commercial painter.

Preschoolers share a third room, separated from the toddler room by a low partition that allows caregivers to easily monitor activities.

## Special Issues in Infant/Toddler Care

In caring for the very young infant, there are several critical issues that arise: the question of whether early care may interfere with how infants form attachments to their parents, problems of separation from the parents, and how the infants as toddlers develop a sense of identity.

**Attachment Issues** Over the past 20 or so years, there have been many studies of **attachment**. One of the crucial issues in infant/toddler care is whether the children involved will establish bonds with working parents. Studies have shown that infants do bond with their parents, and in centers where they are consistently assigned to one caregiver for extended periods of time, infants will establish secondary bonds with that caregiver. This is why in some infant/toddler centers,

**attachment**—the child's bond with a teacher or caregiver, established over time through personal interaction. A child's primary attachment is usually to her parents.

▶ **Figure 12-2**
In this family care home, everything is within reach of older infants and toddlers.

a caregiver will move with the child from the infant to the toddler room. Watson (2003) writes, "When primary caregivers are responsive and sensitive to children's needs, these supportive experiences allow children to develop secure attachments and view relationships as reciprocal and cooperative." She continues to explain that as these attachments are developed, children acquire the ability to trust and enlist help from adults, in support of the child's learning and development.

In other words, infants secure in their bonds to parents and caregivers will be able to resolve the Erikson task of learning to trust and learn to ask for help from significant adults in their lives by age three, as Burton White (1975) has suggested.

**Separation Issues** Historically, mothers stayed home, and those who worked were frequently regarded negatively. Many mothers approach the use of child care with feelings of guilt, even though family finances may dictate that they work. Added to this is *society's* condemnation of working mothers—especially those with infants—and parents' concerns about how to find a caregiver they can trust in a quality care setting.

Dombro and Lerner (2006) mention that some parents, usually mothers, become concerned that their children will form a primary attachment to their respective caregivers rather than to them. Sharing care with another can and does provoke strong feelings, and Dombro and Lerner caution caregivers to:

◆ Be aware of the impact that their words and actions can have on others.

◆ Help families recognize the central, forever roles they play in their child's life. Assure families that no one can take their place.

◆ Acknowledge the feelings that caring can stir up; these can sometimes be difficult to admit and handle.

◆ Communicate respectfully and effectively.

◆ Understand, appreciate, and address differences.

In addition, they recommend the following:

◆ Good infant and toddler programs assign a primary caregiver to each child. In the former student's home-based child care center, the mother had the primary care of a newly enrolled, two-month-old infant. At nine months, when the child was crawling, she enrolled a second, very young infant (six weeks old). The daughter had the primary care of the second infant and the mother retained the primary care of the older one.

◆ Caregivers should have formal and informal communication with parents about the details of the child's day, to help form viable partnerships. A notebook—mentioned before, with notations of feeding, sleeping, and diaper change times—that goes back and forth between caregiver and parent is certainly one way of maintaining formal contact. As the infant grows, notations can include such milestones as turning over, sitting up, walking, and so on. Taking a few minutes to converse when the infant is brought in or picked up allows for informal communication.

◆ Low staff turnover is essential to building emotional trust between caregiver and infant and between caregiver and parent.

**The Issue of Identity Formation** If, as research states, a baby is emotionally part of his parents, just as he was physically a part of them prior to birth, how does an infant/toddler center deal with the child's developing sense of being *separate* from the parent—his sense of identity? Lally and Mangione (2006) believe that infants develop a sense of self during their first 2 years. "How they are treated and what they are allowed to do or not to do is incorporated into the infant's developing self." They assert that the way in which adults respond to the infants' needs impacts the child's **identity formation**. In addition, "because security, exploration, and identity formation manifest themselves differently during the infancy period," adult responses must fit the child's developmental stage (Lally & Mangione, 2006).

**identity formation**— the way in which a young child separates from his parents and establishes his own character traits and personality.

▶ **Figure 12-3**
Books are placed in a rack that toddlers can access easily.

Lally and Mangione (2006) further agree on the need for responsive infant/toddler care. They assert that infants learn in a holistic way, in that they are continually learning. Furthermore, infants rapidly move from one developmental stage to another. It therefore is essential that caregivers be responsive to infants and toddlers. Caregivers should allow the children to make their own choices as to what toys they want to play with and what books to peruse (see Figure 12–3) or which puzzles to reconstruct, to guarantee their optimal development.

## Infants and Toddlers with Special Needs

Batshaw (Batshaw, Pellegrino, & Roizen, 2008) points out that in the United States, 6.9 babies out of 1,000 died during their first year of life in the year 2000. The most common causes were related to prematurity. However, if you are placed in an infant/toddler center, you are more likely to see children whose mothers were substance abusers during pregnancy than you are to see infants with more serious medical needs. As newborns, infants may have had to be withdrawn from the drugs the mother was using. Frequently, a mother abuses more than one substance, and it is often difficult to know which are involved.

Children born to mothers who are substance abusers are often placed in foster care, with a trained foster mother who knows how to care for babies with special needs. "Many of these children qualify for early intervention services . . . [and] the short-term effects of intervention are encouraging in terms of gains in language acquisition and socialization skills" (Batshaw, Pellegrino, & Roizen, 2008).

Batshaw then affirms:

◆ the effectiveness of early intervention

◆ the mandate of the law that special needs children be included with their non-disabled peers

◆ the need for families to have access to services like quality care, education, and special intervention

◆ the fact that increasingly diverse populations of infants and toddlers present great challenges to child care and educational systems

◆ the need for action to support child care and education, in meeting the challenges of diversity and inclusion

◆ the need to validate the quality of infant/toddler programs, and that these should support full inclusion

◆ the necessity for child care, health care, and education to be integrated, and for individualized care and education to be provided to all infants, toddlers, and their families

◆ to this end, the need for collaboration among the different fields of early childhood mentioned above

◆ the right for all infants, toddlers, and family members to child care, education, and intervention, to be delivered by trained personnel, with appropriate certification or licenses, who are adequately compensated (Sexton, Snyder, Sharpton, & Stricklin, 1993)

## Infants Born to Teenage Parents

DeJong and Cottrell (1999) state that child care programs for children born to teenage parents must have some extra features not found in most infant/toddler care settings. She stresses that teenage parents present unique challenges. One frustration for the teacher occurs when the parent appears to be disinterested in her child. Another happens when "a teen appears to compromise the needs of her infant to get on the good side of her boyfriend or when she repeatedly brings an unclean baby or dirty bottles to the center." DeJong and Cottrell assert that they have found Erikson's model of social-emotional development helpful (see Chapter 6). They have noted that many of their teen mothers had not resolved earlier stages of development, especially trust.

DeJong and Cottrell believe then that the major goals of programs for these special parents must be to help them:

◆ Stay in school, to earn a high school diploma or its equivalent.

◆ Continue their post-secondary education.

◆ Improve their parenting skills.

◆ Reduce repeat pregnancies.

◆ Deliver normal-birth-weight babies, of at least 5.5 pounds.

## STUDENT TEACHING WITH INFANTS AND TODDLERS

An infant/toddler center is an entirely new world, one that is completely different from the preschool environment. Every infant/toddler center is operated a little differently. However, most centers have similar regulations regarding children's health, caregivers' health, feeding, and diaper-changing procedures. A student teacher should request a staff handbook. Read it before you go to the center. Be prepared to ask questions about anything that you do not understand. Babies need consistency, and it is important that you be able to fit into the center routines as quickly as possible. Most importantly, relax and enjoy the children!

## APPROACHING AND WORKING WITH VERY YOUNG CHILDREN

When working with infants and toddlers, remember that every child is an individual. Even tiny infants have preferences. They may prefer to sleep on their sides rather than their backs, although because of the possibility of **sudden infant death syndrome (SIDS)**, the American Pediatric Association urges parents to place their newborns on their backs. Some infants like a special blanket or soft toy to hug when they nap; others like a pacifier. Some infants may like to be burped over your shoulder, rather than across your knees. When caring for infants, take a minute to try and find out what some of their preferences may be.

When working with children of this age, remember:

◆ Your size may be frightening to a child.

◆ Keep confidential material to yourself. Medical, financial, personal, and family information is privileged information that helps you understand the child more completely.

### Working with Infants

Children need to hear your voice; talk to them and softly sing lullabies to them (Honig, 2005). They need the social contact that only another person can provide. Hearing language is also how children learn to talk. Be sure to use clear, simple language. *Speak softly.* Voice tone and volume greatly affect small children. If you speak in a loud, excited voice, the children are very likely to become loud and excited in response.

**sudden infant death syndrome (SIDS)—** where death of an infant occurs without warning, generally during the first three months of life and for which there is no known cause.

Sharing music can be a playful, energizing experience: Think of songs by Raffi, Dan Zanes, Laurie Berkner, and Ella Jenkins. On the other hand, cradle songs or lullabies can calm and soothe children and help them relax and sleep (Honig, 2005). In an earlier study, Kemple, Batey, and Hartle (2004) mention that "infancy and early childhood are prime times to capitalize on children's musical spontaneity and to encourage their natural inclinations to sing, move, and play." Play, according to these authors, is the vehicle through which young children best learn, and music and play are difficult to separate, as both are interactive, social, creative, and joyful.

*Encourage anticipation* by telling children what you are going to do. Say, "Now we are going to change your diaper." They will respond and cooperate when you let them know what to expect.

Try to *be at eye level* with children. Sitting or kneeling on the floor brings you closer to their line of vision. *Make eye contact.* When bottle-feeding, playing, diapering, and the like, look directly at children. Meet and hold their gaze when talking to them, and *smile.* You like to have people look at you; babies undoubtedly feel the same way.

*Move slowly* around infants. Young children do everything in slow motion. They often get upset and overstimulated when adults run around them excitedly. Young infants need time to understand the changes that are happening. Be affectionate and warm but *do not hover.* Be ready to hug, hold, and comfort when they need it, but let them be free to explore. Young children need to be able to move around and experience their environment. They need to find their own solutions to problems whenever they can. Let children experiment with toys and invent new uses for them. Intervene only when they are likely to get hurt, are obviously in distress, or are too frustrated to cope.

Becoming independent, competent, and self-sufficient is hard work; children need loving, secure adults and a safe place to begin the process. *Encourage babies to help you* in care giving. You need to dress them, change them, and feed them. However, they will help if you let them. Recognize their attempts to participate, and encourage them. Allowing them to help does not take much longer, and the rewards are many times greater.

There has been an increased use of signing with infants as a result of current attention to infants' and toddlers' communication and pre-reading skills (Meyer, 2005). Early childhood infant educators are much more aware of infants' attempts to communicate with nonverbal hand, arm, facial, eye, and body movements or expressions. Almost all adults realize that arms extended upward means a child wants to be picked up; most adults know to watch children's eyes to find out what has attracted their attention. Skilled caregivers working in infant centers may understand each infant's unique and individual signing attempts, and then imitate and pair the child's signs with simple words or phrases (e.g., "bottle" or "ball, you want the ball?"). Meyer writes that babies as young as 6 months are able to learn and use basic signs to tell their caregivers that they would like milk, food, or a diaper change. This gives infants the knowledge that they are indeed communicating, for their signs elicit caregiver actions.

Researchers believe this signing interaction does not inhibit but rather enhances the infants' and toddlers' eventual use of words. Acredolo and Goodwyn (2000) found that successful signing by babies stimulates brain development, particularly in areas involving language, memory, and concept development.

## Working with Toddlers

Toddlers are a very special group. They are just beginning to understand that they are people (see Figure 12–4). They are seeing themselves as separate from their parents for the first time. They are compelled to explore and understand their environment (see Figure 12–5). They must assert themselves as individuals. If you can recognize their need to be individuals without feeling personal insecurity, you will have made a giant step in dealing effectively with them.

*Student Teacher Quote*—"One of my friends said I'd never want children of my own if I worked at a toddler program. Wrong! It made me want children of my own even more."

**Briana DeLong, Center for Infants and Toddlers, Pleasanton, CA**

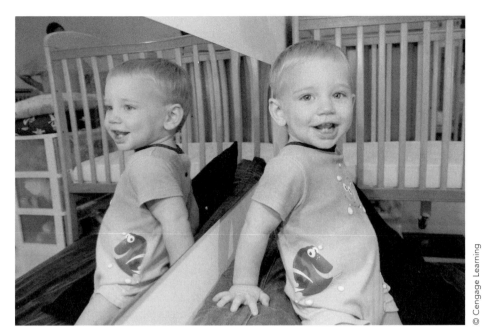

▶ **Figure 12-4**
This toddler sees himself as a separate individual.

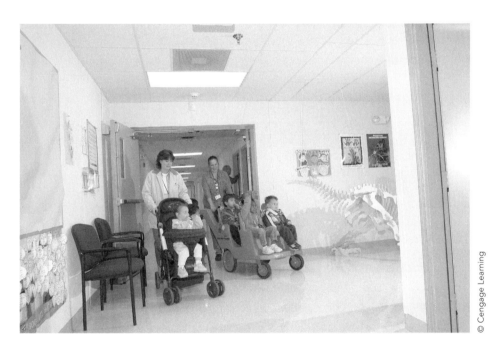

▶ **Figure 12-5**
Going on a long walk may require special equipment, and lots of teacher help.

Toddlers, more so than infants, will challenge your authority. They may test you until they can feel secure in your response. You will need to call on all your reserves of strength, firmness, patience, and love to deal with them. They are loving, affectionate, giving, sharing, joyful, spontaneous people; take pleasure in them.

You may find some of the following ideas helpful when working with toddlers. Read the suggestions and think about them. Try to put them into practice.

- *Make positive statements.* "Feet belong on the floor." When children hear the words *don't* and *no* constantly, they begin to ignore them.

- *Give choices only when you intend to honor them.* If Johnny's grandmother said that her son must wear his jacket when playing outside, do not ask Johnny, "Do you want your jacket?" Instead, say, "Your grandma wants you to wear a jacket today." If you give a choice and the toddler tells you no, you are already in a conflict that you could have avoided.

◆ *Avoid problems by being alert.* Watch for signs that a child may be getting too frustrated to handle a situation, or that a fight over a toy is about to start.

◆ *Use distraction* whenever possible. If you see two children insisting on the same toy, see if the children can work it out themselves. If not, try to interest one of them in something else. You might point out a toy just like it or remind them of another enjoyable activity.

◆ If an argument does erupt, *avoid taking sides.* Help both children understand how the other child feels.

◆ *Encourage the use of words* to handle situations. Encourage the children to name things, to express happiness, sorrow, excitement, and other emotions.

◆ *Let the children talk.* Correct grammar and pronunciation will come later. Practicing verbal expression is the most important thing.

◆ *Act on your own suggestions.* If you say, "Time to clean up. Start putting the toys away," the children are more likely to follow your suggestions if they are accompanied by actions.

◆ Make *alternative suggestions.* If some children continually ignore safety rules or disturb others, suggest an alternate activity the child likes; suggest taking turns; suggest cooperation, or remove the child from the activity. Be firm but calm.

◆ *Do not take the children's reactions personally.* You may hear: "I don't like you!" Say: "I know you are angry. It's okay to be angry." Toddlers respect fairness and desperately want limits that they can depend on.

◆ *Do not make promises you cannot keep.* Just say that you will have to ask if you do not know if something is allowed or possible. Toddlers understand that.

## GENERAL RULES AND REGULATIONS

The physical setting and philosophy of a center will determine how various routines are carried out. Centers usually have specific rules and routines regarding health and safety, medications, emergencies, feeding, diapering, and naps.

### Health and Safety

◆ Smoking is not allowed in infant/toddler centers.

◆ Coffee, tea, and other beverages should only be consumed in staff areas.

◆ Never leave a child unattended on a changing table or in a high chair.

◆ Do not leave children unattended inside or outside. They can easily injure themselves.

◆ Ill infants should not be in the center. Infants who have bad colds, fevers, or contagious diseases are usually cared for at home.

◆ If you are ill, you should not be in the center. You will not be efficient if you are not feeling well. In addition, your illness may spread to the children. If you contract a contagious illness, notify the center immediately.

◆ Wash your hands often. The most important health measure you can take is to wash your hands before and after diapering or cleaning noses and before feeding a child.

◆ Watch for signs that a child may not feel well. Some symptoms are digging at or pulling ears, listlessness, glassy eyes, diarrhea, and limping.

◆ Parents should be given the names of any facility or child care home that specializes in caring for sick children, including infants and toddlers.

## Medication

Normally, only a regular staff person will be allowed to give medication. You should be aware of medication schedules for the children. But you also need to be aware of the effects that medications may have on the children. They may become sleepy, agitated, or may even have an allergic reaction. You must be alert to changes that may occur when medicine is given and communicate these to the staff. (Staff must be given written parental/guardian permission and directions regarding any medications to be given to an infant.)

## Emergencies

If a child experiences a health or safety emergency:

◆ *Stay calm.*

◆ Speak calmly and quietly to the child.

◆ Alert the staff that an emergency has occurred. They should be able to administer the appropriate first aid measures until the child can see a physician.

◆ Help calm the other children. They will respond to the situation the same way that you do. If you are agitated and upset, they will respond to your feelings; likewise, if you remain calm, they usually will also.

## Feeding

◆ *Wash your hands. Again!*

◆ Read the child's chart to see what kind of food, expressed breast milk, or formula to give and how much. (Remember: Do not feed a child from a baby food jar; use a dish or disposable cup [see Figure 12–6]. Saliva, which contains bacteria, will get in the jar and spoil the remaining food.)

◆ Gather all the things you need for feeding: bib, washcloth, spoons, sponges, and so on. It may be helpful to bring one spoon for you to feed the child and a spoon for the infant to "help."

◆ Tell the infant what you are going to do. Let her anticipate being fed.

◆ Settle the child comfortably. You may want to make sure the child has a clean, dry diaper before feeding so she will be more comfortable and attentive.

◆ The child will let you know when more food is desired. When she opens her mouth, respond by feeding.

◆ Talk to the child. Eating is a time to enjoy pleasant conversation and socialization, as young children like being talked to. You can talk about the food, its texture, color, temperature, and taste. Eye contact is important.

◆ Encourage the child to help feed himself. It is a little messier, but it means more independence later.

◆ If the child refuses to take the last ounce of a bottle or the last little bit of solid food, do not push it. Children know when they are not hungry.

◆ Be sure to burp bottle-fed children when they need it. You may want to check with the child's caregiver for any special instructions.

◆ When the baby is finished, wash her face and hands. Again, tell her you are going to do this and encourage the child to take part in this activity. Be gentle with the washcloth.

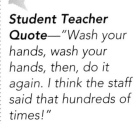

▶ **Figure 12-6**
In this toddler center children are encouraged to serve themselves.

© Cengage Learning

◆ Take off the bib and put the baby down to play.

◆ Clean up. Be sure to wipe off the high chair, the tray, the table, and the floor. Put dishes and bottles in the sink.

◆ Record what and how the child ate.

## Diapering

◆ Gather everything you need to change the baby: diapers, clean clothes, baby wipes, medicated ointment (if needed), and anything else that may be required.

◆ Tell the child what you are going to do. Set the child on the diaper table.

◆ Keep one hand on the child at all times.

◆ Take off the wet diaper and clean the child thoroughly with a warm, wet cloth. Apply any ointment according to the parent's instructions.

◆ Talk to the child about the process. Talk about being wet, dry, and clean. Describe the process of dressing and undressing; you can talk about the baby's clothes and body parts. Involve the baby in the process. Ask the child to lift the legs or give you an arm to put through the sleeve. (Note: How diapers are changed also gives children messages about their sexuality. If you are relaxed and casual about changing them and washing their genital areas, children get the message that they are okay.)

◆ Put the child in a safe place. Dispose of the diaper and soiled clothes according to the directions you are given.

◆ Clean the changing table using a germicidal solution.

◆ Wash your hands. Clean changing tables and clean hands help prevent the spread of disease.

◆ Record the diaper change. Be sure to note bowel movements. Make a note of any diarrhea, constipation, diaper rash, unusually strong urine odor or color, or anything else that seems out of the ordinary.

## Toilet Learning

Toilet learning is too frequently treated with embarrassment in parenting books, and meager research has been done on the topic. Many parents and caretakers do not understand that although bladder and bowel control is a skill, it may not be taught; it is learned.

Infants begin life with automatic emptying of the bladder and bowel. Bladder capacity is so small that wetting may occur every hour or so. Automatic emptying is triggered by the filling of the bladder or bowel, which sets off rhythmic contractions over which the infant has no control.

It is not until the nervous system matures during the first year or two that infants and toddlers show awareness of the sensations of a full bladder or bowel. What behaviors would alert you to this?

◆ a look of concentration while all activity stops

◆ crossing the legs

◆ fidgeting

◆ holding onto the crotch

◆ less frequent wetting

◆ regularity you can count on

◆ a keener awareness of body functions

◆ a sudden dislike of things messy

◆ a more sensitive sniffer

◆ use of relevant vocabulary

◆ improving communication abilities

◆ some self-dressing skills

◆ an interest in the habits of others

Conscious holding of urine is helped by a gradually increasing bladder capacity. By the second year, capacity has usually doubled, and the frequency of wetting is about every 2 or 3 hours. Emptying is still automatic and dependent on a full bladder or bowel. When parents or caregivers boast that toddlers at 14, 18, or 21 months are toilet trained, be aware: this is more often an indication that the adult recognizes the signs of impending need and places the child on the potty than it is an indication that the child has learned how to use the toilet.

In some cultures, parents support their infants in toilet use at very young ages. This is accomplished "through close observation, physical contact, emotional support, mutual trust, and reading non-verbal cues" (Baba, 2003). When parents place their infants in an infant care center, their expectations may be that caregivers will continue to support the infants' toilet use. This can lead to misunderstandings if caregivers and parents have different perceptions about the time for toilet learning. Caregivers should be sensitive to the point of view of parents and try to honor their requests. At the same time, caregivers must be honest about their own needs and time restrictions. Open communication between caregivers and parents is essential.

By age three, most children have learned to resist the emptying of their bowels until it suits them. At this age also, most children have learned to hold urine for a considerable time when the bladder is full. This holding ability requires conscious control of the perineal muscles, which are used in the same way as the bowel sphincter. At this age, however, accidents often occur because children do not have total control over urine release. This becomes obvious when the child who has just been taken to the toilet and not urinated goes back to play and immediately wets.

During the fourth year, most children have acquired conscious control over both bowel and bladder muscles. But it is important to remember that full control is not completely accomplished until about six years of age, when starting the urine stream from a partially full bladder becomes possible.

Learning bladder and bowel control is far from simple. Think of what children must learn:

◆ to remove and replace pants

◆ to use toilet tissue

◆ to flush the toilet, eventually

◆ to wash and dry their hands upon completion

In spite of these complexities, most children acquire toileting skills with a minimum of help (see Figure 12–7).

## When Should Toilet Learning Begin?

Caregivers must acknowledge that toilet learning will be most successful when the child shows clear signs of recognizing bladder or bowel tension. These signs vary from child to child; you will be able to recognize them after they have occurred several times, just before the child has wet or had a bowel movement. Look for any of the following signs, mentioned earlier: stopping what he is doing and concentrating, crossing his legs as if trying to prevent himself from wetting, beginning to fidget, pulling at you, making sounds of distress or using baby words such as *wee-wee*, or putting his hands on his crotch as if he feels his bladder is about to empty.

▶ **Figure 12–7**
By repeatedly flushing the toilet, this toddler is becoming familiar with the sound of the toilet.

© Cengage Learning

Sparrow (2004) cautions about being aware of when a child needs more time to learn, stating that caregivers and parents should look to see if the child does the following:

♦ stands at the potty chair and urinates on the floor, or takes off his diaper and soils the chair

♦ appears comfortable with, or indifferent to, a soiled diaper

♦ wants to keep a diaper on and fights efforts to remove it

♦ hides before soiling herself; this shows she is aware of her body functions but is not ready to involve a caregiver with them

♦ withholds bowel movements

♦ becomes frantic when his skin makes contact with a toilet seat, or when he hears a toilet flushing and sees a bowel movement disappear

Sparrow (2004) also provides caregivers with five training tips:

1. Parents can invite the child to pick out her own potty chair; caregivers may allow her to choose which potty to use.

2. Choose a potty that sits on the floor. She will see this as her own potty and may even want to pull it around behind her.

3. With boys, add plastic urine deflectors, which are meant to direct a boy's urine into the potty. Remember, though, children can be hurt by the deflectors when they sit on the potty.

4. If she's interested, let the child sit on the potty in her diapers or clothes. This will help her become accustomed to the routine. Be aware that a cold potty can inhibit the child.

5. As the child sits on the potty, let him sit for only as long as he chooses. If he wants to run off, let him. He may need some time to get used to what it feels like.

## How Do You Handle Accidents?

The number one rule to remember is that *accidents are inevitable*. Treat accidents matter-of-factly: Wash your hands, change the child's pants, and clean him without showing any irritation. Afterwards, wash your hands again, and disinfect any surfaces contacted by soiled clothing or hands. If you miss a child's cue, or do not move fast enough to help the child urinate or defecate in the potty, compliment the child on his ability to try to get your attention. Recognize that some accidents may be your fault, not the child's.

Many people will give you advice about toilet learning. Your cooperating teacher may follow a routine of taking toddlers to a potty chair at regular intervals. Even if you know that most toddlers do not acquire complete control until 4 to 6 years of age, you can go along with the center's policy; regular toileting helps those toddlers with regular rhythmicity acquire control at an earlier age than those with an irregular rhythmicity (see Figure 12–8). If a parent complains that her child was "toilet trained" before she placed him in the child care center and is angry because your cooperating teacher has asked her to bring in diapers, let the cooperating teacher handle the problem. If the parent tries to involve you, defer to center policy. Be patient with those parents who keep their child in diapers at age three. Perhaps as busy, working parents, they find it easier than to try to learn the subtle cues the child may be providing.

## One Final Word on Toilet Learning

Most children learn by example. As a two-year-old learns to use the toilet independently, she becomes a role model for other children. In a family-type center with a mixture of ages, older children act as role models for the younger ones. Parents also become role models for their children at home. Treat toilet learning like the natural process it is and do not worry about the three-year-old who is still having daily accidents.

© Cengage Learning

▶ Figure 12-8
This girl is learning to use the toilet.

Check for problems such as constipation, diarrhea, painful urination, and so on. Check for any dietary-related difficulties; a diet low in fluids and fiber will often be to blame for constipation. Above all, relax and do not make a big deal about toileting. All children will learn eventually, with or without formal teaching.

## Biting

Next to toilet learning, probably no other behavior causes as many difficulties for teachers and caregivers than does biting. Ramming, Kyger, and Thompson (2006) find that biting "is a typical, frequent phenomenon in toddlers." They state that it is related to stress experienced by the child, especially if the child is a three-year-old. Gillespie and Seibel (2006) assert that biting occurs when the child becomes frustrated and loses the ability to self-regulate. They suggest that caregivers can help children learn how to self-regulate by:

◆ observing closely

◆ responding to individual needs

◆ providing structure and predictability

◆ arranging developmentally appropriate environments

◆ defining age-appropriate limits

◆ showing empathy and caring

Other guidelines include:

◆ Understand that aggression occurs most often because the toddler is unable to express wants, needs, or feelings in words.

◆ Make a determination of what situations lead to the child's biting. Intervening and suggesting to the child that she can use words will help. Actually saying what you think the child is thinking also works, especially with a child who does not have many words in his expressive vocabulary.

◆ Remember that redirection and distraction can be very effective with toddlers.

◆ Respond when biting occurs by giving a firm, clear message that the behavior is not acceptable. Use the same words on each occasion: "No biting, John," or "Biting is not allowed, Keisha."

- ◆ Remove the biter to a short time-out after the incident.
- ◆ Console the child who was bitten.
- ◆ Note whether the biting appears to be related to teething; try offering the child a teething ring or a soft, pliable plastic toy to chew.
- ◆ Deal with biting immediately. Asking a parent to talk about biting at home is ineffectual. Toddlers cannot remember carry-over instructions.
- ◆ Remember that toddlers need a lot of time and repetition to learn new behaviors. You may want to keep a record of how many times a day the biting occurs and at what times of day.
- ◆ Ask for the parents' help to reinforce substitute behaviors for biting when the child is at home.

What should you tell parents about biting incidents? In a student teaching assignment, defer to your cooperating teacher; she will know what to do. She is likely to do the following:

- ◆ As briefly as possible, tell the parents of the child who was bitten what happened. Do not tell the parent the name of the biter.
- ◆ Ask the parents of the biter if he has bitten anyone at home. It is important to determine whether the behavior occurs only in the child care setting or if it also happens at home.
- ◆ Enlist parents' help in eliminating the behavior. Suggest that parents teach the child to use words, not teeth. Teach the parents to use the same phrases that are used at the center: "Biting is not allowed." Consistency is the key.

## Using Conflict Resolution with Toddlers

When dealing with conflict between toddlers, Ramming, Kyger, and Thompson (2006) suggest that, before intervening, caregivers should look at what is happening. How aggressive are the toddlers? Is the conflict emerging or has it already escalated (see Figure 12–9)? Given toddlers' immature social development, they feel that conflict is inevitable and that caregivers' approaches to resolving conflict should be on prevention. By taking time to assess where the toddlers are in the *process* of a conflict, caregivers will understand better how to react. Can the caregiver prevent whatever conflict might erupt? Once conflict has appeared, which intervention strategies work best?

Among the suggestions provided are:

- ◆ Remain at the children's eye level.
- ◆ Watch and wait before interceding.
- ◆ Use *I* messages.
- ◆ Move closer to the conflict.
- ◆ Use language that tells the toddlers what you see happening.
- ◆ Prevent injury by interceding quickly when necessary.
- ◆ Provide just enough help to allow toddlers to solve their own dilemmas.
- ◆ Be available to comfort each child by remaining at the child's level, squatting, with your arms open.
- ◆ Stay until toddlers disengage from the scene.
- ◆ Model gentleness to the aggressor.
- ◆ Offer yourself, instead of objects, for comfort; offer your lap to a child seeking comfort.
- ◆ Continue to verbalize what you see going on by using active, reflective listening.

Do not try to fix the problem, and do not overreact; above all, do not expect a toddler to respond in more mature ways.

▶ **Figure 12-9**

Strategies for caregivers to use when toddlers come into conflict with each other. Reprinted by permission of D. A. Da Ros and B. A. Kaach, and ACEI. Copyright© 2001 by ACEI.

| | | | Process of Conflict | | |
|---|---|---|---|---|---|
| | **Potential Conflict** | **Emerging Conflict** | **Engaging Conflict** | **Struggling Conflict** | **(Disengaging) Resolving Conflict** |
| **Toddler Behavior** | Aggressive acting Child in close proximity to other children | Two toddlers in opposition over object Dissipate/escalate | Toddlers fully involved Engage in physical contact Not at maximum level | Emotionally invested in process (crying, yelling) Actively engaged in physical contact Tug-of-war Climatic Stakes are high | Win, lose, or draw Emotional process is diffusing Anticipate Disengaging |
| **Caregiver Strategies** | Keenly observe More proximal | Assess at child's eye level Analyze Remain neutral Nonjudgmental | Watching and waiting Keep safe Allow natural consequences Remain neutral, attentive, focused | "I" messages; use singular pronouns Verbalize what is happening (sportscasting) Prevent hurting Available to each Keep own emotions in check Model gentleness | Provide help for them to problem-solve Available to each Do not leave scene until a toddler leaves Model gentleness Verbalize affect, emotions |
| | | | Level of Intrusiveness | | |
| | **Least intrusive** | | **Moderate** | | **Interactive** |

## Nap Time

Young children vary considerably in their nap times. You must be alert to signs of sleepiness in order to prevent a young child from becoming overtired. Toddlers usually learn very quickly to adjust to the nap schedule of the program. Watch for yawning, rubbing of eyes, pulling of hair, thumb sucking, and disinterest in toys or people. All these are signs that a young child may be ready for a nap.

Before putting a child down to nap, check his schedule. Make sure he is dry and not due to be fed soon. You may want to feed a child a little ahead of schedule if he appears sleepy. Make sure you have a clean crib and blanket (see Figure 12–10). Also, check to see if the child has any special toy he likes to sleep with.

A child who is new to the center may be reluctant to take a nap. This may be because the child is in an unfamiliar place that is full of strangers. Check to see if the child prefers to sleep on her back, side, or stomach, but remember: as a precaution against SIDS, most infants are placed on their backs to sleep. If the parent assures you that the infant prefers sleeping on his stomach, be sure that no smothering hazards exist, such as a pillow in the crib, a stuffed toy, or too soft a cover too close to the baby's face. Many older infants and toddlers enjoy sleeping on their stomachs.

Naptime is a part of the curriculum in an infant/toddler center.

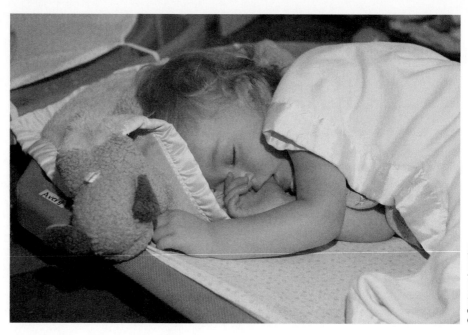

You may find it helpful to sing softly, rub the infant gently on the belly, or provide a rocking motion to help the child settle down to sleep. Dimming the lights may help calm the child. Many times, all the excitement of the center and the other children makes it difficult for babies to sleep. Be patient but firm.

Do not feel as though you have failed if you do not get instant success. Ask staff for suggestions. Infant center personnel are usually more than willing to answer questions, listen to concerns, or offer suggestions.

## CAREGIVING AS A TEACHING ACTIVITY

Consider the following skill areas, usually included in the preschool program: motor, cognitive, language, social, sensory, self-esteem, and mathematics. All these are encountered during routine caregiving activities. Bauer, Fortin, and McPartlin (2006) argue for a new model for infant curriculum development, composed of four building blocks:

- ◆ personal relationships
- ◆ classroom environment
- ◆ family connections
- ◆ caregiving routines

Think about caregiving routines and about what aspects of an infant curriculum are involved when you *change a diaper*:

| Caregiver Action | Curriculum Area |
|---|---|
| ◆ You talk to the child, stating what is going to happen. The child is developing a sense of sequential events. | language development<br>mathematics<br>social development |
| ◆ You take off the child's diaper and let the legs move freely. The child feels the air on the body. | motor development<br>sensory stimulation |
| ◆ You tell the child that the diaper is wet or contains a bowel movement. | cognitive development<br>sensory stimulation |

© Cengage Learning

◆ You wash the child with a washcloth or baby-wipe. You apply diaper rash medication if necessary. You talk about how this feels.

sensory stimulation
language development
cognitive development

◆ You put a new diaper on the child and possibly, new clothes. The new diaper is dry and feels more comfortable.

sensory stimulation
language development
cognitive development

◆ You talk about what is happening, encouraging the infant to help you by lifting the legs, putting out an arm, and so on.

language development
motor development
social development

◆ The infant is now more comfortable and probably happier. You have had an opportunity for a special one-to-one experience with the child. For a few minutes of a busy morning, the infant has your complete attention.

self-esteem
sensory stimulation
social development

What about *feeding?*

◆ You know it is time to give a bottle or feed a child. You tell the child you are going to prepare the food. You are again helping the child develop a sense of sequence of time.

mathematics
language development
social development

◆ The young infant may be just starting to eat or just learning to eat from a spoon; the older infant may be using fingers or learning to use a spoon. How special he feels when he succeeds!

motor development
language development
self-esteem

◆ You sit with the child or a small group of children while they eat lunch. You talk about what they are eating, about how the food tastes, its texture, and color. A child who does not like peas may be encouraged to try three peas or two pieces of carrot.

social development
language development
cognitive development
sensory stimulation
mathematics

◆ The bottle-fed child or slightly older infant has your total attention. You talk to the child. You make eye contact while feeding the infant, holding him close and safe.

self-esteem
language development
sensory stimulation

◆ After the child has eaten, you wash his face and hands with a warm, wet cloth. First, the right hand; then, the left. The older child may be able to help you.

sensory stimulation
language development
cognitive development
motor development

Diapering and feeding are just two examples of the many routines that happen in an infant center. Think of how many things are happening to a child during these routines. Think about what else is happening. What other messages is the infant receiving? Think about bathing and dressing to go outside. What about nap time? What kinds of things could you do that would make nap time smoother? What can you do to make each routine a more complete experience for each child?

# A CURRICULUM FOR INFANTS AND TODDLERS

A good infant/toddler curriculum meets children's early developmental needs within a responsive, play-based environment (Bergen, Reid, & Torelli, 2009). It takes into consideration "broader family, and societal influences that affect infant and toddler development and learning" (Bergen et al., 2009).

A question often raised by people who are unfamiliar with infants and toddlers is "What do you mean when you say you *teach* them? Don't they just play?" Yes, they do play—that's how they learn. Many people—including parents—underestimate just how much their children learn during their first years of life. Geist (2003) looks at how infants and toddlers explore math through play activities, how children's behaviors relate to mathematics, and what you as a teacher can do to enhance these learning experiences.

Parish, Rudisill, Schilling, McOmber, Bellows, and Anderson (2006) stress how important it is to ensure that toddlers have ample opportunity for active, physical play in a safe environment. They decry the current problems of inactivity and its relationship to obesity in young children and suggest that centers and preschools provide a variety of physical activities. Some activities take place in large groups, but others occur through individual opportunities to explore attractive equipment, such as a climbing structure and tricycles, or toys, such as balloons, balls, cups, and other available materials at your center or school.

Segatti, Brown-DuPaul, and Keyes (2003) maintain that even very young children problem solve. An infant who accidentally creates a noise with a rattle may then purposefully make the sound over and over. Older infants take much joy in playing peekaboo with an adult, and they may deliberately hide a toy under a scarf for the sheer excitement of finding it again and again. Through trial and error, toddlers may discover that while one child cannot push a wagon up a small incline, two can. Yet another may find out that if she spins around with a bubble wand, the bubbles rush out more rapidly than if she stands still. "In quality programs teachers stimulate development by recognizing and encouraging spontaneous problem solving" (Segatti et al., 2003).

Butler (2004) emphasizes the need for older infants and toddlers to be active. She urges teachers to get down on their knees and play with children, sing with them, and read with them, even if reading is not sequential and the child continually turns to a favorite picture in the story book.

Quann and Wien (2006) write about the ability of infants and toddlers to show empathy for one another. They define *empathy* in very young children as the "capacity to observe the feelings of another and to respond with care and concern for that other." They note that in the laboratory school where Quann worked, three different forms of empathy were observed: *proximal empathy,* where a child shows concern for a classmate who is close by; *altruistic empathy,* where a child offers concern in response to another child in distress, who is not nearby; and *self-corrective empathy,* where a child offers concern in response to something he or she has done that has caused distress to another.

## NAEYC's Developmentally Appropriate Practice in Infant and Toddler Programs

Editors Copple and Bredekamp's (2009) *Developmentally Appropriate Practice in Early Childhood Programs: Third Edition* contains a section devoted to appropriate practices in infant and toddler settings. They received permission from Zero to Three to reprint the section on development in the first 3 years, which can be found in the above-named publication as Part 2: "Developmentally Appropriate Practice in the Infant and Toddler Years—Ages 0–3" (Zero to Three, 2008).

This introduction is followed by an extensive list of examples of *Developmentally appropriate* practices, *in contrast* to inappropriate ones. Some examples of these practices follow:

*Relationship between caregivers and child*

<u>Developmentally appropriate</u>

There is sufficient continuity of care to ensure that every infant and parent can form a positive relationship with one or two primary caregivers.

Caregivers spend most of the day holding or touching infants in one-on-one interactions that are warm and caring. Caregivers stroke and pat infants and talk in a pleasant, calm voice, making frequent eye contact.

<u>In contrast</u>

Infants are shifted from group to group or cared for by whichever adult is available at the moment. Caregivers leave infants for long periods in cribs, playpens, or seats. They follow "no touch policies," ignoring the importance of touch to children's healthy development.

Caregivers interact with infants harshly or impersonally, or they ignore infants' cues that they do not want to be held or touched. Or they give more attention and warmth to certain children (e.g., in family care, favoring their own child).

*Sensory environment*

<u>Developmentally appropriate</u>

The play areas offer children a variety of touch experiences (e.g., soft and hard areas, different levels).

<u>In contrast</u>

There is no carpeting and no contrast between soft areas and harder ones.

The play areas are sterile, designed for easy cleaning but lack different textures or levels.

*Play spaces*

<u>Developmentally appropriate</u>

Caregivers put infants in cribs mainly to sleep, not to play. During play periods, they place babies on firm surfaces where they can move freely and safely.

<u>In contrast</u>

Babies are confined to cribs, infant seats, or playpens for long periods (e.g., for caregivers' convenience or "to keep infants safe").

*Exploration and play*

<u>Developmentally appropriate</u>

Caregivers value infants' exploration and play. They observe what each child is doing or focusing on, comment verbally on the play, and provide a safe environment for it. This quiet support encourages children's active engagement.

<u>In contrast</u>

Infants are interrupted; toys are dangled, put into their hands, or whisked away. Caregivers impose their own ideas on the play without regard to the child's interests, or they play with the toys themselves while the child merely watches.

*Reciprocal relationships with families*

<u>Developmentally appropriate</u>

Caregivers communicate daily with parents in a warm, honest, and respectful way to build mutual understanding and trust, which help in resolving any issues that may arise.

<u>In contrast</u>

Caregivers communicate with parents rarely or only when there are problems or conflicts.

Other headings include such topics as routines, the relationship between caregiver and child, and policies. For more complete information, please read the section in the NAEYC publication mentioned previously.

Lally (1999) identified three stages of development for infants and toddlers that educators and student teachers may find helpful. These are:

◆ birth through 8 months—*the early months*

◆ eight- to eighteen-month-olds—*crawlers and walkers*

◆ eighteen-month-olds to three-year-olds—*toddlers and two-year-olds*

Lowman and Ruhmann (1998) remind practitioners that toddler environments should not be scaled-down versions of preschoolers' classrooms. Classrooms that could be best described as being saturated with sensorimotor activities are more developmentally appropriate. Lowman and Ruhmann recommend a simplified arrangement, with four activity areas:

**1.** large motor zone

**2.** dramatic-play zone

**3.** messy zone

**4.** quiet zone

*Multi-S environments*, a term coined by Lowman and Ruhmann, include simplicity, seclusion, softness, sensory features, stimulation, stability, safety, and sanitation.

## ACTIVITIES IN THE INFANT/TODDLER CENTER

Play can usually be divided into two types: *social play*, in which a child interacts with an adult or another child; and *object play*, in which the child interacts with an object or toy. Children of all ages engage in both types of play and the following guidelines hold true for any child.

### Effective Social Play

◆ Activities for infants are not preschool activities that are geared down. Infants are a specific age group, and they need specific activities.

◆ Play *with* children, not *to* them. Try to interact, not entertain. The adult can initiate the activity but should wait for the child to respond.

◆ Involve different ways of communicating in your social interactions: looking, touching, holding, talking, rocking, singing, and laughing. Give infants a lot of different social responses to learn.

◆ Be sensitive to infants' signals. If they are interested, they will laugh, coo, look, smile, and reach. If tired or disinterested, they may fuss, turn away, or fall asleep.

◆ *Talk* to infants. Children learn speech from the moment they are born. The more language they hear, the more they will learn. Name actions, objects, and people.

◆ Offer new ways of doing things. Demonstrate how something works. Encourage persistence. Do not direct children as to the "right" way to use a toy; let them explore and experiment. Obviously, if some danger is involved, use your judgment and intervene when necessary.

◆ Be sensitive to variations initiated by the child, and be ready to respond to them.

A child can use play materials either alone or with an adult. Adults should use judgment in the choice of materials presented to each age group. A toy that a two-month-old might enjoy might not be appropriate for a nine-month-old. When offering materials to the children, remember:

◆ Toys and materials should encourage action. Materials should not just entertain but elicit some action.

◆ Toys should respond to the child's action. When the child pushes or pulls a toy, the toy should react. The ability to control parts of one's world, to learn cause and effect, is an important part of learning at this early age.

◆ Materials should be versatile. The more ways a toy can be used, the better it is.

◆ Whenever possible, toys should provide more than one kind of sensory output. For example, a clear rattle lets the child see, as well as hear, the action.

Play and playthings are an important part of the environment. Do not believe that constant stimulation is the aim. Even very young infants need time to be alone and to get away from it all. It is important to be sensitive to the infant's cues about feelings to help avoid overstimulation and distress.

The following are some activity ideas for infants 1 to 12 months old. Remember that some activities are appropriate for many ages.

◆ Change the infant's position for a different view.

◆ Use bells, rattles, and spoons to make noise.

◆ Exercise the infant's arms and legs.

◆ Put large, clear pictures at eye level for the infant to look at.

◆ Imitate the sounds the infant makes.

◆ Put toys slightly out of reach to encourage rolling over and reaching.

◆ Take the babies outside on warm days. Let them feel the grass and see trees and plants.

◆ Call the children by name.

◆ Play peekaboo with the children.

◆ Make puppets for children to look at and hold.

◆ Let children play with safe, unbreakable mirrors.

◆ Play games and sing, using parts of the body. Make up songs about feet, hands, noses, and so on.

◆ Show children how to bang two toys together.

◆ Let the child feed herself. Give peas, diced cooked carrots, or small pieces of fruit to practice with (see Figure 12–11).

◆ Play patty-cake and sing *Row-Row-Row Your Boat*. Encourage children to finish the songs for you.

◆ Listen for airplanes, trucks, cars, dogs, and the like, outside, and call the children's attention to them.

◆ Roll a ball to the child and encourage the child to roll it back.

◆ Play music for the children; encourage them to clap along.

◆ Have hats for the children to wear. Let them see themselves in the mirror.

◆ Read to the children. Point out the pictures; encourage the child to point to them.

◆ Let the children play with different textures.

◆ Put toys upside down and sideways. See how the children respond to the changes.

◆ Show the children how to stack blocks.

▶ **Figure 12-11**
Allow toddlers to practice feeding themselves.

© Cengage Learning

© Cengage Learning

▶ **Figure 12-12**
Infants and toddlers enjoy outdoor exploration.

◆ Let children play with measuring cups and spoons in water, sand, or cornmeal.

◆ Play follow-the-leader.

◆ Make an incline for the children to roll objects down.

◆ Have children set the table with plastic cups and dishes.

◆ Hide a clock or toy under a towel and see if one of the children can find it.

◆ Let children finger paint with nontoxic paint.

◆ Let them go barefoot in sand and grass, so they can feel the textures (see Figure 12–12).

◆ Encourage children to help put their toys away.

◆ Let them practice opening containers (e.g., plastic margarine bowls). Put a toy in the container to encourage them to open it.

◆ Make toys for the children; be inventive, and let your imagination go! Remember that toys should have no sharp edges, and they should be too large to fit in babies' mouths.

Infant activities gradually become more and more complex as children mature. Usually, by 12 to 14 months, the child is walking and beginning to talk. An infant at this age is quite accomplished mentally. He understands that objects are separate and detached. The infant rotates, reverses, and stacks things, and places them in containers and takes them out again, to further consider their separateness.

Projects for toddlers can be more complex in response to their increased mental and physical abilities. Small-group activities can usually be tried with some success. When working with toddlers and planning activities for them, remember that the activities should be kept as simple as possible. And *plan ahead*. Anything that can go wrong will. Bring everything needed to start and finish the project with you.

Following are some ideas you might want to try with toddlers. Watch the children and see what you think they might enjoy.

◆ *Easel painting* (one-color paint; mix with small amount of liquid soap to make it easier to wash the paint out of clothes).

◆ *Waterplay.* Use measuring cups for pouring.

◆ *Coloring.* Use a limited number of large-size crayons and a large sheet of paper. For a change, try covering the whole table with paper.

◆ *Collage.* Try using starch and tissue paper with paintbrushes.

◆ *Finger painting.* For a change, try yogurt or pudding, but be sensitive to the feelings of parents who do not want their children to play with food.

◆ *Paint on cloth* pinned to the easel. It makes a great gift for parents.

◆ *Flannelboard stories.* Keep them short and graphic.

◆ *Bubble blowing.* This should be done sitting down. Emphasize blowing through a straw. Use a cup with water and soap. Collect *all* straws; they can be dangerous if a child falls on them. Note: A small slit cut near the top of the straw prevents a child from sucking up soapy water.

◆ *Gluing.* Use torn paper, tissue, magazine pictures, and the like. Avoid small beans, peas, and so on, which could be swallowed or put up noses.

◆ *Modeling dough*, made with salt, flour, and nontoxic coloring.

◆ *Hand and footprints.*

◆ *Body tracings.*

◆ *Paint a large cardboard box*; cut shapes in the sides. Children can climb through the sides after they paint it.

- *Go on a sock walk.* Have children remove their shoes (with parent permission) and go for a walk in the yard. Look at the seeds and other interesting items collected on the bottoms of the socks. Place any seeds collected on a wet sponge and watch them sprout in a few days. (More suitable for older toddlers.)
- *Do simple shape rubbings.* (More suitable for older toddlers.)
- *Make simple roll-out cookies,* or use frozen dough for the children to roll out and cut with cookie cutters.
- *Music.* Try drums, rhythm sticks, clapping games, and simple exercises to music.

Recent findings about music suggest that it may help the brain make connections, thus enhancing the child's ability to learn. Honig (2005) suggests that singing simple melodies is very soothing to babies; use the nonsense syllables they use. Do not be afraid to use a simple tune, like *Twinkle, Twinkle, Little Star. Happy Birthday* will work, too. Do not worry that you do not have a beautiful voice. Babies love all rhythmic, musical sounds. You do not even have to be able to carry a tune—infants will not care! You can also use a tape, CD, or MP3 player to play music softly in the background as infants and toddlers play.

Use music to announce transitions. Sing *Now We're Going out to Play* to the tune of *Mary Had a Little Lamb* and repeat it each time you go out. Soon you will find the children singing along with you (Kemple, Batey, & Hartle, 2004; Honig, 2005).

## CHILD'S PHYSICAL ENVIRONMENT

As a student teacher—the new adult at your placement site—you will need to study both indoor and outdoor space. Try to answer the following questions:

- Are there as many play spaces at any one time as there are children enrolled in the program?
- Are the outdoor spaces safe?
- Are climbing structures high enough to challenge the children but low enough, and cushioned underneath, so falls will not hurt or injure any child?
- Are there enough wheeled vehicles for the number of children who want to ride them?
- Is there a "road" for the wheeled vehicles to follow? Are traffic rules made clear and enforced?
- If there is a sandbox, is there a cover?
- Are water tables set away from major play areas but close to the water supply?
- If a splashing pool is used, is it located near the water supply and sufficiently far from the rest of the play area, to prevent children from being splashed who do not want to be wet? Is the pool drained at night and stored?
- Are there outside and inside water fountains? Are these at child height?
- If cups or plastic glasses are used, are they disposable or personalized, to minimize the spread of germs?
- Are there child-sized toilets or potty chairs? Are they easily accessible to children learning to use the toilet? Are they out of the way of crawlers? Are they disinfected frequently and always after bowel movements?
- Is there a sink for washing hands by the diaper changing table? Is there a sink in the staff bathroom area for washing hands after toileting? Is clean, dry toweling available?
- Do staff wash their hands before preparing food?
- Are children directed to wash their hands before eating (see Figure 12–13)?

▶ **Figure 12-13**

Encouraging children to develop a regular routine of hand washing is all part of the student teaching experience.

© Cengage Learning

## Infant and Toddler Language Development

It is never too early to read to children. Just the sound of the voice, the lilting quality of speech, and the caregiver's proximity ultimately aid in language acquisition. Initially, one may just point to pictures and name objects for children. Later, explanations can be expanded and children can be asked for feedback. Although it is never too early to read, it is important to gauge reading level and length of time spent on one activity according to how the children respond.

Ability to concentrate varies dramatically among children. However, it is true that very young children generally have very short attention spans. The ability to focus on a given object or activity increases dramatically in the first 3 years. Studies show that the observing child is participating and learning, even while not physically involved in the activity.

▶ **Figure 12-14**

Sharing a book with a toddler.

© Cengage Learning

Heavy cardboard books, designed for small hands, are excellent, easily handled manipulatives, and a wonderful way for children to have their first experiences with reading. Simple board books, with brightly colored pictures, and simple, repetitive story lines are best. *Brown Bear, Brown Bear, What Do You See?* is a good book for babies and toddlers, as are *Goodnight Moon*, *Guess How Much I Love You*, and *The Three Little Kittens*. Parents can point you to other good titles, as can your local children's librarian, especially newly published books or ones on special topics. The following are helpful guidelines for toddler reading activities:

◆ Read to a young child when you are in the mood to do so.

◆ Choose a book that is not only appropriate for the child but is also one you like.

◆ Remember that timing is important. A fussy baby or a busily playing toddler will not be interested in a book at that moment.

◆ Establish a special reading time.

◆ Position the child so that pictures can be seen easily. Many children enjoy sitting on your lap or cuddling next to you in an easy chair (see Figure 12–14).

◆ Allow the child to help you, and do not worry if they turn more than one page at a time or want to start in the middle of a favorite book. One toddler, whom we both know, wanted the same book read every day, for weeks, until he had committed it to memory!

- ◆ Point to and identify things in the pictures as you read.
- ◆ React positively to the child's attempts to name objects, turn pages, and verbalize.
- ◆ Use your voice as a tool; vary pitch, speed, rhythm, even loudness. Do remember, though, that a quiet voice is often best.
- ◆ Be responsive to the children; listen to their comments.

One surefire activity of interest to children of any age is music. Simply singing can create great excitement and provides tremendous opportunities for learning. Music uses words that are the same with every repetition, even with minor variations. Children learn words to songs more easily within the pattern of melody, rhythm, and rhyme, which enhances their language development. The use of props at music time reinforces learning. Songs incorporating body parts and movement bring forth squeals of delight from children. In the context of music, even the shy child is more readily drawn out and more willingly participates.

## AWARENESS OF YOUR OWN NEEDS AS A CAREGIVER

We have taken the preponderance of this chapter to discuss elements of caregiving essential to the optimal development of very young children. In reading and thinking about all these elements, you might have wondered if and why children ever turn out all right. How can any caregiver provide enough essential nurturance without smothering for good outcomes? Amidst wondering all this, you might also ask: "What about me as the provider? How can I take care of myself?"

The child care profession is notorious for low wages, long hours, and difficult assignments. Historically, providers have received little respect, few benefits, and not much money.

Although everyone talks about children representing the future, children can be the first to lose in times of economic hardship. Although the importance of the early years is widely acknowledged, we see poor allocation of resources to early childhood endeavors.

Fortunately, in recent years, more effort has gone into the area of early childhood development, the provision of child care, and the education of children in the early years. The early childhood education profession is also increasingly espoused by informed, educated, and intelligent providers. We must view ourselves as professionals, present ourselves to the world as professionals, and expect to be accepted as equals in a world of professionals. To accomplish this, we must first learn to value ourselves.

In your relationships with parents and coworkers, believe in your professional status and behave accordingly. Making yourself knowledgeable, keeping yourself interested, and treating your infant charges, their parents, and your coworkers sensitively and ethically will reap great rewards for you in how all these people respond to you in turn. Continue to educate yourself, not only by participating in classes and reading, but by remaining open to the different experiences of the different families in your center, the individual children, and the other staff members. A willingness to be aware of different needs and different capabilities in those around you is a hallmark of professionalism.

In the course of each day, as well as in a global sense, we as caregivers also must learn to take care of ourselves. Just as infants must be given opportunities to balance activity with periods of rest, providers must have opportunities to make choices in their activities, locations, and levels of stimulation. There are countless activities that potentially enhance any given domain of development. As the caregiver, select the one you can enjoy for that day. Children understand that the needs of their caregivers vary. They can, to a limited extent, moderate their levels of noise, activity, and curiosity if they understand that these conflict with the needs of their caregiver.

Perhaps most importantly, take your responsibilities seriously, but do not take responsibility for those elements of your job that you cannot change. Almost every child care center has dysfunctional families in attendance, and every center has its own internal challenges. Part of being a professional is the recognition of these challenges, the willingness to work to resolve what is in your power to change, and the ability to accept those aspects that are not changeable.

## Consistent Care

For the babies, consistent and responsive care is more complicated. If possible, infants should have the same caregiver for most of their time in child care. If it is absolutely necessary to have multiple caretakers, the child should be well acquainted with any secondary caregivers before her primary caregiver leaves. Any person involved with a group of children should have a thorough familiarity with the facility, its policies, and any program components.

Regular, routine care is essential for infants. Routines provide comfort and security for children, especially the very young. Learning and positive growth experiences are only possible when stress is at a minimum, and routine reduces stress for children. This does not mean that we should avoid novelty entirely. However, novel situations should occur in a context of predictability.

One of the most essential predictable elements must be that caregivers respond to the needs of the infants. Most early childhood experts agree that it is impossible to spoil a child before 6 months to a year of age (Bowlby, 1982; Elkind & Weiner, 1978; Spock & Rothenburg, 1992; White, 1975; Quann & Wien, 2006). White does not believe you can spoil a baby in the first 7 months of life. In fact, he strongly suggests that caregivers typically respond to a baby's crying in a natural way. Elkind and Weiner (1978) cite research studies indicating:

> [P]arents who respond to their infants' cries are likely to provide conditions of warmth and nurturance that will stop the crying, enable their children to feel secure, and make them less likely to cry or demand unreasonable attention in the future.

They go on to contrast the children of unresponsive parents; these children tended to fuss and cry a great deal later on.

Bowlby (1982) talks about spoiling in relation to attachment. He states:

> [N]o harm comes to [the child] when [the mother] gives him as much of her presence and attention as he seems to want. Thus, in regard to mothering—as to food—a young child seems to be so made that, if from the first he is permitted to decide, he can satisfactorily regulate his own "intake."

To echo these experts, a caregiver should respond promptly to calls for attention, attempt to discover the cause of discomfort or need, and if there is no serious problem, comfort the child. Only if she clearly cannot make an effective intervention after trying the above should she allow a young infant to "cry it out" (White, 1975).

For older children, too, responsiveness can only assist in nurturing a positive developmental outcome. The basic sense of trust comes out of having one's needs taken seriously and having them responded to appropriately. Not only will responsive care create trust for the caregiver but also the child will feel valued and validated, resulting in a positive sense of self-esteem. Elkind (2003) decries the misunderstandings about play that too many parents seem to hold. He maintains that the best way to prepare a child to face hardship is to provide a loving, nurturing environment in which she can develop self-esteem and trust in her caregivers. He concludes:

> As teachers of young children, we need to resist the pressures to transform play into work—into academic instruction. We encourage

true play by making certain that we offer materials that leave room
for the imagination—blocks, paints, paper to be cut and pasted—and
that children have sufficient time to innovate with these materials.
(Elkind, 2003)

Responsive care does not apply only to the crying infant. It is equally important
for the exploring, curious, learning toddler. Thus, responsiveness also applies to
awareness of developmental level; current level of functioning; and knowledge of
appropriate tasks, objects, and expectations for given ages.

## SAFETY

Probably the first element parents look for in a care situation is safety. Every parent and provider has heard countless times of the importance of childproofing
their space. Gerber (1971) advocates total noninterference with infants' exploration whenever possible, and this is possible, she says, only by providing a
totally safe, childproof environment geared to the developmental levels of the
children.

Among the essential considerations in childproofing are:

◆ Dangerous objects are not present or are locked up; these objects include sharp
  or breakable items, chemicals (drugs, cleansers, cosmetics), plastic bags, balloons, or other items that can cause suffocation. Furniture is sturdy, and bookcases are fastened to the wall so that the children learning to walk will not pull
  them down on themselves when using them for support or when attempting
  to climb them.

◆ Electrical sockets are plugged with childproof inserts; electrical appliances cannot be pulled down or turned on by children.

◆ Heaters are safe to walk on or touch, or are covered with a safety grate.

◆ Windows, drawers, and doors are latched with childproof latches.

◆ The facility is clean and well maintained; if used, rugs are fastened down and
  regularly vacuumed.

◆ Staff members do not drink hot liquids that can spill on children or that children can consume.

◆ Staff members are vigilant about activities of children, rather than conversing
  among themselves.

◆ Caregivers are aware of health hazards and infectious diseases, and take routine
  steps to minimize the spread of illness. It is an undervalued health fact that
  merely washing hands each time a diaper is changed or a nose is wiped can
  cut illness, or exposure to illness, by over 75 percent. Regularly wiping door-
  knobs, washing toys, and minimizing the use of baby bottles in the play area
  can likewise cut illness for both providers and children.

◆ Staff exercises awareness of contagious illnesses and their symptoms, with rigid
  attendance guidelines for children exhibiting those symptoms.

◆ Lists of toxic plants should be readily available, particularly if the center has
  either indoor or outdoor plants within a child's reach.

◆ Lists of parent emergency numbers, paramedics, and poison control centers
  should be posted in locations readily available and known to staff. Emergency
  treatment consent forms must be on file for each child, with guidelines about
  parental preferences.

◆ Lists of child allergies and medical conditions should also be readily available
  to staff.

◆ Food service should take into consideration potential spoilage of dairy products if left unrefrigerated or if mixed with even miniscule amounts of saliva.

## ▶ SUMMARY

In this chapter, we discussed why there is a need for quality infant and toddler care. We also mentioned some of the characteristics of quality programs. The research tends to reveal more positive outcomes of early care, especially in regard to later social adjustment, and cognitive and language development.

Infant and toddler center routines and procedures depend on the philosophy and physical setting. Every center has guidelines for caregivers' behaviors. Knowing guidelines and fitting quickly into center practice are prime student teacher goals.

Learning takes place during each child's encounter with a caregiver. Caregivers can develop many skills for the child's benefit. Many action activities and experiences planned for this age group incorporate reciprocal responses from adults and play objects. The roots of independence and verbal ability develop as do individual preferences.

## ▶ HELPFUL WEBSITES

**http://www.acf.hhs.gov/**
U.S. Department of Health and Human Services. Search for information on Early Head Start.

**http://www.zerotothree.org**
Zero to Three. Investigate their journal and other publications.

**http://www.naeyc.org**
National Association for the Education of Young Children. Select infant and toddler readings.

**http://www.nccic.org**
National Child Care Information and Technical Assistance Center. Find the online library.

**http://www.ehsnrc.org**
Early Head Start National Resource Center. Supports high-quality services to Early Head Start and Migrant Head Start.

**http://www.fpg.unc.edu**
Frank Porter Graham Child Development Institute. A multidisciplinary institute at the University of North Carolina at Chapel Hill, whose mission is to cultivate and share the knowledge necessary to enhance child development and family well-being.

 Additional resources for this chapter can be found by visiting the companion website at *www.cengage.com/education/machado.*

## ▶ SUGGESTED ACTIVITIES

**A.** If you have not worked or done student teaching in an infant/toddler center, visit one for an hour. List all staff behaviors that protect children's health or safety. Report your findings to the group.

**B.** In groups of three to four, discuss infant/toddler care for teenage parents. Decide what type of care would best suit the teenage parents in your community. Report your ideas to the class.

## ▶ REVIEW

**A.** List three characteristics of a quality infant/toddler center.

**B.** Describe how student teachers are expected to behave during emergencies.

**C.** List ways a caregiver could promote learning when bathing a 15-month-old child.

**D.** Select the answer that best completes each statement.
  1. The factor that may best limit the spread of infection is:
    a. periodic caregiver screening
    b. hand washing
    c. the use of spray disinfectants
    d. the use of clean sponges
  2. When feeding a young child:
    a. Watch for signals that indicate the child is full.
    b. Make sure the child finishes a small serving.
    c. Expect him to try a little of everything.
    d. Eat along with the child.
  3. Telling infants that it is time to change their diapers is:
    a. ridiculous and silly
    b. difficult
    c. not important
    d. important

4. An important part of student teachers' work in an infant and toddler center is:
   a. recording care specifics and asking when in doubt
   b. watching first, rather than pitching right in
   c. moving quickly and efficiently
   d. telling parents how their children are acting

5. If an infant or toddler is using a toy incorrectly:
   a. Demonstrate the proper usage.
   b. Ask another toddler to show how to use it correctly.
   c. Leave the child alone if it is not dangerous.
   d. Talk about the right way to use it.

## ▶ REFERENCES

Acredolo, L., & Goodwyn, S. (2000). *Baby minds: Brain-building games your baby will love to play.* New York: Bantam Books.

Baba, S. (2003, Spring). Diversity corner: Toilet learning in different cultures. *SMAEYC Newslink* [Newletter published by the San Mateo Association for the Education of Young Children], 2.

Batshaw, M.L., Pellegrino, M.D., & Roizen, N.J. (2008). *Children with disabilities* (6th ed.). Baltimore, MD: Paul Brookes Publishing Co.

Bauer, D., Fortin, S., & McPartlin, D. (2006, Spring). Solving the puzzle of infant curriculum: A model for infant curriculum development. *ACEI Focus on Infants and Toddlers, A Quarterly Publication for the Education Community, 18*(3), 3–8

Bergen, D., Reid, & Torelli, L. (2009). *Educating and caring for very young children. The infant/toddler curriculum* (2nd ed.). New York: Teachers College Press.

Bowlby, J. (1982). *Attachment and loss, 1* (2nd ed.). New York: Basic Books.

Butler, S. (2004, November/December). Play with me, sing to me, read to me, me: Fostering the development of toddlers through lots of activity. *Early Childhood News,* 28–31. Stout, WI: University of Wisconsin-Stout.

Carlson, F. M. (2005, July). Significance of touch in young children's lives. *Young Children, 60*(4), 79–85.

Copple, C., & Bredekamp, S. (Eds.). (2009). *Developmentally appropriate practice in early childhood programs* (3rd. ed.). Washington, DC: National Association for the Education of Young Children.

Da Ros, D. A., & Kaach, B. A. (2001, Fall). Assisting toddlers and caregivers during conflict resolutions: Interactions that promote socialization. *Childhood Education, 75*(1), 14–19.

DeJong, L., & Cottrell, B.H. (1999, January). Designing infant child care programs to meet the needs of children born to teenage parents. *Young Children, 54*(1), 33–39.

Dombro, A. L., & Lerner, C. (2006, January). Sharing the care of infants and toddlers. *Young Children, 61*(1), 29–32.

Elkind, D. (2003, May). Thanks for the memory: The lasting value of true play. *Young Children, 58*(3), 46–51.

Elkind, D., & Weiner, B. (1978). *Development of the child.* New York: John Wiley.

Geist, E. (2003, January). Infants and toddlers exploring mathematics. *Young Children, 58*(1), 10–12.

Gerber, M. (1971). *Resources for infant educarers.* Los Angeles: Resources for Infant Educarers.

Gillespie, L. G., & Seibel, N. L. (2006, July). Self-regulation: a cornerstone of early childhood development. *Young Children, 61*(4), 34–39.

Gonzalez-Mena, J. (2004, September). What can an orphanage teach us? Lessons from Budapest. *Young Children, 59*(5), 26–30.

Gonzalez-Mena, J., & Chahin, E. (2004, November). What's best for babies? Beyond right and wrong to different: Comparing philosophies of infant-toddler care. Paper presented at the *National Association for the Education of Young Children Conference,* November, 2004.

Honig, A. S. (2005, September). The language of lullabies. *Young Children, 60*(5), 30–36.

Kemple, K. M., Batey, J. J., & Hartle, L. C. (2004, July). Music play: musical play and exploration. *Young Children, 59*(4), 30–37.

Lally, J. R. (1995, November). The impact of child care policies and practices on infant/toddler identity formation. *Young Children, 51*(1), 17–22.

Lally, J. R., & Mangione, P. (2006, July). The uniqueness of infancy demands a responsive approach. *Young Children, 61*(4), 14–20.

Lowman, L., & Ruhmann, L. (1998, May). Simply sensational spaces: A multi-S approach to toddler environments. *Young Children, 53*(3), 32–36.

Meyer, D. (2005, August/September). The use of American sign language with infants and toddlers. *Early Childhood News,* 38–39. Stout, WI: University of Wisconsin-Stout.

National Institute of Child Health and Human Development. (1996). Characteristics of infant child care: Factors contributing to positive caregiving. *Early Childhood Research Quarterly, 11*(3), 378–394.

Parish, L. E., Rudisill, M. E., Schilling, T., McOmber, K. A., Bellows, L., & Anderson, J. (2006, May). Healthy today and tomorrow: three strategies that work. *Young Children, 61*(3), 32–38.

Petersen, S., & Wittmer, D. (2008, May). Relationship-based infant care: Responsive, on-demand, and predictable. *Young Children, 63*(3), 40–42.

Quann, V., & Wien, C. A. (2006, July). The visible empathy of infants and toddlers. *Young Children, 61*(4), 22–29.

Ramming, P., Kyger, C.S., & Thompson, S.D. (2006, March). A new bit on biting. The influence of food, oral motor development, and sensory activities. *Young Children, 61*(2), 17–23.

Reinsberg, J. (1995, September). Reflections on quality infant care. *Young Children, 50*(6), 11–14.

Segatti, L., Brown-DuPaul, J., & Keyes, T. L. (2003, September). Using everyday materials to promote problem solving in toddlers. *Young Children, 58*(5), 12–16, 18.

Sexton, D., Snyder, P., Sharpton, W. R., & Stricklin, S. (1993, Annual Theme Issue). Infants and toddlers with special needs and their families. *Childhood Education, 69*(5).

Sparrow, J. D. (2004, April/May). Getting ready for potty training: Let your child lead the way in learning. *Scholastic Parent & Child, 11*(5), 63–64.

Spock, B., & Rothenburg, M. (1992). *Baby and child care.* New York: Dutton.

Watson, M. (2003, July). Attachment theory and challenging behaviors: Reconstructing the nature of relationships. *Young Children*, 58(4), 12–20.

Wingert, P., & Brandt, M. (2005, August 15). Reading your baby's mind. *Newsweek*, 33–39.

White, B. (1975). *The first three years of life.* Englewood Cliffs, NJ: Prentice-Hall.

Zero to Three. (2008). Developmentally appropriate practice in the infant and toddler years—Ages 0–3. Development in the first three years of life in *Developmentally Appropriate Practice in Early Childhood Programs Serving Children from Birth through Age 8* (3rd ed.). Washington, DC: National Association for the Education of Young Children.

# Appendix

## INTRODUCTION

The materials in the Appendix complement the materials in the chapters listed but are auxiliary. You may find some selections more useful than others.

## CHAPTER 1

### Summary of portfolio issues and questions

**The characteristics of a useful portfolio are:**

**A clear purpose**

—To demonstrate progress toward applying competencies
—To facilitate student growth and reflection
—To provide supporting documents for articulation purposes

**Integration between coursework and fieldwork**

—Both processes and product are documented
—Student selected examples of applied theory are included
—Shows growth over time in the knowledge base

**Multiple sources of information**

—Attestations from instructors, supervisors, parents, and children may include evaluations
—Artifacts from courses and field experiences may be included
—Reproductions, including photographs, videos, and audio tapes, provide tangible evidence of skills

**Authenticity: a direct link between instruction and evidence**

—A road map such as a table of contents or preface is provided describing the organization of the portfolio
—Captions describing each document, its context, and the reason for including it are essential
—Course syllabi, including objectives and transcripts, detail training received

**Dynamic assessment: capturing growth and change over time**

—Reproduction from each practicum, fieldwork, and student teaching experience is provided
—Selected papers over the course of study are included
—Attestations from others reveal teacher strengths

**Student ownership**

—Personal statement clarifies ideals
—Philosophy of education for young children is included
—Selection of a style of organizing the portfolio and items to be included is chosen by the student, with appropriate guidance

**Multiple purposes: student growth and reflection, assessment and evaluation, and program evaluation**

—Identifies student strengths and weaknesses for setting goals with advisor support
—Facilitates peer support and feedback in regular portfolio sessions

—Provides feedback to instructors on the efficacy of instruction in a given course and in a program as a whole, particularly in the area of applying theoretical knowledge

—Offers tangible evidence of the degree of mastery of competencies, for purposes of articulation or transfer to more advanced study; reduces needless repetition of materials

—Shows degree of understanding of and experience with special needs, multicultural, and bilingual populations

Adapted from Turner, P. (Ed.). (2002). *La Ristra: New Mexico's comprehensive professional development system in early care, education, and family support.* Santa Fe, NM: Children, Youth and Families Department, State of New Mexico. Reprinted with permission.

# CHAPTER 2

## NAEYC CODE OF ETHICAL CONDUCT AND STATEMENT OF COMMITMENT

**Revised April 2005**

### A position statement of the National Association for the Education of Young Children

Endorsed by the Association for Childhood Education International

### Preamble

NAEYC recognizes that those who work with young children face many daily decisions that have moral and ethical implications. The **NAEYC Code of Ethical Conduct** offers guidelines for responsible behavior and sets forth a common basis for resolving the principal ethical dilemmas encountered in early childhood care and education. The **Statement of Commitment** is not part of the Code but is a personal acknowledgement of an individual's willingness to embrace the distinctive values and moral obligations of the field of early childhood care and education.

The primary focus of the Code is on daily practice with children and their families in programs for children from birth through 8 years of age, such as infant/toddler programs, preschool and prekindergarten programs, child care centers, hospital and child life settings, family child care homes, kindergartens, and primary classrooms. When the issues involve young children, then these provisions also apply to specialists who do not work directly with children, including program administrators, parent educators, early childhood adult educators, and officials with responsibility for program monitoring and licensing. (Note: See also the "Code of Ethical Conduct: Supplement for Early Childhood Adult Educators," online at www.naeyc.org/about/positions/pdf/ethics04.pdf.)

### Core values

Standards of ethical behavior in early childhood care and education are based on commitment to the following core values that are deeply rooted in the history of the field of early childhood care and education. We have made a commitment to

• Appreciate childhood as a unique and valuable stage of the human life cycle

• Base our work on knowledge of how children develop and learn

• Appreciate and support the bond between the child and family

• Recognize that children are best understood and supported in the context of family, culture,* community, and society

• Respect the dignity, worth, and uniqueness of each individual (child, family member, and colleague)

• Respect diversity in children, families, and colleagues

• Recognize that children and adults achieve their full potential in the context of relationships that are based on trust and respect

---

* The term *culture* includes ethnicity, racial identity, economic level, family structure, language, and religious and political beliefs, which profoundly influence each child's development and relationship to the world.

## Conceptual framework

The Code sets forth a framework of professional responsibilities in four sections. Each section addresses an area of professional relationships: (1) with children, (2) with families, (3) among colleagues, and (4) with the community and society. Each section includes an introduction to the primary responsibilities of the early childhood practitioner in that context. The introduction is followed by a set of ideals (I) that reflect exemplary professional practice and by a set of principles (P) describing practices that are required, prohibited, or permitted.

The **ideals** reflect the aspirations of practitioners. The **principles** guide conduct and assist practitioners in resolving ethical dilemmas.* Both ideals and principles are intended to direct practitioners to those questions which, when responsibly answered, can provide the basis for conscientious decision making. While the Code provides specific direction for addressing some ethical dilemmas, many others will require the practitioner to combine the guidance of the Code with professional judgment.

The ideals and principles in this Code present a shared framework of professional responsibility that affirms our commitment to the core values of our field. The Code publicly acknowledges the responsibilities that we in the field have assumed, and in so doing supports ethical behavior in our work. Practitioners who face situations with ethical dimensions are urged to seek guidance in the applicable parts of this Code and in the spirit that informs the whole.

Often "the right answer"—the best ethical course of action to take—is not obvious. There may be no readily apparent, positive way to handle a situation. When one important value contradicts another, we face an ethical dilemma. When we face a dilemma, it is our professional responsibility to consult the Code and all relevant parties to find the most ethical resolution.

### Section I

#### Ethical Responsibilities to Children

Childhood is a unique and valuable stage in the human life cycle. Our paramount responsibility is to provide care and education in settings that are safe,

* There is not necessarily a corresponding principle for each ideal.

healthy, nurturing, and responsive for each child. We are committed to supporting children's development and learning; respecting individual differences; and helping children learn to live, play, and work cooperatively. We are also committed to promoting children's self-awareness, competence, self-worth, resiliency, and physical well-being.

### Ideals

I-1.1—To be familiar with the knowledge base of early childhood care and education and to stay informed through continuing education and training.

I-1.2—To base program practices upon current knowledge and research in the field of early childhood education, child development, and related disciplines, as well as on particular knowledge of each child.

I-1.3—To recognize and respect the unique qualities, abilities, and potential of each child.

I-1.4—To appreciate the vulnerability of children and their dependence on adults.

I-1.5—To create and maintain safe and healthy settings that foster children's social, emotional, cognitive, and physical development and that respect their dignity and their contributions.

I-1.6—To use assessment instruments and strategies that are appropriate for the children to be assessed, that are used only for the purposes for which they were designed, and that have the potential to benefit children.

I-1.7—To use assessment information to understand and support children's development and learning, to support instruction, and to identify children who may need additional services.

I-1.8—To support the right of each child to play and learn in an inclusive environment that meets the needs of children with and without disabilities.

I-1.9—To advocate for and ensure that all children, including those with special needs, have access to the support services needed to be successful.

I-1.10—To ensure that each child's culture, language, ethnicity, and family structure are recognized and valued in the program.

I-1.11—To provide all children with experiences in a language that they know, as well as support children in maintaining the use of their home language and in learning English.

I-1.12—To work with families to provide a safe and smooth transition as children and families move from one program to the next.

NAEYC Code of Ethical Conduct  **3**  Revised April 2005

## Principles

**P-1.1—Above all, we shall not harm children. We shall not participate in practices that are emotionally damaging, physically harmful, disrespectful, degrading, dangerous, exploitative, or intimidating to children. *This principle has precedence over all others in this Code.***

P-1.2—We shall care for and educate children in positive emotional and social environments that are cognitively stimulating and that support each child's culture, language, ethnicity, and family structure.

P-1.3—We shall not participate in practices that discriminate against children by denying benefits, giving special advantages, or excluding them from programs or activities on the basis of their sex, race, national origin, religious beliefs, medical condition, disability, or the marital status/family structure, sexual orientation, or religious beliefs or other affiliations of their families. (Aspects of this principle do not apply in programs that have a lawful mandate to provide services to a particular population of children.)

P-1.4—We shall involve all those with relevant knowledge (including families and staff) in decisions concerning a child, as appropriate, ensuring confidentiality of sensitive information.

P-1.5—We shall use appropriate assessment systems, which include multiple sources of information, to provide information on children's learning and development.

P-1.6—We shall strive to ensure that decisions such as those related to enrollment, retention, or assignment to special education services, will be based on multiple sources of information and will never be based on a single assessment, such as a test score or a single observation.

P-1.7—We shall strive to build individual relationships with each child; make individualized adaptations in teaching strategies, learning environments, and curricula; and consult with the family so that each child benefits from the program. If after such efforts have been exhausted, the current placement does not meet a child's needs, or the child is seriously jeopardizing the ability of other children to benefit from the program, we shall collaborate with the child's family and appropriate specialists to determine the additional services needed and/or the placement option(s) most likely to ensure the child's success. (Aspects of this principle may not apply in programs that have a lawful mandate to provide services to a particular population of children.)

P-1.8—We shall be familiar with the risk factors for and symptoms of child abuse and neglect, including physical, sexual, verbal, and emotional abuse and physical, emotional, educational, and medical neglect. We shall know and follow state laws and community procedures that protect children against abuse and neglect.

P-1.9—When we have reasonable cause to suspect child abuse or neglect, we shall report it to the appropriate community agency and follow up to ensure that appropriate action has been taken. When appropriate, parents or guardians will be informed that the referral will be or has been made.

P-1.10—When another person tells us of his or her suspicion that a child is being abused or neglected, we shall assist that person in taking appropriate action in order to protect the child.

P-1.11—When we become aware of a practice or situation that endangers the health, safety, or well-being of children, we have an ethical responsibility to protect children or inform parents and/or others who can.

## Section II

### Ethical Responsibilities to Families

Families* are of primary importance in children's development. Because the family and the early childhood practitioner have a common interest in the child's well-being, we acknowledge a primary responsibility to bring about communication, cooperation, and collaboration between the home and early childhood program in ways that enhance the child's development.

### Ideals

I-2.1—To be familiar with the knowledge base related to working effectively with families and to stay informed through continuing education and training.

I-2.2—To develop relationships of mutual trust and create partnerships with the families we serve.

I-2.3—To welcome all family members and encourage them to participate in the program.

---

* The term *family* may include those adults, besides parents, with the responsibility of being involved in educating, nurturing, and advocating for the child.

I-2.4—To listen to families, acknowledge and build upon their strengths and competencies, and learn from families as we support them in their task of nurturing children.

I-2.5—To respect the dignity and preferences of each family and to make an effort to learn about its structure, culture, language, customs, and beliefs.

I-2.6—To acknowledge families' childrearing values and their right to make decisions for their children.

I-2.7—To share information about each child's education and development with families and to help them understand and appreciate the current knowledge base of the early childhood profession.

I-2.8—To help family members enhance their understanding of their children and support the continuing development of their skills as parents.

I-2.9—To participate in building support networks for families by providing them with opportunities to interact with program staff, other families, community resources, and professional services.

## Principles

P-2.1—We shall not deny family members access to their child's classroom or program setting unless access is denied by court order or other legal restriction.

P-2.2—We shall inform families of program philosophy, policies, curriculum, assessment system, and personnel qualifications, and explain why we teach as we do—which should be in accordance with our ethical responsibilities to children (see Section I).

P-2.3—We shall inform families of and, when appropriate, involve them in policy decisions.

P-2.4—We shall involve the family in significant decisions affecting their child.

P-2.5—We shall make every effort to communicate effectively with all families in a language that they understand. We shall use community resources for translation and interpretation when we do not have sufficient resources in our own programs.

P-2.6—As families share information with us about their children and families, we shall consider this information to plan and implement the program.

P-2.7—We shall inform families about the nature and purpose of the program's child assessments and how data about their child will be used.

P-2.8—We shall treat child assessment information confidentially and share this information only when there is a legitimate need for it.

P-2.9—We shall inform the family of injuries and incidents involving their child, of risks such as exposures to communicable diseases that might result in infection, and of occurrences that might result in emotional stress.

P-2.10—Families shall be fully informed of any proposed research projects involving their children and shall have the opportunity to give or withhold consent without penalty. We shall not permit or participate in research that could in any way hinder the education, development, or well-being of children.

P-2.11—We shall not engage in or support exploitation of families. We shall not use our relationship with a family for private advantage or personal gain, or enter into relationships with family members that might impair our effectiveness working with their children.

P-2.12—We shall develop written policies for the protection of confidentiality and the disclosure of children's records. These policy documents shall be made available to all program personnel and families. Disclosure of children's records beyond family members, program personnel, and consultants having an obligation of confidentiality shall require familial consent (except in cases of abuse or neglect).

P-2.13—We shall maintain confidentiality and shall respect the family's right to privacy, refraining from disclosure of confidential information and intrusion into family life. However, when we have reason to believe that a child's welfare is at risk, it is permissible to share confidential information with agencies, as well as with individuals who have legal responsibility for intervening in the child's interest.

P-2.14—In cases where family members are in conflict with one another, we shall work openly, sharing our observations of the child, to help all parties involved make informed decisions. We shall refrain from becoming an advocate for one party.

P-2.15—We shall be familiar with and appropriately refer families to community resources and professional support services. After a referral has been made, we shall follow up to ensure that services have been appropriately provided.

**NAEYC Code of Ethical Conduct**     **5**     Revised April 2005

## Section III

### Ethical Responsibilities to Colleagues

In a caring, cooperative workplace, human dignity is respected, professional satisfaction is promoted, and positive relationships are developed and sustained. Based upon our core values, our primary responsibility to colleagues is to establish and maintain settings and relationships that support productive work and meet professional needs. The same ideals that apply to children also apply as we interact with adults in the workplace.

#### A—Responsibilities to co-workers

**Ideals**

**I-3A.1**—To establish and maintain relationships of respect, trust, confidentiality, collaboration, and cooperation with co-workers.

**I-3A.2**—To share resources with co-workers, collaborating to ensure that the best possible early childhood care and education program is provided.

**I-3A.3**—To support co-workers in meeting their professional needs and in their professional development.

**I-3A.4**—To accord co-workers due recognition of professional achievement.

**Principles**

**P-3A.1**—We shall recognize the contributions of colleagues to our program and not participate in practices that diminish their reputations or impair their effectiveness in working with children and families.

**P-3A.2**—When we have concerns about the professional behavior of a co-worker, we shall first let that person know of our concern in a way that shows respect for personal dignity and for the diversity to be found among staff members, and then attempt to resolve the matter collegially and in a confidential manner.

**P-3A.3**—We shall exercise care in expressing views regarding the personal attributes or professional conduct of co-workers. Statements should be based on firsthand knowledge, not hearsay, and relevant to the interests of children and programs.

**P-3A.4**—We shall not participate in practices that discriminate against a co-worker because of sex, race, national origin, religious beliefs or other affiliations, age, marital status/family structure, disability, or sexual orientation.

#### B—Responsibilities to employers

**Ideals**

**I-3B.1**—To assist the program in providing the highest quality of service.

**I-3B.2**—To do nothing that diminishes the reputation of the program in which we work unless it is violating laws and regulations designed to protect children or is violating the provisions of this Code.

**Principles**

**P-3B.1**—We shall follow all program policies. When we do not agree with program policies, we shall attempt to effect change through constructive action within the organization.

**P-3B.2**—We shall speak or act on behalf of an organization only when authorized. We shall take care to acknowledge when we are speaking for the organization and when we are expressing a personal judgment.

**P-3B.3**—We shall not violate laws or regulations designed to protect children and shall take appropriate action consistent with this Code when aware of such violations.

**P-3B.4**—If we have concerns about a colleague's behavior, and children's well-being is not at risk, we may address the concern with that individual. If children are at risk or the situation does not improve after it has been brought to the colleague's attention, we shall report the colleague's unethical or incompetent behavior to an appropriate authority.

**P-3B.5**—When we have a concern about circumstances or conditions that impact the quality of care and education within the program, we shall inform the program's administration or, when necessary, other appropriate authorities.

#### C—Responsibilities to employees

**Ideals**

**I-3C.1**—To promote safe and healthy working conditions and policies that foster mutual respect, cooperation, collaboration, competence, well-being, confidentiality, and self-esteem in staff members.

NAEYC Code of Ethical Conduct · 6 · Revised April 2005

I-3C.2—To create and maintain a climate of trust and candor that will enable staff to speak and act in the best interests of children, families, and the field of early childhood care and education.

I-3C.3—To strive to secure adequate and equitable compensation (salary and benefits) for those who work with or on behalf of young children.

I-3C.4—To encourage and support continual development of employees in becoming more skilled and knowledgeable practitioners.

## Principles

P-3C.1—In decisions concerning children and programs, we shall draw upon the education, training, experience, and expertise of staff members.

P-3C.2—We shall provide staff members with safe and supportive working conditions that honor confidences and permit them to carry out their responsibilities through fair performance evaluation, written grievance procedures, constructive feedback, and opportunities for continuing professional development and advancement.

P-3C.3—We shall develop and maintain comprehensive written personnel policies that define program standards. These policies shall be given to new staff members and shall be available and easily accessible for review by all staff members.

P-3C.4—We shall inform employees whose performance does not meet program expectations of areas of concern and, when possible, assist in improving their performance.

P-3C.5—We shall conduct employee dismissals for just cause, in accordance with all applicable laws and regulations. We shall inform employees who are dismissed of the reasons for their termination. When a dismissal is for cause, justification must be based on evidence of inadequate or inappropriate behavior that is accurately documented, current, and available for the employee to review.

P-3C.6—In making evaluations and recommendations, we shall make judgments based on fact and relevant to the interests of children and programs.

P-3C.7—We shall make hiring, retention, termination, and promotion decisions based solely on a person's competence, record of accomplishment, ability to carry out the responsibilities of the position, and professional preparation specific to the developmental levels of children in his/her care.

P-3C.8—We shall not make hiring, retention, termination, and promotion decisions based on an individual's sex, race, national origin, religious beliefs or other affiliations, age, marital status/family structure, disability, or sexual orientation. We shall be familiar with and observe laws and regulations that pertain to employment discrimination. (Aspects of this principle do not apply to programs that have a lawful mandate to determine eligibility based on one or more of the criteria identified above.)

P-3C.9—We shall maintain confidentiality in dealing with issues related to an employee's job performance and shall respect an employee's right to privacy regarding personal issues.

## Section IV

### Ethical Responsibilities to Community and Society

Early childhood programs operate within the context of their immediate community made up of families and other institutions concerned with children's welfare. Our responsibilities to the community are to provide programs that meet the diverse needs of families, to cooperate with agencies and professions that share the responsibility for children, to assist families in gaining access to those agencies and allied professionals, and to assist in the development of community programs that are needed but not currently available.

As individuals, we acknowledge our responsibility to provide the best possible programs of care and education for children and to conduct ourselves with honesty and integrity. Because of our specialized expertise in early childhood development and education and because the larger society shares responsibility for the welfare and protection of young children, we acknowledge a collective obligation to advocate for the best interests of children within early childhood programs and in the larger community and to serve as a voice for young children everywhere.

The ideals and principles in this section are presented to distinguish between those that pertain to the work of the individual early childhood educator and those that more typically are engaged in collectively on behalf of the best interests of children—with the understanding that individual early childhood educators have a shared responsibility for addressing the ideals and principles that are identified as "collective."

NAEYC Code of Ethical Conduct 　　7　　 Revised April 2005

### Ideal (Individual)

**1-4.1**—To provide the community with high-quality early childhood care and education programs and services.

### Ideals (Collective)

**I-4.2**—To promote cooperation among professionals and agencies and interdisciplinary collaboration among professions concerned with addressing issues in the health, education, and well-being of young children, their families, and their early childhood educators.

**I-4.3**—To work through education, research, and advocacy toward an environmentally safe world in which all children receive health care, food, and shelter; are nurtured; and live free from violence in their home and their communities.

**I-4.4**—To work through education, research, and advocacy toward a society in which all young children have access to high-quality early care and education programs.

**I-4.5**—To work to ensure that appropriate assessment systems, which include multiple sources of information, are used for purposes that benefit children.

**I-4.6**—To promote knowledge and understanding of young children and their needs. To work toward greater societal acknowledgment of children's rights and greater social acceptance of responsibility for the well-being of all children.

**I-4.7**—To support policies and laws that promote the well-being of children and families, and to work to change those that impair their well-being. To participate in developing policies and laws that are needed, and to cooperate with other individuals and groups in these efforts.

**I-4.8**—To further the professional development of the field of early childhood care and education and to strengthen its commitment to realizing its core values as reflected in this Code.

### Principles (Individual)

**P-4.1**—We shall communicate openly and truthfully about the nature and extent of services that we provide.

**P-4.2**—We shall apply for, accept, and work in positions for which we are personally well-suited and professionally qualified. We shall not offer services that we

do not have the competence, qualifications, or resources to provide.

**P-4.3**—We shall carefully check references and shall not hire or recommend for employment any person whose competence, qualifications, or character makes him or her unsuited for the position.

**P-4.4**—We shall be objective and accurate in reporting the knowledge upon which we base our program practices.

**P-4.5**—We shall be knowledgeable about the appropriate use of assessment strategies and instruments and interpret results accurately to families.

**P-4.6**—We shall be familiar with laws and regulations that serve to protect the children in our programs and be vigilant in ensuring that these laws and regulations are followed.

**P-4.7**—When we become aware of a practice or situation that endangers the health, safety, or well-being of children, we have an ethical responsibility to protect children or inform parents and/or others who can.

**P-4.8**—We shall not participate in practices that are in violation of laws and regulations that protect the children in our programs.

**P-4.9**—When we have evidence that an early childhood program is violating laws or regulations protecting children, we shall report the violation to appropriate authorities who can be expected to remedy the situation.

**P-4.10**—When a program violates or requires its employees to violate this Code, it is permissible, after fair assessment of the evidence, to disclose the identity of that program.

### Principles (Collective)

**P-4.11**—When policies are enacted for purposes that do not benefit children, we have a collective responsibility to work to change these practices.

**P-4.12**—When we have evidence that an agency that provides services intended to ensure children's well-being is failing to meet its obligations, we acknowledge a collective ethical responsibility to report the problem to appropriate authorities or to the public. We shall be vigilant in our follow-up until the situation is resolved.

**P-4.13**—When a child protection agency fails to provide adequate protection for abused or neglected children, we acknowledge a collective ethical responsibility to work toward the improvement of these services.

# Glossary of Terms Related to Ethics

**Code of Ethics.** Defines the core values of the field and provides guidance for what professionals should do when they encounter conflicting obligations or responsibilities in their work.

**Values.** Qualities or principles that individuals believe to be desirable or worthwhile and that they prize for themselves, for others, and for the world in which they live.

**Core Values.** Commitments held by a profession that are consciously and knowingly embraced by its practitioners because they make a contribution to society. There is a difference between personal values and the core values of a profession.

**Morality.** Peoples' views of what is good, right, and proper; their beliefs about their obligations; and their ideas about how they should behave.

**Ethics.** The study of right and wrong, or duty and obligation, that involves critical reflection on morality and the ability to make choices between values and the examination of the moral dimensions of relationships.

**Professional Ethics.** The moral commitments of a profession that involve moral reflection that extends and enhances the personal morality practitioners bring to their work, that concern actions of right and wrong in the workplace, and that help individuals resolve moral dilemmas they encounter in their work.

**Ethical Responsibilities.** Behaviors that one must or must not engage in. Ethical responsibilities are clear-cut and are spelled out in the Code of Ethical Conduct (for example, early childhood educators should never share confidential information about a child or family with a person who has no legitimate need for knowing).

**Ethical Dilemma.** A moral conflict that involves determining appropriate conduct when an individual faces conflicting professional values and responsibilities.

### Sources for glossary terms and definitions

Feeney, S., & N. Freeman. 1999. *Ethics and the early childhood educator: Using the NAEYC code.* Washington, DC: NAEYC.
Kidder, R.M. 1995. *How good people make tough choices: Resolving the dilemmas of ethical living.* New York: Fireside.
Kipnis, K. 1987. How to discuss professional ethics. *Young Children* 42 (4): 26–30.

The National Association for the Education of Young Children (NAEYC) is a nonprofit corporation, tax exempt under Section 501(c)(3) of the Internal Revenue Code, dedicated to acting on behalf of the needs and interests of young children. The NAEYC Code of Ethical Conduct (Code) has been developed in furtherance of NAEYC's nonprofit and tax exempt purposes. The information contained in the Code is intended to provide early childhood educators with guidelines for working with children from birth through age 8.

An individual's or program's use, reference to, or review of the Code does not guarantee compliance with NAEYC Early Childhood Program Standards and Accreditation Performance Criteria and program accreditation procedures. It is recommended that the Code be used as guidance in connection with implementation of the NAEYC Program Standards, but such use is not a substitute for diligent review and application of the NAEYC Program Standards.

NAEYC has taken reasonable measures to develop the Code in a fair, reasonable, open, unbiased, and objective manner, based on currently available data. However, further research or developments may change the current state of knowledge. Neither NAEYC nor its officers, directors, members, employees, or agents will be liable for any loss, damage, or claim with respect to any liabilities, including direct, special, indirect, or consequential damages incurred in connection with the Code or reliance on the information presented.

### NAEYC Code of Ethical Conduct Revisions Workgroup

Mary Ambery, Ruth Ann Ball, James Clay, Julie Olsen Edwards, Harriet Egertson, Anthony Fair, Stephanie Feeney, Jana Fleming, Nancy Freeman, Marla Israel, Allison McKinnon, Evelyn Wright Moore, Eva Moravcik, Christina Lopez Morgan, Sarah Mulligan, Nila Rinehart, Betty Holston Smith, and Peter Pizzolongo, *NAEYC Staff*

# Statement of Commitment[*]

As an individual who works with young children, I commit myself to furthering the values of early childhood education as they are reflected in the ideals and principles of the NAEYC Code of Ethical Conduct. To the best of my ability I will

- Never harm children.
- Ensure that programs for young children are based on current knowledge and research of child development and early childhood education.
- Respect and support families in their task of nurturing children.
- Respect colleagues in early childhood care and education and support them in maintaining the NAEYC Code of Ethical Conduct.
- Serve as an advocate for children, their families, and their teachers in community and society.
- Stay informed of and maintain high standards of professional conduct.
- Engage in an ongoing process of self-reflection, realizing that personal characteristics, biases, and beliefs have an impact on children and families.
- Be open to new ideas and be willing to learn from the suggestions of others.
- Continue to learn, grow, and contribute as a professional.
- Honor the ideals and principles of the NAEYC Code of Ethical Conduct.

---

[*] This Statement of Commitment is not part of the Code but is a personal acknowledgment of the individual's willingness to embrace the distinctive values and moral obligations of the field of early childhood care and education. It is recognition of the moral obligations that lead to an individual becoming part of the profession.

## Ethical Responsibilities to Practicum Sites

Some knowledge and skills needed by early childhood educators can only be acquired through direct experience in early childhood settings. Therefore, early childhood adult educators rely heavily on placements in programs at practicum sites, where students can apply what they have learned, get feedback from children and adults, and reflect on their experience.

### Ideals

I–2.1 To provide practicum experiences that will positively support the professional development of adult students.

I–2.2 To foster collegial and collaborative working relationships with educators who work in practicum settings.

I–2.3 To be respectful of the responsibilities, expertise, and perspective of practitioners who work with students in practicum settings.

I–2.4 To recognize the importance and contributions of practicum staff members in the professional development of students.

### Principles

P–2.1 We shall place students in settings where staff are qualified to work with young children, where mentors have experience and training in supporting adult learners, which to the greatest extent possible reflect the diverse communities in which our students will be working.

P–2.2 We shall clearly state all parties' roles and responsibilities and prepare students, mentors, and administrators for practicum experiences. We shall provide appropriate support for all parties' efforts to fulfill their roles and meet program expectations.

P–2.3 When we have concern about a program in which we place students, we shall address that concern with the classroom teacher or program administrator. If the concerns relate to the health or safety of children, see the applicable sections of the NAEYC Code: P–1.11 and P–4.9–12.

P–2.4 We shall ensure that qualified personnel conduct regular supervision of practicum experiences in order to support professional development of adult students and monitor the welfare of children.

P–2.5 We shall honor confidentiality and guard the privacy of teachers and clientele at practicum sites.

P–2.6 We shall teach adult students that they have a professional obligation to honor confidentiality and shall make every effort to ensure that they guard the privacy of the program, its teachers, and clientele.

> From the National Association for the Education of Young Children, the National Association of Early Childhood Teacher Educators, and the American Associate Degree Early Childhood Teacher Educators. (2004). *Code of Ethical Conduct: Supplement for Early Childhood Adult Educators*. A joint position statement, reprinted with permission from the National Association for the Education of Young Children.

## CHAPTER 3

## COMPETENCIES IN DEVELOPMENTALLY APPROPRIATE PRACTICE

A. Teachers respect, value, and accept children and treat them with dignity at all times.

B. Teachers make it a priority to know each child well.

1) Teachers establish positive, personal relationships with children to foster the child's development and keep informed about the child's needs and potentials. Teachers listen to children and adapt their responses to children's differing needs, interests, styles, and abilities.

2) Teachers continually observe children's spontaneous play and interaction with the physical environment and with other children to learn about their interests, abilities, and developmental progress. On the basis of this information, teachers plan experiences that enhance children's learning and development.

3) Understanding that children develop and learn in the context of their families and communities, teachers establish relationships with families that increase their knowledge of children's lives outside the classroom and their awareness of the perspectives and priorities of those individuals most significant in the children's lives.

4) Teachers are alert to signs of undue stress and traumatic events in children's lives and aware of effective strategies to reduce stress and support the development of resilience.

5) Teachers are responsible at all times for all children under their supervision and plan for children's increasing development of self-regulation.

C. Teachers create an intellectually engaging, responsive environment to promote each child's learning and development.

1) Teachers use their knowledge about children in general and the particular children in the group as well as their familiarity with what children need to learn and develop in each curriculum area to organize the environment and plan curriculum and teaching strategies.

2) Teachers provide children with a rich variety of experiences, projects, materials, problems, and ideas to explore and investigate, ensuring that these are worthy of children's attention.

3) Teachers provide children with opportunities to make meaningful choices and time to explore through active involvement. Teachers offer children the choice to participate in a small-group or a solitary activity, assist and guide children who are not yet able to use and enjoy child-choice activity periods, and provide opportunities for practice of skills as a self-chosen activity.

4) Teachers organize the daily and weekly schedule and allocate time so as to provide children with extended blocks of time in which to engage in play, project, and/or study in integrated curriculum.

D. Teachers make plans to enable children to attain key curriculum goals across various disciplines, such as language arts, mathematics, social studies, science, art, music, physical education, and health.

1) Teachers incorporate a wide variety of experiences, materials and equipment, and teaching strategies in constructing curriculum to accommodate a broad range of children's individual differences in prior experiences, maturation rates, styles of learning, needs, and interests.

2) Teachers bring each child's home culture and language into the shared culture of the school, so that the unique contributions of each group are recognized and valued by others.

3) Teachers are prepared to meet identified special needs of individual children, including children with disabilities and those who exhibit unusual interests and skills. Teachers use all the strategies identified here, consult with appropriate specialists, and see that the child gets the specialized services she requires.

Reprinted with permission from the National Association for the Education of Young Children.

Bredekamp, S., & Copple, C. (Eds.). (1997). *Developmentally appropriate practice in early childhood programs* (rev. ed.) Washington, DC: National Association for the Education of Young Children.

# CHAPTER 5

## BEHAVIOR MODIFICATION

In terms of behavior modification, it is important to be objective. The term has acquired a negative connotation that is unfounded. Everyone uses behavior modification, whether it is recognized or not, from turning off the lights when children are to be quiet to planning and implementing a behavior modification plan. In any plan, there are seven steps.

1. Keep a log of observations on the child. Really look at what the child is doing. Do this at least five times a day, for at least three days in a row (see Figure AP–1).

2. Read your observations; look for patterns. Is this child predictable? Does he usually have a temper tantrum around 9:30 AM? Does the child often fight with another in late afternoon?

3. Look for the reinforcers of the behavior noted in your observations. Does the child misbehave in order to get attention from the adults in the room? Do friends admire the behavior?

4. Decide on a schedule of reinforcement after finding the current reinforcer.

5. Implement the new reinforcement schedule. Give it time. Many teachers fail to use a reinforcement plan for a long enough period of time. Try a minimum of two weeks to two or three months. Behavior that has taken two or three years to develop will not change in a week.

6. Keep a second log of observations. On the basis of your study of the initial observations, analyze this second series and note whether your reinforcement schedule has worked.

7. Stop your planned reinforcement schedule. See if the child goes back to the former pattern of behavior. If so, go back to the second step and start over.

Look at the second and third steps. You have completed your observations, and now you need to find the reinforcers of the observed behavior. The behavior must bring some kind of reward to the child. As the teacher, your job is to discover what the reward is.

Many student teachers fail to understand the nature of the child's reward system. You look at what an adult perceives as negative behavior (hitting another child, for example), and you may decide to institute a schedule of reinforcement or a behavior modification plan without taking that first step: understanding why the child hits.

Study Step 4, planning a reinforcement schedule. Look at the child in the sample log in Figure AP–1. Assume that the description of behavior is typical of Maria's everyday behavior.

In your analysis of the log, what do you see? Three questions have been raised: Is Maria fairly new to the school? Does she have a hearing problem? Is she bilingual or does she have limited understanding of English? The answers to these questions come during the discussion of observations. Yes, Maria is new to the school. This is only her second week. No, she does not have a hearing problem, but she is bilingual. In fact, the cooperating teacher suspects that Maria may be less bilingual than her mother claims.

What has reinforced Maria's behavior? First, she is unfamiliar with English. Second, her cultural background is different. Girls of Hispanic background are often expected to be quiet, helpful around the house, and obedient to their elders. Certainly, this explains Maria's behavior because she willingly helps with cleanup.

What are appropriate goals for Maria? Assume that you and your cooperating teacher decide that the most appropriate goal is to help Maria feel more comfortable in the room and that adult approval is the most logical reinforcer to use. Your reinforcement schedule might start by greeting Maria at the door every day when she arrives. Smile at her and say, "Buenas dias, Maria. It's nice to see you today." Take her by the hand and go with her to a different activity each day. If Maria seems uncomfortable changing activities so often, stay with the activities she enjoys at first.

▶ **Figure AP-1**
Anecdotal record form

| Student Teacher: | | | |
|---|---|---|---|
| Name of School: | | Date: | |

| Identity Key (do NOT use real name) | Description of What Child is Doing | Time | Comments |
|---|---|---|---|
| M. – Maria<br>T. – Teacher<br>ST. – Student Teacher<br>J. – Janine<br>S. – Susie<br>B. – Bobby<br>Sv. – Stevie | M. arrives at school. Clings to mother's hand hand, hides behind her skirt. Thumb in mouth. | 9:05 | Ask T. how long M. has been coming. I bet she's new. |
| | M. goes over to puzzle rack, chooses a puzzle, goes to table. Dumps out, and works puzzle quickly and quietly. B. & Sv. come over to work puzzles they've chosen. | 9:22 | Her eye/hand coordination seems good. |
| | M. looks at them, says nothing, goes to easels, watches S. paint. S. asks M. if she wants to paint. M. doesn't answer. | 9:30 | I wonder why M. doesn't respond. Ask T. if M. has hearing problem. |
| | M. comes to snack table, sits down where T. indicates she should. Does not interact with other children at table. | 10:15 | Is M. ever a quiet child! |
| | M. stands outside of playhouse, watches S. & J. They don't ask her to join them. | 10:47 | She looks like she'd like to play. |
| | M. goes to swings, knows how to pump. | 10:55 | Nothing wrong with her coordination. |
| | During Hap Palmer record M. watches others, does not follow directions. | 11:17 | Hearing? Maybe limited English? (She looks of Spanish background.) |

Introduce her to the other children at the activity she chooses. Take advantage of the fact that Susie is one of the more mature, self-confident children in the room, and quietly ask her to include Maria in some of her activities. Instead of allowing Maria to watch Susie paint, go to Maria with her painting smock, put it on her, and suggest that she try the activity. When she does pick up the brush and experiment with painting, compliment her action.

Do not worry about Maria's lack of knowledge of the English language. When Maria hesitates, use pointing and naming to help her. Accept the fact that she may always be a shy child; do not push her to be outgoing if that is not her nature.

Continue these activities each day. After a few weeks, make another set of observations, though you may not need this step, as you may already see the difference; still, it is good practice to do the second observation, just to check on your feelings. It is more than likely that Maria is already greeting you with a smile as she enters, and that she is beginning to play with Susie and some of the other, more outgoing children.

Do you believe that changing Maria's behavior was easy? A more difficult example could have been chosen. However, cases like Maria's are common, and many children enjoy a period of watching and listening before joining in activities. You should become aware of these common problems in order to become sensitive about your potential power in the classroom. The word *power* is deliberately being used because, next to the parents or primary caretakers, you, as teacher, are the second most important person in the child's life. You have a tremendous potential for influencing the child.

*Assertion* is defined here as behavior through which a child maintains and defends his or her own rights and concerns. Assertive behavior reflects the child's developing competence and autonomous functioning and represents an important form of developmental progress. Assertiveness also affords the young child a healthy form of self-defense against becoming the victim of the aggressions of others.

*Cooperation* is defined here as any activity that involves the willing interdependence of two or more children. It should be distinguished from compliance, which may represent obedience to rules or authority, rather than intentional cooperation. When children willingly collaborate in using materials, for example, their interactions are usually quite different than when they are told to share.

# CHAPTER 7

## DEVELOPMENTAL CHECKLIST

Name: _____ Birth date: _____

| | | Present | Date Observed |
|---|---|---|---|
| I. Infants | | | |
| 3 Months | **Motor Development** | | |
| | Neck muscles support head steadily | | |
| | Moves arms and legs vigorously | | |
| | May move arm and leg on one side together | | |
| | On stomach, holds chest and head erect 10 seconds | | |
| | When picked up, brings body up compactly | | |
| | May bat at objects | | |
| | Reaches with both arms | | |
| | **Perceptual Development** | | |
| | Follows slowly moving object with eyes and head from one side of body to other | | |
| | Looks at fingers individually | | |
| | Stops sucking to listen | | |
| | Visually seeks source of sound by turning head and neck | | |
| | Hands usually held open | | |
| | **Social Development** | | |
| | Smiles easily and spontaneously | | |
| | Gurgles and coos in response to being spoken to | | |
| | Responds to familiar faces with smile | | |
| | Protests when left by mother | | |
| | Cries differentially when hungry, wet, or cross | | |

| | Present | Date Observed |
|---|---|---|

Cognitive Development

| | | |
|---|---|---|
| Begins to show memory; waits for expected reward, like feeding | | |
| Begins to recognize family members and others close to her | | |
| Explores own face, eyes, mouth with hands | | |
| Responds to stimulation with whole body | | |

**6 Months**  Motor Development

| | | |
|---|---|---|
| Rolls from back to stomach | | |
| Turns and twists in all directions | | |
| Gets up on hands and knees, rocks | | |
| Creeps on stomach; may go forward and backward | | |
| Balances well when sitting, leans forward | | |
| Sits in chair and bounces | | |
| Grasps dangling object | | |
| May sit unsupported for 30 minutes | | |
| Rolls from back to stomach | | |

Perceptual Development

| | | |
|---|---|---|
| Holds one block, reaches for a second, looks at a third | | |
| Reaches to grab dropped object | | |
| Coos, hums, stops crying in response to music | | |
| Likes to play with food | | |
| Displays interest in finger-feeding self | | |
| Has strong taste preferences | | |
| Rotates wrist to turn and manipulate objects | | |
| Often reaches with one arm instead of both | | |
| Sleeps through the night | | |

Social Development

| | | |
|---|---|---|
| Prefers play with people | | |
| Babbles and becomes excited during active play | | |
| Babbles more in response to female voices | | |
| Vocalizes pleasure/displeasure | | |
| Gurgles when spoken to | | |
| Tries to imitate facial expressions | | |
| Turns in response to name | | |
| Smiles at mirror image | | |
| Disturbed by strangers | | |

Cognitive Development

| | | |
|---|---|---|
| Remains alert two hours at a time | | |
| Inspects objects for a long time | | |
| Eyes direct hand for reaching | | |
| Likes to look at objects upside down and create change of perspective | | |
| May compare two objects | | |
| Has abrupt mood changes; primary emotions: pleasure, complaint, temper | | |

**9 Months**  Motor Development

| | | |
|---|---|---|
| Crawls with one hand full | | |
| Turns while crawling | | |
| May crawl upstairs | | |
| Sits well | | |
| Gets self into sitting position easily | | |
| Pulls to standing | | |
| May pull self along furniture to walk | | |

Social Development

| | | |
|---|---|---|
| Eager for approval | | |
| Begins to evaluate people's moods | | |
| Imitates play | | |

| | Present | Date Observed |
|---|---|---|
| Enjoys peekaboo | | |
| Chooses toy for play | | |
| Sensitive to other children; may cry if they cry | | |
| May fight for disputed toy | | |
| Imitates cough, tongue clicks | | |

**Cognitive Development**

| | Present | Date Observed |
|---|---|---|
| Uncovers toy he has seen hidden | | |
| Anticipates reward | | |
| Follows simple directions | | |
| Shows symbolic thinking/role-play | | |
| May say *dada* and/or *mama* | | |
| Grows bored with same stimuli | | |

## II. Toddlers

### 12 Months

**Motor Development**

| | Present | Date Observed |
|---|---|---|
| Can stand, cruise along furniture, and may walk unassisted | | |
| Pivots body 90 degrees when standing | | |
| If walking, probably prefers crawling | | |
| May add stopping, waving, backing, and carrying toys to walking | | |
| Climbs up and down stairs, holding hand | | |
| May climb out of crib or playpen | | |
| Gets to standing by flexing knees, pushing from squat position | | |
| Lowers self to sitting position with ease | | |
| Makes swimming motions in bath | | |
| Wants to self-feed | | |
| May undress | | |

**Perceptual Development**

| | Present | Date Observed |
|---|---|---|
| Reaches accurately for object as she looks away | | |
| Puts things back together as well as takes them apart | | |
| Builds tower of two to three blocks after demonstration | | |
| Uses hammer and pegboard | | |
| Likely to put one or two objects in mouth and grasp a third | | |
| Cares for doll or teddy bear, such as feeding, cuddling, bathing | | |
| Enjoys water play in bath or sink | | |

**Social Development**

| | Present | Date Observed |
|---|---|---|
| Expresses many emotions | | |
| Recognizes emotions in others | | |
| Gives affection to people | | |
| Shows interest in what adults do | | |
| May demand more help than needed because it is easier | | |
| May refuse new foods | | |
| Resists napping, may have tantrums | | |
| Fears strange people, places | | |
| Reacts sharply to separation from mother | | |
| Distinguishes self from others | | |

**Cognitive Development**

| | Present | Date Observed |
|---|---|---|
| Perceives objects as detached and separate, to be used in play | | |
| Unwraps toys | | |
| Finds hidden object, remembers where it last was | | |
| Remembers events | | |
| Groups a few objects by shape and color | | |
| Identifies animals in picture books | | |
| Responds to directions | | |
| Understands much of what is said to him | | |
| Experiments with spatial relationships: heights, distances | | |

|  | Present | Date Observed |
|---|---|---|
| Stops when told *no* |  |  |
| Points to named body part |  |  |

**18 Months**      Motor Development

| | | |
|---|---|---|
| Walks well, seldom falls |  |  |
| Sits self in small chair |  |  |
| Walks up and down stairs one step at time, holding hand of adult or rail |  |  |
| Enjoys push toys |  |  |
| Likes to push furniture |  |  |
| Enjoys pull toys |  |  |
| Enjoys riding toys she can propel with feet on the ground |  |  |
| Strings large beads with shoelace |  |  |
| Takes off shoes and socks |  |  |
| Swings rhythmically in time to music |  |  |
| Follows one- or two-step directions |  |  |

Perceptual Development

| | | |
|---|---|---|
| Demonstrates good eye-hand coordination with small manipulatives |  |  |
| Will look at picture book briefly, turns pages, but not one at a time |  |  |
| Enjoys small objects she can manipulate |  |  |

Social Development

| | | |
|---|---|---|
| Makes distinction between *mine* and *yours* |  |  |
| Makes social contact with other children |  |  |
| Smiles and looks at others |  |  |
| May begin to indicate what he wants by talking, pointing, grunting, and body language |  |  |

Cognitive Development

| | | |
|---|---|---|
| Plays with blocks, can build tower of two to three blocks without model |  |  |
| Can sort by colors and shapes |  |  |
| Remembers where she put a toy, even the next day |  |  |

**III. Two-Year-Olds**

Gross Motor

**2.0 Years**

| | | |
|---|---|---|
| Runs well without falling |  |  |
| Kicks ball without overbalancing |  |  |
| Goes up and down stairs alone, two feet per step |  |  |
| Jumps from first step, one foot leading |  |  |
| Stops when running to change direction |  |  |
| Propels self on wheeled toy with feet on floor |  |  |
| Catches large ball by body trapping |  |  |
| Jumps 8 inches to 14 inches |  |  |

**2 ½ Years**

| | | |
|---|---|---|
| Walks several steps tiptoe |  |  |
| Walks several steps backwards |  |  |
| Walks up stairs alternating feet |  |  |
| Stands on balance beam without assistance |  |  |
| Throws objects and tracks visually |  |  |
| Bounces ball, catches with both hands |  |  |
| Bends at waist to pick up object from floor |  |  |
| Jumps over string two inches to eight inches high |  |  |

Fine Motor

**2.0 Years**

| | | |
|---|---|---|
| Turns knob on TV, toys |  |  |
| Turns doorknobs, opens door |  |  |
| Builds three- to five-block tower |  |  |
| Holds pencil in fist, scribbles, stays on paper |  |  |
| Puts ring on stick |  |  |
| Strings one-inch beads |  |  |
| Puts small objects into container |  |  |

|  | Present | Date Observed |
|---|---|---|
| Paints with whole arm movement |  |  |
| Folds paper in half |  |  |
| Removes jar lids |  |  |
| Builds seven- to nine-block tower |  |  |
| Completes simple inset puzzle |  |  |
| Traces circle |  |  |
| Paints with wrist action |  |  |
| Uses spoon without spilling |  |  |
| Holds glass, cup with one hand |  |  |
| Makes small cuts in paper with scissors |  |  |
| Places six pegs in pegboard |  |  |

**2 ½ Years** (left of the fine-motor list above)

### Language and Speech

**2 ½ Years** Receptive

| Receptive | Present | Date Observed |
|---|---|---|
| Understands most commonly used nouns and verbs |  |  |
| Responds to two-part command |  |  |
| Enjoys simple storybooks |  |  |
| Points to common objects when they are named |  |  |
| Understands functions of objects (e.g., cups are for drinking) |  |  |
| Understands 200 to 400 words |  |  |

| Expressive | Present | Date Observed |
|---|---|---|
| Verbalizes actions |  |  |
| Uses two- to three-word phrases |  |  |
| Asks what and where questions |  |  |
| Makes negative statements |  |  |
| Labels action in pictures |  |  |
| Approximately 50-word vocabulary (at two years) |  |  |
| Answers questions |  |  |

| Speech Sounds | Present | Date Observed |
|---|---|---|
| Substitutes some consonant sounds (e.g., *w* for *r*, *d* for *th*) |  |  |
| Articulates all consonants with few deviations, *p, b, m, w, h, k, g, n, t, d* |  |  |

| Psychosocial Skills | Present | Date Observed |
|---|---|---|
| Sees self as separate person |  |  |
| Conscious of possessions, understands *mine* |  |  |
| Shy with strangers |  |  |
| Knows gender identity |  |  |
| Watches others, may join in play |  |  |
| Begins to use dramatic play |  |  |
| Helps put things away |  |  |
| Participates in small-group activity (sings, claps, dances) |  |  |
| Says *no* frequently, obeys when asked |  |  |
| Understands and stays away from common dangers |  |  |

| Cognitive Skills | Present | Date Observed |
|---|---|---|
| Responds to three-part command |  |  |
| Selects and looks at picture books |  |  |
| Given three items, can associate which two go together |  |  |
| Recognizes self in mirror |  |  |
| Uses toys symbolically |  |  |
| Imitates adult actions in dramatic play |  |  |

| Self-Help Skills | Present | Date Observed |
|---|---|---|
| Can undress |  |  |
| Can partially dress |  |  |
| Gains mastery over toilet needs |  |  |
| Can drink from fountain |  |  |
| Washes and dries hands with assistance |  |  |

| | | Present | Date Observed |
|---|---|---|---|
| | **IV. Three-Year-Olds** | | |
| | **Gross Motor** | | |
| 3.0 Years | Runs smoothly | | |
| | Walks down stairs, alternating feet | | |
| | Climbs ladder on play equipment | | |
| | Throws tennis ball three feet | | |
| | Pedals tricycle | | |
| | Can execute one or two hops on dominant foot | | |
| | Can make sharp turns while running | | |
| | Balances briefly on dominant foot | | |
| 3 1/2 Years | Stands on either foot briefly | | |
| | Hops on either foot | | |
| | Jumps over objects six inches tall | | |
| | Pedals tricycle around corners | | |
| | Walks forward on balance beam several steps | | |
| | **Fine Motor** | | |
| 3.0 Years | Uses one hand consistently in most activities | | |
| | Strings 1/2-inch beads | | |
| | Traces horizontal/vertical lines | | |
| | Copies/imitates circles | | |
| | Cuts six-inch paper into two pieces | | |
| | Makes cakes/ropes of clay | | |
| 3 ½ Years | Winds up toy | | |
| | Completes five- to seven-piece inset puzzle | | |
| | Sorts dissimilar objects | | |
| | Makes ball with clay | | |
| | **Language and Speech** | | |
| | **Receptive** | | |
| | Understands size and time concepts | | |
| | Enjoys being read to | | |
| | Understands *if, then,* and *because* concepts | | |
| | Carries out two to four related directions | | |
| | Understands 800 words | | |
| | Responds to questions | | |
| | **Expressive** | | |
| | Gives full name | | |
| | Knows sex and can state girl or boy | | |
| | Uses three- to four-word phrases | | |
| | Uses *s* after nouns to indicate plurals | | |
| | Uses *ed* after verbs to indicate past tense | | |
| | Repeats simple songs, finger plays | | |
| | Speech is 70 percent to 80 percent intelligible | | |
| | Vocabulary of over 500 words | | |
| | **Speech Sounds** | | |
| | *f, y, z, ng, wh* | | |
| | **Psychosocial Skills** | | |
| | Joins in interactive games | | |
| | Shares toys | | |
| | Takes turns, with assistance | | |
| | Enjoys sociodramatic play | | |
| | **Cognitive Skills** | | |
| | Matches six colors | | |
| | Names one color | | |

| | Present | Date Observed |
|---|---|---|
| Counts two blocks | | |
| Counts by rote to 10 | | |
| Matches pictures | | |
| Classifies objects by physical attributes, one class at a time (e.g., color, shape, size) | | |
| Stacks blocks or rings in order of size | | |
| Knows age | | |
| Asks questions for information (*why* and *how*) | | |
| Can "picture read" a story book | | |

Self-Help Skills

| | | |
|---|---|---|
| Pours well from small pitcher | | |
| Spreads soft butter with knife | | |
| Buttons and unbuttons large buttons | | |
| Blows nose when reminded | | |
| Uses toilet independently | | |

V. Four-Year-Olds

4.0 Years

| | | |
|---|---|---|
| Walks down stairs, alternating feet, holding rail | | |
| Stands on dominant foot five seconds | | |
| Gallops | | |
| Jumps 10 consecutive times | | |
| Walks sideways on balance beam | | |
| Catches beanbag thrown from a distance of three feet | | |
| Throws two beanbags into wastebasket, underhand, from a distance of three feet | | |
| Hops on preferred foot for a distance of one yard | | |

4 ½ Years

| | | |
|---|---|---|
| Walks forward on line, heel-toe, for a distance of two yards | | |
| Stands on either foot for five seconds | | |
| Walks upstairs holding object in one hand without holding the rail | | |
| Walks to rhythm | | |
| Attempts to keep time to simple music with hand instruments | | |
| Turns somersault (forward roll) | | |

Fine Motor

4.0 Years

| | | |
|---|---|---|
| Builds 10- to 12-block tower | | |
| Completes three- to five-piece puzzle, not inset | | |
| Draws person with arms, legs, eyes, nose, mouth | | |
| Copies a cross | | |
| Imitates a square | | |
| Cuts a triangle | | |
| Creases paper with fingers | | |
| Cuts on continuous line | | |

4 ½ Years

| | | |
|---|---|---|
| Completes 6- to 10-piece puzzle, not inset | | |
| Grasps pencil correctly | | |
| Copies a few capital letters | | |
| Copies triangle | | |
| May copy square | | |
| Cuts curved lines and circles with 1/4-inch accuracy | | |

Language and Speech

Receptive

| | | |
|---|---|---|
| Follows three unrelated commands | | |
| Understands sequencing | | |
| Understands comparatives: big, bigger, biggest | | |
| Understands approximately 1,500 words | | |

Expressive

| | | |
|---|---|---|
| Has mastery of inflection, can change volume and rate of speech | | |
| Uses sentences with five or more words | | |
| Uses adjectives, adverbs, conjunctions in complex sentences | | |

| | Present | Date Observed |
|---|---|---|
| Speech about 90 percent to 95 percent intelligible | | |

Speech Sounds
    *s*, *sh*, *r*, *ch*

Psychosocial Skills

| | | |
|---|---|---|
| Plays and interacts with others | | |
| Dramatic play is closer to reality with attention paid to time and space | | |
| Plays dress-up | | |
| Shows interest in sex differences | | |
| Plays cooperatively | | |
| May have imaginary playmates | | |
| Shows humor by silly words and rhymes | | |
| Tells stories, fabricates, rationalizes | | |
| Goes on errands outside the home | | |

Cognitive Skills

| | | |
|---|---|---|
| Points to and names four colors | | |
| Draws, names, and describes picture | | |
| Counts three or four objects with correct pointing | | |
| Distinguishes between day and night | | |
| Can finish opposite analogies (brother = boy; sister = girl) | | |
| Names a penny in response to "What is this?" | | |
| Tells which of two is bigger, slower, heavier | | |
| Increased concepts of time; can talk about yesterday, last week, today, and tomorrow | | |

Self-Help Skills

| | | |
|---|---|---|
| Cuts easy food with knife | | |
| Laces shoes, does not tie | | |
| Buttons front buttons | | |
| Washes and dries face without help | | |
| Brushes teeth without help | | |
| Toilets himself, manages clothes by himself | | |

VI. Five-Year-Olds

Gross Motor

5.0 Years

| | | |
|---|---|---|
| Stands on dominant foot 10 seconds | | |
| Walks backward, toe to heel, six steps | | |
| Walks downstairs carrying object without holding rail | | |
| Skips, jumps three feet | | |
| Hops on dominant foot for a distance of two yards | | |
| Walks backward on balance beam | | |
| Catches ball with two hands | | |
| Rides small bike with training wheels | | |

5 ½ Years

| | | |
|---|---|---|
| Stands on either foot 10 seconds | | |
| Walks backward for a distance of two yards | | |
| Jumps rope Gallops, jumps, runs in rhythm to music | | |
| Roller skates | | |
| Rides bicycle without training wheels | | |

Fine Motor

5.0 Years

| | | |
|---|---|---|
| Opens and closes large safety pin | | |
| Sews through holes in sewing card | | |
| Opens lock with key | | |
| Completes 20- to 25-piece puzzle, not inset | | |
| Draws person with head, trunk, legs, arms, hands, eyes, nose, mouth, hair, ears, fingers | | |
| Colors within lines | | |
| Cuts cardboard and cloth | | |

| | Present | Date Observed |
|---|---|---|
| **5 ½ Years** Builds Tinkertoy structure | | |
| Copies first name | | |
| Copies rectangle | | |
| Copies triangle | | |
| Prints numerals 1 to 5 | | |
| Handedness well-established | | |
| Pastes and glues appropriately | | |
| Cuts out paper dolls, pictures from magazine | | |
| **Language and Speech** | | |
| **Receptive** | | |
| Demonstrates preacademic skills, such as following directions and listening | | |
| **Expressive** | | |
| Few differences between child's use of language and adults' | | |
| Can take turns in conversation | | |
| May have some difficulty with noun-verb agreement and irregular past tenses | | |
| Communicates well with family, friends, and strangers | | |
| **Speech Sounds** | | |
| Can correctly articulate most simple consonants and many digraphs | | |
| **Psychosocial Skills** | | |
| Chooses own friends | | |
| Plays simple table games | | |
| Plays competitive games | | |
| Engages in sociodramatic play with peers, involving group decisions, role assignment, fair play | | |
| Respects others' property | | |
| Respects others' feelings | | |
| **Cognitive Skills** | | |
| Retells story from book with reasonable accuracy | | |
| Names some letters and numbers | | |
| Uses time concepts of yesterday and tomorrow accurately | | |
| Begins to relate clock time to daily schedule | | |
| Uses classroom tools such as scissors and paints meaningfully | | |
| Draws recognizable pictures | | |
| Orders a set of objects from smallest to largest | | |
| Understands why things happen | | |
| Classifies objects according to major characteristics (e.g., apples and bananas can both be eaten) | | |
| **Self-Help Skills** | | |
| Dresses self completely | | |
| Ties a bow | | |
| Brushes teeth unassisted | | |
| Crosses the street safely | | |
| Dries self after bathing | | |
| Brushes hair | | |
| Ties shoes without assistance | | |
| **VII. Six-Year-Olds** | | |
| **Gross Motor Skills** | | |
| Walks with ease | | |
| Runs easily, turns corners smoothly | | |
| Gallops | | |
| Skips | | |
| Jumps rope well | | |

| | Present | Date Observed |
|---|---|---|
| Throws overhand, shifts weight from back to front foot | | |
| Walks length of balance beam: | | |
|     forward | | |
|     backward | | |
|     sideways | | |
| Rides bicycle | | |
| Uses all playground equipment: | | |
|     Swings herself | | |
|     Uses a merry-go-round | | |
|     Climbs on outside climber | | |
|     Swings by arms across ladder | | |
| Other skills | | |
|   Writes name, address, phone number | | |
|   Reads *I Can Read* books | | |
|   Can count to 100 | | |
|   Can retell story after having read it | | |
|   Understands concept of numbers 1 to 10 | | |
|   Understands concept of one more, one less | | |
|   Can complete simple arithmetic problems, addition and subtraction | | |
|   Can write simple story | | |
|   Can illustrate a story appropriately | | |
|   Plays cooperatively with others | | |
|   Stands up for herself | | |

**VIII. Seven-Year-Olds**

| | Present | Date Observed |
|---|---|---|
| Performs all gross motor skills well except for mature, overhand ball throwing | | |
| Knows when to lead and follow | | |
| Knows what he does well | | |
| Knows when to ask for help | | |
| Can draw diamond | | |
| Draws house with straight chimney | | |
| Enjoys card games such as Rummy, Crazy 8's, Hearts, Old Maid | | |
| Enjoys organized sports activities such as kickball, soccer, baseball, track, swimming | | |
| Enjoys reading | | |
| Enjoys games such as checkers, Parcheesi | | |
| Willing to tackle new problems | | |
| Eats well-balanced diet | | |
| Has solid peer relations | | |
| Is responsible | | |
| Writes legibly | | |
| Can articulate most speech sounds without distortion or substitution | | |

**IX. Eight-Year-Olds**

| | Present | Date Observed |
|---|---|---|
| Able to use mature, overhand ball throw | | |
| If given opportunity for practice, can perform all gross motor skills well, including the mature overhand ball throw | | |
| Enjoys organized sports activities, may want to play on a team, is developing a sense of industry, and an *I can do* attitude | | |
| Knows what she can do well and when she needs help | | |
| Enjoys reading | | |
| Enjoys games with rules | | |
| Is able to master pronunciation of all phonemes and most graphemes of the English language | | |
| Enjoys word-play games, such as puns and double entendre | | |
| Has solid peer relationships | | |
| Is able to assume responsibility for his actions | | |
| Willing to try out new activities | | |

| | Present | Date Observed |
|---|---|---|
| X. Nine-Year-Olds | | |
| Masters all arithmetic operations | | |
| Understands concepts of reversibility | | |
| Thinks logically if provided with concrete situations and/or manipulatives | | |
| Able to conserve mass, length, area, weight, among other operations | | |
| Forms classification hierarchies | | |
| Able to transfer learning from one situation to another | | |
| May be entering a growth spurt characterized by rapid long-bone growth (especially girls) | | |
| May develop secondary sex characteristics | | |
| Understands negatively worded questions, such as | | |
| "The only factor *not* in the sequence of events . . ." | | |
| "Which one of the following is *not* . . ." | | |
| and double-pronoun referrents, such as | | |
| "She baked her the birthday cake." | | |
| "He accidentally hit him with the ball." | | |
| Enjoys the company of peers | | |
| Groups into informal "clubs" | | |

## Individual Learning Plan for 2-year-old Alan

A student teacher may be asked to prepare an individual learning plan for one child/student that coordinates with a learning plan developed by the supervising teacher. Below is one prepared for a two-and-a-half year old with language difficulties who attends a state preschool program in the mornings.

1. Activity Title: Watching a Live Bird

2. Curriculum Areas: Science and language arts (vocabulary)

3. Materials needed: Live bird in cage. Table or counter for cage.

4. Location and set-up for activity: Birdcage with parakeet will be set in corner of room where two counters come together. This will keep the cage safer than if placed on a table, and the counter is at eye-level for children so they can easily see the cage and bird.

5. Number of children and adults: Alan and student teacher.

6. Preparation: Talk about pets with Alan. (Ask him if he has any pets. I know he has a dog and two cats.) Ask him if he knows what a bird is. Tell him that I have a surprise for him.

7. Specific behavioral objective: Alan will watch the parakeet for at least 3 minutes. He will be able to call the bird a parakeet and say its name, Ernie. (Long-range objective would be for Alan to feed the bird and give him water.)

8. Developmental skills needed for success: Willingness to watch and listen quietly.

9. Procedure: When Alan comes to school Tuesday, greet him at door and remind him about the surprise you promised. Take his hand and lead him to the corner where the birdcage is sitting. Ask Alan if he knows what is in the cage. Anticipate that he will know "bird." Tell him that this bird is called a parakeet and that the bird's name is Ernie. Ask him to repeat "parakeet" and "Ernie." Ask Alan what color Ernie is. Anticipate that he knows that the color "green." If he doesn't say "green," remind him that Ernie is green. See what else is green and remind Alan that he knows what color "green" is: green like the grass, for example, or green like Tony's shirt.

10. Discussion: Covered in Step 9, "Procedure."

11. Apply: Later in the day, ask Alan what kind of bird is in the birdcage. Ask him the bird's name. (I anticipate that Alan will be intrigued with the bird and that he will want to come over several times to watch Ernie, if only for a minute or two.) Each time, I will name the type of bird and repeat Ernie's name. I think Alan will know both "parakeet" and "Ernie" before he goes home.

12. Cleanup: Not necessary. I will keep the birdcage clean.

13. Terminating statement: Probably not necessary. Otherwise, I'll remind Alan that Ernie is a parakeet and suggest that he might want to see a book about birds (I've brought in several) or play the lotto game.

14. Transition: See #13.

15. Evaluation—Activity, Teacher, Child: I am hoping, of course, that this will be a great success for all children but especially for Alan. I'll write the evaluation after Ernie is brought in.

# Glossary

## A

**acceptant**—the quality of accepting each and every student but also differentiating between acceptance of a child's value as a fellow human being and his behavior, which may or may not be acceptable.

**accreditation**—an official form of approval granted from a review board stating that a learning institution has met specific requirements.

**active listening (with adults)**—the process of putting into your own words a message you received from another based on your understanding of what you thought you heard.

**affective**—caused by or expressing emotion or feeling.

**aggression**—behavior deliberately intended to hurt others.

**allergies**—physiological reactions to environmental or food substances that can affect or alter behavior.

**anxiety**—a general sense of uneasiness that cannot be traced to a specific cause.

**Asperger's syndrome**—one of the autism spectra but generally seen at less severe levels. Children with Asperger's often remain in regular classrooms with a sensitive teacher who recognizes the frequently seen delay in the child's social development and subsequent difficulties with peers.

**assertive discipline**—a form of behavior management used primarily in elementary schools. The consequences of behavior are clearly stated, understood by children, and consistently applied.

**assessment**—the act of appraising, judging, or evaluating another's efforts, performance, or actions.

**at-risk children**—because of adverse environmental factors, for instance, poverty or low birth weight, children are considered at risk for developmental delay and/or for doing poorly in school.

**attachment**—the child's bond with a teacher or caregiver, established over time through personal interactions. A child's primary attachment is usually to her parents.

**attention deficit disorder (ADD)**—a disorder that causes children to have difficulty sustaining attention in the classroom and concentrating on an assigned task for any length of time.

**attention-deficit/hyperactivity disorder (ADHD)**—Like ADD, it causes attention problems and an inability to sit still and concentrate for long. Children with ADHD are said to "bounce off the walls."

**authoritarian**—characterized by or favoring absolute obedience to authority, therefore the classroom is teacher oriented.

**authoritative**—substantiated, supported, and accepted by most professionals in the field of early childhood education, or having an air of authority.

**Autism spectrum disorder**—a persuasive developmental disorder usually seen with qualitative impairments in communication, social interactions, and restrictive or repetitive patterns of behavior that first occur before the age of three.

**autonomy**—the second stage of development described by Erik Erikson, occurring during the second year of life, in which toddlers assert their growing motor, language, and cognitive abilities by trying to become more independent.

## B

**behavior management**—a behavioral approach to guidance, holding that the child's behavior is under the control of the environment, which includes space, objects, and people.

**behavior modification**—the systematic application of principles of reinforcement to modify behavior.

**behaviorism**—a theoretical viewpoint, espoused by theorists such as B. F. Skinner, that behavior is shaped by environmental forces, specifically in response to reward and punishment.

**biases**—particular tendencies or inclinations, especially ones that prevent impartial consideration; prejudices.

**bibliotherapy**—the use of books that deal with emotionally sensitive topics in a developmentally appropriate way to help children gain accurate information and learn coping strategies.

◆ **359**

## C

**charter school**—schools exempt from some local and state regulations. They can be chartered by a school district, a state board of education, a post-secondary institution, or a chartering agency. Some charter schools are publicly funded, while others are privately funded by businesses and corporations.

**checklist**—a method of evaluating children or teachers that consists of a list of behaviors, skills, concepts, or attributes that the observer checks off as the child or teacher is observed to have mastered the item.

**Child Development Associate (CDA)**—an early childhood teacher who has been assessed and successfully proven competent through the national CDA credentialing program.

**classroom management**—consists of supervising, planning, and directing classroom activities and the room environment. It also involves making time-length decisions, providing appropriate direction, and guiding child behavior to enable children to live and work effectively with others.

**collaboration**—parents and teachers working together for the ultimate good of the children or students.

**communication**—giving or receiving information, signals, and/or messages.

**competencies**—the knowledge and skills desired in education professionals in various staffing positions in early childhood care.

**computer literacy**—familiarity with and knowledge about computers.

**confidentiality**—the requirement that results of evaluations and assessments be shared with only the parents and appropriate school personnel.

**conflict resolution**—promoting child-child or child-adult problem solving through verbal interactions, negotiation, compromise, and the use of acceptable physical tactics. It may include teacher support and assistance.

**congruent**—refers to the similarity between what a person (the *sender*) is thinking and feeling and what that person communicates; behaving in agreement with or as a reflection of inner feelings and values.

**conservation**—the ability, usually acquired during the concrete operational phase, to recognize that objects remain the same in terms of size, volume, and area despite perceptual changes.

**constructivism**—a term relating to constructivist theory based on the belief that children construct knowledge for themselves rather than having it conveyed to them by some external source. This theory is often attributed to the work of Jean Piaget.

**curriculum**—overall master plan of the early childhood program, reflecting its philosophy, into which specific activities are fit.

## D

**Developmentally Appropriate Practice in Early Childhood Programs (DAP)**—guidelines developed by the National Association for the Education of Young Children, as a response to the growing trend toward more formal, academic instruction of young children. The primary position of the guidelines is that programs designed for young children should be based on what is known about their development. DAP also reflects a clear commitment regarding the rights of young children, to respectful and supportive learning environments and to education preparing them for participation in a free and democratic society.

**didactic**—often applied to teaching materials, indicating a built-in intent to provide specific instruction.

**disposition**—a consistent inclination or tendency.

## E

**empathy**—the ability of a person to put himself in the child's place, to understand why she is acting as she is.

**empowering**—helping parents and children gain a sense of control over events in their lives.

**equilibration**—according to Jean Piaget, the state of balance that each person seeks between existing mental structures and new experiences.

**evaluation**—making a *judgment* concerning a relative value, worth, usefulness, productivity, effectiveness, or another quality or element.

## F

**feedback**—information given and deemed to be a true and accurate account of what happened. May be evaluated as positive, negative, or otherwise by the informant or listener.

**flexible**—willing to yield, modify, or adapt; change or create in a positive, productive manner.

## G

**gifted children**—children who perform significantly above average in intellectual and creative areas.

**goals**—overall, general overviews of what student teachers expect to gain from the program. The term goals is frequently used to refer to curriculum goals or to concepts children are to learn.

**group times**—also called *circle* or *story* times; time blocks during the day when all of the children and teachers join together in a common activity.

**guidance**—ongoing process of directing children's behavior based on the types of adults children are expected to become.

# I

*I* **messages**—Thomas Gordon's term for a response to a child's behavior that focuses on how the adult feels rather than on the child's character.

**identity formation**—the way in which young children separate from their parents and establish their own character traits and personality.

**idiosyncratic**—a characteristic peculiar to an individual.

**ignoring**—a principle of behavior management that involves removing all reinforcement for a given behavior to eliminate that behavior.

**inclusion**—a term that has widely replaced the term "mainstreaming" and that emphasizes placement of the child with special needs in the regular classroom with, perhaps, greater assistance from special education services.

**Individual Education Program (IEP)**—with children with special needs, an individual education program that states the short-term and long-term learning objectives, how they will be accomplished and by whom, and applicable dates. It must be approved by both parents and school.

**Individualized Family Service Plan (IFSP)**—required initially by the 1986 Education of the Handicapped Act Amendments and reaffirmed by IDEA; the IFSP is often developed by a transdisciplinary team that includes the family, any needed specialists, such as a physical therapist, a language therapist, an educator, who cooperatively determine goals and objectives that build on the strengths of the child and family.

**industry**—the fourth stage of development described by Erik Erikson, starting at the end of the preschool years and lasting until puberty, in which the child focuses on the development of competence.

**initiative**—identified as the third developmental stage of three- to five-year-old children by Erik Erikson and involves their desire to do something by themselves.

**instructional objectives**—aims or goals, usually set for an individual child, that describe in very specific and observable terms what the child is expected to master.

# J

**journal**—a written, pictorial, audio, or computerized record of experiences, occurrences, observations, feelings, questions, work actions, reflective thoughts, and other happenings during student teaching.

# L

**learning disability**—a condition thought to be associated with neurological dysfunction and characterized by difficulty in mastering a skill such as reading or numerical calculation.

**least restrictive environment**—a provision of Public Law 101-476, that children with disabilities be placed in a program as close as possible to a setting designed for children without disabilities, while being able to meet each child's special needs.

**lesson plans**—the working documents from which the daily program is run, specifying directions for activities.

**logical consequences**—Rudolf Dreikurs's technique of specific outcomes that follow certain behaviors and are mutually agreed upon by teacher and children/students.

# M

**Maslow's Hierarchy of Needs**—a theoretical position that attempts to identify human needs and motivations. It describes the consequences of need fulfillment and the consequences of unmet needs on growth.

**mentoring**—guidance by an experienced and trusted teacher who is frequently paired with a new and inexperienced teacher or aide, and who assists the new teacher with ideas and advice.

**modeling**—in social learning theory, the process of imitating a model.

**Montessori equipment**—early childhood learning materials derived from and part of the Montessori approach.

# N

**National Association for the Education of Young Children (NAEYC)**—largest American early childhood professional organization, which deals with issues of children from birth to age eight and those who work with young children.

**National Council for Accreditation of Teacher Education (NCATE)**—an organization that accredits colleges, schools, or departments of education in higher education programs at the baccalaureate and advanced degree levels in the United States.

# O

**objectives**—aims; specific interpretations of general goals, providing practical and directive tools for day-to-day program planning.

**observable behavior**—actions that can be seen rather than those that are inferred.

**observation**—the process of learning that comes from watching, noting the behavior of, and imitating models.

**one-day wonders**—preplanned and often prepackaged collections of materials that student teachers can easily set up or use on the spur of the moment to engage young children.

## P

**parent cooperatives**—programs staffed by one professional teacher and a rotating staff of parents.

**pendulum effect**—a phenomenon observed especially with children in therapy for the treatment of depressive disorders. Children swing from non-expression of emotions to explosive outbreaks.

**practitioner**—person engaged in the practice of a profession or occupation, in this case, early childhood education. Other terms used: educator, teacher, assistant teacher, aide, student teacher.

**professionals**—individuals engaged in occupations considered learned endeavors, such as law, medicine, or as in this text, education.

**professional ethics**—beliefs regarding appropriate occupational behavior and conduct as defined and accepted by recognized professionals in that occupation.

**professional portfolio**—a representative collection of your student teacher accomplishments.

## R

**reflective teaching**—a serious effort to thoughtfully question teaching practices, perceptions, actions, feelings, values, cultural biases, and other features associated with the care and education of young children.

**reliability**—a measure indicating that a test is stable and consistent, to ensure that scoring variations are due to the person tested, and not the test.

**role model**—a person whose behavior is imitated by others.

## S

**scaffolding**—a teaching technique helpful in promoting language, understanding, and child solutions that may include supportive and responsive teacher conversation and actions following child-initiated behavior.

**schedule**—a planned series of happenings for a specific time period to accommodate needs and goals.

**self-concepts**—perceptions and feelings that children may have about themselves, gathered largely from how the important people in their world respond to them.

**self-control**—restraint exercised over one's own impulses, emotions, or desires.

**separation anxiety**—emotional difficulty experienced by some young children when leaving their parents or other primary caregivers.

**specific behavioral objectives (SBO)**—clearly describes observable behavior, the situation in which it will occur, and the exact outcome or the criteria of successful performance.

**stereotype**—a simplified conception or image of a person or group based on race, ethnicity, religion, gender, or sexual orientation.

**stress**—internal or external demand on a person's ability to adapt.

**sudden infant death syndrome (SIDS)**—where death of an infant occurs without warning, generally during the first three months of life, and for which there is no known cause.

**syntax**—involves the grammatical rules that govern the structure of sentences.

## T

**team teaching**—an approach that involves co-teaching, in which status and responsibility are equal rather than having a pyramid structure of authority, with one person in charge and others subordinate.

**terminating statement**—a summary or recap of what has been discovered, discussed, experienced, enjoyed, and so on, after a learning activity.

**theme approach**—a popular approach to child program planning that involves a course of study with identified child activities focused on one subject, idea, or skill such as butterflies, friendship, biking, or a picture book.

**time-out**—a brief social isolation and temporary suspension of technique in which the child is removed from the reinforcement and stimulation of the classroom usual activity, used at times by some educators to decrease young children's undesirable behavior.

**time sampling**—a quantitative measure or count of how often a specific behavior occurs within a given amount of time.

**trust**—the first stage of development described by Erik Erikson, occurring during infancy, in which the child's needs should be met consistently and predictably.

## Y

**you message**—Thomas Gordon's term for a response to a child's behavior that focuses on the child's character (usually in negative terms) rather than on how the adult feels.

## Z

**zone of proximal development (ZPD)**—in Vygotsky's theory, this zone represents tasks that a child cannot yet do by herself but that she can accomplish with support of an older child or adult.

# Index